The DIARY of
George Templeton Strong

★ ★ ★

THE CIVIL WAR

1860—1865

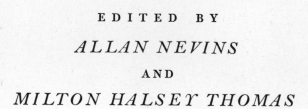

EDITED BY

ALLAN NEVINS

AND

MILTON HALSEY THOMAS

THE MACMILLAN COMPANY

New York : 1952

CONTENTS

Dramatis Personae   *page ix*

   1860   *page 1*
ADELINA PATTI · DARWIN'S *ORIGIN OF SPECIES* · THE DEMO-
CRATIC SCHISM · VISIT OF THE PRINCE OF WALES · LINCOLN'S
ELECTION · SOUTH CAROLINA SECEDES

   January–May, 1861   *page 83*
EFFORTS AT SECTIONAL COMPROMISE · CONFEDERATE DEFI-
ANCE · FORT SUMTER FIRED UPON · THE NORTHERN UPRISING ·
ENTHUSIASM IN NEW YORK

   May–December, 1861   *page 149*
CONFLICT GROWS AND SPREADS · THE SANITARY COMMISSION IS
ORGANIZED · THE BATTLE OF BULL RUN · GREAT BRITAIN'S ATTI-
TUDE

   January–July, 1862   *page 199*
NORTHERN ARMIES MOVE SLOWLY · FORT DONELSON AND SHILOH ·
FAILURE OF McCLELLAN'S PENINSULAR CAMPAIGN · THE SANI-
TARY COMMISSION MEETS OFFICIAL OBSTACLES

   July–December, 1862   *page 242*
MORE NORTHERN REVERSES · SECOND MANASSAS · LEE'S INVA-
SION OF MARYLAND · EMANCIPATION PROCLAMATION · CONGRES-
SIONAL ELECTIONS

   January–July, 1863   *page 285*
NORTHERN REVERSES · COPPERHEAD ACTIVITIES · TROUBLE WITH
ENGLAND · STANTON'S OPPOSITION TO SANITARY COMMISSION ·
GETTYSBURG

July–December, 1863   *page 334*

THE DRAFT RIOTS IN NEW YORK · TURN OF THE WAR IN FAVOR OF
THE NORTH · BATTLES OF CHICKAMAUGA AND LOOKOUT MOUN-
TAIN · UNION MILITARY SUCCESSES IN THE WEST

January–June, 1864   *page 388*

GRANT ASSUMES COMMAND · BATTLE OF THE WILDERNESS · SHER-
MAN'S MARCH BEGINS · SANITARY COMMISSION'S METROPOLITAN
FAIR · HAMMOND'S COURT-MARTIAL

June–December, 1864   *page 456*

LINCOLN'S CAMPAIGN AND REËLECTION · GRANT'S SUMMER RE-
VERSES AND AUTUMN SUCCESSES · SHERMAN TAKES ATLANTA

January–May, 1865   *page 537*

BATTLES BEFORE RICHMOND · FIVE FORKS AND APPOMATTOX ·
END OF CIVIL WAR · ASSASSINATION OF LINCOLN · THE WHITE
HOUSE FUNERAL

Appendix   *page 603*

Index   *page 605*

ILLUSTRATIONS

Front endpaper:
The Seventh Regiment Marching Down Broadway to Embark for the War. "The roar of the crowd was grand and terrible." Wood-engraving from *Harper's Weekly*, 4 May 1861.

STRONG AT FORTRESS MONROE   80
"Dinner table in [Col. Abram] Duryee's Camp, near Fort Monroe, June 4 '61". From a stereoscopic photograph in the Diary, identified by Strong as follows: *Seated*, Capt. Dumont, G.T.S., the Surgeon, Dan Messenger, "Smith," Curtis, Lieut. Dumont, Lamson, Boyd; *Standing*, The contrabands Julius Caesar and Wilson, and the Quartermaster.

PHILIP KEARNY · ROBERT ANDERSON · JOHN POPE ·
   GEORGE BRINTON McCLELLAN   81
Photographs by E. & H. T. Anthony. *Collection of Allan Nevins.*

THE GREAT UNION MEETING, UNION SQUARE, 20 APRIL 1861   112
"Few assemblages have equalled it in numbers and unanimity." From a stereoscopic photograph by E. & H. T. Anthony. *Courtesy of the New-York Historical Society.*

MAKING HAVELOCKS FOR THE VOLUNTEERS   113
"Some thirty ladies . . . met here to make what they call 'Havelock caps' for the Seventh . . ." (29 April 1861). Wood-engraving from a drawing by Winslow Homer in *Harper's Weekly*, 29 June 1861.

EXECUTIVE COMMITTEE OF THE U.S. SANITARY
   COMMISSION   208
Dr. William Holme Van Buren, Strong, The Rev. Henry Whitney Bellows, Dr. Cornelius Rea Agnew, and Wolcott Gibbs. Photographed in February or March 1864 by Mathew B. Brady. *Courtesy of the New York Academy of Medicine.*

SUMMER GROUP AT CORNWALL-ON-HUDSON, NEW YORK,
   1863   209
Seated: Miss Rosalie Ruggles, Harris, Miss Gertrude Stuyvesant, Miss Coles, Mrs. George T. Strong, Miss Hattie Church. *Standing:* James F. Ruggles, Miss Louisa Anderson, four not identified, Miss Kitty Dix. From a photograph in the Diary.

GEORGE TEMPLETON STRONG, 28 NOVEMBER 1860   240
From a photograph in the Diary.

U.S. SANITARY COMMISSION HEADQUARTERS, 823 BROAD-
   WAY, NEW YORK   241
From a photograph in the Sanitary Commission Archives, New York Public Library.

EDWIN McMASTERS STANTON, Secretary of War   304

WILLIAM ALEXANDER HAMMOND, M.D., Surgeon General, U.S.A.
From photographs by Mathew B. Brady in the Library of Congress.

LINCOLN VISITING McCLELLAN AT ANTIETAM, 4 OCTOBER
   1862   305
From a photograph by Mathew B. Brady in the Library of Congress.

SANITARY COMMISSION HEADQUARTERS, GENERAL
   HOSPITAL, GETTYSBURG, JULY 1863   336
Photograph by Tyson Brothers, Gettysburg, Penn., in Sanitary Commission Archives.

SANITARY COMMISSION LODGE FOR INVALID SOLDIERS,
   374 NORTH CAPITOL STREET, WASHINGTON
Photograph in Sanitary Commission Archives, New York Public Library.

THE DRAFT RIOTS AT NEW YORK, JULY 1863   337
SACKING BROOKS BROTHERS' CLOTHING STORE, CATHERINE AND CHERRY STREETS
LYNCHING IN CLARKSON STREET
DRAGGING COLONEL O'BRIEN'S BODY THROUGH THE MUD
POLICE CHARGING THE RIOTERS AT THE *Tribune* OFFICE.
From wood-engravings in *Harper's Weekly*, 1 August 1863.

SANITARY COMMISSION DINNER TO SECRETARY SEWARD   432
From the Diary.

FREDERICK LAW OLMSTED and FREDERICK NEWMAN
   KNAPP   433
Wood-engravings from Katharine Prescott Wormeley, *The Other Side of War* (Boston, 1889).

THE ARCHITECTS OF VICTORY   464
ULYSSES S. GRANT. Photograph by F. Gutekunst, Philadelphia.
WILLIAM T. SHERMAN. Photograph by Brady.
PHILIP H. SHERIDAN. Photograph by Brady.
GEORGE GORDON MEADE. Photograph by Brady. *Collection of Allan Nevins.*

PROGRAM OF THE THIRD AMATEUR DRAMATIC PERFORM-
   ANCE FOR THE BENEFIT OF THE U.S. SANITARY COM-
   MISSION, 18 APRIL 1864   465
From the Diary.

SALMON PORTLAND CHASE   528
Photograph by Brady.

CHARLES SUMNER
Photograph by Silsbee, Case & Co., Boston. *Collection of Allan Nevins.*

HORACE BINNEY, Jr.   529
CHARLES JANEWAY STILLÉ
From photographs in the Sanitary Commission Archives.

Bishop THOMAS MARCH CLARK of Rhode Island
From a photograph in the Library of Congress.

JOHN STRONG NEWBERRY, G.T.S., and CORNELIUS REA
   AGNEW   560
From a photograph in the Diary, taken at a meeting of Sanitary Commission officers at Washington in October 1863.

STRONG'S CARD OF ADMISSION TO LINCOLN'S FUNERAL   561
From the Diary.

LINCOLN FUNERAL PROCESSION ON PENNSYLVANIA AVENUE
From a photograph by Brady in the Library of Congress.

Rear endpaper:
U.S. Hospital Steamer *R. C. Wood*. Photograph from the Sanitary Commission Archives.

DRAMATIS PERSONAE

CORNELIUS REA AGNEW. Surgeon-General of New York when the war began, Dr. Agnew (just past thirty at the time) took charge of the New York State Hospital for Veterans, and managed it with great skill. He became a prominent member of the Sanitary Commission, and Strong found comfort in his zeal and expertness. In 1864, too, as an alumnus of Columbia, he lent a hand in the movement for the School of Mines.

GEORGE C. ANTHON. The close-knit triumvirate of Anthon, Charles E. Strong, and the diarist persisted. Though his war activities took so much of Strong's time and energy, he still found hours to spend with "G.C.A.," whose temperamental vagaries were often trying in the nerve-straining days, but whose loyal friendship was nonetheless a comfort. Anthon was also devoted to Mrs. Strong, sharing her interests in music and art; he frequently escorted her to opera and concert when her husband was busy with Sanitary Commission or Trinity Church affairs.

ALEXANDER DALLAS BACHE. This great-grandson of Benjamin Franklin, head of the Coast Survey since 1843, was made vice-president of the Sanitary Commission. Strong liked the eminent scientist, but Bache was too conscious of his high official position to make a sternly courageous member; and the diary shows that his health failed in 1864.

FREDERICK A. P. BARNARD. When Strong refused to be considered for the presidency of Columbia College, this former president of the University of Mississippi was easily elected to the place (1864). A son of Massachusetts and of Yale, Barnard was then fifty-five. He was deaf as a post, and prosily loquacious. But Strong was convinced from the outset that he was a man of vision, judgment, and courage, and never had reason to change the opinion.

HENRY W. BELLOWS. Unitarian pastor and prime mover in the creation of the United States Sanitary Commission. Aware that the Army Medical Bureau must totally fail to meet the emergency, he took a committee to Washington on May 16, 1861, and held conferences with Lincoln,

Winfield Scott, Secretary of War Cameron, and other notables. The result was Lincoln's approval of the Sanitary Commission scheme June 13, 1861, with Bellows as President. This diary, under date of April 4, 1864, contains an incisive characterization of Bellows. He had his foibles, including vanity, but he was "public-spirited and unselfish, farsighted and wise."

AUGUST BELMONT. Banker, Democratic leader, former diplomat, and patron of the arts, this agent of the Rothschilds played a part in politics which Strong found detestable. A party of his is described here (February 18, 1863) for the shindy that marked it. On September 6, 1864, Belmont assured Strong that he was confident McClellan would be elected over Lincoln.

MARSHALL S. BIDWELL. Strong's old law-partner continued to divide his time between practice and his labors for the American Bible Society and various philanthropies. Much as the diarist admired Bidwell's talents, experience, and public spirit, he found the dark pessimism of the man almost insupportable.

HORACE BINNEY, Jr. The Civil War brought Strong and his cousin-by-marriage into much closer relation than they had known through exchange of family visits. Like the diarist, eleven years his junior, Binney took time from his busy law practice, in which he was associated with his father, to work for the Union cause in many ways. He became a member of the Sanitary Commission in the summer of 1861, to Strong's satisfaction; organized the Philadelphia auxiliary group, brought Philadelphia's leading professional and business men to the support of the work, and exerted a steadying influence on the whole undertaking. Strong wrote that "he was so simple, modest, and retiring that few recognized the value of his quiet, hard work for the country."

AMBROSE E. BURNSIDE. His loss of the battle of Fredericksburg was—as this diary shows—a terrible blow to Northern morale. Strong liked his frank admission that he was unequal to the command of the Army of the Potomac, and found him a man of pleasant social qualities. At the house of Charles E. Strong (February 11, 1863) he heard Burnside try to lay the blame for his signal defeat on one of his generals.

Bishop THOMAS MARCH CLARK. Protestant Episcopal Bishop of Rhode Island at this time. A churchman of abounding vigor, whose hearty good sense, broad sympathies, and eloquent tongue made him a strong member of the Sanitary Commission. He knew President Lincoln well enough to tender him advice, and he had the ear of other high government officers. Strong liked him for his brains, energy, and "lively talk."

JOHN J. CISCO. New York attorney, Assistant Secretary of the Treasury under Salmon P. Chase, and vestryman of Trinity; a man of ability and influence.

General GEORGE WASHINGTON CULLUM. A West Pointer and an expert on fortifications, who served under General Halleck in Washington from November 1, 1861, to September 6, 1864. He was a routine member of the Sanitary Commission of whom Strong held no exalted opinion.

JOHN A. DIX. The General was a man whom Strong almost unreservedly admired. The diary records most of his important activities—his part in organizing the Union Defense Committee in New York in 1861; his rapid organization of regiments for the front; his command in Maryland in the critical days after Bull Run, when that state was precarious; service at Fortress Monroe; and his measures as head of the Department of the East after the Draft Riots.

MORGAN DIX. Strong was deeply gratified when the young assistant rector of Trinity Church was unanimously elected to the rectorship on the death of the Rev. William Berrian in November, 1862, and a month later to Berrian's place on the Columbia College board of trustees. The Rector's sister, "the handsome, buxom, bouncing . . . Miss Kitty," pleased the diarist, too; in fact, he liked the whole Dix family.

THOMAS EGLESTON. Strong's ardent desire to see Columbia College expand into a university made him a sturdy champion of the plan for a School of Mines which Egleston (then at the Smithsonian Institution) published in 1863. From the partnership of four men, Egleston, Charles F. Chandler, Francis Vinton, and Strong, the School was born. A graduate of Yale and the Ecole des Mines in Paris in 1860, Egleston was in his early thirties at the time. The diary throws much light on his unselfish devotion to the great undertaking.

HAMILTON FISH. As former governor and senator, and as scion of two wealthy and aristocratic families, the Fishes and the Stuyvesants, Hamilton Fish was a man of power and influence. But Strong found him too cautious, chilly, and precise-minded to be agreeable, and thought him lukewarm in the Union cause—indeed, in every cause. In a memorable description of the meeting at the Union League Club in celebration of the victorious conclusion of the conflict, Strong presents Fish in an unpleasing light.

WOLCOTT GIBBS. The close friendship between Strong and Gibbs grew closer still when the chemist (who also had a medical degree) became a member of the executive committee of the Sanitary Commission. It was Gibbs, too, who deserved most of the credit for the idea which flowered into the Union League Club in New York, which Strong helped to establish. Until 1863 he held a chair in City College; then he went to Harvard.

WILLIAM ALEXANDER HAMMOND. It required a mighty battle on the part of Bellows, Olmsted, Strong, and other leaders of the Sanitary Commission to place Hammond in the office of the Surgeon-General of the United States. Accepting this post in April, 1862, he carried out his duties with such vigor that he quickly made an enemy of the equally imperious Secretary of War. The diary relates at length how when Stanton resolved to decapitate Hammond, the Sanitary Commission fought for its appointee. "But we shall fail," Strong dolefully wrote. "Stanton is a strong man. He has made up his mind to commit this injustice, and we can hardly prevent him." In August, 1864, Hammond was dismissed from the army.

ELISHA HARRIS. This Vermonter had practised medicine in New York and been superintendent of the quarantine hospital on Staten Island. As an expert in camp sanitation and quarantine practice he was a useful member of the Sanitary Commission. Strong liked him. He was conscientious, hardworking, and longwinded. After the war he published a good book on the control of infectious diseases in camps, transports, and hospitals.

MURRAY HOFFMAN. One of Strong's favorite companions and friends, though a much older man. He was a graduate of Columbia and an active layman of the Episcopal Church. After long practice in New York he was judge of the·superior court from 1853 to 1861. Though born nearly twenty years before Strong, he outlived the diarist.

FRANCIS LIEBER. The Civil War gave national and international scope to Lieber's political wisdom. He was consulted by the Union government in the formulation of rules of war, and his opinions were adopted. The War Department's General Orders No. 100, "Instructions for the Government of Armies in the Field," was an issue in revised form of

Lieber's most famous treatise on this subject. Nothing of the kind existed in any language before this publication. It was accepted by military authorities of other countries and became the basis of international rules for the conduct of war.

ABRAHAM LINCOLN. Nothing in the wartime diary is so striking as the change in Strong's attitude toward the President. At first, like Dr. Bellows and others, he doubted Lincoln's equipment for his tremendous responsibilities. "O for a day of the late Andrew Jackson!" he sighed at a moment of apparent presidential irresolution. But the wisdom, courage, and vision of the great national leader gradually impressed Strong, until at the end he concluded that Lincoln was a statesman of the highest power—as great as, and perhaps greater than, Washington. Several meetings with Lincoln are described, and Strong does far better than most observers in rendering the President's pronunciation.

GEORGE BRINTON McCLELLAN. Strong liked McClellan's integrity and his "uncommon faculty of brilliant silence." He thought the man a good general, but in the political field he condemned him emphatically. "A poor citizen," ran his verdict at one point; and at another, in February, 1863, "he has done the state some service, but is now doing it vast mischief." Strong thought McClellan's campaign for the presidency in 1864 a national calamity.

GOUVERNEUR M. OGDEN. One of the most important of the Columbia trustees, and as treasurer of the college, a watchdog on its expenditures; the diary reveals him as conservative, intelligent, and gloomy.

FREDERICK LAW OLMSTED. Left his work with Central Park to become General Secretary of the Sanitary Commission, and intermediary between it and the high Washington officials. Being responsible for the efficient operation of the Commission, he selected personnel, supervised preparations to meet medical needs, coordinated the various parts of the great machine, and in fact oversaw all details. He was a man of initiative, patience, endless energy, and foresight, but not tact. His decisive acts, stubborn insistence on having his own way, and intensity of temper made enemies.

FITZ-JOHN PORTER. Strong reached the conclusion that he had probably been guilty of misconduct in the battle of Second Manassas, and that he deserved his court-martial and dismissal. "What floored Porter was the McClellan letter and McDowell's evidence," he wrote early in 1863.

SAMUEL B. RUGGLES. Strong's influential father-in-law, busy in many public fields, remained well throughout the war. He conferred often with his friend Seward and lobbied for important legislation. In 1863, going to Berlin to attend an International Statistical Convention, he used the opportunity to promote the Northern cause in Prussia. Like Strong, he became a warm admirer of Lincoln, and when the President was shot made a statement remarkable for so kindly a man: "The one consolatory fact connected with Lincoln's death is that he cannot pardon his murderer."

WILLIAM H. SEWARD. The Secretary of State appears repeatedly in the diary, not always in an impressive fashion. We are told of a notable dinner party given by Ruggles in Washington in 1863 at which Seward talked continuously from half-past five until eleven.

CHARLES JANEWAY STILLÉ. One of the most active men in the Sanitary Commission, and later its historian. This cultivated Philadelphia lawyer and writer, who became provost of the University of Pennsylvania, gave his whole energies to the Union cause. He wrote a telling pamphlet, "How a Free People Conduct a Long War" (1862), which was circulated in hundreds of thousands of copies; and Strong tells how its fame led the Lincoln Administration to consider making him head of a Bureau of Emancipation.

CHARLES E. STRONG. Upon the cousin and partner of the diarist fell the heavy burden of the Wall Street law office whenever the combined needs of the Sanitary Commission, Columbia College, and Trinity Church absorbed nearly all of George Templeton Strong's energies. The diary reflects the almost perfect harmony of opinion and outlook between the two men.

ELLEN RUGGLES STRONG. The diarist's pride in his wife reached even greater heights as the war revealed unsuspected qualities in her. She threw herself wholeheartedly into war work and when, in the spring of 1862, she won her husband's reluctant permission to serve on some of the Sanitary Commission's hospital ships in Southern waters, she astonished him by her physical endurance and her executive ability as much as she worried him with her disregard of danger. "What a plucky little thing she is!" he wrote; and how proud he was of her "stepping naturally into command of our volunteer corps of nurses" on the ships. Mrs. Strong made frequent and protracted visits to Washington during these years, meeting notable personages and getting an inside view of the political machinery.

GULIAN C. VERPLANCK. As lawyer, political veteran, and litterateur, nobody in New York was more warmly liked than Verplanck; but as the bitterness of the conflict grew, his Copperhead tendencies led to his deposition from the presidency of the Century Club—a step which Strong half approved, half lamented.

FRANCIS VINTON. This highly educated and fluent preacher, who had begun life as a soldier, might have been a bishop of Indiana, but preferred to become assistant minister of Trinity. Though his reputation for eloquence attracted large audiences, Strong writhed under the inanity and wretched taste of many of his sermons.

THE PRINCE OF WALES (later Edward VII). His visit in 1860 turned New York society topsy-turvy and produced an epidemic of tuft-hunting that disgusted Strong. Dr. Vinton of Trinity Church proved particularly obsequious, and even the rugged Peter Cooper fawned upon the royal guest.

RICHARD GRANT WHITE. The Shakespearean critic helped Strong judge a contest for the best patriotic song in 1861, drilled with the diarist for a time in the New York Rifles, and was active in the Sanitary Fair which Mrs. Strong helped supervise. But Strong, though frequently having White at his house, somewhat distrusted him as "a decorated, flamboyant gent."

1860

ADELINA PATTI · DARWIN'S *ORIGIN OF SPECIES* · THE
DEMOCRATIC SCHISM · VISIT OF THE PRINCE OF WALES ·
LINCOLN'S ELECTION · SOUTH CAROLINA SECEDES

*A*s the year 1860 opened, the antagonism between the North and South
seemed fast ripening toward a breach. The Speakership contest still
dragged on in Washington; moderate leaders all over the North were organizing Union meetings to express their alarm; and while Northern free-soilers
demanded the exclusion of slavery from all the territories, the Southern extremists called for the enactment of a Slave Code which could protect slave-
owners in each territory until it adopted its own constitution and was admitted as a state. Congress presented a chaotic spectacle, the three parties
spending their energy in vituperation and wrangling, and ignoring the business of the nation. Not until January was almost over was a Speaker elected
—Pennington of New Jersey, a staunch Republican of Whig antecedents.
Even then sectional passions continued to run high. The Kansas question was not
yet settled, and Democratic leaders had given notice that President Buchanan
would veto a bill for admission under the free-soil Wyandotte Constitution;
personal affrays between Congressmen were still reported; the New York
Tribune was selling enormous numbers of a pamphlet summary of Helper's
book for twenty-five cents; and a Congressional committee was probing the
John Brown affair and stirring up feeling by hearing a long list of witnesses.
Europe, since the peace of Villafranca, was fairly quiet—so quiet that the
Prince of Wales would soon appear in Canada and the United States. Perhaps
the greatest sensation of January was a horrible catastrophe at Lawrence,
Massachusetts, on the afternoon of the 10th. The great Pemberton mill col-
lapsed in a sudden crash while some six or seven hundred operatives were at

work; and about two hundred persons, many of them girls, were either crushed to death or roasted alive in the flames which soon swept the wreckage.

January 1, SUNDAY.   New Year's Day. God prosper the New Year to those I love. Church with Ellie and Johnny; an effective sermon by Higby. Thereafter we took a cold "constitutional" up the Fifth Avenue to Forty-second Street, a rather vigorous winter day, still and sharp. Tonight is overcast, with promise of snow tomorrow.

January 5.   With Ellie to the Artists' "Reception" in Dodworth's Rooms; a vast crowd. Discovered Mrs. D. C. Murray and Mrs. John Weeks, General Dix, Wenzler, Stone, Rossiter, Mrs. Field (commonly distinguished as "the murderess," being mixed up a little with the Duc de Praslin affair),[1] the Rev. Mr. Frothingham, Lewis Rutherfurd, and others. Many bad pictures on the walls, and some few good ones. Eastman Johnson and Charles Dix are making progress. Wenzler has a lovely portrait of one of Dr. Potts's daughters. Stone's portrait of my two little men was there, and people praised it—to *me*.

Monday the second was kept for New Year's Day. It was a fine specimen of crisp frosty weather, with a serene sky and a cutting wind from the northwest. I set forth at eleven o'clock in my own particular hack, *en grand seigneur*, and effected more than twenty calls, beginning with Mrs. Samuel Whitlock in 37th Street. My lowest south latitude was Dr. Berrian's and the Lydigs'. There were no incidents. Bishop Potter's drawing-room was perhaps the dullest place I visited. The Bishop is always kindly and cordial, but nature has given him no organ for the secretion of the small talk appropriate to a five minutes' call. He feels the deficiency and is nervous and uncomfortable. Very nice at Mrs. George F. Jones's, and at Mrs. William Schermerhorn's. At Mrs. Peter A. Schermerhorn's, in University Place, I discovered the mamma and Miss Ellen, both very gracious. At Mrs. William Astor's, Miss Ward (the granddaughter of the house; Sam Ward's daughter by his first wife) talked of her friend Miss Annie Leavenworth. . . . Mrs. Edgar was charming in her little bit of a house, the "Petit Trianon." Poor Mrs. Douglas Cruger seems growing old, is less vivacious and less garrulous. At Mrs. Serena Fearing's I was honored with a revelation of the baby that was produced last summer.

---

[1] Henry M. Field, brother of Cyrus W. and David Dudley Field, had married (May, 1851) Laure Desportes, who was innocently involved in the famous Choiseul-Praslin murder case in France. Rachel Field has told the story in *All This and Heaven Too* (1938).

Pleasant visit to Mrs. Christine Griffin, née Kean—where little Miss Mary was looking her loveliest. That little creature will make havoc in society a year or two hence, when she "comes out." She is very beautiful and seems full of life and intelligence. Mrs. Isaac Wright in Waverley Place, with her brood of four noble children rampaging about her, was good to see. . . .

Home at six, tired after a pleasant day's work. We had a comfortable session at dinner with Dr. Peters and Mrs. Georgey Peters, Miss Annie Leavenworth, Miss Josephine Strong, Walter Cutting, Richard Hunt, Murray Hoffman, George C. Anthon, Jem Ruggles, and Jack Ehninger. Dinner was successful.

January 7. Walked uptown with George Anthon, who entertained me with the biography of his runaway cousin, Miss "Unadilla" Elmendorf, and incidents of the elopement, which is chronicled in newspaper paragraphs as a "marriage in high life." The girl is illegitimate, and her Lochinvar a noted swindler of tailors and hotelkeepers and a parasite of opera troupes, but full of talent and impudence. He made his way into the barbarous State of Virginia to report John Brown's execution for *Frank Leslie's* or some other newspaper when almost—or quite—every other reporter was repulsed and excluded by the natives.

January 9. To Columbia College meeting, Lafayette Place, at two in the afternoon. . . . I moved that Lieber's opening lecture of his present Law School course be printed, which was carried.

Thereafter to Tenth Street Studio Building to call on Leutze; I spent an hour with him pleasantly. I saw his "Battle of Princeton" picture, and another, a Venetian scene—masqueraders in a gondola, the Bridge of Sighs overhead, the corpse of a state criminal just brought out into another boat, upon which the riotous festive party comes suddenly and unawares. This latter picture is unfinished, but will be among the best things Leutze has done.

January 10. House of Representatives not yet organized, no Speaker elected and government at a deadlock. Members spend their time during the interval between the ballotings in speech-making about John Brown, fugitive slaves, Hinton Rowan Helper's *Impending Crisis*, and the irrepressible nigger generally. That black but comely biped is becoming a bore to me. No doubt he is a man and a brother, but his monopoly of attention is detrimental to the rest of the family; and I don't believe he cares much about having his wrongs redressed or his rights asserted. Our politicians are playing on Northern love of justice and a more or less morbid Northern philanthropy for their own selfish ends by putting themselves forward as Cuffee's champion. But the South is so utterly barbaric and absurd that I'm constantly tempted to ally myself with Cheever and George Curtis.[2]

January 11. News today of a fearful tragedy at Lawrence, Massachusetts, one of the wholesale murders commonly known in newspaper literature as accident or catastrophe. A huge factory, long notoriously insecure and ill-built, requiring to be patched and bandaged up with iron plates and braces to stand the introduction of its machinery, suddenly collapsed into a heap of ruins yesterday afternoon without the smallest provocation. Some five or six hundred operatives went down with it— young girls and women mostly. An hour or two later, while people were working frantically to dig out some two hundred still under the ruins, many of them alive and calling for help, some quite unhurt, fire caught in the great pile of debris, and these prisoners were roasted. It is too atrocious and horrible to think of.

Of course, nobody will be hanged. Somebody has murdered about two hundred people, many of them with hideous torture, in order to save money, but society has no avenging gibbet for the respectable millionaire and homicide. Of course not. He did not want to or mean to do this massacre; on the whole, he would have preferred to let these people live. His intent was not homicidal. He merely thought a great deal about making a large profit and very little about the security of human life. He did not compel these poor girls and children to enter his accursed mantrap. They could judge and decide for themselves whether they would be employed there. It was a matter of contract between capital and labor; they were to receive cash payment for their services. No doubt the legal representatives of those who have perished will be duly paid the fractional part of their week's wages up to the date when they became incapacitated by crushing or combustion, as the case may be, from rendering further service. Very probably the wealthy and liberal proprietor will add (in deserving cases) a gratuity to defray funeral charges. It becomes us to prate about the horrors of slavery! What Southern capitalist trifles with the lives of his operatives as do our philanthropes of the North?

January 17, TUESDAY. Mr. Ruggles is quite ill at Lockport (Governor Hunt's), so ill that Mrs. Ruggles and Miss Bostwick go thither tomorrow. He went to Buffalo, last Thursday was a week, to attend to some railroad receivership and caught severe cold on the journey. Our cars

---

[2] The Rev. George B. Cheever, author of *God Against Slavery* (1857); George William Curtis, now attacking slavery in his speeches and writings.

in wintertime, with their sloppy floors, red-hot stoves, and currents of chill air from opened doors and windows, are perilous traps for colds and inflammations. He took refuge at Governor Hunt's after two or three days of indisposition, which he was obliged to neglect, and was threatened with congestion of the lungs. He is reported by telegraph "mending slowly" but has been heavily dosed with anodynes and other vigorous medicaments that have weakened and depressed him. We have but just learned how seriously ill he has been, and Ellie feels quite uneasy, but I hope without sufficient cause.

January 19. Mr. Ruggles reported by telegraph "improving," but not strong enough to travel.

January 20. Anxious about Mr. Ruggles at Lockport. A telegram from Jem, received just before dinnertime, announced that "the physicians thought" him improving slowly, which was satisfactory enough, but for the inference, strained perhaps, that Jem did *not* think so.

January 22, SUNDAY. This afternoon lots of people called to ask for news of Mr. Ruggles. I saw D'Oremieulx, D. B. Fearing, and Miss Mary Morris Hamilton. . . . Afterwards George Anthon came in . . . also Dr. Peters. I stated to the doctor what I know of Mr. Ruggles's case, and his prognosis was, on the whole, decidedly encouraging. He thinks the nervous and cerebral trouble in a patient of Mr. Ruggles's peculiar temperament (especially after treatment with narcotics and quinine) likely to occur after any acute attack of disease, and not grounds for serious apprehension.

January 25. Wolcott Gibbs called by appointment tonight. We microscopized energetically, and the performances terminated with a very modest supper of chicken and hock. Gavitt was to have joined us but made default. We studied the Ross 1/12 objective and examined the circulation in the tail of a tadpole and a kitty fish, which I brought uptown with me from the little aquarium shop in Fulton Street this afternoon. Results were satisfactory. My binocular is unquestionably an acquisition. It shews certain structures better than the Ross instrument.

The Rev. Mr. Bellows, who called at breakfast time this morning to ask after Mr. Ruggles, is my authority for the following diplomatic

Scene at the Tuileries. A State dinner. The Honorable Mr. Mason, F.F.V., (our Minister to France), and Don Somebody, the Spanish Ambassador, glowering at each other across the table, during intervals of deglutition, each timidly desiring to establish himself in rapport with the other.

Spain. Breaking the ice: "Parlez-vous français, M'sieu Masón?"

America. With effort: "Ung Poo." (A pause) "Permit me, Sir, to ask whether you speak the English language?"

Spain: "Small." (Conversation closes.)

February 2. After dinner with Ellie to No. 24, where I left her, and then seeing a glow in the southern sky over the roof of the Union Place Hotel, I started in pursuit of the fire. I dog-trotted to Grand Street before I found it. A great tenement house in Elm Street near Grand burning fiercely. Scores of families had been turned out of it into the icy streets and bitter weather. Celtic and Teutonic fathers and mothers were rushing about through the dense crowd in quest of missing children. A quiet, respectable German was looking for his two (the elder "was eight years old and could take care of himself, but the younger had only nine months and couldn't well do so"). I thought of poor little Johnny frightened and unprotected in a strange scene of uproar and dark night and the glare of conflagration and piercing cold, and of Babbins, and tried to help the man but without success. There were stories current in the crowd of lives lost in the burning house; some said thirty, others two. The latter statement probably nearer the truth. Steam fire engines are a new element in our conflagrations and an effective one, contributing to the *tout ensemble* a column of smoke and sparks, and a low shuddering, throbbing bass note, more impressive than the clank of the old-fashioned machines. . . .

There is a Speaker at last. Sherman withdrew, and the Republicans elected Pennington of New Jersey (Bill Pennington's father), who seems a very fit man for the place. Reading Agassiz's *Essay on Classification.* Rather hard reading for anyone not thoroughly learned in a score of -ologies. But I can see and appreciate its general scope and hold it to be a very profound and valuable book.

February 3. Last night's Elm Street fire was a sad business. Some eighteen or twenty people perished. There was another fire in Lexington Avenue (dwelling houses) due to these pestilent furnaces. Two factories have just been blown to bits in Brooklyn by defective or neglected steam-boilers, with great destruction of life. We are still a semi-barbarous race. But the civilizing element also revealed itself this morning at the Tombs, when Mr. Stephens was hanged for poisoning his wife. If a few owners or builders of factories and tenement houses could be hanged tomorrow, life would become less insecure.

February 6, MONDAY. Just from opera, *Puritani,* with Ellie and Mrs. Georgey Peters and Dr. Carroll. Little Patti, the new prima donna, made a brilliant success.[3] Her voice is fresh, but wants volume and expression as yet; vocalization perfect. . . .

Columbia College meeting at two P.M. Resolved to appropriate the President's house and Professor Joy's to College purposes, turn them into lecture rooms, and so forth. A good move. It is contemplated to build a new house for the President on Forty-ninth Street, which I think questionable. I brought up some matters connected with the Law School, which went to the appropriate committee, and instigated King to introduce the question of suppressing these secret societies, which do immense mischief in all our colleges. John Weeks has just taken a young brother of his from Columbia College and sent him into the country, because he found that the youth belonged to some mystic association designated by two Greek letters which maintained a sort of club room over a Broadway grocery store, with billiard tables and a bar. Whether it be possible to suppress them is another question. Result was that King is instructed to correspond with the authorities of other colleges and see whether any suggestions can be got from them and whether anything can be done by concerted action. . . .[4]

February 10. Opera tonight with Ellie and Mrs. Georgey Peters and her papa; *Der Freischütz* in an Italian version. The Germanism of that opera is so intense that any translation of its text is an injustice to Weber's memory, but its noble music can afford to be heard under disadvantages. Max was Stigelli, and very good. Agatha (Colson) was respectable. She knew how her music ought to be sung and tried hard, but had not the vigor it demands. Caspar (Junca) was pretty bad.

Query: if there ever existed a Caspar who could sing "Hier in diesem Jammerthal" as it ought to be sung, or an Agatha who could do justice to the glorious allegro that follows her "leise, leise, fromme Weise"? I enjoyed the evening, also Wednesday evening, when we had Charley Strong and wife in "our box" and heard *The Barber*, delightfully rendered. Little Patti made a most brilliant Rosina and sang a couple of English songs in the "Music Lesson" scene, one of them ("Coming through the Rye") simply and with much archness and expression. This little debutante is like to have a great career and to create a furor in Paris and St. Petersburg within five years. . . .

[3] Adelina Patti, now about to enter her eighteenth year, had made her operatic debut in New York in 1859.

[4] Fraternities were well planted at Columbia. Alpha Delta Phi had been chartered there in 1836, and three other fraternity chapters had been organized in the 1840's. Francis Henry Weeks took his degree at Williams College in 1864.

Last night I attended W. Curtis Noyes's first lecture before the Law School of Columbia College.[5] It was carefully prepared, and (to my great relief) honored by an amply sufficient audience. The lecture room was densely filled, and Oscanyan told me sixty or seventy were turned away. We may have to resort to the Historical Society lecture room (in Second Avenue).

There is much less talking of politics now that a Speaker is elected. I think a cohesive feeling of nationality and Unionism gains strength silently both North and South, and that the Republican party has lost and is daily losing many of the moderate men who were forced into it four years ago by the Kansas outrages and the assault on Sumner. If the South would spare us its brag and its bad rhetoric, it would paralyze any Northern free-soil party in three weeks. But while Toombs speechifies and Governor Wise writes letters, it's hard for any Northern man to keep himself from Abolitionism and refrain from buying a photograph of John Brown.

Southern chivalry is a most curious and instructive instance of the perversion of a word from its original meaning; *lucus a non lucendo* seems a plausible derivation when one hears that word applied to usages and habits of thought and action so precisely contrary to all it expressed some five hundred years ago. Chivalry in Virginia and Georgia means violence to one man by a mob of fifty calling itself a Vigilance Committee, ordering a Yankee school mistress out of the state because she is heterodox about slavery, shooting a wounded prisoner, assailing a non-combatant like Sumner with a big bludgeon and beating him nearly to death. Froissart would have recognized the Flemish boor or the mechanic of Ghent in such doings. Sir Galahad and Sir Lancelot in the *Morte d'Arthur* would have called them base, felon, dishonorable, shameful, and foul.

Burke announced sixty years ago that "the age of chivalry" was gone, and "that of calculators and economists had succeeded it." Their period has likewise passed away now, south of the Potomac, and has been followed by a truculent mob despotism that sustains itself by a system of the meanest eavesdropping and espionage and of utter disregard of the rights of those who have not the physical power to defend themselves against overwhelming odds, that shoots or hangs its enemy or rides him on a rail when it is one hundred men against one and lets him alone when

[5] William Curtis Noyes (1805–1864), one of the foremost New York lawyers, and owner of a magnificent law library, had distinguished himself in numerous cases; notably in the prosecution of the Wall Street forger Huntington, and in protecting the New Haven Railroad stockholders from the consequences of Schuyler's embezzlement.

evenly matched, and is utterly without mercy for the weak or generosity for the vanquished. This course of practice must be expected of any mere mob when rampant and frightened, but the absurdity is that they call it "chivalry." There was something truly chivalric in old John Brown's march with his handful of followers into the enemy's country to redeem and save those he held to be unjustly enslaved at peril of his own life. For that enterprise he was hanged, justly and lawfully, but there was in it an element of chivalry, genuine though mistaken, and criminal because mistaken, that is not to be found in the performances of these valiant vigilance committeemen.

February 17. Old Stephen Whitney dead, leaving (some say) fifteen millions behind him.[6] That may be exaggerated, but he was close-fisted enough to have saved up thirty without doing the least good to himself or anyone else. His last act was characteristic and fitting. He locked up his checkbook and died.

D. Appleton & Company had issued Darwin's The Origin of Species *in 1859; and it forthwith encountered the warm approbation of a large group of scientists, and the fierce antagonism of most clergymen and religious editors. During the 1840's the works of the English Tractarians had provoked a bitter controversy; since then the writings of Strauss on Christianity had created a tempest in the limited American circles which knew them through George Eliot and others; but the storm of indignant abuse which fell upon Darwin and his American publishers exceeded all precedent. The publishing house was deluged with hundreds of threatening letters. A distinguished clergyman wrote William H. Appleton that divine wrath would be visited upon him in this world and through all eternity. The Appletons pointed out that giving their imprint to a volume did not necessarily mean that they gave it their approval. Nevertheless, they became keenly interested in the new scientific works of Darwin, Herbert Spencer, Huxley, Tyndall, and other Englishmen, and with E. L. Youmans as adviser were soon specializing in their publication. Strong's notes on Darwin are an interesting evidence that his ideas —though combated by Agassiz and others—exercised considerable influence in the United States even before the Civil War.*

[6] Moses Y. Beach's *Wealthy Citizens of New York* (1845) had listed Whitney, a merchant, cotton speculator, and real estate investor whom it described as "a very shrewd manager and close in his dealings," as worth ten millions and standing next John Jacob Astor in wealth.

February 18. Spent this evening diligently cutting the leaves of Darwin's much discussed book on *The Origin of Species* and making acquaintance with its general scope and aim. It's a laborious, intelligent, and weighty book. First obvious criticism on it seems this: that Darwin has got hold of *a* truth which he wants to make out to be *the* one generative law of organic life. Because he shews that the fauna and flora of a group of islands lying near a certain continent are so like those of that continent, though differing specifically therefrom, and so unlike those of other regions more remote, as to make it probable that they are the offspring of the continental species modified by the altered conditions of their new habitat, he considers himself entitled to affirm that *all* beasts, birds, and creeping things, from mammal to medusa, are developments from one stock, and that man is the descendant of some ancestral archaic fish, with swimming bladder improved into lungs, that flying fish have by successive minute steps of progress through countless ages become albatrosses, and flying squirrels bats. But I suspect that He who created and upholds this great marvelous system of various harmonious life is not obliged to conformity with any *one* Law of Creation and preservation that Darwin's or any other finite intellect can discover.

Darwin asks rather large concessions. You must begin by giving him thousands of millions of millions of years (that Johnny Strong would be puzzled to read were they expressed in Arabic numerals) for the operation of his Law of Progress, and admit that the silence of the stratified record of those ages as to its operation and existence may be explained away; and then, the want of affirmative evidence to sustain his theory being accounted for, he can make out a plausible case for it by suggesting that "it may have been"; "why should not"; "we may suppose that," and the like.

The period required for the production of the whole animal world from a single parent stock (and he holds that both the animal and vegetable races have one common primeval parent, a diatom, I suppose) by the working of his imaginary law of natural selection is even beyond the all but inconceivable procession of ages which he concedes that his theory calls for. Let us see. We have records of the condition of animal life in certain of its departments that go back to the earliest picture writing of Egypt and become more and more abundant and minute as they approach our own days. Those of the last two hundred years are copious and elaborate. During the last fifty, a mass of evidence has been collected that could hardly be read through in one lifetime. The superficial area covered by investigations thus recorded in our own day is immensely great; that is, 25,000 miles of European coast line alone, studied almost inch by inch, every zoological province of all the earth's surface investigated (though, of course, not exhaustively) by inquisitive travelers and men of science. Practical men, stimulated by hope of profit in money, have been working hard and intelligently to modify existing breeds or species by changing all their original or natural relations to climate, food, and habit, and perpetuating as far as they could every improvement in the breed artificially or accidentally produced. But no symptom of the change of one species to another has been produced or has occurred within the historic period. There is not even a legend of the ancient identity of lion and eagle, no tradition of a period before horse and ass; geese and ducks were distinct animals. No development of new organs or new functions by any animal is anywhere recorded or traceable. Scientific breeders after centuries of vigilant work have produced various types of horse, sheep, pigeon, and so forth; but these several types lose their respective peculiarities, unless their purity be carefully maintained. (Note Darwin's statement about the tendency of peculiarities of the rock pigeon, the original progenitor, to recur in the fancy breeds, pouter and tumbler and so forth.) The area covered by scientific research and by experiments in breeding for the last century is equivalent (in considering Darwin's theory) to scores of thousands of years of recorded observation in a single district. But however this may be, man's experience for, we will say, only four thousand years furnishes no instance of the development of new functions or new organs by any animal or vegetable organism.

February 25. Efficient in Wall Street. Pio Nono, "the Pope, that pagan full of pride," is on bad terms with the Eldest Son of the Church, that unprincipled Ghibelline, Louis Napoleon. Unless the Ravaillacs and Jacques elements are extinct, Louis Napoleon may be in danger.

February 29. Went alone to Philharmonic rehearsal at Academy of Music. Watched Hazeltine and pretty Helen Lane billing and cooing just in front of me to the very appropriate accompaniment of Beethoven's lovely D Symphony. A sentimental gent would say that the handsome young couple and the glowing joyous music of that brightest of all Beethoven's greater works were each a sort of commentary on the other. Then I went to 24 Union Square and saw Mr. Ruggles, who left Lockport Monday, spent a day at Albany, and reached New York this morning. I paid him another visit this evening. He has convalesced rapidly and looks better than I expected to see him. I feared this perilous illness might have left him with energies impaired and faculties blunted, but he is quite himself, full of life and vigorous thought. He is not without his hobby, namely: there is, or seems to be, a political reaction against sectionalism, John Brownism, Higher Lawism, and the like. This is, therefore, a good opportunity to assert the claims of the church as a conservative law-loving institution against Calvinism and the ultra Protestant notions it has produced; to tell Union men throughout the country that they belong in the church; to define the limits of authority and private judgment in political ethics. A clear statement of all this might effect a great deal just at this time and would come with a certain authority from the committee appointed by the last general convention of which Mr. Ruggles is chairman.

Monday, Jem and George Anthon dined here, and we heard *Martha*, which is a very pretty opera. Last night I attended Noyes's second lecture before the Law School; crowded, like the first. That people should go away from a law lecture in New York for want of seats is without precedent. This school is the only one of our seeds of post-graduate instruction that survives and grows, our only university nucleus. If Betts and Ogden were less hopelessly inert, it might be developed into usefulness on a large scale.

March 2, FRIDAY.   Stopped at Barnum's on my way downtown to see the much advertised nondescript, the "What-is-it."[7] Some say it's an advanced chimpanzee, others that it's a cross between nigger and baboon. But it seems to me clearly an idiotic negro dwarf, raised, perhaps, in Alabama or Virginia. The showman's story of its capture (with three other specimens that died) by a party in pursuit of the gorilla on the western coast of Africa is probably bosh. The creature's look and action when playing with his keeper are those of a nigger boy. But his anatomical details are fearfully simian, and he's a great fact for Darwin.

March 3.   George Anthon called in Wall Street, and before going uptown, we stopped at Barnum's. The "What-is-it?" is palpably a little nigger and not a good-looking one. There are other animals in the establishment much more interesting; for example, a grand grizzly bear from California, a big sea lion, a very intelligent and attractive marbled or mottled seal (*phoca vitulina?*), a pair of sociable kangaroos, and (in the

[7] This "What-is-it?"—shortly to be viewed by the Prince of Wales—became the most famous circus freak in America. Often called "the missing link," he was really a Negro of distorted frame and cone-shaped head named William H. Johnson, who survived until 1926.

happy family cage) an armadillo, a curious spotted rodent said to be
Australian, two fine owls, and so forth.

March 4, SUNDAY. . . . Church this morning. Higby preached. Not up
to his average. Mr. Derby and Hoffman sat with us. Talked to Professor
Lieber who came home with us. In correspondence with him for a day or
two past. He's a troublesome subject. His sensibilities are lacerated because
he fears he "is to be a mere adjunct of Dwight's" in the Law School, and he
intends to decline all further share in its duties. Sorry to lose him. But he
ought to see that the school cannot be established and will not win students
unless training in practically useful and profitable knowledge (such knowledge of the Revised Statutes and Wendell and Cowen and Hill as it is
Dwight's office to impart) be its prominent feature. Lieber's political
philosophy and spirit of laws and Nairne's legal ethics must be gradually
worked into the system. If we make them essential and obligatory portions
of the course at once, we shall simply frighten students away and dwarf or
destroy the school, as a yearling baby would be stunted or killed by a diet
of beef and madeira. . . .

March 5. . . . Did little in Wall Street. Columbia College trustees met
at two P.M. and accomplished little, except to decide on building a president's house on the college grounds, which might better have been left
undone. Mr. Ruggles appeared at the meeting, unexpectedly and perhaps
rather imprudently. . . .

March 6. . . . Looking further into Darwin's *Origin of Species* this
evening. Though people who don't like its conclusions generally speak
of it as profound and as a formidable attack on received notions, I timidly
incline to think it a shallow book, though laboriously and honestly written.

Darwin cannot understand why Omnipotent Power and Wisdom should
have created so many thousand various types of organic life, allied to each
other by various complex relations and differing in points of detail for which
we can assign no reason. He wants to shew that the original creative act was
on the smallest scale and produced only some one organism of the humblest
rank but capable of development into the fauna and flora of the earth,
from moss to oak and from monad to man, under his law of progress and
natural selection. To him, as to the physicists of the last one hundred
years, the notion of a supernatural creative power is repugnant and offensive. He wants to account for the wonderful, magnificent harmonies and
relations of the varied species of life that exist on earth by reducing the
original agency of supernatural power in their creation to a minimum. This
feeling sticks out at page 483, where he asks triumphantly, Do people

"really believe that . . . certain elemental atoms have been commanded suddenly to flash into living tissues?" (That passage is the keynote of the whole book.)

I must say I find it just as easy to answer that question in the affirmative as to admit that certain elemental atoms of lime, silex, carbon, oxygen, hydrogen, and so forth are daily and hourly "commanded to flash into" organic wood fibre, cellulose, parenchyma, and so on. The latter miracle is being performed on the largest scale this minute wherever vegetation is in progress; the former seems to occur only at long intervals. I can see no other distinction between them. One is familiar to our senses, the other is proved by deduction. They are a priori equally credible, or incredible, whichever Mr. Darwin pleases. The inorganic world has its own internal harmonies and relations quite as distinct and unmistakeable as the organic. But no law of progressive development can be inferred from them. Mr. Darwin would not venture to maintain that iodine and bromine are developments of chlorine or vice versa, that some one little dirty, obscure or obsolete element was parent and progenitor of osmium, iridium, ruthenium, and all the rest of the platinum group. Very possible that these so-called elements may be hereafter decomposed and proved to be composite, but we have no right to assume that they will be, and until analysis reduces the inorganic world to a series of compounds of only two primal entities, it will testify against Darwin's theory.

March 10. Dr. Cogswell's ghostly experience at the Astor Library is worth recording, but I wait for a more authentic report from K. Armstrong or Murray Hoffman.[8]

March 12, MONDAY. The night is damp and cloudy and raw as raw can be. Old Sands's spook is walking through the Astor Librarie. It lounges in the alcoves, it yawns and vainly looks for something entertaining in the outsides of the books. It is wholly out of business; it has but a choice of bores. The streets are chill and dreary, closed are the playhouse doors. It walks the Astor alcoves, having naught else to do. It is staring at shelf B 30, blasé and tired and blue.

Three several nights last winter the doctor caught it there. (He is a powerful scholar, as the ghost was well aware.)

"Mr. Sands," said Dr. Cogswell, "permit me, sir, to say, you have no business here tonight, and you must go away.

[8] Joseph Green Cogswell, now nearing seventy-five, who as head of the Astor Library occupied rooms there, had reported an interview with the ghost of the late Austin L. Sands, wealthy merchant and insurance man.

"The library's closed at five P.M. Its rules I must maintain. I must insist that you withdraw, and don't come back again.

"Why do you call this time of night and keep me out of bed? You never came in while living, and you shan't come now you're dead."

The ghost looked stern at the doctor. The doctor looked straight back, ready to fire off his Hebrew, and his Cælosyriac.

The ghost became embarrassed. It could think of nothing to say. Being in a false position, it quietly went away. It was glad to try the vanishing dodge, and it silently vanished away.

That's the true narrative of the apparition of Austin L. Sands, Esq., deceased, to Cogswell at the Astor Library on three several occasions, as detailed by him to Mrs. Burns and Hoppin, and so forth, at D. B. Fearing's dinner table. Cogswell has been working at the catalogue late at night, is nervous and shakey, and quite an old man now. So he is a likely subject for spectral illusions. I don't understand that he tells the story as anything more than an instance of hallucination. He has gone South to recruit and returns next Saturday. Some say that on one of their three interviews, the ghost answered Cogswell's vigorous allocution by saying that it came there "for variety."

March 14. Philharmonic rehearsal at three-thirty. Beethoven's *D Symphony*. Ellie joined me there (Academy of Music). . . .

The D Symphony is gorgeous. Pages of bosh might be written about it. It does not impress one with a sense of uncanny supernatural power, such as one feels in the *Eroica*, the A Symphony, and the C minor, but it is clear, healthy, genial, and sunshiny throughout; and in that respect is above all the three, except, of course, the C minor, in which doubt and darkness are so magnificently developed into light and victory. . . .

March 17. Rumors thicken of a movement to turn out some or all of Trinity Church vestry next Easter Tuesday. It's a coalition of St. John's Park lot owners with aggrieved assistant ministers. Morgan Dix's elevation has affronted them all, and Vinton, Ogilby, and Higby think they have special gravamina besides. I will cheerfully subscribe a trifle toward the expenses of any movement to turn out myself, if my proposed substitute be of average respectability. The office is no sinecure. Committee business consumes much time. Business relations with clergymen are bad for a layman; weaken his faith in the institution of the church and his respect for the clerical office. Higby and Ogilby, lobbying for more money and saying sharp, uncharitable things when they fail, tend to "disillusionate" a vestryman and degrade the clergy in his estimation. The priestly office is de-

graded with the individual, illogically but inevitably. I can't go to Trinity
Chapel and parade up and down the aisles with my official penny-grabbing
plate, without an unpleasant sense that Higby's sharp, shrewish wife and
plain-spoken daughters are looking at me as that horrid Strong, who is one
of the close-fisted set that won't let Pa have the money he wants, and that
nice Mrs. Hobart, true to her wifely instincts, feels aggrieved because I
helped to promote Dix over her husband's head. Consciousness of this
has turned the scale and kept me at home more than once when I should
have gone to church. So I've not the least objection to being turned out,
but there is little chance the opposition ticket will succeed. Bleecker and
John R. Livingston are probably doing what they can to help it, but neither
can do much, and I'm satisfied we ought to drop Bleecker.

March 19.   George Wood died yesterday. A very great lawyer, with
an intellect that worked slowly but most effectively, like a heavy siege
gun. Any sharp-witted man could outmanoeuvre him at *nisi prius*, but
with time for preparation and on a question of principle, he was irresistible.

March 22.   Went after dinner through the snowstorm to hear Bradford's Law School lecture "On the Historical Connexion of Civil with
Common Law"; a scholar-like performance, but I wish Bradford pronounced
his Latin quotations better.[9] On my way home found the St. Denis Hotel
(corner Broadway and Eleventh Street) on fire; crowd, clamor and excitement. The fire was in the roof, made little show and was probably soon
put out by the overwhelming force of engines. . . .

I think we are to be administrationed into a second Mexican War.
Judge Daly lectured at Law School Tuesday night on maritime law, very
fairly.[10] He has read and studied and worked since he came to man's
estate, but the want of early education and culture cannot be supplied, and
shews itself in little aberrations from the line of correct diction and relevant
thought.

March 24, SATURDAY.   With Ellie this morning at Academy of Music
and heard the lovely D Symphony rehearsed. How much thought and work
are embodied in its transcendent larghetto! That movement seems as if it
might have been written as the musical exposition of some poem, or
story—an impression Beethoven's music seldom produces on me. There
is a *special* character about the sentiment of its phrases and their grouping

[9] Alexander Warfield Bradford (1815–1867), former surrogate for the city and
county of New York, was particularly erudite in church law.

[10] This, of course, was the eminent Recorder Charles P. Daly (1816–1899), who
rose from cabin-boy at sea to be head of the city bench in New York.

that suggests correspondence with or illustration of some series of varied incident or imagery; something of Goethe's or Schiller's, perhaps, but I cannot guess at the key. It might be *The Winter's Tale* or *Merchant of Venice*, or the like. These plays are of about the degree of intensity embodied in this movement.

March 27.   Tonight at Noyes's Law School lecture in Lafayette Place. The "Law of Lights" its subject. Noyes has been so busy with his "omnibus" New Haven Railroad case that he could not prepare for a third lecture on colonial jurisprudence. . . . I inspected St. George's chapel in Beekman Street this morning; my first visit for about twenty-five years. It is a very shabby church, undoubtedly. No doubt its Rev. Rector Mr. Brown cleans the pews and sweeps the gallery.

March 29.   Conferred with Dan Messenger and with Albert Mathews. Messenger is to go to Rome and Florence after his work is finished at London. While at Florence, he will probably be requested by Dr. Crane of the United States Army and others of Mrs. Captain Brannan's family to look into the truth of this strange story of her recognition at Florence last February by a Mrs. Carpenter of Philadelphia. Mrs. Brannan disappeared mysteriously a year or two since. Was last seen at Staten Island leaving a ferryboat and entering a carriage that was to take her home. She was not very young, nor particularly attractive; had no lover that any one knows of, and her habits were very quiet and domestic. It has been taken for granted that she was foully made away with, perhaps by her hack driver, but the most diligent investigation by policemen and detectives was fruitless. These Carpenter people know her perfectly well, it seems, saw her more than once at Florence, accosted her at last and demanded of her what she meant by being there and alive, when her remains ought to be mouldering to dust in Richmond County. She fled in great agitation. Shortly thereafter they received a letter signed by another name, but purporting to come from Mrs. Brannan, begging that they would keep her resurrection quiet.

Very puzzling. But it may be a case of mistaken identity. A certain considerable proportion of the English and American lady-sojourners in Florence, being stopped suddenly in the street and asked, "Why did you leave your husband?" would find the position embarrassing. The letter may have been written for the purpose of keeping the Carpenters under their mistaken impression. But in any view of the case, it is a dark and mysterious transaction that stimulates one's curiosity. . . .

Then with Ellie to a grand dinner at Edmund Schermerhorn's bachelor establishment in the old Great Jones Street house. We were twenty. I took in Mrs. William Astor; Edmund on the other side, and little Mrs. Lewis Jones opposite. Got through the evening decently well. Mrs. William Astor (who was a daughter of Abraham Schermerhorn's) is pleasant. The rest were Dan Fearing, Mrs. Sheldon, Jemmy Otis, Neale, Edward Jones, sumptuous Miss Lily Mason (Henry Mason's daughter), young Bowdoin, Miss Stuyvesant, nice Miss Ellen Schermerhorn (who attends Philharmonic rehearsals and "loves" the D Symphony), and so on.

Tuesday afternoon word was brought to Charley (at the office) that a lady wanted to see him downstairs. He responded to the summons, and as he didn't come back, I took it for granted that it was Mrs. Charley who had carried him off to pay a bill. But it was poor Mrs. Bob LeRoy. She had just arrived from Philadelphia and walked to Wall Street from the ferry, carrying her poor little carpet-bag, unescorted. Charley took her up town to Jullien's Hotel in Washington Place, left her there, and went after Bob, who was lying on a sofa at the New York Club in drunken slumber. Bob was horrified when called in to face his wife. He would go straight out of town, to his sister's (Mrs. DeKoven's) by the very next train, would set out at once and *walk* there, if Charley would only go back and say he had not been able to find him. But Charley was inexorable and lugged Bob off. He encountered no reproaches, was not scolded. His poor wife only said, "Robert, my dear husband, why have you been staying all this time away from your wife and child?" Poor Bob could only answer, "I suppose you know why." And the loyal little woman said, "If you *were* desperate and reckless, to whom should you have come but to your wife?" and then Bob burst into a passion of penitent tears and maudlin self-reproach. He has not been sober for three weeks, and is half-maddened by incipient symptoms of delirium tremens. Was to have gone home to Philadelphia with his wife yesterday, but was too faint and ill. He may leave today. . . .

Sic transit: "The glories of our birth and state are shadows, not substantial things." Ten years ago, poor Bob was *the* great match whom scores of mammas were watching and way-laying. He had great wealth in prospect, wit, talent, information, a fine person, family, the best social position. Everyone thought Miss Amelia Lewis the luckiest of girls. Then came a brief period of splendid entertainments in his Twenty-second Street house, Mrs. LeRoy, a leader of New York society, "walking in silk attire," admired and envied and courted. And now poverty and disgrace, with scarce a gleam of hope. His father, old Black Jake, impoverished, dropped by every one; Bob a pauper, drinking himself to death. To be sure, he might live in a house in some pleasant village of Vermont or Connecticut, live there in state and rear a family to usefulness and honor, on his $2,000 income. He could amuse himself with his rod and gun, work at natural history (which he affects), microscopize, furnish papers for periodicals (*Harper's* and others), and be the cock of the village. But he is too far gone, I fear. His only chance is in his wife's influence. That is still controlling so long as he is in her presence. His recognition of her worth is almost the only right feeling that seems left to him. He told Charley with much feeling that she had not uttered a word of reproach or complaint. But the moment he is out of her sight, her influence ceases, and he thinks only of the present moment, poor fellow. He inherits Black Jake's blunted moral sense and want of self-control, and is not like to inherit much besides. The sins of the fathers are visited on the children in their hereditary proclivities to sin and weakness under temptation.

April 1. . . . Wolcott Gibbs unanimously elected a trustee of Astor Library, vice Washington Irving.

Bob LeRoy has gone to Philadelphia at last. His brother-in-law, De Koven, writes to Charley Strong that old Black Jake talks of withholding Bob's allowance of $1,000 per annum, and means to pay it only in case it can be raised from certain promising old assets of his exploded stock-broking firm. This would reduce Bob's income to less than $1,000 (of the Broadway property settled on his wife) and would bring matters to a crisis. He must either work in earnest or drink himself to speedy death with cheap liquor. . . .

April 2, MONDAY. To Trinity Church vestry meeting tonight. As I railroaded homeward at ten, there was much people in and around the *Tribune* office, waiting, no doubt, for returns of today's Connecticut election; the first gun fired in the presidential campaign. . . .

April 4. Met Ellie at the Academy of Music at three-thirty P.M. and heard the Philharmonic rehearsal of the Ninth Symphony. . . . Begin to appreciate the Ninth Symphony. Strange I should have so missed its real character, and overlooked so many great points when I heard it last. An immense, wonderful work; really among Beethoven's greater symphonies. Embodies as much thought and labor as almost any two of them together.

April 6. This being Good Friday, we went to Trinity Church. Even standing room could hardly be found. The aisles were crowded. As we could neither see nor hear, we came away before the sermon. The choral service, faintly heard, was impressive. Mere curiosity, no doubt, attracts many to the church. It is becoming fashionable to go down to Trinity and hear Vinton intone, but the weekday festivals often are far more generally recognized and more fully attended in every church than they were of old. . . . Home at ten. Found George Anthon here, bilious. He goes with Bever to a place called Milford in Pennsylvania on the Erie Railroad after trout. Death of Paulding,[11] and of Samuel Gouverneur Ogden (Mrs. Mowatt-Ritchie's father), one of the Shedden witnesses last fall, at eighty-one.

April 11. Went this evening to a "private view" of this year's Academy of Design exhibition, on a ticket sent me by Stone. The "private view" is more public and crowded and gives one less chance to see the pictures than any view one can take by day or night at any period of the annual exposition. There was a dense crowd tonight, and one could see nothing satisfactorily, but my first impression of this year's exhibition is favorable. It is certainly better than that of 1859.

Thence to a party at Mr. Ruggles's to celebrate his sixtieth birthday. It was very pleasant. Lots of notabilities attended. I discovered three ex-governors (Fish, King, and Hunt), General Scott, who was gracious, Dr. [Isaac I.] Hayes, the North Polar notability (who seemed clear-headed and capable), Dr. Hawks and Dr. Lieber, President King, the illustrious Bancroft, George Schuyler and wife, and Miss Mary Hamilton, Van Brunt ("on Spires"), De Trobriand, and others. The convives belonged mostly to the paleozoic period, contemporaries of their sexagenarian host; but the more recent strata were fairly represented.

April 13. Downtown after a solitary breakfast. Walter Cutting called to inform me that I had been unanimously elected by some convention or synod of men about town as one of a board or committee of twenty, which is hereafter to take charge of polite society, regulate its interests, keep it pure, and decide who shall be admitted hereafter to "Bachelors' Balls" and other annual entertainments. The committee is perpetual and fills its own vacancies. It is to pass on the social grade of everybody, by ballot—one blackball excluding. Outsiders have no voice and nothing to do but to be thankful for the privilege of paying an initiation fee and annual subscription, if we concede them that privilege. Very funny work for me to be concerned in; but I'm in good company. My colleagues are Judge Pendleton, Charles King, Hamilton Fish, Anson Livingston, John Astor, William Schermerhorn, and others of the same sort. Probably the whole project will come to nothing. . . .

---

[11] James K. Paulding (1778–1860), author of the novel *The Dutchman's Fireside* and much satirical and political work.

Tonight to Nairne's lecture at the Law School, one of his courses on ethics; subject, "The Ground of Moral Obligation." Very high-toned and quite forcible. Coleridgean in doctrine. Attendance slim, but mostly law students with pens and notebooks. Saw C. Wright. Tells me the Law School bill is through both houses, and signed. So we of the Law Committee of Columbia College are authorized to manufacture attorneys and counselors. Pity that nasty little New York University Law School of Judge Clerke's and P. Y. Cutler's should have got a little bill through, prescribing a shorter term of attendance.

Heard a good thing of John Van Buren's today.

Scene, Downing's Oyster Cellar. John Van Buren at the counter devouring his shilling's worth of bivalves. Dirty little ——, who has recently tried a case with John in which he was beat, and which he made a personal matter against John and John's client, steps up beside him, resolved to say something crushing.

Pettifogger *loquitur*. "Mr. Van Buren, is there any client so dirty that you wouldn't undertake his case?"

John Van Buren (swallows his oyster unmoved and looks over his shoulder at Pettifogger with an expression of concern). "Why, what *have* you been doing?"

Exit Pettifogger. . . .

April 14. Entered my appearance at Trinity Church as attending Mrs. Berrian's funeral, and then slipped out and joined Ellie, George Anthon, and Murray Hoffman at the Academy of Design. . . . Exhibition better than that of 1859. More landscapes than portraits, and almost as many genre pictures. Some of these last have decided merits; three or four little things by Eastman Johnson especially. Ehninger does himself credit and has improved. . . . Leutze's five pictures (the Princess Elizabeth in prison *tempore* Maria Regina, and Braddock's Defeat) do no justice to his talent, such as it is. There is a marvelous pre-Raphaelite Romeo and Juliet picture by some English artist, with all the faults of that school and some of its good points. In landscape, Durand is much as usual; Mignot very good; Jem Suydam far advanced beyond anything he has exhibited hitherto. Nothing from Church or Kensett ʰhat I remember. One good marine picture by Charles Dix, a colorful Pike's Peak picture by Bierstadt, not bad at all, and so on. . . .

I think there is nothing in the collection but journeyman's work, better or worse. Eastman Johnson's pictures alone strike me as possibly of higher grade. Their commonplace subjects are treated with genial and poetical feeling. They are fine in drawing and above the average in color. May's picture is another exception perhaps, but his subject, "Italian peasants," is so suggestive of conventionalism and formalism that one can hardly decide. The exhibition certainly presents fewer flagrant outrages on art than any I remember.

April 15, SUNDAY. Drove to Trinity Church this morning with Ellie and Johnny and resumed possession of the old pew in the north aisle. Very full congregation, and of every degree from the Astor-oid type down to the English or North-Irish emigrant family party. Choral service was impressive.

April 16. Augustus Perkins of Boston, just returned from Philadelphia, gives Charles E. Strong a very black report of poor shipwrecked Bob Le-Roy. A day or two after Bob reached Philadelphia, symptoms of delirium tremens set in. He saw people dodging him about the house, and so forth. His pretty little wife stood it for a night or two (he grew more wild and unmanageable at night) and finally had to send for Perkins, who slept a couple of nights in his room. He grew more and more ungovernable, tried to throttle Perkins in his sleep, and had to be sent to the Philadelphia Hospital at last, where he spent a week in a padded room. He is now slowly convalescing and watching for chances to smuggle in a surreptitious drink. Physicians report the case hopeless and consider him past the point of possible reformation.

April 17. After an apology for a dinner, I went to [Arnold] Guyot's lecture at the Law School. Well attended and very hot; lecture original and interesting. Thereafter discoursed with Guyot, whom I like, and General Scott, the most urbane of conquerors. Curious it is to observe the keen, sensitive interest with which he listens to every whisper about nominations for the coming presidential campaign.

The Charleston Convention will nominate Douglas, I think. Then comes the sanhedrim of the undeveloped Third Party. It is not at all unlikely Scott may be its nominee. In that case, it is possible the Republican Convention may adopt him. I wish things might take that course, but hardly hope it. Neither Douglas nor Hunter nor Banks suits me.

April 18. After energizing in Wall Street with reasonable diligence, met Ellie at the Academy of Music and heard the second rehearsal of the Ninth Symphony. It clears and brightens wonderfully on nearer acquaintance. After dinner we called for Mrs. Georgey Peters, and with Willy Alston to the Academy of Music again. Ellie enjoyed the evening and seems nowise fatigued. Opera was *Sonnambula*; small beer after Burgundy. Bellini's pretty melodies are "easy things to understand," but how flat and feeble and pale and unreal and Rosa–Matilda-esque they sound when one is fresh from trying to dig into that compact conglomerate of intensities, the Ninth Symphony! Samuel T. Coleridge, in his *Table Talk*, mentions some concert he had attended, and how he didn't like some piece by Rossini: "It sounded to him like nonsense verses. But he could hardly contain himself when something of Beethoven's was played." Coleridge was no special amateur of music, and does not seem to have cultivated his feeling for it.

April 21.   Letters from Robert LeRoy and his wife at Philadelphia are not encouraging as to the future of that unfortunate fellow. He writes of penitence, of the terrible lesson he has had, of reformation, and of work, to be sure. I dare say he was sincere when he did so. But there's no reliance to be placed in what he says or writes, for his self-determining power, if he ever had any, is utterly gone.

April 23.   No news of any action by the Democratic Charleston Convention. Douglas, the little giant, said to be losing ground.

April 26.   No Democratic nominee from Charleston, yet. Two to one on Douglas, I say.

The Democratic National Convention had met on April 23 at Charleston, a most unfortunate place for a gathering which badly needed a calm and conciliatory atmosphere. From the outset it was plain that the Douglas men from the North and West, believing in popular sovereignty, would not yield to the fire-eaters from the Cotton States who demanded that slavery be protected in the territories by a federal code. It was equally plain that the Southern extremists would not recede from their demand. Though the Douglas forces had a majority of the delegates, their opponents controlled a majority of the states (seventeen out of thirty-three) and were hence able to dominate the committees, and to name the chairman of the convention. The first great battle occurred in the platform committee. Here the Southern fire-eaters or pyrophagi, *as Strong calls them, adopted a majority report which declared that a territorial legislature had no power to abolish or impair slavery, and that it was the duty of the national government to give slavery, when necessary, its positive protection. The minority of Northern men in the committee reported a moderate plank reaffirming the popular sovereignty doctrine enunciated by the party four years earlier, and pledging the party to support the Dred Scott decision. When the two reports came up for debate, Yancey of Alabama bitterly reproached the*

Democrats of the North for declaring that slavery was wrong; they should have asserted "that slavery was right and therefore ought to be protected." Pugh of Ohio, as Douglas's spokesman, at once defiantly announced that the Northern Democrats would never make such a statement. "Gentlemen of the South," he shouted, "you mistake us—you mistake us; we will not do it!"

Strong's belief that Douglas would be nominated rested on the fact that he was much the strongest candidate the Democratic Party could nominate, and that if placed upon a moderate platform he would almost certainly win. But the Southern extremists would not listen to reason. On Monday the 30th, the convention adopted the Douglas platform, 165 to 138. The Southern delegates were almost solidly opposed to it. At once the chairman of the Alabama delegation rose and announced that his state would leave the convention. It was followed, as Strong notes below, by the withdrawal of six more states—the whole Cotton Kingdom. The convention then began balloting for a candidate. But although Douglas repeatedly obtained a majority of the votes, he could not attain the necessary two-thirds; and the gathering adjourned to meet in Baltimore on June 18th. The Cotton States seceders agreed to hold their own convention a few days earlier in Richmond. It was plain that the schism in the Democratic Party could not be healed.

April 27.   Little or nothing to record. Fine Day. Rumor this afternoon of schism in the Charleston Convention, certain Southern delegations of *pyrophagi* seceding. Not impossible, nor unlikely if the Convention refused to put the ultra proslavery plank of a slave code for the territories into its platform, and so throw away all chances of carrying any one Northern state. But I hope it's untrue, and that this congregation of profligate wire-pullers will mature its plans for the next campaign without any open rupture. For if disunion tendencies within the Democratic party are stronger than the cohesive power of public plunder and can disintegrate the party itself, it's a bad sign for our national unity.

April 30, MONDAY.   Everybody talks of the great Heenan and Sayers prize fight in England—the "international" fight—and of the American champion's unfair treatment. It occupies a much larger share of attention than the doings of the Charleston Convention, the results of which may be so momentous.

May 1, TUESDAY. . . . Some eight Southern delegations have seceded from the Charleston Convention. It refused to make a slave code for the territories an article of faith, and hence this schism. So the great National Democratic party is disintegrated and dead; broken up, like so many other organizations, by these pernicious niggers. It is a bad sign.

May 2. . . . Tonight, Professor Dwight and Gouverneur Ogden here, a sub-committee of the Columbia College Law committee, settling the form of the Law School diploma, under the Act of April 7th, and arranging other matters. There is hope that we can get a fraction of the graduating class to attend a third year, and we must set up another degree, "Master of Laws" perhaps, or some such thing, to be conferred on those who do so.

Rumor that old broken-down "Black Jake" LeRoy is about to marry some deluded young country girl of his Columbia County villagery. DeKoven says he never conceived of anything worse than this old rake's devilish malignity and bitterness against poor Bob, his only son, and for whose faults and excesses and fall he is so largely responsible. He exults over Bob's excesses and disgrace and distress, and "only hopes he may actually *see* him in the gutter some day"! Think of poor Bob, decidedly first among our "eligible," *the* great prize for which match-making mammas were ready to scratch out each other's eyes, and of poor Bob, 1853–57, with his splendid house and grand parties and lovely wife, and then think of Ellen and Mrs. Eleanor and Miss Cary clubbing together to send poor Mrs. Bob clothes to wear and raiment for the baby she expects in June!—and of Bob himself, sodden with drink, afraid to face his wife, and submitting to be rated and bullied by the few friends that still consent to recognize him. The true history of the LeRoys for the last ten years would make a brilliant "sensation" novel.

May 3. . . . The Democratic Convention has dissolved and dispersed *without nominating anybody*. It is to assemble again at Baltimore in June.

May 7. . . . Thank God for Ellie's safe *accouchement* . . . a man-child . . . a ten-pounder . . . with well-developed lungs. . . . Lewis Barton Strong is not an ill-sounding name.

May 11. . . . Stopped at Law School on my way down, with Mr. Ruggles, and conferred a little with the graduating class. The young men have expressed the wish to have a sermon preached to them before their Commencement (the 23d instant) on the duties of their profession; very becoming and graceful, especially as it is quite spontaneous. Hawks was applied to, but after nibbling a little at the invitation, declined it. He is lazy, and it may be, too, that he himself was aware that the subject demanded heavier metal than his smooth, wordy rhetoric. So the class instructed us to apply to Vinton, and we called at Trinity Church after service. Vinton sees plainly enough that it is an opening not to be despised, and accepts readily. . . . Afterwards with Lewis Rutherfurd and William Betts, about degrees to be conferred at this Law Commencement. We propose to LL.D. Judges Ingraham, Woodruff, and Daly, who have consented to act as a committee to examine the essays and examination papers and award the prizes. *Vivat* the Law School! I hope to make a great deal out of it.

The Baltimore Convention of conservative fogies and fossils nominates Bell for President and Edward Everett for Vice-President. Not of much practical importance probably, but I for one am tired of talk about niggers and feel much inclined to vote for anybody who promises to ignore that subject.

May 15, TUESDAY. . . . Universal sympathy for poor Fowler, except from a very few Buchananizing Democrats. Isaiah Rynders has not yet succeeded in arresting him, and probably won't succeed if he can help it.

On May 13, as Strong here indicates, rumors had spread through the city of a heavy defalcation in the New York post office; and the city was soon horrified to learn from federal officials that Postmaster Isaac V. Fowler had indeed absconded, owing the government more than $155,000. Fowler was a genial, popular man, with what the Tribune *called "a showy figure and a constitution of iron." He had taken an important part in Democratic politics, and had abetted Buchanan in his warfare upon the followers of Stephen A. Douglas. Besides taking the moneys of the post office, he had borrowed large sums from friends, and had been associated with Secretary of War Floyd (who was more than suspected of corruption) in the sale of military sites. Speculation on the stock exchange and general improvidence had swallowed up all that he had received, and he fled with but a few thousands. As the United States Marshal, Captain Rynders, made no very energetic effort to apprehend him, he made good his escape.*

Meanwhile, Republican delegates were gathering in Chicago, and on May 16 their national convention met in the great temporary structure or "wigwam" built for the occasion. Seward of New York, Lincoln of Illinois, Chase of Ohio, and Bates of Missouri all had enthusiastic supporters. At the outset the contest was regarded as one of "Seward against the field," but it was soon plain that the real struggle was between Seward and Lincoln. Of the two,

Seward had far the greater political experience and far the more public support. But he was regarded by many voters in the critical states of the East and Middle West as too extreme on the slavery question; his apparently radical views, summed up in his recent speech on the "irrepressible conflict," had damaged his prospects. Moreover, many people in New York—as Strong well knew—had been repelled by Seward's selfishness, and by his identification (though personally quite honest) with some men who had fished assiduously for public contracts and offices. Lincoln was not regarded as too radical; he had no bad party connections; and he commanded the warm support not only of the Illinois and Indiana delegates, but of the tumultuous crowds that filled and surrounded the "wigwam." On May 16 George Ashmun of Massachusetts became permanent chairman; on the 17th the platform was reported, and —after Strong's friend George William Curtis had made a notable speech in favor of reasserting the principle that "all men are created equal"—was adopted. On the 18th, the third day of the convention, the balloting began.

May 16. Chicago Convention is in full boil and bubble. Strong opposition to Seward, but he will be nominated at last. That wily old Thurlow Weed, the most adroit of wire-pullers, seldom fails when he takes hold of a case in earnest.

General Dix is to be Fowler's successor in the post office. Butterworth of the assay office will decline the appointment.

May 18. The Supreme Court at General Term this morning decided that the law passed for the benefit of the New York University is unconstitutional and refused to admit a batch of graduates from that learned institution without another examination under the auspices of the Court. We shall present a clearer case in certain points, but I have no doubt they will treat our diplomas with like contempt. I think they are manifestly wrong, and it may be worth our while to carry the question to the Court of Appeals, so that it may be settled one way or the other. If the Act of April, 1860, don't give us this privilege, Judge Parker's Albany Law School ought not to enjoy it under a like act passed some years ago.

Tonight at William Schermerhorn's for private theatricals; Sandeau's *Mlle. de la Seiglière,* translated by William Schermerhorn, who with Miss Laura Pell, Mr. and Mrs. Alfred Schermerhorn, Willy Cutting, Thorndike, and a son of Mrs. Augustus Schermerhorn, played it very fairly. Cutting and Thorndike were a little wooden. Mr. and Mrs. Alfred Schermerhorn acted with ease and spirit, being used to it, but pretty, fair-haired Miss Laura (whose first appearance it was, and who had had only a fortnight's time to prepare, as substitute for Mrs. Lewis Jones) covered herself with glory.

May 19. Thy Nose, O W. H. Seward, is out of joint! The Chicago Convention nominates Lincoln and Hamlin. They will be beat, unless the South perpetrate some special act of idiocy, arrogance, or brutality before next fall.

Lincoln will be strong in the Western states. He is unknown here. The *Tribune* and other papers commend him to popular favor as having had but six months' schooling in his whole life; and because he cut a great many rails, and worked on a flatboat in early youth; all which is somehow presumptive evidence of his statesmanship. The watchword of the campaign is already indicated. It is to be "Honest Abe" (our candidate being a namesake of the Father of the Faithful). Mass-meetings and conventions and committees are to become enthusiastic and vociferous whenever an orator says Abe. But that monosyllable does not seem to me likely to prove a word of power. "Honest Abe" sounds less efficient than "Frémont and Jessie," and that failed four years ago.

May 20, SUNDAY. Dwight is to move tomorrow at General Term for an order admitting our Law School graduates under the Act of '60. He read me his points, which are about as conclusive as anything in English. I have the opinion of the court on the university application, and a most shallow and flippant production it is. The legislature is bad enough, but our courts are little better. Witness the arrogance with which these three judges, two of them second-rate lawyers, and the third (Leonard) a tenth-rate, groggy attorney, overrule and nullify an act of the legislature, without even hearing counsel. They ought to be impeached. Dwight's motion will be denied, of course, and its denial won't do us much harm. A bench adorned by Leonard and others naturally dreads an educated bar, and instinctively discourages whatever tends to raise the professional standard from its present zero point of utter degradation.

May 21. Trustees of Columbia College met at two in the afternoon and pushed through a good deal of business, chiefly relating to the Law School, very harmoniously. Ordronaux was reappointed; Lieber and Nairne were formally attached to the School. All details referred to the Law Committee. General satisfaction with the progress and prospects of the School, which is certainly prospering beyond my hopes. This late decision of Sutherland, Mullin, and Leonard at General Term had got

into the papers and is generally discussed and condemned. It is spoken of
as a decision against the College (though, in fact, against this nasty little
sham Law School of Cutler's and Judge Clerke's) and advertises us most
effectively.

May 23, WEDNESDAY.   Tonight the first Law School Commencement
at the Historical Society Hall in Second Avenue; it went off very well.
Duffie as Chaplain of the College opened the solemnities of the evening.
Dwight made a brief statement of the history and the prospects of the
school. The President conferred degrees (including an LL.D. to Judges
Ingraham, Woodruff, and Daly, who have worked hard and cheerfully in
examining the essays and papers submitted to them, and the like honor to
Professor Dwight). Bidwell delivered an address to the class, of about an
hour, and very creditable. Judge Ingraham announced the award of the
prizes, and one Hutchings of the graduating class delivered a valedictory
that was full of faults—verbose, florid, slip-slop, crude, and so forth—but
shewed decided ability, nevertheless. Its substance was far from commonplace; the orator had read and thought, and his notions were vigorous
and true. The Commencement went off as well as possible. I have great
hopes of this embryo school. Shirked the symposium at President King's.

May 26.   Our late Law School operations are talked about and
approved. We have got an order duly entered denying our motion in the
case of young Cooper (son of William B. Cooper), who doesn't want to
open an office at once. Most of the others have been tested by the Supreme
Court examiners, James T. Brady, John Burrill, and Malcolm Campbell,
a very young man and a pet of Sutherland's. A batch of a dozen was
examined Thursday afternoon, and I meant to attend; but the majority
of them were below the average of the class. All the third-rate graduates
were there (with one exception, fortunately); and when the examiners
took their seats, I fled the arena, foreseeing defeat and annoyance. I hear
that they did not distinguish themselves, but I do not know the result.
It would be most unfortunate if any failed to pass. They are necessarily
weak on questions about practice, and the manner of the examiners is
peremptory and hostile—quite unlike Professor Dwight's searching but
kind and patient queries. . . .

Consummated today a very weighty business—the transfer to me by
Mr. Ruggles of $110,000 real estate, subject to encumbrances (by mort-
gage) of much larger amount; that is, his Atlantic Dock stores. I paid
$1,200, which is about $1,199 more than the present market value of the
property. . . . These stores were reconveyed to him by Frank Griffin's

estate; he secured the Griffin estate and other creditors by mortgage, leaving certain other debts of comparatively small amount unsecured. Among them are claims of John Harriot and Robert Henry, builders. He has been keeping these down ever since, reducing them by payments from time to time out of his professional earnings. But Harriot & Henry have recently commenced a suit or suits for the balance due them, and hope to screw Mr. Ruggles into getting an advance from his friends, which he declines to ask. Under a judgment they might force this property to a sale and sacrifice the lien of the second mortgages, which will be secure if the property is nursed a few years longer. So I have taken it. I don't expect to see my $1,200 again very soon, but I dare say I shall be annoyed by stories about a conveyance from father-in-law to son-in-law intended to hinder and delay creditors.

May 28, MONDAY. The park below the reservoir begins to look intelligible. Unfinished still, and in process of manufacture, but shewing the outline now of what it is to be. Many points are already beautiful. What will they be when their trees are grown and I'm dead and forgotten?

One thinks sometimes that one would like re-juvenescence, or a new birth. One would prefer, if he could, to annihilate his past and commence life, say in this A.D. 1860, and so enjoy longer acquaintance with this era of special development and material progress, watch the splendid march of science on earth, share the benefits of the steam engine and the electric telegraph, and grow up with this park—which is to be so great a fact for the young men and maidens of New York in 1880, if all goes well and we do not decompose into anarchy meanwhile. The boy of that year is likely to have larger privileges and a better time than were conceded to the boy of 1830. Central Park and Astor Library and a developed Columbia University promise to make the city twenty years hence a real center of culture and civilization, furnishing privileges to youth far beyond what it gave me in my boyhood.

May 30, WEDNESDAY. Invited to be a vice-president of a great Republican ratification meeting tomorrow night. Declined on the plea of "engagements," but the truth is I do not know whether I am a Republican at all.

May 31, THURSDAY. Seward's special friends grumble at Lincoln's nomination, but seem disposed to support it in good faith. It looks to me as if "Honest Abe" were going to run well. The Democrats must patch up their domestic difficulties, and select a strong and available candidate, or they will be beat.

June 1, FRIDAY. Pleasant beginning of another summer. Light showers at noon, and the afternoon a little too cool and breezy. But Ellie enjoyed her drive in the new park and her stroll through the "Ramble." We were an ample carriage-load—poor Miss Annie Leavenworth, Mr. Ruggles, Ellie, I, Babbins, and Johnny on the box. Mr. Ruggles dined here. . . .

Poor Ike Fowler said to be at Havana. Old associations make me share most fully the general sympathy for him in his fall and exile, but it does seem strange that nobody speaks of him as criminal; that one hears no denunciation of his crime, in stealing $158,000 of somebody's money. Everybody says "poor Fowler," "what a pity," "I'm very sorry for Fowler," and the like, just as if this catastrophe were a case of misfortune, the failure of a trader or speculator. Can a community maintain itself long without revolution, being so utterly wanting in perception of the difference between night and morning?

June 4, MONDAY. . . . Columbia College trustees met at two in the afternoon; barely a quorum. What an inert, blasé, non-feasant set they are! Resolutions allying us with the College of Physicians and Surgeons passed *sub silentio*. Lewis Rutherfurd looked volumes of homeopathy and hydropathy and medical progress, but kept his peace. So we have our Medical School now as well as our Law School, and begin to look like a real university. . . .

June 6. Summer begins to pronounce itself. Was industrious in Wall Street and stopped on my way uptown at Barnum's. That specimen of showmen has resumed his functions, and his ancient and seedy museum is instinct with new life. The old wax figures are propped and brushed up and some of the more conspicuously mangy of the stuffed monkeys and toucans have disappeared. There is a colossal fat boy on exhibition (a real prodigy of hideousness), in addition to the miraculous calculator and the "What-is-it?" I went to see the aquaria. Sundry splendid tropical things from the Gulf of Mexico have been introduced there. . . .

June 8. With Ellie tonight, Charley, and Mrs. Eleanor at opera; *Lucrezia Borgia*. Duke and Duchess (Cortesi) good; the Gennaro bad.

Townsend Harris's treaty of 1858 with Japan had called for the visit of a Japanese delegation to America for the exchange of ratifications. Some seventy Japanese were therefore brought to the United States on an American warship. They aroused great curiosity, for few occidentals had ever seen an inhabitant of the hermit empire; and as they visited the principal cities of the

East, for Congress had appropriated funds for their entertainment, they were welcomed by great crowds. The procession up Broadway which Strong here describes was one of the most important features of their reception. Everywhere the courtesy and intelligence of the visitors produced a favorable impression.

But a much more important visit was at hand. The Prince of Wales, later Edward VII, a rosy-cheeked youth of attractive demeanor, was about to make a twenty-nine-day tour of the country. He slept in the White House; he planted a tree at Washington's tomb; and he attended balls, concerts, and dinners. He was received with great cordiality by everybody but the Irish; the Sixty-ninth Regiment in New York under Colonel Corcoran declining to parade in his honor. Much of the deplorably exaggerated interest taken in his reception sprang from the fact that the list of guests at the various balls he attended indicated who was "in society" and who was not. The Prince was much liked, and his visit did something for Anglo-American cordiality— which had been a little ruffled by the great prize-fight noted above. Heenan, the American champion, had met the British favorite, Tom Sayers, in a bare-fisted battle which was stopped by the crowd in the thirty-seventh round. The match was declared a draw, but most Americans believed that Heenan, the "Benicia Boy," had really won it.

June 16, SATURDAY.　From early morning (or at least from the earliest hour of which I am personally cognizant) the town was all agog about the Japanese ambassadors. Streets were already swarming as I went downtown. Hardly an omnibus but was filled full. Every other person, at least, was manifestly a rustic or a stranger. Flags everywhere. Small detachments of our valiant militia marching, grim and sweaty, to their respective positions. Dragoons, hussars, and lancers, by twos and threes, trotting about with looks of intense uneasiness. The whole aspect of things indicated some great event at hand.

I left Wall Street at about two-thirty, intending merely to walk uptown and observe the humors of the dense crowd that lined both sides of Broadway, for I was so sick of talk about the Japanese that I vowed that I would not see them. But I met young Dudley Field, who kindly insisted on my taking advantage of certain eligible windows in his office on Broadway. There I found his sister, Miss Jenny, Miss Laura Belden, Judge Sutherland and Judge Leonard, Gerard, and one or two more, with strawberries and ice cream, and so forth, and saw all the show to great advantage.

Quite an imposing turnout of horse, foot, and artillery. Ditto of aldermen in barouches and yellow kids, trying to look like gentlemen. The first-chop Japanese sat in their carriage like bronze statues, aristocratically calm and indifferent. The subordinates grinned, and wagged their ugly heads, and waved their fans to the ladies in the windows. Every window in Broadway was full of them. The most striking object was the crowd that closed in and followed the procession. Broadway was densely filled, sidewalks and trottoir both, for many blocks, and mostly with roughs. But the police kept good order. I made my way uptown through side streets with difficulty, for they were thronged with currents of sightseers flowing off from the great central canal, and of loafers, slinging along with the characteristic loaferine trot to get ahead of the procession and have another look at the Japs. . . .

Two old fools, Samuel Neill and Tom Bryan, have been making themselves ridiculous by going to North Carolina in this weather and fighting a duel. The former, they say, has a bullet hole through the arm. They got into a squabble "late at e'en, drinking the wine" at the Union Club, over the weighty question of Garibaldi's nationality. One said he was a Scotchman, and the other said he wasn't, and they punched each other's heads without being able to settle it that way. Garibaldi, by-the-by, holds his own. Success to him, filibuster as he is. There are limits even to conservatism.

Professor Dwight has been heard at length in our Law School appeal by the Court of Appeals, which held a special evening session for that purpose. Judge Denio and O'Conor and others say it was a very able argument. . . .

Was at the Savings Bank Thursday afternoon, taking Hamilton Fish's place as attending trustee. His daughter, Miss Sarah, has just married one Sidney Webster, and the Governor had to do the honors of the wedding reception.

There is talk of the Democrats nominating Judge Nelson. I'd gladly vote for him, especially so against "Abe," whose friends seem to rest his claims to high office chiefly on the fact that he split rails when he was a boy. I am tired of this shameless clap-trap. The log-cabin hard-cider craze of 1840 seemed spontaneous. This hurrah about rails and rail-splitters seems a deliberate attempt to manufacture the same kind of furor by appealing to the shallowest prejudices of the lowest class. It ought to fail, and I hope it may; but unless the Democrats put up a strong man, it will succeed.

June 20. Attended the British Consul this morning, closing a commission to take testimony for the Court of Sessions.[12] Talked with him about the proposed visit of the Prince of Wales. Archibald seems to have been called on by his government to advise whether the Prince, if he come here, shall accept the invitation of the city government or decline it and travel through the country incognito. He wanted to know what I thought about it, and I decidedly recommended that this royal imp should visit us as an English gentleman or nobleman, and accept no public hospitalities, for the tender mercies of the Common Council are cruel. But Mr. Archibald thinks otherwise, and he may be right. A frank acceptance by the Prince of any civility paid him by our public functionaries, such as they are, would flatter the public vanity and bring us closer to England. . . . Crowd at the Metropolitan Hotel all day, except at intervals when dispersed by a shower. People stand and stare at the windows for a vision of some ugly Mongol mug protruded for a moment and then withdrawn.

June 21. This evening with Mr. Ruggles to Dr. Gilman's, Thirteenth Street, to meet sundry of the professors of our Medical College and consider whether any kind of scientific post-graduate course can be evolved out of nothing by concerted action between Columbia College and this, its new ally. President King and Torrey were there, and the Medical College was represented by Gilman, Parker, Delafield, Clark, Dalton, and other medicine men, generally of high caste. We talked the matter over and agreed to meet again a fortnight hence. Something may come of it, but my expectations are moderate. The Medical College building, at the corner of Twenty-third and Fourth Avenue, is convenient and accessible, but we want men of larger calibre than Joy, McCulloh, Dr. Delafield, and Dr. Parker. . . .[13]

[12] E. M. Archibald had been the able British consul since 1857.

[13] Willard Parker (1800–1884), for whom the Willard Parker Hospital for Infectious Diseases in New York is named, had studied in Europe and held chairs of anatomy and surgery in several medical schools in this country before he joined the faculty of the College of Physicians and Surgeons as professor of principles and practice of surgery (1839–1870). Edward Delafield (1794–1875), ophthalmologist and surgeon, founded the New York Eye and Ear Infirmary in 1818. He occupied the chair of obstetrics and diseases of women in the College of Physicians and Surgeons from 1825 to 1838, and was president of the College from 1858 to 1875. Alonzo Clark (1807–1887) held the chair of physiology and pathology in the College of Physicians and Surgeons from 1848 to 1855, when he became professor of pathology and practical medicine in the same school. John Call Dalton (1825–1889) was the first physician in America to devote himself exclusively to experimental physiology and related sciences. His studies with Claude Bernard in Paris turned his ambition from practice to teaching, and he

The Democratic Baltimore Convention is still sitting, and none the easier for sitting. The great old Democratic Party is *in articulo mortis*; its convention is abolishing of itself, and just on the eve of suicide by dismemberment and disintegration, after the manner of certain star-fishes (*vide* Gosse). If Douglas be nominated, a Southern limb drops off. If any other man is nominated, a Northwestern ray or arm secedes. Southern swashbucklers demand an ultra-nigger platform that would cost the party every Northern state; unless it be adopted, they will depart to put on their war paint and whet their scalping knives. The worst temper prevails; delegates punch each other and produce revolvers. In short, a wasps' nest divided against itself is a pastoral symphony compared to this Witenagemot. Its session has abounded thus far in scandalous, shameful brutalities and indecencies that disgrace the whole country and illustrate the terrible pace at which we seem traveling down hill toward sheer barbarism and savagery.

The Convention has made little progress yet—has not even succeeded in defining its own identity. Its throes and gripings have thus far been on the question whether certain chivalric delegations that seceded at Charleston shall be received back digested and assimilated, or rejected as foreign matter. The New York delegation seems to hold the balance of power. After Douglas, Dickinson and Horatio Seymour are talked of; I could vote for the latter. There is a Nelson movement, too, silent as yet, but growing.[14] But the elements of the Convention are in unstable combination, and it is likely to decompose with an explosion like chloride of nitrogen, or disintegrate like a Prince Rupert's drop, on the slightest provocation before it nominates anybody. And, if one half of its bullies and blackguards and Southern gentlemen will make free use of their revolvers on the other half, during the general reaction and mêlée that is like to accompany the act of decomposition, and will then get themselves decently hanged for homicide, the country will be safe; and millions yet unborn will bless the day when the Baltimore Convention of 1860 exploded and the Democratic Party ceased to exist.

If there were a real ruler now to march into this congregation of politic knaves and hang a dozen of the worst cases, with their bowie

introduced the experimental method in teaching of physiology, thus opening a new era in medical education. He occupied the chair of physiology in the College of Physicians and Surgeons 1855–1883, and served as president 1884–1889.

[14] Strong's unwillingness to vote for the politician Daniel S. Dickinson (1800–1866) is understandable. The movement for Justice Samuel Nelson of the Supreme Court (1792–1873) developed no strength.

knives round their necks, and set the rest to hard labor on public works for a term of years!!! What a subject he would be for a biography by Carlyle! But there is no such luck. Whatever may be the result of this Convention, the Democracy has disgraced itself and damaged itself beyond cure. I half expect that Republicanism and Abe Lincoln will sweep every vestige of that party out of existence.

June 23. Mr. Ruggles came in this evening and reports that the rump of the Convention has nominated Douglas. Afterwards came Walter Cutting, very kindly offering me tickets for the grand ball Monday night in honor of the Japanese embassy. Tickets are in great demand and hardly to be got by any one who has not an uncle or a confederate in the City Councils. It will be a showy and lavish entertainment, but neither Ellie nor I care to assist. Have encountered attachés of the embassy twice, looking over books and buying largely at Appleton's new store. They seem intelligent and observant, talk in soft oriental whispers, and contrive to make themselves understood by Kernot and Allen and the other salesmen. Books on the industrial arts, geographies, atlases, and high-colored lithograph illustrations interest them especially. They buy largely, also, of children's books, and say "new language—child's book—very good."

June 26, TUESDAY. At Columbia College Commencement this morning in the Academy of Music, the first commencement I've attended for years. I was on the stage officially with about a dozen of the trustees. . . . I sat through two hours of it and then slipped off with John Astor and came to Wall Street. The house was a pretty sight from the stage, densely filled, mostly with feminine young America; parquet and boxes and balcony were flower beds of sweet young faces and summer bonnets.

Uptown again early for Belmont's matinée. Little Miss Laura Belden came to go with us; and while we waited in the front parlor for Ellie to perfect her toilette, made me her confidant in the kindest and prettiest way. She is engaged to Dudley Field. If Dudley has sown all his wild oats, he may make Miss Laura a good husband. But there is room for misgiving.

Then to Belmont's. Splendid house—probably the most splendid and showy in the city. The picture gallery is a great feature. Every room fragrant with flowers. Mrs. Belmont (Commodore Perry's daughter) received her guests most graciously and gracefully. She is very beautiful and stately, certainly among the loveliest of our New York duchesses. There was a vast crowd. The first-chop Japanese made their appearance at about four o'clock, looking impassive and insensible, and were duly cultivated and admired by everybody.

June 27. Ellie went to the Astor Library today at two, and had the felicity of an interview with these same magnates who visited the library by invitation, only John and Willy Astor, Wolcott Gibbs, and one or two trustees being admitted. She reports their manners to be notably gentlemanlike and dignified. . . .

Tonight from six till after ten at the annual meeting of trustees of Theological Seminary, which adjourned to tomorrow, when a deal of important business must be done. I regret I cannot attend. This is a crisis in its affairs, which have been ill-managed for many years past. Its financial condition is shaky. There have been bad investments and improvident expenditures, which seem to have used up all its personal assets. Abel T. Anderson, treasurer, is held by certain of the trustees to have exercised his official functions unwisely. He will not be reëlected. If he were a Japanese treasurer, he would commit hara-kiri and disembowel himself. . . .

July 4. "The day was ushered in," as the newspapers say, with the usual racket, which has not yet abated. I lounged downtown after breakfast, and made an expedition to Jersey City; partly for want of something to do, and partly to give Miss Rosalie Ruggles the latest news from Barrington. A sweltering hot day it has been, as I found out on my walk home after lunching at Delmonico's.

After dinner, I strolled out again and found my way to the North River, in the region of Bank Street, where the *Great Eastern* lies.[15] She loomed up colossal in the twilight. It was too late to ask for admission (price, one dollar). So I walked home again. Looked in at the "Palace Garden" in Fourteenth Street and "looked" out again very speedily. It was hotter than the hot street and presented no attractions but colored lamps, a dismal orchestra, and an occasional skyrocket.

July 5. . . . Visited the *Great Eastern* this afternoon. Visitors seem few. She is an enormity. But the bulk of the ship impresses me less than that of the titanic engines. I dived into their depths by the help of certain slippery cobweb iron ladders. The huge cylinders and piston rods are awful to behold, even in repose. This big ship, with all her apparatus of engines, telegraphs, corrected compasses, and what not, is the incarnation

---

[15] The *Great Eastern*, a British liner designed by Russell Scott weighing almost 19,000 deadweight tons, the leviathan of her day, had reached New York, June 28, to find the shores black with throngs excited over her arrival. In the first five days 143,764 people paid to visit her.

(or inferration) of a good deal of thought, study, and experiment by quite a number of generations. Such a result is not developed out of the coracle of our barelegged, woad-stained ancestors, *tempore Julius Caesar*, by a single step. . . .

July 9, MONDAY. . . . I went up the river to Hudson, by the *Rip Van Winkle*, Friday afternoon, and took the Hudson and Berkshire road at five the next morning. Breakfasted at West Stockbridge and reached Great Barrington at ten-thirty after two most preposterous stoppages of some three hours.

Found Ellie and the children well and happy; Lewis—God save his Majesty—growing visibly from week to week. Certain drives and rambles, and church Sunday morning. . . .

July 10. Evening at Dr. Gilman's in Thirteenth Street for a second consultation with our new allies of the College of Physicians and Surgeons about the projected Scientific School—the last hope of our "Columbia College Scientific Post-graduate Course." Dr. Torrey, Mr. Ruggles, William Betts, and myself represented Columbia; Gilman and Delafield, Parker, St. John, and others of the Medical College faculty propounded their scheme. It promises well and may be nursed into vigorous life. The proposed course includes zoology, geology, and physiology. A year hence, we may add applied chemistry and engineering. We were all of one mind. William Betts takes hold very cordially. A special meeting of our board is to be called for the 19th instant. We signed a requisition to Governor Fish at Newport to summon it for that day. Ogden will oppose, of course, *virtute officii*, as treasurer and *advocatus diaboli*, but I think we shall put it through.

July 19. Very muggy. Worse than anything this summer. Not early downtown, detained by dyspepsia. Special meeting of Columbia College trustees was called for two P.M. to consider the overtures of our Medical College allies. No quorum, only ten present. We talked them over informally. The plan did not find favor. Ogden, our treasurer, opposed every plan that involves outlay, *ex officio*. He made a very clear and satisfactory statement of receipts and expenditures, showing a balance of several thousand dollars on the wrong side of the account for our next financial year. Governor Fish and John Astor were, on the whole, disinclined to disburse $2,500 on a doubtful experiment, at least until more Botanic Garden lots are leased. Cannot say they were wrong. Walked down to Pike's after we separated, and then came home. Miss Rosalie called to ask after Ellie and the babies. I took a cup of coffee. Horace

Binney came in and spent half the evening, and Dr. Gilman, to whom I had to report the failure of his scientific lecture project.

July 22, SUNDAY.   Hot day and a hot night, but breezy and tolerable enough. Quite refreshing after the three days of suffocating sultriness we have just passed through. . . .

Reading Ruskin's *Modern Painters*, volume five and last. Less vigorous than the other four. Effort at fine writing is manifest, and a "sensation" style; that is, a style that aims at astonishing the reader or stimulating his curiosity, and does not seek exclusively to convey the writer's meaning with the maximum of clearness and brevity, which I suppose to be the sole office of language and test of "style." A feeling of despondency and doubt is very manifest. He thinks the prospects of Christendom and its civilization discouraging, and the real value of discussions about art questionable.

July 25.   Just from Laura Keene's with Charley Strong; *Our American Cousin*, revived. It retains its popularity. The house was full and enthusiastic. With all its extravagance and absurdity, the piece has strong points.

August 3.   Am elected to the New York Club! I shall not probably trouble the clubhouse much except during summer solitude, when it may be a little less disgusting than Delmonico's. Dinner at any restaurant is a bore. Yesterday I dined at Dr. Peters's; Fred Snelling and Dr. Alexander Mott also present.

August 8.   Here is a specimen of our political morals. General [John A.] Dix, Ike Fowler's successor as postmaster, says he was called upon the other day by a delegation of prominent Democrats and requested to dismiss one of his subordinates for saying that "in his opinion Fowler was little better than a thief." As Fowler is an absconding defaulter whose deficit is between $100,000 and $200,000, Dix declined compliance.

August 15.   Find myself on a committee headed by General Scott and William B. Astor to get up a "banquet" for Lord Renfrew, alias the Prince of Wales, when and if his Lordship's Grace's Highness comes to this city.

August 16.   Made my debut in the New York Club this afternoon. Dined there with Charles Strong better and more cheaply than at Delmonico's. One enjoys, moreover, a sensation of being nobby and exclusive when one dines there, which ought to promote digestion, but it has failed to do so this time, for I'm dyspeptic tonight with cephalalgic tendencies. Saw but a few men there, including Bill Pennington, who was a

little tight and exuberantly cordial. My respect for the Club has greatly
increased since Baron Rothschild's friends had to withdraw his name,
because the Baron, though illustrious and a millionaire, was immoderately
given to lewd talk and nude photographs. I did not give the Council
credit for moral courage enough to deny him admission.

After dinner George Anthon came in and we went to Niblo's Pantomime and Horse-Opera. I came off before the performance was over,
finding two hours of it sufficient. In *Cinderella* some two score very little
children took part, some mere toddlers, and some very lovely. Poor little
souls!—it's a horrid, murderous sacrifice of childhood. But I suppose the
sin rests on that convenient scapegoat, the abstraction we call "society."
I paid my fifty cents (or rather my dollar for an orchestra seat) like others,
and so contributed, as much as any one person commonly contributes, to
maintain this child-slaughtering system. But I really did not know or
suspect, nor had I reason to suspect, that the entertainment I was
"patronising" was to be provided, in part at least, at such terrible cost.

September 4.   This morning a Trust Company meeting. Afterwards
a session of our Prince-Catching Committee; some fifty present. We
determined to enlarge our numbers to four hundred. Old Peter Cooper
was in the chair and distinguished himself by invariably taking the question on the wrong motion, in spite of the whispered remonstrances of the
secretary, Maunsell Field.

September 6.   Prince of Wales. Papers full of his movements—*ad
nauseam*. He is in hot water just now with the Orangemen of Upper
Canada, whom he refuses to recognize as Orangemen; that is, as a proscriptive, vindictive faction. His guardian, the Duke of Newcastle, would
not let him land at Kingston, where the reception prepared for him was
exclusively Orange and anti-Catholic. So the insulted Protestantism of all
Upper Canada is in an uproar, and denounces his Royal Highness's
tutors and governors. That feeling may appear even during the Prince's
visit to this country, for our Know-Nothing lodges are, in fact, offshoots
of Orangeism. But their influence and importance are next to nothing
now, at least as compared with what they were of old.

Apropos of this theological subject, a Congregational "religious"
newspaper of Boston announces with great satisfaction and complacency
that Theodore Parker was killed by certain religious and orthodox
women of that city, who prayed systematically that the mischief of his
preaching might be stopped somehow. They heard with amazement and
awe that his lungs had become affected and reverently recognized the

tubercular deposits on those maleficent organs as a gracious response to their prayers. Hardly credible, but true and (as the *Tribune* suggests) alarming. Against what or whom will this death-dealing "circle" or coterie next direct its prevailing prayers? . . . Praying people to death is ugly work for Christian women.

September 12, WEDNESDAY.   Last Friday to Great Barrington. . . . Left Great Barrington at ten-thirty this morning. Very chill and savage easterly rain storm. Solaced myself with a novel of Wilkie Collins's, *The Woman in White*, and Dumas's *Mille et un fantômes*. The former is of a class now uncommon, a novel depending for its interest mainly on an artistically constructed plot, attracting its reader by an elaborate puzzle which can be resolved only by those who read on to the last chapter.

September 13.   Dined at New York Club with Charles E. Strong and Henry Fearing. Thereafter we inspected the grand procession of the "Wide-Awakes," a new notable club organization of the Republicans. It extends through these Northern states, is semi-military, and is intended (as people say) to keep order at Lincoln's inauguration (he will certainly be elected) in case Governor Wise and Mr. Yancey and other foolish Southern demagogues try to make a disturbance. This procession, which we watched in Astor Place and the Bowery, was imposing and splendid. The clubs marched in good order, each man with his torch or lamp of kerosene oil on a pole, with a flag below the light; and the line was further illuminated by the most lavish pyrotechnics. Every file had its rockets and its Roman candles, and the procession moved along under a galaxy of fire balls—white, red, and green. I have never seen so beautiful a spectacle on any political turnout.

September 14.   Went with George Anthon and Walter Cutting to the opera. Heard three acts of *Martha* in the Cutting box. Patti and Brignoli did fairly. House full, but strangers mostly. Music is pretty, but not very strong.

Last night's Republican turnout is the town talk. Everyone speaks of the good order and the earnest aspect of the "Wide-Awakes," and likens this to the "Tippecanoe and Tyler too" gatherings of 1840. Certainly, all the vigor and enthusiasm of this campaign are thus far confined to the Republicans. Their adversaries are disorganized, divided, and discouraged. In this state, there is a fusion (worse confounded) of the Union Party (Bell and Everett) with the Squatter Sovereignty Democrats (Douglas and Johnson), and a sort of feebly coherent composite electoral ticket. . . . They are trying to coalesce with the Breckinridge people so as to include in one ticket all the anti-Lincoln elements. But that seems as yet beyond the powers of political synthesis.

So we have three parties in this state, *videlicet*:

1. "Honest Abe" Lincoln's party.
2. The Fusionists, whose ticket is twenty-five Douglas and Johnson, and ten Bell and Everett, and who are engineered by Washington Hunt and the New York *Express* and patronized as well-meaning people, but soon to fail, by the New York *Herald*.
3. Breckinridge and Lane's party, consisting mainly of federal office-holders.
4. No. 4, "Sham" Houston's party, has dissolved, that hero having magnanimously withdrawn.

I don't know clearly on which side to count myself in. I've a leaning toward the Republicans. But I shall be sorry to see Seward and Thurlow Weed with their tail of profligate lobby men promoted from Albany to Washington. I do not like the tone of the Republican papers and party in regard to the John Brown business of last fall, and I do not think rail-splitting in early life a guarantee of fitness for the presidency.

I could vote for Bell and Mr. Orator Everett. But I can't support them in their partnership with Douglas, the little giant, for I hold the little giant to be a mere demagogue. As to Breckinridge, the ultra Southern candidate, I renounce and abhor him and his party. He represents the most cruel, blind, unreasoning, cowardly, absolute despotism that now disgraces the earth, Garibaldi having probably squelched poor little Neapolitan Bomba before this date. Freedom of speech and of thought is extinct south of the Potomac. Life and property are as insecure there as in Paris in 1793 or in the Kingdom of Dahomey. Witness the atrocities daily perpetrated, for example, in Texas, where white men are being hanged and niggers burned by terrified Vigilance Committees, self-appointed and irresponsible, on the strength of legends about "one hundred bottles of strychnine" to be used by some nigger toxicologist to "poison the wells" of a whole county. These grisly antics of insane Southern mobs and the idiotic sanguinary babblings of Southern editors and orators tempt me to become a disunion man. Alliance with communities so lawless—more than semi-barbarous—seems degrading to the comparatively civilized North.

October 1. The Prince's ball next week's the chief topic of the town. The King of Naples has run away and Garibaldi triumphs. The House of Bourbon is on its last legs. John Jay has been making a row in the diocesan convention with a speech on the slave trade, which Mr. Ruggles says was very able. George Anthon suggests an alteration in the prayerbook for the benefit of the "Church South," namely, in the prayer for persons going to sea.[16] Instead of "these Thy servants," add "These our servants," and instead of "conduct him in safety to the haven where they would be," read ". . . the haven where they *wouldn't* be" (if they could help it, that is). . . .

October 2. Diligent day. Having been put on the reception committee for the Prince of Wales's ball, I attended a meeting thereof. There were Hamilton Fish, Luther Bradish, Perit, Maunsell Field, Minturn, Cisco, and myself. There was severe prosing on "nice sharp quillets" of etiquette. Bradish and Field were uncommonly solemn and impressive. With what manner of reception shall we receive General Scott? "Can he be separated from his military family?" There's the rub. Shall we ten reception committeemen dress alike? Shall it be white vests and black cravats or vice versa? Are silk vests considered provincial in Paris? What manner of gloves prevailed at the Tuileries when Governor Fish was there last, and what light is thrown on the whole subject by Bradish's little souvenirs of court society at the several capitals of Europe? Cisco and I are a sub-committee on the carriages that are to convey His Royal Highness and suite from the Fifth Avenue Hotel to the Opera House. O happy carriages, and horses too much blessed! I am a Committee of One to provide drinks for the special consolation of His Royal Highness in a small withdrawing room to be consecrated to that use. The Prince is said to be partial to sherry and seltzer water.

October 5, FRIDAY. Wednesday night with Ellie, Miss Leavenworth, and Cameron to Tiffany's shop in Broadway, where I had engaged a second story window. We inspected the grand National Wide-Awake torchlight procession. It was brilliant and successful. It was more than two hours in passing, and its most pleasing feature was the rear-rank of the last division. These demonstrations of the prevailing Republican party are elaborate and splendid, but cold and mechanical. One misses the spontaneous hullabaloo and furor of the Harrison campaign. Even in '56 there was more enthusiasm. Of course, the corresponding depression on the other side is deeper yet. It is conceded that neither of the opposing candidates stands the smallest chance of election by the people. So Douglas men, Bell men, and Breckinridge men are all equally dumpish, and any excitement about fusion is impracticable. You can get up a hurrah for the

---

[16] That is, for the slaves now being run in from Africa.

gallant Smith or the "ga-lorious" Jones, but not for a mere abstraction for the generalization of Smith and Jones.

Much occupied with divers matters growing out of the expected advent of our "sweet young Prince." "Long may he wave," but I wish he were at home again with his royal mamma, and I hope the community won't utterly disgrace itself before he goes away. The amount of tuft-hunting and Prince-worshiping threatens to be fearful; and, I don't know how it happens, but I fear my share in the demonstration is to be much larger than I expected or desired. The Reception Committee met today and passed on divers weighty matters. It is proposed that we "wait on the Prince" the evening before the ball, which seems to me a very superfluous work of supererogation. All we can say or do is to express the hope that His Royal Highness finds himself pretty well, considering, and I think His Royal Highness will be inclined to take it for granted that we hope so, whether we call or not.

Maunsell Field's exertions and labors over the arrangements for the ball are most arduous. He works all day and nearly all night and will break down if he isn't careful. Honorable Luther Bradish has been *sold* with a grave suggestion that the Reception Committee wear small-clothes and silk-stockings, and was much exercised thereby. On reflection, he thought it might be, on the whole, highly becoming and proper. It seems a place on this committee is a much coveted place of honor. I was selected after great consideration. Very much obliged.

His Royal Highness is to attend services at Trinity Church on the 14th, "The First Sunday after the Ball" and the 18th after Trinity. The vestry met specially yesterday and a committee of arrangements was appointed: the Rector, Dunscomb, Hyslop, Cisco, and myself. The committee met this afternoon, and I walked up with Cisco, stopping at Mathews's to arrange about the binding of a special prayerbook for His Royal Highness's pew, with an inscription alluding to the former munificence of the British Crown to Trinity Church (Berrian suggested "his royal ancestors," forgetting that His Royal Highness is descended neither from William and Mary nor from Queen Anne), and at Gimbrede's about printing tickets of admission. We must admit by tickets or let the church be filled up with a mob, but I should much prefer to dispense with them.

October 9, TUESDAY.   Tomorrow we shall hear of today's state election in Pennsylvania. Its result, if favorable to the Republicans, will be decisive, and one may in that case predict Lincoln's election by the people with entire confidence. What will little South Carolina do then? If she doesn't

secede, she will be utterly ridiculous. She will have to make her choice
between the guilt of treason and the contempt of mankind. . . .

October 10.   Republicanism triumphant in Pennsylvania and by majorities that transcend the wildest prophesyings of the *Tribune*. So the question
is settled and Honest Abe will be our next President. Amen. We may as
well ask the question at once whether the existence of the Union depends
on the submission to the South.

October 11.   I begin to be weary of this "sweet young Prince." The
Hope of England threatens to become a bore. In fact, he is a bore of the
first order. Everybody has talked of nothing but His Royal Highness for
the last week. Reaction is inevitable. It has set in, and by Monday next,
the remotest allusion to His Royal Highness will act like ipecac. It has
been a mild, bland, half-cloudy day. By ten o'clock, people were stationing
themselves along the curbstones of Broadway and securing a good place
to see the Prince. What a spectacle-loving people we are! Shops were
closed and business paralyzed; Wall Street deserted. I spent the morning
mostly at the Trinity vestry office, signing tickets, and so forth. We had
to pass on a bushel of applications for admission next Sunday. Lots of
Fifth Avenueites sent in letters, tendering a private carriage for the
conveyance of His Royal Highness to church, with a postscript asking for
a "few" tickets. Corporators of Trinity Church bluster about their rights
and insist on reserved pews. I fear we are a city of snobs.

I lounged uptown at two o'clock, feeling my way through the crowd
that filled Broadway. Omnibusses and carriages were turned into the side
streets and all Broadway was one long dense mass of impatient humanity.
All the windows on either side were filled. Temporary platforms crowded,
at five dollars a seat. It was beyond the Japanese demonstration, though
Mr. Superintendent Kennedy assured me the other day that the Prince
of Wales would be less popular than Tommy.

At three, I went into the New York Club and took a seat with Charley,
Seton, Pinckney, Stewart, Jem Strong, Bankhead, and others, at a convenient window. We watched and waited, and united in denunciation of
F. Wood, Mayor, whom we assumed to have got the Prince in his grasp
and to be detaining him with a speech at the City Hall. It was six o'clock
and quite dark before the head of the procession reached us. We saw a
six-horse barouche pass. We hurrahed. Ladies in the opposite windows
waved their handkerchiefs. Little boys in the street hay-hayed. Elder
loafers yelled, and the Prince was gone. Keen-sighted and self-confident
men insisted that they had actually seen someone in scarlet uniform bowing

his acknowledgments, but their assertions inspired no confidence. It was too dark to distinguish colors.

I fought my way home through the crowd. We dined at seven. Ellie and Johnny had "seen" the royal procession at Mrs. Cutting's in Fifth Avenue, and Babbins at Union Square.

October 13, SATURDAY. From any more princes of the blood, *libera nos Domine*. May this nice-looking, modest boy find his way home, or at least to our boundaries, with all convenient speed.

I've been in hard work about His Royal Highness for forty-eight hours. I'm weary of His Royal Highness. . . . The Ball is over, thank Heaven, but the Trinity Church reception and services tomorrow are still to be. What they will be, time must tell. I've made the most minute, definite arrangements with Mr. Kennedy and Sergeant Cropsey and the sextons and their aids, but I fear the crowd will out-general me. And I cannot be at the church till the services are actually commencing, for the destinies compel me to accompany or escort the royal party, our guests; and Hyslop and Dunscomb, who will be at the church from nine (when the doors open) till the Prince arrives, are timid and imbecile. I'd give a great deal if tomorrow's august transaction were done and well done.

Mr. Ruggles took Ellie and me, also Mrs. Hunt, to the Astor Library yesterday morning. Only two or three onlookers were present; Mrs. Schuyler and Mrs. John Sherwood. We waited and waited, lounged through alcoves, looked with vain longings at the titles of nice books. The trustees of the library were biding their time below, waiting to pounce on His Royal Highness the moment the sound of his chariot wheels should be heard. At length, about eleven o'clock, a noise of much people was heard without—a hooray—an opening of the police-guarded door, feet on the stone staircase, and then a vision of a girlish-looking young boy walking swiftly through the library with Dr. Cogswell, followed by the hairy-faced Duke of Newcastle with Mr. S. B. Ruggles and by William Astor, Carson Brevoort, and others of the library trustees escorting Lord Lyons and a lot of peers and honorables beside. They inspected the premises in double-quick time, and at the head of the staircase on their way out, His Highness shook hands with Cogswell and thanked him very briefly, simply, and nicely, just as any untitled gentleman would have done (think of it!), and the royal party was gone.

I spent a few minutes in looking at some of the special treasures of the library—the First Folio Shakespeare, the *editio princeps* of Homer, and so on, and then went down to Wall Street. . . .

At eight to the Academy of Music. The doors were not yet opened to the common herd, but my exalted official position on the committee admitted me by the royal entrance on Fourteenth Street. The house looked brilliant, blazing with lights and decorated with great masses of flowers. My post was with Charles King, Ben Silliman, and Cyrus Field in the room appointed for the reception of invited guests generally. Certain other committees had interfered with our arrangements in an unwarrantable and unconstitutional manner. The consequence of this outrage was (as we had distinctly foreseen and predicted) that the great majority of the invited guests found their way to "the floor" for themselves without being conducted thither by any legitimate organ. Our duties were therefore light. We "received" a few South American and Portuguese diplomats and General Paez and Major Delafield and Captain Cullum and sundry army and navy people and a score of city militia, colonels in most elaborate uniforms, and Mayor Wood (I had a very intimate talk with that limb of Satan); and at ten we adjourned to the special reception room and joined Hamilton Fish and old Pelatiah Perit (who looked like a duke in his dress coat and white cravat), and Peter Cooper, who looked like one of Gulliver's Yahoos caught and cleaned and dressed up.

In came the royal party at last, with the Reception Committeemen, who had been assigned the pleasing duty of escorting them. We were presented to His Royal Highness *seriatim.* I had supposed that shaking hands with a Prince of Wales was indecorous, and that a bow was the proper acknowledgment of introduction to so august a personage; but when the Prince puts out his hand, or extends and proffers his fingers like anybody else, it seems ungracious to decline the honor and say, "Sir, I am so well bred as to know my place, and I am unworthy to shake hands with a descendant of James I and George III and a probable King of England hereafter." I think of having my right-hand glove framed and glazed, with an appropriate inscription.

Fish had assigned to each of the committee the duty of conducting one of the Prince's suite into the ballroom, and I was charged with Lord Hinchinbrooke. I had implored Fish to bear in mind that most of our committee (myself included) were unable to distinguish dukes from mere honorables and asked him to be sure to introduce each notable to his committeeman godfather (*vide* programmes of autos-da-fè). But he forgot to do so, and we marched into the ballroom in a very promiscuous way—Fish escorting Monseigneur, Peter Cooper tagging after them, and the rest like a flock of sheep—and took our place at the head of the room;

that is, the east end. Orchestra plays "God Save the Queen," followed by "Hail Columbia!" Aspect of the house and the crowd brilliant and satisfactory. I fall into talk with a pleasant-looking Englisher, and introduce myself. He proves to be Englehart, the Duke of Newcastle's private secretary, and an amiable, agreeable man.

A space in our front was kept clean by the Floor Committee, and through this the crowd began to defile, Fish presenting them as they passed and people making "murgeons and jenny-fluxions" to H.R.H. George Anthon passed with Ellie. . . . I was pointing out notabilities to Englehart and the Honorable Mr. Somebody, and just indicating John Van Buren as the son of one of our ex-kings, when there was a dull, ugly, jarring report, quickly followed by another of the same sort. Everybody started and peered in vain over the heads of the densely packed crowd, and wondered what it was. But there was no panic and no rush. Presently we learned that the temporary flooring had given way in two places; over the stage a couple of beams broke, causing the reports we had heard. Ellie went down into one of the pits and was frightened, but did not lose her footing, nor her self-possession.

Of course, people crowded away from this dangerous region in all directions. The promenade became impracticable, and the Prince and his suite and most of the committee retreated to the reception and supper-rooms. A large space was presently roped off, including the two chasms in the floor, and revealing the scandalous, criminal negligence with which the work of constructing the supports had been done. A score of carpenters and policemen and the illustrious Brown were energetically repairing the damage within fifteen minutes after the accident. But there was a general sense of failure and calamity. Everything looked bilious. Everyone said the whole floor was unsafe. There could be no dancing; the ball was a disgraceful fiasco. I explained to many persons that the Reception Committee had nothing to do with the arrangements of the house. Meantime, the carpenters were working for their lives. Brown peering down into the oblong hole looked as if engaged in his ordinary sextonical duties at an interment. . . .

By midnight damages had been repaired and dancing set in. People streamed over every part of the floor the moment the Prince appeared on it. Danger was forgotten. His Royal Highness's partners, Mrs. Goold Hoyt, Miss Lily Mason, Mrs. John Kernochan, and others, were among our prettiest women. Mrs. Governor Morgan, with whom the Prince opened the ball officially, is elderly and stout, but presentable enough. It is said that she had been taking dancing lessons for the last fortnight, rubbing up her old steps, and that when the quadrille commenced, she timidly inquired, "Your Royal Highness, isn't it time for us to *balancer*?" Miss Helen Russell was overpowered when the Prince was presented. Her voice failed her for fear, and she astonished H.R.H. with a series of contortions and muscular twitchings before she succeeded in articulating an audible word. So they say; I saw little of the dancing. The way people crowded round was snobbish and rude and indecent, and I kept on the outskirts, where I loafed and lounged dejectedly. . . .

While the Prince was waiting for Mrs. Camilla Hoyt, his partner, Walker, the Presbyterian bookbinder, bustled up with a young woman under his arm, introduced himself, and proceeded, "The lady with whom Your Highness was to dance doesn't seem to be ready; allow me to introduce my daughter." The Prince said, "Yes, the crowd is very dense," or some such thing, and evaded this ambitious plebeian rather gracefully for so young a person. Ellie heard this *propriis auribus*. She was presented to the Illustrious Stranger and discoursed with him and danced in the same "Lancers." I had a very pleasant talk with Mrs. Colonel Scott, and was introduced to Millard Fillmore, who is well-bred and cordial, but I spent most of the evening, or night rather, dawdling about and wishing it were over.

Got home at daylight, weary and worn after nearly nine hours spent in a new pair of patent leathers. Very tired. If H.R.H. appreciate my exertions, he will send me the Victoria Cross or make me a duke *in partibus*, at least.

This evening at Mr. Ruggles's awhile and saw part of the Firemen's procession pass up the Fourth Avenue. It was very brilliant, with torches, colored lights, and so forth. On Madison Square, where they no doubt displayed all their resources of Roman candles and portable fireworks, it must have been a really attractive spectacle.

October 14.   Laus Deo, this day is over, and the services at Trinity Church were marked by no gross indecency.

It was a cold, gray, bleak morning. The afternoon and tonight wet and stormy. Called for Cisco at nine-thirty and went with him to the Fifth Avenue Hotel as committee to show our august friends the way to church. Shown to their parlor. Lord Lyons and others of the suite came in, and then the Prince of Wales, looking boyish, feminine, and modest, but remarkably courteous and self-possessed. He stopped the Earl of St. Germans, who was introducing me, and said, "O, I met Mr. Strong at the ball Friday night." He is, no doubt, under orders to be studiously polite and make a good impression, and has had the printed list of the Reception Committee before him, on which my distinguished name appears. We talked a little for ten minutes or so about the weather, and the voyage to West Point tomorrow, and the scenery of the Hudson, and our fall foliage. The Duke of Newcastle came in. He looks like a duke of the tenth century, a vigorous hirsute *Dux* rather than a starred and gartered duke of these days. The Prince said, "It's ten o'clock, and it won't do to be late at church." So we marched downstairs and entered our barouches, the police keeping back the crowd that filled Twenty-third Street. Cisco wanted me to take a seat in the Prince's carriage, as senior in the vestry, but as he evidently coveted that distinction, I declined it, and drove down in Carriage No. 2, with St. Germans, General Bruce, and Major Teesdale. My anticipations were dreary, but I found myself at once on terms of pleasant acquaintance, I could not tell how, with these well-bred, easy-mannered aristocrats. Major Teesdale looks like one of Leech's "heavy swells" in *Punch*, and is taciturn. The other two were very agreeable persons. They asked many questions about matters and things—the American church, the endowment of Trinity Church, education, public and private, and answered queries of mine about the universities and the relations of the colleges to them. They were, of course, polite enough to commend everything they had seen here, or at least to make no criticism on their reception; and they spoke so warmly and earnestly that I think they felt what they said. Unless they are uncommonly good actors, I am sure they are gratified by our ovation. Noticed particularly General Bruce's manner and expression when I said something about the unanimity and the depth of the popular feeling. Nothing could have been more cordial and genuine and kind.

We reached Trinity Church and found a great crowd at the gates, kept back by Superintendent Kennedy's myrmidons. Dunscomb and Hyslop received the visitors. I think Dunscomb had prepared a speech. He bowed and hummed and choked, *more solito*, and Lord Lyons observed sotto voce, "I suppose we may as well move on." So we went up the middle aisle and were spared the infliction. The church (all but the middle aisle) was packed. I saw no indecorum. H.R.H. and suite took the front pews on the south side of the middle aisle; the vestry sat on the north side. I had secured a good place for Ellie and for Mr. Ruggles and Mrs. Governor Hunt and others on the north side of the south aisle just behind the Royal pew. . . .

As soon as [the services] were over, H.R.H. got up, looked warily down the aisle to see whether the coast was clear, and then pegged out of church as fast as his legs would carry him, instead of staying, as I thought he would, a few minutes after service. He showed much practical sense thereby. We followed and reëntered the carriages as before. The crowd was very dense and occupied the whole street as far as the park. With a score of mounted police to help, it was not easy to get through. It was a vociferous crowd and cheered vehemently. . . . There were lines of people waiting all along Broadway to Fourteenth Street, two or three deep, and all cheering, the better class of men raising their hats as the Prince passed by.

We left the party at Archibald's (the Consul's in Fourteenth Street) where they were to lunch or dine, and I took leave of my three and of Dr. Acland and Mr. Englehart very pleasantly, and walked home with Cisco.

So that matter is over. My judgment of the future King of England, from the little I've seen of him, is that he is not remarkably bright or forward for his years, and that he has been carefully trained to remember the duty of courtesy to all classes. Everyone has some little instance to tell of his good-breeding, under difficulties at the ball, when he must have been sorely tried by the well-meant gaucheries of a few and the unpardonable flunkeyism of others. Today, when he got out of his carriage and bade Cisco goodbye, he added a request to bid Mr. Strong goodbye and thank him for his attention in accompanying me, or some such thing. Many young Americans of eighteen would have forgotten this little civil formality. . . .

His visit has occasioned a week of excitement beyond that of any event in my time, and pervading all classes. Its permanent effect, if any, will be good here and in England. The unanimity of the feeling is wonderful, when one thinks of twenty years ago. The protest of certain militia companies of Irishmen against parading to do honor to a Saxon and an oppressor of Ireland is the single exception. I've not heard a single growl or sneer about the fuss we have been making over this young man, who is no better than anybody else, after all, or anything tending that way even remotely.

October 19. Play-going with Ellie tonight at the Winter Garden; *Guy Mannering*. A dramatic distortion of the novel. Miss Charlotte Cushman was the Meg Merrilies, supported by the worst sticks I ever saw on any stage. She is called very great in this role, and the discriminating Dr.

Carroll thinks it equal to any of Rachel's. She certainly makes up as the grisliest of hags. Her performance is intense and carefully studied. A few points in which Scott's words were preserved were effective and beautiful. Her attitudes are remarkably grotesque and striking. But it was almost all overdone and untrue. She was a Hecate, or Waldfrau, perhaps, but not Walter Scott's Meg, nor any other possible woman. . . .

Lincoln's election seems to be conceded. Fusionism has lost all heart. What will happen when this result is announced? There is much stir and swagger and note of preparation among the fire-eaters. Can they overcome the conservative feeling and the common sense that doubtless exist at the South, even in South Carolina itself, and carry on an overt act of secession and treason? There is ground for anxiety. Republicans laugh at the vaporings of our Southern friends. I devoutly hope the result will justify their unconcern. It is easy to show that secession would be an act of madness and folly, but we know there are fools and madmen south of the Potomac, and they may do sore and irremediable mischief to us, their wise brethren at the North. . . .

October 22.   Our little Prince sailed . . . Saturday, and got safely out of our hands. Inferences from the phenomena that accompanied his visit are: (1) No community worships hereditary rank and station like a democracy. (2) The biggest and finest specimens of flunkeyism occur in the most recently elevated strata of society, as for example, Cooper: the "self-made millionaire glue-boiler," Leary: the fashionable hatter's son, and others. (3) Under all this folly and tuft-hunting there is a deep and almost universal feeling of respect and regard for Great Britain and for Her Britannic Majesty. The old anti-British patriotism of twenty years ago is nearly extinct. . . .

I've nearly made up my mind to deposit a lukewarm Republican vote next month. It is a choice of evils, but we may as well settle the question whether a President can or cannot be chosen without the advice and approval of the slaveholding interests; whether 300,000 owners of niggers have or have not a veto on the popular choice. The question must be settled sooner or later, and we may as well dispose of it now. It is impossible for me to vote the Fusion ticket and thereby strengthen the show of the mischief-making demagogue Douglas, or of Breckinridge, the ultra-nigger-driver and demisecessionist. But I may vote for the ten Bell and Everett electors on that ticket, scratching off the rest.

October 23.   Fine day. Tonight's anti-Lincoln or Fusion Torchlight procession was "a big thing." It was more numerous than any political

demonstration I have ever witnessed. It began to pass No. 24 Union
Square (where I joined Ellie) a little before ten. We got tired of lanterns,
Roman candles, red shirts, and the like by a little after eleven, and came
home. The rear-guard had not then reached Union Square. We could see
the distant line of lights still flowing down Fourteenth Street. It's now a
quarter past twelve, and band after band is still audible as the procession
goes down Fourth Avenue. Its route was up Broadway, through Fourteenth Street to Fifth Avenue, through Fifth Avenue to Twenty-sixth
Street, and then down Fourth Avenue and the Bowery. The Fusionists
have certainly turned out in great force. (There goes "Dixie's Land";
another band is passing the corner.) There were delegations from Brooklyn, Newark, Paterson, and other cities, but this city furnished the great
majority, and this certainly looks as if the Fusionists' boast of 40,000
majority in the city and county of New York might be justified. Here
come more drums.

Talked with Mr. Ruggles about this crisis. He is constitutionally
timid when people are angry and excited and Southern bluster has somewhat impressed him. Perhaps his anxiety is well grounded, for blusterers
may be mischievous. Both North and South seem to him deeply diseased
with sectional animosity, and he thinks the Cotton States may probably
commit some overt act of treason and secession when Lincoln's election
is announced. Stocks have fallen heavily today.

October 24, WEDNESDAY. The Board of Brokers is in decided panic.
Stocks are going down. Cause, the anticipation of trouble growing out of
Lincoln's election. The government loan, just taken at a premium, is a
strong indication the other way, especially as Southern bankers bid for it;
but a few timid capitalists here are unquestionably converting their securities, and Kearny tells me the deposits in the Trust Company are unusually heavy. There is heavy money-pressure at the South. But that is
one of the ordinary fluctuations of trade, due to causes outside of politics,
and has not yet reacted on us here.

Walter Cutting was very atrabilious—his prophesyings were full of
woe. Joseph Lawrence of the United States Trust Company says that they
have been refusing Southern stocks as collaterals for several days. He and
other leading financiers say that, though secession would produce a general
fall in values here of twenty-five per cent, at least, it is better for us to test
the question at once and submit to that fall, if so it must be, than continue
exposed to these panics and fluctuations, which must occur at short intervals while the question remains open.

People begin to look grave and talk anxiously about our prospects. Will this have any serious effect on the vote of New York and Pennsylvania? Panic and pressure in New York and Philadelphia will not have made themselves felt throughout the country in time to influence the elections. Had they occurred earlier, they might have determined the result, for comparatively few Republicans love niggers enough to sacrifice investments for their sweet sake.

October 25. We have reason to be unsettled and alarmed. A large and influential Southern party is working hard for disunion, and in South Carolina, at least, is strong enough to overawe and silence the sensible and conservative minority. Lincoln's election will certainly be followed by a revolutionary movement there. Then we shall see. If no other state join her in secession and if she have time to cool down and recover her senses before any actual collision, and if no accident complicate the situation, this dangerous point may be weathered. But if things take another turn, the black year of 1860 will long be remembered. At best, we must expect an ugly shock and an anxious time before this year is ended.

October 27. Today's special rumor is of a scheme of disunion, fathered by the Hon. Howell Cobb of Georgia, Secretary of the Treasury, who is now favoring us "mudsills" of New York with his presence and talking sedition. His plan is said to be the secession of all the Southern states and of the commercial portions of the Middle and New England states. New York, I suppose, is to be divided by a line crossing the Hudson at West Point. This is lunacy incredible of a man who goes at large. But, I fear there is no doubt that this Honorable Cobb, one of our highest officers of state, is in shameful alliance with the most advanced destructives and secessionists of the South, and stands ready to become a traitor upon the first eligible opportunity for treason. There is reason to fear that our disgraceful old chief magistrate, James Buchanan himself, is in the hands of men like Cobb and ready to become their instrument.

Even anti-Republicans seem to find this a little too much to bear. The attempt to bully us is barefaced. If these threats are in earnest, they will drive all the North into earnest, resolute resistance, with very little distinction of party. If they are merely part of the electioneering programme of the administration and the South, it is a rash and indiscreet programme. The crack of the plantation whip is too audible.

Caleb Cushing foreshadowed something like this in a speech last summer, when he said in effect that Abolitionists need not suppose the civil war which their fanaticism was bringing upon the country would be remote and confined to the South. "No, we will begin it here, in the streets of Boston." But the dream of setting up insurrection against our "State Sovereignties" of New York and Massachusetts in enthusiastic loyalty to the "peculiar institution" and the nigger-owning aristocracy is too extravagant to be entertained by any sane man not under the influence of whiskey, opium, or hasheesh.

October 28. The talk today is that Fusionism may carry this state after all. Then the election goes into the House and would be long contested before a majority could unite on any one of the three. Excitement would be prolonged and sectional fury intensified. I don't feel like voting for Lincoln, but I should be sorry to see New York frightened into voting for anybody else, even if the inevitable crisis were thereby postponed to 1864. It may as well be met now; and were Lincoln to be beat, I believe the Southern states would go into convention, nevertheless, so scared and angry are they.

Old Mrs. Hayward of South Carolina is at the New York Hotel in deep affliction and alarm because it is well known that "the abolitionists" have consigned large invoices of strychnine and arsenic to the slaves of her neighborhood. So Mrs. S. B. Ruggles reports, who saw her yesterday.

Mrs. Sally Hampton spoke the other evening at Mrs. Peters's of Dr. Lieber's having lately presided at a German Republican meeting at Cooper Institute. "So unfortunate for his son" (in business at Columbia or Charleston), "he was doing so well, and, of course, this ruins all his prospects at the South"!!! This is tyranny beyond King Bomba. If severance come, we must console ourselves for its calamity by remembering that we are freed from a most disreputable partner.

The Hon. Cobb, at Duncan, Sherman & Co.'s office, has been openly damning the blindness and stupidity of the capitalists who have taken the United States ten million loan at a premium, and declaring it is not worth fifty cents on the dollar. (So Charley Strong reported on respectable authority.) Pretty talk for a Secretary of the Treasury! I guess he put this loan into the market just at this time in the expectation it would not be taken, and hoping to make capital out of its failure for his own clique of traitors.

October 29. No new features in today's political talk. Perhaps the Fusionists are rather more confident, though the *Herald* gave the latter up for lost a week ago. I hear it said today that New York, New Jersey, and Pennsylvania will vote anti-Republican, which I doubt most omnipotently. There is at least an even chance that we are now on the eve of a great public disaster, a calamity to the whole civilized world. Submission by the North would not avert it long if the Southerners are as unanimously in folly as they seem to be, and I'm not sure the North can submit to be rough-ridden any longer without disgrace.

October 31, WEDNESDAY.   Am just from *Der Freischütz* with Ellie and Mrs. Georgey Peters. The lovely phrases of the finale are not quite out of my ears yet. Formes was Caspar; Stigelli, Max; and Fabbri the heroine. The best performance of the opera I have seen. The Fabbri misconceived her part, took everything too slow and spoiled the glorious allegro of the "Wie nachte mir der schlummer" scene by breaking it up into little bits of light and shadow instead of giving us the sustained rush of joyous melody which Weber meant it to be, and which she could have made it if she tried. But in that scene, perhaps, and in Caspar's drinking song certainly, Weber overrated the capacities of voice, energy, and expression. No mortal ever existed who could render them as they should be rendered and do full justice to their intensity. . . .

No change in the aspect of political matters. Samuel J. Tilden has come out with a letter (anti-Republican) that shows far more depth and ability than I've given him credit for. He has passed for a commonplace, clever, political wire-puller, but he deals with this great question in a statesman-like way. Southern papers and stump orators continue in a blatant way. Fortunately a deal of mischievous gas is liberated and made audible which might be energetic for evil were it pent up. . . .

Republicans refuse to believe secession possible (in which I think they are wrong), and maintain that were it accomplished, it would do us no lasting mischief. I am sure it would do fatal mischief to one section or another and great mischief to both. Amputation weakens the body, and the amputated limb decomposes and perishes. Is our vital center North or South? Which is Body and which is Member? We may have to settle that question by experiment. We are not a polypoid organism that can be converted into two organisms by mere bisection. China is a specimen of that type, but we claim higher rank. Bisection is disaster and degradation, but if the only alternative is everlasting submission to the South, it must come soon, and why should it not come now? What is gained by postponing it four years longer? I feel Republican tonight.

November 2.   Sent Ellie to the opera in charge of her brother Jem and sallied out for a debilitated stroll. Found a great Wide-Awake demonstration in progress; inspected them in Fourteenth Street. Seward was making a speech in "Palace Gardens," and the crowd there was dense, the

Gardens packed full and impenetrable. The show in the street was brilliant—rockets, Roman candles with many colored fire balls, Bengal lights, the Wide-Awakes with their lanterns and torches, and "I wish I was in Dixie." I adjourned to Broadway in front of the New York Hotel to see the procession pass. The Southerners of the hotel groaned and hissed, and the Republican mob in and about the Lincoln and Hamlin headquarters across the street cheered and roared, and the din was deafening. But there was no breach of peace. . . .

Think I will vote the Republican ticket next Tuesday. One vote is insignificant, but I want to be able to remember that I voted right at this grave crisis. The North must assert its rights, now, and take the consequences.

Think of James J. Roosevelt, United States District Attorney, bringing up certain persons under indictment for piracy as slave-traders to be arraigned the other day, and talking to the Court about the plea the defendants should put in, and saying that "there had been a great change in public sentiment about the slave trade," and that "of course the President would pardon the defendants if they were capitally convicted." !!! Is Judge Roosevelt more deficient in common sense or in moral sense? If we accede to Southern exactions, we must re-open the slave trade with all its horrors, establish a Slave Code for the territories, and acquiesce in a decision of the United States Supreme Court in the Lemmon case that will entitle every Southerner to bring his slaves into New York and Massachusetts and keep them there. We must confess that our federal government exists chiefly for the sake of nigger-owners. *I can't do that.* Rather let South Carolina and Georgia secede. We will coerce and punish the traitorous seceders if we can; but if we can't, we are well rid of them.

If I looked remarkably like Kossuth or Mazzini, I could nevertheless travel through Austria with no danger beyond that of a few days' detention, at the end of which, my identity being proven, I should be dismissed with apologies and an indemnity. But I happen to be mistaken for John Jay at least once a week, and it would therefore be utter madness for me to visit that section of our free and happy republic that lies south of Mason and Dixon's line. Before I had traveled half a day's journey through that sunny and chivalric region, some gent who had visited New York would spot me as a damned abolitionist emissary. I should be haled forth from my railroad car and hanged on the nearest palmetto tree.

November 4, SUNDAY.   Mr. Ruggles had a long private talk yesterday with General Scott, some portion whereof he imparted to me, including matters I don't care to write here. The General is loyal and union-loving, intensely and without reservation. He wrote to the War Department October 27 or 28, calling attention to the inadequate garrison of Fort Moultrie, only about one hundred men instead of the eight hundred or one thousand required to work its guns, and to the unprotected state of other Southern forts and arsenals, but he has received no answer. Ingraham, appointed some three months since to command of the Home Squadron, is a South Carolina man.

If old Buchanan be really playing into the hands of secessionists, and if disunion come next week, as I think it will, and if his non-feasance enable the fire-eaters to take possession of Fort Moultrie or any other federal fortalice, there will arise from all the North (and, I trust, from no small portion of the South), a reactionary indignant cry for vengeance against traitors in high places that will make old Buck's neck feel insecure for a season.

November 5. With William Schermerhorn to Columbia College Board meeting at two o'clock. Unusual amount of business, mostly unimportant. Treasurer's report. Report from a Committee on Tutorships; we decided to appoint three. . . .

I confidently predict that Lincoln will be elected by the people, and that South Carolina and Texas, and probably Georgia and Mississippi, will thereupon be foolish enough to commit themselves to revolution, which will be a grave calamity. Also that Governor Wise will make several great speeches, and make himself singularly ridiculous. Also, that there will be Northern men enough interested in Southern trade to paralyze our Northern protest against treason and disunion, and that their special organ will be the New York *Express*.[17] Also, that Southern conservatives will be crushed and silenced, though in a majority, and that the Reign of Terror in the Carolinas, Georgia, and other states will be so strengthened that it may become intolerable and be thrown off. I fear the question may have a grim solution in an uprising of the slaves, from Richmond to Galveston, stimulated by their masters' insane talk about the designs of the Black Republican party.

November 6, TUESDAY. A memorable day. We do not know yet for what. Perhaps for the disintegration of the country, perhaps for another

[17] James Brooks's *Express*, founded in 1836 and now supporting Douglas, was a peace-at-any-price organ, reflecting the views of many merchants; in 1861 its defense of the South almost provoked mob violence.

proof that the North is timid and mercenary, perhaps for demonstration that Southern bluster is worthless. We cannot tell yet what historical lesson the event of November 6, 1860, will teach, but the lesson cannot fail to be weighty.

Clear and cool. Vote very large, probably far beyond that of 1856. Tried to vote this morning and found people in a queue extending a whole block from the polls. Abandoned the effort and went downtown. Life and Trust Company meeting. The magnates of that board showed no sign of fluster and seemed to expect no financial crisis. Uptown again at two, and got in my vote after only an hour's detention. I voted for Lincoln.

After dinner to the Trinity School Board at 762 Broadway. Thence downtown, looking for election returns. Great crowd about the newspapers of Fulton and Nassau Streets and Park Row. It was cold, and I was alone and tired and came home sooner than I intended. City returns are all one way, but they will hardly foot up a Fusion majority of much above 25,000. Brooklyn said to be Fusion by 14,000. An anti-Lincoln majority of 40,000 in New York and Kings, well backed by the river counties, may possibly outweigh the Republican majorities in the western counties, but that is unlikely. The Republicans have gained in the city since 1856, and have no doubt gained still more in the interior.

The only signs of excitement and enthusiasm that I saw were in the crowd about the Bell and Everett headquarters (in Broadway below Pine Street).

Election day, as Strong indicates, passed without disturbance in New York; the press even found it dull. Lincoln's election was so universally expected that no one could feel very much excited. As the returns were telegraphed in, it became plain that he had won an overwhelming majority in the electoral college, where he had 180 votes, Breckinridge 72, Bell 39, and Douglas 12. But he had only a plurality of the popular vote, which stood Lincoln 1,866,452; Douglas 1,376,957; Breckinridge 850,082; Bell 588,879. Lincoln had carried all of the free states except New Jersey, where he divided the electors with Douglas. In New England, New York, and Pennsylvania his majorities were impressive. But the most striking feature of the election was the heavy popular vote that Douglas, with the Buchanan Administration and the South opposing him, polled. The question now in everybody's mind was as to the course of the South. Already, on November 5, Governor Gist of South Carolina had recom-

mended to the legislature that if Lincoln were elected, it should provide for a
convention to decree the secession of the state from the Union. And on election
night the crowds in Charleston cheered the news of Lincoln's triumph as the
harbinger of a new Southern confederacy. But Strong remained hopeful.

November 7.   Lincoln elected. Hooray. Everybody seems glad of it.
Even Democrats like Isaac Bell say there will be no disturbance, and that
this will quiet slavery agitation at the North. DePeyster Ogden's nerves
are a little unstrung, but they are never very steady.

Republicans have carried every state on which they counted, except
New Jersey, and it may be they have carried that, too. They have a very
fair show in Delaware!!! Wilmington gives them a majority. Kentucky,
Virginia, Maryland, and Tennessee are believed to have gone for Bell, a
sore discouragement to the extremists.

Telegrams from the South indicate no outbreak there. There is a silly
report from Washington that Governor Wise contemplates "a raid" on
that city at the head of a ragged regiment of rakehelly, debauched Virginians. He has few equals in folly, but this story is incredible. I wish it
was true and that he would proceed to do it. Nothing could make Southern
ultraism more ridiculous. I would not have him hanged for his treasonable
attempt, but publicly spanked on the steps of the Capitol.

The next ten days will be a critical time. If no Southern state commit
itself to treason within a fortnight or so, the urgent danger will be past.
Now that election is over, excitement will cool down rapidly, and even
South Carolina will not secede unless under excitement that blinds her to
the plain fact that secession is political suicide.

If they were not such a race of braggarts and ruffians, I should be sorry
for our fire-eating brethren, weighed down, suffocated, and paralyzed by a
nigger incubus 4,000,000 strong, of which no mortal can tell them how they
are to get rid, and without a friend in the world except the cotton buyers
who make money out of them, and the King of Dahomey. The sense of the
civilized world is against them. They know that even the manufacturers
and traders who profit by them condemn the institution on which their
social system rests. And now their own country decides against their real
or imaginary interests, and gives a judgment which they consider (and
perhaps correctly on the whole) to be a censure, and which many of them
suppose commits the government to a policy hostile to them and endangering their peace and safety.

November 8. . . . News from the South comes only in brief, but is all one way. Wrath and fiery hatred and malice, privy conspiracy and rebellion, treason and secession, seem the popular doctrine and sentiment in all the Cotton States, and even in North Carolina and Virginia. Colonel Scott (the General's son-in-law), who is a quiet, thoughtful, judicious man, tells me he expects serious trouble in South Carolina and Alabama at once, but he is not sure it will involve the neighboring states.[18] *Per contra*, men like old Stevens, John C. Green, Bidwell, and others, see not the slightest ground for apprehension.[19]

November 9.   Much gasconading from the sunny South, condensed in telegraphic reports fortunately. "Palmetto Flag" raised, great speeches, fuss and fury, messages from governors, conventions called, Collector of Charleston resigning, "secession inevitable," and so on. It's a critical time, but things are not so bad as I expected they would be three days after Lincoln's election.

November 10.   Trinity Church Committee on St. George's chapel this afternoon. Gouverneur Ogden tells me Betts wants his salary raised to $1,000 as clerk of Columbia College on the strength of our benefaction to the treasurer (Gouverneur Ogden). They are equal in meanness and rapacity. Trustees of a religious or charitable organization should be prohibited from receiving pay for services in any capacity. They should be men who can and will give their time and labor for the public good without reward. If the College needs a financial agent who will make the management of its property his chief business, it should select him from among business men outside the board. If Betts is to have $1,000 for keeping our minutes, each of his colleagues is entitled to $500 per annum, at least, for attending meetings and serving on committees. . . .

News from the South continues to be menacing and uncomfortable. I think the storm will blow over and die away without uprooting anything, but it is a critical time. A trifle may fatally complicate the situation. . . .

November 11, SUNDAY.   Miss Puss at tea tonight; afterwards Charley, D'Oremieulx, Dr. Carroll, Jem Dwight, Hoffman, Jem Ruggles, and George Anthon. Political crisis thoroughly discussed. General disposition to concede the right of secession and to regard it with indifference and

[18] Henry Lee Scott, who married Winfield Scott's daughter Cornelia, was a North Carolinian. He had just been retired as Inspector-General in command of the forces in the city of New York.

[19] John A. Stevens was president of the Bank of Commerce; John C. Green was also a banker, and a merchant in the China trade; he is best remembered as a benefactor of the New York Society Library and New York University, and as the philanthropist who endowed the John C. Green School of Science at Princeton.

contempt. I hold secession unlawful and most calamitous, but the South is likely to do this wrong and folly and mischief if it find the North acquiescent and good-natured. I'm sorry, however, to find so many Northerners holding the Union so cheap.

November 12.   No material change in the complexion of Southern news. Unless writers of telegraph items lie loudly, secession is inevitable. There is uneasiness here, but mainly as to the possibility of a tight money market from the financial crisis Southern folly is bringing upon the South, which must inevitably react on us more or less. People generally treat the political peril with what seems to me unaccountable indifference. This financial crisis is already beginning in Charleston and Mobile. Suspension of specie payments seems close at hand. They have overtraded, and their crops are short, and they would have been hard up had Lincoln been defeated, and obliged to do their uttermost to get the hogs and housing they need to carry them through the winter. But now that Lincoln is elected and their terrorists are roving about confiscating Northern property and repudiating Northern debts, their credit is paralyzed and they are in danger of a general smash. It would injure us, of course; it may bring them to their senses, or it may make them desperate and reckless.

November 13.   Stocks have fallen heavily today, and I think they will fall much lower before this game is played out.[20] One can buy in yet more profitably a fortnight hence. Southern securities are waste paper in Wall Street. Not a dollar can be raised on them. Who wants to buy paper that must be collected by suit in the courts of South Carolina and Georgia?

November 15.   Tonight I heard Lieber's lecture at the Law School. Matter good and well arranged; manner bad—dreamy, dozy, and maundering. . . .

No material progress in the political crisis. Stocks have rallied a little here. Perhaps the febrile symptoms and cerebral disturbance of the South seem a shade easier. But the reign of terror in South Carolina continues unmitigated. Mrs. Sally Hampton, now in New York, wants to go home to Columbia, S. C., or thereabouts, and requires an escort, of course. Her husband can't come North without exposing himself to a conviction of "incivisme," and Mr. George Baxter, her papa, cannot go South without danger of being tarred and feathered as a Northerner and a possible Abolitionist. So Mrs. Sally Hampton and her three pretty babies still abide in Second Avenue. Willie Alston and Pringle meant to spend another

---

[20] Many business men thought the panic worse than in 1857; and numerous firms failed as their Southern paper became worthless.

month here, but their neighbors write them that they must come home. Their loyalty to the South will be suspected if they keep away. So they return, reluctantly. . . .

We are generally reconciling ourselves to the prospect of secession by South Carolina, Georgia, Alabama, little Florida, and perhaps Mississippi, too. We shall be well rid of them. Perhaps the prevalence of this feeling— the cordial consent of the North—will keep them from seceding. I think these porcine communities incline to run out of the Union merely because they think we want to keep them in. One should never pull a pig in the direction one wants it to travel. They have long governed us and controlled our votes by the threat of secession. They naturally think secession will be a crushing calamity to the North and the severest punishment they can inflict on us for electing Lincoln.

November 17. Things in general look bluish-gray. Prophesyings of panic and crisis, and of still worse calamity, are heard in our streets. But people try to amuse themselves; for example, Henry Fearing has just been giving a sumptuous dinner to a dozen men at the New York Club, and Giraud Foster is to give another at the Union. Charles E. Strong, Jem Strong, and H. H. Ward as umpires are to decide which dinner was the more brilliant success, and the giver of the second best pays for both. A very pleasant transaction, no doubt, but just at this time it impresses me disagreeably. It seems like some gorgeous *Heliogabalic Convivium* of the days when the Empire was in decadence. . . .

Memoranda of the crisis. Stocks fell heavily today. The Trust Company declines receiving deposits payable on demand, or for less than six months. A Charleston savings bank has decided to act on a by-law or a provision of its charter authorizing it to insist on ninety days' notice of every draft. Doubt and distrust reign in Wall Street. The best paper is negotiated with difficulty. William and Edmund Schermerhorn, Edward Bancker, and other croakers think we are drawing near to the worst period of crisis and depression this city has ever known. Mr. Samuel B. Ruggles confidently expects another suspension of specie payment before next spring, perhaps before January. *Per contra*, John A. Stevens is sure this flurry will be over, and everything in its normal stride again within thirty days. Everyone admits that our financial condition was never sounder than at this time. But a vague apprehension of some undefined change and revolution has destroyed confidence in securities and property of every kind.

November 19, MONDAY. A most gloomy day in Wall Street. Everything at a deadlock. First-class paper not negotiable; demand for money greater than in October, 1857. Stocks falling. It's said the banks resolved today to buy three millions of exchange on London. This may probably see the machine going again, for the time at least, and enable the West and South to begin moving their grain and cotton. . . .

Very few now deny the probability of secession by the Cotton States, and South Carolina is given up as hopeless. Our national mottoes must be changed to *"e pluribus duo"* (at least) and "United we stand, divided we stand easier." It is generally conceded, moreover, that if federal coercion be applied to a single seceding state, the whole South will range itself against the government.

November 20. Wall Street was a shade less disconsolate this morning. Stocks rallied at the First Board but began to waver and fall again at the Second. The banks cannot bring about a decisive reaction; the disease is too deep-seated.

The revolutionary movement in South Carolina and the Gulf States seems, on the whole, to be gaining strength and consistency. No signs yet of any "sober second thought." Conservatism and common-sense (if any be left in the Cotton States), are still intimidated and silent. Probably the Border States, led by Virginia, will try to mediate and pacify. Dissolution of the Union and re-opening of the slave trade would be disastrous to them, so they naturally desire to make peace. But their mediation will probably be upon the basis of recognition by the North of the extremest Southern exactions (slave trade excepted). The North must consent that slavery be introduced into the territories; Massachusetts, Vermont, Wisconsin, and other states must repeal their "personal liberty" laws that interfere with the Fugitive Slave Law. That plan will not work. Those state laws ought to be repealed, but the South has no right to demand their repeal and make their enactment an excuse for treason, because they are utterly unconstitutional and mere nullities, and no one doubts the United States Supreme Court would so adjudge them.

If these traitors succeed in dismembering the country, they will have a front place in the Historical Gallery of Celebrated Criminals. No political crime was ever committed as disastrous to mankind and with so little to provoke or excuse the wrong as that which these infamous disunionists are conspiring to perpetrate. . . .

November 22. Wall Street has breathed more freely these two days. News this afternoon that all the banks from Charleston to Philadelphia have suspended. I don't know that we need suffer in consequence.

November 23. Mrs. Carson of South Carolina (daughter of Petigru of

Charleston) dined here; conversable, agreeable, and handsome in a mature style. Also Mr. and Mrs. D. C. Murray, Wickham Hoffman, George F. Allen, and Mr. Ruggles. We had much pleasant talk, though the one engrossing subject of the time was excluded, for the sake of our South Carolinian convive. Mr. Ruggles and Allen remained after the rest had gone.

November 24. Stocks all up today and Wall Street very jolly. But they will go lower yet, and Wall Street will look more blue than it has looked these thirty years before A.D. 1860 is ended.

Dr. Peters, and George Anthon, and Charley Peters dined here. After dinner with Ellie and George Anthon to Academy of Music on Robert Cutting's invitation to the rehearsal of *La Juive*; Stigelli, Fabbri, Anna Bishop, Formes, and others. A pleasant and sunny evening. Opera in *dishabille*, and a splendid revelation of Bohemia.

November 25. The Supreme Court in this district has at last reluctantly concluded that it won't do to nullify the decision of the Court of Appeals, reversing their order in the Law School case; so Mr. H. W. Cooper will be sworn in whenever he pleases.

November 26. Today's newspapers indicate no new symptom in our sore national sickness. The tide is still rising, I think, in all the Cotton States. Reaction and ebb are sure to follow, but they may come too late. This growing excitement may do irreparable mischief before it dies out and reaction sets in. The country may be overwhelmed by a flood of disaster and disgrace before the tide begins to fall.

November 27. Nothing new in Wall Street, except that stocks are all down again. Secession certainly gains favor at the South, and grows more threatening every day. But there are symptoms of backing down at the North. There are demonstrations toward repeal of the obnoxious "personal liberty bills" of certain Northern states. It seems likely that Republican leaders and wire-pullers have concluded on a policy of concession and conciliation. I hope it may be in time to prevent terrible mischief.

These "personal liberty laws" are unconstitutional and void. They are mere nullities, and do no harm to the South. What one nigger has South Carolina lost by the legislation of Vermont or Wisconsin? The clamor about them is a palpable humbug. Still they ought to be repealed, being wrong in spirit and interest.

November 28. No political news of importance. The progress of events has startled and staggered some of our notables, who were laughing secession to scorn a fortnight ago. John C. Green, for one, "never dreamed these Southerners would go so far." I think, from all indications, that the Republican leaders are frightened and ready to concede everything, to restore the Missouri Compromise line and satisfy the fugitive slave remedies of the South. A movement that way has certainly begun. But it may be too soon for the North and too late for the South. Suppose it prevail. How will it be received in Massachusetts and Western New York? Will Republicans feel that they have been sold by their leaders, and recalcitrate into more intense anti-Southern feeling? I think they will and that many Republicans will enroll themselves as Abolitionists. But if this crisis pass over without disruption and ruin, if our national life endure another year, I think a strong Union party will come into being and control extremists, South and North both.

November 29. Thanksgiving Day. No political news today. Congress meets Monday. Mr. Ruggles's friend, Senator Dixon,[21] is in town on his way to Washington. Horribly frightened. Connecticut expects him to do something in the Senate, and he is anxiously enquiring, "What shall I do to be saved from the humiliation of admitting that I'm unequal to my high place?"

Tom Corwin was in town Tuesday night with the draft of some "Bill of Rights" which he means to propose, affirming the rights which the South pretends to believe endangered.

There's a bad prospect for both sections of the country. Southern ruffianism and brutality are very bad, but the selfishness, baseness, and corruption of the North are not good at all. Universal suffrage has been acquiesced in for many years. It is no longer debated. But it's at the root of our troubles. What we want is a strong government, instead of a "government of opinion." If there be disunion, a strong government will be demanded and will come into being somehow, both North and South. Democracy and equality and various other phantasms will be dispersed and dissipated and will disappear forever when two hostile families of states stand side by side, and a great civil war becomes inevitable. To which party will God give a great general, when that crisis is upon us?

December 1. Sorry to learn that the Vermont legislature refuses to repeal its personal liberty bill.

A money indemnity for run-away niggers might satisfy the South (if it wanted to be satisfied), but I fear no such arrangement is practicable. Every worthless Cuffee and superannuated Dinah south of the Potomac

[21] James Dixon (1814–1873), Republican Senator from Connecticut.

would be somehow exported into the free states within a year and would have to be paid for.

One hears queer talk in these days of excitement. That white-cravatted, conservative, old, quiet Dutchman, Edward Bancker, thinks every man ought to be hanged that voted for Lincoln, and "means to go South and shoulder a musket." So he tells me, but I think fear for the future of his bank stocks and real estate has slightly deranged his mind, for he is said to have experienced some slight aberrations a few years since, when he had a fierce quarrel with a neighbor about a right of way on Staten Island. Willy Cutting talks mysteriously of an organization to revolutionize the city immediately upon the secession of the South. New York and Brooklyn are to be a free port, and with one or two adjoining counties, Westchester and Kings, I suppose, to constitute an independent principality. Mayor and Common Council to be kicked out, if not hanged, and suffrage to be confined to owners of $5,000 worth of property. A promising prospect.

Why *do* the people so furiously rage together just now? What has created our present unquestionable irritation against the South? What has created the Republican party?

Its nucleus was the abolition handful that has been vaporing for thirty years, and which, till about 1850, was among the more insignificant of our *isms*. Our feeling at the North till that time was not hostility to slavery, but indifference to it, and reluctance to discuss it. It was a disagreeable subject with which we had nothing to do. The battles in Congress about the right of petition, and the Giddings business, made little impression on us. But the clamor of the South about the admission of California ten years ago introduced the question of slavery to the North as one in which it had an interest adverse to the South. That controversy taught us that the two systems could not co-exist in the same territory. It opened our eyes to the fact that there were two hostile elements in the country, and that if we allowed slaves to enter any territorial acquisition, our own free labor must be excluded from it. The question was unfortunate for our peace. But we might have forgotten it had not S. A. Douglas undertaken to get Southern votes by repealing the Missouri Compromise. That was the fatal blow. Then came the atrocious effort to force slavery on Kansas by fraud and violence, with the full support of old Buchanan and his Southern counselors, the brutal beating of the eloquent and erudite Sumner with the cordial approbation and applause of the South, the

project to revive the slave trade, and (a little earlier) a sentimental ro-
mance, *Uncle Tom's Cabin*, that set all Northern women crying and
sobbing over the sorrows of Sambo. The Fugitive Slave Law stimulated
sectional feeling by making slavery visible in our own communities, and
above all, the intolerable brag and bluster and indecent arrogance of the
South has driven us into protest against their pretensions, and into a
determination to assert our own rights in spite of their swagger.

December 2, SUNDAY. At supper, Mrs. Carson of South Carolina,
and one Lowndes (a very nice fellow), and Lawrence Williams, Murray
Hoffman, and his brother Wickham, Walter Cutting, George Anthon,
Mr. Ruggles, Dr. Peters, William Chrystie, and one or two more.

Lowndes is quite a young man. Seems a specimen of South Carolinian
conservatism. Is engaged as assistant to Petigru in codifying the laws of
his state, but favors disunion decidedly. His talk is temperate but unintelligible. I could make no sense of it, and suggestions that I took to be
truisms seemed to strike him as speculative novelties he was unwilling
to admit. I fear Northerner and Southerner are aliens, not merely in
social and political arrangements, but in mental and moral constitution.
We differ like Celt and Anglo-Saxon, and there is no sufficient force in
"a government of opinion" to keep us together against our will. . . . A
move toward concession and conciliation will undoubtedly be made in
Congress at once by Republican leaders, and will probably prevail. But
it is too late for the South and too soon for the North. The utmost I hope
is that the offer and its contemptuous rejection will put South Carolina
hopelessly and visibly in the wrong, strengthen Union men in the other
Cotton States, and disgust Virginia and Kentucky.

These Southern heretics would be inexhaustible mines of fun, were
the position a little less grave. For example, Governor Gist of South
Carolina writing a grand revolutionary message and recommending all
sorts of measures for "national" defense and "national" finance and so
on, and the enlargement of the State Lunatic Asylum! "National," indeed!
The whole white population of that dirty little spiteful district is con-
siderably less than that of Brooklyn, less than the increase of this city and
county of New York since 1855.

December 4. Interview with Bob LeRoy. Another chapter has opened
in the disastrous history of his family. His father, flagitious old Black
Jake, took a young wife last June—an attractive, refined, well-educated
girl of twenty or thereabouts, daughter of a used-up, insolvent Claverack
lawyer. She sold herself to the old beast for the sake of her family. She

was soon told by the "housekeeper," Mary Ann (a retired strumpet, and formerly in the service of the distinguished Fanny White) that she must not presume on her position, and that if she did so, she should be turned out of doors. The poor wife made some feeble appeal to Black Jake, but without effect, and seems to have acquiesced in her degraded position. This Mary Ann and her husband James (Black Jake's body-servant and confidential adviser) hold Black Jake under their absolute control. Then the lady was reported *enceinte*, over which fact her husband exulted in a style more vehement than refined. A week ago, she was ill, afflicted, it was said, with a disease to which any woman who had married Black Jake would be exposed, and threatened with miscarriage. According to Bob and the Rev. Mr. DeKoven, she died Sunday soon after taking medicine from the hands of this man "James," and was buried yesterday. Bob had seen the nurse, who came to town last evening and who declares there was foul play, and that the physician says she was poisoned. Bob goes to Hudson tonight, resolved on investigation, exhumation, and other steps. If he can get these filthy parasites out of his father's house, his position will be improved. From what he told us, I guess the case was either puerperal convulsion in premature confinement, *or* strychnine poisoning; probably the former.

President's message appears today, and is gobbled up with avidity by everyone. Weak, of course, but perhaps the "Old Public Functionary's" positions are, on the whole, discreet and sensible. The federal government is too notoriously weak to menace with effect. Had Buchanan said, "Secession is treason, and treason is a capital crime, and we have a federal judiciary established for the purpose, among others, of punishing crime, and an executive to hang whomsoever the judiciary shall adjudge worthy of hanging," his position would have been more consistent. But I incline to think it's practically the best thing a *commonplace* president could have said at this crisis. . . .

No concession will avail now, I fear. The Cotton States want to set up for themselves and they will do it.

Buchanan's message to Congress, delivered December 3, was the fruit of anxious thought and numerous Cabinet sessions. He declared that the national crisis had been caused by incessant Northern agitation for the abolition of slavery, which imperiled the security of the slaveholding states. "Many a matron throughout the South retires at night in dread of what may befall her and her children before the morning." The South, he remarked, should have been left alone. He went on to state that the recent presidential election did "not of itself afford just cause for dissolving the Union." The South, in justice to the nation, ought to await some overt act against its institutions before it resorted to secession; it could trust to the facts that the President's power was limited, and that Congress and the Supreme Court had shown themselves friendly to Southern rights. Moreover, the President asserted, secession was unconstitutional, and the Union was rightly perpetual. Under the supreme-law clause, the national government acts directly upon the people, and "the Constitution is as much a part of the constitution of each state and is as binding upon its people as though it had been textually inserted therein." But after denying that secession was either just or valid, Buchanan went on to state that the federal government could do nothing to prevent it. The national government had no rightful power to make war upon a state; and if it did attempt coercion, the resulting civil conflict would cost "a vast amount of blood and treasure" and would make future reconciliation "impossible."

Strong's disgust with this message was shared by most Northerners. But as yet no state had actually left the Union, and Buchanan believed that a conciliatory policy might yet arrest the disruption of the nation. That is, he felt it possible that if the government used only moderate measures, the upper South and Border States would remain in the Union; and that the Cotton States, seeing they could be left alone, would draw back. In any event, he was determined that the first violent step, the "overt act," should not be the work of the federal government. Winfield Scott, in a letter of October 29th to the President, had recommended that six of the forts in the South be garrisoned at once to prevent secessionist elements from taking them over. But Buchanan negatived this proposal. His policy, in the face of Southern preparations for secession and civil war, remained feeble until his cabinet was revolutionized by the resignation of Southern members and the advent of two strong Northerners, E. M. Stanton and John A. Dix. The best that could be said for his course was that it maintained an atmosphere of peace while various leaders made an effort for compromise.

December 5. President's message finds little favor here, or any-where. It's a bad time. This nation is manifestly "coming in two," or three, or more. Hopes of a Congressional compromise diminish. I have lost faith in the magic words, "somehow or other," on which I've thus far relied for a solution of the problem.

From DeKoven I hear various facts and circumstances that make it probable old LeRoy's wife had foul play. Probably she was not buried Monday, for her physician declared she should not be until after an investigation. The movements of her husband, Black Jake, were strange and suspicious a day or two before her death, but he may have acted under the direction of his two servants, James Watson and Mary Ann, who have a hold on him in some mysterious way. Mary Ann was the maid of the first Mrs. LeRoy at the time of her death.

There is yet another tragedy at hand in that unhappy family. Poor, pretty, impoverished little Mrs. Bob LeRoy has been troubled for some time by a tumor in the breast, which her physicians have been trying to reduce by pressure and other measures. Van Buren and Metcalfe now pronounce it cancer and fatal. They discourage any resort to surgery. The poor little woman bore the announcement bravely, only begging her husband might not know it yet, lest it should drive him back into his old habits.

December 6, THURSDAY. Very gloomy day downtown. "Secession" by Southern madmen felt to be inevitable and civil war sure to follow it, within the year. Forebodings grow more grave every day. The only man I know who pretends to think we shall get through this crisis is Willy Duncan (Duncan, Sherman & Co.). He thinks the money pressure in the Cotton States is going to be so severe as to bring the Bobadils and copper captains to their senses.

December 7. Stocks fell badly today, and the difficulty about exchange has returned, having been merely palliated by the action of the banks.

A committee is appointed by the House of Representatives to concoct a compromise and save the Union. It will fail. These Cotton States are acting under the influence of spite, envy, and panic fear all combined. They want no compromise. But the Republican leaders probably design to put the North right on the record by proposing liberal concessions, knowing that the South will refuse them. An abstract or summary of the President's message is much quoted. Seward has the credit of it. "No state has the right to secede, unless it wants to. The Executive is bound to coerce a seceding state, unless the Executive be opposed in its efforts to do so." Don't believe Billy Seward ever said so good a thing. . . .

Bob LeRoy has returned from his father's, after a feeble, superficial enquiry into the circumstances of his step-mother's death, and inclines to no further investigation. The physician, who was at first clamorous for a post-mortem examination, has changed his mind, and is quite satisfied there is no reason to suspect foul play. Bob has talked with her mother and sister, who seem to shrink from the question and are unwilling to have it raised.

Perhaps Old Black Jake's brutality, as detailed by himself to Bob, is enough to have killed this unfortunate girl. He is certainly by far the worst man I know. He combines more of beast and fiend than any person of whom I ever heard, except possibly a few Roman emperors in the decadence of the Empire, and a few Frenchmen of the Revolution. He converts me to the modern theory of "moral insanity." So has that venerable skeptic, Count Gurowski, been recently forced to admit one proposition of Christianity, a future state of rewards and punishments. He says, "The slavery secessionists and disunion men demonstrate the necessity of a Hell."

December 8. No special progress today in this our Revolution. Stocks rally a little. I'm satisfied from my talk with clubmen tonight that the North will ratify no compromise about the territories. Perhaps it may consent to restore the Missouri line, though even that concession is doubtful. But it will not admit that slavery exists wherever the federal government rules and that the nation recognizes slavery among its institutions.

December 9. Mr. Ruggles is on his Pacific Railroad hobby, and riding it hard. He is likely to publish certain views about it that are original and forcible and most appropriate and salutary just now. He's a very large pattern of a man.

December 10. Stocks went down today. But there seem to be gleams of light opening on us, permanent or transitory. Tonight's *Commercial* says the tide has turned; the "seceding states" will merely send commissioners to Washington to negotiate for a dissolution of the Union, and the whole treasonable movement will be procrastinated and postponed and come to naught. Perhaps. Time will tell.

I'm satisfied, too, that secession of the Cotton States alone will do us little harm. If we hold Fort Moultrie and other posts, the federal revenue will not suffer. If South Carolina and Alabama choose to decline a United States postal service and representation in Congress, I don't perceive that they will thereby hurt us much. We need not make war on them. Should we find it necessary to do so, they are weak and vulnerable and powerless for aggressive hostility. It seems questionable whether England and the other powers of Europe would feel inclined cordially to recognize a state or confederacy founded on the one idea of slavery and the extension of slavery as entitled to a place in the family circle of Christian nations. Toombs, Rhett, Wise, Yancey & Co. think they can control Christendom because the South produces cotton. They forget that it is quite as important to Charleston and Mobile that cotton be sold as it is to Lancashire and Lowell that cotton be bought.

December 12. Talked with Governor Fish. There are authentic reports of the gravest financial pressure and prospect of famine before three weeks in South Carolina, and so on. Fish thinks that hard times will rather weaken the Union men. Fusionists will attribute the calamity to the North and "the damned Union," and the ignorant, half-savage "poor whites" will believe them.

Thence to a state dinner at William Astor's (Jr.), Thirty-fourth Street and Fifth Avenue; about twenty. Ellie and I, Mr. and Mrs. Rives, Mr. and Mrs. John Astor, Mr. and Mrs. William B. Astor, Suydams, Belmonts, Duncans, Major Van Burens, Robert Hones, R. B. Minturns. I took in Mrs. Rives and had a pleasant time with her and our host. (She was Miss Barclay; her husband [Francis R.], William C. Rives's son. Their wedding was the day after ours, May 16, 1848.) . . .

The "LeRoy poisoning case" has got into the papers, thanks to Black Jake's folly. People were full of it at Astor's dinner table this evening. He sent for physicians from this city to exhume the body and make an examination (a proceeding, by the by, that looks as if Watson, who has him under control, did not fear inquiry); whereupon the coroner took the case out of the doctors' hands and summoned a jury. There is strong feeling against Black Jake in Hudson and Claverack, but mainly because of his rumored cruelty and brutality to this unfortunate young girl. The notion prevails there that she died of syphilis.

Charley has seen Judge Sutherland (whose wife is nearly related to the deceased Mrs. LeRoy) on his own responsibility, not on behalf of Bob LeRoy or Dr. DeKoven, and apprized him of the statements made by the nurse. Sutherland is not on the bench today, and has gone, I suppose, to Columbia County. He says she was a most charming and refined young woman. The physicians sent for by Black Jake were the same who lately conducted the post-mortem of his quondam concubine, Mrs. Blankman, alias Fanny White. The coincidence is partly funny, partly hideous and revolting.

Our political prospects are not brightening in the least.

December 13. George Anthon dined here. Then with him to Canterbury Hall, Broadway, a queer place. No women in the audience, which was made up mostly of raffish men drinking lager at little tables and smoking. The performances (ballet-gymnastics, singing, and so on) were respectable enough. Perhaps the ballet dancers' skirts were half an inch shorter than in *Robert le Diable* at the Academy of Music. There was some very fair comic singing (by one Ogden, *not* Gouverneur), and good music by a small orchestra.

Visit from that dirty brute Hogg. Also from the Rev. Mr. DeKoven, in a most tremulous twitter about the inquest at Hudson and the effect on his wife of any public scandal implicating her father. Consoled him by offering to bet ten to one against any evidence of poison being produced; also, by the suggestion that Black Jake's reputation could not be damaged by the clearest proof that he was accessory to any conceivable crime or enormity—in which Dr. DeKoven acquiesced.

Colonel Henry Scott tells me Major Anderson has only forty available men, at most, in Fort Moultrie. The War Department has sent him no orders. If he is repairing the works and so on, as the newspapers say, he is acting on his own responsibility. In other words, our disgraceful executive has been and is playing into the hands of traitors. That Buchanan might be hanged under lynch law almost reconciles me to that code.

Things look black. But I don't repent of my vote for Lincoln. It contributed to an experiment that tests our Boiler, and it must have undergone that same test very soon had Lincoln been defeated. The question may as well be settled at once whether we have a national government that can sustain itself under pressure, or a mere sham government that must perish whenever a set of semi-barbarous Southerners pronounce against it, with or without reason.

December 15, SATURDAY. This has been the gloomiest day yet. Mr. Secretary Cass has resigned, following the example of Mr. Secretary Cobb, whom no one regrets in the least.[22] General Scott has been in council with the Cabinet, giving advice that old Buchanan declines to adopt, namely, that the garrison of Fort Moultrie be strengthened. The necessity for reinforcements there is most urgent and the duty to send

[22] On December 14 Secretary of State Cass, after a vain effort to get Buchanan to reinforce the Charleston forts, resigned. Howell Cobb, Secretary of the Treasury, had already made his exit in order to help speed the secession of Georgia. Jeremiah S. Black of Pennsylvania was advanced from the post of Attorney-General to that of Secretary of State, and at once took a strong stand in defense of the Union. After a brief trial of a weak Marylander, Philip F. Thomas, Buchanan appointed John A. Dix—another militant Union man—to the Treasury.

them with the least possible delay as clear as the sun. Is old Buchanan imbecile, or a traitor? Or does he calculate profoundly on uniting the whole North in one flame of indignation against South Carolina by tempting the Charleston militiamen and mob to make a rush on the forts and destroy Major Anderson and his little party of less than fifty available men? The folly of his non-feasance, too! With these forts decently manned, the commerce of Charleston is under control, Federal revenue secured at that port, and South Carolinian treason paralyzed. If her chivalry attempt a siege, one month's experience of its cost would bring that Bedlamite state to its senses, like a bucket of cold water on the head of a patient in hysteria. The experiment of war could not be tried under conditions more auspicious for the Union and more sure to convince the South of its folly. Yet old Buchanan leaves Anderson and his party unsupported, with orders to defend the fort as best he may. When the calamities that seem at hand are upon us, Buchanan will hardly be able to live at the North. He will have to emigrate below the Potomac and become a "poor white" dirt-eater of the pine-barrens. Perhaps the South will tolerate the presence of a Northerner who has made himself infamous and become a fugitive and an exile by knuckling to Southern dictation. But perhaps it won't. It may hang Mr. Buchanan and tar and feather him and expel him from Southern soil as being a mere proselyte of the Gate, not a thorough-going Southerner. I don't know where the poor wretch can go with safety after dissolution is established.

Today's feeling is that secession is inevitable; that Virginia and Kentucky and the other Border States must follow their sisterhood on the Gulf, and that civil war is at hand. The prospect of conciliation by any Congressional action seems fading away.

Were we only united and unanimous here at the North, I should welcome the prospect of vigorous war on Southern treason. But we are discordant, corrupt, deeply diseased, unable to govern ourselves, and in most unfit condition for a war on others.

December 16, SUNDAY. Trinity Church, taking Hoffman with me. Vinton preached. Stopped at the post office, but found no letter there. I hoped to have received notice of Ellie's safe arrival at Washington. This evening I dined with Dr. Peters; Walter Cutting, Dr. Carroll, and Fred Snelling convives. Of course we talked of politics. Nobody talks of anything else. There is a disposition to censure the Republicans for their obstinate silence in Congress. It is said they ought to try to pacify the South by avowals of a conservative and friendly policy.

December 17, MONDAY. Murray Hoffman dined with me. Meant to have seen Booth in *Hamlet* after dinner, but we found ourselves comfortable where we were, procrastinated, and didn't go. . . .

The South Carolina convention has met and is to adjourn from Columbia to Charleston, being driven away by an epidemic . . . of small pox. Pickens is elected governor of that insolent commonwealth. He seems committed to secession and treason now, but when he crossed the Atlantic a few months ago with Mr. and Mrs. Philip Allen, he said his object in coming home was to tell his fellow citizens that they were making themselves the laughing-stock of Europe. This foul disunion disease is frightfully contagious, however (like other cachetic, asthenic distempers, jail fevers, and the like), and Pickens may have caught it. It's making steady and rapid progress in Virginia, Kentucky, Tennessee, and every slaveholding state. William Chrystie thinks, however, that Pickens's movements are those of a captain whose company is running away, and that he is trying to get ahead of the runaways that he may head them back.

Seward in town yesterday. Report of schism in Republican party of this state. A lot of extreme Free-soilers headed by Horace Greeley and including D. D. Field and Austin Stevens, Jr., pronounce against Seward and Thurlow Weed, and mean to establish an Albany newspaper organ in opposition to Weed's. Wade held forth in the Senate today against secession, "with much applause from the galleries," according to this evening's *Commercial*. The District of Columbia is Republicanized, a natural result of Lincoln's election. General Scott is at Washington, urging the President to reinforce the handful of men that garrisons Fort Moultrie, but in vain. Depression today deeper than ever. Most people give up all hope of saving the government and anticipate general bankruptcy, revolution, mob-law, chaos, and ruin.

The defeated Fusionists are holding meetings and deprecating the wrath of South Carolina. Their supplications are vain. The only thing they can say to the South with good effect is that they and their organs (*Herald* and *Express*) have been lying about the Republican party all through the campaign, for party purposes, and that the Republicans are not Abolitionists and do not seek to raise the Negro to social and political equality with the white man. But this they won't say. They might refer to the fact that of the 32,000 who voted for Lincoln in this city only 1,600 voted for the Negro suffrage amendment to the Constitution, and that in the Republican state of New York that amendment was defeated by 100,000 majority.

The principal hope for a compromise which would avert secession centered in a Senate "Committee of Thirteen," which included the moderate Crittenden of Kentucky, several Southern extremists like Robert Toombs and Jefferson Davis, and several free-soil Northerners like William H. Seward and Ben Wade. But the committee accomplished nothing. Crittenden had a plan by which slavery should be prohibited in all the national territory north of the old Missouri Compromise line of 36°30', but given federal protection south of that line; future states either north or south of the line might come in with slavery or without it, as they should decide for themselves; the Fugitive Slave Act should be vigorously enforced; whenever local sentiment prevented its enforcement, an indemnity should be paid the owner; and Congress should call upon the states to repeal the personal liberty laws. But the Republican leaders, with Lincoln foremost, refused to accept a plan which would sanction the existence of slavery in any national territory as yet unorganized as a state. They had just won an election on that issue, they contended. Moreover, they feared that the Crittenden plan would stimulate the South to attempt the conquest of Cuba and Mexico, thus acquiring more land for slavery expansion. The committee broke down in its efforts and reported no plan. Southern members also objected to certain features of the Crittenden scheme, and they declared that Republican acquiescence in any plan was a sine qua non *of Southern adherence to it.*

December 18. Columbia College meeting at two o'clock, which soon adjourned. . . . Stocks rose this morning, and everybody seemed cheerful and hopeful. There were encouraging indications in the action of Congress yesterday. Governor Fish was oracular but inclined, on the whole, to think affairs improving a little. That rather questionable Mr. F. P. James, who voted Fusion and has extensive business affiliations in every Southern state, told me his letters satisfied him that secession would end in a "fizzle"; and that if the North didn't back down, the South would have to do it within thirty days or starve. But this evening's news doesn't look well. The secession distemper is spreading fast in the Border States. Ellie mentioned in her letter that Reverdy Johnson had expressed to her great apprehension as to the course of Maryland; and Virginia, Kentucky, and Missouri are evidently uncertain and wavering now. If the Border States go, they take the national capital with them!

There is a growing disposition here to offer liberal concessions to the South; and if they be rejected, to make WAR on Southern rebellion with all the resources of the North. And that's the true talk for the times.

Suppress the sedition of Massachusetts and the treason of North Carolina with impartial rigor, and so avert our death as a nation.

December 19. Nothing new today about our national convulsion. Perhaps our prospect may be a shade less blue. Ellie's letter says little of state affairs. She's enjoying the most delightful time at Washington. I see no hopeful symptoms that have any material significance.

December 20. Lawrence Williams and George C. Anthon dined here. Murray Hoffman came in, and our session lasted till near midnight. Talked of little but North versus South, secession, coercion, Buchanan, Fort Moultrie, and so on. . . .

Things certainly a very little brighter. Action of the Georgia legislature conservative, as far as it goes, and the Charleston Convention, instead of adopting a Declaration of Independence at once, is twaddling with feeble prolixities over twopenny preliminary details as if it dreaded to approach the main question. This eruption has certainly spread fearfully through the great Border States within the last fortnight; but there are just the faintest indications that it is beginning to dry up and disappear in the region where it first broke out. Perhaps it's merely a rash that must run its course, and will leave the nation healthier and stronger. God grant that so it may be!

Many people look radiant today—Moses H. Grinnell, Royal Phelps. Even poor Bancker has emerged from the pit of his despair. Lawrence Williams, who has great intelligence and sagacity for so young a man, is clear there will be no secession, unless by poor little sulking South Carolina; and that if she sulk out by herself, she must eat humble pie and come back within six months. If this movement come to nothing, the Southern secession brag game will hardly be tried again. The South must either secede and try to set up for itself or admit that its predominance and control in our national councils have departed, never to return. Secession is madness and ruin, so they have but a choice of evils. It's their misfortune that they are pledged to a system that is against their own material interests, and of which the Gulf States, at least, cannot possibly get rid. It compels them to elect between humiliation and suicide, so I don't wonder they are savage and dangerous.

December 21, FRIDAY. Jem Ruggles dined here. George Anthon came in and they carried me off to Laura Keene's to see an idiotic production called *The Seven Sisters.* It's the most incoherent nonsense, with a few funny points. Asa Trenchard and Lord Dundreary from *Our American Cousin* are reproduced in it by tolerable imitators of Jefferson and Sothern.

. . . That termagant little South Carolina has declared herself out of the
Union, and resolved to run away and to the sea.[23] How many of the
Southern sisterhood will join the secession jig she thus leads off remains
to be seen. It strikes me that this proceeding, strictly considered, does not
take the soil and the people of South Carolina out of the federal jurisdiction at all, but if it have any legal validity or effect whatever, simply
amounts to a resignation of the qualified sovereignty heretofore enjoyed
by that state, and converts what was the State of South Carolina into the
Territory of South Carolina. It belonged and still belongs to the national
government; if it repudiates and resigns the title, duties, and dignity of
a state, what can it be but a territory? That its foolish inhabitants want
to be called an Empire or a Herzogthum or a Tribe makes no difference.

This proceeding surprises nobody and makes no sensation. It's a
grave event, and may well bring tremendous calamity upon the country.
It's a grave affair for any family if one of its members goes mad. But as
an offset, we have the influx of gold from England and the growing hopes
that Northern cities will get through the winter without the panic and
crisis and uprising of hungry mobs that our Southern friends complacently
predict.

The speeches in the seceding convention seem amazingly weak,
muddled, and prolix, coming from orators at treason-heat. No great men
appear as yet in the Southern Revolution. I suppose the leaders are of
ability not much below the average; but their proceedings (as reported)
look puerile. They resolve themselves out of the Union, and then it
seems to occur to them for the first time that they have (nominally at
least) annihilated all their postal system and abolished all commercial
relations with every port of every civilized country on earth, and they
begin pottering' about keeping up the present system for the time and
making arrangements with the federal government; in other words,
most unfortunately, with Buchanan (I omit the adjectives that *should*
precede his dirty name, for decency's sake). O, for an hour of Andrew
Jackson, whom I held (when I was a boy and he was "taking the responsibility") to be the embodiment of everything bad, arrogant, and low.

Prospects of compromise in Congress rather diminish. I fervently
hope ample concessions may be tendered to the South; concessions that
will more than satisfy all the complaints of Toombs and Yancey. I could

[23] The South Carolina Convention, meeting in Charleston, on December 20 unanimously adopted its ordinance of secession. On December 20 and 24 elections in
Mississippi and Florida chose conventions committed to secession.

almost say that I hope those concessions may be contemptuously rejected, which is nowise improbable, and that the case may thereupon be brought to a practical issue.

December 22. Today has been warm and wet. Anxiety about political matters does not diminish, but Wall Street is rejoicing in rising stocks, and easy money-market, and returning confidence in our commercial soundness.

Had a couple of hours confabulation with Mr. Ruggles. He is exulting over the passage of the Pacific Railroad Bill through the House and figures up ten majority in the Senate. It may be Pacific indeed! Louisiana and Texas will pause before they walk out of a Union that wants to spend $36,000,000 on them. The still larger outlay for the northern road will ensure the loyalty of Missouri, and at all events the North, West, and East will be bound up with Oregon and California, whatever the South may do. He is keenly and intensely gratified, too, by the introduction of his name into the bill as a corporator by general concurrence when it was in its last stages and its supporters had resolved to permit no amendment in any one feature.

At about sunset of the day on which Clan Carolina "seceded," the ayes and noes were being called on the question of appropriating ninety-six millions for a great national work! Mr. Ruggles says he went out on one of the Capitol terraces or porticos and saw the sun going down in splendor after a stormy day, and that it was *the* moment of his whole life. He saw the Pacific Coast in the glow and glory of the western sky, and saw, moreover, the sign and token that a great nation was saved. . . .

Thank Heaven, Ellie did not pay her respects to our latter Arnold, the traitorous Old Public Functionary, who lives (on the public money) in the White House.

The State Convention of South Carolina had met at Columbia on the 17th, but as Strong notes, a smallpox scare had caused it to adjourn to Charleston, where the delegates were tumultuously welcomed. In this city the secession ordinance was passed December 20, as noted above, by all of the 169 members of the convention. On the day before Christmas a "declaration of independence" was added, South Carolina resuming her "separate and equal place among the nations." In following this headlong course, the South Carolinians had been encouraged by commissioners from Mississippi and Alabama, who promised that their states would fall into line. The Charleston convention appointed

DINNER IN CAMP OF DURYEE'S ZOUAVES, FORTRESS MONROE, 4 JUNE, 1861

STRONG IS SEATED SECOND FROM LEFT

PHILIP KEARNY

ROBERT ANDERSON

JOHN POPE

GEORGE BRINTON McCLELLAN

agents to visit other Southern States and try to persuade them to join a great
Southern Confederacy, the future of which it painted in the most alluring
colors. Such a Confederacy would stretch its arms over a territory larger than
that held by any power in Europe; and "with a population four times greater
than that of the whole United States when they achieved their independence of
the British Empire; with productions which make its existence more important
to the world than that of any other people inhabiting it; with common institu-
tions to defend and common dangers to encounter," it would at once become a
great nation. South Carolina also sent three commissioners to Washington,
with orders to arrange a division of public property and a cession of the United
States forts in the harbor. All eyes were now drawn to these forts. Moultrie
was exposed to an easy attack on the land side; and Major Robert Anderson,
who perceived that the Confederates were preparing a seizure, on December
26th removed to Fort Sumter. A groan went up from the whole North as the
palmetto flag was raised over Moultrie and the federal custom house and post
office in Charleston.

December 23, SUNDAY. Fine weather. With Ellie and Johnny to
Trinity Church. Miss Rosalie joined us there; came home with us to
dinner and spent the night here. After the prayer for the President of the
United States, the Rev. Vinton read us the Bishop's pastoral letter on the
national crisis. A good sensible bread-and-milk-poultice document. His
sermon was on the same subject, and rather vigorous. . . . This morning's
Herald reports that despatches have been received at Washington that
Fort Moultrie is to be stormed by the young men and braves of the
Charleston tribe without delay. . . . I disbelieve the report . . . but I was
glad to hear from Williams that even with a garrison of only sixty-five,
the fort is safe against a *coup de main.* . . .

December 27. Great News! . . . Last night Major Anderson secretly
moved his command from Fort Moultrie to Fort Sumter, which is isolated
in mid-channel and commands Fort Moultrie and is able to resist all the
armies and navies of South Carolina, even with its present garrison. He
fired Fort Moultrie and some say blew it up, spiked the guns, and doubtless made it innocuous. An excellent move, no doubt due to Scott. It
postpones actual collision and saves the lives probably of Anderson and
his little handful of men. . . .

During these four days people have been settling down to the conviction that all the Slave States will go out, that the South will make an

attempt on Washington, and that civil war is certain. All which is not cheering at all. . . .

December 31. . . . It seems now that Major Anderson's transfer of his command to the safer position of Fort Sumter was without express orders and on his own responsibility. The Secessionists denounced the movement as a breach of faith on the part of the Administration and demanded his recall, or that he be ordered back into Fort Moultrie. Mr. Secretary Floyd, with or without Buchanan's concurrence, had promised the Charleston people that there should be no change in the position of this handful of government troops. . . . He insisted that Anderson be censured and sent back to Fort Moultrie or that the garrison be withdrawn altogether. But even Buchanan and his cabinet could not swallow this dose of baseness, so Floyd has resigned and the country is well rid of him. . . .

EFFORTS AT SECTIONAL COMPROMISE · CONFEDERATE
DEFIANCE · FORT SUMTER FIRED UPON · THE NORTHERN
UPRISING · ENTHUSIASM IN NEW YORK

*W*hen New Yorkers celebrated New Year's Day after their traditional
fashion, hope of a peaceful solution was steadily growing weaker. The
venerable John J. Crittenden, after seeing the Senate reject his compromise
based on the prohibition of slavery north of 36°30′ but its maintenance in
federal territories south of that line, proposed on January 3 that his plan be
submitted to the voters in a great referendum. This came to nothing; the idea
of a referendum was strange, and the principal Republican leaders would have
nothing to do with Crittenden's scheme. As the year opened, South Carolina
stood alone in secession, but it was plain that other states (despite strong
minorities opposed to secession) would soon follow her. On January 9, Mississippi took the plunge; on the 10th, Florida imitated her example; and Alabama,
urged to the step by Yancey and other fire-eaters, immediately joined the group.
Before the month ended, Georgia and Louisiana fell into line; and the six
states which had thus defiantly aligned themselves against the Union elected
delegates to a convention which met at Montgomery, Alabama, on February 4
to form a Southern Confederacy. All eyes North and South were then fixed on
the Border States. Strong read the future correctly when he took the view that
an armed collision was inevitable, that little South Carolina had aroused a
spirit that could not be laid, and that the revolution must terminate in eventual
civil war. But firm and sagacious action in Washington might yet save some
of the Border States for the Union and open the war under favorable conditions.

Like most Northerners, in the first days of the new year Strong felt a
short-lived elation in Buchanan's seeming abandonment of vacillation for a

display of real strength. The reorganization of the Cabinet, following the withdrawal of Cass and several Southern members in December, brought in a number of strong Unionists, who for a time perceptibly stiffened Buchanan's stand. As noted above, John A. Dix became head of the Treasury, and Jeremiah S. Black head of the State Department, while the belligerent Edwin M. Stanton was made Attorney-General. With their encouragement, Buchanan on January 8 sent a message to Congress which had the right ring. It declared that no state had the power to secede, and that the national government had both the right and the duty to use military force defensively against those who resisted federal officers or attempted to seize federal property. But when the unarmed Star of the West, *sent with men and munitions from New York to reinforce Fort Sumter, was fired upon by the guns of South Carolina, she turned back without delay; no additional move toward reinforcement was made. The Buchanan Administration simply marked time while Southern Senators and Representatives withdrew from Congress, while the Confederacy framed a constitution, and while numerous arsenals and forts in the South were seized. Naturally Strong and others were disgusted by the seeming feebleness of the government. The "wretched old Chief Magistrate," the "O.P.F." (Old Public Functionary or Old Pennsylvania Fossil), came in for endless abuse from all sides. But actually he had little choice, and he was playing a more consistent part than men realized then or for decades to come.*

Humiliated by the apparent weakness of the federal tie, by the "impotent and despicable" role of the Administration, and by the confusion, factionalism, and disheartenment of the people, Strong looked about eagerly for some tokens of rising vigor and energy. His journey to Washington early in the year was partly for purposes of observation, partly to help his father-in-law, S. B. Ruggles, push the project for what ultimately became the Union Pacific Railroad. He did not look in vain. New York and Washington had plenty of invertebrate men, to be sure, but the heart of the intelligent masses was sound. Before January ended he was able to record some encouraging street-talk, and to declare that the folly of the Southern "conspirators" had done more for the Abolitionist cause in ninety days than John Brown, Harriet Beecher Stowe, and Wendell Phillips, with their associates, could have done in a hundred years. This was true. The business leaders of New York City, even those favorable to the South, had been roused to almost unanimous indignation by the secessionist movement. The Journal of Commerce *reported on January 5 that "a large class of conservative men" in the city were ready to take "a decided stand should South Carolina persist in a belligerent course." The popular reception given to Lincoln when he passed through New York indicated a new tone of feeling; and the best men of all parties, as Strong approvingly notes, applauded the firm language of the First Inaugural. As late as March 12, Strong was still humiliated by the spectacle of "a weak, divided, disgraced people"—but the electrifying response to the firing on Fort Sumter swept away all his despondency.*

January 2, WEDNESDAY. Reports from Washington indicate that our wretched old Chief Magistrate begins to exhibit symptoms of a backbone at last. He may perhaps be beginning to understand that he has played into the hands of Southern traitors long enough, and that theirs is too hard a service. It is rumored today that Major Anderson is to be reinforced and that certain ships of war are under sailing orders for Charleston Harbor. Too late, I fear.

I spent yesterday at home. Some eight or ten dined here, and others came in afterwards. It was a pleasant evening. Bob LeRoy appeared very well. The inquest in Columbia County on poor Mrs. "Black Jake" LeRoy is going on, and the testimony thus far looks bad. It convicts Black Jake of the vilest, beastliest tyranny and brutality and strengthens the suspicion of poison.

January 11, FRIDAY. Much to write, too much for one who was up at 4:30 this morning and has travelled a quarter of a thousand miles since daybreak. Even the most insignificant memoranda of these revolutionary days may be worth preserving. We are making history just now fearfully fast.

Thursday, the third, [took] Jersey City ferry and railroad for Philadelphia at eleven A.M. Disgusting steady rain, dull headache. An uninteresting, monotonous ride at best, but most dreary when all the country looks waterlogged and as if deliquescing into primæval chaotic bog, when the very ducks and geese gaze at the traveller with a mute appeal for pity and warm towels, when all one's feelings are harrowed up by sympathy for his unhappy fellow creatures condemned to live in the dismal farmhouses and village homes that are visible from the railroad cars. Reached Philadelphia at three o'clock; Girard House. Most lonely and doleful drive thereto from the railroad depot through miles of monotonous, dirty streets. Rain held up in the evening, and I found my way to Horace

Binney's in South Sixth Street, where I was most kindly received by Horace and Mrs. Eliza and poor Julia Johnson, and urged to take up my quarters with them.[1]

Friday, the fourth. . . . [Took] the railroad for Baltimore at noon. . . . I found William H. Aspinwall on the train at Baltimore, bound for Washington on a Union-saving expedition. Showed me letters from Petigru and others at Charleston, indicating an uncomfortable state of affairs in that metropolis. Washington and Willard's Hotel at 6:15 P.M.; supper. Call on Mrs. Senator Dixon of Connecticut, with Mr. Ruggles, and also on General Scott. Long live the old General!

Saturday. With Mr. Ruggles, inspecting exterior of Treasury, Patent Office, and so forth, and to the Capitol. Settled ourselves in Senate Chamber, first calling on Seward at his house, and calling also on Mr. Speaker Pennington in his gorgeously gilt-and-mirrored Speaker's room. Seward opened the Pacific railroad question in a dignified, statesmanlike speech (which Mr. Ruggles wrote in our little parlor last night). There was opposition from Missouri, from the extreme factions South, of course, and from the Northwest, which wants a route yet farther north. Rice of Minnesota objected and opposed, with a dirty appeal to Southern prejudice and passion for which he ought to be burned in effigy from Boston to St. Paul's. It went off at last without any decisive vote. I left the Senate in disgust and adjourned to the Smithsonian, preferring stuffed penguins and pickled lizards to the dishonest gabble of the Senate Chamber.

Much impressed by the amplitude and grandeur of all the federal buildings, and by the splendid marbles and frescos of the Capitol. We cannot *spare* these structures quite yet. If a partition of federal property is inevitable, let us give South Carolina *all* the pictures in the rotunda, and Clark Mills's equestrian statue of Andrew Jackson. The Smithsonian collections are most fascinating. . . . Evening—with Mr. Ruggles to Seward's. Sat an hour or two with him and Preston King, talking crisis and compromise. Both Senators most jolly, genial, good-natured, and

[1] This was Horace Binney, Jr. (1809–1870), son of the eminent Pennsylvania attorney and himself a successful lawyer since his admission to the bar in 1831, three years after graduation from Yale. He had married Strong's cousin, Eliza Johnson. With their mutual interests in the law, literature, and political affairs, the two men had much in common. At the outbreak of the war, Binney threw himself into activities in support of the Union with a fervor equal to Strong's. He soon became a leading and, Strong later wrote, a steadying member of the Sanitary Commission, president of the Philadelphia Associates of the Commission, and in 1862, chief founder of the Philadelphia Union League Club. Their war-time collaboration deepened the relationship between the diarist and his cousin-by-marriage into an intimate friendship.

free from care, laughing at the vagaries of Toombs and Iverson, talking of conciliation and arrangement as likely to be effected, perhaps—but not worth much effort.

Sunday, the sixth.   To church at St. John's. Sat in Seward's pew by his invitation. The Senator did not appear. Reverend Smith Pyne was emphatic and spasmodic in the pulpit. Afterwards, called on us Captain Lewis (of the Navy Yard), Thayer (*Evening Post* correspondent), Stewart, Henry Edwards of Keene, New Hampshire (a nice sensible old gentleman), and others. Many rumors and reports, mostly lying.

Monday. . . . To the Senate Chamber. Very earnest and patriotic speech from Crittenden; labor thrown away. To the House; nothing of much interest there. Heard of the death of William Kent and of the Rev. Henry Anthon. He died Saturday morning after severe suffering patiently endured. I hoped he might yet recover, for Fish, who arrived Saturday night, reported that he was a little better Friday afternoon. Prof. Hackley of Columbia is gone, too. Congestion of the brain. . . . There are men whose death would have been a heavier loss.

Tuesday, the eighth.   Neither House in session. . . . With . . . Senator Anthony of Rhode Island to Navy Yard; Captain Lewis, Dahlgren guns, Maynard rifles, fuses, percussion caps, and so forth; all the processes of the foundry and the laboratory duly expounded. Our four hours' scientific session succeeded by a most hospitable lunch. Lewis a decided trump. . . .

Wednesday.   Rain; Senate again; message from President. Bitter, acrimonious conversational debate on questions growing out of it between Preston King, Jefferson Davis, and others. "Jim Lane" savage and insolent; Wigfall of Texas venomous as one of his copperhead congeners.[2] Little hope of any amicable settlement. Pacific Railroad came up and I came off, desponding. Evening, another alarm of fire; fires occur every night. . . . Rumors are rife of an attack on the city by a Virginian mob. People are sending off their families to Philadelphia and New York. These incendiary fires are supposed to be part of the revolutionary programme. But old Scott has the case under advisement; that may avert any attack. Burglars are apt to postpone their visit when they know the family expects them. Scott tells Senator Foster that he expects three companies of light artillery from Fort Leavenworth, and one or two of infantry, also the sappers and miners from West Point, to arrive in Wash-

[2] That is, James H. Lane (1814–1866), Senator from Kansas, and Louis T. Wigfall (1816–1874), Senator from Texas; respectively a Republican and a Democratic fire-eater.

ington within a week. With this force as a nucleus, the militia of the District will be of service. If more men be wanted, "I shall write to my friend General Sandford of New York, who has considerable military capacity, and request him to send me the Seventh Regiment. That regiment, sir, can be relied upon. It will stand being brick-batted without drawing a trigger till it is ordered to fire!"

Thursday. Great news at the breakfast table. Steamer *Star of the West*, carrying reinforcements to Major Anderson, fired upon by the savages of South Carolina. Rumor No. 2 was that she had nevertheless made her way into Charleston harbor and fulfilled her mission. Rumor No. 3 (unfortunately correct) that being without heavy guns, she had turned tail and steamed out of the harbor. This will produce great excitement and strengthen the Union feeling all through the North. At Senate heard Jefferson Davis talk treason awhile. Thence to Smithsonian with Eliot and Judge Huntington of the Court of Claims. Spent four hours there, with Professor and Mrs. [Joseph] Henry, not unprofitably. Growing cold and windy.

Evening. Charles Sumner (the Martyr) called to see Mrs. Eleanor; Hawkins, member of Congress from Florida (an unhanged traitor), came to see Mr. Ruggles.[3] The two pairs sat at opposite corners of our little parlor, discoursing *sotto voce*. I was introduced to Hawkins, and had to take his hand, which I dropped with all convenient speed, and then retired to a convenient position, where I waited to see whether the gallant Floridian would not rise up suddenly and scalp the Massachusetts man. But there was no breach of the peace. Sumner tells me he has read the notes of Seward's great conciliation speech soon to be delivered and that it will be effective and conclusive. Much is expected from Seward, but I do not believe he can say anything that has not been said before.

This (Friday) morning, breakfasted by gas-light, a late supper rather than a breakfast, and was off at a little before six, with Mr. Ruggles, Dr. and Mrs. Peters, and Mrs. Eleanor. Lovely cloudless sunrise, clear and cold. But the sky was soon covered with grey frosty fog that became a heavy and uniform cloud and developed into a snowstorm at Philadelphia. Bitter cold ride. Steamboat at Amboy, and a hearty supper. Home at seven; all well, thank God. Ellie has gone to musical party at Mme. de Trobriand's.

[3] George Sydney Hawkins (1808–1878), a native of New York State now serving his second term in Congress from Florida.

A visit to Washington gives one no special insight into national affairs. People there are eager for New York papers to tell them what the government did or talked about the day before. But my prognosis is unfavorable. Virginia and Kentucky and Tennessee will secede (i.e., rebel) and Maryland will follow Virginia. War seems inevitable. We cannot let the rebels occupy the national capital without a struggle.

Have been much with James W. Beekman; Union-saving and anti-Republican; wealthy and money-loving. But he avows himself ready to spend his last dollar in upholding the territorial integrity of the Union. A significant fact.

January 14.   The *Star of the West* has returned to this port with a big shot-scar in her timbers and does not seem likely to revisit the waters of Charleston just at present. The nation pockets this insult to the national flag; a calm dishonorable, vile submission. But it's wise to postpone actual hemorrhage as long as may be. "Something may turn up."

Seward's long-expected speech is a fine essay. Does him great credit. He's a man of higher faculty than I took him to be. People are disappointed that he proposes no panacea. How could he? The whole subject is talked out. General Dix went to Washington this morning to open his portfolio as Secretary of Treasury. He had a conference with an informal meeting of bank presidents and capitalists Saturday, and was told that if the government meant to sustain itself and not to acquiesce in its own disintegration and decomposition, it could have all the money it wanted. Dix's appointment inspires confidence. He is honest, and though reluctant to take responsibility, will not decline it when it comes.

January 15.   Nothing new from Washington, or from the insurgents of the South, except that the Old Pennsylvania Fossil is rumored to have relapsed into vacillation and imbecility. It seemed a week ago as if he were developing germs of a backbone. Had this old mollusk become vertebrate, the theories by Darwin and the "Vestiges of Creation" would have been confirmed.

Rumors multiply and strengthen of an organization in this city intended to give aid and comfort to Southern treason by getting up such disturbances here as will paralyze any movement to strengthen the government by men or money. The programme is (as reported) a nocturnal insurrection by an armed mob, taking possession of the armories of the several militia corps, breaking into the banks, and sacking the houses of conspicuous Republicans. I know (from T. Bailey Myers) that the editor of the Washington *Constitution* (a renegade Englishman) is privy to this plot, and I have the best moral evidence that Delaplaine ("Ikey Pig"), a Congressman-elect from this city, favors it.[4]

Treated myself to a "Maynard Carbine" ($47.50) this afternoon.

January 17. Nothing special to note in the history of the revolution now in progress. There are slight indications of reaction and common sense at the extreme South, with decided symptoms of growing fever in the Border States. I fear we are a decomposing nation. Justice Weeks asked me to meet a few gentlemen of the neighborhood at his house to talk over the expediency of organizing and drilling a special police corps for our own defence, in view of possible outbreaks here. Called on Mr. Superintendent Kennedy this afternoon to take his opinion about it.[5] He discourages the plan. Expects no disturbance, thinks the police able to quell any anarchical demonstration, distrusts all amateur organizations. The regular army always distrusts volunteers.

January 19, SATURDAY. The general feeling today is that political news looks better and brighter. There is evidence that neither Georgia, Alabama, nor Mississippi is unanimous in rebellion. Even under the present epidemic of treason and reign of terror, there is a strong minority (at least) in each of these states that has thus far been silent; that has not voted or has voted against what they call secession. Reaction, and the pressure of calamity (both inevitable), may strengthen this inert and suppressed anti-secession party, wake up the whole people to the true state of the case, and bring the conspirators, who have raised this storm for their own selfish ends, to a stern reckoning. Indications from the Border States are encouraging as far as they go. Crittenden has taken decided ground in the Senate, and says the Union must be preserved, peaceably or forcibly, according to circumstances. . . .

The insecurity of property in all Southern ports seems to be driving all imports and exports away from them and into Northern ports through inland lines of river and railroad. This tendency is likely to increase. Rumors (true or false) of Southern legislation repudiating debts and confiscating property will keep capital away from Mobile and New Orleans. And suppose those cities be declared no longer ports of entry??? !!!

Lieutenant Lawrence Williams dined here with Miss Rosalie this afternoon. Had a talk with him after I returned from the Schermerhorns'.

[4] William M. Browne had gone from the New York *Journal of Commerce* to edit the Washington *Constitution*, and was hand-in-glove with Southern secessionists; Isaac C. Delaplaine (1817–1866), a graduate of Columbia College, had just been elected to Congress as a Fusionist Democrat.

[5] John A. Kennedy, Superintendent of Police.

He has changed from a mercurial boy, the cadet of 1852 at West Point, to an intelligent, candid, strong-headed young man. Though a Virginian, he's not a Southern fanatic. He says the South is wrong and the North right; the North is strong enough to conquer the South if it come to a civil war. But he insists, very forcibly, that, since the South is manifestly mad and mischievous, the North should give way on a question of mere abstraction (viz., the territories) for the sake of peace and to save the country from ruin.

January 21. Everybody, even Daniel B. Fearing, is full of confidence that the national disease has passed its crisis. I cannot see any reason for thinking so. The revolution seems to me still in full progress. The conspirators of South Carolina and other states have raised a spirit of treason they cannot lay if they would. Many of them intended only a gigantic game of brag, but they have gone a little too far. The ignorant barbarians of their own states, hearing only one side of the question, believe all that Toombs, Yancey, & Co. have been saying, though it was said merely to frighten the North.

I fear we are two peoples, unable to live in peace under one feeble "federal" government. . . .

January 22. Nothing hopeful in today's political news. The Border States will assuredly drift into rebellion within six weeks. And here we all sit and prophesy and philosophize and speculate, doing nothing to avert the ruin that impends. But what can we do? What can *I* do? What could I do were I Webster and Clay combined? Concession to these conspirators and the ignorant herd they have stimulated to treason would but postpone the inevitable crisis a year or two longer. The South can be permanently pacified only in one way. The masses of the North must declare slavery just, beneficent, and expedient, and allow every Mississippian who chooses to visit New York to bring his niggers with him. Not merely his niggers; his rights over them according to his own slave code must accompany him, and be recognized and enforced by the courts and sheriffs of every Northern state. That's what these madmen demand of us, and civil war is the alternative. Their suicidal frenzy tempts me to believe in Wendell Phillips and Captain John Brown (hanged a year ago, and justly hanged, as I've always supposed). This madness of slaveholders looks as if slaveholding were doomed. . . .

January 23. At Philharmonic rehearsal (Academy of Music) on my way uptown this afternoon. Began with a well-known symphony of Haydn's (in F or B flat), the best among the few of his symphonies I have had opportunity to hear; every movement most genial and delicious. How honest, healthy, and true is all his music! Upon my word, I seriously think that the general neglect of his works by musical people, and the general preference, for example, of Beethoven's intensities to the pure, kindly, and vigorous heartiness of Haydn, is a symptom of the moral disease that oppresses this generation, and strictly analogous to the Byronism and Wertherism that have now nearly disappeared. Of course, Beethoven is the greater or the stronger composer. So Byron is stronger than Cowper. But if we know of two men only this, that one delighted in Cowper and the other in Byron, I think we should infer that the former was the healthier-minded of the two. . . .

No political news today. The Border States will get no concession from Congress. They will secede (that is, their inhabitants will rebel against the national government) within sixty days. Civil war is inevitable.

January 24. The affairs of the nation are as they were. No change. One story is that Seward and others have given satisfactory assurance to the leaders of Virginia and Kentucky that everything will be arranged as soon as Lincoln is inaugurated, that the Republicans are holding back only that Lincoln's Administration may have the credit of settling matters, and that they have a perfect understanding with prominent men in the Border States. All which I incline to disbelieve.

The toxicological experts who have been testing the viscera of poor Mrs. "Black Jake" LeRoy find no strychnine, arsenic, or other drug. Medical chemistry has no tests for brutality and tyranny, however concentrated and murderous.

January 25. News today is that the Kentucky legislature has refused to call a convention, but that is too good to be true. It has probably tabled the subject, in hope of action by Congress before March 4. Also, that the State of Mississippi continues to take indecent liberties with boats going down the river. They are brought to by cannon shot and examined before they can pass Vicksburg. Fire away, O valiant State of Mississippi! This may bring on the trial of strength (that seems inevitable, anyhow) on an issue and in a form that will *not* unite every Southern state as "coercion" by the army and navy of the United States probably would. The people of the Northwest will probably take the matter into their own hands, and in that event, Louisiana and Mississippi will be wiped out. Kentucky, Tennessee, and Missouri will not sympathize strongly with the Southern side of that controversy. And its result may teach all the slaveholding states a useful lesson as to their own real weakness.

January 26. Things look a little better today. Loyalty still asserts itself in Kentucky and Maryland, with prospect of success, though Virginia seems less promising. People begin to talk of disruption as likely to make the North richer and more prosperous. Capital will desert these combustible, extra-hazardous, seceding communities, they say; and the trade of New Orleans and Mobile will transfer itself to Northern ports. Perhaps so; symptoms of that change have already shown themselves, unquestionably. But money cannot pay for our national disgrace. Every citizen of the United States is humiliated and lowered in his own estimation and that of the civilized world by the part his national government has played in this great crisis. It has not only avowed itself impotent and despicable, but it has been, at least, conniving at the vilest conspiracy since Catiline's; or rather, all things considered, the vilest conspiracy with the basest motives and the largest aim of mischief to mankind on record anywhere. As much depravity may be found in the pages of the Newgate Calendar, but the range of the conspirators has been far more limited. History may possibly record other political crimes, contemplated or consummated, of equal maleficence and evil magnitude, but it records none committed on so slight inducement and for ends so base. . . .

Floyd's revelations, in his after-dinner speech at Richmond, are appalling to every sane man's moral sense. I rejoice to learn that a District of Columbia Grand Jury has indicted him for malversation in office as a party to the late frauds on government. I have long believed him utterly profligate and corrupt, independently of his participation in this treasonable disunion movement. In this Richmond speech he calls Jefferson Davis "the bright Saladin of the South." Can people who utter such embodiments of concentrated ipecacuanha, people who talk such heroic doses of tartar emetic, and those who hear and applaud them, live in peace and quietness under the same government with reasonable beings?

Whatever may be the result of all this, "We the People" are disgraced and degraded in the eyes of all Christendom by the events and by the disclosures of the last three months. If these be legitimate fruits of democracy "after its kind," Heaven preserve and strengthen all despots! But I hope they are the fruits, not of our national institutions, but of our national ulcer—slaveholding, which blunts the moral sense, and from time to time turns the brain of every community affiliated with it. The slaveholding interest has controlled the government from the first. It is mainly responsible for this our national infamy. If disunion become an established fact,

we have one consolation. The self-amputated members were diseased
beyond immediate cure, and their virus will infect our system no longer.

January 27, SUNDAY. . . . Tonight, Mr. Ruggles, D'Oremieulx, Williams, Hoffman, and others at supper. Mr. Ruggles has come from western
New York; reports it unanimous on the issue of government or no government and ready to fight. Not absolutely unanimous, because the Hon. Washington Hunt of Lockport is probably weak-backed, or so I infer from Mr.
Ruggles's cautious expressions of dissent. . . .

Walter Cutting very lugubrious and despondent this evening. Nothing
but ruination before us, and all because those damned Republicans will
tender no "compromise," and sit still while the Border States are gravitat-
ing into secession. But is any compromise or pacification desirable until
we have ascertained whether we have or have not a government? Is not
our first business now to see that the law of the land is executed and
Abraham Lincoln, Esq., duly inaugurated March 4? Would not "concession" *now* be an admission that what we have called the federal "government" is and has been all along a mere sham, scarecrow, and practical
nullity, unable to assert its own existence as against a seditious minority?

Things look bad. Diagnosis is very unfavorable in Virginia. Kentucky
and Maryland cannot be expected to stand firm if Virginia fall, as I predict
she will within thirty days. I remember this black bugaboo of "disunion"
ever since I was old enough to understand the words "United States."
But till within the last ten years, it was, to me, a mere possibility of
disaster, a question for college debating societies. I fear that ugly spectre
has risen—too soon—and that we have got to deal with the awful question
of a dissolution of the Union *now* and *here*.

January 29.   John Austin Stevens, Sr., of the Bank of Commerce,
has authentic, private, confidential information that Seward, Crittenden,
Hunter of Virginia, and Douglas agreed last night on certain "conciliatory"
measures, and the whole slavery question is settled. No four and no forty
politicians can settle that question. The Cotton States have settled it, and
have settled themselves, too. As I heard a rather seedy gentleman observe
in the crowd at the Post Office yesterday, "The Lord will begin teaching
them fellows down there pretty soon." The folly of Southern conspirators,
and the madness to which they have stimulated the ignorant, half-civilized
herd of their own states, have done more for Abolitionism in these ninety
days than a score of anti-slavery societies and a regiment of John Browns,
Wendell Phillipses, and Mrs. Beecher Stowes could have achieved in a
century.

January 31. Last night at William Astor's. Great crowd. I spent a pleasant evening enough. Fernando Wood in a white cravat was remarkable to behold. His invitation was a tribute by his millionaire host to the dangerous democracy, like the distinguished consideration shown by Isaac of York to Front de Boeuf and the Grand Master. Our Fernando has just married a "genteel" wife, to be sure (No. 4, I believe), and has his opera box, and is trying for a "social position." But I do not think I should invite him to this house were I twenty William B. Astors, or had he married twenty Miss Drake Millses.

People generally talk rather despondently today. No wonder. All the indications are that this treasonable inflammation—*secessionitis*—keeps on making steady progress week by week. A little prophylactic treatment before November 6 (reinforced garrisons and the like), or even six weeks afterwards, would have checked it and confined it to the insignificant spot of chronic ulceration where it originated, South Carolina. But there was no such treatment, for the sufficient reason that government was in the hands of the cabal that desired its destruction; the doctors were in the interest, not of the patient, but of the disease. Old Dr. Buchanan does not certainly know yet whether he wants to see his patient perish, or be cured by remedies alien to his school. So the inflammation is gaining ground every day in the Border States. The chances are against Virginia's continuing loyal to the Union. Farther south it has already produced morbid structural changes that only the knife can remedy. Six states are out of the Union, if legislation can take them out, and their delegates meet next Monday in treasonable convention to organize a new "Confederation."

One's opinions change fast in revolutionary times. Three months ago, I thought with horror and incredulity of the chance that poor little South Carolina might be mad enough to "secede" alone. Now I am content to let her go, and carry all the Gulf States with her to chaos and the devil, if Maryland, Virginia, Kentucky, Tennessee, and Missouri will but be true to themselves and to the Union, or rather (it's the better word) to the *nation.* Let the barbarians of Mississippi and Alabama rebel if they like, and call it "secession." We can get on without them. The national councils are well rid of their representatives. The Northwest will take care that its great outlet into the Gulf is unobstructed. Woe to Natchez and Vicksburg and New Orleans if it be blocked! We need not attempt to reconquer and retain the territories of the new Southern Confederacy. It cannot sustain itself long. It must soon decompose into anarchy. The United States will gradually establish itself in possession again by a protectorate, and what were once the Gulf States will be the Gulf Territories. It is all plain sailing if we can but keep the Border States in line.

February 2. Warm, wet, and sloppy. Philharmonic rehearsal this morning with Ellie; concert tonight by myself. Betook myself to the sky-gallery, which, I observe, is favored by Scharfenberg and others, as the best place in the house for those who go to hear. Lots of Germans there, "professionals" apparently, following the orchestra through copies of the score.

Schumann's Symphony (No. 3, E flat, opus 97) was effective, the second movement especially. There may be gleams in it of real life, of something above mechanism. If not, *life* is most cleverly and dexterously simulated. The Haydn Symphony (No. 2, in B flat) is most genial, beautiful, and pellucid. What is there in music much lovelier than the *adagio* and the delicious, kindly, joyous *minuetto*, so full of exuberant, rollicking, healthy fun?

Wagner's *Tannhäuser* Overture, particularly unlike anything Haydn ever thought of, but a very substantial composition beyond all gainsaying, closed the concert. . . .

Nothing special from the Southern Rebellion. But we have been uncommonly blue today, perhaps because of this nasty humid weather. Within a very few days there is like to be a trial of strength between the traitors of South Carolina and Anderson's seventy men in Fort Sumter. It cannot be postponed very long. The sooner it comes the better, I suspect. But there will be "a murder grim and great" when it does come, and North and South will instantly flash into crystallizations of hostile steel.

February 4. Just from an unpremeditated evening at opera with Ellie and Miss Rosalie; sat in parquette. *Barber of Seville* nicely done by Brignoli and his company. . . .

Everybody bluer and blacker every day. Governor Fish believes the story in today's *Times* that Fort Sumter has been privily reinforced by men conveyed thither in small boats from the *Brooklyn*. I do not. It seems feasible enough, but it is a move beyond the capacity of our disgraceful Administration.

This is an important day. The seceding states meet in convention to form an Algerine Confederacy, and Virginia elects a convention to decide whether that grand old state shall or shall not abide by the Union. I have little hope of her. This seems the hour of darkness. Jem Strong says the motto of the new-born nation of South Carolina should be "Pickens and Stealins." . . .

The Rev. Dr. Seabury has put forth a book maintaining the right to hold slaves on religious and ethical principles.[6] It looks sound and sensible. The complaint of Christendom and of all humanity against the South is not founded on their exercise of that right (though most people take for granted that it is a wrong), but on the diabolical peculiarities of the Southern system—separation of families and the like—which I suppose to be mere accidents of slaveholding, not of its essence. . . .

One evening at Washington last month, sitting with the ladies in our little parlor, I picked up a sheet of note paper and scribbled a communication to the Charleston *Mercury*, signed "a friend to the Sunny South," or some such thing, about gun cotton, and how cotton was king in war as in peace, and how cotton when immersed in equal parts of fuming nitric acid and sulphuric acid of sp.gr., I forget what, with about a dozen decimals, became a substitute for gunpowder. I didn't dream that any news—paper (unless it might be one published for the delectation of a lunatic asylum) would print this palpable gas and bosh; and I thought no more about it, until last night, when Charley [Strong] showed me a paragraph in the Sunday *Times*, from which it would seem that the *Mercury* accepted and published this as the bona fide suggestion of a friend.

February 5. Virginia certainly seems to have done better than I hoped. Not merely in the Panhandle and West of the Blue Ridge, but even in Eastern Virginia, the counties that lie around Richmond and Norfolk, the so-called "Union Party" (that is, the opponents of immediate secession, those who want to wait for a "compromise") has prevailed. Seward told D. H. Haight last week that he pledged his honor as a man and his capacity as a politician that all this agitation should be ended within sixty days. So Haight tells Charley. If Seward said so, he is either the grossest of fools, the most astute of politicians, or the boldest of political liars— perhaps with good intent.

February 6. Everybody in high glee today. The *immediate Secessionists* of Virginia defeated by some 40,000 majority as estimated. How ready we are to take hold of every little symptom of recovery and make more than the most of it! This result doesn't show that Virginia decides for the Union, by any means. She merely postpones rebellion for a month, in hope of concession. But we have been firing a hundred guns in honor of Virginia, and all Wall Street is confident we are out of trouble now, and that the Border States are all safe. This is premature and absurd. But the Virginia news is good as far as it goes. It is the first hopeful sign that has

---

[6] Dr. Samuel Seabury (1801–1872) had just published *American Slavery . . . Justified*, an unfortunate expression of his ingrained conservatism.

been seen since November, the first streak of blue sky since the storm set in; important not only as indicating the strength of the quasi-conservative feeling in that state . . . but also in its influence on the North. So long as our Southern news was all one way, nothing but fury, hatred, and malice, overt acts of treason, insolent challenges to Civil War, it was hard for any of us possessing even the rudiments of a backbone to tolerate talk about conciliation and concession. But the most important and influential of the Southern communities now tells us, in substance, that though irritated and affronted and strongly tempted to rebel, it yet prefers on the whole to follow the destinies of the nation, and that it will uphold and abide by our national unity if the North will but make some conciliatory move.

This alters the aspect of the controversy. To be sure, the North is entitled to say it has done no wrong and contemplates none, that it has only exercised the right of a majority to control a republican government, that it is not bound to make concessions because a factious and lawless minority threatens treason and rebellion. The North is right, and its legal position is unassailable. But it may fairly concede something to its weaker brethren if in the full tide of their wrath, however groundless and irrational, they avow themselves desirous of peace and compromise. This action of Virginia's changes my view as to the course Republicans in Congress should take. I now think they should be diligent in devising measures to satisfy the South, so far as they may without sacrifice of principle. "*Beati pacifici*" is now my motto in the controversy.

February 7. Indications of the state of affairs at Washington are discouraging. Republicans seem indisposed to make any offer of conciliation, and I fear the Border States will demand concessions the North cannot grant.

February 8. Standing Committee of Columbia College met at Gouverneur Ogden's office; Ogden, Robert Ray, Betts, Zabriskie, and myself. Only routine business done. We are like to have a crisis with President King. His house on the college grounds is nearly finished. It was built with regard to the demands of his immense family, and the plans were submitted to him and his household and amended and at last cordially approved by him and them. Now I hear that Mrs. King and the young ladies vow and declare they will not give up their pleasant, accessible, provisional abode in Fourteenth Street for solitary exile in the high northern latitudes of the college. King intimated at a recent meeting of the board that if the house was ready for him next first of May, he should not then be ready for the house. The devices and bequests of the late lamented [Nicholas] Low [King's father-in-law] have produced appreciable results. I think the board will hold, unanimously, that the President must occupy the house we have built for him with his knowledge and concurrence, or resign his seat. Should he resign, who shall be his successor?

Dr. Francis is dead—of a carbuncle, I understand.[7]

February 10, SUNDAY.   Reverend Alexander Vinton preached at Trinity this morning. He is "called" by St. Mark's to succeed Reverend Henry Anthon.

Great news yesterday afternoon. Georgia has seized five New York vessels by way of reprisal for our stoppage of arms en route for that rebellious community. This is a calamity. It will strengthen the anti-conciliation party at the North. Tomorrow morning's *Tribune* will make the most of this last manifestation of Southern madness. The seceding states (from South Carolina to Louisiana) seem to have formed a "Confederacy" on the basis of the Constitution of the United States. . . .

Northern forbearance is nearly exhausted by successive outrages. War is inevitable, and it will be war in earnest. The savages of the South will give no quarter and ignore the amenities of civilized warfare. We shall have to fight them with their own weapons. We shall be arming and drilling slave regiments within a year, and making fortified breaches in the levees of the Mississippi to drown out New Orleans.

February 13.   Ash-Wednesday. After dinner, Ellie read Haydn for me, and Ehninger and George Anthon came in for a few minutes. Jack thinks he and his associates (eighty or thereabouts) who have been diligently drilling for six weeks, will not be required at Washington on March 4 after all. Probably he's right. Seizing that city by a *coup de main* was certainly on the conspirators' programme, but Scott's preparations to receive them and the unexpected attitude assumed by the Border States have brought that project to naught. The electoral votes were counted today, and as I hear no extras in the streets, they were probably counted in due form, and the result announced without disturbance. This was the critical day for the peace of the capital. A foray of Virginia gents, with Governor Wise at their head and Governor Floyd at their tail, could have done infinite mischief by destroying the legal evidence of Lincoln's election (after they had killed and beaten General Scott and his Flying Artillery, that is). . . .

[7] John W. Francis, M.D. (1789–1861), now best remembered for his *Old New York*, had been a landmark in city life; "learned and jolly," as Philip Hone called him.

This revelation of the gallant Floyd's gigantic larcenies must weaken the cause of secession, for many Southerners possess a moral sense and must distrust a leader who steals.[8] Certainly, Floyd & Co. have done more villainy on smaller provocation than any gang on record. The deluded mobs of Charleston and Savannah have some excuse for their criminal outrages. There is none for the Floyds, Cobbs, Davises, and other false prophets who have deliberately stimulated their ignorance to crime by malicious lies, and who have stuck at nothing from theft to treason and civil war, that they might hold political power a little longer. These men want hanging—badly. But they will reap deadly fruit yet from their own treason. The devil they have raised will turn and rend them, unless he be laid at once, and that is beyond the magic of Jefferson Davis.

February 15.   Northeast gale and rain all day. To Columbia College this morning with William Schermerhorn, attending examination. Performances in Davies's and Peck's rooms brilliant. In Anthon's (Rhesus) as usual; that is, creditable to his drilling. In McVickar's also as usual— that is, bad; the professor maundering about the evidences, the students indifferent and uninterested and answering no question more than half way, making at best only a vague, shadowy approximation to what was called for. Nairne was examining on Logic, and the atmosphere of his room was that of McVickar's, perhaps a trifle less languid.

February 18.   No political news. Lincoln is making little speeches as he wends his way toward Washington, and has said some things that are sound and creditable and raise him in my esteem. But I should have been better pleased with him had he held his tongue altogether. He enters New York tomorrow afternoon. Broadway will be less crowded than it was when the Japanese embassy came, but his advent will make people turn out in great force, if it be a pleasant day. . . .

February 20.   The nation still very sick, but no worse. Secession has run its course and reaction has set in. Missouri votes strongly for the Union. Even Arkansas tends the same way. There would no doubt be like symptoms in the Gulf States but for the reign of terror there, and had they not committed themselves so deeply in the first hot stage of secession fever. It would certainly come, sooner or later, in South Carolina itself, but before it can have time to develop itself, a collision is inevitable. That will postpone the return of common sense indefinitely. Fort Sumter cannot

[8] It had just been learned that $870,000 of state bonds in the Indian Trust Fund of Floyd's Interior Department had been embezzled; and if Floyd stole nothing himself, his laxity or connivance helped others to steal large sums from the government.

long be left without reinforcement, and federal revenue must be collected at Southern ports. Unless these things, and others, be done, we virtually confess and declare that our national existence is a mere name, without the power of self assertion that gives national dignity to the smallest German Grand Duchy. If the federal government have no constitutional power to repress the treason of a minority, it may as well disintegrate at once and let the counterfeit sovereignty, "the likeness of a kingly crown," that has imposed on all the powers of Christendom so long, be swept into the rubbish bin of history at once, as a detested and acknowledged humbug. Though the original secession epidemic has, I think, exhausted itself, we have yet to see what Virginia, Tennessee, and other states will do when the contest begins between the federal government and the rebellious slave states. Which side will they take???

Lincoln arrived here yesterday afternoon by Hudson River R. R. from Albany. I walked uptown at 3:30. Broadway crowded, though not quite so densely as on the Prince of Wales's *avatar* last October. The *trottoir* well filled by pedestrians (vehicles turned off into side streets), and sidewalks by patient and stationary sight-seers. Above Canal Street they were nearly impassable. At St. Thomas's Church I met the illustrious cortege moving slowly down to the Astor House with its escort of mounted policemen and a torrent of rag-tag and bobtail rushing and hooraying behind. The great rail-splitter's face was visible to me for an instant, and seemed a keen, clear, honest face, not so ugly as his portraits. . . .

February 21.   This evening at R. B. Minturn's, a masculine soirée, one of the series of "Thursday evening parties" . . . made up of reputable fogies, ancient and medieval. Millionaires, like William Aspinwall, John D. Wolfe, Russell; political notabilities, as Governor Fish, Augustus Schell, Evarts, Judge Roosevelt; great scholars, like George Bancroft and George Folsom, and Dr. [James] Wynne. There were Bishop Potter, also, and Dr. Bellows, Captain Benham of the United States Engineer Corps, Maunsell Field, and that florid donkey Alfred Pell, George Schuyler, Daniel Lord, Colonel James B. Murray, C. E. Habicht, Abram S. Hewitt, and others.

February 23, SATURDAY.   Yesterday's anniversary celebrated with greater emphasis than ever before, at least in my day. Great parade, and great crowd of lookers-on, packing Broadway from City Hall to Fourteenth Street. The Seventh and other regiments marched well and looked imposing. There were signs of enthusiasm, unusual in the phlegmatic street gatherings of New York.

Extras out at noon today. How a plot for Lincoln's assassination was revealed at Harrisburg late last night; how his railroad train was to have been thrown down an embankment by obstructions on the rails or undermining the track between Harrisburg and Baltimore; how Lincoln thereupon left it privily, disguised "in a Scotch cap and long military cloak," and traveled all night and reached Washington at an early hour this morning. That is fact.[9] The conspiracy story sounds a little romantic. But our Southern fanatics are capable of any enormity. I have said, all along, that there was at least an even chance of an attempt to take Lincoln's life before the 4th of March. It's to be hoped that the conspiracy can be proved beyond cavil. If it cannot be made manifest and indisputable, this surreptitious nocturnal dodging or sneaking of the President-elect into his capital city, under cloud of night, will be used to damage his moral position and throw ridicule on his Administration.

Other political news indefinite. Schism in Republican party seems widening. The New England States, Preston King of New York, and the New York *Tribune* are making war on Seward and striving to exclude him from prominent place in Lincoln's Cabinet. He is a compromiser; they are uncompromisers. "Confederate States of America" are organizing—on paper. Their leaders crave a strong government. But how can they get it, without compromising the sacred right of Secession? General Dix is winning honor and applause in his position at Washington. He shows more pluck and vigor than I gave him credit for.

February 26. Political affairs progress with mingled indications of good and of evil. There has been an election in the savage commonwealth of Arkansas; result uncertain. That there is any doubt about it, is a strong and comfortable symptom that the treason-eruption has run its course and passed its maximum virulence, for Arkansas is constitutionally predisposed to whatever things are unlovely, lawless, and of ill report.

It appears that Abraham Lincoln sympathizes with Seward and the

[9] The plot and the night journey were facts, but not the disguise. Lincoln, warned by the detective Allan Pinkerton that his safety could not be guaranteed if he made an open daylight crossing from one Baltimore station to another, was fully justified in expediting his journey. It is now known that enemies had plotted to kill him on the cross-city ride. He arrived in Washington when last-minute efforts at compromise were still being made by Senator Seward, by Representative Thomas Corwin, head of the House Committee of Thirty-three, and by an unofficial Peace Congress of elder statesmen of moderate views, presided over by ex-President John Tyler. But the tide of secession had swept too far to be halted, and Jeff Davis's government declared that it would insist on absolute independence.

Republican Right, and not with Greeley and Sumner and the Extreme Left. Glad of it.

General Twiggs has suddenly become exceedingly infamous. He has surrendered to the Nation of Texas all the military property, movable and removable, which the U.S.A. entrusted to his keeping. Faith and honor and common honesty are rare in the Gulf States just now! No revolution, no great political movement ever combined so much and so various crime, dirty and bold, sneaking and insolent, as this, unless there be a parallel case in the history of France, or that of the Roman Empire in its days of rotting. Southerners have lost all moral sense. Their nerves of moral sensation seem smitten with paralysis. Their "chivalry" exults in treachery, bad faith, oppression of the weak, and every thing that distinguishes the churl from the knight. . . .

Let us keep the comparatively humane and civilized Border States true to their allegiance, if we can, by any compromise or concession, but let us extend no olive branch to the Algerines of the Gulf. We are well rid of them. Let Government collect its revenues at their posts, and be thankful that they have renounced, in their fanaticism and folly, the right to be represented in its councils by delegations of traitors and ruffians (like Toombs and Yancey and Davis and the late-lamented Preston S. Brooks) and the privilege of helping to disgrace and afflict us with such portentous national calamities as James Buchanan, now President of the U.S.A.

Old James Buchanan, the "O.P.F.," stands lowest, I think, in the dirty catalog of treasonable mischief-makers. For without the excuse of bad Southern blood, without passion, without local prejudices, and in a great degree by mere want of moral force to resist his confessedly treasonable advisers, he has somehow slid into the position of boss-traitor and master-devil of the gang. He seems to me the basest specimen of the human race ever raised on this continent.

February 27. Important news from Washington. The Council of Notables, commonly described as "The Peace Congress," has agreed on a scheme of compromise at last and submitted it to Congress. Its main feature seems to be the re-establishment of the Missouri Compromise line, and it restricts future acquisitions of territory. D. D. Field and W. C. Noyes seem to have opposed it stoutly, so it's evidently distasteful to the Republican Left. It is not at all clear that it can get such a majority in Congress and in the states as will be needed to make it an amendment to the Constitution. Probably there will be a hard battle on the question of its ratification, and I suppose it will be the duty of conservative and patriotic men to support it. But concession, right or wrong, to the demands of this blustering faction is painful. . . .

Letter from Charley today, written Monday evening. He's disgusted with the crowd of office-seekers and unfragrant Western men at Willard's. Thinks Lincoln a smart country politician and Mrs. Lincoln a very vulgar old woman, and so forth. He is assured "on the best authority" that ample provision has been made for reinforcing Fort Sumter.

March 1. Coming from opera tonight, on foot and without overcoat, I found myself irrigated by a fine summer shower. Yesterday afternoon, I presided over the close of the system on which the business of the Bank for Savings has been done for more than forty years, and at ten this morning opened the bank for business under the new rule, and stayed half an hour, and spent another hour there before closing at 2 P.M., as a supernumerary assessor to James de P. Ogden, our new salaried "comptroller." The new system will make the duties of "attending trustee" practically nothing. At present, he is bound to do nothing but sign checks, and it will soon be found that that office can be executed more conveniently and with equal safety by the functionaries of the bank. I am very glad to be relieved from the annual fortnight of drudgery, and especially from the handling of pass books, many of which look and smell as if smallpox and malignant dysentery were concentrated in the filth of their covers. . . .

March 2. Thank God the disgraceful reign of James Buchanan draws near its close. . . .

We have relapsed into gloom, and are once more talking despondingly of "what Virginia will do" and which way the Border States will go. The prospect that Congress will do nothing to appease them (and Congress is even now just passing out of legal existence), and the prevailing belief that ultra-Republicanism is to be strongly represented in the new Cabinet, seem to be doing grave mischief. There is a new hand at the bellows of sedition in Virginia and Maryland, and those states are doubtful again. So say newspaper correspondents and telegrams and editors. Perhaps they lie, to frighten the North. I hope so, but these are sad and troublesome times.

The alarm of this morning made a ten-strike in the stocklist. Everything went down. Border State stocks gave way by five per cent. No wonder. I wouldn't touch them if they fell fifty per cent lower.

Much depends on the tone of Lincoln's Inaugural next Monday. But I doubt if words will do much good now, however pacific, fair, and reasonable. Kennedy told me this afternoon (at the Bank) that he had seen private despatches assuring him it would be a conciliatory and emollient paper. But the general belief is it will announce Lincoln's intention to uphold the law; to reinforce Fort Sumter, now actually besieged (and its garrison likely to get no quarter if its far outnumbering besiegers prevail); to retake the other forts now in the hands of the rebellion; and to collect federal revenue, by blockade or otherwise, at every Southern port. How can Lincoln say anything else, if he allude to the subject of secession at all, and how can he ignore it without shame? The logic of the situation is inexorable, and war is the only possible deduction from the premises. Civil war is at hand; within a week, if the fire-eaters of Charleston take the initiative and open their batteries on Fort Sumter, which they are like to do at once on reading a virile and honest Inaugural—and within sixty days, anyhow.

Were we at the North only united, of one mind, loyal to government, I should not fear civil war. But there are the New York *Express* and the New York *Herald*, and the like. The Cuttings are exposing themselves to remark by wild ultra-Southern talk. My old friend, Walter Cutting, in the opera house lobby last night, "hopes for civil war. Sooner it comes the better. If people will not compromise, one party or the other must be exterminated. That's all there is about it, now." He, for one, is ready to go in for a fight and to give up all he's worth in the world and his life, too, to exterminate those d—d Abolitionists. . . .

March 4, MONDAY. Feverish anxiety in Wall Street. News from Washington awaited impatiently. Everybody longing for the Inaugural. Natural enough. We are on the edge of the crisis now.

At twelve appeared an *Evening Post* Bulletin. "Great excitement in Washington. The President up all night. Great efforts to make him alter his Inaugural. The president firm." That is, Weed and perhaps Seward want Lincoln to say nothing about enforcing law. Also, there was a rumor of the rebel batteries opening on Fort Sumter, but discredited.

Next, at half-past one, was a bulletin that the Senate has passed by a $\frac{2}{3}$ vote the proposed Constitutional amendment (already adopted by the House) prohibiting Congress to interfere with Niggerdom in the states.

Met Walter Cutting, who says the "feeling is a little better," and that Thurlow Weed has telegraphed to buy stocks. Pierre Marié confirms this. But the Machiavellian Thurlow Weed's telegrams are not like those of common people. D. B. Fearing bewails the fate of his country in despondent platitudes. Woe to the man he buttonholes.

At two P.M., extras. Lincoln in triumphant progress along Pennsylvania Avenue from Willard's Hotel to the Capitol. All well. Vast crowd. Great cheering. No row.

Walked uptown with George Anthon. Encountered Ellie in carriage. Joined her; drove through Central Park, and Anthon dined here. First half of Lincoln's Inaugural in second edition of evening papers. Sent out for a later edition after dinner, but in vain. I like the way this document opens. . . .

Thank God, a most critical and perilous point is safely weathered. The new government has been installed with all the formalities, and without bloodshed. And old Buchanan is no longer a Public Functionary.

March 5. Weather grows cold again. Much wind and dust. People differ about Lincoln's Inaugural, but favorable criticism preponderates, though stocks have gone down. At Trust Company Board this morning. Kernochan[10] and other ultra "conservative" Southronizers approved and applauded it as pacific and likely to prevent collision. Maybe so, but I think there's a clank of metal in it. It's unlike any message or state paper of any class that has appeared in my time, to my knowledge. It is characterized by strong individuality and the absence of conventionalism of thought or diction. It doesn't run in the ruts of Public Documents, number one to number ten million and one, but seems to introduce one to *a man* and to dispose one to like him. That is its effect on Augustus Clason, for example, a strong Southern Democrat.

The absence of fine writing and spread-eagle-ism is a good sign. Its weak points, I think, are its discussion of the political authority of the Supreme Court of the United States and its admission that the North condemns slaveholding as a moral wrong. That is unfortunate in a paper intended (among other things) to strengthen the hands of Union men at the South. We Northerners object to slavery on grounds of political economy, not of ethics. . . .

March 6. . . . The Inaugural is generally approved by Democrats as well as by Republicans. I think it is going good even at the South, though Southern politicians denounce its "coercion" spirit and vapor horribly. Indications in Virginia and elsewhere are favorable today. There is a story this evening that Crittenden has been nominated to the vacancy in Supreme Court of United States. Too good to be true. It would be a wise, statesmanlike measure, hardly to be expected from a party Cabinet.

[10] Joseph Kernochan, as a partner in Parish & Company, had grown rich in Southern trade.

Punch suggests "Slave-ownia" as the name of the new nigger-driving nation on the Gulf. As the United States of America has long been familiarly impersonated by the endearing title of "Uncle Sam," the new schismatic Confederacy (C.S.A.) will probably be known as "Uncle Sambo."

March 7.   Exceeding cold and windy. Charley returns from Washington full of news and incidents of the momentous ten days now last past. Of course, he has talked to everybody, seen everything, found his way into every place. No time to record details. His report of the aspect of things, as seen from Willard's and Pennsylvania Avenue, is decidedly favorable. The Inaugural has done good. Army and navy men from Virginia and even from the rebel states say they will abide by the flag of the United States and the doctrine of the Inaugural, whatever their states have done or may do; for example, Captain Lewis of the Navy Yard, whose allegiance was very shaky two months ago. Men of the Border States are encouraged and sanguine.

Wigfall of Texas said in Charley's hearing on Monday that he was disgusted with his Southern friends. They had sworn that Lincoln should be killed, and now he was peaceably inaugurated after all. He was tempted to say he would have nothing more to do with such a d—d set of humbugs.

Crittenden is hopeful, even confident. If we can drag through the next thirty days without bloodshed at Fort Sumter or elsewhere, all may be well. Seward's policy has been to procrastinate, to gain time, to wait; and that will be the policy of this Administration. He urged it daily on Charles F. Adams, while the House Committee of Thirty-Three was sitting, and he was quite right. Government is weak and must postpone a trial of strength, in hope that something may turn up.

Trinity Church Standing Committee this afternoon. Chess with Johnny after dinner. Then to George F. Allen's in 24th Street. He, Rutherfurd, and I are a committee on the College course and have a difficult and responsible work before us. . . .

Mrs. Charles E. Strong, I believe, claims the credit of having saved the Corwin Resolution, which scraped through the Senate by a vote of precisely $\frac{2}{3}$. She bullied Anthony or Simmons or Foster or some other Senator into changing his vote. . . .[11]

March 9.   To New York Club. Spent an hour with Tom Meyer, John

[11] Thomas Corwin, chairman of the Committee of Thirty-three seeking a solution of the crisis, had presented a report embracing a series of conciliatory propositions. His proposed constitutional amendment safeguarding slavery in the states where it already existed passed the Senate 24 to 12.

J. Townsend, Cutting, Christie, and John Sherwood. Townsend just returned from Savannah, Mobile, and North Carolina. Though ultra-Republican, he seems astonished and cowed by the depth and unanimity of the secession feeling at the South and thinks secession must be recognized, Fort Sumter abandoned, and the Cotton States left in peace to go to chaos their own way. Unfortunate, if true.

There are certainly indications the other way—indications faint and perhaps unreliable of reaction setting in and Union men taking heart, even at Charleston, of financial pressure becoming intolerable, and of emigration from the Cotton States. There are contradictory reports as to the effect of the Inaugural, but it seems on the whole to have made a favorable impression.

Foster has moved the expulsion of the chivalric Wigfall, Senator from Texas.[12] Wrote Ellie this morning to give Foster my personal thanks as for a personal favor. Wigfall's presence in the Senate Chamber, after his audacious, insolent utterances of treason in his official place, is an affront to every citizen of the United States.

The Border States seem convalescing. Even North Carolina refuses to call a convention.

March 11, MONDAY. General Dix tells me they have advices at Washington that the United States flag is flying on every tavern in North Alabama. Also that the control of West Point was on the programme of Buchanan's traitorous Cabinet, and that they came very near getting it into the hands of men pledged to secessionism and prepared to use its men and matériel in aid of an expected revolutionary anti-Lincoln demonstration in this state!

Today's great news is that government contemplates withdrawing Major Anderson and his command from Fort Sumter! It is said they can not maintain themselves there without supplies more than twenty or thirty days longer, and that the batteries in Charleston Harbor are *now* (thanks to old Buchanan's imbecility or treason) so strong that supplies and reinforcements cannot be thrown in without some 10,000 men and a strong naval force. We have not got the men or the ships, and they cannot be got for months. What is to be done? Withdrawal, surrender, "calm, dishonorable, vile submission," seems the only course we have left. But it will be a sore occasion for South Carolinian bullies to bluster and blaspheme. They will laugh consumedly over their whiskey.

If newspaper reports be true, the surrender of Fort Sumter is inevitable.

[12] That is, L. S. Foster (1806–1880), Republican Senator from Connecticut.

The surrender may do good at the South, possibly. Some say it will break the neck of "secession" in South Carolina itself, and ruin every secessionist leader. But it will stir up corresponding exasperation at the North, strengthen the Greeley wing of Republicanism, and weaken the conservatives whom Seward leads. The proposition is generally received with favor here. It will be otherwise received in New England and the West, I think! I recognize it as a stern necessity, but as a deep humiliation withal, as an unavoidable submission to gross personal insult from Jefferson Davis and Governor Pickens and their crew of "chivalric" bullies and braggarts.

The political entity known as the United States of America is found out at last, after imposing on the community of nations for three-quarters of a century. The bird of our country is a debilitated chicken, disguised in eagle feathers. We have never been a nation; we are only an aggregate of communities, ready to fall apart at the first serious shock and without a centre of vigorous national life to keep us together.

March 12.   Murray Hoffman dined here, and we went downtown to the plebeian Stadt Theatre in the Bowery, where we saw *Orpheus in der Unterwelt*, a funny extravaganza that has had a great run in Paris. Music by the celebrated Offenbach, whoever he is; rather piquant and Frenchy. It includes one or two appropriations from Haydn, scraps of Volkslied (for example, "Guter Mond du gehst so stille"), and lovely larcenies from the *Zauberflöte*.

Nothing definite about Fort Sumter, but the impression grows stronger that its surrender is unavoidable and that government has not the means to hold it. Lincoln's Administration cannot fairly be held responsible for this national disgrace. Traitors—Floyd, Cobb, & Co.—have been diligently paralyzing our national strength for months, if not for years. Their successors in office cannot undo the spell at once.

But, whoever may be responsible for the calamity, this is a time of sad humiliation for the country. Every citizen of what has heretofore been called the Great Republic of America, every man, woman, and child, from Maine to Texas, from Massachusetts to California, stands lower among the inhabitants of this earth tonight than in March, 1860. We are a weak, divided, disgraced people, unable to maintain our national existence. We are impotent even to *assert* our national life. The country of George Washington and Andrew Jackson (!!!) is decomposing, and its elements reforming into new and strange combinations. I shall never go abroad. That question is settled. I should be ashamed to show my nose in the meanest corner of Europe. Naples and Florence and Milan, now triumphantly asserting their national life and unity, are entitled to look down on Boston and New York. All my right, title, and interest in the Fourth of July and the American Eagle and the Model Republic can be bought at a "low figure."

I'm tempted to emigrate, to become a naturalized British subject and spend the rest of my days in some pleasant sea-side village in the southern counties of old Mother England. It's a pity we ever renounced our allegiance to the British Crown.

March 13. No political news today. Some say the talk of evacuating Fort Sumter is a ruse to disarm South Carolina and facilitate the introduction of reinforcements. I fear it covers no such politic purpose.

March 14. . . . To Mr. Ruggles's to ask Mrs. Ruggles to be kind enough to look after the babies a little, while I go to Washington for Ellie (letter this morning from her; O.K.), and then to the New York Club. Messenger, Clarence Cram, Thorndike, Bob Benson, Lafitte, and others. Thorndike expatiated on Church's iceberg picture, not yet quite finished. It will be another sensation, [a] $20,000 work, like "The Heart of the Andes," but it will be clever and far from commonplace.

March 15. Have been spending the evening with George F. Allen over College business. He is sagacious and thoughtful, and among the most genial and attractive men I know. We have to revise the proposed "Statute" defining the college course. There are two points that require attention: 1. The Higher Mathematics. Rutherfurd wants them cut out or made optional, which amounts to the same thing. 2. Nairne's course. I am clear we should suppress his Empirical Ontology, and *Hickok*, and Philosophy of the Will and ditto of the Affections, and cobwebs and moonshine and Scotch metaphysics; also, his Principles of Aesthetics. Our average boys are utterly unripe for these abstractions. We should substitute definite, tangible History of Modern Literature and History of Philosophy, ancient and modern. . . .

Political affairs unchanged. There is only one hope left us now, and that is revolutionary reaction in the seceded states against the conspirators who have dragged them into rebellion. But there is no symptom that way. To be sure, there may be unseen tendencies toward it, repressed by the Reign of Terror there established, and it may be the stronger when it breaks out at last. But we have no ground for supposing that any such feeling exists. Everything there (except in the feeble, thinly-populated regions of Northern Alabama and Georgia) indicates unanimity in treason.

March 19, TUESDAY.　Home again after my tour to Washington, *once capital de facto* of our nation.

At Jersey City ferry 6:30 A.M. Saturday. A bleak, grey morning. Streets shrouded in snow that fell Friday night. Into the railroad cars and away. Sun broke out and clouds vanished. Philadelphia, Wilmington, Baltimore, were successively passed without the minutest material for a journal paragraph, and our locomotive screeched over its advent at Washington at six o'clock P.M. Proceeded to Willard's, where I found Ellie and Mrs. D. C. Murray and Jem Ruggles in full go. There was a reception at the National Hotel that evening in honor of Mrs. J. J. Crittenden's departure. Mrs. Murray assisted; Ellie stayed at home. The reception seems to have been a specimen of the vilest American spread-eagle taste, justifying Dickens in *Martin Chuzzlewit*.

Hotel lobbies crawling with office-seekers. Germans from the Northwest in great force. Anthony Bleecker is struggling for the United States marshalship of this district, but will struggle in vain; New York politicians give him little countenance.[13] If that prize fail him, he will jump at any crumb or bone of patronage from the Executive table. Poor Anthony Bleecker!

Oscanyan, our Columbia College Law School janitor, wants a diplomatic position in Mesopotamia, or that neighborhood. I know not precisely where. (Probably the consul-generalship at Alexandria, salary $3,500, which Thayer of the *Evening Post* seems to have secured.) Gave him the benefit of my political influence, for so inefficient a janitor may make a brilliant diplomat, and I cheerfully contributed my mite to relieve the Law School of a sweeper and maker of fires who knows so little of his profession.

Sunday was cloudy and cold. To St. John's Church with Ellie. Reverend Smith Pyne, whom his parishioners call "Pitch Pine," preached in his usual key. His sermon was spasmodic, but of more than average depth. I rate the Reverend Smith Pyne rather high among preachers. Long walk thereafter with Jem in the grey evening, inspecting Mills's bronze equestrian Washington in a gale of wind. Afterwards discoursed with Senator Foster, Mr. and Mrs. Bigelow Lawrence, Fry of the New York *Tribune* staff (very clever, and I think consumptive; he's after some diplomatic post and relies much on his terrible cough, the result of speech-making over much of New York and Ohio in the last campaign).[14]

[13] Anthony J. Bleecker was one of the leading Republican merchants; he did not become marshal.

[14] William H. Fry had been music critic of the New York *Tribune*.

Monday, walked alone to that hideous unfinished Washington Monument. Then with the ladies to Senate at one P.M. Very cold and beginning to spit snow. Routine business ended. J. C. Breckinridge opened with an insidious, mischievous speech, asking information as to Lincoln's policy, deprecating "coercion" as sure to drive every "Border" State out of the Union, and deploring the obstinate refusal of the North to make concession. Hale replied in slang-whanging stump-orator style. He is more effective than J. C. Breckinridge and made several telling points. He had a small passage of arms with the irrepressible Wigfall of Texas.

Senate went into executive session at half-past three. Galleries were cleared, and we emerged from the Capitol into a snow storm. Secured a hack for the ladies, and went at five to a little dinner at Sanford's (the ex-attaché). There were Ellie and I, Truman Smith, Mr. Secretary Cameron, Senators Anthony of Rhode Island and Baker of Oregon. Sanford is to be Minister to Belgium.[15] Pleasant session, but these great men had no light to throw on the mysterious situation of affairs. Even Cameron professed to know nothing about Lincoln's plans and policy; an official white lie, of course, which nobody was expected to believe. They all predict that the Border States will slough off, Virginia first of all. Those states merely weaken and paralyze us. I begin to think they had better go and make no long tarrying; that free states cannot dwell together in unity with slaveholding states.

The talk about a strong and growing Union Party in Virginia and Kentucky is delusive. This so-called Union Party says in substance: "If government will sit quite still while its territory is surrendered, its flag insulted, if it will give up its forts, and let its property be stolen and its revenues cut off by traitors and rebels, without resistance, then we will stay in the Union, at least until we change our minds. Otherwise, hurrah for secession and the Confederate States of Slave-ownia!" On these terms, the Union is not worth saving.

March 20. No material change in the political situation during these few days. The quasi-Union party in Missouri and Arkansas seems dominant. In the Slave-ownian Confederacy, it becomes plainer every day that secession is the act of an oligarchy, and ignores or contradicts and overrides the "self-evident truths" of all the Democratic platforms of the last half century. The non-slaveholders and poor whites, who do the hurrahing and the lynching, are blindly assisting at their own political

---

[15] Henry S. Sanford (1823–1891), of a wealthy Connecticut family, had been secretary of legation in Paris.

THE GREAT UNION MEETING, UNION SQUARE
20 APRIL 1861

MAKING HAVELOCKS FOR THE VOLUNTEERS

DRAWING BY WINSLOW HOMER

annihilation. Lord Davis (they have baptized a recently launched war-scow or canoe the "Lady Davis" in honor of Mrs. Jefferson Davis) means to rule his people. That prince and his chivalric pals have no notion of submitting constitutions to a popular vote. Not they. Alabama and Mississippi newspapers begin to recalcitrate a little, but it will be in vain. Democratic theories of universal suffrage and the Rights of the People stand no chance against resolute men who have attained power and mean to keep it in times of revolutionary excitement. If the Southern Confederates hold together long enough to take definite political form, their government will be that of a strong, unscrupulous aristocracy. Malcontents will be promptly silenced or hanged, and even the sacred fundamental constitutional right of secession will not be exercised without serious danger and embarrassment.

March 21.   We were blue in Wall Street. Something must be done about our most injudicious tariff, lest the South get the better of us and absorb the commerce and imports of New York and Boston.

I see no indications thus far of vigor or sagacity in the new Administration. There are vague rumors of a proclamation that is to be issued within a few days, and that will produce a great effect. We shall see.

March 22.   Bigelow Lawrence isn't Secretary of Legation after all. Some Illinoisome individual gets that post. William H. Fry has lost the Paris secretaryship (under Dayton), and of all people in the world, Bill Pennington takes it. Nobody more surprised than he is, for he had made no application for it. Probably his father, the ex-Speaker of the House, put in a claim on his behalf. Bill is a jolly good fellow, but will make a remarkable diplomat. He speaks no French, but he swears wonderfully in strong, nervous Saxon, and can drink any three Frenchmen drunk and sober again. This is all today's political news. We generally predict today that there will be no war after all.

March 28.   Mr. Ruggles and Murray Hoffman dined here. Bigelow Lawrence goes to Florence as Consul General or something of the sort, and William H. Fry is to be Secretary of Legation at Turin.

March 30.   At Century Club tonight (afterward for Ellie at Mrs. Tighe's), and converse with Lieber and Verplanck and others. . . . Lieber referred to Hoffman's story that seemed so to delight him last Sunday night, a story of Richelieu's time, and a singular instance of a lively faith. It is this. There was to be a solemn procession through the streets of Paris, escorting the thaumaturgic and healing relics of St. Martin. All the lame, blind, and paralytic beggars got, or got carried, into alleys and byeplaces off its route, lest they should be healed against their will of the diseases by which they made their living. Lieber matches this with the story of a Mexican girl who was certain she could cure any disease by securing the intervention of the Madonna. She had found out how to do it infallibly. If the Madonna hesitated, she just took away the Bambino, and the Madonna had to come round.

Omnibussed downtown this morning with Senator Foster and his charming wife, shopping through the town on their way home to Norwich. The new Administration disappoints Foster. What he said implies that he holds Lincoln & Co. unequal to the crisis. I fear he is right.

April 5. No material change in public affairs, or if any, for the worse. Secession fever certainly gaining in Virginia. Rumors of a projected outbreak or revolutionary *coup d'état* at Richmond. A dash at Washington is again talked of as likely to be tried. Then, of course, comes war, at once, and on what seems a tolerably plain case—bloodshed in an open rebellion against both state and federal authority. But would even this aggression stiffen up the spiritless, money-worshipping North? Strange the South can't kick us into manliness and a little moderate wrath. Southerners rule us through our white slaves of Fifth Avenue and Wall Street.

There are symptoms of a decisive move by the Administration. Great stir in army and navy. Governor's Island, Fort Hamilton, and Brooklyn Navy Yard full of business. Troops moving, no one knows whither. Ships getting ready for sea in hot haste and sailing with sealed orders, some say for Fort Pickens (Pensacola), and others for Fort Sumter. Abandonment of Fort Sumter is *not* determined on, according to present reports; and Pensacola is to be reinforced anyhow. Bellicose rumors abound today. Colonel Keese and Colonel Henry Scott were off early this morning, I hear. Curtis tells me they were very doleful and despondent half an hour or so at Dr. Van Buren's Thursday evening party. Forsyth, one of the "C.S.A." Commissioners, was expected, but was summoned to Washington by his colleagues yesterday afternoon. All this looks as if things were coming to a crisis.

Virginia will secede within three months. Amen! We cannot live together. Her dictatorial arrogance is unbearable. Let her go in peace, if that be possible. Rhode Island election a Democratic victory. Democratic gain in Connecticut. Thus are we divided and paralyzed. Per contra, the nucleus of a quasi-Union party seems to exist in certain districts of Slaveownia itself; that is, in Northern Alabama and Mississippi. . . .

April 6, saturday. *Evening Post,* second edition, says advices have been received at Washington that Major Anderson has been notified by the circumambient traitors of Charleston to vacate Fort Sumter within forty-eight hours, or in default thereof, to take the consequences. The third edition says that *firing has commenced.* Maybe so, maybe not. Any newspaper rumor is probably a lie; the general presumption is against it. But the South Carolinians are doubtless advised of the stir and preparation here, and this may have precipitated the crisis. We shall not be long in suspense. The prevailing opinion today has been, however, that the troops we are sending off from Governor's Island and Fort Hamilton are destined neither for Sumter nor Pickens, but for Texas, to strengthen the hands of Governor Samuel Houston.

Poor Ellie suffering all day from another of these unaccountable headaches.

Century tonight. Monthly meeting. Edward Cooper[16] talking the wildest secessionite doctrine, under a heavy fire of common sense and common honesty from George Allen, Professor Lieber, and Dr. Bellows. The political and private ethics of that school (wherein Floyd and General Twiggs are chief teachers) may be chivalric; they are certainly amazing. They result in this proposition: "No faith is to be kept with heretics." And all are heretics who are unsettled as to the right and the expediency of owning another man's wife and children.

Here is a Southern editor elaborately eulogizing the "Honorable" ex-Secretary Floyd. "But for Floyd's vigilance and sagacity, the whole secession movement would have been a failure. General Scott's plan of reinforcing Fort Moultrie would have killed it dead. But Floyd's official position under Buchanan enabled him to embarrass and prevent the execution of the plan, and he did so very gallantly and chivalrously, keeping the secessionist leaders constantly advised of what the Cabinet was doing or contemplating. Praise and glory to the gallant, true-hearted Floyd!" That is to say, Floyd is to be honored and exalted because he did his utmost to aid and encourage certain traitorous enemies of the Union, while he was a sworn officer of the Union and receiving its pay. . . .

The "decisive move" by the Administration of which Strong speaks was really under way. As early as April 4, Lincoln had decided that he must send a relief expedition to Fort Sumter in Charleston Harbor and another to Fort Pickens in Pensacola Bay, these being the only major forts in the seceded states

[16] Son of Peter Cooper; a Democratic politician and future mayor.

left in Federal hands. The President had avoided any effort to repossess the numerous posts and fortified places already lost, including Fort Moultrie at Charleston, Fort Pulaski at Savannah, Fort Morgan at Mobile, and the nineteen army posts given up to the Texas authorities by General David E. Twiggs while Twiggs still wore his United States uniform. But he wished to maintain the status quo, and Sumter would have to be evacuated unless stores of food were taken to it. Days and nights of incessant labor got the Pickens expedition ready to sail from New York on the 6th. The Sumter expedition was also to leave on that date, but was delayed, and in consequence of bungled orders was not accompanied by the frigate Powhatan *as Lincoln had intended. It was not until April 9 that it made a start, and the lack of a powerful warship seriously crippled it.*

Men like Strong in the North regarded the provisioning of Fort Sumter as a test of Lincoln's announcement in his inaugural that no further surrenders of national forts would take place. Radical Southerners, on the other hand, regarded it as an act of aggression which must be met with force. Lincoln took pains to see that the government of South Carolina was notified in advance of the expedition, with information upon its pacific character. But the moment news of the movement reached the South, it was taken as a defiance and a threat. The Confederate Cabinet was called in an excited consultation; and as the relief expedition of three vessels under Captain Gustavus V. Fox slowly voyaged southward, the Secretary of War at Montgomery ordered General Beauregard in Charleston to demand the evacuation of Fort Sumter. If this be refused, he added, "reduce the fort." On the night of April 11, four Confederate officers carried word of these instructions to Major Robert Anderson, commanding the fort. In reply, Anderson promised to evacuate Sumter by noon on the 15th unless he received controlling instructions or additional supplies prior to that date. The supplies were now at hand, while Lincoln's determination not to evacuate was well known. At 3:30 on the morning of April 12, therefore, Beauregard's aides served notice upon Anderson that the Southern guns would open in one hour. Precisely on time, the firing began—and with it four years of war.

April 8, MONDAY. With Charley Strong at the Brooklyn Navy Yard this afternoon. A large force sailed on Saturday for parts unknown, but there is still great bustle and activity there, getting the *Wabash* and other ships ready for sea. Went on board the old *North Carolina* and came off after an interesting two hours, convinced that something is about to be done. . . .

April 9.   Great anxiety for news of our armada, by this time in Southern waters, and general gratification, even among the more moderate Democratic malcontents, at this vigorous move, the first sign of national self-assertion. Many believe the fleet destined for Charleston harbor, and that Fort Sumter is not to be given up after all. At the Law School to-night George Allen, Professors Lieber and Bidwell, President King, and others were jubilant over this indication that our great Union, so bragged of for so many years, is not to perish without a struggle.

April 10.   This morning's *Tribune* and *Times* announce positively, and as if by authority, that the fleet has gone to Charleston and that Fort Sumter is to be reinforced. Then shall we hear stirring news! But is this force strong enough? It is only about 2,000 men, and the talk has been that 20,000 were needed. Perhaps the Administration counts on a repulse as a tonic and stimulant to the North, but I trust there will be no repulse. God forbid that this effort, forced on the country after long forbearance to maintain the sanctity of law and the authority of government, should be defeated.

April 11.   Nothing from the seat of war (wherever that is) except a rumor that Jefferson Davis orders Charleston to make no opposition to the introduction of provisions into Sumter. A politic move, for everything depends on being strictly right on the particular issue in which the first blood is drawn, and many Democrats and Border State men would say the South was wrong in refusing to allow the *status quo* to be maintained by a supply of food to Anderson and his little force. . . .

Dined at William B. Astor's. Dinner given to the worshipful judges of the Court of Appeals, now in session here. There were also Evarts, Charles O'Conor, John Carey (Rev. Mr. Arthur Carey's brother, and one of George Anthon's class in Columbia College, and now Astor's son-in-law, whom I've not seen for twenty years), Governor Fish, Judge Pierrepont, Dr. Rae of Arctic notoriety (who expatiated on flavor of raw walrus blubber warmed at a lamp), and Judge Daly. Mrs. Astor and Miss Maggy Ward gave us the light of their countenances. It was pleasant enough, but their Honors, from Judge Davies *up*, are a little slow.

April 12, FRIDAY.   *War* has begun, unless my extra *Herald* lies, and its Charleston despatch is bogus. Busy downtown. . . . Walked up with George Anthon. Evening papers told us nothing material from the South. With Ellie to dinner at Mrs. Annie Cameron's (64 Fifth Avenue) . . . .

Came off at the earliest possible moment, leaving Ellie there, and went to Dr. Berrian's. Committee met there to consider the amount to be allowed by Trinity Church for support of St. George's Chapel. We were a discordant committee, and after much prosing decided that as we could not agree on anything, we had better call a special meeting of the vestry for Tuesday night and leave the question for them to settle.

Walked uptown with Gouverneur Ogden and that wooden-headed Dunscomb. The streets were vocal with newsboys—"Extry—a *Herald!* Got the bombardment of *Fort Sumter!!!*" We concluded it was probably a sell and that we would not be sold, and declined all invitations to purchase for about four blocks. But we could not stand it longer. I sacrificed sixpence and read the news to Ogden and that galvanized pumpkin Mr. Dunscomb by the light of a corner gas lamp. The despatch is a column long, from Charleston, in substance to this effect. The rebel batteries opened on Sumter at "twenty-seven minutes after four" this morning. Major Anderson replied only at long intervals till seven or eight o'clock when he began firing vigorously. At three P.M. (date of telegram) he had produced no serious effect. "No men hurt" in the rebel batteries. No impression made on the "floating battery." Fort Sumter suffering much. "Breaches, to all appearance, are being made." The *Harriet Lane* in the offing, but no other government ships on hand. "Troops are pouring in," and "within an area of fifty miles, where the thunder of the artillery can be heard, the scene is magnificently terrible." That magnificent and terrible sentence sounds as if it belonged to a genuine despatch from the South. Yet I doubt its genuineness vehemently. I can hardly hope that the rebels have been so foolish and thoughtless as to take the initiative in civil war and bring matters to a crisis. If so, they have put themselves in a horribly false position. The most frantic Virginian can hardly assert that this war is brought on by any attempt at "coercion."

April 13.   Here begins a new chapter of my journal, entitled WAR— EXSURGAT DEUS *et dissipentere inimici ejus, et fugerunt qui oderunt eum a facie ejus. Amen!*

This morning's papers confirmed last night's news; viz., that the rebels opened fire at Sumter yesterday morning. During the day came successive despatches, *all one way*, of course, for the Charleston telegraphs are under Charleston control, and in addition to the local taste for brag and lying, there are obvious motives for a high-colored picture of damage done the fort. It tends to prevent reinforcement by any supplementary expedition that might be extemporized if the parties appeared to be at all equally matched.

In substance, the despatches say that firing ceased at six P.M. yesterday, but shells continued to be thrown into the fort all night at intervals of twenty minutes. Cannonade resumed this morning with brilliant success. The fort on fire. "Flames bursting from the embrasures." Raft outside and men passing up water. Great havoc among them. Two explosions in the fort. Major Anderson "believed to be gradually (!) blowing it up." Nobody hurt in the rebel batteries. No impression made on that formidable battle-scow "the Floating Battery." Major Anderson has ceased firing. Then came a fourth edition of the *Evening Post*, with a despatch that he has surrendered. This was while I was at the New York Club. On coming home, I find Ellie in possession of a still later *Herald* extra. The ships are engaged with the batteries; (this we had earlier). Two are sunk. The rest are shelling the city, which is on fire. I take this last item to be invented for the sake of stimulating wrath and fury in the Border States.

To shell Charleston, the ships must have worked their way into the harbor and passed Sumter. If so, they must have silenced the batteries and been able to throw supplies into the fort, which is hardly to be hoped. Had they done so, the object of the expedition would have been accomplished. And I doubt whether they would have fired on the city under any circumstances. But that damnable little hornet's nest of treason deserves to be shelled. It's a political Sodom. . . .

So Civil War is inaugurated at last. God defend the Right.

The Northern backbone is much stiffened already. Many who stood up for "Southern rights" and complained of wrongs done the South now say that, since the South has fired the first gun, they are ready to go all lengths in supporting the government. The New York *Herald* is noncommittal this morning. It may well be upholding the Administration and denouncing the Democratic party within a week. It takes naturally to eating dirt and its own words (the same thing). Would I were in Sumter tonight, even with the chance of being forced to surrender (seventy men against seven thousand) and of being lynched thereafter by the Chivalry of Charleston. The seventy will be as memorable as the "four hundred" of the Light Brigade at Balaklava, whatever be their fate.

It is said the President will assume the right to call for volunteers, whether the law give it or not. If he does, there will soon be a new element in the fray; viz., the stern anti-slavery Puritanism that survives in New England and in the Northwest. Ossawattomie John Brown would be worth his weight in gold just now. What a pity he precipitated matters and got himself prematurely hanged!

April 14, SUNDAY. Fine day. Morning *Herald* announces *Surrender of Fort Sumter* and great jubilation in Charleston. To Trinity Church with Ellie and Miss Rosalie and Johnny. On our way back, I made a detour to the *Tribune* office. The whole story discredited there. Lots of private despatches quoted, inconsistent with surrender, and tending to show there had been no serious fight.

Mr. Ruggles dined with us. This evening Dr. Rae and his pretty wife were here by appointment, with their two young friends from England. . . . There is no doubt that Fort Sumter has surrendered. Despatches received by Mrs. Anderson, Cottenet, and others settle that point. But no reliable details of the transactions have reached us. If it be true, as Charleston telegrams assert, that after forty hours' firing "no one is hurt," *Punch* and the *Charivari* have an inviting topic for jokes at our expense. . . .

From all I can learn, the effect of this on Democrats, heretofore Southern and quasi-treasonable in their talk, has fully justified the sacrifice. I hear of F. B. Cutting and Walter Cutting, Hewitt, Lewis Rutherfurd, Judge Vanderpoel, and others of that type denouncing rebellion and declaring themselves ready to go all lengths in upholding government. If this class of men has been secured and converted to loyalty, the gain to the country is worth ten Sumters. CAM, heretofore strongly Southern in his talk, was declaring his readiness this evening to shoulder a musket in defence of Washington. That is the next point to be thought of. "He is the true Pope who lives in the Vatican." It must be defended at any cost.

At Trinity Church today, Vinton read the prayer, "In time of war and tumults," and the Amen of the white-robed choir boys was emphasized by a suggestive trumpet-stop coloring from the organ.

April 15. Events multiply. The President is out with a proclamation calling for 75,000 volunteers and an extra session of Congress July 4. It is said 200,000 more will be called within a few days. Every man of them will be wanted before this game is lost and won. Change in public feeling marked, and a thing to thank God for. We begin to look like a United North. Willy Duncan (!) says it may be necessary to hang Lincoln and Seward and Greeley hereafter, but our present duty is to sustain

Government and Law, and give the South a lesson.[17] The New York *Herald* is *in equilibrio* today, just at the turning point. Tomorrow it will denounce Jefferson Davis as it denounced Lincoln a week ago. The *Express* is half traitorous and half in favor of energetic action against traitors. The *Journal of Commerce* and the little *Day-Book* show no signs of reformation yet, but though they are contemptible and without material influence for evil, the growing excitement against their treasonable talk will soon make them more cautious in its utterance. The *Herald* office has already been threatened with an attack.

Mayor Wood out with a "proclamation." He must still be talking. It is brief and commonplace, but winds up with a recommendation to everybody to obey the laws of the land. This is significant. The cunning scoundrel sees which way the cat is jumping and puts himself right on the record in a vague general way, giving the least possible offence to his allies of the Southern Democracy. The *Courier* of this morning devotes its leading article to a ferocious assault on Major Anderson as a traitor beyond Twiggs, and declares that he has been in collusion with the Charleston people all the time. This is wrong and bad. It is premature, at least. . . .

Expedition to Governor's Island this morning; Ellie and I, Charley Strong and wife, Dan Messenger, Christie, Miss Kate Fearing, Tom Meyer, and one or two more. Officer of the day was Lieutenant Webb of Maine, whose guests we were. He treated us most hospitably, and had out the band, playing an hour or two for our delectation. Its programme included that jolliest of tunes, "Dixie Land," and "Hail Columbia." We took off our hats while the latter was played. Everybody's patriotism is rampant and demonstrative now. About three hundred recruits on the Island, mostly quite raw. I discoursed with one of them, an honest-looking, simple-minded boy from somewhere near Rochester, probably some small farmer's son. "He had voted for Abe Lincoln, and as there was going to be trouble, he might as well *fight* for Abe Lincoln," so he enlisted two weeks ago. "Guessed they were going to get some hard knocks when they went down South, but then he had always kind o' wanted to see the world—that was one reason why he 'listed."

Great activity on the Island. Guns and all manner of warlike munitions and apparatus are being shipped, generally for Pensacola.

[17] William B. Duncan, a conservative Democratic merchant, had been one of the business leaders who, in 1860, tried to fuse the Douglas, Bell, and Breckinridge parties to defeat Lincoln and thus "save the Union."

April 16. A fine storm of wind and rain all day. The conversion of the New York *Herald* is complete. It rejoices that rebellion is to be put down and is delighted with Civil War, because it will so stimulate the business of New York, and all this is what "we" (the *Herald*, to wit) have been vainly preaching for months. This impudence of old J. G. Bennett's is too vast to be appreciated at once. You must look at it and meditate over it for some time (as at Niagara and St. Peter's) before you can take in its immensity. His capitulation is a set-off against the loss of Sumter. He's a discreditable ally for the North, but when you see a rat leaving the enemy's ship for your own, you overlook the offensiveness of the vermin for the sake of what its movement indicates. This brazen old scoundrel was hooted up Fulton Street yesterday afternoon by a mob, and the police interfered to prevent it from sacking his printing office. Though converted, one can hardly call him penitent. St. Paul did not call himself the Chief of the Apostles and brag of having been a Christian from the first.

This and other papers say the new war policy will strangle secession in the Border States. But it seems to me that every indication from Virginia, North Carolina, and elsewhere points the other way. No news from Slave-ownia today, but most gladdening reports from North, West, and East of unanimity and resolution and earnestness. We are aroused at last, and I trust we shall not soon relapse into apathy. Ellie indisposed again. I begin to be seriously uneasy about the constantly recurring attacks of slight illness—headache and the like—that have visited her of late.

Trinity Church Vestry tonight; special meeting on St. George's Chapel and a very long debate. The appropriation required is large ($6,000 per annum, at least), and in moving it, I premised that the whole question turned on the ability of the vestry to spend that sum. If they have it to spare, the Chapel can be maintained, otherwise not; and a smaller appropriation just keeping up the establishment in its present dead-alive condition would do no good and be simply throwing away so much money, besides bringing a certain amount of discredit on Trinity Church. A smaller appropriation was moved as a substitute and carried by a large majority, Swift and I voting in the negative, with three or four others. . . .

Thence to New York Club. Our talk was of war. Subscribed to a fund for equipment of the Twelfth Regiment and put down my name for a projected Rifle Corps, but I fear my near-sightedness is a grave objection to my adopting that arm. I hear that Major Burnside has surrendered his treasurership of the Illinois Central Railroad and posted down to Rhode Island to assume command of volunteers from that state. Telegram that 2,500 Massachusetts volunteers are quartered in Faneuil Hall, awaiting orders.

GOD SAVE THE UNION, AND CONFOUND ITS ENEMIES. AMEN.

April 17. Dull weather, but it has cleared up tonight. No material change in the complexion of affairs, except that a crisis is drawing very near in Virginia and Kentucky. I count on the loyalty of no Border State, except Maryland. We are on the eve of a civil war that will be bitter and bloody, and probably indecisive.

There was a slight outbreak here today. I was sitting in my office at three o'clock when I heard unwonted sounds in Wall Street, and looking out, saw a straggling column of men running toward the East River. My first notion was that they were chasing a runaway horse, but they soon became too numerous to be engaged in that. They halted in front of the *Journal of Commerce* office and filled the street densely for about a block.[18] There were outcries, which I could not distinctly hear for a minute, and then the American flag was hung out from a window, and the crowd sent up a cheer that stirred one's blood a little, and the surface of the black mass was suddenly all in motion with waving hats. Then a line of policemen came down the street on a dog-trot, and the crowd thereupon moved promptly up Wall Street again, cheering lustily.

They were mostly decently-dressed people, but with a sprinkling of laboring men. I understand they paid a like domiciliary visit to the *Express*, the *Day-Book*, and the *Daily News*, requiring each to put up the flag.[19] They intended to call on the New York Hotel, it is said, but Cranston was forewarned and the American flag was flying from its roof as I came uptown.

April 18. Fine day; drizzly evening. Journalizing is a serious job just now. We are living a month of common life every day. One general proposition to begin with. My habit is to despond and find fault, but the attitude of New York and the whole North at this time is magnificent.

[18] Gerard Hallock's *Journal of Commerce*, long proslavery in tone, had been outspoken in favor of letting the South secede in peace. It argued that two American nations, one free and one slave, might live amicably together.

[19] The *Day-Book*, conducted by John H. Van Evrie, had been violently proslavery and pro-Southern; the *Daily News*, controlled by Ben Wood, a brother of Mayor Fernando Wood, and the *Express*, owned by James and Erastus Brooks, had been only less offensive.

Perfect unanimity, earnestness, and readiness to make every sacrifice for the support of law and national life. Especially impressive after our long forbearance and vain efforts to conciliate, our readiness to humble ourselves for the sake of peace. Still, I expect to hear only of disaster for a long while yet.

The morning papers give us Jefferson Davis's proclamation of reprisals on Northern commerce. Letters of marque are to be issued to any piratical Spaniard who will accept them. Very well. Then we shall have no scruples about retaliating on Southern property, which is peculiar for possessing a capacity for being invited to go away, and legs to take itself off, and arms wherewith to use such implements as may aid it in so doing, if opposed. Davis's proposed privateers can take their prizes into no civilized port. They will have to sink, burn, and destroy. Every maritime power in Christendom will make common cause against them and his "Algerine" Confederacy.

With Bidwell on reference in Carter v. Taylor. Little progress. Went to the [City] Hall. The [Sixth] Massachusetts Regiment, which arrived here last night, was marching down on its way to Washington. Immense crowd; immense cheering. My eyes filled with tears, and I was half choked in sympathy with the contagious excitement. God be praised for the unity of feeling here! It is beyond, very far beyond, anything I hoped for. If it only last, we are safe.

The national flag flying everywhere; every cart horse decorated. It occurred to me that it would be a good thing to hoist it on the tower of Trinity—an unprecedented demonstration, but these are unprecedented times; not only good in itself, as a symbol of the sympathy of the Church Catholic with all movements to suppress privy conspiracy and sedition, but a politic move for Trinity Church at this memorable hour of excitement. Somewhat to my surprise, General Dix, Cisco, Skidmore, Swift, and Gouverneur Ogden cordially concurred with me and signed a note to Dr. Berrian, asking his permission to hoist it.

Posted up to the Rector's in Varick Street, but he was out. Again at four, but he was not very well and could not see me. So I left the note and announced that I should call tomorrow morning for an answer. I expected a negative answer, supported by platitudes of fogyism, easily to be imagined. But while I was at dinner came a note from the Rector, who "very cheerfully" complies with our request. Hurrah for Dr. Berrian! His consent to this is the strongest indication yet of the intensity of our national feeling just now. May we dare to hope it will last?

Ellie dined at her father's. I dined here with Miss Rosalie and the children. Jem Ruggles (corporal or sergeant in the Seventh Regiment), received an appointment on General Hall's staff a week ago, and had intended to resign out of the regiment and be henceforth Judge Advocate with the rank of a Major. But the Seventh is ordered to Washington and he has wisely and rightly got leave of absence as staff officer and decided to go South in the ranks. I am proud of my brick of a brother-in-law.

After dinner, at eight o'clock, to Fifth Avenue Hotel. Its halls crowded. Excited individual mounts a pile of trunks and says: "Gentlemen, some of us are going to the Brevoort House to call on Major Anderson. Who'll go with us?" General yell and rush. Excited individual proceeds, "I saw Major Anderson this afternoon. He stands by the national flag while it floats, and will go to its funeral when it's buried." Universal roar. Then a tramp down Fifth Avenue to Brevoort House, at the corner of Fifth Avenue and Eighth Street. Cheers for Anderson and groans for James Watson Webb of the *Courier and Enquirer*. Anderson was not there, was dining at William H. Aspinwall's in Fourteenth Street. Another trot (with an attempt to sing "The Star-Spangled Banner," but the musical training of this community is imperfect). I fear the advent of this roaring mob frightened the ladies of Dr. Metcalfe's household a little. I saw them peering through the parlor windows. But Major Anderson was not there, and I abandoned his pursuit and betook myself to the New York Club.

He and his command arrived here today in the *Baltic*. I saw her come up the bay from the battlements of Trinity Church tower, where were Reverend Ogilby, Cutler the organist, and several others. Strong feeling for Anderson and against Colonel Webb for his scandalous attack on Anderson in the *Courier*. The mob that cheered for Anderson tonight groaned savagely against the *Courier*. . . .

April 19.   Busy this morning in pursuit of a flag for Trinity Church steeple. Hunted through the city with Vinton in vain; went off on my own account and secured one at last (20 by 40) from Robert B. Minturn, who was most kind and obliging. He went to one of his ships with me and insisted on sending up riggers to help Secor's people hoist it. At half-past two, it went up; the chimes saluting it with "Hail Columbia," "Yankee Doodle," and "Old Hundred," and a crowd in Wall Street and Broadway cheering. Higby, Vinton, and Ogilby led the cheers. The flinging out of the flag, the clang of the bells, and the enthusiastic cheering, gave me a new sensation. I am amazed by the strong feeling of gratification strengthened by surprise that this little flourish called out. The solution is, probably, that the ideas of Church and State, Religion and Politics, have been practically separated so long that people are specially delighted with any manifestation of the Church's sympathy with the State and recognition of our national life on any fitting occasion. This flag was a symbol of the truth that the Church is no esoteric organization, no private soul-saving society; that it has a position to take in every great public national crisis, and that its position is important. Some sense of this truth must have been at the bottom of the many emphatic expressions I heard this afternoon (from strangers) of approval of the flag-raising on Trinity spire; for example, "Are they really going to hoist the flag on the steeple, Sir? —Well, now, I tell you, that's the *biggest thing* that's been done in New York in my time!"

Thereafter uptown with George Anthon; Broadway crowded. Established ourselves in an upper loft of a carpet-store near Spring Street. After long waiting and watching, the Seventh Regiment appeared, far up Broadway—a bluish steel-grey light on the blackness of the dense mob that filled the street, like the livid ashiness of the clouds near the horizon just before the thundershower breaks. As they came nearer and passed by, the roar of the crowd was grand and terrible. It drowned the brass of the regimental band.

George Anthon dined here. Evening spent in listening to Scharfenberg and a dozen "professional" people rehearsing Haydn's lovely Mass No. 2 for our next "concert."

Thereafter to New York Club. There has been serious disturbance in Baltimore. Regiments from Pennsylvania or Massachusetts assailed by a mob that was repulsed by shot and steel. . . .[20] It's a notable coincidence that the first blood in this great struggle is drawn by Massachusetts men on the anniversary of Lexington. This is a continuation of the war that Lexington opened—a war of democracy against oligarchy. God defend the Right, and confound all traitors. Amen and Amen.

Mr. Ruggles here tonight, just after an interview with Major Anderson, whose quiet dignity and unassuming manner impress him much. Anderson attends the great Union meeting tomorrow, when the flags of Moultrie and Sumter will be displayed.

[20] The Sixth Massachusetts was attacked on April 19 by a mob in Baltimore and had to fight its way from one railway station to another; an unarmed body of a thousand Pennsylvania volunteers at the same time had to return to the Susquehanna.

April 20, SATURDAY.   Another intense day. Morning news: Blockade of Southern ports proclaimed. Gloomy reports from the South. Railroad bridges and telegraph wires down from Philadelphia to Washington. The Seventh Regiment and other troops at Philadelphia unable to move. Baltimore mob furious and determined that troops shall not go through. No despatches from Washington. People talked darkly of its being attacked before our reinforcements come to the rescue, and everyone said we must not be surprised by news that Lincoln and Seward and all the Administration are prisoners. We feel a little better tonight, but without any very definite reason.

Could do nothing in Wall Street, though many things there require attention. Walked uptown at two. Broadway crowded and more crowded as one approached Union Square. Large companies of recruits in citizen's dress parading up and down, cheered and cheering. Small mobs round the headquarters of the regiments that are going to Washington, staring at the sentinel on duty. Every other man, woman, and child bearing a flag or decorated with a cockade. Flags from almost every building. The city seems to have gone suddenly wild and crazy.

The Union mass-meeting was an event. Few assemblages have equalled it in numbers and unanimity. Tonight's extra says there were 250,000 present. That must be an exaggeration. But the multitude was enormous. All the area bounded by Fourteenth and Seventeenth Streets, Broadway and Fourth Avenue, was filled. In many places it was densely packed, and nowhere could one push his way without difficulty. This great *amoeba* (to speak microscopically) sent off its *pseudopods* far down Broadway and Fourteenth Street and in every cross street. There were several stands for orators, and scores of little speechifying ganglia besides, from carts, windows, and front stoops. Anderson appeared and was greeted with roars that were tremendous to hear. The crowd, or some of them, and the ladies and gentlemen who occupied the windows and lined the housetops all round Union Square, sang "The Star-Spangled Banner," and the people generally hurrahed a voluntary after each verse.

Mayor Wood, the sagacious scoundrel, committed himself by a straightforward speech. Reverend old Gardiner Spring, who opened one of the many *centres* of the meeting "with prayer," came out soundly and manfully in a little introductory allocution. In substance: "Many of you know my opinion about issues heretofore existing between the North

and South. That opinion is unchanged. But the controversy is now between Government and Anarchy, Law and Rebellion."[21]

Major Anderson spent an hour at Mr. Ruggles's before I got there.
Ellie and Miss Rosalie are enthusiastic about him. . . . Anderson tells
Ellie we must not underrate the rebel army. It is brave and desperate and
well drilled. Ours includes some dead wood, but theirs is young and fresh
and vigorous.

Should Providence send them a great general, woe to the North! But
I do not expect that Providence will. We have four advantages, viz.,
money, numbers, the navy, the sympathy of Christendom. They have one
vital disadvantage, viz., niggers; and another, the utter want of mechanical skill and educated labor.

This battle will be *à l'outrance*; that is certain now. And I predict
that within twelve months a company of "John Brown Zouaves" or
"Harper's Ferry Liberators" or the like, will be organized in New England
or Western New York. For these Southern madmen are driving us
straight into Abolitionism.

April 21, SUNDAY. Fine spring day. With Ellie and Miss Rosalie
and Johnny to Trinity Church. Drove down Bowery, Broadway being
packed full of people. . . . Major Anderson was there, with his quiet,
self-possessed, intelligent look and penetrating eyes. People crowded
about him after service; and though I should have been glad to be presented, I was disinclined to bore a brave man and increase the pains and
penalties of heroism.

The Epistle for the Day was a coincidence. The Lesson (beginning
with 9th verse of 3rd chapter of Joel) yet more appropriate. It was electrifying. "Prepare War: wake up the mighty men: let all the men of war
draw near . . . let the weak say, I am strong . . . Beat your plowshares
into swords . . . Multitudes, multitudes in the Valley of Decision, for the
Day of the Lord is near in the Valley of Decision . . . Egypt shall be a
desolation and Edom shall be a desolate wilderness . . . because they have
shed innocent blood in their land."

The Lesson would have been yet more germane to the present distress had it commenced a verse or two earlier: "And they have cast lots
for my people, and sold a girl for wine, that they might drink."

[21] Spring (1785–1873), pastor of the Brick Presbyterian Church, one of the most
active and influential churchmen in the country, had been a strong sympathizer with
the South. He now became a fervent supporter of the Union, and later this spring persuaded the Old School Presbyterian Assembly to pass resolutions pledging allegiance
to the national government.

Walked uptown with Johnny through the crowd. At Leonard Street or thereabouts we met one of our regiments marching down Broadway to take steamship for Washington. At Canal Street, we were told two others had turned off there from Broadway. I had taken it for granted the men we saw were the three regiments that set off today. If not, we have sent off some four thousand men. Of those I saw, perhaps a third were unarmed and in citizen's dress, perfectly raw recruits. But it's believed they can be equipped and armed when they reach Washington. Arms have been withdrawn from Harper's Ferry during the last month and transferred to Carlisle Barracks. Another Massachusetts regiment is said to have passed through the city early this morning and yet another to have arrived here at 7 P.M. Hurrah for the old Bay State! She is first in the field in 1861 as she was in 1776. Boston is reported in white heat over the murder of Massachusetts soldiers by Baltimore plug-uglies. Governor Andrew's despatch to the Mayor of Baltimore, "praying" that their bodies may be laid out, packed in ice, and "tenderly" sent to Boston, is a model specimen of condensed telegraphic composition. Nothing could be better.

It seems settled tonight that our Seventh Regiment has got to Annapolis, by steamboat from Philadelphia by way of Havre de Grace. It must then march some thirty miles across country before it can report at Washington. I discredit the rumor of a telegram this evening that they are at Bladensburg, almost within rifle-cannon range of Washington.

The manifestation of patriotic feeling in New York after the firing on Fort Sumter had been (as Strong indicates) truly wonderful. As a prominent merchant wrote Gideon Welles on April 15: "There is but one feeling here now, and that is to sustain our flag and the government at all hazards." The diarist's father-in-law, Ruggles, was conspicuous when the Chamber of Commerce on April 19, in the largest meeting it had ever held, pledged support to the Administration. The huge mass-meeting in and about Union Square next day, addressed in four sections by four different groups of speakers, was described by the Tribune *as "the greatest popular demonstration ever known in America." It appointed a Committee of Safety, out of which emerged the Union Defense Committee, a powerful and efficient body headed first by John A. Dix, and when he went to the front, by Hamilton Fish.*

The exigencies of the time were tremendous. Communication with Washington was precarious, and fear existed that the capital might be seized by

Confederate forces; arms, ammunition, and other supplies were lacking; dis-ciplined and well-equipped troops were not to be found. By a hasty bond issue the city raised a million dollars for war purposes, while leading businessmen contributed several hundred thousand more. Troops were hurried southward, and new volunteer regiments were hastily organized and drilled. On April 19, the day that the Baltimore mob attacked the Sixth Massachusetts, killing and wounding forty men, the Seventh Regiment of New York militia was sent off. Regarded by many as the finest body of men in the country, it marched down Broadway "through that tempest of cheers two miles long," and reached Philadelphia to find that railroad bridges had been burned between that city and Baltimore. Taking the transport Boston down Chesapeake Bay, the Seventh Regiment reached Annapolis early on Monday, April 22, and before noon of the 25th were in Washington. For nearly a week the capital, cut off from the North, had been the prey of gloom and apprehension; but the dark clouds rolled away as the magnificent regiment, with flags and music, passed up Pennsylvania Avenue to the White House—this time through a tempest of cheers one mile long, for half of Washington turned out to applaud. Strong's brother-in-law was with the force, and his friend Theodore Winthrop, marked for death in an early battle of the war.

Lincoln had called for 75,000 troops, and New York's quota was seventeen regiments; but it was manifestly important to raise and drill much larger bodies of men. By the end of 1861, the Union Defense Committee in the metropolis had acted so energetically that it placed sixty-six New York regiments in the Union armies. Though Strong was well past fighting age, he put his shoulder to the wheel by helping organize and train the New York Rifles. Their committee on organiza-tion, in fact, met in his library on the night of April 21, with himself as chair-man. It included Lieutenant Dick Smith, formerly instructor at West Point, Nathaniel Prime, and young men of the Delafield, Livingston, and other promi-nent families. They went to work in earnest and were soon whipping a regi-ment in shape. But Strong's true sphere of wartime usefulness was to lie else-where, and he was not to be long in finding it. During the winter of 1854–1855 the British and French troops in the Crimea had suffered so terribly from disease and neglect that the British Government in April, 1855, sent out a Sanitary Commission which was given plenary authority to take any and all measures for improving the health of the troops, both in the camps and the hospitals. This body, assisted by the publicity given to Florence Nightingale's work in the

Scutari hospitals, brought about a beneficent revolution. Now it appeared that a body of somewhat similar character was needed in the United States. During April, May, and June in 1861 regiment after regiment arrived in the Washington area under conditions which presented a real emergency. Frequently they made their journey in cattle-cars, dirty, crowded, and unprovided with food and drink. After long waits on sidings, many would arrive in Washington sick and exhausted. In this wretched state, they would find that little or no preparation had been made for their reception; and they often had to stand for hours in a broiling sun or a drenching rain while their commissaries and quarter-masters made ineffectual efforts to relieve them. When at last they found their way to the camps, they were given unpalatable and unwholesome rations, and they slept on bundles of rotten straw, covered with thin, shoddy blankets. Some experienced officers, seeing the lack of sanitary facilities in most of the camps, predicted that fifty per cent of the volunteers would be killed or incapacitated by disease before the end of the summer. Before April ended, one of Strong's friends, the Rev. Dr. Bellows, was being enlisted in a movement to apply preventive measures; and Strong himself was soon thereafter brought into the organization.

April 22.   Nothing tangible today, except the report that a special messenger from the President has reached Philadelphia with instructions to the Governor of Pennsylvania, and with the statement that the capital is considered secure at least against a *coup de main*, until the Northern reinforcements arrive. This agent got through Maryland with difficulty, disguised as a Methodist preacher. All telegraph wires are cut and railroad bridges broken between Philadelphia and Washington. The North and its millions are cut off from their capital by the mob of Baltimore. That city seems in absolute anarchy. It should receive a severe lesson. When the first indispensable point of reinforcing Washington is attained, the next will be to secure the line of communication. I trust the railroad line will be then promptly repaired and held, and that Baltimore will be told that so many thousand Northern troops will march through her streets on such a day; and that if they are molested, they will withdraw until Fort McHenry shall have wiped out the city, and then resume their march.

The position of the Seventh Regiment not yet ascertained. It is probably in Washington before this.

Hard at work this morning over organization of our proposed corps. Meeting of the Bar at three, which I could not attend, for there was a special meeting of Savings Bank trustees. Something a little like a run, and authority wanted to sell stocks. I hear the Bar meeting was large and enthusiastic, and subscribed $25,000 to uphold the government. Tonight an adjourned meeting at Thorpe's of the proposed Volunteers' Association. Great crowd, unfortunately, and everything going wrong. A day lost, at least. Everything deferred to an adjourned meeting tomorrow night, when the question of fusion with another organization, got up by Lloyd Aspinwall, is to be considered.

Barlow married Miss Arabella Griffith at St. Paul's Chapel Saturday evening, left her at the church door, and went to Washington yesterday.[22]

I have done this people injustice in my thoughts. We are *not* utterly corrupt and mercenary.

April 23. Broadway packed full as I walked downtown and up again. The Sixty-ninth and Eighth Regiments marched down at about four. The former is the Irish regiment, Colonel Corcoran's, and there were a large infusion of Biddies in the crowd "sobbing and sighing." Both regiments looked as well as one has a right to expect of levies raised on such short notice. A large portion in citizen's dress and without arms, but seemingly respectable material. The uniformed companies looked and marched well. At the corner of Rector Street and Broadway, I saw part of another regiment (I forget its number) raised by that notable alder-manic bully, Bill Wilson. They didn't clearly know what regiment they were told they belonged to, but said they were "Billy Wilson's crowd." A desperate-looking set. It's said that when they were told they were to have not only the regulation arms but revolvers and bowie knives, too, they danced and yelled with delight: "We can fix that Baltimore crowd! Let 'em bring along their pavin' stones; we boys is sociable with pavin' stones!"

After breakfast to J. Cooper Lord's, across the Square, where the joint committee on Lloyd Aspinwall's cavalry and artillery project and our infantry project met to confer on the proposed constitution. Beside our committee, there were Lloyd Aspinwall, Dan D. Lord, Potter, and others of that party. We were harmonious enough. They stuck me in the chair, and our constitution was approved with a trifling alteration for the better. The rest of the morning spent in the same business, conferring with Prime, Ellery Anderson, Talmage, and others. After dinner to

[22] This was Strong's friend Francis Channing Barlow, law-partner of George Bliss, Jr., who enlisted as a private and rose to be major-general, specially distinguishing him-self at Gettysburg and Spottsylvania.

adjourned meeting at Delmonico's; well attended, and its action business-like and without speechifications or much parliamentary red-tapeism. We declined a fusion with Aspinwall's horse and heavy guns on the ground that time will be gained if each perfect its own organization separately, and then come together on terms of equality instead of spending time on debates about matters of detail. Reasonable enough, but Aspinwall went off in a slight huff. I know him little, but he seems rather weak, vain, and dictatorial. We also ordered 400 Enfield rifles, the order to go out by tomorrow's steamer, for they cannot be got here, and adjourned to tomorrow night for business and (thank God) for DRILL, at last, if drill-masters can be secured in time. Adjourned at half-past ten and hurried up to Governor Dix's in Twentieth Street, where was a small masculine gathering "to meet Major Anderson." They were at supper and beginning to thin out, but the Major had not gone, and I had the great pleasure of being presented and of saying to him in a bungling way what every loyal man that meets him wants to say. Discoursed, also, with D. D. Field, M. H. Grinnell, R. B. Minturn, Judge Roosevelt (now a renegade proselyte from secessionism and treason), Dr. Higby, Dr. Ogilby, and others. . . .

Everyone's future has changed in these six months last past. This is to be a terrible, ruinous war, and a war in which the nation cannot succeed. It can never subjugate these savage millions of the South. It must make peace at last with the barbarous communities off its Southern frontier. I was prosperous and well off last November. I believe my assets to be reduced fifty per cent, at least. But I hope I can still provide wholesome training for my three boys. With that patrimony they can fight out the battle of life for themselves. Their mother is plucky and can stand self-denial. I clearly see that this is a most severe personal calamity to me, but I welcome it cordially, for it has shown that I belong to a community that is brave and generous, and that the City of New York is not sordid and selfish.

"Hear *THIS*, ye old men, and give ear all ye inhabitants of the land. Hath *this* been in your days, or even in the days of your Fathers?" New York lavishly tendering life and money to sustain a righteous cause, and without one dissenting voice from Forty-ninth Street to the Battery!

In the City Hall Park a line of light wooden barracks is being rapidly run up, from its lower apex, opposite the Astor House, to Chambers Street. A camp was being laid out this morning on the Battery. This is for the Fifth Regiment. . . .

April 24. . . . Mr. Derby, Mr. Ruggles, and George Anthon dined here, and a letter came in from Jem Ruggles, dated at Annapolis, yesterday, 5:30 P.M. The Seventh are in good spirits and eager for a brush with the Rebels. Their voyage was a bore, but not so bad as it might have been. Provisions not first rate. People of Annapolis not positively hostile. The men have not taken off their clothes since they left New York. Reports of hostile parties outside Annapolis prepared to dispute the road to Washington. Nobody knows whether they are to go ahead or wait for reinforcements. The Regiment wants to march at once. The *Baltic* said to be just coming up with reinforcements. That's the substance of the letter. . . .

After dinner, to the old New York Club House at the corner of Astor Place and Broadway, where we began drill at last. Got on well, and the meeting was satisfactory. Our association has grown to near 200. I've found out what "Eyes Right!" means. I've long wanted to know the purport of that familiar but mystic phrase.

Thence to the New York Club, and thence home. Assisted at initiatory steps for a general club meeting to expel its Southern members (poor, fat Willy Alston included) as guilty of treason. Of course, the movement will be resisted as introducing a political test. But this is no political issue. The question now is not what shall the nation do?—but shall the nation live or perish? The Club must decide whether it will endorse and uphold men who are doing their utmost to destroy our national existence.

April 25. Our "New York Rifles" met at 7:30 at rooms hired for the evening, a loft at 814 Broadway. It was crowded, so two squads adjourned to the old club house at the corner of Astor Place, where we were drilled more than two hours. Everybody awkward, but earnest and diligent. Then we marched back. I was solemnly elected president of the association till our military commandant shall be chosen, and got through my duties decently well, I believe, keeping the mob of men in tolerable order, though all were on their feet, having nothing but the floor to sit down on.

Captain Lewis of the Washington Navy Yard has resigned. A very base and cowardly proceeding, which I fully expected. Lawrence Williams will doubtless go after him now that Virginia (its genteel eastern quarter, at least) is in rebellion. Is it not wonderful that any relation, social or domestic, with a slave-driving community should so paralyze the moral instincts of men like these, who pride themselves on their special sense of obligation to duty, fidelity, loyalty? They desert the nation that has educated and fed them in its hour of peril. If they are not traitors, they are sneaks.

We have given up our musical party, the second rehearsal for which was to have been held tomorrow night. This is no time for "parties." We shall want all our spare cash, and perhaps a little more, before we have established the proposition that the people of the United States constitute a great nation, and not merely a great mob.

There are signs of amazement at the South at our general rally here in support of law and order and national life. Charleston and Mobile and New Orleans scarcely realize it yet. They have counted on the support of Northern capital and on a strong revolutionary "Democratic" party here. Their miscalculation is natural enough. Twenty days ago—no longer— I thought as they have thought, that the North would be divided and paralyzed whenever the struggle should begin.

April 26. No authentic, official, reliable statement even yet that our Seventh Regiment and other reinforcements have reached Washington, but it is generally believed they have got there safely.

New York Rifles from 7:30 to 10:30. Met at our new rooms, hired for a month in the new building (Henry Mason's) at the corner of Broadway and Fourth Street. My squad of 100 or thereabouts was marched to Washington Parade Ground, where we were drilled and marched by "Captain Levy," a very efficient and authoritative drill officer, for an hour and a half. I confess myself tired and footsore.

April 27. I think the Administration is working out its difficult problem wisely and energetically.

The Seventh has undoubtedly reached Washington in safety. That seems settled, at last.

Saw Horace Binney, Jr., this morning, convalescing from a low typhoid fever of forty days, and on his way to Providence and farther north for a restorative holiday. He reports the national spirit in Philadelphia no less earnest than in New York.

Here the flag is on every public building, every store, every private house almost. The roof of No. 74 East Twenty-first is to be honored by a flagstaff and a big flag next Monday. The supply of bunting has been far short of the demand, and the stars and stripes multiply slowly, but steadily. The example set by Trinity Church on 19th instant has been followed. The steeple, tower, or pediment of every church building, almost, displays the national colors, and symbolizes the sympathy of the Church Catholic (and of the Church dissenting and schismatic) with law and order and national life. . . .

Army and Navy officers (Virginians mostly) who are resigning their

commissions just now, most indignantly censured, and even by men like
Walter Cutting. Their resignations should not be accepted; they should
be put under arrest and tried for their lives by court-martial as spies and
traitors.

April 28, SUNDAY.   Not much news. Reaction in Maryland strengthening itself rapidly. The leaders in that state want to rebel and to have Jefferson
Davis to rule over them, but are terrified by the great unanimous rising
of the North, and by the certainty that Baltimore will be razed if necessary.
No wonder they are scared. I look with awe on the national movement
here in New York and through all the Free States. After our late discords, it seems supernatural. . . .

I hear of no exceptions to the general fervor of loyalty in this state.
But George Anthon brings from Mrs. Christine Griffin reports of individual instances of dissent at Newport, Rhode Island, and how they were
received; e.g., Reverend L. P. W. Balch undertook to improve the service
last Sunday by praying "for the Presidents of the United States," and
then proceeded to preach a sermon in favor of rebellion. His congregation
rose up, and people said, "Stop that!" "No!" and the like. He went on,
however; whereupon certain of his vestry walked up the aisle, lugged him
out of the pulpit, and marched him out of church.

"Poke" Wright called at Mrs. Lawrence's (the widow of "Don't
Give Up the Ship" Lawrence) and found that elderly lady scraping lint
with a carving knife, and her sweet little granddaughter, Miss Mary
Griffin, making up an American flag. Wright said some flippant irrever-
ence about the flag, whereupon the grandmamma told him no one should
speak with disrespect in *her* house of the banner under which her husband
had fought and died, charged on him with her carving knife, and drove
him out with directions not to call again; whereupon, being in the street,
he was seized by certain chance passengers who had witnessed his expulsion, and was required to go down on his knees and hurrah for the flag,
waved by pretty little Miss Mary from the front window. This incident
may be funny, but it signifies nothing, for Wright is notoriously a donkey
and habitually affects a silly dissent from every prevailing sentiment.

Also, William Beach Lawrence has had his nose pulled by one Kinsley
for talking sympathy with South Carolina.[23] That is satisfactory, if true.

[23] Lawrence (1800–1881), attorney, expert on international law, and one-time lieu-
tenant-governor of Rhode Island, thought slavery an economic necessity, denounced
the abolitionists, and demanded that the Southern States be allowed to leave in peace.

His respectable and wealthy nose has been saving up for that experience these twenty years. . . .

April 29. Fine day. Busy in Wall Street. Saw a letter from Jem Ruggles written in the Senate Chamber on the desk of a seceded Georgian Senator. He writes in the best spirits. Wrote a letter to him, and sent him on a couple of cases of claret. Some thirty ladies, Mrs. Peters, Mrs. Alfred Schermerhorn, Miss Lizzy Clark, Mrs. Parkyn (who was Miss Fanny Rogers), and I know not who all beside, met here to make what they call "Havelock caps" for the Seventh; that is, white coverings for the military cap and for the back of the neck as a protection against heat. Tonight Ellie and Miss Rosalie at work on the same business in the front parlor, while the Celtic handmaidens of the house plied their needles in the blue room.

On my way uptown saw the "Fire Brigade of Zouaves" on their march to the steamer, escorted by the whole fire department. This is Colonel [Elmer] Ellsworth's regiment, about 1,100 strong, armed with Sharps's rifles and revolvers. They are a rugged set, a little above Billy Wilson's corps in social status, generally men and boys who belong to target companies and are great in a plug-muss. They were coming down Chatham Street and hurrying up Broadway. At the Astor House, they halted and received a flag. Mrs. J. J. Astor had presented them with another. I got on top of an omnibus and inspected them. The crowd was immense and the cheering uproarious. These young fellows march badly, but they will fight hard if judiciously handled. As a regiment of the line, they will be weak, but they are the very men to deal with the mob of Baltimore.

After dinner, drilled severely for two hours and more, perspiring and blundering, but making some little progress. The "New York Rifles" prosper and receive large and steady accessions. . . .

April 30. Lawrence Williams here at breakfast time, and dined with us. He is very unhappy, but declares he has no intention of resigning. Growls and carps at the Administration (but all army and navy men do that always) and is plainly dissatisfied, uncertain, and unsettled. Naturally enough, poor fellow, with his unconscious education in Southern notions about state sovereignty, and all his kinsfolk and old associates urging him to join them in rebellion, disguised as an assertion of state rights. He deserves credit for standing firm thus far, but I confidently predict that sixty days hence he will be in arms against the national flag he has sworn to follow. So malignant and mortal is the moral atmosphere breathed by every officer who comes from a slave state. He tells me that Captain Lewis is hard at work in the Navy Department of the Rebels, and that his kinsman, Colonel [Robert E.] Lee, did not throw up his commission without severe struggle and distress. Lee refused even to invite Williams to follow him—told him to follow the dictates of his own conscience.

New York Rifles tonight, corner Fourth Street and Broadway. Did not drill, being engaged in committee business. Recruits come in quite fast enough. We enlisted William Astor, Daniel Huntington (the artist), and Tom Cooper, among others.

No material news today, except that Baltimore and Maryland seem to have reacted into loyalty and submission to law, under pressure of our vigorous demonstrations of national life on their Northern borders. This fact is significant. It shows what the last Administration might have done five months ago by a little self-assertion, and how much of our present distress is due to the collusion or inertia of old Buchanan and his Cabinet of traitors. Who knows what the resolute attitude of government may effect even yet? I think that the presence of a national force maintaining national rights would awaken a National or Union party in every Southern state—even in South Carolina. . . .

May 2.   No material news. Rumors of any amount of "Confederate" troops assembling at Richmond or elsewhere for a march on Washington, but all confused, contradictory, and contradicted. But we should act as if these rumors were true. Beauregard and Bragg and other traitors are brave, intelligent, and enterprising. The unanimous uprising of the North against their treason makes them desperate. They must make some bold and vigorous move at once or perish.

Many people detect signs today of a collapse at the South. Except in Maryland, I see no sign of any such thing, unless it be in the intensified Billingsgate of Southern newspapers. The fiercer virulence of their scolding *may* indicate fright. It certainly shows amazement at the attitude taken by New York and by other commercial centres heretofore abjectly submissive to Southern dictation. The Richmond *Enquirer* expatiates on "execrable New York," that Sodom ungrateful for the Southern custom that has built it up. It thinks the Seventh Regiment viler and baser than all the regiments of Massachusetts, because it once visited Richmond and was hospitably received there, and nevertheless sets out "to cut the throats" of Virginians; whereas the Massachusetts people cannot help being born on Cape Cod. It talks of Scott, the Arch Traitor, and Lincoln, the Beast, and so on.

May 3.   Dull, cold day, deliquescing at last into cold, drizzling rain. Very diligent in Wall Street. Drilled in an upper loft of 31 Broad Street an hour and a half under Ashley, an efficient drill master and a gentleman-like man. Dined at John Astor's, with Vice-President Hamlin, General Wool, Major Arnold (one of Wool's aids), Simeon Draper, Moses H. Grinnell, Bancroft Davis, George Schuyler, George Bancroft, William M. Evarts, William B. Astor, Charles King, Isaac Bell. Bell was a rank traitor sixty days ago.[24] He is very loyal now, but lets drop an occasional sneaking phrase of covert depreciation of our national reaction. I do not trust him in the smallest degree. Our dinner-table talk was all of the war and its prospects. We generally agreed that it is to be a sharp struggle in which we must use all our energies, but that the South is paralyzed when its ports are blockaded and that it has not the resources to keep up an efficient military organization very long; that it will have to concentrate itself for one aggressive movement on the North—at Washington or some other point—and collapse utterly if it fail. I hope that time may verify our predictions.

Hamlin impresses me favorably, though he pronounces *NOW*, "Ne-a-ow." He seems a vigorous specimen of the pure Yankee type. His complexion is so swarthy that I cannot wonder at the demented South for believing him a mulatto. General Wool is quiet, dignified, and courteous.

May 4.   No national news of much importance today. There are signs, more or less reliable, of collapse and intimidation in Virginia and Maryland. A strong party in Kentucky and western Virginia seems certainly arming for the nation and against state secession. The twenty days within which the President's proclamation called upon all rebels to disperse expire tomorrow, and there are vague rumors of decisive steps thereupon to be taken. We shall see. We are generally hopeful and in high spirits today. But our levies are very raw; the rebel commanders have the energy and freshness that belong to revolutionary leaders. Worse than the loss of three pitched battles would be overtures of compromise and negotiation from the swindling chivalry—"the felon knights" of Jefferson Davis's Round Table. That would divide and weaken us again. I fear the subtle, knavish, desperate leaders of the South have some such move in reserve.

May 6, MONDAY.   No material change in the aspect of affairs. Mary-

[24] Bell was a merchant in the cotton trade, and Democrat of Southern sympathies, who in 1859 had helped found the Democratic Vigilant Association to defend Southern rights and combat Sewardism.

land seems coming out right. The movement in its legislature for a Committee of Public Safety with dictatorial powers has failed. Government is moving troops on the railroad communications of Baltimore, and seems to have a plan of operations and to be carrying it out with energy. It is said tonight that the governor of Virginia, Letcher, has put forth some kind of rebellious or secessionist manifesto that will precipitate crisis and collision in that state. Be it so. Western Virginia will have something to say on that question.[25]

May 7. To New York Club, where I signed a call for a general meeting to consider the case of its Southern members. Thus much is plain. Either those of our number who have left the city in the Seventh and other regiments for the purpose of killing all they find in arms against government, or those who are arrayed against government and ready to kill the former, are guilty of a crime: namely, unlawful homicidal intent, and ought to be summarily expelled. But the question of fact remains and is embarrassing; for example, Willy Alston's acceptance of a commission in that nasty little rebellious army of South Carolina rests wholly on rumor.

May 8. News today is of decided "secession" in Arkansas and Tennessee. In the latter state, there will be an earnest and numerous minority, at least, recalcitrating against treason, with Andrew Johnson at their head. I care little about this. Though Kentucky and Tennessee are grand states, and each can send into the field an army far more formidable than can be raised among the poor whites of the Carolinas and the Gulf States, I would rather both should be openly arrayed against us than that they should continue to paralyze us by standing undecided. Fear of affronting the Border States has kept us hesitating far too long already. When every slave state has cast its lot with the woman-flogging Sepoys of the South, the nation will breathe more freely and act more decisively. Arkansas amounts to little or nothing. In Kentucky, Major Anderson's prestige and his appointment to the command of the volunteers assembling in that state will have great effect.

May 9. At Trinity Church Standing Committee meeting, I brought forward informally, for discussion, my plan for an appropriation by the vestry in aid of the Ladies' Association of the parish for the manufacture of clothing and hospital furniture, to which I'm instigated by Mrs. John Astor. I shall carry it through, I think. Gouverneur Ogden supports it. Verplanck (who is growing senile, I regret to say) demurs on some in-

---

[25] The Virginia Convention had voted an ordinance of secession, 88 to 55, on April 17, but it did not go before the people for ratification or rejection until May 23.

comprehensible ground. Skidmore hesitates. Dunscomb, that chief of
noodles, objects because relieving the wounded is "humanity" and the
Church holds its property in trust for Christianity! Also because "Secessionists" may set the church and chapels on fire in revenge. In fact, since
the flag was hoisted on Trinity steeple, he has ordered Meurer the sexton
to admit no more visitors there, lest they should surreptitiously set said
steeple (which is built of red sandstone) on fire. I think Dunscomb is the
most perfect specimen of an absolute dolt I ever knew.

Tonight, at drill room; committee business, and so on. Colonel Alden
speaks highly of our proficiency, considering the little time we have spent
in drill. Then to New York Club. Rumors there of 4,000 Secessionists
occupying Arlington Heights, which story I doubt omnipotently. But a
collision is drawing near, beyond all question, and I greatly fear the result
of the first exposure of our new levies to fire. For they have been mostly
men of peace, unlike the Southern Sepoy (whether of "gentleman" caste,
or dirt-eater), who habitually carries his knife or revolver. Our many
reports of Southern movements are discordant, and severally unreliable,
but they indicate, on the whole, and pretty certainly, a convergence of
rebels from the Carolinas and the Gulf States to Virginia. If there be
means to feed them, they must be assembling there in formidable masses.
Davis cannot afford to wait. With his ports blockaded, he must strike a
decisive blow at once, or suffocate. To us, every day without actual
battle is great gain. We are organizing and drilling and converting our
recruits into soldiers, and we can go on for six months without feeling
the cost.

Drums audible in Fourth Avenue. Hurrah! No doubt the Vermont
Regiment, expected here tonight.

May 11.   Fine day. Nothing memorable in Wall Street. Walked uptown with George Anthon, stopping at Tiffany's and Ball & Black's to
look after Ellie's usual 15th May anniversary present. Necessarily economical this year.

The *Evening Post* contains a first-rate puff of the New York Rifles.
To their drill room after dinner; spectator of drill and attending to business. Then to New York Club. The proposed expulsion of traitors, like
Major Deas (who was in treaty, by his own admission, for an appointment
in Jefferson Davis's army before resigning from that of the United States)
creates much talk. Many of our members are sadly gelatinous, emasculate,
and feeble. . . .

May 12, SUNDAY.   News by the morning papers looks well (*Tribune* and *Times* appear every morning in the week now) though there is not much of it. The independent movement of Western Virginia in protest against the proslavery mania of the Tidewater counties seems extensive and distinctly pronounced. Some seventy counties to meet in convention; loyalty and nationality decidedly predominant west of the mountains. This movement seems most important and I trust the Administration will foster and strengthen it judiciously and vigorously. They talk, it seems, of secession from the state and of forming a new state, "New Virginia," or "West Virginia." That won't do at all. They are entitled to call themselves Virginia without prefix, for the fanatics of Richmond are in rebellion against their own state laws. Eastern Virginia is in revolution, with no color of legal right. Wise, Letcher & Co. stand where Governor Dorr of Rhode Island stood twenty years ago. This decided action in Western Virginia has its weight, too, as indicating the probable disposition of that broad strip of nominally slaveholding but practically free territory that slopes southward through east Kentucky and Tennessee into north Georgia and Alabama. Should the people of that tract declare for the nation, or even stand divided and undecided, the phalanx of rebellion is pierced and broken.

May 13. . . . Another street fight in St. Louis; its mob fired on by the United States volunteers in a passionate, undisciplined way. Not only the mob, but the volunteers, suffered from the firing. The German element seems conspicuous among the Missouri loyalists. This will appeal strongly to Germans, not only North, but in Southern States; for example, Texas, where are large and prosperous free-soil German settlements. It will probably be felt along the Rhine and the Danube, and bring us experienced volunteer officers who have seen service. This war will soon be universally recognized as waged by an effete corrupt aristocracy of slave breeders against the cause of Progress, Democracy, Free Thought, and Equality (for which, by the by, I have no great respect, though I certainly prefer them to the semi-barbarous system of Mississippi and South Carolina), and the sympathies of Christendom will begin to array themselves against Southern treason.

May 14. Unsettled weather, the early afternoon clear and hot. Spent the morning with Bidwell in Robinson's office. Argument on the objections to Burrowes's deposition in the Carter case. Shall not be surprised if we have to send the commission back for reëxecution, Burrowes having made defective answer to one or two interrogatories. Thereafter Maunsell Field seized on me to say I had been appointed (query, by whom?) on a committee to issue proposals by advertisement and award a prize for a national hymn or popular and patriotic song appealing to the national heart. Was such a thing ever heard of before???!!!

Went to meeting in Chamber of Commerce building. Field was there, Arthur Leary, Brodhead, George William Curtis, the Howadji, and Richard Grant White. Talked it over and adjourned to Thursday night. General Dix, Cisco, Charles King, Hamilton Fish, and others, are of the committee, so I shall be ridiculous in decent company.

"Wanted, by the American Nation, a Marseillaise. Any poet having one to dispose of will please apply to etc., etc., at etc., etc., on or before etc., etc." Or, "$250 reward. A Tyrtaeus is urgently required by the people. If he be about anywhere, he will please call on etc., etc., by whom a reasonable compensation for his services, not exceeding the amount above named, will be promptly paid."

May 15. Nothing from Washington today that need be recorded. Rumor that Mr. John A. Washington proposes to resurrectionize the bones of General Washington from their resting place at Mt. Vernon, and carry them beyond the reach of national law. It would be a characteristic transaction and worthy the Sepoy chivalry. The chivalric Mr. John A. Washington makes large money profit, in the first place, out of the grave of the great head of his unworthy family, by selling Mount Vernon to a "Ladies' Association" for $200,000, cash down. Then he steals the body. Next, I suppose he will proceed to raise another $200,000 on it. (Barnum would buy it at something like that figure.) Why shouldn't he? Medieval princes used to pledge the relics of St. A. and St. B. when they wanted a loan. Many capitalists would advance money to the rebels of Virginia were George Washington's coffin and its contents hypothecated as security.

We are a little uneasy today about the position England may take. Will she insist on a supply of cotton for her factories and side against whatever interferes with it? Time must tell. I believe in the instincts of the people of England. England cannot be against us in this struggle.

May 18. No events in today's papers, and people begin to grumble about inaction. They are impatient for a new excitement, which will come soon enough. May it not come in the form of consternation at calamity! I am well satisfied with the conduct of affairs. Government is moving and working *ohne Hast, ohne Rast*. Of course, both parties gain strength by time, but we gain two per cent while the rebels gain one. Every day a battle is postponed seems worth a thousand men to the nation. General Dix, with whom I talked this afternoon, seems sanguine.

The fright and fury of the rebels shows clearly in the Billingsgate of Southern papers. Bad language has never been uttered on so grand a scale. Lincoln is a "beast" and a "baboon"; Scott a "miscreant" and an "arch-traitor"; all Northern soldiers "hireling cutthroats," "ruffians," and "scoundrels." . . . As I fully believe that Southern rebels will fight bravely, I cannot understand their scolding and bragging so horribly. The sublime swagger of their talk cannot be matched in history, except by the state papers of China. Meanwhile, the blockade has reached Charleston harbor. Baltimore is coerced into loyalty, and General Harney is vigorously upholding the authority of government in Missouri. *Deus salvam fac Rempublicam!*

May 20. A cold storm all day, now just clearing off. Visit in Wall Street from Alden, discoursing on business of the New York Rifles. Then to a meeting of Columbia College trustees at Law School; after which I talked with [President] King, who like Alden, has just returned from Washington, where they have been in conference with General Scott, Seward, Lincoln, and other magnates.

They agree in the impression they received as to the probable course of the campaign; namely, Norfolk to be attacked within a day or so—the movement to commence tomorrow, probably. Then the summer to be devoted to the assemblage and organization of great masses of men at suitable points from Cairo to Washington, the defensive line being possibly pushed a little farther in front of Washington. With the first black frost of autumn that restores salubrity to the sunny South, two great columns to be set in motion down the Mississippi Valley and along the Atlantic seaboard. The programme looks sensible and promising. Both King and Alden report Scott clearheaded and sanguine, though somewhat shaky on his legs. How he must wish himself twenty years younger! Seward told King he thought there would be no serious fighting after all; the South would collapse and everything be serenely adjusted. Seward pushes consistency to fanaticism.

The Seventh Regiment is in fact much dissatisfied with Colonel Lefferts and thinks him wanting in energy and in personal pluck.

May 22. Fine day. Accomplished a little in Wall Street. On my way uptown, saw the Troy Regiment (I think) march down Broadway toward the South. Uniformed, not thoroughly drilled, but mostly rugged young farmers with a few rough loutish Germans and Celts. Home. . . . Then to Richard Grant White's with Gentil. We three are Executive Committee of our Company. Then to the New York Club, where I waited till late for adjournment of the Council, wishing to learn their decision on the proposal that they present charges against Major Deas. They sat long, tried to dodge the question by various devices, and the motion to present was lost on ayes and noes, eight to six. The affirmative vote was, I'm told, Henry Cram, Charley Strong, George Anthon, John Sherwood, Russell, and Charley Hoffman. On the result being announced, duplicates of the charge and specifications were handed in, signed by Henry Cram, Charley Strong, and myself as members of the Club, which very politic move checkmated the majority and compelled the Council to call a general meeting of the Club to pass on the question whether Deas shall be expelled as a traitor or no.

Chief talk of today the attitude of England as displayed by the utterances of the *Times*, and by Lord John Russell; the rebels "to be recognized as belligerents." Disappointment and exasperation are universal and deep.[26] The feeling of cordiality toward England—of brotherhood, almost of loyalty, which grew out of the Prince's visit last fall (how long ago that seems!)—is utterly extinguished. England, the ally of free institutions throughout the world, the great exemplar of a law-abiding nation; England, that has been twitting us with our toleration of slavery for fifty years past; England turning against us in this great uprising of democracy against the treachery of politicians and oligarchs—in the struggle between law and anarchy—in the rebellion of a cruel, merciless, semi-barbarous mob of slave-owners against our national life! It is monstrous and incredible. We are too fast; we are judging England prematurely. When these utterances of English sentiment appeared, it was still uncertain whether the nation had vigor enough to assert its own existence. Washington was still in most imminent danger. Harper's Ferry and the Norfolk Navy Yard had just been successfully abandoned, and that was all we had to show. The unexpected national uprising at the North was not yet distinctly pronounced. London saw only a united, vigorous South and a North paralyzed by discord.

Let us hope the great English people will be true to its traditions and its better instincts, when it sees more clearly the attitude of both sections of our country. But if not, if England be in truth a nation of shop-keepers, if I have always been wrong in my estimate of her place in the history of

[26] The British Government, to the great disappointment of both South and North, issued on May 13 a proclamation of neutrality. Its action was perfectly correct, and the treatment of the Confederate States as a belligerent was in fact a necessity, since President Lincoln's proclamation of the blockade on April 19.

this age, if she be willing to ally herself with the cause of chaos against that of harmony, of anarchy against order, of slavery against freedom, because "Cotton is King" and she dreads pecuniary damage from a short supply of cotton—if the England of Milton and Coleridge and Tennyson be in truth so disposed, let us accept the fact and prepare for war with England as the European champion of Nigger Slavery, and for all the ruination and disaster incident thereto. Thus much is clear: England's uncertain attitude just at this moment, even should it be promptly changed for a worthier position, costs us at least two thousand men and ten millions of money in the encouragement it gives Rebellion.

May 23. . . . Law School Commencement tonight at Historical Society room, corner Second Avenue and 11th Street. Very respectable audience. Professor Dwight delivered an excellent introductory address, introducing the candidates for degrees. . . . Then came Judge Murray Hoffman's address to the graduating class, by far the finest production of the kind I ever heard, most forcible and beautiful, and far above what I supposed to be his capacity. . . .

May 24. A large force marched from Washington last night, secured Arlington Heights, and pushed on to Alexandria, which was occupied without serious resistance. Colonel Ellsworth's Regiment of Firemen Zouaves headed the column. Ellsworth entered the principal hotel of the place, the "Marshall House," and himself hauled down the rebel flag flying over it, and was thereupon or soon thereafter shot by a concealed assassin, said to have been one Jackson the hotel-keeper. That flower of Sepoy chivalry was promptly knocked on the head. Colonel Ellsworth was a valuable man, but he could hardly have done such service as his assassin has rendered the country. His murder will stir the fire in every western state, and shows all Christendom with what kind of enemy we are contending.

I am glad that further summary vengeance was not taken, though military usage would have justified it. Forbearance has been our rule, and should be, for a season yet. But treachery, poisonings, and assassinations will make forbearance a crime before many months are gone.

It seems that Corcoran's Irish Regiment is entrenching itself on Arlington Heights; the Seventh, near "Columbia Spring." . . . We have from five to eight thousand men in or about Alexandria, throwing up fieldworks and expecting an attack from a rebel force supposed to be moving from Culpeper County. I rejoice in the fieldworks. In a contest between raw levies, the party that fights under protection of ditches and embankments must prevail. Murray Hoffman and Mr. Samuel B. Ruggles dined here. Evening with "New York Rifles," and afterwards at Club. Presided over meeting of our company. Gentil and Richard Grant White elected first and second lieutenants; election of captain postponed.

May 25.   Found a letter in Wall Street from Horace Binney, in great perturbation about the deficiency of arms in Pennsylvania. Made enquiry at the shops and found, as I expected, that they can furnish none for thirty days, at least. The best offer I got was 100 Sharps's Rifles at $45, and 2,000 very untrustworthy altered United States muskets which one would not like to fire till he had received plenary absolution and the last sacraments. Called on Union Defense Committee. It thinks Philadelphia should have been more provident and looked out for itself more promptly. So it should, but *tua res agitur cum proximus ardet Ucalegon.*[27] Philadelphia is between us and the rebellion, and the arming of Philadelphia is emphatically our affair. . . .

At eight P.M. to meeting of New York Rifles at Hope Chapel. Alden called us to order and asked me to preside as his deputy. We sat till half-past ten, debating whether we should organize under the state militia laws. Almost unanimous disposition to do so, and reference to a Committee of One (the commandant, to wit), to report to an adjourned meeting next week.

May 26, SUNDAY.   Today's event was Colonel Ellsworth's funeral; attended, I hear by a vast, grim, silent crowd. Beside the driver of the hearse sat Private Brownell of Ellsworth's regiment (who shot down and bayonetted his commandant's assassin), bearing his rifle with fixed bayonet and the rebel flag which Ellsworth had hauled down. This close juxtaposition of the murdered colonel with the bayonet that was red with his murderer's lifeblood forty-eight hours ago was hardly appropriate to the solemn decencies of a funeral, but certainly picturesque and significant —a stern symbol of the feeling that begins to prevail from Maine to Minnesota. . . .

Colonel Alden called after dinner and spent an hour discussing our proposed military organization. Tells me he talked over this movement on Alexandria with General Scott a week ago. Scott was then doubtful

[27] Here Strong has tinkered with Virgil's *Aeneid*, II, 311–312, and come up with a hexameter of his own: "It's your business when the house of your neighbor Ucalegon is on fire."

whether he had force enough and decided not to move forward till he was so strong as to make success certain. He is a cautious general, and most economical of men; expends lives as reluctantly as a miser parts with dollars. The object of this demonstration is to secure the "Manassas Gap Junction" and cut off the communications of the rebel advance at Harper's Ferry.

May 28. At drill room tonight. Attendance smaller. Many are offended by what they consider the "intemperance" of Barnes's and Barnard's speeches at our meeting Saturday night. They think there is a plan to entrap them into militia service, and they resign. This is unfortunate.

Colonel Baker's California regiment (several hundred of its rank and file at least), quartered in a lower story of our building, is most mephitic.[28] I never knew before what rankness of stench can be emitted by unwashed humanity. Some foul infectious disease might well break out among the wretches who spend their days and nights in this deadly atmosphere. It poisons the whole building and, of course, prevails in a concentrated form in the story they occupy, where it is absolutely stercoraceous and of ammoniacal intensity—nauseous and choking. It half strangles me as I go upstairs.

[28] Edward D. Baker (1811–1861), English-born Senator from Oregon, raised a "California regiment" in New York and Pennsylvania, and spent the summer training them.

MAY–DECEMBER
1861

CONFLICT GROWS AND SPREADS · THE SANITARY
COMMISSION IS ORGANIZED · THE BATTLE OF
BULL RUN · GREAT BRITAIN'S ATTITUDE

*O*n *May 29, Strong journeyed to Washington, partly on legal business and partly to inquire into the wants of the New York regiments in that area and at Old Point Comfort and near Norfolk. As yet no serious fighting had taken place either east or west. Virginia and Tennessee had joined the Confederacy, but despite the efforts of secessionist governors, both Kentucky and Missouri were mainly with the Union. The loyal party in Missouri, led by Frank P. Blair and supported by General Nathaniel Lyon, had dealt heavily with Confederate plotters in St. Louis and Jefferson City. But it was not until June 17 that the battle of Boonville made the position of Missouri fairly secure; and it was not until late June that McClellan invaded western Virginia with about twenty thousand men and there fought a successful campaign of a month. The most spectacular movement of May was that by which, on the morning of the 24th, Federal troops crossed the Potomac and violated the "sacred soil" of Virginia. Alexandria was hastily evacuated by a small Confederate force as a Michigan regiment and the New York Fire Zouaves entered. The commander of the latter, Colonel Elmer Ellsworth, whom Lincoln knew and loved, was shot by the keeper of the principal hotel for cutting down a Southern flag which floated over that building. As Strong has indicated, the death of this knightly young man, who had a host of friends all over the North, gave the whole country a sense of bereavement. As soon as the Union troops had occupied Alexandria and Arlington Heights, General Winfield Scott launched a column to threaten Harper's Ferry, where the Confederates had seized the arsenal and valuable stores. In due time, on June 15, this important post fell into Union hands.*

But meanwhile the health and welfare of the fast-gathering host of Northern troops had aroused much anxiety. Small groups of women in various cities were forming societies to supply nurses, to purchase clothing, medicines, and comforts for the sick and wounded, and to furnish other necessities. Near the close of April, the Rev. Dr. Bellows and a well-known physician, Dr. Elisha Harris, met accidentally in a New York street and discussed the general question of military sanitation and health. They talked with others. Presently a call was sent out for a general meeting at Cooper Institute to deal with the work of relief in the army, nearly a hundred of the most influential ladies of New York signing their names. The result was the formation of the Women's Central Association of Relief. A group of physicians and surgeons connected with the New York hospitals also held meetings; so did a "Medical Association for Furnishing Hospital Supplies." It became evident that a conference would have to be held with the army authorities. All the various associations therefore combined to send a delegation of four men—Dr. Bellows, Dr. Harris, Dr. W. H. Van Buren, and Dr. Jacob Harsen—to Washington. This body, reaching the capital on May 16, found everything in confusion. The Medical Bureau of the army, then headed by Acting Surgeon-General R. C. Wood, was manifestly incompetent to meet the demands made upon it. Pressure was at once brought upon Wood to consent to the creation of a great volunteer auxiliary organization. Strong's own view of the reasons why such an organization was needed is forcefully stated in a letter he wrote his friend Francis Lieber on July 12, 1862. It appears in an appendix to this volume.

May 29, WEDNESDAY.   Off by early train after very early breakfast. Fine day; Wickham Hoffman joined me at the Jersey City depot. No incidents of travel; Baltimore, that nest of traitors and assassins, was traversed in peace. There were crowds at the corners of the streets watching the trains. They were looking out for the troops that were in a train we passed on a turn-off at Havre de Grace. But the crowd was silent and innocuous, for Fort McHenry is now strongly reinforced and Federal Hill is white with the tents of government troops. At Washington in due season, and to Willard's Hotel; densely crowded. We had to put up with one room, a very good one, however, on the second floor. The corridors downstairs are packed with a mob of civilians, army officers, motley militia men, and loafers of every class. The little reception parlor on the side street is the headquarters of

Colonel Somebody (D'Utassy, I believe) of the "Garibaldi Guard," a very promising corps, and that end of the first floor passageway is permanently occupied by a guard of swarthy Italians and Hungarians.

Called on sundry people with letters and cards and lodged our pasteboard successfully with all but Mr. Secretary Blair, who was on his own front "stoop" and could not be escaped. We bored him about twenty minutes, not more. He tends a little to prose, but is courteous and intelligent. His talk is encouraging. He thinks there is little fight, if any, in the blustering fire-eating elements of the South; its bar-room swashbucklers will collapse whenever they are resolutely met. And this element constitutes, he thinks, two-thirds of the secession force. We were presented to Mrs. Blair, a lady-like person from New England.

Met Dick Smith, whilom of West Point, who marched me into General Sandford's parlor, where I had some talk with that chieftain and with Clarence Brown and Aleck Hamilton (not James A.'s Aleck, but John C.'s), who are on his staff. Heard all about the Alexandrian movement, for the execution of which Sandford takes much credit to himself. I hear Scott ranks him high for a "trainband" general, experienced only in marches down Broadway. I called with Hoffman at Scott's quarters. Saw Schuyler Hamilton, one of his aids, but did not disturb the meditations of the wily old Lieutenant-General, who lies there like a great spider in the center of his net, throwing out cords that will entangle his buzzing blue-bottle of an antagonist, if all go well.

Many New Yorkers at Willard's. Clarence Cram, Sam Neill, Willy Cutting, and others are begging for commissions. The honorable F. B. Cutting is diligently backing his son's petition; he has already secured a lieutenancy for Hayward Cutting, his youngest son. The Cuttings begging office from Lincoln, and these offices of all others, are a goodly spectacle to those who remember their extravagant, treasonable talk of sixty days ago and ever since last November. Many Republicans are soured by seeing a share of public patronage given to late-converted ultra-Southern Democrats. But the Administration is right. All party lines are wiped out now.

Dan Messenger, Judge Cowles, and others are after jobs in the Civil Service. The Rev. Dr. Bellows is concerned with the proposed Sanitary Commission. President Felton, Peirce, and Emory Washburn of Harvard, and Leutze are lookers-on.

May 30. Afternoon, parade and review of newly arrived regiments. Garibaldi Guard, Colonel Blenker's Germans (very promising corps both), the New York Ninth in their effective black and red uniform, and a fourth that I've forgotten (the "Brooklyn Zouaves")[Fourteenth New York].

May 31.   Drove with Hoffman, Dan Messenger, and his friend Charley Smith of Boston to Long Bridge. Our pass was inspected, and we went on. We invaded and (I suppose) "polluted" the Sacred Soil of Virginia. But it is so lacerated and insulted already by entrenchments, that our intrusion was a trifle. A very formidable *tête-du-pont* is in progress at the Virginia end of the bridge, and swarming with working parties. It is not armed yet, nor near completion, and it will need 2,000 men and upwards to occupy it when completed. Thence drove southwards, passing camps of New Jersey, Massachusetts, and other regiments, challenged every half mile, at least, by sentries and required to show our passes. Michiganders just outside Alexandria (fine looking fellows), and Pennsylvanians in the town. They do not seem to me very promising material. We drove to the famous Marshall House where Colonel Ellsworth was assassinated. It's a second-class hotel. Admitted with difficulty and formality; passes countersigned by the "provost-marshal." Explored the house, which is being carried off by relic hunters in little bits. Flag-staff is nearly cut through; stair-banisters, all gone; pieces of floor and stairs gouged out. Ordered dinner at Mansion House and drove a mile and a half northwest to Shooter's (or Sutter's) Hill, where Ellsworth's regiment (the New York Firemen Zouaves) is encamped and working at entrenchments, covering the extreme right of our line. Unfavorably impressed by the Zouaves. The men "sassed" the officers and the officers seemed loose in their notions of military subordination. One of them, a captain, and a rather scrubby specimen of a fire-company foreman in regimentals, said, "I guess we'll have the Colonel we want" (Ellsworth's successor); "if we don't, we'll let them fellows know we're about. We're firemen, we are." Probably a few of the Zouaves will have to be court-martialled and shot before the regiment can be relied on. With or near them are some Massachusetts soldiers and one of Sherman's light batteries. . . .[1]

Returned from Alexandria by a back road, visiting the camp of the New York Twelfth in a secluded, picturesque place, surrounded by woods and enlivened by a rattling stream. The regiment is quartered partly in bush huts, partly in an old tumbledown cotton factory, built forty years ago and never worked from that day to this. . . .

We then visited all the lines south of Long Bridge. Spirit and temper of

[1] Thomas W. Sherman (1813–1879), a Rhode Island veteran of the Mexican War, still in the regular army, had been ordered to assist in the defense of Washington.

the men clearly good. Equipment imperfect in many particulars, but I heard no grumbling. One fact is apparent and unmistakable, that discipline and actual service produce good manners. We were challenged and called on to produce our passes a score of times, and the sentinels (except perhaps certain of the Massachusetts boys) were common men enough, country laborers or city roughs. But we experienced no incivility, even of manner. They scrutinized our passes, asked questions sometimes, but were always respectful and courteous, and generally dismissed us with a sort of apology for our detention and some reference to their orders as leaving them no discretion.

We recrossed the Long Bridge and drove to Colonel Burnside's Rhode Island camp, far away on the outskirts of the City of Distances, somewhere northwest of the Capitol.[2] It's a model of neatness and order, with every provision for health and comfort; by far the most sensibly arranged camp I've seen. The huts are well built and ventilated, with convenient bunks, and a covered porch for the mess table. Talked with Goddard and other Providence millionaires who are serving in the ranks, and saw their evening parade, which was creditable and closed with an evening service by chaplain. Chapter in the Bible and extempore prayer. It suggested a field-preaching in the days of Lauderdale and Claverhouse, and though Puritanism is unlovely, the Rhode Island boys will fight none the worse for this daily inculcation of the truth that they are fighting for the laws of God and not merely for those of Congress. Thence to Burnside's quarters. He seems one of the strongest men I've seen in command.

June 1, SATURDAY. Spent the morning at War Office on business. Visited the Capitol, Smithsonian, and so on, with Hoffman. The Capitol has suffered no damage from its occupation by the Northern hordes. Its beautiful frescos are unscathed by the mudsills who were quartered there. Dined with [Henry A.] Wise of the navy; Mrs. Wise is a daughter of Edward Everett. Wise is extravagantly funny. He is now in a prominent and responsible position in the Department. After dinner, walked with the lady and her nice children, and N. P. Willis, in the grounds back of the White House, listening to the Marine Band. Loungers numerous and the crowd bright with uniforms. Firing heard in direction of Alexandria. Excitement, rumors of battle, and rapid dispersion of the audience. It was probably a salute. Returned to Wise's, and escorted Mrs. Wise to

[2] Ambrose E. Burnside (1824–1881) had organized the First Rhode Island and led it to Washington; he prided himself on the fine condition of his regiment, which Lincoln repeatedly visited in camp.

reception at Secretary Blair's. Pleasant enough; Seward, General Mansfield, Hamilton, Trowbridge, and others.

Called on Bache this morning and on Trowbridge.[3] Coast Survey office full of business. Surveys of southern ports not yet published are so far advanced that they can be made useful to the blockading squadrons, and copies are being got up and issued with all possible despatch. At two, I happened to see the prisoners brought in who were taken at the Fairfax Court House skirmish Thursday night. They were in a covered waggon, escorted by dragoons, revolver in hand, on their way to Mansfield's headquarters.

This was a dashing little affair, though General McDowell tells me it was injudicious and might have turned out very badly. Fifty United States dragoons . . . were making a reconnaissance, when they were fired on by a rebel guard of two men. They shot one and captured the other, who was interrogated and said there were about 100 men in the village. Relying on this, the dragoons rode in, and found themselves in presence of from 1,000 to 1,500 men. Their treacherous informant was shot down at once and very properly. This I heard in confidence. They charged and dispersed the rebels, rode through the streets more than once under fire from windows and from behind fences, and came off at last with trifling loss and several prisoners. The rebels fired quite wildly. The prisoners begged and cried and knelt and seemed to expect instant military execution. One of them (a son of Colonel Washington who was lost on the *San Francisco*) was seized by the hair of his head and dragged across the pommel of a saddle and carried through the village with the charging dragoons. He took oath of allegiance very promptly when it was tendered him, declaring he was a Union man, coerced into the rebel service, and was liberated by Mansfield and provided with some cloak or overcoat to cover his rebel uniform. . . .

June 2, SUNDAY. Drove with Hoffman to Arlington House, the hereditary mansion of that fine old fellow, Colonel [Robert E.] Lee, now unhappily a traitor. A splendid place amid beautiful grounds, through which we strolled a while. The sentinels refused us admission to the house and we were walking back to our carriage when General McDowell came riding up the road with his tail of staff and orderlies. He hailed me, dismounted, took us through the house, and was very kind and obliging. It's a queer place, an odd mixture of magnificence and meanness, like the

[3] Alexander Dallas Bache (1806–1867), superintendent of the Coast Survey; his assistant, William Petit Trowbridge (1828–1892), was later professor in the Columbia School of Mines.

castle of some illustrious, shabby, semi-insolvent old Irish family; for example, a grand costly portico with half-rotten wooden steps. Hall decorated with pictures, battle-pieces, by some illustrious Custis or other (fearful to behold); also with abundant stags' skulls and antlers. Thence to the camp of the Sixty-ninth, Colonel Corcoran's regiment. Inspected their battalion drill; rather rough. Then visited the New York Twenty-eighth and Fifth Regiments a little in advance, supported by the United States Dragoons, who charged through the streets of Fairfax Court House. Trained soldiers are easily distinguished from even the best volunteers. There was a little bugler of fifteen perhaps, a Brooklyn boy, whose narrative of the fray was spirited and modest. . . . The officers of the Twenty-eighth would not let us drive to Georgetown by the Chain Bridge. It was too hazardous. Rebel pickets were within a mile or two of the road, so we returned by the rope ferry. Orders were issued tonight by telegraph for a general advance. This I had from Wise. But they were countermanded.

Monday morning Hoffman returned to New York. At two I railroaded to Baltimore with Dan Messenger, Smith, and one Lamson of Boston, who is applying for a commission; a very good fellow he seems to be. We had agreed to visit Old Point Comfort and pay our respects to General [Ben] Butler and Colonel [Abram] Duryea. From depot to wharf, where we embarked in the *Adelaide*, heavily laden with stores for Fort Monroe, but built for first-class summer passengers to the fashionable hotel at the Point—the "Hygeia Hotel," a Baltimorean Newport in former days. Only half a dozen passengers with us; one a Virginian who wanted to get to Norfolk to look after some property there, and professed himself, in talk with us Union men, to be a sort of Union-lover, of a cold-blooded, anti-coercion type. A very fat and funny old fellow he was, Jenison by name. He was just from Harper's Ferry, where he had friends to see him through. Reports the rebel force at Harper's Ferry undisciplined and insubordinate, the officers and men "all mixed up together." Says he saw a captain enter a bar-room in great excitement and address himself to his commandant. "Colonel, what in H—— shall I do with the boys? They say they won't drill this morning." Colonel replies, "O, well, get two or three of them to turn out, and then I guess the others will come in by degrees." . . .

June 4.   Out of my stateroom early enough to see the sun rise, red and angry. Landed at Old Point and went into the moated fort, an extensive and formidable stronghold. The runaway niggers who have sought refuge there, and have been received by Butler as contraband of war, were bricklaying a structure that is to be a bakery and toiling at piles of sandbags.

Most of the officers to whom we had letters were absent on scouting parties. Introduced to Colonel [Charles] Dimmock and to General Butler. Lamson had a mission to Butler of complaint and remonstrance from Governor Andrew of Massachusetts about the commissariat and a shipload of provisions sent on by the market men of Boston (fresh meat and ice) that has been lying off the fort for ten days, and nobody the better for it. Butler met the complaint with clearness and decision. He's a rough, clear-headed, energetic man, I think. Gave us a pass that carried us across the causeway and bridge that connect Fort Monroe with the mainland of Virginia and hits the camps of Allen's regiment (Troy) and of Colonel Duryea's Zouaves, the "red-legged devils" of whom even Virginia secessionists stand in awe. They are among the best regiments I have seen.

Talked with Colonel Duryea, Hamlin (the adjutant and a six-footer), Captain Dumont, and others. Several companies off on scouting expeditions to Fox Hill and elsewhere, and many rumors of battle. . . . In this camp were five contraband niggers, with whom we held converse and exchanged views. "Why, sar," said Julius Caesar, "I didn't run away from my Massa, sar. He run away from *me*, sar."—"I heard the Northern gen'lmen were favorable to the colored population, sar, so I thought I'd come over here, sar."—"My friends whar I come from, sar, are all right, sar. They've been expecting the Northern gentlemen down here ever since Massa Lincoln was elected, sar."—"They wanted us to go to York [that is, Yorktown] to make the batteries, but I said, I'd never had no arms all my life and I thought I shouldn't be exactly handy with 'em, sar."

We started with Hamlin and Lieutenant Boyd for a walk to Hampton through the woods. Met a detachment of Duryea's marching in, footsore after a long nocturnal march in quest of fugitive rebels. Woods and meadows glowing and fragrant with honeysuckle and wild roses and all manner of wild flowers. Called at ex-President Tyler's country house and entered it through a cellar window.[4] He was out. He and all his family fled with precipitation some ten days ago. Signs of hasty, terrified flight abounded in the house; bureau drawers pulled out and left on the floor, unimportant papers scattered over the floor. I secured two or three scraps of the Tylerian correspondence.

[4] This was ex-President John Tyler's house "Sherwood Forest." Tyler, after the failure of compromise efforts in Washington, urged the secession of Virginia, and proposed that Southern troops hasten to occupy Washington. He sat first in the Provisional Congress at Montgomery and then was elected to the Confederate House in Richmond.

Mallory's house was abandoned, too, but apparently in less haste.[5] All the upstairs rooms were left locked and continue inviolate. There were stories in camp of vandalism at Tyler's—fine statuary destroyed and furniture cut up. They proved unfounded. The furniture was uninjured. The "statuary" was certain cheap plaster casts. Those in the parlors were intact and still covered by their gauze drapery. Two, in niches on the narrow stairway, had been knocked down and smashed, probably by Tyler's people lugging down the Tyler trunks and boxes.

We went from Tyler's to Hampton Creek. The bridge was burned by the rebels and we paddled across. The town of Hampton is beyond our pickets and I thought our visit imprudent, but we got off unscathed and uncaptured. The town is deserted by all but its niggers. Houses and stores are all closed and abandoned. Only two white men left, one a very jolly Irishman, and the other probably a rebel spy. . . . Hampton niggers generally a jolly set of fellows. Discoursed with one or two families that reminded me of Eastman Johnson's "Old Kentucky Home" picture.

Great vigilance against depredation and violence by our men. Hamlin hauled up one of Allen's lieutenants for breaking into a store to get a barrel of nails for the woodwork of a battery, though under his colonel's orders, and made him deliver a written acknowledgment of the seizure to the long, lantern-jawed Virginian above-mentioned as probably a spy.

Back to camp through a thundershower that wet us through. Dined with Dumont, Hamlin, and others very pleasantly. We contributed the drink— a basket of champagne and other liquors brought with us from Washington. Got on board the *Adelaide* again at five. . . .

Wednesday morning. Baltimore at seven. Strolled through the city with Lamson. Market very fine. Train at about ten. Comfortable day's ride and home at half-past eight.

June 8, SATURDAY.   Stephen A. Douglas dead. A loss to the nation, perhaps.[6] Certainly unfortunate for him that he should have had so little time left him to undo the mischief of his past career.

June 9.   Wickham Hoffman has been appointed to a nominal position

[5] That is, the house occupied by Stephen R. Mallory, Confederate Secretary of the Navy, who had been busy at Norfolk trying to create an iron navy, and whose efforts bore fruit in the ironclad *Merrimac*.

[6] Douglas, who had done his utmost during the campaign of 1860 to expose and thwart the disunion conspiracy, and who had recently been rallying the North to suppress the rebellion, died of typhoid fever in Chicago on June 3, 1861; a heavy loss to Illinois and the nation.

on Governor Morgan's staff as a volunteer aide, with the duty of looking after the material wants of our New York regiments at Washington and Old Point Comfort. Gibbs is on the Sanitary Commission that undertakes a like office as to all the volunteer force. I suggested to them both that they should appoint certain men here (and in Boston and other cities) a committee to raise funds in aid of their mission. The "Union Defense Committee" won't do.

June 12. This evening Mr. Ruggles, the Rev. Dr. Weston, George Allen, and half a dozen others met here to consider about organizing an association or committee to help the government provide for the material wants of the New York regiments at Old Point Comfort and elsewhere. We organized ourselves, and with some little prospect of doing good service. There is much money here that is impatient to burst out of private pockets into the hands of any honest body of trustees for the public good. But [Simeon] Draper & Co. have made the "Union Defense Committee" to stink in the nostrils of all good citizens.

June 13. Lovely weather. No material news. Washington reported in great agitation about a threatened advance of Beauregard with 60,000 men. Has he got them? Nobody can tell. According to the authentic newspaper statements of the last thirty days, there must be not less than two millions of rebel soldiery in Virginia by this time. I fear there is no doubt that poor Theodore Winthrop fell in that miserably managed skirmish at Bethel. Very sad for his sister, Mrs. Laura Johnson. He was a plucky, enterprising fellow, who might have made himself a name.[7]

June 14. This afternoon's papers report the rebel army at Harper's Ferry blowing up bridges and abandoning the position. It looks authentic, and perhaps it is; but philosophic skepticism as to all news is the proper temper now. This is important if true. The retreating rebels will doubtless fall back on the entrenched camp at Manassas Junction, and the force there may then feel strong enough for a dash at Washington. Who can tell? But the demonstrations of loyalty in Western Virginia are most encouraging. We are raising regiments there which with McClellan's command threaten the flank of any aggressive move by the rebels.

[7] The novelist and essayist Theodore Winthrop, who had recently been Ben Butler's military secretary at Fortress Monroe, fell victim to a Confederate sharpshooter at Big Bethel on June 10, 1861. His fame was more secure than Strong realized. Though he had as yet published little, he left the manuscripts of three successful novels, *Cecil Dreeme*, *John Brent*, and *Edwin Brothertoft*, and of two books of travel and adventure, *The Canoe and the Saddle* and *Life in the Open Air*; all five of which, issued in the years 1861–1863, produced a lasting impression.

Visit from Ashley this morning. I'm appointed paymaster of the New York Rifles. Till we are duly enrolled in the state militia we are only playing soldier, so my appointment and office have little worth.

This morning's *World* has a telegram about the Sanitary Commission and its appointment by the President: Professor Bache, Wolcott Gibbs, the Rev. Dr. [Henry W.] Bellows, Dr. [William H.] Van Buren, Dr. [Samuel Gridley] Howe of Boston, and others—and George T. Strong of New York. I have heard nothing of my appointment from any other quarter, and never dreamed of any such thing. I can hardly believe this. So many scores of men arc better qualified and more conspicuously fitted for the place and more likely to be thought of. *Vides, mi fili, quam parva sapientia. . . .*

The Sanitary Commission had sprung into formal existence on June 9. Dr. Wood, as head of the Medical Bureau of the Army, had at first taken a hostile attitude. But the able delegation which the several relief organizations of New York sent to Washington had irresistible arguments at their command. They pointed to the gross neglect of sanitation in the camps; the scandalous lack of materials and nurses to care for the wounded in any great battle; and the necessity of setting up some body to utilize the contributions which the people were anxious to make for the well-being of the troops. At first they hoped for a Sanitary Commission which (like the British commission in the Crimea) would have plenary power to carry its recommendations into effect. When Dr. Wood declared that his Medical Bureau would never consent to such a plan, they modified it. Wood then gave way, and on May 22 wrote a letter to Secretary of War Cameron asking for the appointment of "an intelligent and scientific commission" to cooperate with the Bureau in applying the best modern doctrines with respect to the diet, hygiene, and hospital care of the troops. Much tedious negotiation followed. Finally, on June 9 Cameron appointed Bellows, Bache, Gibbs, Van Buren, Wood, and others to the Sanitary Commission. They organized June 12, choosing Dr. Bellows president, and at their second meeting they elected Strong to membership, appointing him treasurer of the Commission— an onerous post.

June 21, FRIDAY. The Sanitary Commission has sat in permanence; the morning and evening sessions today lasted eight hours. Yesterday's were nearly as long, and we dined at the Rev. Dr. Bellows's in Twentieth Street. He's our president, Professor Bache vice-president. We have elected Olmsted (superintendent of Central Park, and author of certain valuable books of Southern travel) secretary and general agent to reside in Washington, and a member of the Commission. I like him much.[8] There are also Dr. [Cornelius R.] Agnew, Bache, Dr. [John Strong] Newberry of Cleveland, Wolcott Gibbs, Dr. Van Buren of this city, and one or two more. We have planned much work and done a little.

Poor Theodore Winthrop's remains passed through the city today on their way to New Haven. In Missouri, General Lyon seems to have gained a decided success, routing a large rebel force at a place called Boonville. The traitorous governor of that state has fled to parts unknown. Nearer home, there has been another blunder by a militia commander, at Vienna (near Fairfax), losing us a dozen men and upwards. They were in a railroad train which was fired on by a battery in ambuscade, according to the favorite tactics of Southern chivalry. Beauregard seems to be making some kind of forward movement from Fairfax and Manassas Junction, and the newspapers predict a great battle very shortly.

Much apprehension about some manoeuvre in Congress at the approaching extra session, to get up a compromise or pacification—a "Crittenden resolution" or some such temporary patchwork of concession. Won't do. The North won't stand it. None will be louder in opposition than a large class of the Democrats of last winter (like F. B. Cutting and Judge Vanderpoel) who were then so clamorous for "conciliation," and so sure that "no troops would be permitted to pass through New York." These men are now at least half-Abolitionist. As to the New York Club, I sent in my resignation last night. I have not heard what was done. It was to be presented if Deas's resignation was accepted by the Council; his, Magruder's, and Fauntleroy's (late of the navy) had been received by Ward and no doubt accepted so as to block action by the adjourned meeting of the Club that should have been held tonight.[9] Wickham Hoffman writes me that

[8] Frederick Law Olmsted (1822–1903), already well known for his invaluable books on Southern conditions, and as superintendent of the newly-planned Central Park in New York, was now well launched on his great career as landscape architect. He had shown marked powers of organization and political management. Dr. Bellows now suggested that he become general secretary, which meant chief executive officer, of the Sanitary Commission. When he accepted and obtained leave of absence from his work with Central Park, he embarked on his greatest single piece of public service.

[9] John B. Magruder, a West Pointer of Maryland family, who had served with much distinction in the Mexican War, had cut a dashing figure in New York and Newport society. Just after Lincoln's inauguration he had resigned from the army and accepted a Confederate commission as colonel. He commanded the force which won the engagement at Big Bethel, but his subsequent career was ill-starred. Strong had no intention of remaining in a club which flinched at the expulsion of such enemies.

Magruder told the officers who went with a flag of truce to recover poor Theodore Winthrop's body that "he hoped Brigadier-General Peirce's misfortune at Great Bethel would not be remembered against him and prevent his being employed to command hereafter." May he laugh on the other side—or on both sides—of his mouth, with a tight halter round his neck, before this game is played out!

June 22. Downtown early attending to proofs of my Sanitary Commission's circular inviting funds. It reads fairly in print. Commission met at twelve and sat till four P.M. at Bellows's house. Bellows goes off for Camp Denison and Cairo with Dr. Newberry on Monday. We meet again at Washington the 10th of July.

Dined at the Union Club, on Dr. Van Buren's invitation, with the New York Commissioners and old Dr. Mott.[10] Much pleasant talk with Bellows and Olmsted. Came away at eight to attend meeting here of our absurd "National Hymn" Committee. (Four or five huge bales of patriotic hymnology were deposited here this afternoon by our express wagon.) There were present Governor Fish, Luther Bradish, John R. Brodhead, Maunsell Field, Dick [Richard Grant] White, and others. Charley Strong happened in and acted as amateur assessor.

We got through possibly a third of our job between eight and twelve-thirty. There are 1,156 "hymns," many of them with music. The great majority of those we opened were consigned to the great rubbish bin (or clothes-basket) after reading the first three lines. A few were put aside as meritorious and worth looking at, and a few others as brilliantly absurd and therefore worth saving. We came across no production to which we could think of awarding a prize.

June 23, SUNDAY. Read today *Observations on Diseases of the Army,* by Sir John Pringle, Bart., 7th Edition, London, 1774. It was lent me by Dr. Peters, and seems a sound, sagacious book, though its details of medical treatment are doubtless obsolete.

No news from the war, except an alleged extract from a Charleston newspaper stating that Beauregard's command at Fairfax or Manassas Junction is among a hostile population that picks off sentries just as the people about Alexandria and Georgetown assassinate our men. Remarkable if true. Virginians and all who belong to slaveholding communities seem an exceptional, abnormal race, unlike anything else in Christendom.

General Dix takes command on the other side of the Potomac in a day

[10] Dr. Valentine Mott (1785–1865) was an authority on surgical anesthesia, on which he wrote a report (1862) for the Sanitary Commission.

or two. . . . Seward is becoming unpopular, or rather odious and offensive, because of stories that he favors peace with the rebellious South and desires to outmanoeuvre Cameron, Chase, and Blair by negotiating a compromise.

June 26.   National Hymn Committee met and had a good time. We disposed of bushels of rubbish. This committee is responsible for the production of an enormous bulk of commonplace, watery versification. Fortunately, two-thirds of the trash is already consumed with fire. But there remains an immense pile of poetry with music to match still to be inspected. It's clear, I think, that we get no national hymn. Perhaps we may secure a dozen bits of second-rate lyric that charitable people may justify us for publishing.

Today spent in diligent service of Sanitary Commission; writing letters and mailing documents all the morning. Our outside Finance Committee of associate members was summoned to meet here this evening. Cyrus Field responded and [John J.] Cisco and Robert H. McCurdy and Charley Strong; no more. But we got on very well, "added to our numbers" very liberally, and adjourned to the Chamber of Commerce Friday afternoon. Charley undertakes to get out notices. This is the real stress of our case. If the merchants and capitalists of New York are prudent enough to sustain the Commission, it will work and will save the nation thousands of men and millions of money within the next three months. If they do not sustain it, the loss is theirs and will be felt in the depression of New York property for ten years to come. An epidemic of camp fever or dysentery or cholera among our volunteer regiments is inevitable within sixty days unless their sanitary system be reorganized, or rather unless a sanitary system be created for them. The highest medical and military authorities at Washington prophesy a loss of fifty per cent by October 1. When this army is destroyed by disease, we shall have to raise another and at a fearful cost. We cannot afford to waste life.

After this financial meeting, Gibbs, Dr. Van Buren, Dr. Agnew, and I adjourned to the library and worked till after midnight on matters referred to us as a subcommittee of the Commission. . . .

Met a volunteer regiment marching down Broadway this afternoon from Clinton and St. Lawrence Counties; fine, stalwart fellows, true Norsemen, though inland, and among the best specimens I've seen of our New York levies. God defend them from the perils of camp disease and of privy assassination by the skulking dog-chivalry of Virginia (whose valor is manifested in picking off a sentinel from behind a tree and then running away).

June 28. Working diligently these two days, mostly on Sanitary Commission business. Last night at Wolcott Gibbs's with Dr. Agnew and Dr. Van Buren, settling the form of printed questions to be addressed to colonels and regimental surgeons as to the condition of camps and quarters, and as to precautions against disease, that will, I think, be unpleasant to answer—that will probably remain unanswered in *saecula saeculorum.* There are indications that the Commission will be sustained by the community. Everybody talks cordial approval, and I have $795 as deposit today, though not a dollar has yet been solicited. People have sent in contributions to that amount unasked, except by our newspaper appeal. . . .

June 29. The distinguished Hurlbut (*vide* this journal A.D. 1857) is arrested as a spy at Atlanta and sent to Richmond for trial.[11] Very odd. He was a vehement Republican in 1856, but a proslavery Democrat in 1860. At Washington last January he was intimate with Southern traitors and said to want a diplomatic appointment in the service of their projected Confederacy. Can he have ratted again and got an appointment from the government on secret service? Not impossible, for he has no principle, and is a wonderfully clever, plausible adventurer.

July 1, MONDAY. General Banks (of Massachusetts) is doing a good work at Baltimore. He has jugged all the traitorous police board of that city (except the mayor) and locked them up in Fort McHenry, along with Kane, their traitorous chief, whom he locked up several days ago. So the city is under something like martial law, a very appropriate treatment.

July 2. After dinner to Richard Grant White's (186 Tenth Street), where were old Verplanck, George William Curtis, and Maunsell Field of the National Anthem Committee. We examined a score or two of efforts that had been laid aside as not manifestly rubbish on our former inspection. Of these, we condemned only about one-half, a very tender and merciful judgment. It is conceded that no one of our 1,275 contributions answers the conditions of our advertisement and deserves the prize, but it is thought we may publish the best of them. Not one seems to me worth preserving, but there may be a dozen or so that the public would buy. . . .

No news today, but confident predictions of an advance from Wash-

[11] William H. Hurlbut (1827–1895), the brilliant blackleg who appears as one of the characters in Winthrop's *Cecil Dreeme,* had gone to the South on a business errand (he was a native of Charleston); and being arrested there, was confined in Richmond until he escaped in the summer of 1862. He was next to be heard of as one of the editors of the New York *World.*

ington on Manassas Junction and Fairfax, in which predictions I put no faith. Dr. Clymer "knows" that Scott is only waiting for Congress to legalize and adopt the volunteers assembled under Lincoln's April proclamation. Then he will at once make a forward shove. James W. Beekman "knows" that the unfortunate clamor of the *Tribune* and other newspapers about inaction and indecision has compelled Scott to order an advance, though against his own deliberate judgment; that six days' rations were to be issued today, and so forth; all which I respectfully disbelieve. Scott is not the man to wait for legal formalities at a crisis like this, or to be driven into premature action by newspaper editorials and public opinion.

July 7, SUNDAY.   Dined at one at Frank E. Howe's down the street, with Governor Andrew of Massachusetts; James T. Brady; his brother John; Mr. Ruggles; and six or eight more, generally Boston men living in New York. Find Andrew a genial, refined person, with good stories to tell. We had a pleasant session, though with free perspiration.

Our host is a good, warm-hearted, energetic fellow, wanting balance perhaps, and always in earnest and without an atom of self-consciousness. He has been agent of Massachusetts to look after the men passing through this city from that state on their way to Washington. . . .

July 8.   No war news today. Indications certainly strengthen of an advance from Washington, and General Patterson may find himself involved in battle on a large scale at some point near Martinsburg, where is a formidable rebel force that seems inclined to make a stand. God grant our first great battle be not a great national defeat.

July 15.   Home again. Thank Heaven, for of all detestable places, Washington is the first—in July, and with Congress sitting. Crowd, heat, bad quarters, bad fare, bad smells, mosquitoes, and a plague of flies transcending everything within my experience. They blackened the tablecloths and absolutely flew into one's mouth at dinner. Beelzebub surely reigns there, and Willard's Hotel is his temple.

Went off with Wolcott Gibbs Tuesday morning and got quarters at Willard's by special favor. Saw Olmsted. Visited our very grand official room in the Treasury Building, with its long, official, green-covered table and chairs ranged in official order around it, and official stationery in front of each chair. One could not sit there a moment without official sensations of dignity and red-tapery.

Wednesday, Thursday, and Friday spent in work. We sat from ten A.M. till about four daily, and then from seven or eight till eleven and later. Dr. Van Buren and Dr. Agnew and the Rev. Dr. Bellows joined us Wednesday morning. Professor Bache, Dr. Wood, and Major Shiras also sat with us, all three interested and useful; Shiras and Wood especially useful as supplying information about the present practical working of our military system, of which none of us (except Dr. Van Buren) know anything at all. We did a good deal of business. Extricated ourselves from an entanglement with that philanthropic lunatic, Miss [Dorothea L.] Dix, appointed four agents, or inspectors, adopted Dr. Van Buren's code of sanitary rules that is to be distributed among the volunteers and my draft of instructions to agents (without material alteration, strange to say), and sundry recommendations to Congress and the War Department, and so on. We attended the Military Committee of the Senate Thursday and Friday at nine A.M. Bellows was chief speaker on our behalf. [Henry] Wilson, fat Preston King, Lane, and that nasty fellow Rice constitute the Committee.[12] They heard us kindly and with interest. We submitted the draft of a bill endorsing our appointment by the Secretary of War, giving our agents rations while in camp, and requiring all officers either to comply with the recommendations of our agents or to assign reasons in writing for declining to do so, and giving our President and Secretary power to frank documents addressed to officers and soldiers. I opposed asking this last privilege and predict it will kill the bill. But the Committee was fully and strongly with us. Preston King and Wilson actually wanted to give us power to suspend any officer who may decline obeying our Sanitary counsel. That would be most odious and dangerous. We protested against being vested with such prerogative of mischief-making. The bill has passed two stages in the Senate unanimously, but I do not expect it will succeed.

Thursday evening I had a pleasant drive for an hour or so with Dr. Wood. Friday afternoon we dined on desiccated meats and vegetables, prepared by Sanderson, and then crossed the Long Bridge and drove about a little, visiting Colonel Corcoran's camp.

I shifted my quarters by a forced march Wednesday at midnight. Willard's functionaries took the liberty of putting a suspicious-looking stranger in my room. There I found him ensconced in a cot and breathing stertorously when I went upstairs for the night. As they would do noth-

[12] Henry Wilson, the distinguished Senator from Massachusetts and future Vice-President, had himself raised the Twenty-second Massachusetts Regiment. Senators Preston King of New York and the demagogic "Jim" Lane of Kansas were both Republicans of the Radical persuasion; Henry M. Rice of Minnesota may have struck Strong as "nasty" because of his Democratic views or because of his frontier manners—he had been an army post sutler and fur trader.

ing about it and declined even giving me a sofa to pass the rest of the night on, I magnanimously paid my bill and packed my trunk, ordered a carriage, and fared forth into the night. Visited every hotel in the city without finding a shelter. Made up my mind I must either sleep under the Treasury portico, enlist, commit a breach of the peace and get lodging in the watchhouse, or engage my coachman to spend the night driving up and down Pennsylvania Avenue. But I did worse. Got in at the National, and was assigned a cot in a large omnibus garret room—one of eight or ten. Worse than my room at Willard's, but then I had no feeling of being imposed upon. Didn't take off my clothes and didn't sleep a wink. My roommates snored. One of them ordered and swallowed three several drinks between daylight and breakfast time; viz., a sherry cobbler, a whiskey julep, and a brandy-smash. His voice and manner were as of one belonging to the better class—a gentleman.

I shifted again that night to Wormley's, a quiet little place in "I" Street, where Van Buren, Agnew, Bellows, Gibbs, and I messed together and fared well.

Saturday afternoon to Baltimore (2:30 train), thence by steamer to Old Point. Of the Commission there were those above named and Olmsted. We took with us also Giraud Foster, Charles Loring Brace, Taylor (a partner of J. C. Bancroft Davis), and the distinguished Russell of the London *Times*. Dr. [John C.] Peters and Dr. Alexander Mott were also on board. Very pleasant run down the beautiful Chesapeake. Talked much with Russell. Clever and well informed. Only drawback, a quiet, unconscious Anglican depreciation of everything outside England. So I heard him in discourse with others; I studiously avoided paying him the homage of a single query as to his opinion of anything here or at the South, and talked of India and the Crimea.

Sunday morning at Fort Monroe. Walked about the works with Russell, who explained the true significance of sundry ravelins and gorges and so on very learnedly. Saw a parade of regulars and one company of volunteers from Lowell, who appear on parade nearly as well as regulars. McChesney's regiment encamped on the parade ground seem a scurvy set. Called on General Butler and on Dr. Cuyler. Butler's friend, Dr. Kimball, took us through the hospital (Hygeia Hotel). Many wounded there from the Bethel blunder, and others who had been picked off while on guard by the chivalry of Virginia; one poor boy of eighteen who ran away from the Sophomore class of Harvard to join Duryea's regiment and got a bullet in the leg at Bethel. All were cheerful, plucky, and grateful for every kind look or word. None seemed to begrudge his lost leg or arm. Sickness, loss of blood, and low diet gave them all a look of refinement—their eyes were large and bright and their complexions clear, and they spoke slowly and low. There were two or three ugly typhoid cases, moreover. Kimball said one of them "might slip through his fingers"; "he had been overlooked a little, and they ought to have begun stimulating twelve hours ago." Our medical associates don't think much of Dr. Kimball. There is a large staff of nurses, seemingly good and attentive, generally from Massachusetts.

General Butler got out a steamboat for us and we went to Newport News. (N.B. Why do we occupy that point? Its land communication with Hampton is not kept up; the two positions are practically insulated, and what do we gain by two weak bases of operation?) Walked through camps there with Lieutenant-Colonel George Betts. Regimental hospitals crowded and bad; camp police generally good. Butler exhibited one of his Sawyer guns (42-pounder) and fired a few conical shells at the rebel batteries opposite and about four and a half miles distant; elevation of the gun from twenty-two degrees to thirty degrees. I think the shells generally fell a half mile short, but they said one or two went into or over the batteries. Steamed back to the Fort. Drove with Gibbs and Bache back to Hampton. Bridge nearly restored, only a few planks to be replaced. Visited Colonel Max Weber, who was civil and brought out some Rhine wine. His soldiers are in high feather. They have planted a battery of two guns on this side that rakes the bridge. Crossed it on foot. Hampton still deserted by its people, a fact that looks bad for our final success, unless by a war of extirpation, but crowded with soldiers, mostly of the Naval Brigade (commonly called Naval Brigands). Just beyond the old church a stockade and trench are in progress, and guns in position. Left the Point by steamer, which waited for us a couple of hours, at eight P.M. and reached Baltimore at half-past eight this morning. Home at nine tonight, having dined in Philadelphia with Van Buren, Gibbs, and others. Ellie went to Savin Rock with the babies Friday afternoon, so I return to a lonely home.

We are in great spirits over McClellan's successes in Western Virginia.

July 17. Attended meeting at the Chamber of Commerce of our Executive Committee of Associates charged with the duty of raising money for us to spend—Morris Ketchum, [George] Opdyke, Mr. Ruggles (chairman), [Marshall O.] Roberts, [George] Hoadly, and others. I presented my report on money received and disbursed, and then followed a long debate on matters of detail, in itself of no importance, but showing that Opdyke wants to be considered *one of the Commission*. He is a pushing, intriguing man, fond of power and position, and might give us trouble were the urgency of the case less manifest.[13] Tonight at Dr. Bellows's with Mr. Ruggles and Agnew, concerting measures. Our prospects are good. We must meet in Washington early in August. . . .

McClellan seems to have crushed treason in Western Virginia. And McDowell's column is in advance on Fairfax and Manassas Junction at last. I fear this move is premature, forced on General Scott by the newspapers. A serious check on this line would be a great disaster.

July 19. Dined with Charley Strong and George Allen at the "Maison Dorée," a new and very nice restaurant established in Penniman's house on Union Square. Called on Dr. Peters, as a private sanitary agent on my own account, also at Mr. Ruggles's. We are all waiting breathlessly for news from the Army of Virginia. Batteries were encountered by the advance yesterday at Bull's Run, three miles this side of Manassas Junction, and there was a sharp skirmish, our advance falling back on its supports at last with a loss of some sixty men. Today, there have been diverse stories of additional fight, stories both good and bad; but the last report is that all are fictions and that things are *in statu quo*. This lack of authentic official reports is no sign of success. We seem on the eve of a general action, but perhaps the enemy is holding Bull's Run to secure a comfortable retreat toward Richmond. He certainly ran away from Fairfax with great precipitation, but I suppose the chivalry will fight pretty well behind entrenchments.

July 22, MONDAY. Good news—certainly good, though it may not prove sufficient to justify the crowing and the capitals of the *Tribune*. It's rather sketchy and vague, and no doubt exaggerated, but there has been fighting on a large scale at Bull's Run. Our men have been steady under fire and the enemy has fallen back on Manassas. This last important fact seems beyond question.

General Johnston seems to have joined Beauregard, giving him numerical preponderance. Patterson does not seem to have followed Johnston up. We attacked yesterday morning, and there was hard fight-

[13] George Opdyke (1805–1880), wealthy dry goods importer and merchant, manufactured arms and uniforms during the Civil War. He was elected mayor on the Republican ticket, serving 1862–1863; we shall meet him again during the Draft Riots.

ing till about half past five. Our right, under Hunter, turned the rebel entrenchments and seems to have repulsed the enemy, where they came out of their cover, and tried to use the bayonet. Hunter is killed or severely wounded. Ellsworth's Fire Zouaves and Corcoran's Irishmen are said to have fought specially well, and to have suffered much. It is rumored that an advance was shelling the batteries at Manassas last night. Not likely.

Thank God for this good news. We shall probably receive a cold-water douche, however, before night in the shape of less comfortable intelligence.

Seven P.M. My prediction about the douche verified indeed! Today will be known as *BLACK MONDAY.* We are utterly and disgracefully routed, beaten, whipped by secessionists. Perhaps not disgracefully, for they say Beauregard had 90,000 men in the field, and if so, we were outnumbered two to one. But our men are disorganized and demoralized and have fled to the shelter of their trenches at Arlington and Alexandria as rabbits to their burrows. All our field artillery is lost (twenty-five guns out of forty-nine!), and if the secessionists have any dash in them, they will drive McDowell into the Potomac.

How it happened is still uncertain. It doesn't appear whether the stampede came of a sudden unaccountable panic, or from the advent of General Johnston on our flank. In this latter case, it was a revival of the legitimate Napoleonic drama: Blücher, General Johnston; Grouchy, General Patterson. But our reports are all a muddle. Only one great fact stands out unmistakably: total defeat and national disaster on the largest scale. Only one thing remains to make the situation worse, and I shall not be surprised if tomorrow's papers announce it. That is, the surrender of our army across the Potomac and the occupation of Washington by the rebels. We could never retreat across the Long Bridge if successfully assailed, even were our men not cut up and crestfallen and disheartened.

Who will be the popular scapegoat? Probably Patterson, perhaps Secretary Cameron, or even General Scott!

Well, *In Te Domine Speravi!* If the North be not cast down and discouraged by this reverse, we shall flog these scoundrels and traitors all the more bitterly for it before we are done with them.

July 23. We feel a little better today. The army is by no means annihilated. Only a small part of it seems to have been stricken with panic. A gallant fight has been made against enormous odds and at every disadvantage. An attack failed and we fell back. *Voilà tout.* Only there is the lamentable loss of guns, some say eighteen, others nearly a hundred.

That cannot be explained away. It's said tonight that Tyler is at Centreville, entrenching himself, so all the ground occupied by our advance is not abandoned. The rebels show no disposition to follow up their advantage or venture outside their woods and masked batteries. The first reports of our loss in killed and wounded are said to be greatly exaggerated.

Why we delivered battle is a mystery. I suppose the *Tribune* and other newspapers teased and scolded General Scott into premature action. Thought him too strong and self-sustained to be forced to do anything against his own judgment by outside pressure and popular clamor.

July 25. These Southern scoundrels! How they will brag over the repulse at Bull's Run, though, to be sure, it's not nearly so bad as our first reports. And is there not good reason to fear that their omission to follow up their advantage by a march on Washington indicates a movement in overwhelming force on the column of General Banks (late Patterson's) or Rosecrans's (late McClellan's)? May we not have another disaster to lament within the next forty-eight hours?

How the inherent barbarism of the chivalry crops out whenever it can safely kill or torture a defenseless enemy! Scrape the "Southern Gentleman's" skin, and you will find a second-rate Comanche underneath it. These felons solaced themselves by murdering our wounded men in cold blood when they found us retiring from the field last Sunday afternoon—and did so with an elaboration of artistic fertility in forms of homicide (setting them up against trees to be fired at, cutting their throats, and so on), that proves them of higher grade in ruffianism and cowardly atrocity than anything our Five Points can show. We *must* soon begin treating the enemy with the hempen penalties of treason.

July 26. The Eighth and Seventy-first Regiments (three-month volunteers) returned today, welcomed by crowds that blocked Broadway. They will be missed at Washington. We feel rather blue today, though without special reason. It seems clear that the loss of the rebels last Sunday was fully as severe as our own. Russell (London *Times*) writes Sam Ward that the Union army "ran away just as its victory had been secured by the superior cowardice of the South." Pleasant! But Russell headed the race.

Bull Run seemed at the time a stunning defeat, but it was actually an indecisive battle which did little to benefit the South save by producing a transient sense of triumph and elation, and very little to injure the North. Indeed, since it

stimulated the Northern people to grimmer and more determined effort, it prob-
ably did the Union cause more good than harm. The story of the battle is
sufficiently familiar. General Irvin McDowell, with an army of about 35,000,
was guarding the southern approaches to Washington from a position at Centre-
ville, some twenty miles deep in Virginia. He was confronted by a slightly
smaller Confederate force under Beauregard. This held Manassas, the impor-
tant junction point where the railroad from the Shenandoah Valley joined the
railroad to Richmond. Old General Winfield Scott opposed any immediate
advance. But the public clamored for action, while many newspaper editors were
anxious to see the army thrown forward into battle before the time of the three-
months volunteers expired. An offensive became almost a political necessity.
Undoubtedly McDowell laid his plans well. But his position was rendered pre-
carious when the Union forces in the Shenandoah allowed General Joseph E.
Johnston to slip away and reinforce Beauregard on the very eve of the combat.
The Union attack began on the morning of July 21, and for a time went well.
The raw volunteers, who fought with surprising steadiness, gained ground. But
in mid-afternoon, after T. J. Jackson's men had stood like a stone wall, the
reinforcements from Johnston enabled the Confederates to carry a key position
(Henry Hill). The Union troops then had to fall back; and a retreat which
began in orderly fashion soon became a pell-mell rout, with officers, men,
stragglers, spectators, correspondents, and Congressmen fleeing in a mass
toward Washington. William H. Russell of the London Times *gave Europe*
an account of the flight which Americans keenly resented, but which in essential
particulars was accurate.

The lack of discipline which the battle revealed was no surprise to members of
the Sanitary Commission. They had been shocked by the want of care, vigilance,
and foresight in the army camps; defects which pointed to a weak military
organization and deplorable faults of administration. Early in July the Com-
mission held a session at which it drew up a series of sensible recommendations.
It urged that rest-rooms be provided near the station in Washington for arriv-
ing and departing soldiers; that arrangements be made to enable soldiers to send
their families all or part of their pay; that a system of military police be insti-
tuted to keep soldiers out of groggeries and houses of ill fame; that rigid rules of
camp sanitation be enforced; and that plenty of fresh vegetables should be
supplied, with really good cooks to prepare them. Strong relates how as early as
June 28 he worked with Wolcott Gibbs and two physician-members upon a form

of questions to be submitted to colonels and regimental surgeons. This list was extended, and immediately after Bull Run was made the basis for a searching inquiry into sanitary affairs, and also into the causes and extent of the demoralization which attended the battle. The facts elicited as to the lack of care and discipline in the treatment of the volunteers were so discreditable to the government that they could not be published at the time. In many regiments the men had given way because of long deprivation of food, exhaustion before the battle, and overtasking as the conflict wore on. Olmsted reported of the woebegone rabble which reached Washington: "Some appeared ferocious, others only sick and dejected, all excessively weak, hungry, and selfish. There was no apparent organization. . . ."

Soon after the battle Strong went to Washington again to look into the condition of the hospitals, now crowded with wounded and sick, and the state of the camps. What he saw was not reassuring, and he returned sad and despondent.

August 2, FRIDAY.   Exceeding sultry. Up before three this morning for the early train. But as the ticket office of that wickedly managed Baltimore & Washington Railroad was not opened till long after the hour for starting, our train got off near half an hour behind time, and missed its connection at Baltimore; so we were detained there till ten o'clock, and might just as well have postponed our arising till six. A most sultry ride. There were Dr. Bellows, Van Buren, George Gibbs, Wolcott Gibbs, and myself. Breakfasted at the Gilman House and dined at the Continental (Philadelphia). Saw Horace Binney at his house a moment. We have elected him and Bishop Clark of Rhode Island full members of the Commission, and I think both will serve.[14] Home at half-past nine.

Washington hotter and more detestable than ever. Plague of flies and mosquitoes unabated.

Went on by night train Saturday. Spent the night filed away like a bundle of papers in one of the "sleeping" (!) car pigeonholes, where I perspired freely all night.

Sunday at the hospitals—two at Georgetown ("Seminary" and "Union Hotel"), and one at Alexandria. Much to write about both, were

[14] Few New England clergymen were as influential as Thomas March Clark (1812–1903), a man of Massachusetts birth and Yale education who, after occupying pulpits in Boston, Philadelphia, and Hartford, had been elected Bishop of Rhode Island in 1854. His powerful physique, learning, strong wit and humor, and broad sympathies made him a highly popular preacher, while he was a fluent and prolific contributor to the religious press. His *Reminiscences* describe fully his work with the Sanitary Commission.

there time. Condition of the wounded thus far most satisfactory. Everything tends to heal kindly. But our professional colleagues say this is deceptive. The time for trouble has not yet come, and hospital disease is inevitable within sixty days. The medical men in charge are doing what they can, but radical changes are needed. The buildings are defective in many points. As at Fort Monroe, the cheerfulness and pluck of the men are most touching. I saw several hideous cases of laceration by Minié balls and fragments of shell, too hideous to describe; but all doing well. One poor fellow (a Glasgow man of the Seventy-ninth named Rutherfurd) was *in articulo mortis* with dysentery and consequent peritonitis. Another died while we were there, after undergoing amputation an hour or two before. One or two typhoid cases looked unpromising.

Visited "Fort Ellsworth," in front of Alexandria. It is finished now and very formidable, easier to defend than to assault. But it seems to me (in my ignorance) insufficiently armed, and commanded, moreover, by the neighboring hills. The chivalry will never try to storm it, but I don't see why they should not shell its defenders out. This seems true also of the most important works at the head of the Long Bridge.

Our session adjourned late last night, having sat, as before, morning and evening. It engrossed all of my time, except that we took two or three drives in what should have been the "cool" of the evening to visit certain regiments that are specially demoralized by the disaster of the 21st, the Seventy-ninth and others.

We did a deal of work. Among other things we recommended the Secretary of War to remove Dr. Kimball (General Butler's amateur interloper) from Fort Monroe, a step which at once put us on intimate cordial and endearing relations with all the Medical Bureau, Dr. Finley included.[15] But we receive no sincere cooperation from our pretended Congressional allies. Senator Wilson seems to have played a double game with us. The President, with whom Professor Bache and Dr. Bellows had a conference Thursday night, is our friend. So is [Montgomery C.] Meigs the Quartermaster-General, with whom I had an interview. He is an exceptional and refreshing specimen of sense and promptitude, unlike most of our high military officials. There's not a fibre of red tape in his constitution. Miss Dix has plagued us a little. She

[15] The Medical Bureau of the War Department had for its head when the war began Surgeon-General Thomas Lawson, who had been in the service with few interruptions since 1809 and was totally unfit for his duties. Dying on May 15, 1861, he was succeeded by Colonel Clement Finley, another veteran of inadequate abilities and training, of whose deficiencies we shall hear much more.

is energetic, benevolent, unselfish, and a mild case of monomania. Working on her own hook, she does good, but no one can cooperate with her, for she belongs to the class of comets and can be subdued into relations with no system whatever.

Long talk with General [Irvin] McDowell. He is sadly depressed and mortified, most unlike what he was a fortnight ago. Says he has nothing to reproach himself with, and that he did his best. He took 31,000 men into the field, and of these the reserve of 1,000 was not under fire at all. The enemy were twice his strength. Colonel Cullum tells me we lost twenty-five guns, just one more than half those that went into action. Though at the head of Scott's staff, he cannot ascertain and does not know what produced this ruinous panic and stampede, or what regiment began it. Nor does he know whether the rebel force in Virginia is 70,000 or over 200,000. History is worth little.

From conversations with eye witnesses, I am satisfied that the rebels treated our wounded men with characteristic barbarity. Dr. Barnes found thirty wounded officers and men whom he had collected in a shady place and left for a few moments (while he went for some surgical implement or assistance to the church that was used as a temporary hospital) bayonetted on his return. Two very intelligent privates of a Michigan regiment now in one of the Georgetown hospitals tell me with all minute details of time, place, and circumstance how they saw rebel soldiers deliberately cut the throats of wounded men.

I return from Washington depressed and despondent. Our volunteer system with its elected colonels and its political major-generals is very bad. We are fighting at sore disadvantage. The men have lost faith in their officers, and no wonder, when so many officers set the example of running away. Of the first three hundred fugitives that crossed the Long Bridge, two hundred had commissions. Two colonels were seen fleeing on the same horse. Several regiments were left without field officers and without a company officer that knew anything beyond company drill. The splendid material of the Scotch Seventy-ninth and the Fire Zouaves has been wasted. Both regiments are disheartened and demoralized. Neither would stand fire for five minutes—they are almost in a state of mutiny, their men deserting and the sick list enlarging itself daily. Why the rebels did not walk into Washington July 22 or 23 is a great mystery. They could have done so with trifling loss.

August 13, TUESDAY. Rumor in evening papers by telegraph from St. Louis that General Lyon's command in southwest Missouri is routed, and the general killed. Wonder when the tide of disaster will turn. But the misfortune may be exaggerated.

August 15. To town this morning, and very busy all day over Sanitary Commission letters and papers to the exclusion of everything else. Three thousand dollars came in from the Mutual Life Insurance Company, of which F. S. Winston is president. I trust we may do some good service to justify the confidence the community reposes in us. . . .

We claim the Missouri battle as a victory, General Sigel having retreated in good order after General Lyon fell and left only a very few guns on the field. If these be victories, may we soon enjoy a few defeats! Lyon is killed, undoubtedly; some say the rebel General Price, too, and that notable land-loafing partisan *knight* of the knife and the revolver, Ben McCulloch. I'm sure I hope both are in Heaven, but I don't feel confident about it. . . .[16]

We are not yet fighting in earnest, *not even yet.* Our sluggish, good-natured, pachydermatous Northern people requires a deal of kicking to heat its blood. Not a traitor is hanged after four months of rampant belligerent rebellion. We must change all this. The Southern oligarchy is making war with hysterical, unscrupulous energy, like France in her unblessed First Revolution. We have got to tune ourselves up to the same pitch, hang rebels, arm their niggers, burn their towns, expel all sympathizers with treason that infest our own borders. . . .

August 16. Two consolatory facts appear. The banks have taken the million loan, and the United States Grand Jury has presented the *Journal of Commerce, Daily News,* and one or two other "sympathizing" newspapers as nuisances. . . .

August 19. Olmsted here (from Washington for a day or two, looking after Central Park), also Drs. Van Buren and Agnew—a Sanitary Council. . . .

Olmsted thinks ill of affairs at Washington. Demoralization, discouragement, desire to get home again, have shown themselves in many regiments. There are mutinous tendencies. We have not yet sounded all the depths of disaster and disgrace. The government seems limp and nerveless and unequal to the crisis. A dozen mutineers, or a score of

---

[16] Brigadier-General Nathaniel Lyon (1818–1861), whose bold steps as supreme commander of Union forces in St. Louis had done much to hold Missouri in the Union, had rashly pushed into southwest Missouri with an inadequate force. At the battle of Wilson's Creek on August 10, he and Franz Sigel were crushed by superior Confederate forces and he was slain. His opponents, Sterling Price and Ben McCulloch, were not hurt.

dozen, if necessary, should be summarily shot at once. Government stocks would instantly rise three per cent, on the strength of that or any other like decided action; for the people feel that government is not making war with all its heart and soul and mind. I almost suspect that it is trying to keep a door open for some compromise or convention. If so, the error is chargeable to Seward. He and Cameron can be spared from the Cabinet. The people themselves are far less fully aroused and in earnest than their Southern enemies. The two surgeons, Winston and Swift, just released from their captivity at Richmond, report to Dr. Agnew that New York and Washington seem to them indifferent and careless in comparison with the fever-heat of Virginia.

August 22. Glad to hear that Dr. Higby, at a meeting of trustees of the Theological Seminary, turned a cold shoulder on his quondam friend Judge Chambers of Maryland, and being interrogated by the latter told him distinctly that he did so because of his disloyal course in that state. Very good for Dr. Higby, with his Southern connections and antecedents. This is a little like the temper that ought to prevail here and that must prevail, if we expect to fight this battle out to any result but national disgrace. The first duty of the government at this time is to hang some highly respectable, gentlemanlike, wealthy, and well-connected person, after due trial and condemnation, for treason. There are plenty of cases within its reach. One such proceeding would do more to consolidate the nation and invigorate its life than all this Cabinet has done since the Fourth of March.

Not much war news. General [John E.] Wool has superseded Butler at Fort Monroe. An important change, that quarter (rather than the Potomac) being the true base of operations for an advance on Richmond. Excitement about a rebel move on Washington has in some degree subsided. . . .

We begin to receive the rebound from England and France of the first news of the Bull Run battle. It is bitterly galling. The nation is disgraced, for a time at least, in the eyes of Christendom. Later reports from Southern newspapers showing that the rebels were absolutely beaten when the arrival of reinforcements turned the tide of battle in their favor, and that their loss exceeded ours on their own showing, may restore our credit a little. But this more accurate statement of the case may come too late to prevent France and England from recognizing the rebellious confederation of our Southern States, and introducing new and serious complications into our national trouble. Who could have dreamed a year ago that England would hesitate one moment as to the side of this controversy entitled to her sympathy and moral support?

August 26, MONDAY.   This evening Gibbs here, Dr. Agnew, and one of our sanitary inspectors, Dr. Douglas. He has been with General Banks's column, now retrograding from Harper's Ferry toward Baltimore (nobody knows why), and gives an encouraging report of its morale and its sanitary condition. Gibbs read me a letter from Dr. Suckley, however, at Alexandria, giving the most deplorable account of our volunteer regiments about Washington; disorganized, demoralized, without spirit, or discipline, or confidence in their officers. He predicts another grand defeat. "Was ne'er prophetic sound so full of woe." Suckley is partial to a grey tone of color and minor keys, but I fear his prophesying is a genuine article. Our volunteer system, with its elective officers, is radically weak.

McClellan sent in his resignation last week, Lincoln having given him a list of subordinates whose appointment was a political necessity. After twenty-four hours' consideration, Lincoln concluded it would not do to let McClellan resign, and withdrew his list of appointees. . . .

August 27.   It is almost time for another great disaster. It will occur in Western Virginia, probably. Can any disaster and disgrace arouse us fully? Perhaps we are destined to defeat and fit only for subjugation. Perhaps the oligarchs of the South are our born rulers. Northern communities may be too weak, corrupt, gelatinous, and unwarlike to resist Jefferson Davis and his confederates. It is possible that New York and New England and the Free West may be unable to cope with the South. If so, let the fact be ascertained and established as soon as possible, and let us begin to recognize our masters. But I should like a chance to peril my life in battle before that question is decided.

Saw the valiant John Cochrane march down Broadway this afternoon at the head of his regiment, a scurvy gang enough.

September 2.   Olmsted writes me from Washington, Saturday, that Russell and English officers sojourning there interpret Beauregard's late movements to mean an attack in force. I doubt whether he can attack our fieldworks successfully, or cross the Potomac at Leesburg or anywhere else without strong odds against him. People say he must make a forward move at any risk for want of provisions and to prevent discord and disintegration within his command, but I do not believe people know much about it. We hear today of a move by General Frémont that looks like war in earnest, at last: a proclamation of martial law in Missouri, confiscation of all rebel property, and freedom to all slaves owned by rebels in that state. A most significant step, and in the right direction, though it may weaken the national cause in Kentucky. . . .

September 3.   Mr. Ruggles and Jem here awhile this evening; Mr. Ruggles in exaltation over George Allen's Flax Cotton. I am going in as director of the company and shall immolate myself in the cause to the extent of two or three hundred. Of course, there will be found a weak point somewhere in the demonstration of facts and figures that Flax Cotton is a "big thing." It's always so, but I will sacrifice a moderate amount for the chance of dealing a blow at King Cotton, though the chance is small.

September 16, MONDAY.   Went thither to Washington by the usual day train Wednesday the 4th. Dr. Bellows and Gibbs were my fellow travellers. Found Bishop Clark there. He is a brick. The Medici, Van Buren and Agnew, arrived next morning and we duly inaugurated our session in the Treasury Building. It adjourned last Thursday night, but the Rev. Dr. Bellows and I stayed one day longer, hoping to consummate certain material reforms (in the Medical Bureau) that seemed all but accomplished. They are only inchoate, however, to this day. Put not your faith in princes, nor in the confidential pledges of secretaries and heads of departments. I experienced little beyond our ordinary routine of a morning session at ten, and an evening session at eight. "The battle" was always coming off tomorrow morning, but it did not come off at all.

Saturday the 7th we all dined at Professor Bache's. Sunday morning I went to the camp of the Rhode Island Second Regiment at "Brightwood." Bishop Clark preached from the top of a military chest or box of pinewood, with the Rhode Islanders and a Massachusetts regiment for audience. A very vigorous, honest, unconventional sermon it was. It was like one of Charles Kingsley's sermons, and it was not thrown away. I saw many a rather dirty handkerchief pulled out.

Monday afternoon, we revisited that camp by invitation. Its Colonel Wheaton of the regulars seems a fine young fellow. Evening parade and evening service, with an address from Dr. Bellows. He told the men, in substance, that there were several ways of serving God, varying according to one's position and surroundings, and that their way, at this particular crisis, was to obey orders and to fight like the devil.

Wednesday afternoon, General [E. D.] Keyes invited us to review his brigade at the race course, just across the Long Bridge. It was a fine sight, the movement of some four thousand men, with bands playing and field and staff officers galloping about. Found an acquaintance in one of the General's aids, young Chetwood, a Columbia College Law School graduate of last year. We were saluted and took off our hats in due military form, and it was all very high and mighty and grand.

There were one or two other pleasant drives on the other side of the Potomac. It is a lovely region, richer, brighter, more exuberant, and better (barring malaria) than Great Barrington. Poor Virginia ought to be the Queen State of the Union, but she is crushed by niggerdom. If this war rids her of that incubus, she will be the centre of western civilization, A.D. 1875.

McDowell dined with us. He is very sore about the Bull Run battle, and insists on talking about it and explaining his defeat. General Tyler went beyond his orders on the 18th, and Butler and Patterson were severally to have moved forward on the fatal 21st, which thing they did not. I like McDowell. A civilian always likes major-generals who, as it were, appeal to him for sympathy and a candid judgment. Shameful that our venomous critics of defeat should say he was drunk at Bull Run. The man is an ultra total abstainer. He invited me to go up in the army balloon with him, and I hope to do so yet. General [Ambrose E.] Burnside tendered the like hospitality to Bishop Clark. The Bishop made an aeronautic assignation with him, which he was prevented from keeping, so the unprecedented conjunction of a balloon and a bishop is still *in fieri*, among the unconsummated concatenations of future time. Burnside is a brick (he and the Bishop roomed together and they seem old friends). He says our men were steadier and fired better than the enemy on the 21st of July, and all was going well and the victory substantially won, when officers and men went suddenly to the rear in the wildest stampede. He remarks further that it was "the worst planned battle he ever saw or heard of." When his brigade was deployed pursuant to orders, he found it at right angles to the line of battle. Curious story of Colonel Slocum, who had been with Burnside in Mexico—a man of peculiarly sanguine temperament and light heartedness. He told Burnside on that Sunday morning, as they were leaving the Council of War, that he was sure he should be hit, and hit twice. He knew he should not come out alive. His prediction was accurate. He was shot twice, in the leg and in the head, and died at Richmond two or three days after the battle.

My former friend, E. K. Smith (of West Point in 1852) is not killed, but only "kilt" by a ball in the shoulder. He is the "General Kirby Smith," it seems, who led up the rebel reinforcement that turned the tides of battle against us.

Debates at this session were livelier than before. We had the question constantly before us, in one form or another, whether we should go on in alliance with the War Department Medical Bureau or denounce their inefficiency. Our government members—Professor Bache, Dr. Wood, Major Shiras, and Colonel Cullum—stood up vigorously for the officials, of course. There was much discussion about a queer, clever report by Olmsted as to the causes of the volunteer demoralization that culminated in the race to Washington after Bull Run. An able paper, certainly, but its publication would have done mischief—would have retarded recruiting.

The "queer, clever report" was the "Report on the Demoralization of the Volunteers," prepared by Olmsted and presented to the Sanitary Commission on September 5, 1861. It is referred to in the preceding editorial note. Stillé, the Commission's historian, was probably right in calling it the first study of the causes of the loss of a battle ever made so thoroughly and so promptly. Within a week after the battle, seven of the Commission's inspectors, provided with a set of seventy-five questions, had interviewed officers and men who had been in the engagement. Their reports, which covered some 2,000 items of information, were carefully analyzed by E. B. Elliott, a Boston life insurance actuary employed by the Commission. The testimony of the soldiers about the conditions under which they had functioned before and during the battle, and the record of the futile attempts the Sanitary Commission had made to overcome official indifference to the dangers inherent in the lack of organization and discipline, were a clear indictment of the War Department's mismanagement. The army's assumption that discipline could not, and need not, be enforced with volunteer troops died abruptly after this experience. Olmsted cited as an example the New York Fire Zouaves, a group of unquestionably brave men but without any understanding of military subordination; they became completely demoralized on the field. At the other extreme, the Second Rhode Island Regiment, whose officers had paid exceptional attention to sanitary details and had enforced strict discipline, acquitted itself with distinction and returned to Washington in excellent condition in spite of heavy losses.

The Commission ordered the report printed for its members only, for whom it served as a guide in planning future activities. Later it was made accessible to the public as Document No. 28 of the Sanitary Commission.

I don't know about Cameron and the War Department, but the inefficiency of the Medical Bureau is criminal and scandalous. Its super-annuated officials are paralyzed by the routine habits acquired in long dealing with an army of ten or fifteen thousand and utterly unequal to their present work. Ten days ago there were not in or about Washington medicines, beds, or hospital provision of any kind for 300 additional patients, though the head of the bureau admitted that any hour might bring on a great battle and 5,000 or 20,000 cases to be provided for. "They could send to New York for medicine," and so on. The fogies of that department manage it in the spirit of a village apothecary. But the day after the skirmish at Lewinsville (last week) some half-dozen wounded men were brought in, and the Medical Purveyor (Dr. Lamb) wrote us that the Medical Department was "out of bandages" and begged for a supply from our storehouse. Old Finley, the head of that office, is utterly ossified and useless. The next available man on the list is our excellent, warm-hearted colleague, Dr. Wood. His main defect is blind, fanatical loyalty to his chief, Finley. If the Commission oust Finley, I doubt whether Wood could be prevailed on to take his place. Dr. Tripler, McClellan's Medical Director, is an energetic, spasmodic, crotchety, genial old gentleman. . . .[17] He might be made to do as head of the Bureau. He would certainly do better than its present wooden head. But Mc-Clellan, in conference with Bellows and Bishop Clark, hinted a doubt of his capacity. He was with McClellan after the little Centreville skirmish, and sat on his horse ten minutes in full view of a wounded man who lay on the ground with a shattered tibia or femur or some such thing, and never offered to dismount. This little omission seems to have settled Tripler in McClellan's estimation.

"We, the Commission" think well of McClellan. His activity and industry and attention to details may not be equivalent to military genius, but are of great practical value nevertheless. He has a talent for silence. Nobody knows whether he has 100,000 or 250,000 men in camp around Washington. I discovered for myself that there were great fieldworks going up on the east side of the city, the Maryland side. They were unknown to the gossipers of Willard's.

I left Washington early Saturday morning by railroad. Stopped at Baltimore. Breakfasted, took a carriage, and visited the new fieldworks

[17] Surgeon Charles S. Tripler acted as Medical Director of the Army of the Potomac from August 12, 1861, until July 1, 1862. McClellan valued him highly as a staff officer.

on Federal Hill and Duryea's red-legged Zouaves (now [Col. G. K.] Warren's, Duryea being a brigadier-general), and drove to Fort McHenry, where I found General Dix in a most jolly frame of mind over his arrest of seceshers. The Maryland legislature is seized and locked up.

September 23, MONDAY. I'm resigned to speedy and total insolvency. War, taxes, and cessation of business will have done their work before long. Poverty will soon drive me to enlist, if patriotism does not; and then, if I survive the war, I will set up a street microscope exhibition. I recur for consolation to the remembrance of my microscopic experiences at Savin Rock. I never bottled so rich a tablespoonful of mud and water as I got from a certain salt-water ditch in the meadow behind the hotel. It produced, *inter alia*, a profusion of that marvellous, self-acting carpenter's rule, *Bacillaria paradoxa*, sliding about in the liveliest way.

Tonight, Bellows, Gibbs, Van Buren, and Agnew were here in the library in council. Slight supper thereafter, with Ellie presiding and very happy. Our reformation of the Medical Bureau does not make headway, but rather drifts to leeward. McClellan is so busy and Mr. Secretary Cameron so slippery that it is hard to get decided action from either. So the Medical Bureau continues to be an invertebrate organism, with Finley for its head. General Frémont seems to have set up a local Sanitary Commission of his own at St. Louis, "to act under the direction of Miss Dix." Success to its action, regular or irregular. There is plenty of work to do. This has doubtless been got up by that indefatigable woman. She is disgusted with us, because we do not leave everything else and rush off the instant she tells us of something that needs attention. The last time we were in Washington, she came upon us in breathless excitement to say that a cow in the Smithsonian grounds was dying of sunstroke, and she took it very ill that we did not adjourn instantly to look after the case.

Bad news from Missouri. Hard fighting at Lexington and Colonel Mulligan compelled to surrender to a much superior force. There is room for doubt, but it is safe to believe reports of disaster. Frémont must look sharp or he will be superseded. Kentucky seems to pronounce distinctly for the nation. That is well, better than I hoped. But this is a doleful time, and I am intensely blue.

September 25. The bad news from Missouri confirmed, of course. Lexington is lost. People lay this to Frémont and hold him responsible for General Lyon's death and all that has gone wrong in the West since he took command of that Department. We pass quick judgment on our military leaders. Two months ago we reposed implicit confidence in Scott and McDowell. Both are condemned now as worthless, and we all swear by McClellan.

September 28. Visit from Bellows before breakfast. Knapp is in town and reports everything at Washington rose-colored; everybody in the best spirits and troops steadily improving in spirit and discipline. The Commission doing good service and in high favor with all military authorities. Olmsted telegraphs that McClellan is going on at once with hospital accommodation for 15,000 men. I think our plan for pavilion hospitals, which was sent off this week, has been adopted by the War Department. . . .

Mr. Ruggles here awhile this evening; that is, till 12:30, discussing a measure to be brought forward in next diocesan convention—some declaration or protest against secession of southern dioceses, or proclamation of the church's loyalty to government. He objects to any action influenced by feelings of personal kindliness toward misguided, deluded, or possibly coerced southern churchmen, and by that unhappy popular notion that "religion has nothing to do with politics," which seems to me practical atheism. Bishop Potter prefers that all action be postponed till next general convention, and so it will be, I suppose.

September 30. Olmsted's letters indicate that excitement and hard work acting on a sensitive, nervous temperament are making his views morbid. He sees only present imbecility and future inevitable disaster. Seems to think the army a mere mob; War Department, paralyzed by corruption; Navy Department, ditto, and so forth.

We do not meet the revolutionary energy of the South with a corresponding intensity and unanimity, but I think the government seems trying to do its work honestly and diligently. . . .

October 2. Higby, an old friend of Frémont's, is inclined to think him unequal to his great place. I fear Higby is right. Frémont's recently published letters are weak. His great published catalogue of his staff, with an "Adlatus" and a "Musical Director," is characteristic of a vain, ostentatious, weak man, intoxicated with the importance of his high position. It is unfortunately very high and important. If we lose Missouri, we lose all that lies west of it, even to the Pacific, and are no longer a continental nation. It looks just now as if we were fast losing Missouri and Kentucky, too.

October 4. Meeting at Dr. Bellows's this evening—the Sanitary Commission; Bellows, Van Buren, Agnew, Gibbs, and that invaluable

Knapp of Walpole, New Hampshire, one of our inspectors.[18] He's of a type rarely met among us; energetic, intelligent, self-sacrificing, but shy and timid when not in his work, and deficient in social self-assertion. Not unlike Tom Pinch in Dickens's *Martin Chuzzlewit.*

Letters indicate that our business at Washington is going on favorably. Our plans for pavilion hospitals seem to have been referred to Tripler by the War Department and approved by him. They will provide for 15,000 men. Tripler tells Olmsted that "for their hospital clothing, he must rely on the stores of the Commission"—a pretty confession, indeed! It is time now for another money-grabbing movement. The influx of cash has become feeble of late, and we must stimulate the current with a few circulars and advertisements.

Frémont is not superseded in the least, nor is he ordered to Washington. That is certain. I think government is right in this. A change of commanders just at this crisis would be *prima facie* wrong. When the storm is at a maximum, it is a bad time to change one's umbrella. And it would seem from the newspapers that Frémont's personal popularity in the West is an important feature of the case. Reports of his removal were ill-received at St. Louis.

October 8, TUESDAY. Olmsted came to town Saturday night, but I have not yet seen him. Dr. E. Harris seems to be doing harm by his private communications with the Medical Bureau and Dr. Tripler about hospital buildings.

October 12. Last evening a Sanitary dinner here; Gibbs, Olmsted, Bellows, Van Buren, Agnew. The session seemed agreeable; lasted into this morning, though only a little way. We were discussing the work we have got to do at Washington next week. We must reinvigorate the movement to turn out Surgeon-General Finley, and we must devise means and employ special agents to make the allotment system more fruitful of results. The health of the army will be improved if pay be more generally sent home to wives or mothers of the soldiers or to savings

[18] Of the early inspectors employed by the Sanitary Commission, Dr. Buell was sent to St. Louis, Dr. Aigner to Cairo, Illinois, Dr. Douglas to the forces of Banks in northern Virginia, and Dr. Tomes and Frederick N. Knapp to the Army of the Potomac. Knapp, whom Stillé, the Commission's historian, called "a large-hearted man, as quick in action as he was generous in impulse," played a leading rôle in the development of the Commission's Special Relief Service, which he initiated in the summer of 1861 when he found sick soldiers abandoned by their comrades in the Washington railroad station and promptly cared for them. As will be seen in the diary, his important work for the Commission later became marred by difficult personal relationships.

banks, instead of being expended in the purchase of bad pies and rot-gut whiskey; and the health of the community will gain in like measure if these remittances can be made more general, for they will go far to avert the disease of pauperism with which we are threatened.

October 13, SUNDAY.   General Burnside is in town. Missed tonight's train to Washington. Says there is to be another reconnaissance in force tomorrow—an offer of battle, which the rebels will not accept. Gunboats and transports have been leaving the harbor yesterday and today to rendezvous at Annapolis and Fort Monroe. Twenty thousand men are said to be ready for embarkation on the Chesapeake.

Dr. Hammond, U.S.A., of Baltimore, is in town.[19] Only an Assistant Surgeon, but he has had intimations from the War Department that the last may be first, and that he *may* take Dr. Finley's place. . . . Dr. Bellows thinks well of him.

Another gap now occurs in Strong's diary, occasioned by a fresh trip to Washington; but he fills much of it by a retrospective survey on his return, under date of October 23. The Sanitary Commission was still faced with a critical situation. General McClellan, to be sure, had ably reorganized the army and was imparting to it a fine spirit of discipline. Frederick Law Olmsted, the capable General Secretary of the Commission, was able to report in September that army regulations were being enforced with ten times the zeal previously used and that the results were excellent. "Even the demoralized regiments, with but very few exceptions, are now in better condition, better spirit, in better health, than they were when they received the order for the advance on Bull Run. The very measures which the Commission urged, which it was said could not be enforced, would not be submitted to, and would be useless with volunteers, are now rigidly enforced, are submitted to with manifest satisfaction by volunteers, and are obviously producing the most beneficent results, and this equally in the new and the older regiments."

[19] Here appears a figure soon to dominate many pages of the diary. William Alexander Hammond (1828–1900), the first eminent American neurologist and a great figure in medical education, had been born in Annapolis and had received his medical training in New York. Entering the army as assistant-surgeon in 1849, he served for ten years at various Western posts. Then he resigned to teach and practice in Baltimore, but on the outbreak of the Civil War again enlisted. After organizing a hospital in Baltimore, he attracted attention by his efficient work as inspector of camps and hospitals under Rosecrans in West Virginia. A man of rugged energy, keen mind, and determined will, he seemed just the person to replace the feeble, petulant Finley.

But prodigious labors remained to be accomplished; and they could hardly be carried through until the head of the Medical Bureau of the Army, Surgeon-General Finley, who was accurately described by Strong as "utterly ossified and useless," could be replaced. His personal character was excellent, his former services creditable. But he had been trained to minister to the medical needs of an army of ten or fifteen thousand men; and he recoiled from the radical changes required for the great hosts now in uniform. A lover of routine and red tape, he resented the interference of this novel and anomalous volunteer agency, the Sanitary Commission. Fortunately the Commission had the warm co-operation of General McClellan. Most of its recommendations this fall—its proposal that the head of the Army of the Potomac be allowed to select his own Medical Director, independent of the Medical Bureau, and its suggestion that McClellan also be allowed to create an "Ambulance Regiment" were of special importance—fell upon deaf ears. The War Department ignored them. As a result, the horrors of the Peninsular campaign the next spring were greatly increased. But McClellan supported the Commission's plan of keeping a staff of expert Inspectors of Camps busy in the field, making sure that proper principles of camp sanitation were observed. Both he and the War Department accepted the Commission's recommendations for the erection of a great system of military hospitals built on the "pavilion plan" and properly staffed. The Commission was accomplishing a great deal.

October 23, WEDNESDAY. . . . The Commission no longer occupies its room in the Treasury, having outgrown it. Government has hired for us, in addition to our storehouse, the old rambling three-story "Adams House" for our offices and council room. It is now being repaired, polished up, and papered, and will make commodious headquarters. We met there. Dr. Wood, an excellent, loyal old gentleman, Bishop Clark, Dr. Howe and Dr. Newberry attended, beside our New York members. Colonel Cullum was out of town, and we saw little of that inveterate red-tapist Major Shiras.

The business before us was to kick out the Surgeon-General; to get our hospital plans approved and the work of erecting them begun; to get increased efficiency put into the allotment system, and so encourage volunteers to send their pay home to their families and check the growth of pauperism instead of spending it in the sutler's tent to the detriment of their own condition, moral and sanitary. We worked efficiently toward these several ends and made good progress, though without absolutely attaining either.

As to our groups of one-story pavilion hospitals, we overcame the protest against their cost by demonstrating that it did not very much exceed the aggregate of exorbitant rents paid for old buildings (unfit for hospital purposes and sure to become pesthouses when it shall become necessary to close their windows), and the expense of alterations and ventilating arrangements that would be defective and insufficient at best.

General Meigs (the ablest man I have seen in Washington) spent a morning with us discussing this and other subjects. He is very uneasy about the iron-plated rebel steamer *Merrimac*; thinks we have only two guns that can make any impression on her, the Union Gun at Monroe and another that is not yet mounted. Expects her to sally forth "on the rampage" in a few days, shell the camp at Newport News, pass Fort Monroe, and play the devil. If he is right and she is invulnerable, there is no reason why she should not steam up the Narrows and lay this city under contribution.

Dr. Tripler was an early convert to the hospital scheme and brought over McClellan. They united in endorsing it to the extent of 5,000 beds, but ask for two groups of buildings instead of five. Tripler says they have not medical officers enough to take charge of more than two. We left the plan approved in writing by General Meigs, General McClellan, Dr. Tripler, and Cameron, and only waiting for Lincoln's endorsement, which Cameron insisted upon because of the large outlay involved. Cameron is sadly wanting in moral courage, and the first question he asks about any measure is, "What will the newspapers say?"

The Surgeon-General question is still undecided. Scott, the Assistant Secretary of War, is earnest for Finley's removal and Hammond's appointment. After the Committee adjourned (Saturday evening), Dr. Bellows and I stayed behind for an interview with Cameron Tuesday night. Cameron talked about the newspapers, demurred and hesitated about removing Finley, though admitting his utter imbecility to be most deleterious just now, and pronounced against Hammond most emphatically the moment he was named. "Whatever he did, he should not appoint *that* man." Some official pique or personal grievance was evidently in his mind. Then I brought up the allotment matter and suggested that the pension agents be charged with the duty of receiving and distributing monies sent home; but Cameron, though admitting the propriety of employing them and the immense importance of the work to be done, was afraid of the newspapers. "There would be a howl" about increasing the patronage of the department; he didn't think he could safely take any action about it. I don't know whether Cameron is corrupt or not, but he is certainly a most cowardly caitiff.

We had an audience of Lincoln from nine to eleven A.M. Thursday (I think it was Thursday). He is lank and hard-featured, among the ugliest white men I have seen. Decidedly plebeian. Superficially vulgar and a snob. But not essentially. He seems to me clear-headed and sound-hearted, though his laugh is the laugh of a yahoo, with a wrinkling of the nose that suggests affinity with the tapir and other pachyderms; and his grammar is weak. After we had presented our views about the Surgeon-General, and after Lincoln had charged us with "wanting to run the machine" and had been confuted, Bishop Clark introduced the subject of exchange of prisoners. Of course, Lincoln replied that such exchange implied recognition of the rebel government as a legitimate belligerent power, and spoke of the flag of truce sent out to recover Colonel Cameron's body after the battle of Bull Run, and of General Scott's reluctance to send it. The General said he had always held that if he fell in battle, he should be quite satisfied to rest on the battlefield with his soldiers.

Poor old Scott, by the way, is sinking. Grows lethargic, sleeps half the day, and entertains certain jealousies of McClellan.[20] His career is finished. Had a talk with poor McDowell. Still sore and morbid about Bull Run.

Another matter was the schismatic St. Louis Sanitary Commission, appointed by General Frémont on his own authority with plenary powers, ignoring our authority derived from the War Department. It's an excellent board of five or six prominent St. Louis men. The Secretary of War, being only too happy to snub Frémont, sent him orders to revoke this appointment or to instruct his local commission to report to us, neither of which he has done yet. Of course, all we want is to keep the peace and secure concert and unity of action; so I telegraphed them to send us one of their number with power to treat and adjust all matters in controversy. They sent us their chief, the Rev. Dr. Eliot of St. Louis, a Unitarian

---

[20] Scott was, in fact, ill as well as aged. On these jealousies, see *McClellan's Own Story*, New York, 1887, p. 136 ff. The Assistant Secretary of War mentioned above was Thomas A. Scott (1824–1881), who had been one of the principal architects and executives of the Pennsylvania Railroad, and who performed invaluable services first under Cameron and later under Stanton.

philosopher and a great man in his own city.[21] He is fluent and plausible, fond of power, and with a mental apparatus constructed on a curiously illogical, feminine plan. He appeared to us Wednesday evening in high wrath at our interference. His dignity was cruelly abraded, and he talked of appeasing it by the sacrifice of the sanitary interests of the Western Division. He and his colleagues would probably feel it due to themselves to abandon their work and leave the field to us. To be sure, we should probably be able to do very little with all the local feeling of St. Louis against us, and so on. We represented that we had no notion of interfering with them, that we only wanted to do what the War Department had entrusted to us all, that no appearance of wrong ought to be done just now to the principles of national unity. He was fractious and petulant, and we spent one evening in a very jolly little discussion, Bellows our chief speaker. Bellows and Eliot are in some sense professional rivals, and clawed each other in an urbane, velvety, brotherly, Christian way. Dr. Vinton (whom we invited to the honors of our sitting as an associate) put in his oar once or twice more efficiently than I expected. James W. Beekman and Dr. [Edward] Hartshorne of Philadelphia were also present as associate members, but said little. I gave Eliot one or two touches on the jaw that seemed to tell. He hauled off a little after midnight much shattered and in an ill humor. But he was in a better frame next day, and I guess our proposition will be well received; namely, to make one of the St. Louis men a full member of the Commission and to let them retain their organization as a local auxiliary board.

There was sharp fighting near Leesburg Monday. We crossed the Potomac and encountered the rebels in superior force. Poor Colonel Baker was killed, and Cogswell of the regulars, who married Miss Susan Lane a year ago, was wounded and made prisoner. General Burnside told me last evening that it was a substantial success; that we have crossed the Upper Potomac and are entrenching ourselves on that side, but have lost three guns, a rifled cannon, and two mountain howitzers, and have

[21] Actually William Greenleaf Eliot was a man of distinction and character. Born in New Bedford, Mass., in 1811, he became a Unitarian minister in St. Louis, established Washington University there, was head of the St. Louis school board, and served many civic and philanthropic enterprises. Cooperating with Frémont in the establishment of the Western Sanitary Commission in September of this year, he gave that body ten years of unpaid labor. Strong may have been misled by his small, frail physique and nervous manner. It is probable that Strong would have found the society of his Anglo-Catholic grandson, T. S. Eliot, more congenial.

suffered a good deal, generally. It is an obscure story as yet. Knapp and Dr. Douglas left Washington at four this morning on horseback with a wagon load of hospital stores, and I came rather near going with them.

October 29. The Grand Armada was still in Hampton Roads Saturday. This pause does not seem strong proof of high military capacity in Commander duPont and General Sherman, but perhaps it is all right. The report that these commanders have been "sowld" by a treacherous official who ran away with the sealed orders in his pocket that show their destination is still current.

It's our great misfortune that the North is not yet thoroughly purged of spies and traitors. I could name a dozen people in this city whom I believe fully capable of conveying intelligence to the rebels. There are commissioned officers of high grade in army and navy whom many distrust; among them, I'm sorry to say is L.W. He is most unjustly suspected, no doubt, but we have colonels and navy captains now in active service who would have no serious objection to seeing the rebels triumphant. . . .

A telegraph operator called on Wolcott Gibbs Saturday with a singular story. He was lounging about the streets of Alexandria on the 21st or 22nd when he heard the familiar tapping of a telegraph, and being a sound-reader, stopped to listen. It was the army telegraph and he heard it tell the story of the Leesburg defeat, and heard, moreover, one or two important orders from headquarters. Most experienced telegraph operators are sound-readers, and this gross want of precaution may account for the rebels having been forewarned of certain intended movements; for example, that on Munson's Hill. The Secretary of War has been duly notified of this.

November 2. Last night a Sanitary Commission meeting at Dr. Bellows's; Van Buren, Agnew, Gibbs, Olmsted, Professor Bache, and myself. I believe the Surgeon-General kicked the Medical Director out of his office, or something of the sort. Very likely Tripler deserved it. General Scott retires and McClellan is Commander-in-Chief. Saw a letter from Washington tonight stating that Colonel [E. D.] Baker had a major-general's commission in his pocket when he fell, that he knew Scott was to retire, that he advanced in disobedience of his orders hoping to gain a brilliant success, and so to be appointed to Scott's place over McClellan's head. It would be incredible but for the fact that he was intimate with Lincoln and is believed to have possessed great influence with him. *Quam parva sapientia,* and so forth! Baker was undoubtedly eaten up by inordinate personal ambition.

November 4, MONDAY. Cullum[22] says Scott actually means to go abroad for the sake of some ailment that he wants treated by Parisian surgery and which Van Buren says can be as well treated here.

This will be an ugly blot at the end of Scott's bright record. Cullum regrets it and has remonstrated in vain. He says Charles King has more influence with the General than any other man. Mr. Ruggles will enlist Charles King in the service. His flight will do us harm abroad. He goes with his daughter and son-in-law, Colonel Henry Scott, who is just put on the retired list because of certain apocryphal piles. Both sympathize with secession. *Punch* will picture the General as a rat leaving a sinking ship.

November 5. Charles King has seen General Scott, who says, "You distress me, sir," and adheres to his fatal determination.

November 6. General Frémont is superseded and notifies his army of the fact in a becoming and dignified general order that is exactly what it should be. I suppose his removal was a necessity, even at this moment, and in the face of the enemy and with mutiny imminent as its consequence. Frémont has undoubtedly shown lack of discretion and foresight. He is in the hands of California gamblers and speculators, many of whom are his creditors. But it was a most lamentable necessity and will probably be followed by the retreat or defeat of his disgusted army. He seems to possess a personal magnetic influence over his subordinates, if he have no other qualification for command.

The criticisms on his memorable proclamation are absurd. I wonder if the government has sent out a real estate agent with the naval expedition to arrange for a temporary hiring of the land on which 15,000 men are to be encamped and has instructed General Sherman not to disembark his troops till a proper ground for their occupation is secured with all respect for the legal and constitutional right of the proprietor? If not, why should it treat rebel slave property with more delicate consideration than other property of rebels?

November 8, FRIDAY. Went to Philadelphia yesterday at two P.M. Steamboat to Amboy with Professor Bache, Dr. Bellows, Olmsted, Agnew, and Van Buren. Detained near Burlington; reached Continental (admirably appointed hotel) at seven P.M., and after gulping down a cup of tea, proceeded to Horace Binney's, who had convened some thirty or

---

[22] George W. Cullum (1809–1892), a West Point graduate now acting as aide to General Scott with the rank of major; now best remembered for his monumental *Biographical Register* of West Point graduates and officers.

forty solid men of Philadelphia, professional and financial, to meet us and consult as to organizing our associates in that city for action in aid of the Sanitary Commission. I knew few of them. There were Caleb Cope, Henry Carey, Judge Hare, Dr. John McClellan (the General's brother), Dr. Meigs, Dr. Gurney Smith, Sam Powel, Dr. ⌈H. W.⌉ Ducachet, Dr. ⌈W. H.⌉ Furness, and others. Bishop Alonzo Potter took the chair, and we of the Commission made statements and explanations. Dr. Bellows, Dr. Van Buren, and Professor Bache delivered themselves very effectively. The result was the appointment of committees, and so forth. It may or may not lead to something substantial. Binney is not well enough to do much work, and Dr. Hartshorne, though very willing, does not look like an efficient man. . . .

Leaving the Jersey ferry boat this afternoon, we met the distinguished Charles Sumner. He says he knows the instructions given to General Sherman as to his relations with the contrabands of the district he is to occupy and all the secret history of their discussion and settlement in the Cabinet, and that they are equivalent to *Emancipation*. We shall see. I put no great faith in Sumner, and we may as well effect our landing and secure our foothold before we consider that question. I observe that the word "contraband" has established itself in a new sense as designating a class of biped mammalia. This we owe to General Butler. "Secesh" is another novelty that may become classical English.

November 9. General Scott sailed for Europe this morning, in spite of remonstrances. I doubt his return. He is very shaky. Received $900.00 for the Sanitary Commission today from the little city of Troy, and more coming.

November 11. Last evening was pleasant. We had at supper George Allen, Mr. Ruggles, Murray Hoffman, Dr. Cogswell, Schroeder (formerly minister to Sweden, a gentlemanlike, agreeable man), Henry Dorr, and Wolcott Gibbs. Schroeder is recommended by Cogswell as his successor in the Astor librarianship.

November 19. No special news these last few days. It would seem that our seizure of Mason and Slidell is within the rules of international law as laid down by British authorities and supported by British precedent. But I fear John Bull will show his horns and that we shall have increased ill-feeling on both sides. Foreign war would be an ugly complication of our internal disease. I have no respect for John Bull any more. He ought to be called John B. Pecksniff.

Dr. Jenkins, just from Washington, tells me McClellan is steadily moving ambulance trains to the front. Arrival from Port Royal today. We have not yet occupied Beaufort.

November 20.   We talk very stiffly about the capture of Mason and Slidell, but I greatly fear that it will give our mean cousin across the water an excuse for quarrelling with us. I am ashamed of England, if the *Saturday Review*, the *Times*, and *Blackwood* be exponents of English feeling.

November 24.   Death of Charles A. Clinton, DeWitt Clinton's son. A genial old fellow, not overwise; whilom clerk of Superior Court when I was a law student.

November 27.   Very diligent on Sanitary Commission affairs. Meeting of New York Commissioners here Monday evening, with Mr. Ruggles as *adlatus*. Have corrected and re-corrected proofs of a begging letter, a mendicatory whine some twenty pages long. Unless we, the Commission, be soon reinforced with money, we must begin to wind up, dismiss inspectors, and go into liquidation. Battle with the Surgeon-General is upon us at last. The *World* of a week ago published an attack upon his inefficiency. The *Times*, instigated, of course, by Dr. [Richard S.] Satterlee, U.S.A., defends him by assuming that the attack came from the Commission (which it didn't; it was Dr. Agnew's own private dab at red tape and mismanagement), and charges the Commission with presumption and ambition in assailing government officials and trying to supersede them. The *World* responded this morning in a damaging way. Other shots will follow, and from heavy ordnance.

November 28.   Were I dictator at this time, my military policy would be: 1. To defend and hold Washington, Western Virginia, Kentucky, Missouri; 2. To make a vigorous demonstration in support of the oppressed loyalty that survives in North Carolina and in Eastern Tennessee; 3. To recover and hold (or destroy with sunken ships) every port and inlet from Hatteras to Galveston. The inland forests of Georgia and Arkansas cannot be overrun and occupied, but the rebels of the South can be locked up and left to suffer and starve till they repent and beg pardon. That is our true policy; coupled with a true and just treatment of Southern niggerdom, that is, a proffer of freedom to every able-bodied slave owned by a rebel, it would kill rebellion slowly but surely.

The Sanitary Commission was making progress, and as Strong's entry above indicates, was also making some enemies. In the latter half of 1861 it organized separate departments to handle the various branches of its work; it put the labor of collecting supplies and money, establishing hospitals, furnishing battlefield relief, and gathering vital statistics on a systematic basis; and it recruited a corps of capable inspectors to serve as its field agents and planners. Upon the quality of these inspectors a great deal depended. "I trust," Strong had written Olmsted on July 8, "you have your eye on a few good intelligent, energetic men, professing plenty of tact and fertile in resources, to act as our agents." Several of the inspectors were men of high distinction; for example, the Rev. Robert Collyer, later a famous preacher—a brawny, great-hearted, iron-willed Yorkshireman, as sagacious as he was indefatigable. The inspection system came to be highly efficient.

But to place the medical and hospital services of the country on an efficient basis, an attack had to be levelled against what Strong called "the rigor mortis of the Medical Bureau" under its incompetent chief Surgeon-General Finley. A newspaper war on the subject began. As the diarist writes, Dr. Agnew struck the first blow with "his own private dab" against the prevailing mismanagement. Dr. Finley's side was taken by a somewhat hysterical young woman of New York named Miss Powell, who liked the old surgeon-general and disliked the incisive Olmsted. She inspired no less a personage than Henry J. Raymond of the Times *(rather susceptible to young women) to defend Finley; the* World *meanwhile battling hammer and tongs for reform.*

December 14, SATURDAY.   England seems wrathful about the seizure of Mason and Slidell, but disposed to admit that we were technically right. Soreness and irritation are increasing and may well lead to war somehow. England's last war was to uphold Mahometanism, her next may be in aid of slavery. It's a mean people.

Signs multiply of an opposition party, founded on anti-slavery feeling stronger than that of the Administration. I am content to leave that very delicate and difficult question in the hands of government, though my instincts seem to tell me that its present policy is weak, vacillating, and timid.

Memorabilia of Washington.   Off early on Friday, the 29th, with Ellie. . . . John Astor was with us, *en route* for Washington to enter on his novel duties as a volunteer aide to McClellan. He is a very fine fellow, were he tenfold a millionaire. Reach Washington comfortably and find excellent rooms, including a nice private parlor, secured us by Mr. Knapp.

Find also that the meeting of Sanitary Commission is adjourned to the following Tuesday. Thus I had a spare day or two to devote to the ladies. Took them to Alexandria and through Fort Ellsworth on Saturday. Next morning we went to St. John's Church, and I dined in the evening with General Keyes and Astor, who lives with him for the present.

There are officers of high position who do not hesitate to denounce General Scott as of lukewarm loyalty and more Southern than national. They say his intimate associates of last winter and spring, up to the very outbreak of the war, were all traitors; men like [Senator James M.] Mason of Virginia. Keyes was dismissed from his staff for advising about the reinforcement of Pickens at the President's request without Scott's privity. It is even said that Colonel Henry Scott disclosed to the rebels an intended move of McClellan's against Munson's Hill, thus enabling them to withdraw without loss, and that McClellan demanded the retirement of both the General and his son-in-law under threat of exposure. Hence the retreat of both to Europe. All this may be true or not, probably not. I do not believe Colonel Henry Scott knew anything about McClellan's plans, and though it is certain his heart has never been in the war, he has always seemed to me a man of the highest honor and principle. I'm almost ashamed to have recorded the existence of so shameful a story.

The next (Monday) morning with the ladies to camp of Sixth Cavalry (Regulars) to see parade and drill. Colonel [William H.] Emory (Bache's brother-in-law), lately suspected of secessionism, in command. Lawrence Williams, major. One of the captains, [Charles Russell] Lowell of Boston, a notably promising officer, admired and commended by the regular brethren as the best appointment ever made from civil life. Clarence Cram is in the same regiment and working hard to fill a position for which his physique and all his former habits rather tend to disqualify him. Last Sunday morning we drove across the river; heard services at a Massachusetts camp. . . . Then to Arlington House, where we had a long talk with General McDowell and Mrs. McDowell, whom I knew a little at West Point ten years ago. She has not gained in personal beauty. Poor McDowell is still sore about Bull's Run, and insisted on shewing us his military maps and how he had ordered one division to advance on this road and another on that, and how they would certainly have cut off and destroyed one of the enemy's advanced brigades of South Carolina soldiers, only they were dilatory in advancing. . . .

The Commission met Tuesday and sat till Saturday night. I remained to help Olmsted with his Report to the Secretary of War, and worked harder than I've done for years, writing steadily from Sunday afternoon till Thursday night every day till midnight, Wednesday evening alone excepted. I traced out most of the ground and left a great pile of crude MS matter for Olmsted to polish into shape and comeliness. It will be an interesting and valuable paper, I think.

The old Surgeon-General has been making war on us through the *Times*. [Henry J.] Raymond is his personal friend. The attack has done us little harm. "Woe unto you when *all* men speak well of you." If one's attack on a hornet's nest be really vigorous and useful, one must expect to be buzzed about, at least, if not severely stung.

Ground for our model hospitals was duly staked out a week ago last Tuesday, but they are not yet begun. Some red-tape tangle interferes.

Health of the army continues tolerably good. But the practice of closing tents tight against cold is producing some little show of pure typhus, and the murderous folly of sending cases of measles and other ailments into the smallpox hospital at Kalorama has naturally infected several regiments with variolous disease. The wretched, inefficient, ill-provided Medical Bureau issued its "last crust" (of vaccine virus, to wit) last Saturday.

Our great want just now is funds for the Sanitary Commission. Its treasury is fast running dry. There are indications that money is beginning to come in more freely, but unless Philadelphia and Boston be prompt and liberal, the Commission will have to wind up its affairs at once.

Opdyke is mayor, Wood having failed of reëlection by a close shave. I have no sort of faith in Opdyke, but he is certainly not proven to be quite as bad as his predecessor.

December 16, MONDAY. This has been a day of perturbation. The rumor of last night's supper table was confirmed by the morning papers. John Bull is rampant about the capture of Mason and Slidell and demands their restoration with an apology. Some think war inevitable. I do not. But I think it probable that within thirty days our chief solicitude will be not the army of the Potomac, but the harbor of New York, and the question whether we can stop iron-plated steamers from coming up the Narrows and throwing shells into Union Square.

It would be an immeasurable calamity, and I fear England is bent on war and cotton, and is merely availing herself of this pitiful technical pretext. If so, the calamity cannot be averted and we must prepare to meet it as grimly as we may. But the bitterness of the blow is in its coming from England and in its shattering so many traditions of loyalty and respect. That England, after all her professions of philanthropy and civilization and humanity and liberation, should turn upon us in our struggle for national life against this foul conspiracy of nigger-breeding, woman-flogging oligarchs, whose sole pretext for rebellion is that they are forbidden to make slavery national and extend its area!

December 19.   Wasted two hours tonight with Dr. Peters in the *Tribune* office, waiting to see Dana—in vain. I want to enlist the *Tribune* against the *Times,* which continues to defend the imbecile Medical Bureau by the dirtiest little suggestions of hostility to the Sanitary Commission. Raymond of the *Times* tells Dr. Agnew frankly and unblushingly that he is obliged to take this position because Dr. Finley is a friend of his. So it seems the Medical Bureau will neither do its special duty and protect our soldiers nor allow a volunteer organization to make up for its shortcomings.

But for the threatened interference of England in aid of the slave-breeding and woman-flogging interests, I should think the national prospects brightening. As it is, they look dark. I fear England wants a pretext for breaking up our blockade of Southern ports and supplying her manufacturers with cotton. So much for British philanthropy and humanity. This generation must pass away before we forget the baseness of England toward her own children in this hour of their trial and distress.

I have always been Anglophile and Anglomaniac, but I am disillusionated now. I feel like repudiating the Archbishop of Canterbury and transferring my allegiance to the Patriarch of Constantinople. I sympathize with old G. C. Verplanck's Democratic father, who doubted in 1812 whether the American people ought to speak English. "Why should they not speak French or Dutch instead of that d—d anti-democratic language?"

December 23.   Vile weather, cold, wet, blowy, rainy, sleety. Walked uptown through it this afternoon in a cantankerous frame of mind, though I was buying Christmas presents. Very busy day, but among my duties was the receipt, acknowledgment, and deposit in the bank of $11,700 and upwards for the Sanitary Commission ($10,000 from Boston, $1,500 from the Pacific Mail Steamship Co., $200 from the generous little city of Troy).

The Washington *Republican* publishes a long, dirty attack on us and our operations, evidently under the inspiration of the Medical Bureau.[23]

[23] This journal, though in no sense an Administration organ, had been established in Washington by certain Republican leaders when it became certain that their party would assume power.

It is so dirty and so manifestly malignant and spiteful that I think we ought not to make any reply. It is evidently from the same person who contributed a couple of articles to the New York *Times* over the signature of "Truth." . . . Pity that Bureau will neither do its official duty nor permit volunteers to help it without throwing filth at them. But I care little about this attack, except so far as it may diminish the influx of funds into our treasury, and we are now strong in money. If we can only secure decent attention by the government to the health of our volunteers, my character and repute may take care of themselves. Damage to them is a very trifling matter in comparison, and I do not expect they will suffer very seriously.

December 29, SUNDAY. Last night, Olmsted, Bellows, Van Buren, Agnew, and Gibbs were here taking counsel and supper together.

News. We surrender Mason and Slidell on the demand of our mean transatlantic cousin. The act will be generally approved, and will raise little or no protest or clamor here, notwithstanding [William H.] Russell's prophecy that the Administration could not stand against the wrath of the mob if it conceded what England so ungraciously demands. We are generally satisfied that the form of their capture was technically wrong, and that we cannot afford a controversy with England just now. The general acquiescence in this concession is a good sign. It looks like willingness to pass over affronts that touch the democracy in its tenderest point for the sake of concentrating all our national energies on the trampling out of domestic treason.

At a bank council last night, it was resolved to suspend specie payments tomorrow morning—a grave fact.

December 31. Poor old 1861 just going. It has been a gloomy year of trouble and disaster. I should be glad of its departure, were it not that 1862 is likely to be no better. But we must take what is coming. Only through much tribulation can a young people attain healthy, vigorous national life. The results of many years spent in selfish devotion to prosperous, easy money-making must be purged out of our system before we are well, and a drastic dose of European war may be the prescription Providence is going to administer.

NORTHERN ARMIES MOVE SLOWLY · FORT DONELSON AND
SHILOH : FAILURE OF McCLELLAN'S PENINSULAR CAM-
PAIGN · THE SANITARY COMMISSION MEETS
OFFICIAL OBSTACLES

———————❧———————

*Though Strong chafed much less than most Northerners, his diary in the
first weeks of the new year reflects the general impatience for an advance by
the Union armies. Since the beginning of November, McClellan had possessed
about 140,000 men in or near Washington, a force which he drilled most
thoroughly. But although the weather remained fine during November and most
of December, he had declined to move forward against the weaker Confederate
forces. Finally Lincoln, who shared the popular irritation, issued his famous
general order for a frontal movement by both the Eastern and Western armies
on February 22. In the East the state of the roads and other factors forbade its
execution, and it was not until early in April that McClellan, who had taken
his army of about 100,000 men to Fortress Monroe, began a cautious march up
the Peninsula between the James and York rivers to reach Richmond. His progress was painfully slow. In the West, fortunately, Grant evinced more energy.
The Confederate line was based upon Fort Henry on the Tennessee River and
Fort Donelson on the Cumberland, only eleven miles apart. During January,
Grant conceived a plan for cutting the line by capturing these two posts, and
thus throwing all western Tennessee open to his army. With the aid of a force
of gunboats he captured Fort Henry on February 6, and Fort Donelson ten
days later, taking more than 15,000 prisoners. John B. Floyd, who had been
Buchanan's Secretary of War, barely escaped. These were the first decided
successes of the war for the North, and they greatly heartened the people.*

*Strong's energies were now largely spent in the work of the Sanitary Com-
mission, which had been carried forward to a point where its future usefulness*

depended upon the reform of the Medical Bureau of the Army. The Commission was doing all that it could independently. It sent agents to accompany the expeditions of Burnside against Roanoke Island, of Sherman against Port Royal, and of Ben Butler against New Orleans; these men, with inspectors and relief officers also supplied by the Commission, doing everything in their power for the health and comfort of the troops. Sanitary Commission stores were judiciously distributed. The Commission had set a number of the most eminent medical men of the country to work on a series of brief treatises furnishing the latest and most expert information on the treatment of disease. But it was clear that while the Medical Bureau continued under an incompetent head, with an inadequate, ill-trained, and elderly staff of surgeons who, for the most part, had stagnated in garrisons for decades, the care of the sick and wounded would be wretched. New personnel was needed at once—officers chosen without regard to the paralyzing rule of seniority, which gave the leadership to old men. In addition, it was important that the Medical Bureau, when once reorganized and invigorated, be granted fuller powers. The Quartermaster's Department of the Army controlled the construction and equipment of the hospitals; the Subsistence Department controlled the supply of food. Yet the Medical Bureau had no control, direct or indirect, over the policy or action of either of these departments. A hurried campaign of education had to be pressed to enlighten Congress upon the defects of the existing system and the need for radical reforms; siege had to be laid to the Military Committees of both houses of Congress; and the aid of the President and Secretary of War had to be enlisted. The attention of the government was engrossed by other subjects which seemed more important, while the old fogies of the Medical Bureau declared that the clamor against the existing defects was greatly exaggerated. But by unremitting effort, Strong (who wrote editorials, buttonholed men of influence, and joined deputations to Washington), and his associates finally achieved the needed reforms.

January 2, THURSDAY.   It was a pleasant day, but in these times one cannot get rid of the presence of national peril. Even when one gives up a whole day to mere amusement, he is haunted by a phantom of possible calamity and disgrace. . . .

William H. Russell of the London *Times* dined at the New York Club last evening on the invitation of Samuel Ward and others. His presence stirred up a little row outside the dining room. Fred Gibert and George Anthon denounced his entertainers' bad taste in extending the hospitalities of the Club to a man who was writing slanders against us and our cause to the most important newspaper in Christendom. The difference was assuaged, I hear, by drinks all round. But we are beginning to hate England and Englishmen, not without reason. The course of the English press has been flagitious, but perhaps the newspapers of England misrepresent the feelings and sympathies of England.

January 9. This evening a meeting of associate members of the Sanitary Commission at the Century Club; about sixty present. A highly respectable lot, including such men as Minturn, McCurdy, Jonathan Sturges, and a large delegation of doctors. Opdyke, our new mayor, presided. There was good discourse from Bellows, Van Buren, Ordronaux, Mr. Ruggles, Dr. Osgood, and others, and we passed, with great unanimity, a series of strong resolutions urging reformation in the Medical Bureau. Adjourned at eleven to a slight refection downstairs.

January 11, SATURDAY. We are expecting decisive news from the West. Movements down the Mississippi and up the Tennessee River and on Bowling Green (Kentucky) seem at hand. Congress will probably make the national paper money a legal tender. This is disastrous for certain classes of the community, including mortgagees like myself. It will probably destroy at least half of what property I possess. Taxes will absorb the other half. Never mind. I shall not complain if the nation be saved. But I miss a great leader, statesman, or general just now.

Saw Dana of the *Tribune* this morning and gave him another roll of manuscript thunder against that wretched Medical Bureau, which he says shall appear editorially.

January 15. The illustrious Hurlbut is released from the Richmond jail in which he has been detained as a suspicious character since last June. Cameron retires from the War Department and Stanton reigns in his place.

January 17. Last night with Van Buren, Agnew, and Gibbs at Dr. Bellows's. [F. S.] Winston, Stewart Brown, Mr. Ruggles, and Dr. Alonzo Clark with us. They (and Robert B. Minturn) are appointed, under the resolution adopted at our Century Club meeting, a committee to visit Washington and press the passage of the Medical Bureau Reform Bill. They seem ready to go, but we shall fail, however strongly backed. Neither Congress nor the President nor the people appreciate the importance of that measure. Nothing but a disastrous epidemic of camp fever, paralyzing the army and carrying death and dismay through the whole community (which the diseased army will infect), can purge their vision. Washington is already full of smallpox and typhoid disease. The fact may tend to wake them up. . . . We are very slow in learning to use the slave population. Paralyzed, I suppose, by fear of offending Kentucky. I should enlist and drill all black volunteers at Port Royal and elsewhere, were I Commander-in-Chief.

From reports by George Schuyler, Judge Daly, and others who have lately talked with generals at Washington, I think it probable there will be an advance and hard fighting before March 1. May God uphold the right! McClellan has a plan, unquestionably. Perhaps he is waiting till Burnside or the Port Royal division shall have cut one of the rebel lines of railroad transportation on the seaboard, and Buell shall have intercepted another in Eastern Tennessee, and the rebels are compelled by want of supplies to abandon their lines at Centreville. The chances are against them if they move forward. They can hardly hope to carry the fieldworks in front of Washington. If they fall back, they will speedily become demoralized and a pursuing army will convert their retreat into a rout. This may be the programme. But suppose we fail to cut these lines of railroad? Suppose the rebel army of the Potomac be still supplied after they are out?

January 20, MONDAY. Tomorrow morning early, or rather, late tonight, I'm off for Washington. We expect to organize a strong lobby there in favor of reforming the Medical Bureau. Delegations from New York and Philadelphia are to meet us there. Nobody has ever heard of the Medical Bureau, but it ought to be an important and respected and well-known bureau, and we hope to make it so. "We" hope, but as an individual, I despond. I have no faith in senators and secretaries and chairmen of military committees.

Evening papers announce a victory in East Kentucky. General [Albin] Schoepf encountered the rebel General [Felix K.] Zollicoffer, and there was a fight from the rising of the sun to the going down thereof. Rebels "effectively defeated." Zollicoffer killed. "Heavy loss on both sides."

Here occurs a gap of more than a week in the diary. Strong was in Washington, where the weather was abominable with fog and drizzle. "Roads across the Potomac impracticable by sightseeing visitors except on horseback; every camp-site reported an area of abysmal mud. An advance impossible just now. Mud of Washington streets in its highest perfection." He resumes the diary with a retrospective survey.

January 29, WEDNESDAY. This has not been a session of the Commission. Bellows, Van Buren, Agnew, and I went on to grease the wheels
of the New York and Philadelphia delegations and help them to urge
reform in the Medical Bureau. The muster was beyond my expectation.
From this city we had William H. Aspinwall, Robert B. Minturn, Stewart
Brown, F. S. Winston, J. W. Beekman, and others. Our Philadelphia
associates sent Judge Hare (Binney's brother-in-law and a notably attractive person), William Welsh, and a platoon of high caste doctors, including John McClellan, Gurney Smith, Stillé, LeConte, and others. We spent
two days mostly in council over the details of sundry bills now before the
Senate or the House, or got up by some of the Medical Bureau, and settled
at last the form of a highly concentrated bill embodying the minimum of
revolution. Thursday the new Secretary of War, Stanton, and General
McClellan spent a couple of hours with us. The General seems entirely
convalescent but looks careworn.[1] Stanton impresses me and everybody
else most favorably. Not handsome, but on the contrary, rather pig-
faced. At lowest estimate, worth a wagon load of Camerons. Intelligent,
prompt, clear-headed, fluent without wordiness, and above all, earnest,
warm-hearted, and large-hearted. He is the reverse in all things of his
cunning, cold-blooded, selfish old predecessor. Cameron looked like a
hybrid between Reineke Fuchs and some large chilly batrachian reptile,
but this is a live man, and of a genial robust Luther-oid type. He is most
fully committed in favor of reform, but doubts whether he can accomplish
anything till Congress acts. He is the most popular man in Washington
now, but will it last? The *Demos* begins to carp at McClellan, its idol six
months ago.

Senator [Henry] Wilson was with us a good deal; professes to be
the special friend and Senatorial agent of the Commission, and as chairman of the Military Committee, he is an important personage. But I
distrust him. He is full of little politic stratagems, lacks straightforward-
ness and sincerity and reliability. He is playing some kind of game with
us, which I do not comprehend.

We had a hearing before the House Committee on Monday, and before
the Senate Committee on Tuesday. Bellows the chief speaker, of course;
he presented the case forcibly and well. Both military committees seemed
impressed, if not convinced. But for my experience of the variety of all

---

[1] McClellan had been confined to bed for three weeks in December and January
with typhoid fever; "very weak and ill," he wrote later, but with "a clear intellect,"
so that he was able to give orders at all times.

assurances from politicians, I should feel sure satisfactory measures would be speedily carried. As it is, I expect nothing. It does seem not improbable, though, that old Finley, the Surgeon-General, will be retired or somehow eliminated. He has no friends that I can discover (except "Miss Powell"), and even the medical staff begin to admit he must be thrown overboard. Who would succeed him? Probably old Dr. Wood. This would be great gain, but Wood is far too old and too far gone in the ossification of routine to be fully fitted for the place.

Bellows and I called on the President yesterday to make the modest proposition that if any bill passed giving him power to appoint (doing away with the fatal principle of seniority), he would hear us before making any appointments. It was a cool thing. Lincoln looked rather puzzled and confounded by our impudence, but finally said, "Well, gentlemen, I guess there's nothing wrong in promising that anybody shall be heered before anything's done." We had the unusual good fortune to catch our Chief Magistrate disengaged, just after a Cabinet council, and enjoyed an hour's free and easy talk with him. We were not boring him, for we made several demonstrations toward our exit, which he retarded severally by a little incident he remembered or a little anecdote he had "heered" in Illinois. He is a barbarian, Scythian, yahoo, or gorilla, in respect of outside polish (for example, he uses "humans" as English for *homines*), but a most sensible, straightforward, honest old codger. The best President we have had since old Jackson's time, at least, as I believe; for Zachary Taylor's few days of official life can hardly be counted as a presidential term.[2] His evident integrity and simplicity of purpose would compensate for worse grammar than his, and for even more intense provincialism and rusticity.

He told us a lot of stories. Something was said about the pressure of the extreme anti-slavery party in Congress and in the newspapers for legislation about the status of all slaves. "Wa-al," says Abe Lincoln, "that reminds me of a party of Methodist parsons that was travelling in Illinois when I was a boy thar, and had a branch to cross that was pretty bad—ugly to cross, ye know, because the waters was up. And they got considerin' and discussin' how they should git across it, and they talked about it for two hours, and one on 'em thought they had ought to cross one way when they got there, and another another way, and they got quarrellin' about it, till at last an old brother put in, and he says, says he,

[2] A slip; Zack was President for sixteen critical months.

'Brethren, this here talk ain't no use. I never cross a river until I come to it.' "

I had a private "sifflication" to present on behalf of one George Dower, the husband of little Lewis's excellent, devoted nurse, Ellen. He was convicted a year and a half ago of manslaughter in causing the death of a seaman, he being mate of a merchant vessel, and sent to Sing-Sing for a term of years. The case is hard and doubtful, and I wanted to get his pardon. The papers were referred to the Attorney-General. "It must be referred to the Attorney-General," said A. Lincoln; "but I guess it will be all right, for me and the Attorney-General's very chicken-hearted!"

February 1.   The "legal tender" feature in the Treasury Note bill vigorously opposed but can hardly be defeated, I fear.[3] Mr. Ruggles keeps up a damaging cannonade against this disastrous, shortsighted project in the columns of the New York *World*. If it pass, the government should at once hire Union Square as a place to stack its paper money, for no building in the city is large enough to hold what will be spawned within three months.

February 4.   Fifty years hence John Brown will be recognized as the Hero or Representative Man of this struggle up to 1862. He will be the Wycliffe of the anti-slavery Reformation. A queer, rude song about him seems growing popular:

> John Brown's body lies a-mouldering in the grave (repeat)
> But his soul's a-marching on.
> Glory Hally Hallelujah,
> Glory Hally Hallelujah,
> But his soul's a-marching on.

February 8, SATURDAY.   Excellent tidings from Tennessee; Fort Henry, a rebel earthwork on the Tennessee River, bombarded and taken. . . . The war news is decidedly encouraging, but we are very blue indeed. Signs of speedy intervention (probably by France with pharisaical England looking cannily on) increase and multiply. The Treasury of the United States is vacuous, and the House has passed the "legal tender" bill. The Senate will not dare to dissent and thereby delay the supply of means. . . .

[3] The House Ways and Means Committee had reported a bill to make $150,000,000 of Treasury notes legal tender in payment of all debts public and private, and Chase, the head of the Treasury, supported it. Despite the opposition of Eastern bankers, merchants, and economists, it became law on February 25, 1862.

If the Virginia roads would but dry up for one week and enable Mc-
Clellan to advance! The chances would be at least three to two in favor
of his defeating the rebel hosts, and that would not only check interference from abroad, but break the backbone of all Secessiondom.

February 12. Laus Deo! The best day we have seen since war began.
The Norfolk papers announce Burnside's occupation of Roanoke Island,
the whole rebel force prisoners, the gunboats captured, and Elizabeth
City abandoned and burned; alleged severe loss on our side, but that is
doubtless magnified by rebel report. Burnside is pushing on, up Albemarle Sound, it would seem. Hurrah for Burnside! Even better than this
is the news from the West. Our gunboats have made their way up the
Tennessee River and into northern Alabama as far as Florence on an
unopposed reconnaissance, and found strong Union feeling manifested at
many points on the river. This seems reliable and is most important. I
did not expect it. Fighting is now probably going on at Fort Donelson
on the Cumberland River, which will probably be a tougher job than its
neighbor, Fort Henry. . . .

Louis Napoleon, in his allocution to his *Corps Législatif* (in "Bed of
Justice" assembled), talks non-intervention. Very good. Monday afternoon, everybody was astounded by the news that General [Charles P.]
Stone had been arrested. He is now in Fort Lafayette, charged, it is said,
with treasonable correspondence. Very marvellous. That there has been
treason somewhere in high quarters is certain, and if Stone be guilty, I
hope he may be speedily hanged. He has had certain strong Southern
affinities, vehement anti-Abolition tendencies, undoubtedly. Having been
under a cloud ever since the Ball's Bluff disaster, for which he was generally held responsible, rightly or wrongly, and sharply censured and
abused by the press and perhaps by his military superiors, it may be—it
is at least conceivable—that he has become disgusted with the cause of
the country and has listened to overtures from old friends in the rebel
army.[4] He was certainly not reputed a rebel when I saw him last June.
People then gave him credit for having saved Washington from an
irruption of wild Virginians, when the city was at their mercy and the
railroad torn up, by his presence of mind and forethought in taking military possession of certain steamboats running on the Potomac.

[4] This arrest was one of the most unjust official acts of the war. Anxious to find a
scapegoat for the defeat at Ball's Bluff, the Joint Committee on the Conduct of the War
seized on some malicious gossip and had this capable and patriotic officer placed in
solitary confinement in New York harbor; the War Department keeping him there
until late summer.

February 17. *Laus Deo* again! We are victorious at Fort Donelson. It was doubted by a few till one o'clock, when the *Commercial* bulletin-board confirmed the tidings (received via Norfolk, Fort Monroe, and Baltimore) by despatches from the West. The fort is taken. We have 15,000 prisoners; perhaps an exaggeration. Rebel loss in killed and wounded, 10,000; doubtless a vast exaggeration. Our loss heavy. Generals Albert Sidney Johnston, Buckner, and Pillow among the prisoners. Floyd said to have stolen away—more rumor. But Judge Daly tells me tonight that Floyd is reported caught. If so, what shall we do with him? Commit him to Barnum's custody as a special deputy United States marshal *pro tem.* for a consideration? He could be most profitably exhibited along with Commodore Nutt and the "What-Is-It?" The point of the exhibition would be intensified by employing a genteel Virginia contraband as exhibitor: "Ladies and Gemmen. Dis here remarkable specimen is Massa Floyd, who"—and so forth.

February 18. Meeting of Executive Committee of Sanitary Commission at Dr. Bellows's at two o'clock. Olmsted with us. We propose now to prepare, at least, to put our house in order, wind up our affairs, and resign. Government keeps no faith with us. From last July till this time, there has been a series of promises unperformed. We got our hospitals erected, to be sure; General Meigs kept his word with us. But that is the single exception. Mr. Secretary Cameron promised and re-promised reforms, but nothing was done. McClellan has promised us general orders "this afternoon or tomorrow," begging us always to tell him what we thought necessary at once, but he has issued nary order on our suggestion. So with Lincoln. So with Stanton. It is nearly a month since he pledged himself, with apparent warmth, to decisive steps that have not been taken to this day. We cannot go on asking the community to sustain us with money as an advisory government organ after six months' experience like this. I heartily approve of the proposition to resign. We have been shielding the Medical Bureau all this time from the hurricane of public wrath its imbecility would have raised by our volunteer work. Active operations are beginning now. The Bureau is still imbecile, notwithstanding all our remonstrances. For our own sake, we had better retire and leave the responsibility where it lawfully belongs.

Tonight with Ellie, Miss Rosalie, and Mrs. D. C. Murray to Gottschalk's concert at Niblo's Saloon. He has great command of the piano and could render real music admirably if he chose to play it. But he prefers pseudo-musical manifestations of physical strength and dexterous manipulation. His feats are surprising. But I think those of the Hanlon brothers and other like athletes more exciting, and those of Herrmann the Prestidigitator more amusing.

February 20. No news, except that General Grant has bagged another batch of 1,000 rebels innocently marching to reinforce Fort Donelson. But the captured General Johnston is not the genuine A. S. Johnston. He is a bogus Johnston, a "Bushrod Johnston" [Johnson] that nobody ever heard of. We have also caught a General Price in Missouri, but the real original Price (who is predisposed to diarrhoea) continues to evade us. We have chased him out of Missouri into Arkansas. There is a singular concurrence just now of reports and rumors, severally untrustworthy and probably unfounded, of things that indicate rebel collapse. Stories, for instance, that Governor [Isham G.] Harris of Tennessee orders all Tennesseans to lay down their arms, that several hundred Virginia rebels are marching to join the Army of the Potomac, that [Charles J.] Faulkner of Virginia has been making speeches against secession, that there are Union demonstrations in New Orleans and at Richmond. These are doubtless fictions, but they are novel fictions, and the appearance of so large a crop of fictions all pointing one way is remarkable.

Mr. Secretary Stanton's letter to the *Tribune* this morning is admirable.[5] No high official in my day has written a dozen lines half as weighty and telling. If he is not careful, he will be our next President! I think the Army of the Potomac is about moving, or trying to move, *non obstante* Virginia mud. The newspapers are goading McClellan, as they goaded Scott and McDowell last July. Heaven defend us from another premature advance and another Bull, or Bull-calf, run back again!

February 22, SATURDAY. Parade, jubilation, universal efflorescence of flags. Little business done in Wall Street. It was deserted by two o'clock, and I walked uptown with George Anthon, struggling through the crowd that obstructed Broadway. Tonight there was a quasi-illumination; in all the houses around Gramercy Park, the front window blinds and shutters were thrown open and the gas lit in every story. Effect quite brilliant. . . .

Yesterday at noon was hanged Gordon, convicted of piracy as a slave-

---

[5] Stanton's letter of February 19 protested against a *Tribune* editorial which gave him excessive credit for the recent victories. Attributing the successes to the gallant soldiers and officers who fought the battles, he declared that new gains would be won "by boldly pursuing and striking the foe."

EXECUTIVE COMMITTEE OF THE SANITARY COMMISSION

VAN BUREN   STRONG   BELLOWS   AGNEW   GIBBS

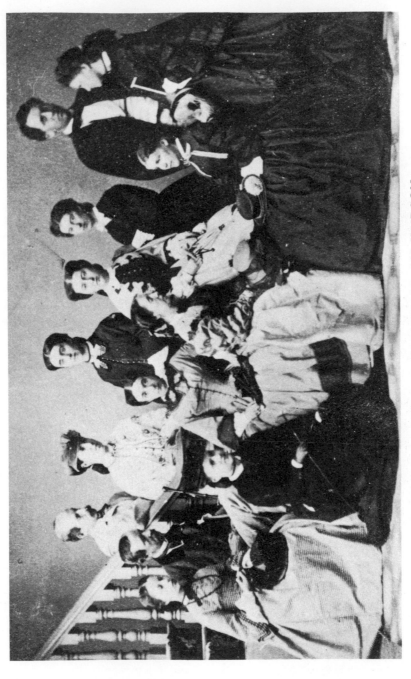

SUMMER GROUP AT CORNWALL-ON-HUDSON, 1863

Seated: MISS ROSALIE RUGGLES, HARRIS, MISS GERTRUDE STUYVESANT, MISS COLES, MRS. G. T. STRONG, MISS HATTIE CHURCH. *Standing*: JAMES F. RUGGLES, MISS LOUISA ANDERSON, FOUR NOT IDENTIFIED, MISS KITTY DIX

trader.[6] *"Vere dignum et justum est, dignum et salutare."* Served him right, and our unprecedented execution of justice on a criminal of this particular class and at this particular time will do us good abroad, perhaps with the pharisaical shop-keepers and bagmen of England itself. Immense efforts were made to get the man pardoned or his punishment commuted. Lincoln told me of them last January. He deserves credit for his firmness. The Executive has no harder duty, ordinarily, than the denial of mercy and grace asked by wives and friends and philanthropes. Gordon, poor wretch, made a very pitiful exit. He went to the gibbet half-dead with a dose of strychnine swallowed with suicidal intent and more than half-drunk with brandy. The doctors drenched him with stimulants and thus kept life in his body for the law to extinguish in due form. *Vivat lex*, and may it promptly exterminate every man who imports niggers into this continent.

February 27. Two significant advertisements in last night's papers from two steamboat lines. They discontinue their trips for the present, because the government has engaged all their vessels. For the Potomac? —or perhaps for the James and York rivers. It's said that heavy reinforcements have been sent to Fortress Monroe. The "mortar fleet" has mostly sailed for some port unknown. So has the Battery. Mrs. [John G.] Foster writes to Ellie, "You know the right wing has commenced moving."

March 16, SUNDAY. To Washington Tuesday, the 4th instant, at eleven o'clock in the evening with Agnew, who watched over my health and comfort kindly and assiduously. Bellows, Bishop Clark, Gibbs, Harris, and others of the Commission were already in Washington. Van Buren did not report himself till Saturday. Our sessions during that week were diligent. We had reports from inspectors, discussion of relations with the government, and of our financial prospects, and so on.

Saturday night at Mrs. Sedgwick's (wife of an Abolition member of Congress from western New York), where were Senator Foster and his wife, Mrs. Kemble and her most charming daughter Mrs. Wister, and others.[7] With the last-named lady I discoursed agreeably to myself, but "her awful mother I had in dread, and likewise my power of conversation was limited," so I exchanged no shots with the tragedienne. This was my only "social" experience.

Sunday came the news that Banks had occupied Leesburg, and a few

[6] Captain Nathaniel P. Gordon had commanded a slave-ship; previous offenders of the sort had escaped justice, but the government was now inexorable.

[7] Senator L. S. Foster of Connecticut (1806–1880); Charles B. Sedgwick of Syracuse (1815–1883); and the famous actress Fanny Kemble (1809–1893), with her daughter, the wife of Dr. Owen Jones Wister of Germantown.

minutes later the disastrous tidings that the *Merrimac* was on the rampage among our frigates in Hampton Roads, smiting them down like a mailed robber-baron among naked peasants. General dismay. What next? Why should not this invulnerable marine demon breach the walls of Fortress Monroe, raise the blockade, and destroy New York and Boston? And are we yet quite sure that she cannot? The nonfeasance of the Navy Department and of Congress in leaving us unprotected by ships of the same class, after ample time and abundant warning, is denounced by everyone.

Tea at Professor Bache's, where were [Edwin] Stevens of the Hoboken Battery and Professor [Joseph] Henry of the Smithsonian. Our talk was of floating batteries and mail-clad steamers, and of the maximum time needed to finish the Stevens battery. Henry approves of its design. He was the minority of the Commission that reported against it. The majority consisted of old bureaucratic fogies unable to receive a new idea unless trepanned for its introduction. Returning from Bache's, Eliot and Dr. Jenkins met me with news of the advent of the *Ericsson, sicut deus ex machina,* and that the *Merrimac,* new-baptized the *Virginia,* is beat back to her den, more or less damaged. We sent Judge [Mark] Skinner of Chicago (one of our new Western colleagues, and a decided acquisition) to the White House, being an old friend of Lincoln's, to make a casual call and fish for authentic news. He brought back intelligence of victory in Missouri, or in Northwest Arkansas. The President produced his telegram from Halleck and read it with this preface: "Here's the despatch. Now, as the showman says, 'Ladies and Gentlemen, this remarkable specimen is the celebrated wild he-goat of the mountings, and he makes the following noise, to wit.' "

Strong showed surprisingly little interest in the great battle between the Monitor *(which he referred to by the name of its inventor) and the* Merrimac *in Hampton Roads on March 9. This first engagement of iron-clad warships was epoch-making in itself, and by intimidating the* Merrimac, *which had destroyed two Northern ships like sitting ducks, the* Monitor *saved the remaining ships of the Union navy in this port and removed the fear of depredations on Northern ports.*

The victory in Arkansas was the defeat of General Van Dorn at Pea Ridge.

Monday morning we had a hearing before the House Military Committee on the bill to reform the Medical Bureau. Bellows blew an effective blast. [Frank P.] Blair and his colleagues seem heartily with us. The bill is a special order for next Tuesday. It has passed the Senate, but with paralyzing amendments we must get striken out. Thence to Bache's.

On our way home, we find a crisis at hand.[8] Army of the Potomac moving at last. All the reserves on this side of the river moving toward the Long Bridge. Artillery from near the Capitol down the Avenue and Fourteenth Street, a long line of rifled guns and caissons. Cavalry from the opposite direction. Regiment after regiment of infantry pouring down Fourteenth Street. These three lines converged at Willard's corner. There was a crowd of lookers-on assembled at that point, but none of the jollity and jubilation that cheered the premature and disastrous advance of July. People looked anxious, and soldiers looked as if they felt there was serious work before them, though rumors were already rife of general flight along the whole line of the rebellion. This was no bad sign. Perhaps the weather helped repress any unseemly manifestations of anticipated triumph, such as tempt the destinies. It was chill and overcast and gusty, with a wan sun struggling through cold, watery clouds. We watched the sky anxiously that night. There were indications of heavy rain early in the evening that suggested soaking bivouacs and roads yet more miry. But the clouds vanished at last, and the stars shone bright, and a drying northwest wind worked diligently on our side. The old English proverb, "a bushel of March dust is worth a King's ransom," which I met somewhere when I was a child and which fixed itself in my memory the more firmly perhaps because incomprehensible, is understood and appreciated now when we see a nation's life depending on practicable roads and the disappearance of mud.

Agnew and Gibbs departed Saturday. On Wednesday, we set forth for Centreville and Manassas and Bull Run. The rebels had abandoned the line they held so long. They seem to have begun retreating before we advanced. "The wicked flee when no man pursueth." Warned by the winds of Heaven that were making the roads of Virginia passable, the rebel host had broken up its cantonments and retired across the Rappahannock. Our party was Bellows, Van Buren, Olmsted, Rogers (of Boston, a wealthy stolid citizen who has left his home and taken up his abode in

---

[8] McClellan began his unhappy Peninsular Campaign by an advance, commencing March 10, 1862, upon Centreville. He writes in his memoirs that this was partly with the hope that he might bring Joseph E. Johnston to battle under favorable circumstances, "but also to break up the camps, give the troops a little experience in marching and bivouac before finally leaving the old base of supplies, to test the transportation arrangements and get rid of impedimenta, and thus prepare things for the movement to the Peninsula."

Washington to work for the Commission without pay), Dr. Chamberlain (one of our inspectors) and myself. The expedition took a carriage (driver Uncle Ned, whose services entitle him to the highest commendation), three saddle-horses, forage for man and beast, blankets, buffalo robes, and one revolver. We alternated between the carriage and the saddle. Left 244 F Street at eight o'clock in the morning Wednesday and crossed at Aqueduct Bridge. Roads miry and abominable till we struck the Alexandria and Fairfax turnpike. It was a bland, sunny day. Dined at Fairfax Court House al fresco. Great accumulation of troops there. It was far the largest exhibition of war I have yet seen. Camp after camp and long lines of brigade drill, and great columns moving over the dreary hillsides. Thence to Centreville over miry roads. Halted there and set off for Manassas. We got separated by mistake. Olmsted, Chamberlain, and Rogers, the equestrians, took the road to Blackburn's Ford. The rest of us, in the carriage, made for the Stone Bridge, plunging through perilous quagmires and vainly looking for our companions. At Cub Run we found the bridge burned and the ford dangerous in the uncertain evening light. No civilian on horseback had passed that way, as we were assured by certain contrabands marching northwards with bundles on their backs. So we reluctantly and anxiously retraced our steps to Centreville, meeting ghostly-looking cavalry pickets going off to their posts over the black plains.

All this region of Virginia is detestable, the meanest and most repulsive portion of this earth I have yet seen. Independent of damage from military occupation, it is nothing but mud, worn-out fields, mangy with broomsedge and sprinkled with ugly "loblolly pines," roads worthy of Chinese Tartary, and squalid houses. Centreville is the *ne plus ultra* of all this and has at present "neither horse meat nor man's meat nor a place to sit down." The one decent house is that of a Mr. Grigsby, an alleged Union man, carried off prisoner by the retreating rebel General Stuart, and of this we took possession. The rebels had cleared out most of its furniture, and our men had been taking liberties with the remnant. His contrabands wanted to have some Northern gen'l'men on the premises as a sort of protection. A couple of reporters were there, and one Alvord, a new government agent. The head of the colored family, "Aunt Polly," did her best for us and eked out our stock of provisions with corn-pone, bacon, and eggs. She is a most favorable specimen of the institution. "Hoped Massa Grigsby and the family would soon come back. Always been like father and mudder to me, sir, never had a hard word from nary one of 'em, sir." We slept in our shawls and overcoats on the floor. Van Buren snored in a steady, severe, classical style; Bellows in a vehement, spasmodic, passionate *sturm und drang* Byronic way, characteristic of the Romantic School.

Up early Thursday morning and drove to Blackburn's Ford. Overcast and chilly. Walked whenever we came to a dry spot. Country covered with dead horses and deserted cantonments. Rebel huts well and substantially built. Stopped at one William Wen's, an abandoned brick house that had been Beauregard's headquarters. He's another "Union man," and has run away to Culpeper. Rummaged the premises and found quantities of military papers which we confided to certain stray soldiers with directions to take them to General McDowell.

Reached Manassas Junction at last. Olmsted met us, bristling with bowie knives and shooting irons picked up on the ground and looking like Robinson Crusoe. They had found shelter, provisions, and blankets in the rebel huts and got comfortably through the night.

What a scene! Acres and acres of huts, some of them burned; the ground literally covered with abandoned baggage and arms, which contrabands were diligently collecting and bundling up in abandoned portmanteaus and chests. Most of the swords and knives had been collected in heaps apparently and burned with other more combustible articles so as to destroy their temper; but many were still intact, and we brought off a supply of trophies. Letters abounded. I could have collected a bushel. Their spelling generally bad. Some of them more obscene and filthy than anything I ever read. One (in vilest spelling) very plucky and manly. All indicate severe distress in secessiondom—want of money and of whatever money can buy.

From Manassas we drove over what these benighted Virginians call a road (in fact, a mere miry wagon track through dismal miry fields), and over the battlefield of Bull Run to the Run itself, which we forded just below Stone Bridge. The bridge had been blown up. We bivouacked, made a fire, and dined on this side, just below the Warrenton turnpike and the ruined bridge, and returned to Centreville and Aunt Polly at dusk. Next morning, we drove into Washington, crossing the Long Bridge before four o'clock in the afternoon.

We have been humbugged by the rebels. Their position at Centreville is strong (reminds one of descriptions of Borodino), but their works on the crest of the hill were flimsy and armed with logs painted black instead of heavy guns. The Manassas redoubts are no better. They seemed to have been armed, but that position has no special strength. We could have carried it last December with ease. McClellan is suffering sorely. He is denounced for inaction, for letting the rebels escape. Mr. Secretary Chase denounces him freely and wants McDowell to supersede him.[9] People talk of this retreat as a great disaster. I think not, unless they lure us into direct pursuit through an exhausted, beggarly country. It certainly lowers their prestige.

March 19, WEDNESDAY.   A brief article in the *Christian Remembrancer* read tonight at the Society Library made me tingle. "On the whole, justice is on the side of the rebellion. Slavery has nothing to do with the war. That arose from selfish legislation by Northern majorities on questions of tariff and protection." (So thinks the English shop-keeper, though he supposes himself to write as churchman and Catholic.) The moral tone of the South is exalted, while the North is base altogether. The church of South Carolina and other Southern States is healthy and vigorous. In the Northern States, it seems numerically stronger, but that is because the corporation of Trinity Church happens to own all the business portion of the great city of New York! And so on. So talks the organ of what is best and most hopeful in England, the mouthpiece of the Catholic-minded party in the English Church!

March 23.   News of action by Parliament on the blockade question most satisfactory. N.B. Gustave Doré ought to produce a picture of the battle at Pea Ridge, Arkansas, where some two thousand Indians, enlisted by the rebels and dosed with whiskey in advance, went utterly wild and shot and scalped both sides indiscriminately.

March 28.   There is uneasy feeling about the conduct of the war. That fatal *Merrimac* is ready for sea again. With a little luck to help her, she may do infinite mischief. Is Congress or the Navy Department accountable for our want of preparation? Somebody ought to be hanged, because we have not six *Merrimacs* now in commission. The Navy Department is certainly responsible for the escape of the *Nashville*, which has run the blockade at Beaufort, North Carolina. At Island No. 10, we are still hammering away. That expedition seems a failure, but as we have not

[9] The evacuation of Centreville by the Confederates revealed that they had successfully bluffed McClellan. With about 150,000 men in recent weeks, he had been held in check by Johnston's force of about 50,000. Chase wrote that "our immense and magnificently appointed army" had been kept at a standstill by a force "not one-third as great in numbers and inferior in almost all other respects," while "the impregnable fortifications, which had been so magnified by our generals, were works of little strength and incapable of withstanding any vigorous assault."

come to close quarters, we have sustained no loss. Then there is no doubt that the great expedition to New Orleans has come to blows with the rebel batteries at the Mississippi before this, and that is a risky, unpromising enterprise, *periculosum plenum opus alia*, with Butler in command. So there are excuses for my feeling blue and anxious.

Van Buren, Bellows, Agnew, Gibbs, Olmsted, and Bishop Clark here last night and well into this morning in debate over the question of resigning our Commission and publicly protesting against the non-feasance of the government. Resolved not to resign but to define our position and try to shield ourselves from blame, stimulate government, and wake up the people by an able manifesto or proclamation. This is unwise for our own sakes, because we shall be held accountable in some degree (however unjustly) for the sickness and suffering with which the army will soon be visited and for the army itself, because we have ascertained after six months' work that we cannot force into official heads the urgent importance of reforming the Medical Bureau. Our resignation might call public attention to the subject and a clamor might be thereby raised to which government could not close its ears. But an elaborate statement will effect nothing, except that it may slightly aggravate uncharitable feeling of the Medical Bureau toward the Sanitary Commission.

Tonight at Agassiz's lecture (Irving Hall) suggesting the outlines of that fearful and wonderful subject, the creative law manifested in the organic world, geological and living.

April 3.   People offer bets that McClellan will dine in Richmond next Sunday. Safe bets to take. He is believed to be at Old Point with 100,000 men. Maybe so, maybe not. The rebels certainly seem abandoning Virginia and concentrating their force in the Southwest.

April 7, MONDAY.   How slowly this great tragedy develops itself to us, the impatient audience! No news today. Yesterday's "most reliable" reports are without confirmation. We do not appear to have taken Yorktown, and McClellan probably dined today outside the city limits of Richmond. Fitz-James O'Brien, who was on [Frederick W.] Lander's staff, has died of lockjaw from a wound received in battle. I forgive him his bad poetry.

April 9.   There has been a great battle indeed in the Southwest, a conflict of two days, closely fought and with varying fortune and by great armies. It seems entitled to a place among the first-class battles of history, and quite above any passage of arms that this campaign had produced. "Pittsburgh Landing," on the Tennessee River, was the field. According to the reports now received, we were outnumbered two to one the first day and pushed back in imminent danger of defeat. On the second day, Grant was reinforced, and after a hard struggle recovered his lost ground, repulsed the rebels, took guns and prisoners, and pursued the retreating enemy. Sidney Johnston is killed and Beauregard minus an arm. So says rumor. Also that the rebels carried off prisoners, General Prentiss among them, and that our casualties are 20,000 and the enemy's 40,000!!! Exaggerated figures, no doubt, but there has certainly been a big fight and "a murder grim and great." It will probably turn out an important national victory with heavy loss, for which *Gratias agimus Tibi*. McClellan does not seem to get on very fast at Yorktown. But our weak spot just now is Norfolk, where the *Merrimac*, with her iron carapace, may do us infinite damage.

The battle of Shiloh (so called from the log meeting-house near Pittsburgh Landing on the Tennessee) was the bloodiest contest fought in the Mississippi Valley during the war. A Confederate army of 40,000 under the gallant Albert Sidney Johnston, eager to wipe out the defeats at Forts Henry and Donelson, fell upon Grant's force of some 33,000 at dawn on Sunday, April 6. For a time they swept all before them. Thousands of panic-stricken new recruits in the Union army fled to the river, where they were sheltered by high bluffs and protected by gunboats. But Grant was undismayed. Heavy reinforcements under Buell arrived at dusk; others came up under Lew Wallace. Next day these fresh troops recommenced the battle and inflicted a heavy defeat upon the wearied soldiers of Johnston, who had been killed on the first day as he rallied his men for a charge.

April 12.   There is no progress at Yorktown. We are in great ferment and fever, nervously looking for news from that place. Broadway is full of people this beautiful moonlight night, collecting in knots at corners, from which one is sure to hear in passing the words *Merrimac* or *Monitor* or Fortress Monroe. I am tired of this state of tension, which has now lasted a year.

But we have gained something already. Emancipation in the District of Columbia has passed both Houses by more than two to one, and unless Lincoln veto the measure, which is unlikely, the nation has washed its hands of slavery. Only the damnedest of "damned abolitionists" dreamed of such a thing a year ago. Perhaps the name of abolitionist will be less disgraceful a year hence. John Brown's "soul's a-marching on," with the people after it.

April 16. We have Grant's report of Pittsburgh Landing. Substantially, as I supposed, an attack repulsed after a narrow escape. Nothing said about guns taken by either party. It seems a victory if holding the field of battle be the test. Its moral effect on the rebels must be disheartening and decomposing. They are not made of the stuff that bears failure well. General [Ormsby] Mitchel is the hero of the hour. His successful cutting of these main railroad arteries through which flows the life blood of the rebellion is a great stroke. He has won a major-generalship. . . .

Lincoln has signed the Emancipation Bill.[10] Has any President, since this country came into being, done so weighty an act? The federal government is now clear of all connection with slaveholding. We are uneasy about McClellan. He is in a tight place, possibly in a trap, and the cabal against him at Washington may embarrass and weaken him. I am sorry to believe that McDowell is privy to it. He knows better, I am sure, but ambition tempts men fearfully.

April 19, SATURDAY. . . . Am just from Van Buren's, where I met Wolcott Gibbs by appointment at half-past nine. The doctor and Dr. Bellows left Washington this morning with tidings of weight. The Commission seems to have achieved at last the work it has been prosecuting for at least seven weary months of hope deferred, of official promises sliding away under its feet like the slopes of a steep sandhill, of repulses, snubbings, and misrepresentation, and of late (in my own case, at least) of disgust and despair: the work of reforming the Medical Department of the army; a bill to increase the efficiency of that rheumatic, lethargic, paralytic, ossified, old institution passed a few days ago under pressure brought to bear on the Congress by the United States and by the public opinion we have been educating. It is our bill, except that it impairs the integrity of "the Corps" by making volunteer brigade-surgeons eligible to the newly-created offices of sanitary inspector, and so on, and in a few minor particulars. We resisted these revolutionary measures before the military committees of both houses. Had the bureau united with us, we could have saved it from what it considers to be disorganization and destruction. But the bureau was inspired by that blind, arrogant old Finley, who ruled it as the last Bourbon ruled France. It fought for its own divine right of imbecile misgovernment and for nothing else. It learned nothing

[10] Before the bill freeing the slaves in the District of Columbia passed, many had doubted whether Lincoln would sign it. As it contained provisions for compensating the owners and encouraging colonization of freedmen abroad, thus applying two of his favorite ideas, he showed no hesitation in approving it.

from the fact that it had become guardian of half a million of men, instead of 15,000; refused to concur in any enlargement of its resources or change in its venerable routine. So, the bill passed, and "the Corps is ruined," according to Dr. Satterlee and Dr. Wood and every army surgeon of twenty years' standing.

This is all by way of prologue to Dr. Van Buren's narrative. The Secretary of War telegraphed for him to come to Washington. (He did not send for Hammond.) Bellows went with him. Van Buren reported at the War Department, and the Secretary asked frankly what he should do with the Medical Bureau. "I have called you into a bad case." "What are the symptoms, Mr. Secretary?" "General imbecility." They had more than one free discussion, and Van Buren submitted a list of names for the new offices with Dr. Hammond at their head, and Vollum and Edwards of the regular corps, and Dr. Lyman and Dr. Clymer of the volunteers, and so on, which the Secretary approved. Then it appeared that Lincoln had been subjected to political pressure and was, moreover, influenced by personal regard for our excellent old colleague, Dr. Wood, who hates Hammond. The medical staff judges of its members by their military record rather than by scientific or professional rank. Bellows tackled Lincoln while he was being shaven [the] next (Thursday) morning and seems to have talked to him most energetically and successfully. He was with the President again last night and was informed that Hammond was appointed. "Shouldn't wonder if he was Surgeon-General already," said the President, and they shook hands upon it. I believed this, coming from Lincoln, but I wouldn't believe it if it came from any other Washington official. "I hain't been caught lying yet, and I don't mean to be," said Abe Lincoln, during their discussion, and such is probably the fact.

Another *Lincoln.* Dr. Bellows, apropos of something he said, advised him to take his meals at regular hours. His health was so important to the country. Abe Lincoln *loquitur,* "Well, I cannot take my vittles regular. I kind o' just browze round." He says, "Stanton's one of my team, and they must pull together. I can't have any one on 'em a-kicking out."

The Sanitary Commission is treated with profound respect by all Washington officials. Our relations with the government are now more intimate than they ever have been. We have *carte blanche* from the War Department as to hospitals at Yorktown.

The bill for which the Sanitary Commission had labored so energetically was finally passed on April 18, 1862: "An Act to Reorganize and Increase the

Efficiency of the Medical Department of the Army." It was not all that Strong and his associates desired, but it marked a tremendous advance. It provided that the Surgeon-General and the higher officers of the Bureau staff were to be chosen from the most competent officers of the whole corps, and were no longer to be selected by the silly rule of seniority. It provided for eight medical inspectors, who were to have very considerable powers of remedying evils. Reforms were effected in hospital administration and in the transportation of the sick and wounded. Finally, the law was so worded that many detailed changes for the better could be instituted by the new Surgeon-General, upon whom fell the task of giving life and vigor to the reorganized system.

So important was the selection of an expert and energetic Surgeon-General that the problem had given Strong and others the greatest anxiety. Fortunately, one of the officers of the Medical Staff had shown such exceptional ability that when the reorganization bill became law the Sanitary Commission had already fixed upon him as the best possible choice. **Dr. William A. Hammond,** *a comparatively young assistant-surgeon in the army, had been busy since the outbreak of the war in organizing general army hospitals at Baltimore, Wheeling, Hagerstown, and Chambersburg. This work had been admirably performed. Inspectors of the Sanitary Commission, visiting the hospitals, spoke warmly of their arrangement, administration, and special features and credited Hammond with the rapid improvement of the patients. The Commission learned that Hammond, who had been born in Annapolis in 1828, had been educated in medicine at the University of the City of New York; that after a short period of general practice, he had entered the army as assistant-surgeon in 1849; that he had served at various frontier stations from New Mexico to Florida; and that while doing so, he had found time to conduct scientific investigations and had published an essay to which the American Medical Association awarded a prize. He had resigned from the army in 1859 to teach anatomy and physiology at the University of Maryland; but on the beginning of the war he promptly reëntered the service. He was thoroughly aware of the defects of the medical service of the army, and cordially agreed with the Sanitary Commission as to the nature of the reforms required. The medical profession of the country was strongly enlisted in his behalf and sent numerous petitions to Washington asking that he be appointed Surgeon-General. Secretary Stanton was not wholly favorable. But, as Strong records, the President commissioned Hammond as Surgeon-General, with the grade of brigadier-general, on April 25, 1862. No better choice could* *have been made—though Hammond's imperious temper and aggressive ways were soon to bring him into sharp conflict with the still more masterful and autocratic Secretary of War.*

April 22, TUESDAY. Walked uptown with Agnew this afternoon. Telegram from Olmsted that the government has put the *Commodore* at our disposal as a floating hospital or sanitary transport. She is at Fort Monroe or Ship Point, and it is thought necessary that Agnew inspect her equipment. He will go if I go with him, and not otherwise, though I shall be the merest cypher of utter uselessness; so I may probably undertake another Southern pilgrimage at six o'clock tomorrow evening. Walked about town tonight, making arrangements therefor. Knapp is at Old Point. This journey is a dismal prospect. If we go to Ship Point, we shall doubtless see much that is interesting and exciting, but there is the painful, mean feeling that one is so far below the men who are perilling life and limb for the country.

April 30, WEDNESDAY. Government changed the arrangements for our floating hospital. The steamship, *Daniel Webster*, Captain Bletham, lying at Alexandria, was turned over to us Friday at six o'clock in the morning.[11] She had been used as a transport and was full of filth, had to be thoroughly disinfected and purified and gutted, berths torn down and new ones put up. Gangs of carpenters were sent down to work night and day and a dozen contrabands, supplied by General [James S.] Wadsworth. They attended to the scrubbing and scraping and whitewashing. Spent Saturday morning on board and went down by steam-tug Sunday morning. We were delayed many hours by failure of supplies. Messengers were sent off to ransack Alexandria for fresh meat. They returned at last after an expedition into the back country, and we steamed down the Potomac at four o'clock in the afternoon, passed Mount Vernon and Fort Washing-

[11] When McClellan moved his army to the Peninsula, a swampy, malarious region, easily accessible by sea, it became evident that some capacious steamers were needed as hospital ships. Fighting shortly began between McClellan's troops and the Confederates under Generals J. B. Magruder and Joseph E. Johnston. At Williamsburg on May 5 a sharp action lasted all day as the Southerners fought a rear-guard battle to protect their retreating trains. The Sanitary Commission had asked Secretary Stanton for some large vessels to be fitted up for the sick and wounded; and the Quartermaster-General was directed to supply ships accommodating a thousand beds. When the *Daniel Webster*, with room for about 250 cases, was assigned to the Commission at the end of April, Olmsted at once took command, supervised her refitting as a hospital, placed stores and medical personnel on board, and took her to the York River, Strong lending him constant assistance. The vessel immediately carried her first load of sick and wounded to New York, and then returned for more.

ton and the Stone Fleet (waiting to be sunk whenever the *Merrimac* shall appear) and anchor off Aquia Creek when daylight fails.

We have on board Olmsted, Agnew, Knapp, Dr. Hartshorne of Philadelphia, Lewis Rutherfurd, and his son "Stuyvy" (guests of the Commission, as is also that florid and gassy gent, Caleb Lyon "of Lyonsdale"), Stillé of Philadelphia, Mrs. Christine Griffin, Mrs. David Lane, Mrs. Howland, and Miss Woolsey, a dozen he-nurses from Philadelphia, and six or eight nice young medical students from New York, who rank as "dressers." Haight, Woodruff, and Conolly seem very fine, intelligent young fellows; also, Dr. Grymes of Washington, a few officers, and some fifty soldiers. These were government passengers. The soldiers were well behaved and orderly. One of the officers, a chaplain from western New York, Cleveland by name, gave us a "service" Sunday night by invitation, the like of which I do not care to hear again. . . .

Toward four o'clock, we open York River and the gunboats that guard it, and then turn off into "Poquossin" [Pequoson] bay (I am not sure I have got its chivalric name right) and enter Cheeseman's Creek after grounding once or twice. It was a goodly spectacle; a narrow estuary, with low-wooded shores studded with tents and alive with moving masses. Some hundred transports congregated on its still waters—sailing vessels and steamers, big and little, of every degree, some of them black with men of [William B.] Franklin's division, which has now been afloat and waiting for a fortnight. As night came on, all these vessels were lit up, and great campfires glared out on either shore, and there were conflagrations (of brushwood and obstructive timber, probably) that reddened the sky. Men were singing on board the transports, bugle calls and drumbeats were all around, and through these noises came every few minutes the boom of a heavy gun from the lines. These sights and sounds were suggestive.

Tuesday morning up by daylight; boat up the creek with Dr. Chamberlain, Agnew, Olmsted, and Dr. Hartshorne of Philadelphia. Landed, after a long row through the congregation of transports with little tugs steaming about in all directions in high pressure, hurry, and feaze. Got horses from Colonel [Rufus] Ingalls and pushed into the luxuriant leafy woods full of swamp, malaria, lovely holly trees, mistletoe, and other novelties. Too much occupied in picking our way to notice these things closely. An interesting little tree lizard prevails there and moves about like a flash. Came upon a regiment of Mainote lumbermen marching in line upon the forest, tree after tree crashing down before them to be made useful as corduroy road. Took to the road at last, an alternation of deep quagmire and perilous corduroy; and after frequent detours through bush and briar to avoid the immense army trains, came out where we looked down on about a square mile of tents and found ourselves at McClellan's headquarters. Conference with Dr. Tripler, utterly and disgracefully un-provided for the work before him. Men are lying on bare hospital floors and perishing of typhoid who could be saved if they had a blanket or a bed, or appropriate food and sufficient stimulants and proper hospital clothing instead of their mud-encrusted uniforms. The region is pestif-erous. As I returned, under a broiling sun that blistered my face, the whole country was sending up a steam that rose some four feet from the ground. By five o'clock there was a cold wind coming from a black cloud that rose behind Fort Monroe, and an icy, deadly, penetrating rain, through which I saw typhoid patients carried ashore to Dr. Cuyler's hospital. . . .

I ascended a high tree by a very dubious ladder and had a view of Yorktown and rebel batteries about a mile off. They were throwing shell every three minutes or thereabouts, but their practice was bad. The shells burst in the air generally about forty-five degrees up. Only one did well, and that burst in a wood on our left, where it no doubt damaged the forest growth of Virginia but accomplished nothing more. McClellan's staff in the best of spirits, confident of success. They say that our batteries when they open will be heavier than those arrayed against Sebastopol, and that one of them, No. 1 on York River, on our extreme right, will be the heaviest ever mounted. The best rebel sharp-shooters are niggers. One of them seems to bear a charmed life and has been very successful. He is known as the "irrepressible nigger" and Berdan's best operators have thus far failed to touch him.[12]

Rode back to the landing alone, the rest of the party proposing to visit "Battery No. 1," and I being compelled to return in time for the one o'clock boat to Old Point so as to be here tomorrow. It was a perilous ride over roads blocked by army wagons and mortars and siege guns going to the front, and with abysses of mud on either side.

May 3. Death of Bruce Schermerhorn, son of Abraham Schermer-horn. He leaves all his property to his sister, Mrs. Astor.[13] Mrs. Suydam

[12] Hiram Berdan, ultimately brevetted a major-general, was colonel of the First U.S. Sharpshooters.

[13] William Astor had married Caroline Webster Schermerhorn. Their son John Jacob Astor, after a career of some distinction, for he was on General Shafter's staff in the Spanish War and invented an improved turbine engine, was drowned on the *Titanic*.

and Mrs. Irving and others are wrathful. I suppose I drew this will in the spring of 1859, but I have forgotten the transaction.

The nation has been making progress. We have occupied New Orleans and thus tied a main artery of treason. Fort Macon has been shelled into surrender. We have taken Baton Rouge. Also there are reports (too good to be true) of Burnside's threatening Norfolk from the rear. The traitor Beauregard is said to be evacuating Corinth.

May 4, SUNDAY. Van Buren, Bellows, and Agnew came in after dinner, and I went downtown with Agnew to see about getting off our thirty nurses and half-dozen doctors and others by this evening's train. This evening appeared Bellows, Van Buren, Agnew, and Gibbs; also, Miss Laura Pell, Mr. Ruggles, Charley Strong, George Anthon, Mignot, a French naval lieutenant whose name I forget, Walter Cutting, Mrs. Carson, Temple Prime, Dr. Lieber, and others; and at supper-time a strong column of young British guardsmen on leave from Canada with Maclure and Kingsland as bear-leaders. They are a pleasant set of fellows; Pakenham, Lord Dunmore, Crichton, Duncombe, and others. Dunmore is descended from the Dunmore of our colonial history, has property in Virginia, is related to Colonel [Robert E.] Lee, and seceshionizes vehemently.[14] Has run the blockade, and has been fêted at Richmond, has talked with the anti-President Jefferson I, who announced this as his view of the Secesh future, viz: recognition "next winter." In case of defeat in the field, a circumambient guerrilla campaign is to last till Lincoln goes out, by which time the exhausted North will be glad to make terms, and perhaps make him president for the sake of conciliation. This Scotch peer is a frank, well-mannered, good-natured boy, who does not in the least understand what he talks about. Chief of a clan, moreover, and plays a fearful imitation of the pipes on our parlor organ, which instrument being out of tune enables him to do so with special accuracy and excruciation. . . .

May 5. Busy day. Part of the morning spent with Gibbs buying hospital stores. This evening awhile at Charley's. Went down to the depot with Ellie and her faithful army and saw them off. About a dozen women go, ladies and their servants, with Bellows as chief pastor. There are Mrs. Bellows, Miss Harriet Whetten,[15] and a daughter of Charles E. Butler's.

[14] This was Charles Murray, Earl of Dunmore (1841–1907), who later made a name for himself as explorer, politician, and author.

[15] Miss Harriet Douglas Whetten is described by Katharine Prescott Wormeley in *The Other Side of War* as a tall, symmetrical woman who played an active and heroic part in the nursing work in 1862.

I send Ellie off with sore misgivings and at her own earnest request, relying mainly on Van Buren's excellent judgment. He thinks there is no exposure and no risk of typhoid or malarial fever. I have armed the little woman with prophylactic quinine. May she get safely home again, and may this crusade plant no seeds of disease in her impressible system.

May 6. Walked uptown with Agnew, stopped awhile at the New York Hospital, and then at Colonel [Zenas R.] Bliss's, where we learned that the *Daniel Webster* had been telegraphed below. Omnibussed at once to Whitehall and found she was lying off Castle Garden. I took a boat. Made a hurried inspection. She came away yesterday morning with 187 sick, of whom four have died. Two more are moribund, if appearances be reliable. Some thirty or forty are convalescent. They are on deck enjoying the tonic northwest wind and bright sunshine and doubtless appreciating the visible signs of home and civilization all around them. In the wards below we found excellent ventilation, no smells, attentive and vigilant officers, comfort and order. But with all this, the bunks of the forward cabin were tragic. Gaunt, wan, wild faces, restless tossing forms, arms that were ready to strike hard for the country against the country's enemy strapped relentlessly to the fevered body. Great big eyes looking at us without intelligence. One poor fellow had just died, and lay with unclosed eyes glaring upwards, as if appealing to the God of Justice for vengeance on those who have brought this murderous war upon us.

I was much gratified by the talk of the soldiers. "Nothing at all to complain of, sir." "Have you been treated as well as you were in your shore hospitals?" "Oh, there ain't no comparison, sir. We've been treated like gentlemen *here*, but in them holes there wasn't nobody to look after us." This is satisfactory; a tangible result that justifies our appeal to the public for aid and support, and the time we have spent in work for the Sanitary Commission.

May 9. Nothing from Ellie, except that I learn tonight that she was established on board the *Knickerbocker* yesterday and in good health and spirits.[16] What a fool I was to let her go off on this cruise!

May 10. The more we learn about the New Orleans fight the better it looks.[17] It seems likely to be remembered as among the more notable

[16] The *Knickerbocker*, a large river steamboat, had been prepared for surgical cases and could carry 300 men. Mrs. Strong, Miss Wormeley, Mrs. William Preston Griffin, and other devoted women served on her.

[17] Farragut's fleet on April 24 successfully ran past the two forts below New Orleans (Fort Jackson and Fort St. Philip), destroyed the Confederate gunboat fleet, and brought his ships and troops into safe waters. Although the passage of this fortified part of the

battles of history, being full of picturesque incidents, such as fire-ships, mortar-boats clothed in leafy branches or with long canes from the swamp and belching out thirteen-inch shells from the recesses of a green bower, and so on. There are fierce displays of individual pluck, too. We have contributed a sensational chapter to the world's history.

May 11, SUNDAY. *Gratias agimus.* God be praised for today's news.[18] Did not go out this morning: sent Johnny to St. Paul's with his grand-mamma and dawdled over books in the library, and snuffling, snorting, sneezing, and choking with this pestilent cold. Soon after dinner, the streets were full of noises, the cry of panting newsboys with their *extrees*. I posted myself at the front door and discoursed with a patriotic old gentleman who recognized me as an enquirer and imparted the news. I don't know who he was, and it made no difference. We waved our hats to passers-by and they waved theirs. The city was jubilant. At last, a youth came along, and I invested in an extra *Tribune*, declining to receive change for my quarter. Read the news, which I had not dared fully to believe till I saw it in print, and executed a war dance round the hall, to Temple's astonishment.

General Wool landed at Willoughby's Point yesterday morning and marched on Norfolk. Lincoln seems to have been with him in person. There was some little fighting and firing and bridge-burning, and Norfolk and the Navy Yard were surrendered. Viele is military governor, and at five this morning the *Merrimac* was blown up. Her destruction and the occupation of Norfolk are two great facts. It is also reported that the *Galena* has advanced up the James River, sunk the *Yorktown*, and captured the *Jamestown*, but this looks less reliable.

May 13. This evening came a letter from Ellie, brought by Mrs. Dr. Bellows. The *Daniel Webster* arrived this afternoon at four, several hours earlier than we expected. Ellie enjoys her Bohemian life, works hard, sleeps profoundly, finds coarse fare appetizing, and has a good time generally. I have brilliant reports of her energy and efficiency in arrangement, of her cordial acquiescence in drudgery. God bless her for her vigorous

---

Mississippi lasted less than two hours, it meant encountering a succession of deadly perils—mortars, heavy guns, fire-rafts, and well-armed gunboats. Farragut at once pushed on and brought the city of New Orleans under his still heated guns. The Union flag soon floated over the public buildings.

[18] The destruction of the *Merrimac* at Norfolk on May 11 opened the James River to McClellan's advance on Richmond; and by May 16 he established a new base of operations at White House, a long step forward. Brigadier-General Egbert L. Viele (1825–1902), whom Strong had known for his engineering work on the plans of Central Park, became military governor of Norfolk.

devotion to this work. May she only get safe home unpoisoned by Southern typhoid.

May 15. After dinner came in Bellows fresh from a row with the Secretary of War about appointments under the Medical Reform Bill, in which Stanton was petulant and insolent and then emollient and apologetic. Bellows thinks he has some cerebral disease. Took a stroll and on my return found Agnew here, and we accomplished a little work. Much gratified by a letter from Raymond of the *Times* apologizing for the attacks that paper made on us last fall and winter, and sending us one hundred dollars as evidence of his conversion. Miss Powell (alias "Justitia") is found out at last and Raymond has thrown her over. Truth is apt to prevail, if one wait patiently. I wish it might prevail *soon* with Charley Strong and George Anthon. I confess to feeling profoundly embittered by having to fight this battle with my two most intimate friends dead against me, readily absorbing and reissuing every lie that official spite sets in motion against us. I fear it will be long before this feeling wears out. Of course, they are entitled to form their own opinions, and so are the people of England, but it will be a weary while before England can be to us what she was a year ago.

Today's news is that General Hunter at Port Royal proclaims a general emancipation in South Carolina, Georgia, and Florida!!! Very strange and startling. John Brown *IS* a-marching on, and with seven league boots.[19]

May 20. Last night at Gibbs's. Executive Committee, Sanitary Commission. Dr. Satterlee with us, and cooperative (!!!).[20] Tonight at Dr. Van Buren's with Agnew. We have decided to set up a local office here with paid agents. Our work has grown too big for us.

Two days later the Commission rented a loft at 498 Broadway, where Strong and his colleagues worked many long hours. In October, the headquarters was moved to 823 Broadway, an address appearing, sometimes just as "823," with almost daily regularity in the diary for the next three years.

May 24. Today's news obscure and parti-colored. Nothing from McClellan except stronger rumors that Secesh is retiring beyond Richmond. From General Banks's column comes a bulletin of "repulse" and

[19] General David Hunter's order of April 12 freeing all slaves in his hands had been followed on May 9 by one liberating all slaves in his Department.

[20] Dr. Richard Sherwood Satterlee (1798–1880), surgeon, who had served capably in the Mexican War, and was now to act as medical purveyor throughout the Civil War. General Scott had supported him as a candidate for the post of surgeon-general.

"with heavy loss" at *Front Royal*, and from Lewisburg (somewhere in West Virginia) another of a successful "affair," and the capture of cannons and stores. Such is war. That Richmond is in a frenzy and fury and desperation, even as a nest of hornets invaded by unfriendly fumes of brimstone, seems certain.

May 25, SUNDAY.   These are critical hours. The rebels are pressing Banks in great force, and he has fallen back from Winchester on Harper's Ferry.[21] We have no details, but it is generally believed that the rebels are doing what an inferior army in a central position ought to undertake against a larger force distributed around the circumference, namely, strike at some one point before it can be strengthened. Their object is probably to annihilate Banks, and then make a rush for Baltimore. There are already signs of outbreak and disturbance in that guilty town, but Secessia will not have exclusive control of its demonstrations of ruffianism this time. Unionist plug-uglies seem to have something to say now. They have been mobbing people and trying to hang them for demonstrations of rejoicing over this rebel advance. A Baltimore regiment (Colonel Kenly's) seems to have suffered severely in the affair at Front Royal reported yesterday, and the friends of these Baltimore soldiers have been infuriated by the exultation of genteel sympathizers with rebellion.

May 28.   We incline to an open rupture with the Secretary of War, in which we should find many backers. Unless the strange movements of the last five days lead to a decisive victory in Virginia, he can hardly keep his place. There is a good deal of evidence that his brain is diseased. His delay in appointing officers under the Medical Bill is paralyzing Hammond and costs the country scores of lives every day. It is a great crime. It is still uncertain whether any nominations have been sent to the Senate. His relations with us convict him of the utmost unsteadiness and capriciousness, if not of bad faith and downright lying. I believe that he means well, but he is impulsive, flighty, and excitable, and so forgets today what he said yesterday, that he errs in endeavoring to attend personally to details he should leave to his subordinates, and that overwork and a sensitive temperament and perhaps disease account for his erratic performances. People

[21] Stonewall Jackson was in the midst of his whirlwind Valley campaign; a campaign in which, between May 19 and June 9, he marched 270 miles, scattered an array of three Union armies aggregating about 50,000 men, and succeeded in his main object of preventing McDowell from joining McClellan before Richmond. On May 22, Jackson had fallen upon Colonel Kenly's force at Front Royal, killing or wounding 154 and capturing 600 out of a thousand men. The Confederate force then advanced to within three miles of Harper's Ferry while Washington trembled.

talk against him almost as freely as they did against Cameron, but unjustly. They overrated him absurdly at first, and now condemn him as knave and fool.

June 1, SUNDAY.   *News.* Corinth evacuated. Does this indicate collapse of rebellion in the Southwest, or transfer of reinforcements to the rebel hordes that defend Richmond? People mostly adopt the former theory, but it is doubtful.

Halleck, put in charge of the Western army after Shiloh, spent more than a month in making a twenty-mile advance to Corinth, Mississippi, that need not have occupied three days. When on May 30 he reached that town, he found that Beauregard had left it and was slowly falling back to new positions. Farragut, as Strong notes, had meanwhile captured New Orleans and the time was ripe for an instant forward push, Halleck marching southward down the Mississippi while Farragut and Ben Butler moved up the river. But Halleck proved strangely inert, doing nothing of any value—and a good deal that was positively damaging—until on July 11 he was summoned to Washington to take general command of all the Northern armies.

Nor was progress more satisfactory in the East. McClellan, after beginning his Peninsular campaign on April 2, wasted more than a month in capturing Yorktown. He then pushed on slowly against Richmond. The Confederates were thrown into grave apprehension. Their Congress adjourned, their archives were packed for removal, and President Davis sent his family off for safety. On May 31st, bloody fighting at Fair Oaks resulted indecisively, and immediately afterward heavy rains stopped all offensive action. McClellan did nothing even after the roads dried, and it was not until June 26 that the struggle recommenced, Lee and the Confederates then attacking fiercely in the first of the Seven Days' Battles. The Union generals seemed singularly inert and nerveless. They might have profited from the bold example set by Stonewall Jackson, who in May delivered his famous series of lightning strokes in the Shenandoah Valley, defeating McDowell, Banks, and Frémont in succession and then rejoining the main Confederate army in front of Richmond. Strong had to face the news of delay and defeat alone, for his wife was with McClellan's army, helping to direct the nursing services. As his diary shows, she went to the front to make inquiries and arrangements, then returned, and on June 15 sailed with a party of nurses on the steamer St. Mark, *equipped by the Sanitary Commission as a hospital ship.*

June 5.   Nothing from the army before Richmond later than Saturday and Sunday last, when the battle of "The Seven Pines" was lost and won, except rumors that our position was unchanged Monday, the second. That was a grim fight. We held our own and did more. Doubtful if we can claim to have done so much, for though we occupied the field we lost guns.

We are not at all jolly today. People complain of McClellan's slow progress and wonder if he is not over-matched. Guess that Beauregard's army has left Corinth only to turn up in overwhelming force on the James River. It's so easy to transport say 60,000 men, with all their supplies, over 1,300 miles of railroad in a single week! The contest in Virginia will be close enough without counting in the Southwest rebellion. Croakers and grumblers abound and cite facts and rumored facts more than enough to justify their chilling talk. But one of them, my excellent old friend of twenty-four years, Mr. S. B. Ruggles to wit, drives me daily to the verge of dementia and fits. He has always been finding fault, justly enough, with the administration of public affairs, and yet declining for some wholly incomprehensible reason to vote and thereby do his share toward mending them. Recent domestic calamity makes his view of our future darker than ever. Though all his feelings are with the national cause, his way of helping the country is to carp at everything that is done, to growl because everything else isn't done, to disbelieve in everybody's honesty and capacity, to predict every conceivable misfortune, to refuse to raise a finger in aid of any movement for the public service, or to give his sympathy to those who do so. He has notions in his head about the legal aspects of this slavery problem, emancipation bills and all that, which are new and valuable. I tell him he would divert his own mind, gain reputation, and do the country service by putting them into form and publishing them, and that I'll be responsible for the printer's bill. But his only answer is, "Oh, dear no! Why should *I* undertake any such thing?"

June 9, MONDAY. . . . News tonight from Charleston papers of a vigorous demonstration Charleston-ward, by way of Stone Creek, getting behind Fort Sumter. . . .

But Richmond—McClellan!!!??? There is the critical position. Success there kills the rebellion, or leaves it only a feeble life, like that of a decapitated hornet, able to sting careless fingers but sure soon to perish innocuously if let alone. Can we hope for the "crowning mercy" of victory there? People are not sanguine about it. They think McClellan too slow and fear Joe Johnston (or G. W. Smith, for they say Joe Johnston was badly wounded at the battle of the Seven Pines or Fair Oaks) has been largely reinforced by fugitives from Corinth.[22] Time will tell. But why does not McDowell move down from Fredericksburg with his 40,000 men, more or less? And why does he visit Washington so often?—to collogue with Stanton and Chase?

June 12. Chief labor of these days has been the equipment of the *St. Mark.* . . .[23] We shall get her off Saturday; not sooner. Ellie is to be on her staff. That seems settled. Her capacity of unselfishness and intense desire to employ it constitute a "call" to this humane and patriotic womanly work—and a loud call, of two hundred trombone power—which I cannot but hear, though unwillingly. She takes with her Annie, her invaluable handmaiden.

June 13. Nothing new. Letter from Olmsted this afternoon at No. 498, ten pages long, giving a fearful, sickening account of the weakness and inefficiency and imbecility of Dr. Tripler and his subordinates on the Peninsula; of carloads of wounded men dumped on swampy river shores without food, medicine, or attendance; of men with fractured thighs lying neglected and forgotten forty-eight hours in two inches of water, struggling to raise themselves so as to pick the maggots from their rotting wounds and fainting after the effort, and yet keeping a good heart through it. God prosper Ellie in her mission! The *St. Mark* sails tomorrow, and she is to report on board at ten o'clock in the morning.

June 15, SUNDAY. With Ellie and Annie to the foot of Rutgers Street. . . . Everything on board looks well, but six of the twenty nurses failed to report. With Ellie are associated Mrs. Dr. Noyes and Mrs. Draper, a very sweet, youthful, and gentle-mannered little woman, hardly twenty, I should think. Came off at eleven and worked in Wall Street. . . .

Dr. Bellows brings back Knapp seriously prostrated by malarial fever. He saw Burnside in Washington, who reports that he was four hours in driving eight miles to McClellan's headquarters in a light wagon with four horses; that he saw two mules perish by drowning in the fluid mire of the road; and that three days of dry weather will bring a crisis and enable McClellan to deliver a battle. It is believed in Washington that McDowell's

[22] At the battle of Fair Oaks on May 31, General Joseph E. Johnston, the Confederate commander-in-chief, was severely injured. His place was taken by General G. W. Smith until June 2, when Robert E. Lee assumed command of the Army of Northern Virginia.

[23] The *St. Mark* was a large clipper ship, which gave spacious hospital accommodations to about two hundred men. Since she had no steam engines and drew too much water to ascend the rivers, she had to be kept off shore as a receiving vessel.

division has joined McClellan. Telegram from Dr. Hammond: "Fifteen thousand men to be provided for in five days; five thousand in New York." This looks like serious work on hand.

June 17. We are generally cast down today; there's villainous news abroad, and worse tidings may come at any moment. Rebel Army in the valley of Virginia largely reinforced (query: from the disintegrated army late at Corinth?). Banks and Frémont in danger once more. Clever raid in McClellan's rear by a party of rebel cavalry that threatened his communications, got up to the Pamunkey River and destroyed transport schooners and a wagon train before it was beat off. This dashing, successful audacity is a bad sign. McClellan seems to make no progress. We feel as if he were paralyzed by Washington intrigue, denying him reinforcements. God forbid. If so, and if a great disaster come of it, Stanton or somebody will be held to a stern account. The disaster seems likely enough, but I have a lively faith in the honesty and single-mindedness of old Abe Lincoln. There will be no personal intrigue in his Cabinet, "not if he knows it."

June 20, FRIDAY. Weather clear and cool of late. Letter from Ellie dated Monday afternoon just this side Old Point. Excellent spirits and no seasickness. Subsequent telegrams say the *St. Mark* is off Yorktown, *en permanence*, as receiving ship. No military news except our occupation of Cumberland Gap, an important point. Hard worked these last few days. Tonight at Gibbs's with Van Buren, Bellows, and Dr. Douglas.

Poor, honest, irascible, feeble old Tripler's nomination as Inspector General unanimously rejected by the Senate. Not surprising, for Senators have been visiting the White House and seeing for themselves what he can accomplish. Letterman and Vollum are to report to McClellan as Medical Director and Inspector. Tripler is relieved, and McClellan's army still more so. Perhaps we are a shade less blue than three days ago, but still very blue indeed. We think McClellan has been reinforced, but that the desperate rebel army before Richmond may make a dash on Washington and develop the latent sympathies of Maryland.

June 22. Received telegram from Olmsted at White House (through Bloor) that the *Daniel Webster* and the *Spalding* sail for New York today with cargoes of sick and wounded and must be sent back at once. "Should not remain overnight." This has kept me employed all day conferring with Bellows and Van Buren. The *Elm City* is also here, having discharged her freight of damaged humanity at Albany, so we have three transports to equip besides the *Euterpe*. Agnew is at the White House doing "exsections" and the like. T. H. Faile, Jr., our volunteer superintendent for New York, went off with him, deserting his post. Bellows goes to Ohio tonight to look after Antioch College, now in financial extremity. I suppose it to be a humbug in collapse, but Dr. Bellows says he must go and look after it, so the duties of the Executive Committee devolve on Van Buren, Gibbs, and myself.

June 23. Tonight to concert at Academy of Music. It was got up spontaneously by the young men of the Mercantile Society Library for the benefit of the Sanitary Commission. Tolerable house. Guess we shall net $1,000 and upwards. The wonderful Seventh Symphony was on its programme, and of course, covered a multitude of sins—solos, vocal and instrumental, *fioriture*, and bosh. The overtures to *Tannhäuser* and *Euryanthe*, also, are not to be heard every night. The symphony was well enough rendered. Its second movement certainly stands alone, unrivalled in its way, as an expression of hopeless supplication in sorrow, of a despairing cry from the depths and from a horror of great darkness. One might write about it for pages, but what he wrote would be nonsense to everyone but himself, so intangible and incommunicable is the message—addressed by the highest musical art to each individual that feels it. Then that grand, mournful march that comes "sweeping by," like tragedy, "with sceptered pall," silencing the festal phrases of the scherzo; the few massive awful chords that connect these two parts of the third movement, and lead the orchestra back from D major to F; the roaring triumphant chaos and anarchy of the fourth movement. What do they all mean? There must be—or must have been once in Beethoven's heart—a key to this wonderful symphony.

Dr. Grymes and Dr. Chamberlain, both just from White House, are prophets of evil. They say McClellan is in sorest need of reinforcement, that McDowell is *not* with him after all we have heard! I feel very blue tonight and as if heavy disaster might be at our doors.[24]

June 24, TUESDAY. Letter from Ellie at Yorktown. Very jolly, but no work yet. To Columbia College meeting at two o'clock. We gave an A.B. "*honoris causa*" to certain of our undergraduates who have left their

[24] Following the battle of Fair Oaks, the very crisis of the Peninsular campaign was at hand in the Seven Days' Battles, a week of almost continuous fighting. McClellan, after many delays and much indecisive fighting, had pushed to the very edge of the Southern capital. The fears of Lincoln and his advisers for the safety of Washington had thus far kept McDowell in northern Virginia. His force was at last promised to McClellan, and one of his divisions, under McCall, actually took its place in the line on June 19. But McDowell's remaining troops remained out of reach; and as McClellan's army resumed its movement forward against Richmond, the situation was suddenly changed for the worse by the junction of Stonewall Jackson's forces with those of Lee. The Seven Days' Battles ended in the retreat of the Union army to the James.

college course unfinished to take commissions in the army. This inspired my patriotic colleague, Martin Zabriskie, Esq., to move that we give that degree to all second lieutenants in all New York volunteer regiments. Fish duly announced the motion, and that it was *not* seconded. I wish I had seconded it, and said a few words concerning the spirit that prompted the mover. *Esprit de l'escalier!*

Thence to No. 498 Broadway. Chaos and confusion. Fifty people waiting, engaged or to be engaged in this, that, and the other steamer, wanting to know when she will sail, when and where they shall report, and nobody able to tell them. Unless we get this office decently organized, I will resign from the Sanitary Commission, for I cannot carry on my work as treasurer in this way any longer.

June 25.   Faint-heartedness still prevails. The President's visit to General Scott at West Point has stimulated the production of most authentic reports and reliable statements, mostly "asthenic" and unfavorable. Today's crop has been erroneous; for example, "McClellan is dead." "He is not dead yet, but dying of dysentery with typhoid symptoms." "A.B. was told by C.D. that he has a letter from his cousin, Major X.Y. on General Z.'s staff, stating that our McClellan has lost his mind and gone crazy with anxiety and excitement." "Lincoln wants Scott's advice about McClellan's successor."

June 26.   At this moment there are newsboys rampaging up the Fourth Avenue shrieking "Extry Something—Great battle at Richmond and defeat of McClellan!". . . Note from Van Buren. Agnew has returned from Virginia. Reports Yorktown hospitals broken up, the *St. Mark* taking on board the worst typhoid cases. Van Buren warned me that he thought Ellie might be endangered by the presence of a concentrated crowd of fever patients. This disconcerted and alarmed me seriously. Telegraphed her at once directly and also through Bloor at Washington. Wrote her by mail and also by the *Spalding*, which returned this afternoon, entreating, conjuring, and commanding her to quit the *St. Mark*, and if there be no vacancy on any less febrile ship to come straight home. This afternoon at No. 498 Broadway. Agnew was there. Encouraging report from him of the condition of the army in all but sanitary respects. Discipline, equipment, excellent. But hospitals are in a horrible state; malarious fever and diarrhea prevalent. Scurvy has appeared unmistakably.

Ellie's account of her interview with the medical officer in charge of the Yorktown hospital Monday or Tuesday is worth noting. Two thousand patients, typhoid mostly, on the hands of this official gentleman and his staff of one "contract surgeon." "How are you off for hospital diet, sir?" "Well, I don't think we have any. The men draw their rations" (salt pork and the like). "Indeed! Why, we have quantities of condensed milk, beef stock, and the like, on the *St. Mark,* and the Commission will no doubt be glad to supply you." "Oh, thank you; it's of no consequence. They generally die in two or three days, and it isn't worth while." "You have stimulants enough, I suppose?" "Oh, yes, that is, we have not got any now. We had so many gallons of brandy, and so on, but I thought they were used up very fast, and I'm glad they are gone. I shan't make requisition for any more." Is not this murderous and horrible? I believe the new inspector, Vollum, has removed this imbecile wretch, whose name was, I think, Wheaton.

June 27. Big dinner at old Dr. Mott's from six to eleven-thirty. Heavy work in this hot weather. Today has been summer full-blown. There were the Surgeon-General, and Drs. Satterlee, Van Buren, Flint, Markoe, Watts, Judge Hilton, and others—about a dozen. Sat next to Hammond. Like him better and better. Full of original thought and plans of vigorous action and organization. Some already carried out. There is a curious blending of coarse and fine grain in his composition. He is considering the question of an act to give the Medical Department its own independent transportation, the want of which seems to me to lie at the bottom of a large portion of its shortcomings. I have been trying to shew Bellows and Van Buren that this should be reformed and the Medical Bureau no longer depend on the Quarter-Master General for conveyance of stores and of sick men, but in vain. As Hammond is disposed to agree with me, I consider him, of course, a man of great practical good sense.

Bad news from Charleston. A decided repulse on James Island after hard fighting and with heavy loss. It looks like the affair of Big Bethel in many respects; may it be the precursor of no Bull Run! General Benham has come to New York under arrest (or perhaps not under arrest, for no one can be sure about anything), having made this attack in violation of General Hunter's orders.

June 30, MONDAY. Five o'clock in the afternoon. The darkest day we have seen since Bull Run. We have rallied a little and picked up a certain amount of hope since noon, but the general feeling is of dismay.

An extra late last night intimated that something of first-rate importance was in progress, disclosure not yet allowed, magnificent results at hand. This morning comes another, stating (let us see how much we can consider established) very hard fighting from Thursday to Saturday and

probably yesterday. McClellan's right wing has fallen back. White
House is abandoned. Transports, and so on, going down the Pamunkey,
and a certain amount of stores abandoned and burned. This is called a
strategic movement; polite language, I suppose, for a retreat. The fighting
has been desperate. My gallant friend Clitz is mortally wounded, his
regiment (the 12th U.S.A.) cut to pieces. Duryea's Zouaves have lost
their colonel (Warren) and many more. Churchill Cambreleng, one of
their captains, is wounded. (I got his father a pass from Hammond this
afternoon.) The rebels no doubt are terribly punished by our artillery.
That is about all. The War Department is "without further information,"
a fearfully bad symptom. It is all obscure. We cannot make out exactly
what's coming, but it has the walk of a defeat and a very bad one. I would
compromise for a drawn battle. . . .

Seward is in town (colloguing with Thurlow Weed and certain governors at the Astor House) and says it's all right and very jolly—his usual
parrot formula. He has no reliable intelligence. The indications taken all
together—the "totality of the symptoms"—are of disaster and ruin.

*Strong was right in his gloomy interpretation of the news. The irresolute
McClellan, who grossly exaggerated the strength of Lee's army, had completely
failed in his Peninsular campaign. On June 27, Fitz-John Porter's troops
magnificently held the greater part of the Confederate army in check in the
sanguinary battle of Gaines's Mill; and if McClellan had used the unemployed
part of his army (no fewer than 55,000 men) in a spirited attack against the
weak Confederate right wing, he could have overwhelmed it and captured
Richmond. Instead, he irresolutely delayed; and at nightfall Porter's line was
broken, and his exhausted men were forced to retreat. At midnight McClellan
wrote Secretary Stanton in a vain effort to shift the blame to the shoulders of the
Administration. "I have lost this battle," he declared, "because my force was
too small." And he added that if he saved the Union forces from capture, no
thanks would be due the War Department: "You have done your best to sacrifice
this army." Lincoln then ordered him to extricate his command, and on June 28
McClellan began his retreat, burning large quantities of stores and exploding
carloads of ammunition. Lee was at first too astonished by the retreat to attack
the Union army, but on July 1st he caught up and delivered a heavy assault at
Malvern Hill, overlooking the James River. It was repulsed, and McClellan
fell back without further molestation to his new base at Harrison's Landing.
The deepest melancholy enveloped the North. A magnificently equipped army,*

which on June 20 had numbered 105,000 men, and which had penetrated almost within sight of the Richmond steeples, had been thrown back in utter discomfiture by Lee's forces of fewer than 90,000. Thousands of lives (McClellan lost nearly 16,000 men in the Seven Days' Battles) and hundreds of millions of treasure had been expended in vain. The faith of the North in McClellan was almost completely shattered.

July 1. Letters from Ellie. She seems to have left the *St. Mark* at Yorktown Thursday and gone up the Pamunkey to the *Knickerbocker* at the White House just in time to assist at the general movement to the rear. She writes in the best of spirits, undisturbed by all the rumpus and hurry about her, and thinking mainly of her work. She is a very great little woman! Heaven send her safe home!

Visit from Professor Lieber. One of his three sons lost an arm at Fort Donelson. Another, Oscar of South Carolina, was badly hit at Williamsburg, fighting in the ranks of the rebellion, and when last heard from, was lying at Richmond attacked by erysipelas, which disease is ravaging the hospitals of that town. His third son is in the Eleventh or Twelfth Regulars, reported much cut up in this last battle; and Lieber called to enquire about passes to Yorktown, and so on. His visit is a specimen of the practical effects of Civil War. Who is guilty of this Civil War, and what punishment do those on whom its guilt rests deserve?

July 2. Thank Heaven, the President has called for a few hundred thousand volunteers to reinforce the army, at last. Would he had invoked them three months ago! We retire, repulsed and beaten, from James Island, and the capture of Charleston is put off to a more convenient season. Things look ill in the West. Our European news is bad. France and England are itching to intervene and sustain the slave-breeding woman-floggers of Charleston and New Orleans and Richmond in their rebellion. I never expected much from France, but the political immorality of England, as revealed by her press, confounds me. I cannot understand or explain it. If her sense of national right and wrong be so utterly perverted as it seems, she will surely be punished before many generations have passed away.

July 3, THURSDAY. Very bad. What news will come tonight no man can tell, but just now (five o'clock in the afternoon) things look disastrous. Fighting continued Sunday and Monday, when our gunboats seem to have done good service once more. McClellan seems now jammed up against the James River, with his left fifteen miles below Richmond, having abandoned siege guns and left his wounded in the field. Worse is behind, no doubt, or the War Department would speak out. That fellow Stanton probably fears the storm a full report will raise about his ears. Has McClellan ammunition and supplies? Can he maintain himself where he is? Has he transportation if he find it necessary to retreat? Isn't it very possible that his whole army may have to surrender? It's an immense disaster, as it stands, and of course, we do not know the worst yet. Intervention now, another war on our shoulders, and disgrace and ruin for the two alternatives to choose between. . . .

Ten-thirty P.M. George Anthon dined with me, and we had a talk afterwards. His cantankerous ways when out of temper with a friend are certainly compensated by unusual frankness and fullness of kind, apologetic, self-condemning talk when the fit is over. I helped the children ignite certain crackers, and so on. It seemed indecent at this period of disaster and anxiety, but I decided in its favor as a patriotic avowal of "Never say die," and "Don't give up the ship," embodied in pyrotechny. During this performance, there came an extra. In substance, McClellan [was] at Harrison's Bar [Landing] . . . on the James River yesterday at five-thirty o'clock. . . .

On the whole, my construction of the result is this. We are beat back by a superior force but not destroyed. The enemy was superior because we have been outgeneralled. The blame rests, probably, on the War Department. The remedy is speedy reinforcement. This call for 300,000 volunteers would have provided the remedy had it been issued two months ago. But it comes too late to meet this crisis. Whether we can spare men from before Washington or get them up from the Southwest in time is a question. The *Evening Post* announces that the *Daniel Webster* arrived at Baltimore this morning with wounded men. God grant that Ellie was on board of her. If so, she will be here tomorrow.

N.B. Johnny has been reading *Oliver Twist*; and, with most intense delight, *Sintram*. Dare I give him *Undine* and *Peter Wilkins*? He approaches a perilous period of life.

July 6, SUNDAY. A cruel hot day. At home and in shirt sleeves getting up a circular or statement asking contributions for the army. No church, I regret to say. Mr. Ruggles came in this evening, just from Washington, where he has been fighting for enlargement of canals as a highway for gunboats, and he is defeated, or rather put off, by a majority small beyond all expectation, so small that the result is a triumph. He came on with sundry officers wounded during the last week of continuous battle before Richmond. They are amazed at the feeling of depression they find here. "We never supposed we were retreating," they say. "We thought we were gaining a victory every day." He reports Seward full of secret policy and mysterious hints and charlatanism. Louis Napoleon is tempted to intervene, according to Seward, because he wants his son recognized as his successor by European powers and thinks he will secure recognition of his dynasty by active hostility to free institutions. It seems an unreasonable, impractical motive, not at all in the style of that most wily and wary potentate. But I see the danger, though unable to detect the motive, unless we gain decisive results within thirty days.

July 7. Broiling. . . . Busy at No. 68 and No. 498 as usual. After dinner to Dr. Van Buren's to consult over proof-sheets. Summoned into the dining-room, where I find the Dr. and Madame, Miss Addie, a quiet young lady of mature years, to wit, eighteen or so (and they say a remarkably nice, thoughtful little personage), and rampagious Miss Sally of ten or twelve, domestically known as "bird o' freedom," with whom I may claim to be on terms of intimacy. After a little talk and an adjournment for awhile to the doctor's office, I loafed uptown with Agnew.

The *Spalding, St. Mark* and *Daniel Webster* arrived full of wounded men. Letter from Ellie this morning dated Friday night; then leaving the *Daniel Webster* for the *Knickerbocker* at Harrison's Point so as to avoid an outside passage and seasickness, the *Knickerbocker* being destined for Washington. Tonight, another hurried pencil note, brought by private hand, dated yesterday, on board the *Knickerbocker* off Fort Monroe. (I am thankful she has escaped assassination on her way down the James River.) Very tired, but quite well (I hope so), and to be at home again tomorrow night at the latest.

July 11, FRIDAY.   Ellie returned by railroad Wednesday afternoon in the best of spirits and good health, except for a slight symptom of "Pamunkeyness" that will not prove lasting or serious, I hope. Has had a jolly time of hard work and useful work amid the tragedies of visible war. No time to write her story. Wish there were, for it's worth recording. She came to Washington from Harrison's Landing on the *Knickerbocker*, a government transport, with Miss [Helen] Gilson of Chelsea, Massachusetts, and a staff of dressers. It was an experiment of her devising. Government and Sanitary Commission had not worked together on the same ship before. The combination succeeded triumphantly. Ellie's tact, sense, good-nature, and energy conquered the U.S.A. surgeon in charge, Dr. Page, at once, and coerced all his official dignity into loyal submission, or rather into hearty, grateful cooperation in the care of his cargo of 500 "cases," mostly bad ones. She had the great satisfaction of producing, from the little stock of Commission stores she brought on board hastily got together at half an hour's notice from the *Daniel Webster*—and . . . while amputations were going on—the bandages and the stimulants of which the surgeon really believed he had not any on board. The little woman has come out amazingly strong during these two months. Have never given her credit for a tithe of the enterprise, pluck, discretion, and force of character she has shewn. God bless her. . . .

John Astor is in town. How he swears when one names the Secretary of War! He for one believes that Stanton wilfully withheld reinforcements from McClellan lest he should make himself too important, politically, by a signal victory. Many, the majority of people, I think, share his belief. Stanton is being awfully rasped and punished; he's the target for a concentric newspaper fire. My faith in the man failed some time ago; it was a lively faith when his career began, but I don't feel quite justified by the evidence in bringing him in guilty of crime so base and so tremendous in its consequences. I have got positions as nurses on the *Spalding*, which sailed today, for Charles Kuhn, who wants to look after his brother Hamilton Kuhn, reported killed (truly reported, I think, but Charles Kuhn clings to a straw of uncertainty), and for a young Coster who is on a similar errand for one of his house now lying badly wounded at Harrison's Landing. We are run down with like applications. Granting these was a bad precedent and opens a door we shall find it hard to close, but we could not resist the appeal.

Nothing notable today. No news. From eight to ten-thirty at Bellows's with Agnew settling sundry matters of importance, particularly as to the organization of our office at No. 498 Broadway and the framing of rules to prevent abuses on our transports.

We have been and are in a depressed, dismal, asthenic state of anxiety and irritability. The cause of the country does not happen to be thriving just now. McClellan's army is safe, but how soon will the James River be closed by rebel batteries and supplies cut off? May he not be compelled to capitulate within ten days? Are not the rebels now moving a column on Washington? Stonewall Jackson is not killed.[25]

[25] Eastern sentiment was now against McClellan's retention at the head of the Army of the Potomac. On July 11, Henry W. Halleck assumed command of all the forces of the United States, with headquarters in Washington. McClellan wished to remain on the James and to renew his operations against Richmond as soon as he could be reinforced. But Halleck decided to order the withdrawal of the army to Aquia Creek, on the Virginia side of the Potomac some seventy-five miles from Richmond, and the

Letters from Olmsted tonight. Not cheering. He writes on the 4th instant on his way to Washington (on the *Wilson Small*) to make a report to the Surgeon-General on the sanitary condition of the army and to plead for reinforcements for Burnside or somebody, and for 50,000 more men. Where can we find them on demand? Why was recruiting stopped? Letterman, surgeon U.S.A.,[26] says our loss is 30,000, residue 60,000. Sanitary aspect of the army very bad. No camp police; no time for it. On the 7th, after his visit to Washington, which seems to have made no impression, he writes in still darker mood. Seems to think McClellan's whole army may be cut off from its supplies and destroyed. Rebels may close up the James River with batteries suddenly opened. (That is certainly our most pressing peril.) Reaction after terrible tension and excitement appears in the army. Officers sneak off and bully their way on board the hospital transports under flimsy pretexts of sick leave. They long to get away on any terms.

July 14. Fiercely hot again. Busy day, drawing rules for the New York agency and for transport service. Trinity Church vestry tonight,

movement began at once. Meanwhile, on June 26 Lincoln had consolidated the forces under Frémont, Banks, and McDowell, with the troops in Washington, into the Army of Virginia under General John Pope. For a short time the boastful Pope now swaggered in the center of the stage.

[26] Jonathan Letterman (1824–1872), surgeon, United States Army, occupies a place in Civil War medical history greater than Strong's references to him indicate. Immediately after graduation from Jefferson Medical College in 1849, he entered the army as assistant surgeon, thereafter serving in the Seminole campaigns and at several Western posts. In November, 1861, he accompanied troops sent from California to New York. As Strong noted on June 20, he succeeded Charles S. Tripler as medical director of the Army of the Potomac, to the immense advantage of that army and of all United States troops. Reporting to McClellan on July 1, he found the army in dire condition: at least a fifth of its personnel was ineffective from sickness; wounded men, hospital tents, ambulances, and medical stores had been abandoned in the retreat; there were no records and no working organization. Letterman's setting up of a temporary hospital at Harrison's Landing, his removal of some 20,000 sick and wounded men to Washington, and his rapid organization of medical service were unprecedented achievements. With the backing of McClellan, he organized an ambulance service which was adopted by the other Union armies and formalized by act of Congress in March, 1864. He set up a field hospital organization that also became standard throughout United States forces; he reorganized the medical supply table, reducing quantities by careful selection; and he vigorously enforced sanitary measures the neglect of which had cost the Union so many fighting men. Letterman's organization of the medical department of the Army of the Potomac brought order out of chaos, saved an inestimable number of lives, and raised field medical service of the United States Army to a peak of efficiency not to be approached again until the first World War.

G.T.S.
28 NOVEMBER 1860

U.S. SANITARY COMMISSION HEADQUARTERS

823 BROADWAY, NEW YORK

but there was only half a quorum, so I lounged, nerveless, sweaty, and blue, up the Bowery, looking at the wonderful social phenomena of that over-populated country, the men, women, and children whereof seem to spend these sultry nights in the streets, squatting on their door-steps or the curb-stones.

We are in the depths just now, permeated by disgust, saturated with gloomy thinking. I find it hard to maintain my lively faith in the triumph of the nation and the law. I fear tomorrow's war-meeting in Union Square will be unlike that of April 20, 1861 (a time never to be forgotten. It was among the most intense and memorable hours of my life). People without virile loyalty are bolder in their talk. Recruiting is dull. . . . It seems to me the great point is to use the new levies to fill gaps in our existing experienced regiments before forming new ones. Three hundred new regiments, with their officers and men all equally raw, will be a mere mob of Bull-Runagates for six months after they are mustered into service. News this morning that the rebels have retaken Murfreesboro, Tennessee, and threaten Nashville. Rumor tonight that Van Dorn has retaken Baton Rouge. Very bad. On the other hand, the government seems waking up to the duty of dealing more vigorously with rebellion by acts of emancipation and confiscation.

MORE NORTHERN REVERSES · SECOND MANASSAS ·
LEE'S INVASION OF MARYLAND · EMANCIPATION
PROCLAMATION · CONGRESSIONAL ELECTIONS ·

*W*hen Lincoln paid his visit of July 8, 1862, to the Army of the
Potomac at Harrison's Landing, home from the Peninsular campaign,
the war seemed at its very crisis. McClellan's reverses had caused great discouragement in the North; gold stood at a premium of seventeen per cent; the
radical Republicans in Congress were vociferous in their denunciation of the
Administration. The time had come when it was necessary to enlarge the objects
for which the North was fighting. Lincoln had insisted—and he continued to
insist for a short time—that the war was being waged to restore the Union, and
for that purpose alone. But a fast-growing proportion of the people and of Congress wished to fight as well for the liberation of the slaves. Congress on July
11–12 passed the Second Confiscation Act, which after sixty days of warning
freed forever those slaves of "rebel owners" who in any way came under the
control of the national government. The day after its passage Lincoln, driving
to the funeral of Secretary Stanton's child, told Welles and Seward that he had
about reached the conclusion "that it was a military necessity, absolutely essential for the salvation of the nation, that we must free the slaves or be ourselves
subdued." A major change in national policy was impending. The greatest event
of the second half of 1862 was to be adoption by the Administration of the
emancipation policy; henceforth the war was to be fought for freedom as well as
the Union. Abroad as well as at home this lifted the Northern struggle to a
higher plane.

July 17. . . . Olmsted arrived this morning from Harrison's Bar on the *Daniel Webster*, sunburnt and worn but in better health and less doleful in his prophesyings than I expected. When Olmsted is blue, the logic of his despondency is crushing and terrible. Lawrence Williams [just from Virginia on sick leave] on McClellan's staff during the week of battle. Perfect confidence in McClellan. Admirable coolness and equanimity throughout. Fighting earnest and desperate on both sides. We can hold our present position and may do well yet if reinforcements come fast enough and if McClellan be not bothered by interference from Washington. Burnside at Newport News with 10,000 to 15,000 men (Williams), 7,000 (Olmsted). Health of the army decidedly improved during last week (Olmsted). Only a few points on the river where serious mischief could be done by masked batteries, and these could be made secure by felling the trees.

Clitz certainly at Richmond. I trust that is true. Lawrence Williams denounces the Administration, Stanton especially, with plainness of speech that does not altogether become a major in the United States Army. He shudders at abolitionists as hydrophobic patients at the sound of falling water. But it is remarkable that his estimate of Lincoln has changed. He doesn't call Lincoln a "gorilla ape" as he did last winter, but relies on him as the only honest and patriotic man in the Administration. Perhaps he is not so far wrong. He introduced the subject of his own arrest last spring; has not even a suspicion of the reason for it. McClellan discharged him as soon as he knew of it. "As to his communicating with the enemy, why, if he were to go over, his own family would be the first to kick him out of Richmond." I do not dream that Williams could be guilty of treason, and I know little of his distinguished F.F.V. relatives. But I think it doubtful whether there are many Southerners who would kick him very hard for any baseness whatever committed in the interest of the South. The cases of Brooks and Floyd are in point.

July 19. Much cooler. Fervent in business (Sanitary Commission) all day. Our affairs are prosperous. R. G. White dined and spent the evening. No events to record, except the occupation of Gordonsville by General Pope's advance. . . .

July 23. . . . There is one piece of good news. Clitz arrived here yesterday on the *Euterpe*, and has gone to his mother's or brother's at Fort Hamilton. He was a prisoner at Richmond and sent down on parole under flag of truce. . . .

July 26, SATURDAY. . . . Clitz's talk has made me blue-black. I greatly fear that we are on the eve of some vast calamity. Why in the name of anarchy and ruin doesn't the President order the draft of one million fighting men at once and the liberation and arming of every able-bodied Sambo in Southronia? We shall perish unless the government begin singing in that very key (of all the sharps). War on rebels as criminals has not begun. We have dealt with these traitors as a police officer deals with a little crowd that threatens a breach of the peace. He wheedles and persuades and administers his club-taps mildly and seldom.

July 31. We still stew. If I have shed no blood in the country's service, I have been liberal with another secretion, sweat, with which I have bedewed the streets and sprinkled my papers, so that I was obliged to protect them with umbrelloid blotting paper. Don't wonder that the national cause, so prosperous in February and March, goes "all agley" in this weather, or rather in that intensified form of summer that now reigns and roasts alive below the Potomac. How can honest Northern men fight when the very marrow of their bones is oozing out at every pore of their bodies? . . .

Charley Strong dined here. Strolled out with him and called for Ellie at No. 24, where she spent the rest of the evening. Long talk with Mr. Samuel B. Ruggles, just returned from a journey west, even to the Falls of St. Anthony. He was full of what he had seen: of the thousands of miles of wheat harvest through which his iron road had carried him, of the enormous resources of the Northwest, of our national wealth and ability to feed the world, of King Cotton dethroned and King Breadstuff crowned as his successor. He has a wonderful way of giving life and poetry and power to the driest statistics.

August 4, MONDAY. . . . Extra tonight. Advance of a column of Pope's army to Orange C.H., and a reconnaissance and little affair of cavalry fourteen miles from Petersburg. Recruiting goes on better than was expected, and there is a little tentative move toward drafting at last. Inaction of the rebels surprises me. Are they weaker than we think, or are they gathering themselves together for some decisive blow where we don't expect them? McClellan's great name is growing very obscure, I regret to say, and we generally doubt whether he is a genuine congener of Napoleon after all. As we deified him without reason, I suppose we are free to reduce his rank whenever we like. Prevailing color of people's talk is blue. What's very bad, we begin to lose faith in Uncle Abe. "Most honest and true, thoroughly sensible, but without the decision and the energy the country wants." Government "does not lead the people; the people has to keep up a toilsome *vis a tergo,* and shove the government forward to every vigorous step." Such is the talk I hear wherever I go. There seems some element of truth in it; but who that is not behind the scenes can tell? Our letter to the President about filling up old regiments before forming new ones is much approved, and the policy it recommends adopted. A most important result, but the good sense of the people had expressed itself very strongly through many channels in favor of that policy, so that we cannot claim the credit of having persuaded the government to adopt it.

August 7.   Broiling hot. Has the South prevailed on the sun to intervene? Busy day, but nothing special. Dined at Maison Dorée as yesterday. Martinez, the proprietor, discovering that I was the individual who had paid him some thousand dollars for beef-stock during the last two months, became warmly interested in us and insisted on getting up a little artistic recherché dinner for us of his own devising. Very pretty little dinner it was, and full of elegant but surprising effects, and the bill was unquestionably reasonable. George Anthon here afterwards.

Bad news today. California steamer *Golden Gate* burned at sea; 180 passengers lost and more than a million of treasure. Nothing from the army. McClellan seems about making an important move; some say a withdrawal from before Richmond to the Potomac, others the transfer of his whole army to the south side of the James River. Nobody knows, and people's speculations are not worth a damaged Delmonico shinplaster. I hope to go to Newport tomorrow afternoon. Van Buren is to operate on poor Clitz's damaged leg tomorrow and extract the ball.

We gradually come round to a better opinion of McClellan's movements during the memorable battle week; incline to believe his march on the James River a most delicate and critical operation, successfully executed under the most disadvantageous conditions, winding up with demoralizing repulse and slaughter of the rebels at Malvern Hill. As to that, Clitz's report of what his former friends (now in the service of rebellion and the Devil) told him seems conclusive. Magruder was drunk or reckless, and pushed column after column into the overwhelming fire of our artillery, which destroyed or disorganized whole brigades.

August 16, SATURDAY.   Weather continues more bearable, but still hot. Busy days. Sanitary Commission work, of course. Everything else is thrown overboard to my loss and damage. But I believe we are doing a considerable amount of service to the country and that we have saved more men than have been lost in any two days' fighting since the war began. Thank God that a miserable, nearsighted cockney like myself can take part in any work that strengthens and helps on the national cause. Should have gone to Newport this afternoon, but that my semi-annual turn of duty at Bleecker Street Bank comes next week, and I must be in town Monday morning. . . .

War news. Important movements of McClellan's army probably in progress. His present position said to be untenable. General Scott tells Charles King (who tells Mr. Ruggles) that no army can exist on the James River after August 15. It must advance, retreat, or perish, poisoned by malaria. Some say the army is transferred to the right bank of the river; others, that it is falling back on Williamsburg and Fort Monroe; others, that it is to be carried to Aquia Creek and Fredericksburg and take a fresh start. Certainly nothing can be more vicious than the present position of our forces in Virginia; our two armies, McClellan's and Pope's, are unable to support each other, while the enemy, though inferior in force, is concentrated between them and can make a dash at either with fair prospect of success. That campaign on the Peninsula seems to have been a great strategic blunder. An enterprising general, willing to risk something on prompt, vigorous offensive movements, might have carried it successfully through and taken Richmond—or he might not. But that is not McClellan's style of work. He means to be safe, and is, therefore, obliged to be slow. His theory of an invasion is to entrench himself, advance five miles, and then spend three weeks in getting up another line of fieldworks. This would be good practice were not time so important an element. Perhaps no one whose *spécialité* is military engineering can be a great captain and handle men in the field with decision and promptitude. Todleben of Sebastopol and Marshal Blücher cannot be combined in the same general. The expert in siege and operations is most valuable in his proper place, but he cannot be a Marshal "Vorwärts" and is very likely to become a Marshal "Rückwärts" if his opponent be enterprising and vigilant.

I fear Lincoln is what Wendell Phillips calls him, "a first-rate second-rate man." Stanton is certainly three parts lunatic. His preposterous order about drafting and persons seeking to evade the draft is decisive as to his fitness for his great place.[1] Under that order, I, being "absent

[1] After Lincoln's call for 300,000 three-year men apportioned equitably among the states, a great exodus to Canada and Europe had been reported. Stanton tried to check it by a stay-at-home order (August 8, 1862), declaring that no citizen liable to be drafted into the militia should be allowed to go abroad and instructing the military to arrest would-be evaders.

from my state" at Newport last Sunday, was liable to be arrested, carried
to Fort Adams, and kept on military duty for nine months, the expense
of my arrest being deducted from my pay. If arrested, I had no opportunity to show that my visit to Rhode Island was in good faith, and without design to evade military service. The letter of Stanton's order made
my presence in Rhode Island cause for nine months' imprisonment at
hard labor. If I am obliged to go to Brooklyn tomorrow to inspect books
and the like, in the county clerk's office, I shall be "absent from my
county" and liable to the same treatment. Stanton's folly and our generous
acquiescence in it are great phenomena.

August 19.   McClellan has gloriously evacuated Harrison's Landing
and got safe back to where he was months ago. Magnificent strategy.
Pity it has lost so many thousand men and millions of dollars. Our repulse
of Breckinridge's attack on Baton Rouge seems to have been creditable.
A superior force beat back after hard fighting. We lost General [Thomas]
Williams, a good officer. He was Major Williams on Scott's staff at
Rockaway and West Point years ago. The rebel iron-clad ram *Arkansas*,
which has given us some uneasiness, blew herself up (or else was blown
up by our incendiary shells, it is uncertain which), and sleeps with her
elder sister the *Merrimac*. McClellan stock is falling fearfully. He is held
accountable for the thousands of lives expended without result in digging
trenches in the Chickahominy swamp and on the James River. Unjustly
perhaps. Stanton may have withheld reinforcements. But generals are
judged by the results of their generalship.

August 21.   We are most anxious about affairs in Virginia. The
streets are filled with rumors of a great disaster to General Pope's command.[2] They cannot be traced and are disbelieved, but these shadows are
too often the forerunners of some calamitous fact. Such disaster is but too
plainly probable, thanks to the refined strategy that has thus far directed
the campaign. McClellan's withdrawal to the lower end of the Peninsula
makes the whole rebel army available for a dash in any direction its
leaders may select. It is set free—disengaged—for offensive operations.
We are not quite sure that their transportation is so deficient as people
think it. If they possess common sense, they will surely move against
Pope with their whole available force, which certainly far outnumbers

[2] Pope's army lay north of the Rappahannock; Lee's army, crossing the undefended
fords of the Rapidan, arrived on the south banks of the Rappahannock on August 20
and spent the next five days seeking an opportunity to cross it in force and turn Pope's
right flank.

his, hoping to crush him and move on Washington before McClellan can join him. This is their hour. The new levies that are daily pouring southward from New York, New England, and the West will soon make offensive movements impossible. They must strike now. Within a week the sediment of McClellan's grand army will be in a position to support Pope, I trust, and to meet the rebels on terms of equality. I have been listening all day for a screech of newsboys proclaiming: "Extry! Got the great battle and the defeat of General Pope." Every hour decisive battle is postponed is great gain for at least a week to come. We want a strong man, a great general, very badly. Such a man would be dangerous, but we want him.

August 27, WEDNESDAY. . . . We seem to be falling back successfully and maintaining our defensive line on the north fork of the Rappahannock. There has been sharp fighting at several points. An enterprising rebel foray seems to have beat up General Pope's headquarters, destroyed supply trains, and carried off important papers and letters.[3] Scandalous and disgraceful, if we have the whole truth. Some considerable portion of McClellan's army has got back to Alexandria or Aquia Creek, and it is probable that the whole Army of Virginia will be concentrated within ten days or a fortnight. . . .

Sunday [at Newport] to Trinity Church. Afternoon walk on the *soi-disant* "Cliffs" with Ellie. Monday, sailboat; Johnny and Temple and Charley Peters and I fished. Result: flounders, blackfish, "scup," alias porgies, no end of little bergalls, and so on. Tuesday, we repeated the experiment on the "north side of Canonicus," some seven miles up the bay, seeking shark with clothes lines and meat hooks. . . .

August 29. . . . At three-thirty to No. 498 Broadway, where I was surprised to meet Dr. Bellows, called to town from the woods of Walpole, New Hampshire, by some clerical duty, and Olmsted on sick leave from Washington. Jaundiced—yellow as butter; the poison of Pamunkey and the James River malaria is in his very bones.

Olmsted reports Stanton hostile to the Commission and refusing to let the government printers work for us any more. We need their service just now to reprint large editions of certain of our documents for the benefit of the new levies. If the Secretary make up his mind to take this position, we can go before the people with very fair prospect of success.

[3] Stuart's cavalry, by a bold raid in the Union rear, had captured Pope's headquarters and seized a despatch-book full of valuable information.

He will hardly venture on a collision with us. Dr. Hammond working vigorously, but in danger of collision with Meigs, which would be a pity.

Dined with George Anthon at Maison Dorée, and thence at nine o'clock to Dr. Bellows's, settling the draft of his report from the Executive Committee to the Commission at its contemplated meeting September 16.

Still these brilliant, dashing, successful raids or forays of rebel cavalry within our lines. They have penetrated to Manassas, destroying supply trains and capturing guns, taking us by surprise. Are our generals traitors or imbecile? Why does the Rebellion enjoy the monopoly of audacity and enterprise? Were I a general, even I, poor little feeble, myopic, flaccid, effeminate George T. Strong, I think I could do better than this. . . .

August 30, SATURDAY.   A noteworthy day for good or evil; we do not certainly know which. The morning papers were not cheerful. We were out-generalled and out-flanked. Washington in danger again, everything bungled and botched. It was clear that both armies had got into each other's rear and were so mixed up that they couldn't be disentangled without breaking something. The rebels were supposed to be making a bold move on the Upper Potomac, said to be fordable now, with designs on Maryland and the back door of the Capital. There was an epidemic of indigo. At three came a despatch from Pope to Halleck. "Terrific battle" that lasted all yesterday on the field of Bull Run. We took the initiative, drove the enemy, and occupy their position. Fitz-John Porter coming up this morning, when we mean to go in again, but we are too tired just now. Our loss say 8,000; rebel loss twice that; a grand victory. God grant this may be true and the whole truth. But I am not prepared to crow quite yet. Pope is an imaginative chieftain and ranks next to Cooper as a writer of fiction. Good news from Bull Run is suspicious *per se*, moreover. I cannot forget the exhilarating intelligence from that locality that reached us on a—in point of fact, on what may be called a former occasion, about thirteen months and nine days ago. I expect to be informed by tomorrow morning's papers that strategic considerations lead General Pope to follow up his victory by skedaddling toward the Potomac at full speed, leaving guns and prisoners in the hands of the enemy. It is a bad sign that we have no extra tonight. If the rebels were beaten yesterday, they ought to be crushed and annihilated today. Their line of retreat is toward the difficult gorges of the Bull Run range of hills.

Once more a terrible defeat had befallen the Union in the second battle of Bull Run or Manassas. John Pope, a West Pointer of Kentucky birth who had done well at Island No. 10 on the Mississippi, had been brought east and put in charge of the new Army of Virginia, made up of the united forces of Banks, Frémont, and McDowell. The commander began his campaign with a boastful general order that deeply offended the brave troops who had fought on the Peninsula. "I have come to you from the West," he declared, "where we have always seen the backs of our enemies; from an army whose business it has been to seek the adversary, and to beat him when he was found; whose policy has been attack and not defense." Even before this piece of brag had been published, McClellan had been reluctant to cooperate with Pope; and Halleck had found it necessary to give him peremptory orders to send troops to reinforce the Army of Virginia. The veterans of McClellan's force, slowly brought back to the line of the Potomac, were sulky and listless. As soon as Lee saw that McClellan's army was being withdrawn from the Peninsula, he resolved to concentrate his forces and overwhelm Pope before the latter could gain strength. His movements were attended by complete success. Lee detached Stonewall Jackson with 25,000 men from his main army and sent him to outflank Pope—the irresistible Jackson by a swift march cutting the railroad and telegraph lines between Pope and Washington and capturing large quantities of much-needed clothing and food. Then on August 29 and 30, while consternation reigned in Washington, Lee and Jackson fell upon Pope's army (superior in numbers, but as yet pitiably ill organized) at Manassas. The Northern general was well served by one corps commander, McDowell, but very badly by another, Fitz-John Porter, who behaved as if he were indifferent and discontented, and failed to give the active assistance needed. After a hard-fought struggle, in which the Union troops suffered much more heavily than the Confederates, Pope was compelled to retreat in confusion. He did not stop until his men were safe in their old entrenchments in front of Washington, which for a time seemed in danger of capture. On September 2, he made a doleful plea to the government. "Unless something can be done to restore tone to this army," he wrote, "it will melt away before you know it." It was plain that Pope was unfit for his place, and Lincoln forthwith placed McClellan again in command of all the troops defending the capital. The hour was one of the bitterest in the whole war, and Strong does not exaggerate the general discouragement and anxiety.

August 31, SUNDAY. Eleven-thirty A.M. Waiting for news. The suspense is trying. Anticipations not brilliant. No further particulars that are at all reliable in morning papers—an ominous stillness. McDowell telegraphs that it's "decidedly" a victory. The adverb produces a negative impression on my mind. . . . Ten P.M. This citizen does not despair of the republic. Most of his friends do. But though things look bad, and there is reason enough for anxiety and apprehension, people are making up their minds to the worst much too fast. I can find no tangible evidence of serious disaster, yet.

At about one o'clock in came Dr. Harris with a telegram from Stanton to the mayor, calling for surgeons to be sent on at once. It is dated yesterday, three-forty-five P.M., but was not received till nine this morning. The Secretary says Friday's battle was a hard one, but the enemy was beaten at all points. It was resumed this (Saturday) morning, and was still going on at the date of the despatch. No suggestion of misfortune. Harris had been working hard and had already secured some thirty surgeons who were to go south by this evening's train. He has considerable capacity for usefulness, in spite of his faults. After conferring with him, I went by appointment to George Anthon's in East Thirty-fifth Street and dined with him, his mamma, Miss Emily, and young Mrs. Reginald Anthon, who evidently contemplates furnishing the nation with a raw recruit before long; and we went after dinner to the upper end of Central Park and walked down. Great progress made since my last visit. The long lines of carriages and the crowds of gents and giggling girls suggested peace and prosperity. There was nothing from which one could have guessed that we are in a most critical period of a great Civil War, in the very focus and vortex of a momentous crisis and in imminent peril of grave national disaster. Being caught in a lively little shower, we walked homeward rapidly and looked out for an extra as we got into the city. But there was none. Took a cup of coffee in the dining room and received George Anthon at about eight o'clock in the evening. He was a messenger of evil. Pope has fallen back on Centreville, if the reports that prevail be reliable. That does not look like decided victory! But the situation is utterly obscure and we can form no opinion about it.

September 3. It has been a day of depressing malignant dyspepsia, not only private and physical, but public and moral. *Egomet Ipse*, George T. Strong, to wit, and we the people have been in a state of nausea and irritation all day long. The morning papers and an extra at mid-day turned us livid and blue. Fighting Monday afternoon at Chantilly, the enemy beat back (more or less), and Pope retreating on Alexandria and Washington to our venerable field-worn fortresses of a year ago. Stonewall Jackson (our national bugaboo) about to invade Maryland, 40,000 strong. General advance of the rebel line threatening our hold on Missouri and Kentucky. Cincinnati in danger. A rebel army within forty miles of the Queen City of the West. Martial law proclaimed in her pork shops. On the other hand, we hear that General [Julius] Stahel and General [Philip] Kearny have come to life again, or were only "kilt," not killed, after all. Everybody talks down McClellan and McDowell. McDowell *is said* to have lost us the battle of Saturday afternoon by a premature movement to the rear, though his supports were being hurried up. He is an unlucky general.

September 4. It is certain now that the army has fallen back to its old burrows around Washington. It will probably hibernate there. So, after all this waste of life and money and material, we are at best where we were a year ago. McClellan is chief under Halleck. Many grumble at this, but whom can we find that is proved his superior? He is certainly as respectable as any of the mediocrities that make up our long muster roll of generals. The army believes in him, undoubtingly; that is a material fact. And I suppose him very eminently fitted for a campaign of redoubts and redans, though incapable of vigorous offensive operations. There is reason to hope that Stanton is trembling to his fall. May he fall soon, for he is a public calamity. McDowell and Pope are "universally despised"; so writes Bellows. Poor General Kearny is dead and no mistake and will be buried in Trinity Churchyard next Saturday; so says Meurer the sexton.[4] He's a great loss. I don't know whether he understood strategy, but he was a dashing, fearless sabreur who had fought in Mexico, Algeria, and Lombardy, and loved war from his youth up. I remember my father talking thirty years ago about young Kearny, who was studying law in his office, and about this strange, foolish passion for a military life. He was under a very dark cloud six years ago and was cut by many of his friends. But, bad as it was, the lady's family were horribly to blame— most imprudent; and Kearny made all the reparation he could. He married her and treated her with all possible affection and loyalty. Whatever his faults, we shall miss him.

[4] The dashing Phil Kearny, riding into the enemy lines at Chantilly, had been killed September 1. Lee, an old friend in Mexican War days, sent the body to General Pope under flag of truce.

Our Sanitary Commission stores were first on the field after the battle of Saturday and did great service, for all the forty-two wagon loads of the Medical Department were bagged by the rebels at Manassas. Dr. Chamberlain, our inspector in charge, was taken prisoner, but the rebels let him go. Stanton is reported rancorously hostile to the Commission; probably because Bellows has talked to him once or twice like a Dutch uncle, with plainness of speech that was certainly imprudent, though quite justifiable.

September 7, SUNDAY. The country is turning out raw material for history very fast, but it's an inferior article. Rebellion is on its legs again, East and West, rampant and aggressive at every point. Our lines are either receding or turned, from the Atlantic to the Mississippi. The great event now prominently before us is that the South has crossed the Potomac in force above Washington and invaded Maryland and occupied Frederick, proclaimed a provisional governor, and seems advancing on the Pennsylvania line.[5] No one knows the strength of the invading column. Some say 30,000, and others five times that. A very strong force, doubtless, has pushed up the Potomac to cut off the rebel communications. If it succeed, the rebellion will be ruined, but if it suffer a disorganizing defeat, the North will be at Jefferson Davis's mercy. I dare not let my mind dwell on the tremendous contingencies of the present hour. It seems to me not quite certain that our next Sanitary Commission meeting will be held at Washington punctually on the 15th!

The nation is rapidly sinking just now, as it has been sinking rapidly for two months and more, because it wants two things: generals that know how to handle their men, and strict military discipline applied to men and officers. God alone can give us good generals, but a stern and rigorous discipline visiting every grave military offence with death can be given us by our dear old great-uncle Abe, if he only would do it. With our superiority in numbers and in resources, discipline would make us strong enough to conquer without first-rate generals, unless an Alexander or Napoleon should be born into Rebeldom.

September 11. Letters from Agnew full of interest. He has been all over our last battlefields under flag of truce; thirty-six hours in the saddle and feels "as if he had a chronic horse between his lower limbs." Our

[5] Lee, learning that Pope had taken refuge within the defenses of Washington, ordered Stonewall Jackson on September 2 to cross the Potomac and lead an advance into Maryland. By September 7 the Confederate army had concentrated at Frederick. On the 15th Harper's Ferry surrendered with 12,000 men and 73 guns.

wounded were left in the field, without shelter, food, or water, from Saturday night till Wednesday morning, because "that scoundrel, Pope" was too busy cooking up his report to think of sending out a flag of truce. Very many perished from starvation and exposure. Our Commission wagons were first on the ground and did good service, thank God; and the relations of our inspectors and agents with the medical staff seem perfectly harmonious. All, from the Surgeon-General down, recognize the value of what we are doing, or rather of what the people is doing through us as its almoner.

Our public interests continue in a state of prostration approaching collapse. We do not know what force the rebels have thrown into Maryland. It is probably large. What a blessing a heavy rain would be that should raise the Potomac above fordable depth! There are clouds in tonight's sky, anxiously watched but probably barren. Newspapers tell us little or nothing about the situation in Maryland. From a letter received by D. B. Fearing from his son, spunky little George Fearing is on Burnside's staff; and from Agnew's letters and from Burnside's telegram to F. B. Cutting today, the following facts are clearly established: McClellan's headquarters were at Rockville Tuesday; Burnside was then at Leesboro; he was at Brookville this morning; he commands our right (40,000 strong?), Sigel the centre, McClellan the left, which, I suppose, rests on the Potomac; no collision as yet; the rebels have *not* occupied Hagerstown.

I suppose we shall soon hear that McClellan has commenced a series of masterly fieldworks and is engaged on an irrefragable first parallel from the Potomac to the Susquehanna, with a series of dashing and brilliant zig-zags toward the enemy. But it is idle to criticize his practice until we can name some stronger and better man to put in his place. It's a controlling fact that the army confides in him, and may mutiny if he be superseded. General Pope's report bears hard on Fitz-John Porter and others; charges them with declining to support him with their commands at critical moments, and seeks to make them responsible for our latest disasters. It's a plausible paper and (were Pope's veracity unquestioned) would be damaging. As it is, the report has generated a swarm of rumors about one general and another committed to Fort Lafayette for treason. Nobody who knows Fitz-John Porter, Franklin, or McDowell (this last affected by rumors for which Pope's report is not responsible) can believe either guilty of positive disloyalty, of conscious, deliberate treason. But may not their partisanship for McClellan have made them unconsciously backward in supporting his rival? *Quién sabe? Weissnix.* Jealousies exist among our generals beyond doubt, though one would think them impossible in a time like this. Their existence is a fearful source of weakness and paralysis.

Among today's rumors is this: that General Halleck has ascertained Mrs. A. Lincoln to be the mysterious channel through which so many state secrets have reached the rebels and enabled them to anticipate our action; that he has formally demanded her exportation from the seat of government; and that her *Durchlauchtigkeit* has been sent off west under military guard. Highly probable, to be sure! But I suppose she may be a very tattling woman. Underbred, weak, and vain she certainly is, by all accounts. She may have talked too freely.

Hurrah! There comes a sound of rain. Sabrina fair, nymph of the Potomac, please listen where thou art sitting and never mind the loose folds of thy amber-dropping hair, but hurry up the floods of thy river and make it impracticable for rebel artillery, if you will have the goodness, marm.

September 13, SATURDAY.   Agnew returned today and was with us this afternoon. Has been several days on the battlefields around Manassas rendering surgical aid, and with McClellan's advance in Maryland organizing our Sanitary Commission supply trains. His report not encouraging. Many regiments are "asthenic" or worn out. Line of march is traceable by the deposit of dysenteric stool the army leaves behind it. Discipline slack and nerveless; swarms of stragglers marauding, or making up select card-parties by the road side. From other sources I hear of alarming demoralization. McDowell's people are said to have fought badly and to have run with great alacrity a fortnight ago. I fear our army is in no condition to cope with Lee's barefooted, ragged, lousy, disciplined, desperate ruffians. They may get to Philadelphia or New York or Boston, for fortune is apt to smile on audacity and resolution. What would happen then? A new and most alarming kind of talk is coming up, emitted by old Breckinridge Democrats (like W. L. Cutting) mostly, and in substance to this effect: "Stonewall Jackson, Lee, and Joe Johnston were all anti-secessionists till the war broke out. No doubt, they still want to see the Union restored. They are personally friends, allies, and political congeners of Halleck, McClellan, F.-J. Porter, and others. Perhaps they will all come together and agree on some compromise or adjustment, turn out Lincoln and his 'Black Republicans' and use their respective armies to enforce their decision North and South and reëstablish the Union and the Constitution." A charming conclusion that would be of our uprising to maintain the law of the land and uphold republican institutions! But we have among us plenty of rotten old Democrats like Judge Roosevelt, capitalists like Joe Kernochan, traders and money dealers like Belmont, and political schemers like James and Rat Brooks, who would sing a *Te Deum* over any pacification, however infamous, and would rejoice to see Jefferson Davis our next President. Perhaps he may be. If he is magnanimous and forgiving he may be prevailed on to come and reign over us. I would rather see the North subjugated than a separation. Disgust with our present government is certainly universal. Even Lincoln himself has gone down at last, like all our popular idols of the last eighteen months. This honest old codger was the last to fall, but he has fallen. Nobody believes in him any more. I do not, though I still maintain him. I cannot bear to admit the country has no man to believe in, and that honest Abe Lincoln is not the style of goods we want just now. But it is impossible to resist the conviction that he is unequal to his place. His only special gift is fertility of smutty stories. *Quam parva sapientia mundus regitur!* What must be the calibre of our rulers whose rule is so disgraceful a failure? If McClellan gain no signal, decisive victory within ten days, I shall collapse; and we have no reason to expect anything of that sort from him.

Rebel ravages in southern Pennsylvania may stir up a general arming and enrolment, but even that would give us only an undisciplined mob for months to come. O Abraham, *O mon Roi!*

There is a break in the diary from September 13 to September 24, during most of which period Strong was in or near Washington. He went south at a time big with critical events. Early in September, Lee, at the head of about 50,000 ill-equipped troops, had crossed the Potomac and invaded Maryland. Thousands of his veterans marched without shoes. Stonewall Jackson won an initial success by capturing Harper's Ferry, and then hurried by forced marches to rejoin the main army under Lee. McClellan, placed in chief command of the Union forces, had at first shown his old tendency toward delay and despondency. But marching to overtake the enemy, he reached Frederick, Maryland, on September 13, and there obtained a copy of a special order issued by Lee four days earlier, laying bare the whole Confederate plan of campaign. The battle of Antietam or Sharpsburg took place on the 17th, McClellan throwing his army heavily against the much weaker army of the Confederacy. According to the generally received figures, the Northern forces numbered 87,000 men, the Southern forces 50,000 or 55,000—but McClellan used only 60,000. The Confederate line resisted valiantly, and both sides suffered grave losses—the North 12,400 killed and wounded, the South 11,200. At the end of the fourteen hours of conflict, McClellan had the better of the day, and if he had attacked with determination on the 18th, he might have won a crushing victory. Instead, he failed to renew the fight, and Lee slipped back across the Potomac. Although Lincoln was grievously disappointed by Lee's escape to safety, he was encouraged by this partial victory to resolve to issue the Emancipation Proclamation. On September 22 he announced his intention to the Cabinet, and the next day his great writ of freedom was published to the world. "God bless Abraham Lincoln!" exclaimed the New York Tribune, which had long pressed for this step. Strong was close to the scene of action in these great days; part of the time, in fact, in an office so near Stanton's that he could hear the worried Secretary swearing fearfully.

September 24, WEDNESDAY.   Spent an hour or two at Dr. Bellows's in council with our Sanitary Commission colleagues. Our affairs are prospering. Agnew's report of personal experience in Maryland confirms mine, or rather vice versa, his being so many times larger. The Medical Department is utterly destitute and shiftless as usual, and now confessedly is leaning on the Commission for supplies and looking to it for help to get forward its own stores, waiving all its official dignity under the pressure of work for which it made no adequate provision and in an attitude of general supplication and imbecile self-abasement. *Times is changed*, and scornful dogs have to eat dirty puddings. The fossil old Bureau is not yet galvanized into life, with all Dr. Hammond's energy. Want of independent transportation seems its main difficulty. Hammond is paralyzed by dependence on the Quartermaster Department. We must try to mend this, even at the risk of alienating General Meigs.

Memorabilia of this Sanitary anabasis. To Washington by the accustomed railroad Monday morning the 15th. Found Wolcott Gibbs and Bishop Clark on the train; also Binney and Judge Hare. At Baltimore we came in contact with extras. Battle in Maryland on the 14th. Rebels routed. Grand victory. The politic city of Baltimore was in a confluent eruption of national flags. We bought fifty cents worth of Baltimore *Clippers* and hurled them out of the car windows at the lonely picket guards all along the Baltimore and Washington Road. But as we drew nearer Washington, the glorious news began to dwarf and dwindle. The rebel army was not absolutely disorganized and still showed fight. There were unpleasant rumors, unreliable of course, that Colonel [Dixon S.] Miles had surrendered Harper's Ferry.

Reached Washington and received excellent quarters from the magnates of Willard's Hotel. Binney and Hare, and McMichael and a lot of others, a committee of Philadelphians to wait on the Secretary of War and General Halleck and secure a military chieftain to secure the defense of Pennsylvania, were very blue. Stanton could not be seen but was heard cussing frightfully in an adjoining apartment. Our session began Tuesday morning and lasted till Friday night. Agnew and Harris were sent off Wednesday, I think, in charge of medical stores for the battlefield. We did a good deal of work. Had an interview by appointment with Gen. Halleck. . . . We walked away from Halleck's quarters in dismal silence and consternation. Van Buren broke it with the words "God help us!" That aspiration was never more appropriate. Halleck is not the man for his place. He is certainly—clearly—weak, shallow, commonplace, vulgar. He is a strong friend of the Commission and ready to do whatever it asks, so I am not prejudiced against him. His silly talk was conclusive as to his incapacity, unless he was a little flustered with wine, an inadmissible apology for a commander-in-chief at a crisis like this. He seemed to think it facetious to keep calling Dr. Bellows "Bishop," maundered about certain defects of discipline which he said prevented McClellan from moving more than five miles a day and Buell more than three—"when he moves at all, that is." Someone suggested an order from headquarters as the appropriate remedy (he might have referred to the army regulations now in force), whereupon Halleck became stately and said he wasn't a writer for the newspapers. "No, sir. No, I thank you, sir. That is not my line. I cannot do that," and so on, in the silliest style. His revelations were most imprudent. "People expect me to send a column to Gordonsville or somewhere and cut off the rebel communications. Where are the men? Only 42,000 left for the defense of Washington today. Government has paid bounties to 350,000 men under the new levy. Less than 75,000 have reached Washington. None at all these last two days. So many at Cincinnati, at St. Louis, and other places—less than 50,000 all told. The governors keep them back till each man has his tin cup and his carpetbag, and then a week longer to enable some politician to make a speech to the regiment and shake hands with every recruit individually." We adjourned formally Saturday morning, after an efficient session. Bishop

Clark was as genial and enlivening as of old. He reports a rebel prisoner received in Governor's Island who was scrubbed for two hours with soap and water before they got down to the shirt he wore in 1860. Someone said that blatant, gassy George Francis Train (now blowing at Willard's) abstains from all stimulants and narcotics, from coffee, tobacco, and alcoholic drinks. The Bishop replied it would be a pity to dilute George F. Train with whiskey. From all accounts, Abe Lincoln is far from easy in his mind. Judge Skinner, who knows him intimately, says he wanders about wringing his hands and wondering whom he can trust and what he'd better do. What's very bad, he has been heard to utter the words "war for boundaries," to speak which words should be death. Heaven help our rulers. Never was so great a cause in the keeping of much smaller men. But I still have faith in Abe Lincoln.

Left Washington at five o'clock Saturday afternoon. Baltimore cars densely packed. I rode on the platform and took a dessert-spoonful of cinders dirt out of each ear on reaching that town. Took a car for Harrisburg at half-past nine and arrived there at two or three o'clock in the morning. Met Binney there and got decent quarters at the Jones House.

Sunday morning proceeded with Binney to the State House; the town swarming with Pennsylvania militia and all the paraphernalia of war. Men were drilling in all the streets. The great battle of Wednesday and the withdrawal of the rebels from Maryland were not yet fully understood, and people looked grave enough. The militia, however, were in good fighting humor and would have done all that utterly green, undisciplined men could do. We found [Thomas A.] Scott, Cameron's former Assistant Secretary, on duty as representative of Governor Curtin, and he ordered out a special train for us. Inspected the surrounding country from the State House cupola. Lovely landscape, broad, pure, peaceful river (most fordable, unhappily, as it might have proved) flowing down through a gap in the northwest line of wooded hills, and all flooded with the misty sunlight of an Indian summerish morning.

Off at about ten o'clock through a fertile, rich, thriving region, full of nice farmhouses, big barns and comfortable villages; a most tempting prey for Lee's hungry battalions. At Carlisle and the other places we passed through the whole population seemed to have turned out with anxious faces—many of the women crying, and no wonder. They were yet uncertain whether the pressing danger of devastation was passed. At Chambersburg we were delayed a couple of hours to await a special train from Hagerstown with Governor Curtin. It is a pretty village enough. Found Dr. Cuyler there. Traversed every street a dozen times in quest of Dr. Crane, an inspector, without success. Here we met a telegram announcing a sort of Ball's Bluff blunder on Saturday. A brigade sent across the Potomac by Porter to feel the enemy had got caught in an ambuscade and was driven back. The 118th Pennsylvania regiment was much cut up. As young Horace Binney is a lieutenant in this regiment, the news gave his father some cause of perturbation, but he bore up bravely.

We got to Hagerstown at nine o'clock. Rooms at the hotels not to be thought of; it was not easy to get inside their doors. Soldiers and officers were bivouacking in the streets. By good luck we found Dr. Hartshorne, who put us *en rapport* with Dr. Dorsey, one of the F.F.'s, and a thorough-going loyalist, and in his comfortable house we were received at once, with a frank cordiality and kindness beyond all my experience. They only knew we were Union men and engaged in some kind of work for the army. I never appreciated the meaning of the word hospitality before. The lady of the house is a most thorough-bred kind of person, with the most charming, genial manner. They have a son in the rebel army! But one must go into the Debatable Land to see full-blooded, genuine Union feeling. Ours at the North is a second-rate article. Mrs. Dorsey told me much of the rebel forces that occupied the town some four days; how dirty and wretched they were, how they scampered at midnight on the news of McClellan's approach, and what a smell they left behind them. Stuart, a chaplain from Alexandria, told her they meant to take Philadelphia—"Philadelphia or death."

Next morning, Monday, I made arrangements to put the Medical Director, Surgeon A. K. Smith, in funds for the immediate equipment of his hospital, and then took an ambulance and drove off over the Sharpsburg turnpike with Binney and Hartshorne and a certain indefatigable Mrs. Harris, rival of Miss Dix and agent of some Philadelphia relief association. We soon entered an atmosphere pervaded by the scent of the battlefield—the bloody and memorable field of Antietam ("Antee'tum") Creek. Long lines of trenches marked the burial places; scores of dead horses, swollen, with their limbs protruding stiffly at strange angles, and the ground at their noses blackened with hemorrhage, lay all around. Sharpsburg, a commonplace little village, was scarified with shot. In one little brick house I counted more than a dozen shot-holes, cleanly made, probably by rifle projectiles. Here and there was seen the more extensive ravage made by an exploding shell. The country is most lovely, like Berkshire County, Massachusetts, only more luxuriant and exuberant.

At Sharpsburg, we found the little church used as a hospital for the 118th Pennsylvania; some fifty wounded lay there on straw. The regiment had suffered badly. Young Binney was safe and off on picket duty. His men spoke of his conduct enthusiastically and said he was the last man to leave the ground. His father fairly broke down under this, and no wonder. In the crowd of ambulances, army wagons, beef-cattle, staff officers, re-cruits, kicking mules, and so on, who should suddenly turn up but Mrs. Arabella Barlow, née Griffith, unattended, but serene and self-possessed as if walking down Broadway. She is nursing the colonel, her husband (badly wounded), and never appeared so well.[6] Talked like a sensible, practical, earnest, warm-hearted woman, without a phrase of hyperfluti-nation. We went to McClellan's headquarters and to Fitz-John Porter's. McClellan has twenty regimental standards and more, and guns, sub-stantial trophies. But for the miserable misconduct that lost us Harper's Ferry, had that unhappy Colonel Miles held out eight hours longer, the rebel retreat would have been a rout. Miles has gone to his account, and whether he was a deliberate traitor or only faint-hearted and incapable will never be known. Left Binney at Sharpsburg, and proceeded in the di-rection of Keedysville and French's Division Hospital, where we stayed two or three hours. Horrible congregation of wounded men there and at Porter's—our men and rebel prisoners both—on straw, in their bloody stiffened clothes mostly, some in barns and cowhouses, some in the open air. It was fearful to see; Gustave Doré's pictures embodied in shivering, agonizing, suppurating flesh and blood.

Walked with Hartshorne over another section of the battlefield, strewn with fragments of shell and conical bullets; here and there a round shot or a live shell, dangerous to handle. We traced the position in which a rebel brigade had stood or bivouacked in line of battle for half a mile by the thickly strewn belt of green corn husks and cobs, and also, *sit venia loquendi,* by a ribbon of dysenteric stools just behind.

It grew dark, and we watched the light signals from a woody hill in the direction of Harper's Ferry, supped on bologna sausage, drove off at last like mad and got back to our hospitable house at Dr. Dorsey's very late, but not too late for a generous and most acceptable tea. . . . Left Harris-burg at eight this morning.

September 27, SATURDAY.   President's Emancipation Manifesto much

---

[6] Francis C. Barlow was promoted to a brigadier-generalship on September 19, 1862, for his gallant service. The severe wound he received at Antietam was healed in time for him to take part in the Chancellorsville campaign in the spring of 1863.

discussed and generally approved, though a few old Democrats (who ought to be dead and buried but persist in manifesting themselves like vampires) scold and grumble. It will do us good abroad, but will have no other effect.

October 3.   A damp, sultry, steaming, unseasonable moonlight night through which I've just taken an active stroll in the mood of a Sioux off on a scalp dance. My condition as to temper has been terrible since I read the afternoon papers. Ellie and Miss Rosalie (who dined with us) can testify to my ferocity. But I pass this over and proceed to the journal proper. We have left Newport bag and baggage and boys, and are at home once more. That is decided cause for congratulation. Went to that wretched place Monday night. The voyage was not unpleasant. Spent three raw, cloudy, cheerless east-windy days there. Lounged on the beach and on the shores of a certain creek. Tuesday spent with Johnny and Temple; Johnny caught no perch, but showed great prowess as a swimmer. Wednesday took out the duo in Nathan's sail boat and fished off the *Dumplings*. Rain and wind. Both boys were sea-sick, but they behaved like little bricks. Many big black-fish captured. Johnny lost a grand eight-pounder just at the gunwale. Dined pleasantly with Charles Kuhn and his piquant little wife. Saw a good deal of Charles Kuhn. His musical furor has not abated, nor have his high notes in Mozart or what-not that he's trying to render—but one forgives everything. . . .

Now for my special present aggravation and irritation. The Triennial Convention of the Protestant Episcopal Church in the U.S.A. is now sitting in St. John's Chapel. Mr. Ruggles is a delegate from this diocese. (So is the Rev. F. L. Hawks.) The afternoon papers announce that some Pennsylvania delegate offered a preamble and resolutions in substance that whereas there is a rebellion against the nation and a schism in the church, therefore, resolved that the church prays that the rebels and schismatics may be brought to a better mind, that the bishops be invited to set forth a form of prayer accordingly, and that the church also hopes and prays that the devices of rebellion and schism be confounded. This motion was tabled two to one after full discussion.

Mr. Ruggles has the House of Bishops and all the convention at No. 24 tonight, and I expected to go there; counted on the evening and looked forward to it. But I could not go anywhere to meet the councillors of the church after this base action of theirs. The position of the people of England toward us, England's utter selfishness and profligacy, gave me one great disillusioning shock a year and more ago. This action, or non-action, of the (*soi-disant*) American Catholic Church gives me another, yet more stunning.

The church in which I was brought up, which I have maintained so long to be the highest and noblest of organizations, refuses to say one word for the country at this crisis. Her priests call on Almighty God every day, in the most solemn offices of her liturgy, to deliver His people from "false doctrine, heresy, and schism," from "sedition, privy conspiracy, and rebellion." Now, at last, when they and their people are confronted by the most wicked of rebellions and the most wilful of schisms on the vilest of grounds, the constitutional right to breed black babies for sale, when rebellion and schism are arrayed against the church and against society in the unloveliest form they can possibly assume—the church is afraid to speak. How would she get on were there a large, highly respectable minority sympathizing with adultery, or homicide, or larceny? Alas, for my dreams of twenty years ago!

I think this shows the existence of a latent anti-democratic or aristocratic feeling as a constituent element of the Protestant-Episcopal or Anglo-American Church. Not a conservative spirit, founded on tradition, inherited from the English Church and dating back to the days of the Stuarts (such as was manifested in 1776), but a revolutionary spirit as against our democratic institutions. It appears in the specially prominent part taken by Southern bishops, presbyters, and leading laymen in the Southern anti-democratic rebellion; and this shameful reluctance of our Northern Council to commit itself against the rebellion points the same way. Were the instincts of the church conservative, they would prompt the most emphatic declaration of sympathy with government. I have no special liking for democratic institutions, but "the powers that be" and that are ordained of God rest on those institutions and the church is bound to uphold them. Her public avowal of lukewarmness in their support puts her back twenty years in influence and popular respect.

October 8, WEDNESDAY.   At Columbia College meeting Monday we made a good move—appropriated money for a fencing school. This is the entering wedge, I hope, for the recognition of physical education. We reorganized the Library Committee, and Anderson, Rutherfurd, and I were appointed.

Canvass for fall elections fairly begun. Wadsworth and Seymour candidates for governor. I hope Wadsworth and the so-called radicals may sweep the state and kick our wretched sympathizers with Southern treason back into the holes that have sheltered them for the past year and from which they are beginning to peep out timidly and tentatively to see whether they can venture to resume their dirty work. The result will be an important indication of the way popular feeling tends to flow. I *think* it will show important progress the right way, but we must not be over-confident. Seymour's election would be an encouragement to Jefferson Davis worth 100,000 men.

Thus ends this volume of my journal, in days that are chilly and grey, but not without gleams of light that promise the return of sunshine. So let us hope, and in that hope, let us work. If we work faithfully, and do our duty in freely putting forth all our resources, we can hardly fail, with God's blessing, to crush the rebellion and vindicate our existence as a nation. God enable us so to do our duty. Amen.

The autumn elections of 1862 were of unusual importance. A House of Representatives had to be chosen, and in view of the widespread discouragement over military defeats and the heavy burdens of the war, a considerable reaction against the Administration was expected. In New York the governorship was at stake. When the Democratic Party, meeting in convention at Albany on September 10, nominated Horatio Seymour for the place, all patriots of Strong's views felt a distinct shock. Seymour had wealth and influence; he had made a creditable record during his previous term as governor; and he represented the old up-state Democracy of Van Buren and Silas Wright. But he had been a fierce opponent of the Lincoln Administration, attacking all its repressive measures as unconstitutional and opposing the emancipation of the slaves. He had said again and again that the North could never subjugate the South. All the dissatisfied and disloyal elements of the state rallied behind him. On the Republican side, Governor Morgan had made it plain that he would not run again. The party hesitated for a time between John A. Dix and General James S. Wadsworth, whose record at Bull Run had been distinguished and who stood for an energetic prosecution of the war. Meeting at Syracuse late in September, the Republican Union Convention nominated Wadsworth on the first ballot by an overwhelming majority. A campaign of great bitterness then opened. The Democrats called Wadsworth "a malignant Abolition disorganizer"; the Republicans declared, in the words of Henry J. Raymond of the Times, *that "every vote given for Seymour is a vote for treason."*

October 15, WEDNESDAY.   Fine day. News is nix. Went to Jersey City this morning to enquire after Mrs. Herman Ruggles, who is probably in

failing health, but is reported better by Miss Rosalie. Van Buren and
Agnew at No. 498 Broadway this afternoon. News today of our second
$100,000 from San Francisco. I deposited the first yesterday. O pleasing
task! We are to send $50,000 to our secessionizing off-shoot at St. Louis,
which is a less agreeable duty. Murray Hoffman dined here, and we went
to Wallack's old theatre, now a German opera house, and heard the *Ent-
führung aus dem Serail* for the first time and under disadvantage, our seats
being within whispering range of the big drum. But many lovely things
were perceptible, as in a glass, darkly. I hope to hear it again. There was
an exquisite tenor solo, a delicious cosy drinking song, and a lovely finale
for the soli and chorus—antiphonal as the Rev. Vinton and his choir boys
at Trinity Church. These came out clearly and well defined; everything
else somewhat blurred.

Bishop Clark dined here Monday with Vinton, Bellows, Van Buren,
Agnew, and Gibbs, and we had a jolly symposium and much good talk,
though gold is nearly at 140 premium and McClellan's army immovable
as the Pyramids. That general has sent for his wife, his mother-in-law,
and his baby, and is going to go into housekeeping, it seems, somewhere
near Sharpsburg. He may move next first of May, but I fear he is settled till
then. Heaven help us! It is good, however, that the elections yesterday
in Pennsylvania and other states seem to show that the spirit of the nation
is unbroken. May the voice of New York next month be in accord with
theirs, and Horatio Seymour, John Van Buren, Fernando Wood, Richard
O'Gor-r-r-man, and the Hon. Washington Hunt (whom as Mr. Samuel
B. Ruggles's friend, I regret to see in such dirty company) experience the
snubbing a loyal people ought to give them!

The house of clerical and lay deputies is still talking and talking over
the great question before it. Ellie goes down to St. John's Chapel every
morning and has a good time. A pew there is like a balcony seat at the
opera. Prelates and presbyters and notable laics pass through the aisle
and stop to gossip a little about the church and the nation. I think the
lower house will express itself more decidedly than seemed possible a
week ago. The House of Bishops has already taken decided action, I hear.
Our very venerable diocesan got up on Monday and moved that no allusion
be made in the "pastoral letter" to the state of the country. He is certainly
quite "gone in the knees," as horse-people say. His motion was tabled.
The Rt. Rev. Hopkins, presiding bishop, brought in the draft of a pastoral
letter that did not suit. He is reputed of low-grade loyalty. McIlvaine of
Ohio proposed and Whittingham of Maryland seconded another draft as

a substitute, which was adopted almost unanimously. This conjunction of McIlvaine and Whittingham, of ultra-evangelical and ultra-Oxford-man, is notable. Times are changed since 1844.

Notable also as a curious coincidence is Dr. Hawks's conspicuous position in this convention as in that of nineteen years ago. Then he was charged with fraud as now with disloyalty. He occupied a large share of time and attention at both these sessions, each more important by far than any other held during the fifth of a century that separates them, and at each his attitude has been apologetic and defensive. In the former, he was using his remarkable faculty of plausible talk to repel allegations of bad faith toward his neighbors at Flushing; now he is trying to make out that he is keeping good faith with his country. He is not on trial now as he was then, but his position is substantially the same. Having resigned the rectorship of Calvary Church and a salary of $5,000, he wants to be recalled. His speeches in convention are addressed to the vestry of that church, and I dare say they will be successful, whatever the convention may decide to do, for members of that vestry are reputed "sympathetic" souls. How Mr. Ruggles, Dr. Higby, and other thoroughly earnest and loyal men can hesitate any longer as to their duty in convention is incomprehensible.

October 17. . . . Election news from Pennsylvania and the West were cold, but I hope the opposition men elected are "War Democrats."

Nothing material from the seat of war, except that McClellan shows signs of life. He has wiggled a little and made a reconnaissance in force as far as Charlestown (the city of John Brown), with loss of one man killed and six missing. Some say this is the beginning of a general advance, forced on him prematurely by the Cabinet and by popular clamor. Last night our Sanitary brethren of the Executive Committee met here, according to rule of rotation, and with the usual slight supper and good talk. Our reverend president has been making a gander of himself, I regret to say, in the course of an address on the war before his Unitarian Convention or Heretical Assenagemote and convocation of philosophical wiseacres now or lately in session here or at Brooklyn or somewhere else. He said much that was good, valuable, and new (to the public, at least), but went out of his way to eulogize the Southern race and is much assaulted and belabored for having done so. He maintained last night, and very plausibly, that he did not go out of his way, and that what he said about the generosity and gentility of Southern traitors and the nobleness of Southern blood was intended to enforce and did enforce his practical conclusion, the necessity for concentrating all our national energies to crush Southern treason. Perhaps.

October 19. Last night with Ellie, George Anthon, and Johnny to Niblo's where we saw Hackett as Rip Van Winkle and as Dr. O'Callaghan in *His Last Legs*. He was funny in both, and the evening was most satisfactory, though it kept Johnny out of his nest till eleven o'clock.

October 23. To Columbia College this morning with George F. Allen in time for chapel. Service satisfactory. Charles Kuhn and Jem Ruggles dined here, and I spent the evening at Dr. Van Buren's. Meeting of Executive Committee of the Sanitary Commission and slight supper thereafter. Olmsted present, also an intelligent, well-mannered Dr. Fowler, a refugee from Montgomery, Alabama. That town cast him out because he was thought overzealous in caring for a hospital full of Union prisoners, of which he was in charge. Sanitary Commission is waxing fat. Its California remittances will foot up not much below a quarter of a million, and may exceed that sum.[7]

Our war on rebellion languishes. We make no onward movements and gain no victories. McClellan's repose is doubtless majestic, but if a couchant lion postpone his spring too long, people will begin wondering whether he is not a stuffed specimen after all. Fat Colonel Burkett tells Augustus King that there will certainly be a grand movement and great results within a week, but I am tired of such talk. One thing is clear: that unless we gain decisive success before the November election, this state will range itself against the Administration. If it does, a dishonorable peace and permanent disunion are not unlikely. The whole community is honeycombed by secret sympathizers with treason who will poke out their heads and flaunt their "red, white, and red" tentacles the moment avowed division of Northern sentiment enables them to do so safely. . . .

October 25. Philharmonic rehearsal this afternoon; Beethoven's Symphony in B flat (No. 2), one of the two that I know but little if at all. I think I had never heard it. Expected little, but it turns out to be a very noble symphony, and for one hour I forgot all about the war and the Sanitary Commission, and was conscious of nothing but the marvelous web of melodic harmony and pungent orchestral color that was slowly

[7] Led by the Rev. Thomas Starr King, Mayor H. P. Coon of San Francisco, Governor F. F. Low, and others, the people of California had rallied impressively to the support of the Sanitary Commission. Of approximately five million dollars collected by the Sanitary Commission during the War, a total of $1,233,830 came from California.

unfolding. Though deep and elaborate, the symphony is very clear, and I swallowed it all without effort on this first hearing. It is Beethoven, every note of it, except perhaps in the first movement, which is Haydn-oid in sentiment. The second movement seems transcendently beautiful; Haydn's purity and heartiness expressed in Beethoven's more copious vocabulary. The scherzo and trio are full of lovely melodic phrases, and the jolliest thing Beethoven ever wrote for an orchestra. . . .

Last night with Murray Hoffman to the German theatre. Heard Boïeldieu's *Jean de Paris* in a German version. That opera has its good points, in the third act especially, but they are too few to compensate one for three hours of mephitic atmosphere and absorption of carbonic oxide into one's blood and bones in that ill-ventilated little theatre.

Today's news is that McClellan is now positively about to advance at last and also that General Curtis has beaten the rebels of North Arkansas once more at Pea Ridge. Also the Rev. Hawks resigns from Calvary Church and makes his hegira to Baltimore this week.

October 29. At Niblo's last night with Ellie and George Anthon; first part of *King Henry IV.* Hackett's Falstaff seems to me beyond criticism, incapable of improvement in a single detail of look, gesture, or intonation—the only perfect impersonation I have ever seen of any character. Such "histrionic art" has real value; it furnishes the best possible commentary on Shakespeare's text. It is wonderful how Hackett can make the part so broadly comic without for an instant forgetting that Sir John is a gentleman in the conventional sense of the term.

October 30, THURSDAY. Private advices from the War Department are that the Virginia rebels are greatly reinforced and that McClellan is to wait a little longer. Alas for next Tuesday's election! There is danger —great and pressing danger—of a disaster more telling than all our Bull Run battles and Peninsular strategy: the resurrection to political life and power of the Woods, Barlows, LaRocques, and Belmonts,[8] who have been dead and buried and working only underground, if at all, for eighteen months, and every one of whom well deserves hanging as an ally of the rebellion. It would be a fearful national calamity. If it come, it will be due not so much to the Emancipation Manifesto as to the irregular arrests the government has been making. They have been used against the Administration with most damaging effect, and no wonder. They have been

[8] That is, Fernando Wood, his brother Ben Wood, S. L. M. Barlow (with his law partner of the firm of Shipman, Barlow, Larocque & Choate), and August Belmont.

utterly arbitrary, and could be excused only because demanded by the pressure of an unprecedented national crisis; because necessary in a case of national life or death that justified any measure, however extreme. But not one of the many hundreds illegally arrested and locked up for months has been publicly charged with any crime or brought to the notice of a Grand Jury. They have all been capriciously arrested, so far as we can see, and some have been capriciously discharged; locked up for months without legal authority and let out without legal acquittal. All this is very bad—imbecile, dangerous, unjustifiable. It gives traitors and Seymourites an apology for opposing the government and helping South Carolina that it is hard to answer. I know it is claimed that these arrests are legal, and perhaps they are, but their legality is a subtle question that government should not have raised as to a point about which people are so justly sensitive.

There go drums through the street. It's a Democratic procession (democratic!) with torches, parading dirty James Brooks's name on a dirty banner. I met this, or its brother, marching down Fifth Avenue on my way to Agnew's, and felt as if a Southern Army had got into New York. . . .

November 3, MONDAY.   At Columbia College meeting this afternoon. It was not long. We had the treasurer's annual report and important questions about the Law School, which were referred to our Law Committee. The School is expanding and thriving. Dwight's salary (from fees) is now more than $6,000, and certain of the last graduating class ask for a third year with some further degree at its close—"Master of Laws" or the like. A most promising sign. That school has thriven beyond the utmost we hoped, thanks to Dwight's admirable talent for teaching. Thence to the Sanitary Commission rooms. About $26,000 more from California! Telegrams announce still further contributions coming. . . .

Tomorrow's prospects bad. The Seymourites are sanguine. Vote will certainly be close. A row in the city is predicted by those who desire one, but it is unlikely, though people are certainly far more personally bitter and savage than at any election for many years past. A Northern vote against the Administration may be treated by Honest Old Abe as a vote of want of confidence. He may dismiss his Cabinet and say to the Democrats, "Gentlemen, you think you can do this job better and quicker than Seward and Chase. Bring up your men, and I'll set them to work." It would be like him. And there is little to choose between the two gangs.

After all, Seymour and his tail want the offices—public pay and public patronage. As governor, Seymour will probably try to outbrag the Republicans in energetic conduct of the war. He cares more for his own little finger than for all the Body Politic, and will be as radical as Horace Greeley himself whenever he can gain by it; that is, whenever popular feeling calls for "radical leaders." As yet, the people are sound. They see that stopping the war now would be like leaving the dentist's shop with a tooth half-extracted. There are traitors, of course, now beginning cautiously to tamper with the great torrent of national feeling that burst out April, 1861. And there is also a great mass of selfishness, frivolity, invincible prejudice, personal Southern attachment, indifference to national life, and so on, quite ready to be used as a mud-bank to dam the flood that broke out so gloriously a year and a half ago.

Have we the people, or have we not, resolution and steadiness enough to fight on through five years of taxation, corruption, and discouragement? All depends on the answer to that question.

November 4, TUESDAY. A beautiful bright day, but destined to be memorable, I fear, for a national calamity. Voted this morning, and did not much beside. Indications at the several polling places I visited in the course of enquiry for my own proper civic locality (which I found at last in East Nineteenth Street) were of a rather light vote; no excitement or disturbance, and a fair prospect for the Wadsworth ticket. Came uptown at four, stopping at No. 823 Broadway. George Anthon and Murray Hoffman, Jr., dined here (roast pig). I spent an hour at Bellows's in session with the Executive Committee, returned here, and with Murray Hoffman and George Anthon took a Fourth Avenue railroad car down to the Park to look for election news. Horace Greeley was in our car and not jubilant at all. We found excited crowds around all the newspaper offices of that region—the *Times*, *Herald*, *Tribune*, *World*; everybody craning over everybody's head to get a glimpse of the bulletins. These assemblages were rather unusually clamorous and demonstrative, and all the feeling displayed was on the Seymour side. "Where's Greeley's 900,000 men?" "General Wadsworth can't run for governor, but he *can* run sometimes." "Bully for F'nandy Wood," and the like. Downtown returns indicate overwhelming defeat, the election of Seymour, and a vote of censure on the Administration by the people of this state. The Seymour majority in the city is claimed to be 31,000. The Democrats carry every ward. Fernando Wood and Ben Wood and Winthrop Chanler are sent to Congress,

Walbridge and Conkling defeated.[9] Brooklyn goes the same way. The western counties may save the state yet, but it's improbable. I think the battle is lost and Seymour is governor. God help us. I believe He will, if we be not utterly untrue to our cause.

The Democrats carried the state for Seymour by more than 11,000 majority, and gained a tie vote in the Assembly—a result which sickened many patriots. Henry J. Raymond of the Times, *agreeing with Strong, termed it "a vote of want of confidence in the President." Nor was the showing in other states much better. The Democrats carried New Jersey; they obtained twenty-five new Congressional seats in New York, Pennsylvania, and Ohio; and in the Congressional elections in Lincoln's own state, Illinois, they overwhelmingly defeated the Republicans. Yet the Border States showed an unexpected loyalty to the Administration, and Lincoln retained control of the House of Representatives by a practical working majority. The Senate was, of course, strongly Republican. The reaction was natural under the circumstances, and it exhibited only a temporary and superficial rather than a permanent and deep-seated discontent with the conduct of the war. Lincoln was not greatly perturbed by it, and Strong's early lamentations were soon proved to be excessive—as he himself acknowledged.*

Yet the North could take little comfort this fall from the military situation, which remained nearly static. Lincoln, after visiting McClellan's well-equipped army of more than 100,000 men early in September, had urged a forward movement. Halleck, too, had written McClellan on October 7: "The country is impatient at the want of activity of your army, and you must push it on." McClellan did cross the Potomac, but he went no farther than to place his forces on the eastern slope of the Blue Ridge. Finally Lincoln, his patience exhausted, took steps early in November to place the army under a more energetic commander.

November 5. As anticipated, total rout in this state. Seymour is governor. Elsewhere defeat, or nominal success by a greatly reduced vote. It looks like a great, sweeping revolution of public sentiment, like general

---

[9] Hiram Walbridge (1821–1870), a merchant who had been in Congress 1853–1855, had run on the Union ticket. Frederick A. Conkling (1816–1891), a brother of Roscoe, who had organized the 84th New York Volunteers, was now in Congress as a Republican, and was an unsuccessful candidate for reelection. Both lived in New York and were personally known to Strong. John Winthrop Chanler (1826–1877), now elected as a Democrat, sat in the next three Congresses.

abandonment of the loyal, generous spirit of patriotism that broke out so nobly and unexpectedly in April, 1861. Was that after all nothing but a temporary hysteric spasm? I think not. We the people are impatient, dissatisfied, disgusted, disappointed. We are in a state of dyspepsia and general, indefinite malaise, suffering from the necessary evils of war and from irritation at our slow progress. We take advantage of the first opportunity of change, for its own sake, just as a feverish patient shifts his position in bed, though he knows he'll be none the easier for it. Neither the blind masses, the swinish multitude, that rule us under our accursed system of universal suffrage, nor the case of typhoid, can be expected to exercise self-control and remember that tossing and turning weakens and does harm. Probably two-thirds of those who voted for Seymour meant to say by their votes, "Messrs. Lincoln, Seward, Stanton & Co., you have done your work badly, so far. You are humbugs. My business is stopped, I have got taxes to pay, my wife's third cousin was killed on the Chickahominy, and the war is no nearer an end than it was a year ago. I am disgusted with you and your party and shall vote for the governor or the congressman you disapprove, just to spite you."

If I am mistaken, and if this vote does endorse the policy of Fernando Wood and John Van Buren, it is a vote of national suicide. All is up. We are a lost people; United States securities, "greenbacks" and all, are worth about a dollar a cord; the Historical Society should secure an American flag at once for its museum of antiquities. I will forge certificates showing that I was not born in America but in *Hingland*—expatriate myself, and become naturalized as a citizen of Venezuela, Haiti, or the Papal States. But I will not *yet* believe that this people is capable of so shameful and despicable an act of self-destruction as to disembowel itself in the face of the civilized world for fear Jefferson Davis should hurt it.

November 8. At Philharmonic rehearsal with Ellie this morning at ten. On my way thence downtown, heard of Dr. Berrian's death last evening. When I met him at Newport last August, he was much broken and unlikely to live many months. He had rallied since then and was not thought in immediate danger till the day he died. Among my earliest recollections is Dr. Berrian perorating blandly in the pulpit of St. Paul's. He always treated me kindly, and after I came into the vestry in 1847, I enjoyed a good deal of his confidence. He was a useful and valuable man to Trinity parish and through it to the diocese, but he was generally held to be the ideal of decent mediocrity, and his name was a convenient and familiar way of expressing the zero point of dull preaching. His sermons were in fact above average merit, which is not saying much for them. Though he never originated a thought, his commonplaces were always reasonable and judicious. He never violated good taste, and his English was accurate. He would have been held a good preacher but for his delivery, which was a monotonous whine. He was most efficient in business and exerted a controlling influence in his own sphere, but worked in such a quiet, "douce" way that few suspected his power. He used this influence wisely, and never (so far as I know) for private and personal ends, and on the whole, Trinity Church will not easily secure a better rector than poor old "Poppy Berrian."

November 10.   The burial was in one of the vaults of St. Mark's Church. Downtown after dinner to Trinity Church vestry meeting; fifteen present. I moved that before organizing we go into an informal ballot for rector, with nominations. Agreed to, the clerk (G.M.O.) putting the question. Result, Morgan Dix 14, and Higby 1 (namely, Dunscomb). We thereupon organized with Dunscomb the warden in the chair, and went into formal ballot. Dix elected unanimously, and a committee of three sent out to notify him. He had been desired to wait in attendance at the Mission Room of St. Paul's, corner of Vesey and Church Streets (as we might require the assistant rector's presence), and was speedily brought in. He said a few words, accepting the place, with the utmost dignity, simplicity, and sincerity of self-depreciation, so sincere and straightforward as to keep all personal considerations quite out of view. And then, after some talking, we adjourned to tomorrow, when the ancient ceremony of "inducting" our new rector is to be performed.

I think our choice was wise. It was certainly spontaneous. There was no lobbying or electioneering. Every one of us voted on his individual conviction, I believe, and without concert. All consultation had been studiously avoided. How could we vote otherwise? There was Higby. His claims were seniority, and a magnificent but unreliable faculty of rhetoric. But he is as unfit for secular business as a yearling child. Hobart is his father's son, but *non compos* for all affairs of this world. Haight is shelved now by disease. Had this vacancy occurred five years ago, he would have filled it, I think. Vinton has no common sense whatever, and as rector would have been incessantly getting the parish into scrapes, while his love of power and exalted estimate of his own rights would have kept him in permanent hot water with his vestry.

November 13, THURSDAY.   Last night's Sanitary session devoted mainly to our relations with the western branches. There are signs of war. The

Cincinnati branch recalcitrates against Olmsted's proposed system of centralization and absolute subordination, and Judge Hoadly goes with Cincinnati. We shall have a row; that branch will lop itself off after the manner of St. Louis, and we shall have to consider whether we have money enough to enable us to occupy that field without its support and with its quasi-hostility. I rather guess we can for a few months at least, thanks to California.

Tuesday at two o'clock we "inducted" the Rev. Morgan Dix according to our corporate usage. The vestry met in the robing room of Trinity Church, came to order, resolved to induct incontinently, and then marched down the north aisle with the Rev. Morgan Dix at our head and all the sextons at our tail, through the north porch and round the tower to the front or "principal" entrance, which was locked. There Dunscomb as warden delivered the key to Dix, with a formal declaration that he thereby transferred the church to his charge as rector. The keys of the chapels were in like manner delivered, and then handed by Dix to the sextons. He unlocked the church door, and we marched back to the robing-room, feeling that we had done something rather striking and effective. The curious crowd that gathered on the sidewalk of Broadway outside the church railings to inspect this mystical process probably supposed we were testing some new patent impregnable anti-burglarious lock. I never witnessed a "livery of seisin" before and gladly keep up any old ceremonial usage, however antiquated and unnecessary. This witnessed our connection with churchmen of 1697, and through them with ages longer past, and so rather impressed me. Dix's election seems pretty generally approved. . . .

California sends $30,000 more to the Sanitary Commission!!!

The war languishes. We are slowly invading Virginia, but there is nothing decisive or vigorous done there or elsewhere. I've a dim foreboding of a coming time when we shall think of the war not as "languishing" and too slow to satisfy our appetite for excitement, but as a terrible, crushing, personal calamity to every one of us; when there shall be no more long trains of carriages all along Fifth Avenue bound for Central Park, when the wives and daughters of contractors shall cease to crowd Stewart's and Tiffany's, and when I shall put no burgundy on my supper table. Much of the moral guilt of this terrible, murderous convulsion lies at our doors. South Carolina would never have dared to secede but for our toadyism, our disposition to uphold and justify the wickedness of Southern institutions. The logic of history requires that we suffer for our sins far more than we yet have suffered. "Without the shedding of blood there is no remission of sins." It is impossible this great struggle can pass without our feeling it more than we have yet felt it. It is inevitable, but in what particular way we shall be visited I cannot foresee.

November 23, SUNDAY. . . . Went to Washington last Monday morning by the seven A.M. train. Bellows, Van Buren, Gibbs, Professor Bache, Binney, and C. J. Stillé were fellow travellers. Dreary, dingy, wet day. No incidents. Got an ill-ventilated, dark, unwholesome room at Willard's Hotel and then went to work and kept at it till Friday night, when we adjourned. A satisfactory and diligent session. I spent all my time between the hotel and the Sanitary Commission office, 244 F Street, except one evening, Thursday, at the Surgeon-General's, where was a little gathering of gentlemen of the Medical Staff and Sanitary Commissioners. Talked with Abbot, Vollum, Gouley, and others, and had a pleasant time enough. Our meetings from ten to two and seven to eleven were most interesting. The reports of inspectors, and so on, submitted and in part read, would make three or four octavo volumes of most valuable information about the progress of the war. Bishop Clark and Judge Skinner of Chicago were absent; Binney present, a most loyal and useful addition to our number. There were also Mr. C. J. Stillé of Philadelphia and Mr. J. Huntington Wolcott of Boston, representing our associates.

Cincinnati sent us two associates, Mr. S. J. Broadwell and Judge or General Bates, to represent the quasi-secession claims of the Cincinnati branch. They favored us with much vehement talk about the relations of East and West and of the Commission and its branches as regarded from an attorney's point of view, but we voted them down unanimously and resolved that the Commission is central, federal, national, and must and will control the action of state organizations calling themselves branches of the Commission. These gentlemen were fluent in talk. They had supposed themselves our equals, but find that they are expected to be mere "hewers of wood," and so on; that is, expected to conform to a general system in the distribution of hospital and other supplies. Had much talk with them, and found them fair but false, governed, perhaps unconsciously, by jealousy of the East. Their principal pretext is the theory that "associate members" of the Commission are full members of the Commission, which mistake may lead to a disastrous schism of the Sanitary church into East and West. We sent a committee to confer with Halleck on the two important points of an ambulance train and independent medical transportation. They had an hour's talk with him that confirmed the impression we received last September that he is second-rate and commonplace. Probably Meigs is the strongest man in the service. Would that he or F. L. Olmsted were Secretary of War! I believe that Olmsted's sense, energy, and organizing faculty, earnestness, and honesty would give new life to the Administration were he in it.

December 2. A long session of the College Law School Committee at Mr. Ruggles's office, conferring with Professor Dwight. That school continues to prosper. It numbers now 135 students and outnumbers the long-established schools of Harvard and Yale. It has been wisely left during its infancy a loose, flexible, undefined, cartilaginous organism, but it is growing to be a big baby and needs phosphate of lime in its bones— a system, that is, and a more formalized existence. Dwight is its vital principle, and we are feeling our way with his counsel toward a scheme of regulations. It would be a delicate and troublesome undertaking were Dwight not the most candid, honest and disinterested of men, a lover of science rather than a lover of self; for the infusion of system into the school will to some extent diminish his prominence and his income both. . . .

Trustees of Columbia College met yesterday afternoon at the Law School, Lafayette Place. Morgan Dix nominated to fill Berrian's place. I resigned off the Standing Committee, Edward Jones having returned from Europe, and nominated him as my successor. There was a good deal of talk about an application for a little money from a Christian Association of undergraduates, but no definite action. For my part, I dislike to see young boys setting up as teachers and "leading in prayer." I don't want to see a line drawn through our undergraduate corps clearly separating saints and sinners. It tends to make the saints pharisees and the sinners reprobate.

At Wolcott Gibbs's last night talking over the scheme of a proposed club to be called the Loyalist or National, or some such thing. Such an organization might make itself most strongly felt. Would I had the time to work at its devising and building and launching, but I haven't.

December 8. Thermometer stood at eight degrees this morning. Columbia College trustees met this afternoon. Morgan Dix unanimously elected to fill Berrian's place. We gave Lieber leave of absence for a month, the Secretary of War and General Halleck having telegraphed him to come to Washington at once. They must want him to advise as a historical expert, either on military usages as to retaliation and other like questions, or on some point of difference with foreign powers.

December 11, THURSDAY. The crisis seems to have come at last. Burnside[10] commenced throwing his pontoons across the Rappahannock at daylight, and being met by a fusillade from the houses of Fredericksburg, opened on that unhappy town with 143 guns from our side of the river. Fredericksburg *fuit*. Meantime, Franklin was effecting a passage some three miles farther down, and gunboats were shelling the rebel right still lower. There the newspaper telegrams of this afternoon stop. We have no news later than noon or thereabouts. This indicates that we have gained no splendid or decisive success. It is consistent with our repulse, with a fall-back by the rebels to a new line, or with the completion of arrangements preliminary to a great battle. We shall see. God help us. I have little faith in the men to whom our destinies seem confided. . . .

Grand meeting got up by our faithful auxiliaries of the "Women's Central Relief Association" to stimulate the contribution of material supplies from this city. Mayor Opdyke presided. Our $25,000 worth of pig silver from Storcy Co., Nevada (!) was duly displayed; a great row of ponderous, massive, 250-pound chunks of pure metal. Not quite pure, however, for they contain a considerable percentage of gold. It was a splendid symbol of the national feeling that reigns in San Francisco, Stockton, Yubaville, Copperopolis, Volcano, and other places, new to geographical science. Would that Cincinnati were half as loyal! I was on the platform with all the nobs from Minturn and Aspinwall and Dr. Mott and General Anderson down to—well, no matter—down to myself. Bellows made the main speech of the evening, expounding the purposes and methods of the Commission, its relations to government on one side and the popular effort to aid the army on the other. He was clear, compact, and forcible; kept the large audience wide awake for about an hour and a quarter, and was briefly followed by Dr. Adams, Dr. Vinton, and Dr. Hitchcock, who were severally more ambitious and less effective. Dr. Bellows has a most remarkable faculty of lucid, fluent, easy colloquial speech and sympathetic manner, with an intensely telling point every now and then, made without apparent effort. A most enviable gift! The meeting was fuller and went off better than I expected.

Last Tuesday night at Bellows's, Sanitary Executive Committee meeting. Another, as usual, yesterday afternoon at No. 823 Broadway, when we

[10] By an order delivered November 7, McClellan was relieved from command of the Army of the Potomac, and Ambrose E. Burnside was appointed in his stead. Burnside, reluctant to supersede an abler officer and conscious that he was unequal to the post, accepted largely because he did not wish the place to go to Hooker.

considered the Hon. George Hoadly's threatening letter from Cincinnati. He is of low grade—a mere philanthropic attorney—but he may be able to do great mischief. So we decided to convene a special meeting of the Commission here next week. Thereafter Osten-Sacken (of the Russian embassy)[11] and Willy Graham and Mr. Ruggles dined here and went with Ellie and Miss Rosalie to hear the *Ballo in Maschera*, at which performance I was, happily, not required to assist.

December 13.   Burnside, having established himself on the right bank of the Rappahannock, seems to have engaged the rebels at nine this morning, advancing his left under General [John F.] Reynolds. The rebels meanwhile have been throwing cavalry round his right, threatening Aquia Creek and the vital umbilical cord of railway on his rear. I knew and predicted they would do it, and I would bet that there is not a gun or a regiment in position to block that old dodge of theirs, so often successful. We know nothing of the progress of the fight. I anticipate only disaster, and an addition to the catalogue of Bull Runs, Big Bethels, and so on already so large. Defeat at this point, with a broad river in our rear, is destruction. But Burnside may be only feeling the enemy.

I have been out exploring for news. There was a bogus extra, but I can get no later intelligence, and dread its arrival. Want of discipline in the army is our great danger, and that is due to want of virility in those who should enforce it—the ultimate cause being the weakness of the President himself. At all our battles, nearly one man out of three has shirked and straggled, and not one man has been shot down by his commanding officer.

Olmsted tells me he called on the President the other evening to introduce some ladies (members of his recent "Honorable Convention" from relief societies all over the country), and Abe Lincoln expatiated on this terrible evil. "Order the army to march to any place!" said Abe Lincoln. "Why it's jes' like *shovellin' fleas*. Hee-yah, ya-hah!" Whereupon one of the ladies timidly asked, "Why don't you order stragglers to be *shot*, sir?" and the query not being immediately answered, was repeated. Olmsted says the presidential guffaw died away and the President collapsed and wilted down into an embodiment of everything weak, irresolute, perplexed, and annoyed, and he said, "Oh, I ca-an't do *that*, you know." It's an army of lions we have, with a sheep for commander-in-chief. O for a day of the late Andrew Jackson!

Other columns are supposed to be cooperating with Burnside's; Sigel's in the direction of Gordonsville, and [John G.] Foster's toward Weldon,

[11] The Baron Osten-Sacken was first secretary of the Russian legation.

or perhaps Richmond itself. His "Army of the Blackwater" is said to be 40,000 strong. There may be good military reasons for this division and separation of our forces. I hope so.

At the Sanitary Commission rooms this afternoon we had Olmsted and Newberry added unto us. We are doing business on a large scale, and must come to the end of our means before many months, unless another California turn up. . . .

Old Gurowski's *Diary*[12] makes some impression on me, due probably, to the intensity of conviction with which he writes, for he records no new facts and no original thoughts. His English is obscure, and his temper, taste, and moral tone are bad. As to his English, want of facility in using that apparatus is quite pardonable in a foreigner, and his temper and taste, however vile, are part of himself. He is an acclimated and naturalized wild-boar from Slavonia, in which region the breed is not yet extinct, and he thinks, writes, and talks like a vigorous Muscovite or Polack porker of the male gender, which he is. He is, moreover, the Thersites of our camps and councils, denouncing and decrying every chief and every measure, but I fear his denunciations are justified, and that Lincoln, Stanton, Seward, McClellan, and all the rest are unequal to their work. God grant Burnside may be an exception.

December 14, SUNDAY.   I think the fate of the nation will be decided before night. The morning papers report a general engagement that lasted all yesterday, with no result but a little advance by part of our line, and heavy loss apparently on both sides. Taken together, the little scraps of fact and incident and humor that have come over the wires look unpromising but they might be much worse.

December 15.   Sultry weather. Nothing definite from the Rappahannock. There was only skirmishing yesterday. Saturday's business seems to have been on a large scale and not successful. Peace Democrats and McClellanites call it a repulse and say that our main body was engaged. We have reports today that Banks, after showing his fleet south of Hatteras, turned short around and has disembarked at Norfolk. . . .

Poor Bayard, killed last Saturday, was to have been married next Wednesday to a pretty girl of seventeen, daughter of the commandant at West Point.[13] Her trousseau was all ready, and Miss Bessy Fish was to

[12] Count Adam Gurowski, the Polish bear, perpetrated three volumes of an abusive diary 1862–1866.

[13] Brigadier-General George D. Bayard, who had taken a gallant part in Virginia operations, was killed at Fredericksburg.

have gone up the river on special service as bridesmaid. Such details help one to appreciate the depth of meaning embodied in the words battle, war, rebellion. Ought we to leave among us men who sympathize with those who have brought these tragedies into our peaceful homes? . . . There is poor Joe Curtis, too, George William and Burrill Curtis's brother, who rose by merit, step by step, from the ranks of the First Rhode Island to its lieutenant-colonelcy.

December 17. Burnside recrossed the Rappahannock, unmolested, Monday night. The operation seems to have been skilfully performed and was ticklish work. Secesh might have smitten us fearfully during its progress. But it is a cognovit. Burnside pleads guilty to failure and repulse. This news, arriving yesterday afternoon, has produced serious depression and discouragement. The battle of Fredericksburg was a defeat with heavy loss, damaging to the national cause. And Banks has not landed anywhere in North Carolina. We are now sure his force is diverted from the vital centre of contest and destined for the extremities—for Florida, Mobile, or Texas. This looks like bad economy of our strength.

The Sanitary Commission sat yesterday morning at No. 823 [Broadway]. Bellows, Professor Bache, Olmsted, Agnew, Gibbs, Van Buren, Binney, Judge Hare, Stillé, dined here yesterday, and Dr. Howe came in *pendente symposis*. It was a satisfactory evening. This morning we resumed our session and adjourned at three o'clock. Our special business has been the Cincinnati imbroglio. We settled this by a reference with power to a committee of heads of western branches. Perhaps our best course, but it will cost our treasury just $50,000 and will not stop the mouths of the Hon. George Hoadly & Co.[14] We had much debate also about the relative authority of the Commission (or Executive Committee when the Commission is not sitting) and our executive officer, F. L. Olmsted, to wit. Were he not among the truest, purest, and best of men, we should be in irreconcilable conflict. His convictions as to the power an executive officer ought to wield and his faculty of logical demonstration that the Commission ought to confide everything to its general secretary on general principles, would make a crushing rupture inevitable, were we not all working in a common cause and without personal considerations.

[14] Judge George Hoadly (1826–1902), a protégé of Chase's who was destined to be a notable reform governor of Ohio, was the chief figure in the Cincinnati branch of the Sanitary Commission.

Perhaps the saddest single battle of the Civil War for the North, the most unjustifiable tragedy, had just taken place on the banks of the Rappahannock. Burnside, a man of fine personal qualities but inadequate to the command of a great army, had advanced to Falmouth and Stafford Heights on the north side of the Rappahannock, overlooking Fredericksburg. Lee's army held the high wooded hills just to the south of the river. On December 12, Burnside crossed the stream, and on the 13th he delivered a series of frontal assaults on the Confederate entrenchments. The stone wall below Marye's Hill was, as the Union leader General Humphreys put it in his report, "a sheet of flame." Joe Hooker, who loved fighting, declared that he could make no more impression on the Confederate line than upon "the side of a mountain of rock." When the carnage ended, the Northern troops had been beaten back with a loss of nearly 13,000 men; the Confederate casualties were not half that number. On the night of December 15, shielded by darkness and a heavy storm, Burnside recrossed the river. He manfully reported to Washington that the blame for the tragedy was entirely his. Heavy as were the army's losses in men, its loss of morale was still graver, for the defeat left it temporarily unnerved. Throughout the North sorrow and anger possessed the popular mind. The press broke out in denunciation of the nation's leadership, and a storm arose in Congress which brought on a Cabinet crisis—a group of Senators demanding that Lincoln get rid of Seward, who was believed to be an ultra-conservative influence. But by skillful management Lincoln remained master of the situation.

December 18. Our loss at Fredericksburg is crawling up to 17,000. It is generally held that Stanton forced Burnside to this movement against his earnest remonstrance and protest. Perhaps Stanton didn't. Who knows? But there is universal bitter wrath against him throughout this community, a deeper feeling more intensely uttered than any I ever saw prevailing here. Lincoln comes in for a share of it. Unless Stanton be speedily shelved, something will burst somewhere. The general indignation is fast growing revolutionary. The most thorough Republicans, the most loyal Administration men, express it most fiercely and seem to share the personal vindictiveness of the men and women whose sons or brothers or friends have been uselessly sacrificed to the vanity of the political schemes of this meddling murderous quack. His name is likely to be a hissing, till it is forgotten, and the Honest Old Abe must take care lest his own fare no better. A year ago we laughed at the Honest Old Abe's grotesque genial Western jocosities, but they nauseate us now. If these things go on, we shall have pressure on him to resign and make way for Hamlin, as for one about whom nobody knows anything and who may therefore be a change for the better, none for the worse being conceivable. *"O Abraham, O mon Roi!"*

December 21, SUNDAY.   Seward has tendered his resignation! Whether it will be accepted and if so, who will succeed him, and whether other changes in the Cabinet are to follow, we don't yet know. Edward Everett and Charles Sumner are named as candidates for the succession. I do not think Seward a loss to government. He is an adroit, shifty, clever politician, in whose career I have never detected the least indication of principle. He believes in majorities, and it would seem, in nothing else. He has used anti-Masonry, law reform, the common school system, and anti-slavery as means to secure votes, without possessing an honest conviction in regard to any of them

December 24, WEDNESDAY.   The little tempest in the Cabinet has cleared up. Nobody resigns after all. Burnside comes out with a frank, honest, manly report, taking on himself whatever blame attaches to the repulse before Fredericksburg. I regret one passage, in which he says he was unwilling to be entrusted with the command of the army when McClellan was relieved, because he felt himself unequal to the place. But the paper as a whole is honorable to him and of good omen for the country. We are sure now of *one* fact, and we are sure of very few. We have one man in high place who is single-minded and unselfish and sincere. His identification is great gain, even admitting his ability to be third-rate.

Christmas is a great institution, especially in time of trouble and disaster and impending ruin. *Gloria in Excelsis Deo et in Terra Pax* are words of permanent meaning, independent of chance and change, and that meaning is most distinctly felt when war and revolution are shaking the foundations of society and threatening respectable citizens like myself with speedy insolvency.

December 27.   Public affairs unchanged. Will Uncle Abe Lincoln stand firm and issue his promised proclamation on the first of January, 1863? Nobody knows, but I think he will. Charles J. Stillé of Philadelphia has published a clever pamphlet, comparing our general condition as to blunders, imbecility, failures, popular discontent, financial embarrassment, and so on with that of shabby old England during the first years of her Peninsular War. He makes out a strong case in our favor. It is a valuable paper, and we must have it reprinted here, for there are many feeble knees in this community that want to be confirmed and corroborated. It had an excellent effect on Bidwell; a bad case of typhoid despondency in a state of chronic collapse and utter prostration. He rallied a little after reading it, and was heard to remark that "we might possibly come out all right after all."

Jefferson Davis's precious proclamation!! Butler and all Butler's commissioned officers to be hanged, whenever caught.[15] Ditto all armed Negroes, and all white officers commanding them. This is the first great blunder Jeff has committed since the war began. It's evidence not only of barbarism but of weakness, and will disgust his foreign admirers (if anything can) and strengthen the backbone of the North at the same time. If he attempts to carry it out, retaliation becomes a duty, and we can play at extermination quite as well as Jeff Davis.

George Wright, who was here Christmas evening, recounted a talk with some South Carolina woman about the policy of forming nigger regiments. The lady was furious. "Just think how infamous it is that our *gentlemen* should have to go out and fight niggers, and that every nigger they shoot is a thousand dollars out of their own pockets! Was there ever anything so outrageous?" "And then," said Wright, "she was so mad that she just jumped straight up and down a minute or two." No wonder. The liberating proclamation we hope for next Thursday, January 1, 1863, may possibly prove a *brutum fulmen*, "a pope's bull against the comet" (a clever mot of Abe Lincoln's), but the enlisting, arming, and drilling of a few thousand muscular athletic buck niggers, every one of whom knows he will be certainly hanged and probably tortured besides if made prisoner, is a material addition to the national force. How strange that patriotic, loyal people should deny its expediency. This generation is certainly overshadowed by a superstition, not yet quite exploded, that slaveholding rights possess peculiar sanctity and inviolability, that everybody who doubts their justice is an Abolitionist, and that an Abolitionist is a social pariah, a reprobate and caitiff, a leper whom all decent people are bound to avoid and denounce. We shall feel otherwise ten years hence, unless subjugated meanwhile by the pluck and ferocity of the slaveholders' rebellion, and look back on Northern reverence for slavery and slaveholders A.D. 1862, even

---

[15] Bitterness between North and South had now reached a high pitch. Southerners deeply resented the execution of William B. Mumford, "the martyr of New Orleans," by order of Ben Butler in May, 1862, for pulling down a Union flag; Butler's "woman order"; and the execution of Missouri bushwhackers. Davis issued various pronunciamentos and threats respecting retaliation, but in no instance did he really apply the *lex talionis*.

after the long experience of war with treason arrayed in support of slavery, as we now regard the gross superstitions of ten centuries ago, or the existing superstitions of the Mandingoes and the Zulu Kaffirs. I trust we may not have to remember it as a signal instance of judicial blindness, a paralyzing visitation of divine vengeance on a whole people at the very moment when their national existence depended on their seeing the truth and asserting it.

December 30.   We know Banks's destination now. He has relieved Butler at New Orleans. Is this wise? Perhaps they expect to take Charleston or Mobile and want Butler to do the same, organizing work there which he has done so successfully at New Orleans. But today's story is that Secretary Stanton goes out and Butler succeeds him. That would be a gain, I think. . . .

There is a report of nineteen colored chattels hanged in Charleston. If true, the presumption is that this large amount of property was thus sacrificed because it exhibited symptoms of contumacy and insubordination, produced by the expected proclamation of January first—day after tomorrow!!! A critical day that will be. Will Lincoln's backbone carry him through the work he is pledged them to do? It is generally supposed that he intends to redeem his pledge, but nobody knows, and I am not sanguine on the subject. If he come out fair and square, he will do the "biggest thing" an Illinois jury-lawyer has ever had a chance of doing, and take high place among the men who have controlled the destinies of nations. If he postpone or dilute his action, his name will be a byword and a hissing till the annals of the nineteenth century are forgotten.

NORTHERN REVERSES · COPPERHEAD ACTIVITIES · TROUBLE
WITH ENGLAND · STANTON'S OPPOSITION TO SANITARY
COMMISSION · GETTYSBURG

*I*ntense gloom filled the North after the disaster at Fredericksburg. But it was somewhat lightened by a partial success which the Union arms soon scored in Tennessee. A Confederate army under Braxton Bragg had advanced from Chattanooga toward Nashville; and on the day after Christmas the Union forces under W. S. Rosecrans moved out of Nashville to meet him. In the stubborn and bloody battle which ensued at Stone's River or Murfreesboro, Rosecrans kept possession of the field. Although he had gained no decisive advantage and had suffered losses of 13,250 against the Confederates' 10,260, Rosecrans was able to assert that he had won a victory; and Lincoln, greatly pleased, telegraphed "God bless you." Halleck went so far as to term Murfreesboro one of the most brilliant achievements of the war. It was certainly not that, but it did so cripple Bragg that the following summer the Union army was able to push forward to Chattanooga.

Discouragement and defeatism again became prominent, however, when early in January news reached the East that Grant's first movement against Vicksburg had ended in failure—Sherman having been repulsed with heavy loss when he attacked Haynes's Bluff above the city. The long casualty lists there, at Murfreesboro, and at Fredericksburg shocked both the East and the West; the pressure of taxation and the growing national debt seemed terrible; money was fast depreciating, and the cost of living bore heavily on workingmen and their families. Copperheads and traitors became bolder than ever. An unhappy part was played meanwhile by such faint-hearts as Greeley, who opened a correspondence with the chief of the Copperhead Democrats, Clement L. Vallandigham,

*and published editorial demands in the New York Tribune for European media-
tion between North and South. The Emperor Napoleon thought he saw his
opportunity. On February 3, he communicated to Secretary Seward an offer to
try to bring the Union and Confederate governments together—which Lincoln,
of course, brusquely declined. In several states, notably Indiana and Illinois,
the anti-war Democrats were so active that the President told Charles Sumner
that he feared the defeatist and seditious elements in the rear more than he did
the enemy in front.*

*It was important to rally the loyal elements of the North in a demonstration
of their strength, and Union meetings were held all over the country. In December, 1862, a Union League Club had been organized in Philadelphia to lend
support to the Administration; and now Strong was among the patriots who
decided that a similar group must be formed in New York. Indeed, he, Wolcott
Gibbs, George F. Allen, and Professor Theodore W. Dwight were the leading
spirits in founding the Club. It took life, as the diary records, early in February
and opened its club house before the middle of May. Strong meanwhile was
neglecting his law practice to labor for the Sanitary Commission, by this time a
powerful and invaluable organization.*

January 3, SATURDAY. The President has signed the bill admitting
"West Virginia" as a state. And be it remembered, with gratitude to the
Author of all Good, that on January 1st the Emancipation Proclamation
was duly issued. The nation may be sick unto speedy death and past help
from this and any other remedy, but if it is, its last great act is one of
repentance and restitution. . . .

Terrific disturbance at the New York Club. Great excitement; duels
and cowhidings confidently predicted by George Anthon and others. The
original eruption occurred on New Year's Eve, when some fifty members
gave a grand supper to their president, my obese classmate Henry Ward.
About four A.M. of January 1, 1863, the assemblage was generally in an
advanced state of intoxication. At or about that time, our friend Major
Larry Williams, two-thirds drunk, made a speech and "offered a toast,"
namely, "The Sermon on the Mount and Washington's Farewell Address
—the law for all American citizens," or with some such finale. Whereupon
Henry Cram, two-thirds drunk, arose and made a speech and denounced
Major Larry Williams as guilty of blasphemy and an insult to the club. . . .

January 7. . . . Rosecrans has certainly gained a victory, if holding the field be a test of victory. The rebels have cut and run. Perhaps, as on former occasions, they have fought as long as they thought expedient, and then retired to some new position, carrying off captured guns to reinforce their ordnance department. However that may be, Murfreesboro was a very earnest struggle while it lasted and involved great consumption of men and of material. It may have been indecisive, but our resources will stand the wear and tear of indecisive conflict longer than those of slavedom, and can be sooner repaired. . . .

January 10. . . . Last night at Dr. Van Buren's for a meeting of the Executive Committee. Letters from Ellie at Washington. She is having a grand time with all sorts of delightful people. She writes that Fitz-John Porter looks jaded, disgusted, blasé, and incapable of enthusiasm in the national or any other cause. He is doubtless sore about his court-martial and General Pope, though he can hardly fail of honorable acquittal.[1] McClellan's letter urging him to support General Pope cordially was a very damaging piece of moral evidence against him, but McClellan testifies that it was written at the President's earnest request—by the President's order, in fact—and thereby neutralizes all unfavorable inferences. I am clear as to Fitz-John Porter's honesty and loyalty, but public affairs generally are awfully obscure and muddled. Can it be possible, as people say, that the government is preventing our generals from gaining a decisive victory for fear of inconvenient anti-Administration candidates for the presidency? God forbid!

January 12, MONDAY. To Trinity Church vestry for night-long session, and much business done. . . . The Rev. Morgan Dix is to move into the rectory next door to St. John's Chapel. There is every indication that we have appointed the right man rector. Nominations for vacancies in the vestry. I brought up John Astor's name again. . . . Won't Dix feel lonesome and eerie in that big rectory, three rooms deep? Were I in his place, I should marry someone at once to secure companionship in the

[1] Fitz-John Porter had been ordered to resign command of the Fifth Corps and meet a court-martial on Pope's charges that the loss of the Second Manassas campaign was mainly attributable to Porter's disobedience and disloyalty. The ensuing trial of December, 1862–January, 1863, ended in a verdict of guilty, and Porter was cashiered January 21, 1863. The controversy over this *cause célèbre* has never ended. Porter was finally reinstated as colonel in 1886. Grant vigorously championed his plea, and the military critic John C. Ropes, among others, has defended him; General Logan and J. D. Cox pressed the case against him. Gideon Welles believed that Porter, as an intimate of McClellan, was so aggrieved by that general's dismissal in favor of Pope that he had no zeal for victory, and that "to some extent" the loss of Second Manassas was traceable to his lukewarmness.

event of a "manifestation" by the late rector, who loved his home on St. John's Park so intensely for thirty years.

January 13. Poor old Professor Jem Renwick died yesterday after several months' illness. How many reminiscences of good-natured absurdity I could contribute to the materials of his biographer![2]

January 16. Night before last at Wolcott Gibbs's, conferring about the organization of our proposed National Club. The Philadelphia Union League has proved successful. Also last night, a meeting of the Executive Committee of the Sanitary Commission. A very moderate supper there must have given me dyspepsia. . . . At the Law School at three, where the College trustees met informally, and thence to Grace Church. Professor Renwick's funeral was largely attended by ancient New Yorkers. I took off my hat to him for the last time as he passed in at the west entrance. He died of pneumonia, and it's said that with characteristic self-reliance (or self-sufficiency?) he decided that his doctors did not understand their business, dismissed them, and treated himself "on philosophical principles," relying mainly on "Russian baths"; that is, an alternation of vapor bath and cold douche, which treatment settled him expeditiously. Perhaps it is not so, but it's like enough, for the questions in nature, art, and science on which Professor Jemmy Renwick did not feel entitled to speak with absolute authority are few and insignificant. . . .

There is talk in the Cabinet of an Emancipation Bureau, which will be needed, if not needed already. Horace Binney was proposed as its chief, but conceded to be past active service, an octogenarian retired from public life. Then they talked of Stillé—"C. J. Stillé of Philadelphia, who has written that admirable pamphlet," and so on. I don't know whether they agreed about anything or anybody, but that Stillé was brought forward and discussed is certain. It's a hopeful sign. It shows that government is feeling about for strong and honest men wholly outside of party lines. Stillé is a quiet reading man, wholly unfit for the difficult and most delicate duties such a position would throw on him. . . . Nevertheless, the fact that he has been talked about for high public office because he has published a valuable paper on a national subject, and for no other reason whatever, is a most weighty fact and full of encouragement. . . . "Gold has risen." It has indeed—to about 150.

[2] James Renwick, the first professor-emeritus of Columbia College, had continued to lead an active life since his resignation as teacher of chemistry and physics ten years earlier; while his three sons had all gained fame—Edward as inventor, Henry as engineer, and James as architect.

January 22. When I came down to breakfast, the morning papers took my breath away with the statement that the court-martial on Major-General Fitz-John Porter finds him guilty of disobedience of orders and neglect of duty, and that the President confirms the sentence dismissing him from service, a disgraced and ruined man. It seems incredible. The court was composed of good men, so far as I know them. Porter has been a favorite with the army; Pope, his virtual accuser, is disliked and despised. This finding is therefore entitled to every presumption in its favor, though so astounding to all who know the accused, as I have known him for twelve years at least.

Everybody expected his triumphant acquittal. All his antecedents made it most improbable he should have failed in the execution of plain military duty. Though I never thought him brilliant or clever, he seemed the embodiment of the ideal of military subordination, discipline, respect for authority. The evidence has been unequally and imperfectly reported in the papers and has seemed of little weight. McClellan's letter to him, when Pope was put in command, begging him to support Pope cordially, was morally very damaging. McClellan testified, to be sure, that he wrote that letter only because the President asked him to do so. But one of the evening papers asks, very pertinently, whether such a letter would not have been treated as an insult by an officer who meant to do his duty and obey the commands of McClellan and Pope with equal alacrity. It is all a muddle as yet.

January 24, SATURDAY. Ellie not home yet. . . . She's disgusted at the fate that has befallen our poor friend Fitz-John Porter—and no wonder. But that affair makes no great stir. Opposition men try to give it a political color, but it won't do. He was tried by West Point officers; many of the witnesses against him were of the same clannish corps. He had no political position or influence that I ever heard of. And then, there is the summary way in which the Administration shelved Frémont. It's absurd to talk of Admiral Byng. What floored Porter was the McClellan letter and McDowell's evidence. The decision may be erroneous, but with these two telling points in its favor, it will be impossible to make Porter a popular martyr. It's a sad business. Right or wrong, we lose what we took to be one of our most reliable men. . . .

The army makes little progress. That's bad. But far worse is the fact that Northern dirt-eaters grow more insolent and shameless every day, here, in New Jersey, in Illinois, and everywhere else, and that there is no national virility anywhere sufficient to intimidate them. Their last dodge, in this city, is to sow distrust of government paper among trades-people and mechanics. For example, Charles E. Strong's oysterman rather demurred to a one-dollar greenback this morning, because the alderman of his ward, who knows what's what, had confidentially advised him that Treasury notes were waste paper.

I begin to doubt whether the Northern people, with so large a per-centage of false, cowardly, despicable sympathizers with Rebellion now prepared to intrigue against our national life, to bow down to the bullies of the South, and to uphold nigger-breeding as the noblest of duties, can be saved, ought to be saved, or is worth the trouble of saving. The most barbarous, brutal Mississippian now in arms against us is a demigod compared with Vallandigham and Fernando Wood and Winthrop Chanler and others, just as the wolf is nobler than the mongrel cur.

January 26. Afternoon papers bring weighty news. Hooker re-lieves Burnside in command on the Rappahannock.[3] Injudicious Hooker! Perhaps he is the fated knight that is to break the spell under which that army has lain enchanted so long. If he fail, a heavy penalty awaits him, the same that has been visited on McDowell, McClellan, Pope, and Burnside. He undertakes the enterprise at the worst possible moment. I cannot guess what he will try to do. But he is a fighting general who goes under fire without taking much thought for his own skin, and will be just as active as Virginia mud permits. Pity his reputation is that of an unprincipled California gambler and *mauvais sujet*. In view of the most grave political or revolutionary complications that are within the range of possibility, the general commanding the army of the Potomac should be a man of high moral tone. The personal honesty and purity of Burnside, McClellan, and Rosecrans, disinterested, high-minded patriots all three, has been an important element in the chances of our national salvation. Franklin and Sumner are also relieved, I fear because more than suspected of deserving Fitz-John Porter's doom.

At 823 Broadway this afternoon and talked with Agnew, receiving

[3] "Fighting Joe" Hooker, a West Pointer of the class of 1837, who had served in the Mexican War and achieved a reputation in California for gambling, drinking, and bad judgment, had served with dash and ability in the Peninsular Campaign and at Antietam. His dashing ways and frank speech gave him popularity with troops and public. When Burnside gave Lincoln the choice of accepting his resignation or reliev-ing Hooker, W. B. Franklin, and other high officers from duty, the President set Burn-side aside and appointed Hooker head of the Army of the Potomac. This was in a letter of January 26, 1863, memorable for the frankness with which it reminded Hooker of both his merits and faults.

his report of the sayings and doings of the Sanitary Commission session at Washington, just adjourned. Olmsted is in an unhappy, sick, sore mental state. Seems trying to pick a quarrel with the Executive Committee. Perhaps his most insanitary habits of life make him morally morbid. He works like a dog all day and sits up nearly all night, doesn't go home to his family (now established in Washington) for five days and nights together, works with steady, feverish intensity till four in the morning, sleeps on a sofa in his clothes, and breakfasts on *strong coffee and pickles*!!! . . .

It will be a terrible blow to the Commission if we have to throw Olmsted over. We could hardly replace him. . . .

Senator Fessenden tells Dr. Van Buren that we need not be uneasy about the regiments to be mustered out of service within a few months on expiration of their enlistments. There will be 300,000 enrolled Ethiops to fill the gap. *Possibly.* My first emotion when I heard of Fitz-John Porter's condemnation was sorrow for the downfall of an old friend, and regret that he should have put himself in a technically false position. But as I look further into the matter, it assumes another aspect, and Fitz-John Porter's name now seems to me likely to hold the lowest place in our national gallery but one—that of Benedict Arnold. Holt's review of the evidence for and against him is crushing.[4]

January 28.   Active snowstorm today. Snow sloppified as it fell, till about three P.M. when the streets began to whiten. Now (ten-thirty P.M.) I hear the tinkle of snow or sleet against the library window panes, the plash of thawing snow from the roof, and the fitful wail of the east wind. The outlook over Gramercy Park is white and ghastly, and carriages roll by with a wintry, muffled sound.

Dr. Bellows got home from our Sanitary Commission session at Washington this morning, and sent for me. Called at his house on my way downtown. Ellie was well and jolly yesterday afternoon and is to return, squired by George Bancroft, tomorrow. (This is confirmed by my daily bulletin from her, received this morning.) Bellows was full (in one sense) of the little dinner this little woman and her father gave Monday to Secretaries Seward and Usher[5] and General McDowell,

---

[4] Joseph Holt, whom Lincoln had appointed judge advocate-general of the army on September 3, 1862, played a conspicuous part in various courts-martial and military commissions and made reports on the alleged Confederate plot in 1861 to seize the capital, on the Fitz-John Porter case, and on other controversial matters.

[5] John P. Usher of Indiana (1816–1889) had just been appointed Secretary of the Interior in place of Caleb B. Smith, resigned.

Judge Loring, Bancroft, Bellows, and others, about a dozen all told. Seward seems to have selected the occasion for a free statement of his past and present views and policy. Talked from half past five to eleven. Nobody could stand against his talk. George Bancroft and Loring "were like shingles under Niagara." Bellows seemed much impressed by it all, and was writing notes and reminiscences, which he means to ask Ellie and Mr. Ruggles to revise, correct, and complete. He thinks Seward's revelations frank and open beyond precedent, and says all their convives agree with him. Seward said he urged Buchanan to hold and reinforce Fort Pickens, but to abandon Sumter, his object and aim being to postpone the inevitable collision till Lincoln should be in power. He thought he had done the country substantial service in two things, namely, in retarding actual conflict some thirty days, and in getting Lincoln inaugurated President of the United States without a shadow of question as to the regularity and legality and technical accuracy of his accession to office. The faintest shade of question on that point would have been felt for generations to come. That's very true. He eulogizes Lincoln without limitation. Thinks him the best and wisest man he has ever known. Perhaps. Lincoln's grade and place in history will not be settled, probably, till fifty years hence. . . .

New York Common Council has passed resolutions eulogizing Fitz-John Porter and declaring his condemnation unjust. The tender mercies of the wicked are cruel. This will do Porter no good.

Inter alia, Seward said that during the hundred days before Lincoln's accession he kept a hundred hired roughs from New York in the Senate gallery to take care of Northern Senators if necessary (which sounds so Munchausenesque that it makes me distrust all the rest); that he was personally more cordially intimate with Davis than any one else in Washington (which is true), and that Davis never dreamed secession would bring war.

January 30.   Eleven P.M. Very active all the morning. At 823 [Broadway] on my way uptown, and at eight o'clock went to Wolcott Gibbs's, a *conciliabulum* having been called to meet there and consider about the National Club. Only some eighteen invited. No one ignored the invitation; everyone came promptly and punctually or excused themselves on good grounds. There were Professor Dwight, Agnew, George Gibbs, the Reverend S. H. Weston, George Anthon, Judge Murray Hoffman, Wolcott Gibbs, of course, Dr. Bellows, George F. Allen, Horatio Allen, Dr. Dalton, William Hoppin, and myself—thirteen. Judge Hoffman presided, and I was secretary. We appointed a committee of three, namely, Gibbs (Wolcott), Dwight, and George F. Allen, to devise and report a scheme of organization, and adjourned to next Friday. Temper of the meeting more than satisfactory. The only point on which there seemed a difference was whether we should make determination to support government through thick and thin a condition of membership. There was sound and sensible talk on both sides of this question. It is plain that no absolutely decisive test can be devised. No one can be expected to pledge himself to uphold whatever any set of men at Washington or elsewhere may hereafter think proper to do, and on the other hand, no one can expect to be admitted to a club designed to sustain government who goes about denouncing the damned idiocy of Secretary this, and the corruption of Secretary that, and the infernal, ruinous imbecility of that wretched old blackguard Abe Lincoln. The Committee on Organization will have to devise some formula for signature by members that will distinguish the *Bianchi* and the *Neri*, the sheep and the goats, with approximation to accuracy.

February 1, SUNDAY. Seward told Mr. Ruggles of an interview with the French Minister, [Henri] Mercier. That diplomat called on the Secretary to say that his Imperial Master had instructed him to make overtures toward mediation and pacification and to enquire whether there could not be peace between North and South on some terms or other. Seward peremptorily declined to entertain the question. The division of the country "was a subject that could not be discussed in his office." "He should write Mr. Dayton tomorrow of the proposition and of his answer and should instruct him to read the letter to M. Thouvenel and inform him that such propositions might be entertained when Louis Napoleon was prepared to consider the dismemberment of France, but not till then!" Good for Seward.

Rumor tonight that the pirate *Oreto*, alias *Florida*, has been caught and sunk, which I disbelieve.

February 3. Life and Trust Company meeting this morning. To a poor man like me the talk of these wholesale moneyers, like old Joe Kernochan and Aspinwall and others, is sublime. With what irreverent familiarity do they talk of millions! At 823 afterwards.

Murray Hoffman dined here and I went at eight to Executive Committee meeting at Dr. Bellows's, where were also Gibbs and Agnew. Among other little matters that came before us was a draft for some $1,100, the third article of the sort received from Honolulu. Agnew says he expects the next big aerolite that arrives will bring us a contribution from American citizens in the moon. The success of this Sanitary Commission has been a marvel. Our receipts in cash up to this time are nearly $700,000 at the central office alone, beside what has been received and spent by auxiliaries, and the three or four millions' worth of stores of every sort contributed at our depots. It has become a "big thing," has the Sanitary Commission, and a considerable fact in the history of this people and of this war. Our work at Washington and at Louisville, our two chief nervous centres, is on a big scale, employs some two hundred agents of every sort, and costs not much less than $40,000 a month.

National affairs seem stagnant, but I suppose we shall very soon hear news of the first importance from Vicksburg and possibly from Rosecrans. I think the national destiny will be decided in the Southwest, not in Virginia. Richmond is an *ignis fatuus*. We have mired ourselves badly in trying to reach it, twice at least, and can apply our strength more advantageously at other points. I am more and more satisfied, as I have been from the first, that our true policy is to occupy every Southern port, to open the Mississippi, to keep a couple of armies in strong and comfortable and healthy positions on the rebel frontier, and then to say to Jefferson Davis, "We are not going to advance into your jungle over your muddy roads. If you want a fight, you must come to us. If you don't want it, stay where you are and let us see which party will first be starved and wearied into submission." We do not need enterprise and dash near so much as resolution and steadiness, perseverance and pluck; the passive pluck that can suffer a little and wait quietly for the inevitable result. Therein this people seems wanting. Perhaps I do it injustice, but all the symptoms of the last four months indicate a fearful absence of vital power and constitutional stamina to resist disease and pain. The way the Dirt-Eaters and Copperheads and sympathizers and compromisers are coming out on the surface of society, like ugly petechiæ and vibices, shows that the nation is suffering from a most putrescent state of the national blood, and that we are a very typhoid community here at the North.

Thank God for the rancorous, vindictive, ferocious, hysterical utterances that reach us from the South—for the speeches and the Richmond *Enquirer* editorials declaring compromise and reconstruction impossible, that "Southrons" would not take back "Yankees" even as their slaves, that Northern Democrats who talk about restoring the Union are fools and blind. Were the South only a little less furious, savage, and spiteful, it could in three months so strengthen our "Peace Democracy" as to paralyze the nation and destroy all hope of ever restoring its territorial integrity. It is strange Jefferson Davis & Co. fail to see their best move. With a few unmeaning, insincere professions of desire for reconstruction, additional Constitutional guaranties, and so forth, they could bring us grovelling to their feet and secure an armistice most profitable to them, most dishonorable and disastrous to us.

February 5.   These be dark blue days. Of course, every man's duty is to keep a stiff upper lip—*fortem in arduis rebus servare montem*—"to talk turkey" about the moral certainty of triumph at last. I do so very valiantly. It's fearful and wonderful the way I blow and brag about our national invincibility, the extent of our conquests during the last twenty months, and our steady progress toward subjugation of the South. It is the right kind of talk for the times, and is more than half true, and has materially relieved the moral and political *adynamia* of at least one man, Bidwell, already. But (between me and my journal) things do in fact look darker and more dark every day. We are in a fearful scrape, and I see no way out of it. Recognition of the "Confederacy" is impossible. So is vigorous prosecution of the war twelve months longer. This proposition is self-evident "if this court understand herself, and she think she do." How can these two contradictions be reconciled? Rabelais furnishes a case equally difficult. Jupiter created a fox that was destined never to be caught, and afterwards, by inadvertence, a dog destined to catch all foxes, so that the Olympian Ledger of Destiny could not be made to balance. If I rightly remember my learned and pious author, Jupiter got rid of the embarrassment by turning dog and fox into two stars, or two constellations, or two stones, which was a mere evasion, and no solution of the great problem he had to deal with. We are in a similar deadlock of contradiction, I fear; North cannot be defeated and South cannot be conquered. (Of course, this is taking the worst view of the case.)

February 9, MONDAY.   Trinity Church Vestry meeting tonight. Long debate on the Theological Seminary. Its application declined, Bradford and Verplanck alone voting in its favor. I dare say this will raise a stiff breeze against us, but how could we do otherwise? We proceeded to fill the vacancies occasioned by the death of Jarvis and Morgan. Astor and John Travers elected. Young is cantankerous and loud against Astor (on account of his father's interest in the "Astor lease" that expires in a year or two) and had to be snubbed a little. He is a great nuisance in the vestry. . . .

At Century Club Saturday night. Went there for the sole purpose of showing a cold shoulder to two or three of its habitués who seceshionize, or, what amounts to the same thing, throw their influence, whatever it may be, into the scale of opposition to the efforts of government to repress rebellion at the South and privy conspiracy sedition and disaffection at the North. Succeeded, I hope and believe, in manifesting to them my desire we may be better strangers. Ned Bell[6] is a jackass, but I am sorry for Macdonough, who ought not, for many reasons, to have allowed himself to be misled into alliance with traitors and into writing smart editorials for the *World* newspaper.

At this meeting of the Club, Judge Daly delivered a biographical eulogium on poor old lately-deceased Jemmy Renwick. Never was one of those too-common efforts to express unreality and exhale an inferior article of offensive gas executed with more infelicitous bungling. Daly's national Celtic gift of fluent rhetorical bosh had deserted him for the time being, and he talked prosy platitudes and damning faint praise so that I and others who knew old Professor Jemmy Renwick twenty-five years ago felt like a current of ice water suddenly poured under our coat-collars down our backs.

February 11. To dinner at Charley Strong's house. Present, Mr. and Mrs. Fred Sheldon, gorgeous Mrs. Ritchie, Miss Georgey Berryman, General Burnside, General [John G.] Parke, Captain [J. P.] Bankhead of the navy. After the ladies withdrew, there was an hour of good healthy talk on the value of unconditional loyalty. Parke was silent and seems insignificant, but Burnside and Bankhead are bricks. The latter is a South Carolinian! Burnside is most honest, noble, and lovable, just what he was a year or sixteen months ago at Willard's Hotel with Bishop Clark. N.B. There are signs of reaction in the anti-Administration party. John Van Buren's speech last night confirms them. Old Democratic leaders begin to see the impossibility of compromise, and that opposition to the war must be their political ruin. Seymour and his pals are said to have decided that honesty is the best policy. The very *Herald* inculcates the duty of upholding the Administration to the end of its term! "Wonders have done ceasing." The *World* and *Express*, however, continue to be coprophagous. Talking of Bishop Clark, that dry, caustic old Sir Mungo Malagrowther, the ingenious H. C. Dorr, says that what the Bishop especially loves and seeks to imitate in the life of our Great Exemplar is

---

⁶ A prominent grain merchant of New York.

this: that "the Son of Man came Eating and Drinking." I note this merely as an exquisitely characteristic Dorr-ism. The Bishop's geniality and healthy enjoyment of the good things of this life are the reverse of ascetic, but they never run into excess, so far as my knowledge and information go.

Burnside said this evening that he fought the battle of Fredericksburg on his own responsibility, and under no orders from Washington; that he considered victory certain, up to the moment when word was brought him that one of our generals (on the right, I think—probably Franklin) *was doing all he could to make the attack a failure*; that his first impulse was to ride off as fast as possible, confront the delinquent, and *shoot him*; but that considering the demoralization it would have produced, and the critical position of the army with a river in its rear, he decided that it would not do and withdrew his columns. I fear Franklin and many of his brethren are, like the late General Fitz-John Porter, bad cases of blood poisoning and paralysis from hypertrophied McClellanism. McClellan has done the state some service, but is now doing it vast mischief—involuntarily and ignorantly, as I suppose. His popularity is unaccountable to me. It must rest on his unquestionable integrity and his uncommon faculty of brilliant silence, for his name is connected with no great victory. This eastern lionizing tour of his, with its addresses and receptions and presentations, will do him no good. It tends to dethrone him.

February 12.   Much talk of diplomatic complications with France. Louis Napoleon itches to have a finger in our pie, but I do not think he is quite ready to "mediate" or to "intervene." It exasperates me to hear the talk even of honest and high-toned people about that scoundrel. They seem to consider smartness, cunning, and success a compensation for treason, perjury, and all manner of wickedness; forgetting what an accursed thing it is to gaze "on prosperous tyrants with a dazzled eye."

February 14, SATURDAY.   I went to a meeting at Charles Butler's, 13 East Fourteenth Street, to organize a Loyal Publication Association, in opposition to the surreptitious workings of the gang of Belmonts and Barlows and Tildens that met the other evening at Delmonico's and were undermined, caught, and haled out into the light by the *Post* of Friday or Saturday evening. It was a rather nobby congregation of forty or fifty, with Charles King in the chair, but there were too many old talking hacks of doubtful antecedents, like Prosper M. Wetmore and Charles

Gould.[7] Perhaps the secretary, John Austin Stevens, Jr., was in the same category. He is certainly smart and active and sly, but this community does not hold him in high favor. W. Curtis Noyes, Lieber, S. B. Crittenden, George F. Allen, Agnew, Charley Bristed, Charles H. Marshall, Butler Wright (a brick), Seth P. Hunt, Jr., Dr. Gray, and others, were present. Much superfluous jaw. They talked about organizing a "Union League" for general purposes, beyond that of publication, and as Stevens called on me by name, I had to get up and jaw likewise, stating as briefly as possible that an organization for general purposes already existed in an inchoate, embryonic, pulpy, gelatinous stage of development; that it might come to something; and that perhaps this meeting might damage the common cause if it should set up an opposition. But for the presence of those two scallywags, Gould and Wetmore, I should have taken the programme of our "Union League" out of my pocket, read it, asked for signatures, and enlisted the whole crowd. As it was, the meeting virtually declined to undertake any office beyond that of printing and distributing loyal documents.

Last evening, we (that is, Bellows, Van Buren, Gibbs, and I, the Executive Committee and others) dined at Agnew's with Dr. Bell, an eminent physician of Louisville and a leading man in his own community.[8] He is here on special hospital inspection duty for the Sanitary Commission, and seems a kindly, cultivated, intelligent person, of white-hot, steel-edged loyalty. He says McClellan is decidedly unpopular with soldiers of our Western Army. (This confirms what Burnside said, that though McClellan possessed the highest qualifications for the conduct of the siege of Vicksburg, he could not be safely sent to the West, because he would not be obeyed.) Bell says Pope is to Western soldiers what McClellan is to Eastern soldiers (!) and he thinks highly of Pope, whom he knows well. "You cannot believe a word he says, and he would rather lie than tell the truth. But that is a constitutional weakness, a monomania.

[7] As early as 1835, Prosper M. Wetmore, a dry goods and shipping merchant, had joined in a public denunciation of abolitionists; he had long been prominent in conservative Democratic councils, and though he had been a member of the city's Union Defense Committee in 1861, he had no enthusiasm for the war.

[8] Theodore S. Bell, M.D. (1807–1884). Professor of medicine and hygiene in the University of Louisville and editor of the *Louisville Medical Journal*; one of Louisville's prominent citizens and participant in many undertakings for the good of the community. Dr. Bell remained steadfastly loyal to the Union throughout the Civil War. President Lincoln sent him a musket inscribed: "From A. Lincoln to Dr. T. S. Bell, for his unswerving loyalty."

He is true and reliable in business and money matters, and probably the best general we have." A curious case, if Bell is right.

Story of the dying soldier to whom a chaplain is reading the Bible. After trying various portions of Holy Writ without exciting much interest, the chaplain goes back to the military narratives of the Old Testament with better success and reads how Samson slew his thousands with the jawbone of an ass. His moribund patient listens with interest and asks with difficult articulation, "Excuse me, stranger, but ain't them despatches signed John Pope?" This newspaper story is true, Bell says. He further reports that Kentucky loyalty, though rare, is intensely savage. Ladies of Louisville are practising with revolvers and breech-loading rifles. The tendency of a slaveholding community to barbarism crops out on both sides the line, among loyal and disloyal alike.

February 16. R. B. Minturn called this morning, about the nascent "Union League." Long talk with him; he is an excellent man, but impracticable and timid. He sees this movement may possibly prove important and wants to be in it, but objects to "signing pledges," thinks we ought to be liberal and admit weak-backed and cold-blooded men to brotherhood with a view to their invigoration and conversion, and wants to confer with W. H. Aspinwall and Hamilton Fish. Minturn, Aspinwall, and Fish would be important allies, but if they cannot subscribe to our programme, I think we do not want them. James W. Beekman came in to talk of the same matter. He is more virile. Though an old proslavery Whig of the *ancien régime*, with pronounced anti-abolition prejudices, he seeks now only to uphold government and help crush the rebellion at all cost, public or private. . . .

Today's news is not from the South, but comes across the Atlantic. Louis Napoleon seems steadily and stealthily picking his way toward recognition or intervention or both, encouraged by the Northern Dirt-Eaters' shameless sympathy with treason. It's a consolation to know that those scoundrels are most assuredly pickling a rod for their own backs. The game of anti-war politicians is always difficult and dangerous. If Seymour, Vallandigham & Co. bring foreign interference upon us, political damnation awaits them deeper than that of the "Black Cockade Federalists" and Hartford Convention men. In England there seems a strong reaction in our favor, mainly among the ungenteel classes. Large meetings applaud the Emancipation Proclamation of January 1. The *Saturday Review* sneers at them in its usual cynical style, ignoring right and wrong in its characteristic refined, cultivated, scholarly, nobby, godless way. These demonstrations will be duly considered by the Machia-vel of the Tuileries before he commits himself, and they will have some influence in the action of Parliament which was to meet on the fourth; but strange to say, they will rather weaken the Administration with the masses here, as being British sympathy with accursed Abolitionists.

February 17. . . . *Orpheus C. Kerr*, second series, is just out.[9] Not quite equal to the first series, of course, but very smart and fresh. These papers are the most brilliant literary product of the war as yet. Their humor is broad and distinctly American, but, unlike most American humor, the reverse of dry. It is rollicking and wet, as if saturated with champagne of a tolerably high grade, Vergenay at least, and perhaps a touch above it. I am not sure but their author, whoever he is (I have for-gotten his name), possesses genius, more or less of the Rabelaisian type, and I predict that these two volumes will not be forgotten A.D. 1900. . . .

The judicious Hooker is said to have prohibited the circulation of the New York *World*, *Express*, and other disloyal and Dirt-Eating papers within the lines of the Army of the Rappahannock. Good for Hooker. I dare say it's "unconstitutional," but I know of nothing so unconsti-tutional as armed rebellion against the Constitution. If the suppression of that rebellion will be aided and expedited by the unconstitutional exclusion of [Manton] Marble of the *World* and [Erastus] Brooks of the *Express* from their right to the "pursuit of happiness" and of profit by the sale of their traitorous demoralizing newspapers in the camps of the national army, I acquiesce in their suppression and exclusion as the lesser of two "unconstitutional" alternatives.

February 18, WEDNESDAY. I will divert myself by recording the shindy at Belmont's *ballo in maschera* last night, as narrated to me by Charley Strong, an eyewitness thereof. This was one of those stupid, diluted masquerades at which all the women are masked and all the men exposed, like a fleet of old fashioned line-of-battleships encountering a squadron of iron-clads. His *Durchlauchtigkeit* the Marquis of Hartington was there, a gawdy young English swell of the Dundreary type, as I hear, with a lady in domino on his arm (who proved to be that handsome

---

[9] Robert Henry Newell, whose pen name was "Orpheus C. Kerr" (1836–1901), brought out three volumes of *The Orpheus C. Kerr Papers*, 1862–1865. Lincoln read Newell with outspoken admiration. The first volume began: "Though you find me in Washington now, I was born of respectable parents. . . ."

secessionizing Mrs. Yznaga).[10] They stopped to speak to General Mc-Clellan, and Charley then observed with amazement that the illustrious lord was parading a showy little *secesh flag*, conspicuously stuck in his buttonhole. After a little polite talk with McClellan, disturbed by no manifestation of disapproval on his part (!), the pair resumed their promenade, and Charley Strong was looking about for Belmont, intending to make representations to him of this impropriety on the part of his guest, when little Johnny Heckscher came along and gave the Marquis a decided jostle or pull, observing at the same time, "It was intentional, sir, quite intentional." The peer said, "Hee-haw-w-w-what's the matter? It's really vewy extawawdinary," and walked on, followed by Heckscher, who repeated his aggressive demonstration, with a like protest against its being supposed an accident, and added, "I want to insult you, sir." The man stammered, decided to leave the lady on his arm in charge of someone else and to go outside the ballroom with Heckscher for an explanation, and Heckscher told him, at last, "If you do not instantly take that thing out of your buttonhole, I'll pull it out." So Great Britain took it out and put it in its pocket, and (I'm told) apologized to Heckscher afterwards, very frankly, on the ground of ignorance and absence of intention to offend. Good for Heckscher, and not very bad for the young Englisher, who had been consorting with W. Duncan and Belmont and naturally thought sympathy with rebellion *the thing* in New York. Pity it's wrong and disreputable to put incidents like this into the newspapers. An ingenious operator could use this affair so as to do much good. McClellan's indifference, the ire of the young lieutenant, discharged for disability from wounds received on the Peninsula, the bloated British aristocrat flaunting a rebel flag in a gorgeous ballroom, crowded with the millionaires of New York—but snubbed and suppressed and driven to apologize! The subject has immense capabilities.

February 19. . . . Story tonight by old Dr. Mott of a certain Judge Johnson of Georgia or South Carolina who came North to be operated on for extensive disease of the jaw-bone, requiring excision. The doctor

[10] Lord Hartington, later the eighth Duke of Devonshire (1833–1908), who was now visiting the United States, was destined to a prominent place in British public life. He held portfolios in several ministries, sent Gordon and Wolseley to Khartoum, and might have been prime minister had he accepted an offer by Lord Salisbury. John Heckscher, named below, was a lieutenant in McClellan's army. William Butler Duncan (1830–1912), who had married a Mississippi girl, was a banker of prominence and later became president of the Mobile & Ohio Railroad.

consented reluctantly, his patient being somewhat run down, but the patient insisted that he was equal to the trial. The doctor urged him to lie down, but the patient insisted on sitting up. The operation lasted half an hour, "and I must say I did it remarkably well." The patient never winced or twitched or murmured, but sat bolt upright with a face like cast iron, though ether was as yet unknown in surgery. It was just over and the last bandage comfortably applied, when he extended his left hand, traced on its palm with the forefinger of his right, clearly and deliberately, the word "death," crossed the "t," and fell back in his chair, dead. Mott told it vividly and effectively. I hope that may not be a fair average specimen of Southern pluck, resolution, and endurance! Dr. Parker observed that if the man had only condescended to shriek and halloo a good deal, he would doubtless have got through well enough, to which proposition Mott assented.

February 24, TUESDAY. . . . We had a meeting of some fifty or sixty "Union Leaguers" at 823 Broadway Saturday night. Besides those heretofore enlisted were George Griswold; Jonathan Sturges; Dr. Lieber (a nuisance); Mr. Austin Stevens, Jr. (Jr. in the superlative degree); F. H. Delano; Dr. Buck; Dr. Parker; Otis D. Swan; Albert Mathews, and others. The meeting was long and earnest and its result unsatisfactory to me. Dr. Bellows went off at half-cock, a way he has, and proposed to substitute the vague, unsubstantial "platform" of the Philadelphia League for ours, which was done accordingly. The rest of our work was comparatively unimportant. They offered me the secretaryship, which I declined, and Otis Swan was elected, a very good man. I tend to become disgusted with the League. James Brooks and Fernando Wood could sign its test of membership conscientiously, if either had a conscience.

February 26. Mr. Ruggles is enthusiastic about Rev. A. Cleveland Coxe, new rector of Calvary Church, and doubtless a great improvement on Hawks.[11]

March 2. Tonight at 823. Meeting of Committee of "Union League." We are sticking in the mud, floundering among diverse theories of what we ought to be: clubhouse or mere association with $25 annual dues? After we have passed a certain point and settled these and other questions finally, no matter which way, we shall begin to develop fast.

No public news of any moment today. This Congress has little more

[11] Arthur Cleveland Coxe (1818–1896), a conservative, dignified, and learned churchman, had been rector in Hartford and Baltimore before coming to Calvary Church. Two years later he was to become Bishop of Western New York.

than twenty-four hours of life left it, and a vast deal of most weighty work to finish up. If the Copperheads undertake to filibuster and retard legislation, they can do fearful mischief before the next midnight; they can paralyze the Administration and kill the country. But I do not think they will try to do it.

March 5, THURSDAY.   Sharply cold for a day or two. At work again in Wall Street, and busily since Tuesday morning. Last evening at meeting of nominating committee of Union League. We make progress toward organization, but far too slowly. This evening at Dr. Bellows's with Agnew and Gibbs. Meeting satisfactory as to work done and supper eaten. We agree fully as to the necessity of a radical change in the relations of the Washington office to the Commission and the Executive Committee. Olmsted is unconsciously working to make himself the Commission. Perhaps he is competent to do all the work of the Commission without advice or assistance. If so, I for one am inclined to withdraw and let him have all the credit of doing it.

Wall Street in great commotion today. Gold suddenly down to near 150! . . . This fall is an important event, probably. It may, however, prove to be nothing but a temporary fluctuation.

War news very little and not good, though people seem generally in a sanguine fit just now. I can't tell why.

March 6.   To 823 again at eight for a meeting of our nascent Union League. Thirty or forty present, among them R. B. Minturn and George Griswold.[12] Both seem inclined to take hold very hard. Leading merchants are essential to our success. We made considerable headway last night; raised annual dues from $10 to $25, and gravitated toward the clubhouse plan, on which alone we can accomplish anything. There was a little scene with John Austin Stevens, Jr., who has been cantankerous and disputatious and obstructive because it was not taken for granted that *he* was to play first violin in our organization. . . .

Old John Anthon died at eleven last night of pneumonia. He was a great lawyer thirty years ago, managing a very large practice with audacity and success. Then he lost money and began to fall away from his high position. His sons turned out badly, and his daughters did not find husbands. Then came the terrible chancery suit of Lewis *v.* Anthon, a bill in equity by client against counsel for relief against assignment by counsel

[12] Men of property and power were determined to make the Union League Club a success. We may repeat that Minturn was a rich shipping and commission merchant, Griswold a wealthy tea merchant.

to client of certain very questionable mortgages on Staten Island property, executed to John Anthon by the Rev. John McVickar, D.D. It was a bad business. Lewis, the client and assignee (a well-known card-engraver in former times), was half-crazed by his losses and devoted himself to the proclamation of his wrongs and the denunciation of his counsel in season and out of season. He succeeded in blackening John Anthon thoroughly and got a decree in his favor from the old vice-chancellor in 1845 or 1846. I remember my father, years ago, quoting someone as saying, "If you will make Charles Anthon President of Columbia College, Henry Anthon Bishop of New York, and John Anthon Chancellor, you will satisfy their aspirations and stop their factiousness."[13]

March 10. A dingy day. Returning from George Griswold's (90 Fifth Avenue) an hour ago, I found with disgust that it was snowing again. . . . Griswold, Minturn, George C. Ward, and I were together as a committee on building for the Union League Club House. We agreed that Henry Parish's house on Union Square would make the best of possible club houses, and I am to get the refusal of it.

March 11. At 823 this afternoon. A curious correspondence sent us by the Surgeon-General. Autograph letter from the President to him, asking him to employ in the hospitals a certain quack named Forsha, proprietor of a certain oil which acts like magic on all wounds and contusions. Another letter to the same effect signed by Blair, Bates, Welles, and others of the Cabinet, and a copy of the Surgeon-General's reply, stating that Forsha is an ignorant pretender, and that if he wants his panacea used by the Medical Bureau he must reveal its ingredients. This does not indicate a profound wisdom in our national councils.

I fear Olmsted is mismanaging our Sanitary Commission affairs. He is an extraordinary fellow, decidedly the most remarkable specimen of human nature with whom I have ever been brought into close relations. Talent and energy most rare; absolute purity and disinterestedness. Prominent defects, a monomania for system and organization on paper (elaborate, laboriously thought out, and generally impracticable), and appetite for power. He is a lay-Hildebrand. There will be a battle when the Commission meets, and incredible as it seems to myself, I think without horror of the possibility of our being obliged to appoint somebody

---

[13] These three brothers were sons of George Christian Anthon, a German who had once (in late colonial days) been an assistant surgeon in the British army. John (1784–1863), who had been graduated from Columbia in 1801, was long one of the busiest attorneys at the New York bar.

WILLIAM A. HAMMOND

EDWIN M. STANTON

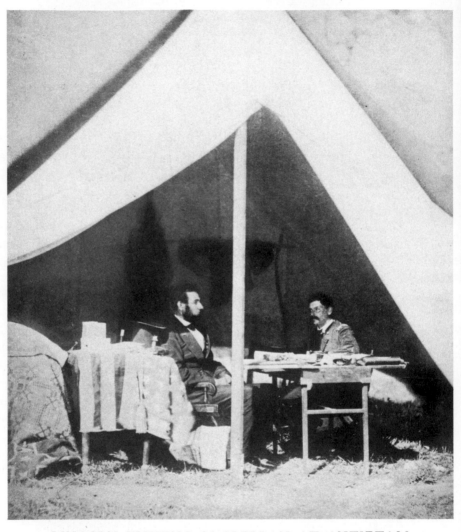

LINCOLN VISITING McCLELLAN AT ANTIETAM
4 OCTOBER 1862

else General Secretary. The Cincinnaughty "branch" seems to have repented and returned to its allegiance.

March 14. . . . George Anthon gives me confidentially the following incident. Phil Anthon, the late John Anthon's third son, who was a rather bad subject, married a lady not in our very best society and whose antecedents were considered by his family so dubious that they dropped him and her. He afterwards died of whiskey and water on the brain, and was buried in the Anthonian family vault in St. Mark's churchyard. This locality was visited by the widow, who planted certain rosebushes and the like around the tomb. When Carpenter, the sexton of St. Mark's, proceeded to dig an access to this vault the other day for the remains of John Anthon, he disinterred a tin seidlitz powder box deposited at the root of these mortuary vegetables and enclosing a letter to Phil from Phil's widow, giving him the latest news of herself and her child and expressing the hope that he, the defunct, is well and comfortable. Human nature is a remarkable institution.

March 15, SUNDAY.   Tonight Mr. Ruggles here, with Murray Hoffman, the rather dilute Dixon, Senator from Connecticut, Judge Shipman, and [George C.] Strong, late adjutant-general on Butler's staff at New Orleans and now promoted to a brigadier-generalcy. We made out our cousinship in the nth degree as descendants of the venerable Elder John Strong, and he seems a man worth claiming as one's kin. Seldom so favorably impressed by a new acquaintance. He told us much that was interesting about Butler's rule at New Orleans: the outrageous indecencies of the rebel women there, and their instantaneous suppression by Butler's much reviled order; the candid admission by leading secessionists that the order was right and necessary, and that they were grateful for it as keeping their wives and daughters from putting themselves in a false and perilous position; the embroilments with foreign consul; the black regiments, and so forth. It was interesting and instructive, but not encouraging as to the present prospects of the national cause, with Banks ruling at New Orleans instead of Butler. But allowance must, of course, be made for his official prejudice in Butler's favor.

March 16.   Committee to nominate officers of Union League Club met at 823 this afternoon; viz., Griswold, R. B. Minturn, Agnew, Wolcott Gibbs, Franklin H. Delano, R. L. Kennedy, and myself. On ballot, Minturn nominated for president. He protested against it, with entire sincerity and frankness, and urged Hamilton Fish. But Fish's place in ichthyology is with that fine, high-flavored East River species known as

Weak Fish. I don't doubt his loyalty, but he croaks and grumbles and desponds and does harm. *Non talis auxilio nec defensoribus istis.* We couldn't take him at any price. We also made up a good list of vice-presidents. . . .

Trinity Church vestry meeting tonight. Much business despatched. We seem to have far more to do than we had ten years ago. A letter came in from that disreputable Copperhead, Fernando Wood, indignantly complaining of the disgraceful neglected condition of Trinity Cemetery, Manhattanville. He has a child and other relatives buried there. Notwithstanding his general scoundrelism, I suppose his complaints well founded.

March 17. Tonight the Executive Committee of Sanitary Commission met and supped at Dr. Van Buren's. Talked mostly of the feud between Stanton and the Surgeon-General, and of measures to restore harmony between them, or to bring the case before the President or before the people. We came to no decision. Stanton seems trying to undermine Dr. Hammond, refusing to let him send an inspector to the West or to go thither in person, and using the general complaint of inefficiency in the Western Department against him. Hammond made a great mistake a year ago, when he generously asked for the appointment of our excellent old friend, Dr. Wood, a fogy of the fogiest type, to his high place in the Medical Department.[14] By virtue of that request, Wood is presiding at St. Louis, and the good old gentleman is [totally unfit] for that work.

March 19. To a state dinner at William Astor's at six. There were Mr. and Mrs. John Astor, Captain Raymond, Tom Bryan, General Marcy, Dr. Agnew, Judge Daly, K. Armstrong, General McClellan, Charles A. Davis, Dr. Parker, Edward Jones, Pen Hosack, Walter Langdon, and myself. Very splendid and sumptuous. It would have been pleasanter had the anecdotes of Daly and Davis been fewer and less long-winded. McClellan kept very quiet. Had a little talk with him after dinner and found him genial and pleasant. We discoursed of West Point in 1850 or 1851 when he was there.

March 20. Meeting at No. 823 Broadway this afternoon; Executive Committee of the Sanitary Commission, and afterwards Nominating Committee of Union League Club. At eight P.M. to a general meeting of the latter at the "Small Chapel of the University." It was harmonious and promising. Report of Nominating Committee confirmed; Minturn presi-

[14] Dr. R. C. Wood, surgeon in the United States Army and acting surgeon-general before Finley's appointment. Franklin Hughes Delano (1813–1893), mentioned above, had married Laura, the daughter of William B. Astor. His marriage was childless, and his niece Sara, wishing to perpetuate his name, called her only son Franklin Delano Roosevelt.

dent and a very respectable catalogue of moneyed men vice-presidents. We may make the thing work. Minturn, George Griswold, Delano, and other strong representatives of capital and commerce are interested and active. Our negotiations with Daniel Parish and Dillon will result in our hiring the hideous but spacious Parish house for one year, with the privilege of four or five, at $6,000 rent, the lessor making all repairs and putting the house into a decent condition as to paint and paper. To furnish and carpet it throughout would cost not less than $20,000, but once in possession, we can make the basement rooms habitable, and with them as our own headquarters, bring in hundreds of new members, whose fees will enable us to fit up the whole house. We may thus associate into an organism some eight hundred or one thousand influential New Yorkians who desire to sustain government against Southern rebellion and Northern sectionalism, and strengthen Northern loyalty to the nation, and stimulate property-holders and educated men to assert their right to a voice in the conduct of public affairs, national, state, and municipal, and do a little something toward suppressing the filthy horde of professed politicians that is now living on us and draining our national life by parasitical suction.[15]

March 23. In the omnibus this morning, my next neighbor, to me unknown, entered into discourse with me on the weather, the state of the country, and the price of gold, with a degree of freedom and facility for which I could not account, till I pulled the check-string and rose to leave the vehicle, when he remarked, with an accent of cordial respect and regard, "Good morning, Mr. Jay."!!! It was a staggering blow, but I controlled myself. Is the establishment of my personal identity hopeless? Must my position before the community continue incurably equivocal? Am I to walk the world all the residue of the days allotted me, half George T.

[15] With Robert B. Minturn as its first president, and a list of vice-presidents which included John A. Dix, Murray Hoffman, George Bancroft, A. T. Stewart, Moses Taylor, and Henry W. Bellows, the Union League Club might now be considered well launched. The first club-house was at 26 East 17th Street, where Broadway and Seventeenth join, overlooking Union Square. Strong was a member of the original admissions committee. The club was unquestionably the child of the Sanitary Commission. Wolcott Gibbs had first conceived the idea of such an organization in the summer of 1862; the election of Horatio Seymour as governor in October, with other Copperhead victories, seemed to make it an imperative necessity; and after Gibbs had consulted Olmsted, who wrote two letters in early November on the objects and methods of the club, Strong lent his assistance and the project was rapidly pushed forward. The second organization meeting was held, on February 6, 1863, at Strong's house, 74 East 21st Street.

Strong and more than half John Jay? Perhaps I was sinfully reliant on
this distinguishing and bristly excrescence. I let it sprout only after serious
deliberation, and after imploring my double-ganger John Jay to affirm
his own separate personality by whiskers, moustache, imperial or any
like badge—after vainly offering to toss with him or fight him, to decide
which of us should make the sacrifice so imperatively required.

March 26.   Gold down again!—139 and thereabouts. *Deo Gratias.*
Fears expressed in the street that it may get below par yet. General tone
of confidence. Government stocks rising. There is ground for this blessed
state of feeling; indeed, it may be said to justify its own existence. Our
great peril has been diffidence and distrust of our own strength. But we
seem a little more sanguine just now than the position and the progress
of affairs entitle us to be. Rebellion is not yet squelched by any means,
and we are not half through our troubles. On the Mississippi, in Tennessee,
at Fredericksburg, and at Charleston, great battles are imminent, and
there are abundant chances of disaster at each point.

April 29.   Story of Senator Dixon calling on the President and suggesting a parallel between secession and that first rebellion of which
Milton sang. Very funny interview. Abe Lincoln didn't know much about
Paradise Lost and sent out for a copy, looked through its first books under
the Senator's guidance, and was struck by the coincidences between the
utterances of Satan and those of Jefferson Davis, whom by-the-by he
generally designates as "that t'other fellow." Dixon mentioned the old
joke about the Scotch professor who was asked what his views were about
the fall of the Angels and replied, "Aweel, there's much to be said on both
sides." "Yes," said Uncle Abraham, "I always thought the Devil was
some to blame!"

April 2.   We have news today of successful fighting in the West,
though not on any large scale, and the rebel foray into Kentucky seems
advancing backward. Report that Burnside is advancing on East Tennessee.
I hope he is. Why that important wedge of loyal territory, penetrating
into the heart of seceshdom, has been so long neglected and its people
left to be harried by beastly gangs of merciless rebel marauders, is (to
me) the one great inscrutable mystery in our conduct of the war. From
Vicksburg and Port Hudson our tidings are bad and indicate probable
failure.

*As Strong has noted, Hooker was now in command of the Army of the
Potomac; an appointment made by Lincoln himself against the wishes of the*

general-in-chief, Halleck. It was a mistaken appointment, and Lincoln sent Hooker a letter which indicated that he was beset by doubts. Hooker, he wrote, had been reported as saying that both the army and the government needed a dictator. "What I now ask of you is military success, and I will risk the dictatorship. . . . Beware of rashness, but with energy and sleepless vigilance go forward and give us victories." Hooker showed marked talent in reorganizing the disheartened army under his command and in raising its morale. Reports of his success in this essential task came north and greatly encouraged the people. Early in April he resolved to take the offensive.He had about 130,000 troops disposed along the North bank of the Rappahannock, as against the 60,000 under Lee on the south bank. On April 27, Hooker began crossing the river for his grand attack, and before the month ended took up what he thought a strong position at Chancellorsville.

Meanwhile in the West the Confederates still held their two fortresses of Vicksburg and Port Hudson on the Mississippi, with the 125 miles of river country between them. The weather this winter had been extremely unfavorable for military operations, constant rain flooding the valley. But as soon as the roads began to dry, Grant ordered McClernand to march his corps southward (March 29), with Sherman and McPherson to follow. At first the progress was slow. N. P. Banks, operating from the South, failed to capture Port Hudson. But on the night of April 16, the Union gunboats, their sides armored, ran past the Vicksburg batteries under a storm of shot and shell and took with them a large body of supplies. It was now possible for Grant's army to strike into Mississippi south of Vicksburg; and one of the boldest campaigns of the war was thus fully launched. With an army of about 43,000, Grant and Sherman had to face Pemberton with a force of 40,000 based on Vicksburg.

April 4, SATURDAY.   Monthly meeting of Century Club tonight was full in spite of the vehement weather, and very pleasant. The only business done was to reject a proposition to build a billiard room, against which Judge Vanderpoel made an energetic protest. In the supper room afterwards I discoursed Verplanck, E. M. Young, Haseltine, Charles Butler, Henry R. Winthrop, James Suydam, Pete Strong, Dr. Lieber, George F. Allen, and others, and turned a cold shoulder on A. R. Macdonough, who's a very uncommonly nice fellow, but writes for the *World* newspaper, according to report. No one in any degree accessory to the daily treason of that infamous paper, even as a mere contributor of opera and theatre criticism, should be cordially recognized by any loyal citizen of the United States. Ned Bell, another of our three or four Century Club secession-ophilous *coprophagi*, was absent. Poor fellow, he had just lost one of his little motherless girls. Abram S. Hewitt and his brother-in-law Edward Cooper were also missing. So the Copperheads and Dirt-Eaters were but feebly represented tonight.

We have not yet opened the Mississippi. Our strategic operations for the reduction of Vicksburg and Port Hudson have failed, and Farragut, now between the two strongholds with only two armed vessels, may be in a tight place. But he can fight himself out of it if any one can.

April 8. . . . The grand meeting of anti-conscription Copperheads at Cooper Union last night was large but not lively. Fernando Wood & Co. were depressed by the Connecticut elections. Very sad that Charles O'Conor should be found in such company.

We are looking for weighty news from Charleston. We *must* be repulsed there, I think (barring miracles), but many sensible people believe that the mass-meeting called for the 11th in Union Square to commemorate that anniversary will have news of the recapture of Sumter to rejoice over. I trust their judgment may be better than mine, and thank Heaven that I have no rudiment of a prophetic gift. May this meeting escape dispersion by a rainy afternoon, and may it not have for its chief office that of trying to stiffen up the backbone of loyalty against the depressing effect of bad news from North Carolina! General [John G.] Foster and his command seem in a tight place, entrenched at "Little Washington," but surrounded and cut off from reinforcements by rebel batteries that command the river and shut off reinforcements from New Berne.

April 9. After dinner, went off by myself to Academy of Music (a thing I have scarcely ever done before), took a parquette seat and heard *Fidelio*, done by Madame Johannsen and the rest of Carl Auschütz's German Company. House was full, interested, unconversational, and applausive. Performance might have been much better, but it was a most satisfactory evening. The music, though rather tough and refractory to one not familiar with it, is very noble. And the opera, dramatically considered, is less base and idiotic than most operas. The grave-digging scene and Leonora's pistol business are effective. They bring water into the eyes of weak people like myself, which hydraulic power is possessed by no other opera I know, except the *Freischütz* and *Sonnambula*.

April 10. At 823 we had a conference with representatives of the Christian Commission. They renewed their propositions of concert in the

matter of supplies which were agreed to four months ago, and then
practically repudiated by these very evangelical gentry. But since then
they have subdivided themselves, it seems, and the New York subdivision
is independent in the field assigned it. The arrangement proposed is
judicious and good, and these two gentlemen, Russell and Bishop, seem
well-meaning. But there is an undercurrent of cant, unreality, or something else, I do not know what, in all their talk, that repels and offends
me. This association, calling itself a "commission" when it is no more a
commission than it is a corporation, or a hose company, or a chess-club,
or a quadratic equation, and thus setting out under false colors and with
a lie on its forehead, seems to me one of the many forms in which the
shallowness, fussiness, and humbug of our popular religionism are constantly embodying themselves.[16]

April 14.   We drift fast toward war with England, but I think we
shall not reach that point. The shop-keepers who own England want to
do us all the harm they can and to give all possible aid and comfort to our
slave-breeding and woman-flogging adversary, for England has degener-
ated into a trader, manufacturer, and banker, and has lost all the instincts
and sympathies that her name still suggests. She would declare war against
us fast enough if she dared follow her sordid impulses, but there are dirty,
selfish considerations on the other side. She cannot ally herself with
slavery, as she inclines to do, without closing a profitable market, exposing
her commerce to privateers and diminishing the supply of breadstuffs on
which her operatives depend for life. On the other side, however, is the
consideration that by allowing piratical *Alabamas* to be built, armed, and
manned in her ports to prey on our commerce, she is making a great deal
of money. It's fearful to think that the sympathies of England—the England of Shakespeare and Hooker, Cowper, Milton, Somers, Erskine, and
others—with North or South, freedom or slavery, in this great continental
battle of her children, are guided by mere considerations of profit and
loss. Anglomaniac Americans, like myself, are thoroughly "disillusionated."

[16] The Christian Commission had been organized by a convention of Young Men's
Christian Associations to minister to "the spiritual good of the soldiers and inci-
dentally their intellectual improvement and social and physical comfort." It was active
in holding religious meetings, erecting chapel tents, distributing Bibles, tracts, and
hymnbooks, and establishing free reading rooms in the camps. It also furnished food,
hot coffee, and stimulants on the battlefield. The Sanitary Commission regarded its
activities with a suspicious eye, and they were marred by a good deal of cant and
narrow dogmatism. But Grant and other leading army officers testified to the good
which it did.

April 21, TUESDAY. Yesterday's mass-meeting of the *other* Union League (Charles Gould's and Prosper M. Wetmore's) on Madison Square, was successful, in spite of the cloudy sky and cold wind. It looked more imposing than that of John Austin Stevens, Jr.'s Union League a week ago. They say the former is a machine run by Seward, and that Chase pulls the wires of the latter, and that each is an organization intended to influence the next presidential election. All stuff and nonsense, probably, but these stories show how watchful we must be in our Union League Club to keep above suspicion of mere political partisanship. Our Committee on Admissions met last night and did not pass Hiram Barney on this ground alone, though I could have given additional reasons for not passing him as fit to associate with high-toned and honorable men. . . .[17]

Dr. [Alden] March, one of our Sanitary Commission inspectors, just from Port Royal, says the First South Carolina is the best regiment he has ever seen—the best disciplined, the most subordinate, and the most pugnacious. It's a regiment of niggers with an infusion of Florida Seminole blood.

April 22. At 823, spent some time with Agnew, just from Hooker's headquarters. He dined with Hooker, who says that he intends to destroy Lee's army or his own within a week. Morale of our people good. Sickness rate low, about seven per cent. Agnew much dissatisfied with the administration of our supply depots and the like connected with this army, and thinks all our agents there but Kerlin and Harris incompetent. There is a set-off in the complimentary and eulogistic resolutions the Ohio legislature has been passing about the Commission.

At George F. Allen's tonight, 42 East Twenty-fourth Street; committee on College course. We agreed on a sensible course for Professor Nairne's department. I wish there were hope that its adoption would make him resign. No danger of that! . . .

Our iron-clads at Port Royal, having repaired damages, are as good as new and ready for another shy at Sumter and Charleston. Strong signs of reaction in England, for her shopkeepers begin at last to perceive that the precedent of neutrality they are setting may be used to their fearful damage the next time they are at war, and that if we had allowed *Alabamas* to be built, equipped, and manned in New York and Boston in 1854,

[17] Barney, a graduate of Union College and a well-known attorney who had begun his career as a free-soil Democrat, was now a Republican, a friend of Salmon P. Chase and of Bryant, and a political enemy of Thurlow Weed. Lincoln's appointment of him to the collectorship of the port, the most important federal office in New York, had attracted much attention and had been regarded as a blow to Weed and Seward.

England would have lost much monish, the only thing England cares for now. So England is beginning to look a little into her shipyards. It is to be noted, moreover, that some six hundred of the French Protestant clergy have united in a remonstrance or protest against any sympathy on the part of "evangelical" Christians with men who set up civil war for the perpetuation of human slavery. Then there is the great fact that Negro enlistments seem cordially approved by the army at the West—at Cairo, Memphis, and elsewhere. Black regiments are (or soon will be) adopted into the national army with as little objection to their color as would be made to the use of a corral of black horses captured from the rebels, and our consent to let niggers enlist and fight is a heavier blow to the rebels than the annihilation of General Lee's army would be.

All these indications forbid us to despair of the republic. But, unlike Seward, I expect no suppression of the rebellion within sixty or ninety days. Nor do I desire it. News of overtures by Jefferson Davis & Co. tomorrow would be worse than news of a great crushing defeat suffered by Hooker, Grant, or Rosecrans. There can be no stable equilibrium and permanent peace till the peculiar institutions of the South have been broken up and ground to powder, and to do this requires at least two more years of war, and perhaps a period of Southern success and invasion of Northern territory, stimulating the North to begin fighting in earnest, which it has not even yet begun to do.

April 23. A Broadway Railroad seems inflicted on us at last. A corrupt bill to establish it was just passing our disgraceful, profligate legislature, under the pilotage of George Law, when the Common Council intervened, seeing that they could make no money out of this Albany job, and authorized the Harlem Railroad Company to lay a track down Broadway. A large force of Celts is tearing up the pavement and laying down sleepers this afternoon at the corner of Broadway and Fourteenth Street. I fear our old familiar Broadway, with its packed omnibusses and difficult travel, is gone. The new regime with its railroad cars may prove more convenient, but I distrust it.

April 24. . . . . Broadway railroad checked by injunction from Supreme Court. Not a checkmate, I fear. Its only visible sign of existence today is a strip of lacerated pavement between Thirteenth and Fourteenth Streets, and a few sleepers and rails lying out in the rain. But this corrupt job will be so lucrative that its consummation is inevitable.

April 25, SATURDAY. Bellows just returned from Washington and General Hooker's headquarters, and told me part of his experiences this afternoon. The War Department has issued an order (No. 87, I think) about the transportation of medical and sanitary stores that seriously curtails the privileges government gives us. I think it was issued inadvertently and in no unfriendly spirit, but Dr. Bellows declares he will resign and make open war on Stanton unless it is resolved or corrected by an explanatory order. He discussed the matter with the solicitor of the War Department (Whiting), an old college friend of his; and in confidential relations with Stanton, Whiting brought the matter before his chief.

Stanton said he had not intended to attack the Sanitary Commission and had not foreseen the injury his order would do the Commission, but that he did not want to revoke or retract anything at its request or to promote its objects. He was no friend of the Commission—disliked it, and in fact, detested it. "But why, Mr. Stanton, when it is notoriously doing so much good service, and when the Medical Department and the whole army confide in it and depend on it as you and I know they do?" "Well," said the Secretary, "the fact is the Commission wanted Hammond to be Surgeon-General and I did not. I did my best with the President and with the Military Committee of the Senate, but the Commission beat me and got Hammond appointed. I'm not used to being beaten, and don't like it, and therefore I am hostile to the Commission."

This is certainly frank. It does not increase one's respect for Stanton, or indicate that he is specially qualified for his great place by peculiar unselfishness or patriotism. It is in fact a *cognovit* on which mankind can enter judgment against Stanton as a caitiff and a scoundrel. But whatever he may do or say, it is our plain duty to make no assault on him and to do nothing that can tend to weaken any one man's faith in the national government. With our money, our affiliated organizations all over the country, our good repute with the people, I believe we could unseat the Secretary of War if Agnew and Bellows and Gibbs and I chose to use the resources of the Commission against him, and that within thirty days. We shall make no such attempt, however, with my consent, but on the contrary, be to his virtues (whatever they are) very kind and be to his failings very blind indeed and stick up for the national government; that is, the present Administration, Stanton and all, through thick or thin.

Stanton must keep his griefs mostly to himself, for Seward told Dr. Bellows that the President and the Cabinet were strong in approval of the Commission; that they had consented to recognize an outside agency and give it a semi-official position very reluctantly, and only because they could not properly say no, and that they had taken it for granted the Commission would collapse and die a natural death within a year after its appointment at latest. But "the Commission has made itself a necessity, and it has done its very difficult and delicate work with so much discretion, tact, and ability, that"—and so forth.

Fine words. I wonder what Seward really knows about the matter.

To the Philharmonic Concert tonight, with Johnny and little Kate, at Irving Hall, which was overcrowded. Programme was the Seventh Symphony; a piano concerto of Mendelssohn's in D (not very impressive on first acquaintance); Gade's "Reminiscences of Ossian Overture," which is generally melodic and suggestive, and in spots decidedly strong, but not worth much as a whole; some more piano (solo) by Richard Hoffman; Beethoven's concerto for cornet-à-pistons(real solid music in large chunks); and Hector Berlioz's pyrotechnic "Franc-Jäger Overture." The children enjoyed the evening and will remember it, I hope. It seemed strange to be listening to the well-remembered phrases of the Seventh Symphony with Charley's little girl (who will be a young lady in a day or two) on one side, and my oldest boy on the other. The music took me straight back to the old times in 1844–1847, when Charley and I heard it together at the ancient "Apollo Room" in Broadway, below Canal Street, and when my Mrs. Ellen (God bless her) and his Mrs. Eleanor were severally young ladies, wholly unknown to us both.

May 1. At the Society Library tonight looking through English magazines and papers. Their misrepresentations about us are amazing and many of their blunders must be dishonest and malignant. *Fuit Anglia*, at least for me. The fair-minded honest old English people, in which I believed so many years so firmly, has ceased to exist—"subjectively," that is.

May 2, SATURDAY. After dinner with Ellie to Chickering's Rooms, northeast corner of Broadway and Fourth Street, the trysting place of a Musicale Club got up by Richard Willis and Scharfenberg for the amateur culture of true music. Found some thirty or forty there: Mrs. R. Willis, little Miss Charlotte Higbee (Angelina Lloyd's daughter); a sweet, stately young Parker granddaughter of old Mrs. Hills; Mrs. Goddard; and Mrs. Charles E. Strong, with others. Programme of the evening something from Rossini's *Semiramide*, and Mendelssohn's *Athalie*. Came off early and went to the monthly meeting of Century Club; Lieber, Carter, George Bancroft, Dorr, Tracy, Henry Winthrop, and others.

Today's news is good, though somewhat obscure. Hooker's great movement across the Rappahannock seems to prosper. Within a week we shall hear of a great decisive battle between Fredericksburg and Richmond. God help us! Amen. There is a report of a demonstration against Richmond by our forces in southeast Virginia at Fort Monroe, Yorktown, and Suffolk. What I most fear is that Hooker is dislocating his army, but the few details given by the newspapers cannot be relied on. Bellows and Agnew estimate him 140,000 strong, and he told them he did not believe he had 80,000 in front of him.

May 4. A mild, showery day. Morning papers tell us nothing, but at ten A.M. the boys are shrieking an extra *Tribune*, with reliable intelligence dated yesterday morning, in substance as follows. Our left across the Rappahannock, occupying Fredericksburg, and the "first line" of works behind it (carried with little loss) and "feeling its way" toward a hypothetical "second line." Our right (and our centre, also, I suppose) at a one-house village called Chancellorsville, around which there was battle. The traitor General Lee held the works behind Fredericksburg with only a rear-guard and had thrown himself in force on Hooker at Chancellorsville or thereabouts. Stoneman is believed to have cut the railroad lines behind the rebel army. If so, Lee's position is most critical. He is likely to be destroyed, unless he gain a decisive victory over our superior force.

Uptown early to Columbia College trustees' meeting, which was unusually efficient and sat till after five o'clock. We went into committee of the whole on that interminable business of the new statutes, and George F. Allen, from our committee "on the Course," presented a series of propositions which were informally approved. We must now go on and frame a "Course" conformable to the theory that seems approved by the board. Our non-committal report on Egleston's dream of a School of Mining and Metallurgy was well received.[18] Allen and Rutherfurd are

[18] This is the beginning of a great story, to be told at length in the diary. The attempt in 1858 to develop university instruction in Columbia had been wholly unsuccessful; the graduate schools of letters, science, and jurisprudence were still-born. The time was not yet ripe. From this effort, however, sprang the long and fruitful connection of Professor Theodore W. Dwight with Columbia as a teacher of law; and the experiment of 1858 probably had much to do with the application of the College of Physicians and Surgeons in 1859 for an alliance with Columbia. Now came a third happy result. The committee on postgraduate instruction had reported favorably in 1859 on a proposal among the trustees for the founding of "a practical school of science." Thus the trustees were predisposed to a favorable attitude when in March, 1863, Thomas Egleston offered a plan for a school of mining, engineering, and metallurgy. Egleston (1832–1900), a graduate of Yale, had studied in the Ecole des Mines in Paris, and then in 1861 had gone to the Smithsonian Institution to take charge of its geological accumulations.

added to the Committee and the whole question referred back to us to settle details. . . .

Telegram at No. 823 this afternoon from Sanitary Commission, Washington office, calling for large supplies of hospital stores.

After dinner to Union League Club House. Agnew, Faile, Gibbs, Swan, and others there. Sought news, but there is none in town. Wall Street this morning; no crowding around newspaper offices. The common talk was that we are doing well, and that Hooker has executed a splendid bit of strategy, with great promise of decisive success. Many expect the annihilation of Lee's army, but the majority are more reasonable. The McClellanites are already laying an anchor to windward as a precaution against the effects of any possible achievement of Hooker's. "Officers and men are so much more experienced now than a year ago" when our *Fabius Minutus* commanded them. "Hooker is not thwarted by government as McClellan was," and so on. The tone of feeling is indicated by a fall in gold. But croakers think Hooker will be cut up, that he has been enticed into a trap and fights with a river behind him, that x plus y men have joined Lee from South Virginia and as many more from Charleston. They dwell, moreover, on a rumor of disaster and stampede in one of our divisions. We have had about two hundred and fifty rumors good and bad, all of them "authentic."

My anticipations are gradually settling downward. I now expect Hooker to fail, though perhaps after punishing the enemy severely. The obstinate silence of the War Department, the absence of official reports, is uncomfortable, and if the rebels be in the tight place in which we suppose them, they will assuredly fight like cornered rats.

May 5. Northeast storm. Details in morning papers of fighting on Saturday and part of Sunday. Very severe and deadly, but we seem to have gained ground, on the whole, taking guns and prisoners and colors, in spite of the dastardly defection of certain German regiments which broke and ran. The best report is that of the *Times*, but its writer is too manifestly a claqueur of Hooker's. . . . This afternoon's papers enlighten us but little.

The battle of Chancellorsville had terminated in another crushing defeat. When Hooker's troops advanced from the area just south of the Rappahannock, they met firm resistance from Lee's troops, who promptly seized the offensive. Hooker was unnerved, and forgetting that his forces were twice as strong as Lee's, fell back. Naturally this unexpected retreat had a demoralizing effect upon the

Union troops. Then Lee and Stonewall Jackson took the bold decision of dividing their small army; and Jackson, with 30,000 men, marched halfway around Hooker's forces in order to fall upon his right flank. The Union generals— Howard as well as Hooker—should have realized that they were in danger of a flanking onslaught; but they fatuously believed that Jackson was in full retreat and trying to save his trains. In mid-afternoon, after covering some fifteen miles, Jackson found himself in a position just west of the Union army; and forming his lines in battle array, he struck with all his might. Howard's Eleventh Corps, holding the right of Hooker's line, was soon in headlong flight. The next morning found Hooker in a state of nervous collapse, utterly unfit for the task of retrieving the half-lost field. He had large forces of unused men whom he might have thrown into the contest, but he made no effort to employ them. By ten o'clock in the forenoon Lee, as he stated in his official report, was "in full possession of the field." On May 6, the Union army, more disheartened than ever, completed its retreat across the Rappahannock. It had lost about 17,300 men; Lee and Jackson had lost about 12,500.

May 6. Storm continues uninterrupted all day, with hard rain and ferocious northeast wind. News *bad.* [John] Sedgwick's division has been pushed across the heights behind Fredericksburg after severe fighting in which it was grievously outnumbered, and seems to have recrossed the river to Falmouth, and then moved up the river to rejoin Hooker. But that can hardly be, for it would leave our vital railroad artery between Falmouth and Aquia at the mercy of the rebel right wing which now holds Fredericksburg. It has been a "dark and dreary" day. We hear tonight that [Samuel P.] Heintzelman is on his way from Washington with 30,000 men to support Hooker, and also that there are indications that Aquia is to be abandoned. Inexplicable, unless Hooker means to change his base to the Orange & Alexandria Railroad and make a dash for Richmond. . . .

Lazed in Wall Street, finding any kind of work impossible. At No. 823 this afternoon. We have sent off Drs. Markoe, Gurdon Buck, and Harry Sands to assist the medical staff and three "dressers" with them. Tonight at Union League Club House, where were about a dozen of us. The second-story rooms are now carpeted and somewhat furnished, and were lit up. The Executive Committee has done its work very well. We discussed arrangements for the opening on the 12th, when there is to be a slight soirée with nothing to eat or drink—also a few little speeches.

It is delightful to perceive that "respectable" Copperheads begin to be aware of this club, and to squirm as if it irritated them somehow. For example, Willy Duncan[19] at the opera last night favored Mrs. Eleanor Strong with his views about it. He thought it very wrong and bad. "No club had ever been established before on a political basis (!!!). It would do great mischief. Great efforts had been made by its leading members to prevail on him to join it, but he had felt it his duty to decline." Very funny; for in all our talk about organization and tests of admission, the name of William Butler Duncan has been familiarly used as a convenient familiar specimen of the class we would not admit on any terms. We have repeatedly named him as a representative and strongly-marked type of the men against whom we are organizing ourselves. I fear he is a snob and a "squirt," the dining partner of his banking house, and the toady of British aristocracy when they condescend to visit New York. This is nearly as bad as Charles Gould's telling William C. Russel that the Union League Club was a most praiseworthy institution, which every loyal citizen of New York ought to join at once. "He (Charles Gould) had done a great deal to set it going and worked for it until he saw it fairly established and likely to succeed, and then he had resigned, because he had so many engagements that he really couldn't"—and so forth. Whereas Charles Gould and Prosper M. Wetmore have from the first been recognized as embodiments of corrupt, mercenary, self-seeking sham-patriotism, and as representing a dirty set of false-hearted hack stump orators and wire-pullers, vigilantly to be excluded.

May 7. Storm continues, but grows less savage. It is cloudy and cold and northeasty, but rain has ceased. Moral coloring of the day livid blue. Failure and repulse again! Hooker has retired across the Rappahannock and is where he was a month ago, but no doubt sorely shattered. It's some consolation, however, to believe that the rebel army has likewise undergone a fearful clawing and suffered more than we have. The worst consequence of this failure is that we lose the faith we felt in Hooker a few days ago, when he seemed likely to be the man we have been so long trying to find. . . .

Coming home, I found Bob LeRoy in the dining room! Talked with him half an hour or so. He looks and talks well. No one could suppose he had so lately experienced delirium tremens and treatment in an asylum. He is

---

[19] The banker William B. Duncan had labored for Buchanan's election in 1856; had endorsed the fraudulent Lecompton Constitution which tried to fasten slavery upon Kansas; and had fought Lincoln's election in 1860.

on recruiting service, lieutenant in a nascent cavalry regiment; is determined to reform, and refused a glass of wine. Poor fellow, may God sustain him in his effort! I believe he is making an earnest, resolute struggle to do right, but the odds are fearfully against him. He fights against inherited proclivities to evil, against habit fortified by prosperous years of self-indulgence, and against a keen sense of disgrace and of a lost social position. If he is saved, it will be by his appreciation of the merit and dignity of that noble little plucky woman, his pretty little wife.

May 8. Went into the new clubhouse with Agnew after we left No. 823 this afternoon, and from its balcony saw the return of that splendid regiment, the New York Fifth, "Duryea's Zouaves" or, rather, of its debris, less than three hundred.[20] A touching sight, when I remembered in what force I saw them march down Broadway two years ago, and that they had been twice recruited since then. They looked rugged, bronzed, and soldierly. The crowd was enthusiastic. Occasionally an officer or one of the rank and file recognized someone on the sidewalk or at a window. The spectacle was a reality and somewhat intense. Its sentiment is in the fourth movement of Beethoven's *Eroica*. I always thought that the meaning of the finale of the *Eroica* and now I'm sure of it.

May 10. A painful piece of information today. The elder Mrs. Ruggles, Ellie's grandmamma, now eighty-three, has been suffering for a year from cancer on the breast. The disease appears to be of an unprogressive type, without symptoms of malignity. An operation is thought inexpedient. But it is draining her vital forces, producing days of exhaustion and pallor, and will terminate her useful busy life, I suppose, within a few months. She's a splendid old lady—the finest specimen I have ever known of geniality, active energy, and unselfishness in extreme old age. I owe much to her vigilant, laborious, cheerful care of Ellie in 1849, when poor Ellie was so desperately stricken by disease and her poor grandmamma so self-sacrificing, efficient, and hopeful—a nurse beyond all price. Her loving diligent service may very possibly have turned the trembling scale and saved poor Ellie's life. We could not expect her to be with us much longer, but it is sad to know that her summons to depart from among us has been issued, and that she must very soon report herself to the Head of the Holy

[20] Colonel and later Brigadier-General Abram Duryea's Fifth New York had fought effectively at Big Bethel, Cedar Mountain, Second Bull Run, and South Mountain. At Second Bull Run, Duryea was twice wounded, and in the Antietam campaign he received three wounds. When a junior officer was promoted over his head, he resigned in January, 1863.

Church Invisible, and be known on earth no more. No. 24 Union Square will not be the same house when she leaves it.

May 12.   Hot, and tonight a lively thundershower. Downtown late and cephalalgic. At No. 823 I find indications that a squabble with the Secretary of War and Dr. Letterman (Hooker's Medical Director) may be at hand. Not an atom of tangible news today, but "it is believed" at Memphis or some other place that General Grant has taken Jackson and thereby made Vicksburg untenable. We shall see. On the whole, we are hopeful and jolly today. Van Dorn's death is established. He was shot by some other gentleman for certain liberties with the other gentleman's wife, a fit conclusion to a life of scoundrelism.[21] It is also established that Stonewall Jackson lost an arm at Chancellorsville. Hooker's advance and Lee's retreat are *not* confirmed.

The Union League Club House was thrown open tonight—"inaugurated," as the newspapers say. Each of our three hundred and fifty members had three tickets and there were invited guests beside, General Wool and his staff, Dr. Vinton, and others. The house was very fairly filled, and was very appropriately and prettily decorated for the occasion under Richard Hunt's artistic supervision. The assemblage was made up of nice people and included many very nice and pretty women. Several persons said it was "brilliant," but I do not precisely know what they meant. Ellie enjoyed the evening hugely. Our president, Minturn, made a little speech and introduced successively George Bancroft and Dr. Bellows, who made each a good and effective fifteen-minute oration. The performance was decidedly successful. Only two Copperheads got in, to my knowledge, Ned Bell and W. H. Appleton, the bookseller. Bell was frightfully out of place. Who could have given him a ticket? Griswold, Delano, and Minturn seemed half disposed to wait on him as a committee and request him to clear out.

Though this organization is not yet beyond a nascent state and has all the perils of infancy to encounter, it seems a promising Babby. If it thrive and grow, it will be useful. But much perseverance in hard work is still necessary to establish it in the position which it aims to occupy. And there are loyal gentlemen in New York who ought to be with us, but are not; for example, Charles E. Strong and George C. Anthon both criticizing twopenny details, and blind, wilfully blind, to the importance of the work.

[21] General Earl Van Dorn, a West Pointer in the class of 1832, who had commanded the Confederate armies in the battles they lost at Pea Ridge and Corinth, and had led the successful raid on the Union base at Holly Springs in December, 1862, was shot May 8, 1863, at his desk in headquarters at Spring Hill, Tennessee.

Both refuse to see the advantage the nation gains by shewing France and England that this war against rebellion is not waged by the rabble of the North, or by politicians, but that the intelligent, cultivated, gentlemanly caste sustains it. These two back out and fail us. So they did in the matter of the Sanitary Commission. I thought myself fairly entitled to count on both as allies and backers, but it seems I was mistaken. Amen.

May 13. Warm day. Afternoon and evening showery. Today's only news is a seemingly trustworthy report that that very salient rebel Stonewall Jackson died last Sunday of pneumonia, which attacked him while weakened by a recent amputation. He seems to have been a brave, capable, earnest man, good and religious according to his Presbyterian formulas, but misguided into treason by that deluding dogma of state allegiance. At half-past two to the Law School, where examination of a large graduating class was begun and continued till near six. Best class yet, I think. Only two failed to do very well. One hundred and sixty names now on the roll, including four third-year students. This school has succeeded beyond my utmost hope—thanks to Professor Dwight's great ability and admirable fitness for his office.

The Confederates had paid heavily for their victory at Chancellorsville. On the night of May 3 Jackson, after sending his army to attack Howard's corps, had ridden beyond the line of battle in order to keep his troops in proper order. As he turned back some of his own men mistook his escort in the gloom for Union cavalry, and fired on his party. Jackson was gravely wounded. Pneumonia set in, and in eight days the indomitable Scotch-Irish leader succumbed. The Confederacy was thrown into mourning; but it was not until other battles were fought—and lost—that it realized the full extent of the calamity. Strong's diary shows that even in the midst of war the North respected the fallen soldier who had so often outgeneralled its own leaders.

Meanwhile, Strong himself was on the eve of an illness which prostrated him from the middle of May to the middle of June, and left a sad gap in his diary.

May 14. Law School examinations again from half-past two till after six. Better than yesterday. The two bunglers (Kenny and Pumpelly) did fairly today. This school is doing great good. I would now pay ten thousand dollars at a venture, if I could so change past time that Dwight and his Law School could have been at work 1838–1841. The most promising men in this class of forty and upwards are an ungainly William Walter Phelps (of Madison Avenue); Erastus B. Rudd, New York; Francis Edward Kernochan (a son of old Secesh Joe Kernochan); and Edmund Wetmore of Utica.[22]

May 17. Mr. Ruggles brings in a comparatively trustworthy piece of information just telegraphed from Washington to one in authority namely, that Stanton resigns and Butler is to be Secretary of War!!! Too good to be true. Also that Sickles (!!!) is to succeed Hooker in command on the Rappahannock. A very doubtful improvement, but there are judicious men who rate Sickles very high.

An unusually weighty and significant article from one of the Richmond papers (*Enquirer* or *Examiner*), reprinted in this morning's *Times*, says in substance: "The Yankees have now made up their minds that this is to be a long war, and they are determined to fight it out to the end. Of course, we shall beat them in every battle, but they can afford to lose five men for the sake of destroying *one* of us. Stonewall Jackson was worth Hooker and his 100,000 men. They threaten us at every point—Virginia, Eastern Tennessee, Vicksburg, Louisiana, North Carolina, Hilton Head, and so forth. Our frontier is too extended to be everywhere adequately defended. Gunboats and cavalry-raids will penetrate the heart of the country, stealing niggers and destroying generally. In short, we are fighting at fearful disadvantage with terrible loss, in spite of our superiority in pluck and in generalship, and the state of things may well continue twenty years longer, for these mean Yankees cannot afford to acknowledge our independence. We draw no inferences, offer no hints, but merely state facts." This was not published, under the traitorous noses of Jefferson Davis and his chief counsellors, without great consideration. What does it mean?

June 15, MONDAY. George Strong, *miserrimiculus, infandum renovat dolorem.* Thank God, I feel a little like myself this morning and seem to see a glimpse of coming emancipation. Last evening I spent two or three hours downstairs. A lot of people came in, and I retreated before ten o'clock and our usual slight supper, tired out. I have gained strength during these last three days, but am still as weak as warm water in its twentieth homeopathic dilution. No wonder, after four weeks of confinement to library

[22] Of these men William Walter Phelps (1839–1894), who was valedictorian of his law class, attained some eminence. Endowed with inherited wealth, important family connections (he married a daughter of the founder of Sheffield Scientific School), wit, and oratorical power, he made his mark as a member of Congress from New Jersey and as minister to Germany. But his close friendship with Blaine subjected him to much attack.

and bedroom, and mostly to bed, thin diet and heroic dosing; two weeks of the four having been, also, a weary period of intense physical pain recurring hourly at least, night and day. This illness began the nineteenth of last month, when I felt utterly prostrate and limp. . . .

As to the war and things in general, much has been going on. I am too flaccid to particularize. This is the first day I've omitted undressing and going formally to bed for four or five hours in the afternoon. There is a dreamy recollection of great news and much jubilation some three weeks ago over Grierson's splendid cavalry raid from the Tennessee frontier all the way to Baton Rouge, and of General Grant's brilliant campaign behind Vicksburg, fighting five battles and taking eighty guns and ten thousand prisoners. Vicksburg had fallen, or was to fall day after tomorrow at latest. But it hasn't fallen, and Grant is laying formal siege to it, an assault having failed. Banks is addressing himself to Port Hudson in like manner. Good prospect of success at both points.

Lee and Hooker both seem moving. Colonel George Ruggles, who is in town organizing and inspecting the new invalid corps, told me last night that Hooker's base of supplies is shifted from Aquia to Alexandria. Lee seems to contemplate either an attack on Washington or an invasion of Pennsylvania.

June 17.   Nothing definite yet as to Lee's programme. Hooker seems to be after him, and troops, such as they are, raw militia mostly, are pouring into Pennsylvania. Our Seventh marched today. Unless rebeldom gain some great decisive success, this move of Lee's is likely to do good by bothering and silencing our nasty peace-democracy. It seems now as if Harrisburg might be defended with success. If we do but carry Vicksburg and Port Hudson, we can well afford to let rebeldom have full swing to burn and plunder for a week or two.

June 24.   Tonight's story is that the rebels are moving on Frederick. *Quién sabe?* Their destination is differently reported every day. It is Harrisburg, Pittsburgh, Philadelphia, Ohio, Baltimore, positively and alternately. Some say Washington. There are indications of strong pressure on Lincoln to restore McClellan. It would be a dubious step. . . .

Nigger regiments seem to stand fire and fight well, an immense point in our favor. It is certainly natural they should exert themselves to avoid being made prisoners! On the whole, things look well, if we can but take Vicksburg and Port Hudson.

June 25.   Wall Street again this morning. This evening, after assisting Johnny and Temple with a few crackers and torpedoes, I went to the

Union League Club, where matters look promising. Over five hundred members now; fifty or sixty present tonight. Adjourned to one of the third-story rooms with Olmsted, Bellows, Griswold, [Dr. B. A.] Gould of Cambridge, and half a dozen more to discuss the project of a weekly paper, independent of mere party politics, and upholding sound principles of loyalty and nationality. What vast good such a paper might do, if honest and able men could be found in sufficient number to form an editorial staff.[23]

According to this afternoon's rumors and despatches, chronicled in the first edition, second and third of the afternoon papers, Lee is aiming at Harrisburg in force. Do not believe he has shewn his hand yet. He is probably watching to strike at any point we may leave uncovered, and helping himself, meanwhile, to the horses and cattle of Pennsylvania by a series of cautious forays right and left. The unpatriotic well-to-do farmers of that region will doubtless suffer some, and it will do them good. The Harrisburgers are shewing themselves uncommonly base, sordid, and spiritless. Pennsylvania is, in fact, the meanest state in the Union. Even in this crisis she is doing little to help herself, and depending on militia from this city, Massachusetts, and elsewhere, out of whom the dirty, drab-colored men of the invaded district are making all the money they can—much too full of their pleasing task to think of enrolling in defense of their own firesides and pigstyes (perhaps tautologous).

June 26.   Visit from Olmsted and Howard Potter, and a long talk about our dream of an honest weekly paper. Potter, William Hoppin, and I are to be trustees of a fund to be raised by subscription, and a strong effort will be made to carry out the design. Griswold puts down $1,000 to begin with.

June 27, SATURDAY.   Tried very hard to be diligent in Wall Street, but had to give it up by two o'clock, completely exhausted.

Lounged awhile at Union League Club tonight. Many there. Despatches and letters from Washington posted on one bulletin board, throwing some light on the "situation" in Maryland and Pennsylvania. Dix has reached Baltimore with ten thousand men and Foster is expected. Everything points to a fearfully decisive battle within a few days on or near the field of Antietam. May God avert a great disaster! I fear Joe Hooker, drunk or sober, is no match for Lee, and that his army, though in excellent

[23] The first mention of an enterprise which, when taken up by Olmsted in conjunction with James M. McKim and others, was to result in the founding of the New York *Nation*.

order and condition, is discouraged by its repeated failures. Should it be badly defeated and disorganized, there is nothing in reserve, and Washington, Baltimore, and Philadelphia will be lost before another army can be raised. Our frivolous, self-indulgent apathy is marvellous.

Rebel pirates are playing the deuce with our commerce. They are now engaged in the chivalric work of burning fishing smacks off Cape Sable. But their sending boats into Portland Harbor and capturing the revenue cutter *Caleb Cushing* does them credit. She was pursued and blown up and her crew brought back in irons, however.

The great turning point of the war was now being reached. On the eastern and western fronts alike the conflict was at its crisis. Lee's army, elated by its smashing victory at Chancellorsville, reached a strength by June 1 of more than 76,000 men and 272 guns. It confronted Hooker's discouraged army of about 105,000 effective men. In Mississippi, meanwhile, Grant by his bold movement to the rear of Vicksburg had shut Pemberton's force of about 30,000 men into that river city; while Joseph E. Johnston, with less than 25,000 men at Canton, was unable to strike at Grant's force of 75,000. Unless the Southern command moved with speed and skill, Vicksburg would soon be lost and the Mississippi throughout its whole length held by the North, shutting off Texas and its valuable food supplies. Some high Confederate officers, including Beauregard and Longstreet, proposed to transfer heavy reinforcements from Lee's army to Tennessee, build up Bragg's command at Murfreesboro to overwhelming strength, crush Rosecrans, and march against Louisville and Cincinnati. This, they said, offered the best hope of drawing Grant off from Vicksburg. But President Davis, anxious to bring about foreign intervention, thought that a victory on Northern soil might achieve this object. Lee, too, preferred operations in the eastern theatre. Ever since the Antietam campaign, the great Confederate leader had believed that another bold strike north of the Potomac might succeed. An invasion of Maryland and Pennsylvania was therefore determined upon; on June 15 the first Confederate troops crossed the Potomac; and by June 25 the whole army was on or over that river and ready to advance on Harrisburg. Hooker followed, keeping between Lee and Washington. Then came the news of George G. Meade's promotion.

June 29, MONDAY.   The hardly credible news that Hooker is relieved and General Meade is in command!!! A change of generals when a great decisive battle seems all but actually begun, and may well be delivered before the new commander is comfortably settled in his saddle! God help us! . . .

People far better pleased with the change of commanders than I expected to find them. Clitz, dining with Henry Fearing at West Point yesterday and, of course, knowing nothing of this change, said that Meade was sure to come out "at the top of the pile" before the war was over.

June 30.   Made my way to Union League Club at nine . . . to keep an appointment for consultation over the proposed periodical, and half a dozen of us adjourned to one of the committee rooms. But it was hot and smelt of fresh paint, and I was faint and sweaty and three-quarters sick, and the effort to follow Olmsted's clear, compact, well-considered statement of plans and probabilities made me desperate and fidgety *"comme un Diable dans un bénitier,"* so I excused myself.

July 1.   At the Union League Club tonight I found a large assemblage; also, sundry telegrams confirming what the newspapers tell us, that Meade is advancing and that Lee has paused and is calling in his scattered columns and concentrating either for battle or for a retreat with his wagon loads of plunder. Harrisburg breathes more freely, and the Pennsylvania militia is mustering in considerable (numerical) force. Much good they would do, to be sure, in combat with Lee's desperadoes, cunning sharp-shooters, and stark, hard-riding moss-troopers.

July 3.   Half-past nine of a muggy morning. We can scarcely fail to have most weighty news before night.

There was a battle at or near Gettysburg on the first, resulting apparently in our favor. We lost a valuable officer in General Reynolds.[24] Fight probably renewed yesterday, but no information on that point. There are no official reports; an unpleasant indication, but the government has maintained the most resolute silence as to all army movements during this campaign. . . .

Evening. No definite news at all. We were told by the bulletin boards at noon that Vicksburg had surrendered, and I believed the story till about one in the afternoon, when it turned out not entirely authentic. Never mind. Do not the *Times, Tribune, Post* and *Commercial* daily certify that the "fall" of Vicksburg is "only a question of time," as distinguished from one of eternity?

[24] Major-General John F. Reynolds, a Pennsylvanian by birth and a graduate of West Point, had been considered by Lincoln for the chief command of the Army of the Potomac. He might have been chosen in Meade's place but that he demanded wide guarantees of freedom of action. He was killed on the first day of Gettysburg as he was leading Wisconsin troops into battle.

July 4, SATURDAY. A cloudy, muggy, sultry Fourth. Awake nearly all last night, tormented by headache and wakened out of each successive cat-nap by pyrotechnic racket. At or soon after daylight, Calvary Church bells began clanging, and cannon firing "a national salute" in Union Square. I arose bilious, headachy, backachy, sour, and savage. Read morning papers. Their news from Meade's army was fragmentary and vague but hopeful. Spent the morning watching over Johnny and Temple, and Johnny's friend, Master Lewis French, firing off no end of crackers, little and big, "columbiads" included. What an infernal noise they make!

At half-past five appeared Walter Cutting with news from the army up to eight last night. There was fighting on the afternoon of the second, renewed yesterday, when the rebels attacked Meade's left centre in great force and were twice repulsed with severe loss. Our cavalry was operating on their flank. Both armies seem to have held their original position. *Gratias agimus Tibi*. This can hardly turn out to have been worse than a drawn battle, and that to an invading aggressive army is equivalent to defeat, as we have good reason to know. Defeat and failure in this desperate undertaking is a serious matter to the woman-floggers. . . .

It would seem that General Daniel Sickles has lost a leg. Wadsworth is wounded. Poor General Barlow (Mrs. Arabella Barlow née Griffith's husband) severely wounded again and probably a prisoner.[25]

July 5. A memorable day, even should its glorious news prove but half true. Tidings from Gettysburg have been arriving in fragmentary instalments, but with a steady crescendo toward complete, overwhelming victory. If we can believe what we hear, Lee is smitten hip and thigh, and his invincible "Army of Northern Virginia" shattered and destroyed. But I am skeptical, especially as to news of victory, and expect to find large deductions from our alleged success in tomorrow morning's newspapers. There has been a great battle in which we are, on the whole, victorious. The woman-floggers are badly repulsed and retreating, with more or less loss of prisoners, guns, and matériel. So much seems certain, and that is enough to thank God for most devoutly, far better than we dared hope a week ago. This may have been one of the great decisive battles of history.

It has been a day of quiet rain. Ellie went to Trinity Church with the

[25] Major-General Daniel E. Sickles, who had offended Meade by taking an excessively advanced position, lost his right leg at Gettysburg; James S. Wadsworth, fighting most creditably as division commander, was little hurt and survived to be slain at The Wilderness. Brigadier-General Francis C. Barlow was shot through the body, left for dead on the field, rescued by the Confederate General John B. Gordon, and restored to the Union forces. He was out of the war for nearly a year.

children. I stayed at home, read, and lay in wait for extras. An extra *Herald* came at noon, another an hour or two later. Both encouraging. At six P.M. appeared Dr. Bellows with a telegram from Olmsted at Philadelphia as follows, to wit: "Private advices tend to confirm report of capture of over fifteen thousand prisoners and one hundred guns. Lee retreating. [Alfred] Pleasanton holds Potomac fords." Olmsted is wary, shrewd, and never sanguine. This despatch was not sent without strong evidence to support it. I carried it down at once to Union League Club and saw it posted on our bulletin board to the intense delectation of a half-dozen people who were hanging about the premises hungering for news.

Mr. Ruggles came in to tea. Afterwards appeared one Hill, of Davenport, Iowa, an ally of Mr. Ruggles in his great ship-canal campaign, and a very intelligent, cultivated person, with no perceptible westernism; also Dr. Peters and Walter Cutting.

At suppertime, ten P.M., a *Tribune* extra. News of victory continued. "Prisoners and guns taken"; x plus y prisoners arrived at Baltimore and "acres of cars" laden with prisoners blocked on the railroad. Lee retreating toward Williamsport. Official despatch from General [William H.] French to General Halleck announcing capture of pontoon train at Williamsport. Significant. The Potomac fords are full just now. Just suppose Meade should bag Lee and his horde of traitors as Burgoyne and Cornwallis were bagged near a century ago. Imagine it! But there is no such luck now.

At half-past eleven, in rushed the exuberant Colonel Frank Howe with a budget of telegrams. Lee utterly routed and disorganized, with loss of thirty thousand prisoners (!) and all his artillery. Details of capture of three or four blockade-running Britishers at Mobile and Charleston I omit as comparatively uninteresting. Now to bed and then for the morning papers. We may be fearfully disillusionated even yet.

July 6. Mugginess continues. Morning papers give us little additional light, if any. Evening papers do. I regret to see no official statement of guns captured. But an extra *Herald* despatch dated at noon today gives us a splendidly colored picture of Lee's retreat and tells how teamsters and artillery men are cutting their traces and riding off for life on their draft-mules; how even [D. N.] Couch's militia regiments are following up the defeated army and bagging whole brigades; and how there is general panic, rout, and *sauve qui peut*. All of which is pleasant to read, but probably fictitious. So is a telegram, no doubt, that I find at Union League Club tonight: "All Lee's artillery captured and thirty thousand prisoners." I take it Lee is badly whipped, but will get across the Potomac with the bulk of his army more or less demoralized. . . .

The results of this victory are priceless. Philadelphia, Baltimore, and Washington are safe. Defeat would have seriously injured all three. The rebels are hunted out of the North, their best army is routed, and the charm of Robert Lee's invincibility broken. The Army of the Potomac has at last found a general that can handle it, and it has stood nobly up to its terrible work in spite of its long disheartening list of hard-fought failures, and in spite of the McClellan influence on its officers.

Government is strengthened four-fold at home and abroad. Gold one hundred and thirty-eight today, and government securities rising. Copperheads are palsied and dumb for the moment at least. S. L. M. Barlow & Co., who are making a catspaw of poor, confiding McClellan and using his unaccountable popularity to stir up disaffection, have lost half their power of mischief. People will soon be cackling, gabbling and gobbling and braying about "George G." as they have been about "George B." George B. is brave, honest, and true, but he has no eye for men, no insight into human character. So he has unconsciously allowed his old friends of days before the war (a long time ago) to use him for their own ends. And as they happen to be Breckinridge Democrats—Constitutional Conservatives—sympathizers and Dirt-Eaters, they have so played him off against the government that he has been for six months past well worth any two rebel generals to the rebel cause. But even their impudence can hardly clamor for his restoration to chief command of the army of Gettysburg. (N.B. I might not object to see him in Halleck's shoes.)

People downtown very jolly today. "This ends the Rebellion." So I was told a dozen times. My cheerful and agreeable but deluded friends, there must be battles by the score before that outbreak from the depths of original sin is "ended." But there does seem to be some kind of obscure Union movement in benighted old North Carolina. Wiseacres profess to know all about it. "Highest authority," "not at liberty to state," and so on, "but I knew it was all arranged with the government through General Foster a week ago" that if General Lee were well licked, North Carolina would secede at once and return to her anxious and heartbroken family. I am not sure I like the prospect. The Returning Prodigal will be represented by a batch of Congressmen swaggering through the corridors of the Capitol with pockets full of revolvers and mouths full of brag and tobacco, ready to play the old Southern game over again. They will fall on their kind old Uncle Sam's neck, of course, and do their best to break it the first time their chivalric sensibilities are stimulated into action, and Uncle Sam will kill the fatted calf and appoint these magnanimous beings Cabinet officers and chairmen of committees on the army. I trust he may not mistake himself for the fatted animal in the pardonable extravagance of his generosity, and so commit national suicide.

The battle of Gettysburg had ended on July 3, when Pickett's charge against Cemetery Ridge broke down with fearful slaughter. Lee expected a counterattack by the Union forces, but it did not come; and after a quiet Fourth, his army that evening began its retreat "under the cover of the night and the heavy rain." Lincoln on the morning of the Fourth had heralded the triumph to the Northern people: "The President announces to the country that news from the Army of the Potomac, up to ten P.M. of the third, is such as to cover that army with the highest honor, to promise a great success to the cause of the Union, and to claim the condolence of all for the many gallant fallen, and that for this he especially desires that on this day He whose will, not ours, should ever be done, be everywhere remembered and reverenced with profoundest gratitude." The Fourth was further signalized by the surrender of Vicksburg. In Pennsylvania Lincoln hoped for a close and destructive pursuit of the fleeing Confederates. He urged Halleck to see that Meade completed his work "by the literal or substantial destruction of Lee's army," when "the rebellion will be over." Halleck, thus firmly and repeatedly prompted by the President, telegraphed Meade to "push forward and fight Lee before he can cross the Potomac." But at the same time he sent despatches of his own informing the general that these directions were "suggestions only," and not orders, and that he was to follow his own judgment. And when Meade, who might have attacked with great effect if not with complete success on July 12 or 13, called a council of his corps commanders, five out of seven advised against a new battle. The result was that on the afternoon of the 14th news came that Lee had brought his whole army intact across the Potomac and was safe. Lincoln's chagrin was intense. He later declared: "Our army held the war in the hollow of their hand, and would not close it." He wrote Meade of his profound disappointment that "your golden opportunity is gone." Strong's diary shows how keenly men of his outlook sympathized with the President's view.

Strong's failure to say anything in particular about Vicksburg also indicates how completely the eastern battle held possession of the minds of New Yorkers.

On the afternoon of July 3, Grant, whose line had steadily closed about the besieged city, and who was ready to begin an assault that the Confederates knew they could never withstand, held a conference with Pemberton, and that evening sent the Confederate general his terms of capitulation. On the morning of the Fourth he was able to telegraph Lincoln: "The enemy surrendered this morning. The only terms allowed is their parole as prisoners of war." Thus closed what was perhaps the most brilliant single campaign of the war. With a loss of fewer than ten thousand men, Grant had inflicted casualties exceeding that number on the Confederates, had captured nearly thirty thousand men and about one hundred and seventy cannon, and had made it possible to seal up the Mississippi River and thus cut the Confederacy in two. Lincoln was soon writing in his famous letter to Conkling: "The Father of Waters again goes unvexed to the sea."

But while these great events were occurring, the city of New York was about to endure the most shameful disorders of her entire history. A Conscription Act had been signed on March 3, 1863, and was now to be put into effect in the metropolis.

July 11, SATURDAY.   The Commission has spent near twenty thousand dollars this week and received as much. It is doing an immense business around Gettysburg. Olmsted reports our losses there inside seven thousand and Bellows twenty thousand!!!

From negative evidence it appears that Lee's retreat was no rout. He shews a firm front at Williamsport and Hagerstown, seeking to recross the Potomac now in high freshet. Meade is at his heels, and another great battle is expected. Olmsted thinks it will be more severe than the last.

I observe that the Richmond papers are in an orgasm of brag and bluster and bloodthirstiness beyond all historical precedent even in their chivalric columns. That's an encouraging sign. Another is the unusual number of stragglers and deserters from Lee's army. Rebel generals, even when defeated, have heretofore kept their men well in hand.

July 12. Despatches in morning papers, though severally worthless, give one the impression when taken collectively that Lee is getting safely across the Potomac and back to Old Virginny's shore, bag and baggage, guns, plunder and all. Whereupon the able editors begin to denounce Meade, their last new Napoleon, as incapable and outgeneralled. . . . People forget that an army of fifty thousand and upward cannot be bagged bodily unless its general be a Mack or a Dupont. But I shall be disappointed if the rebels get home without a clawing.

Draft has begun here and was in progress in Boston last week. *Demos* takes it good-naturedly thus far, but we shall have trouble before we are through. The critical time will be when defaulting conscripts are haled out of their houses, as many will be. That soulless politician, Seymour, will make mischief if he dare. So will F'nandy Wood, Brooks, Marble, and other reptiles. May they only bring their traitorous necks within the cincture of a legal halter! This draft will be the *experimentum crucis* to decide whether we have a government among us.

THE DRAFT RIOTS IN NEW YORK · TURN OF THE WAR IN
FAVOR OF THE NORTH · BATTLES OF CHICKAMAUGA
AND LOOKOUT MOUNTAIN · UNION MILITARY
SUCCESSES IN THE WEST

*The drawing of the names of conscripts under the Draft Act had com-
menced in New York City on the morning of Saturday, July 11. At first
the people seemed to take the draft quietly and good-naturedly; no disturbances
occurred on the initial day. But on Sunday the names of the men selected were
published in the press; and in thousands of homes the meaning of compulsory
service was at last fully appreciated. The foreign-born population of the city,
especially heavy in the Ninth Congressional District, felt that it had powerful
reasons for discontent. For one, most of the foreign-born were Democrats, and
they had been assured by Democratic newspapers and politicians that the acts
of the Lincoln Administration were highhanded, oppressive, and even unconstitutional. For another, the provision by which well-to-do men could hire sub-
stitutes for $300 seemed unjust to the poor. For a third, the Irish and other day-
laborers had felt keenly the competition of Negro freedmen now flocking up from
the South, and many of them were filled with hatred of the blacks. The hardships imposed by the fast-rising cost of living contributed to the general irritation. When Monday the 13th dawned, it was evident that large groups of the
metropolitan population were on the verge of armed resistance to the draft; a
mob soon gathered before the draft headquarters at Third Avenue and Forty-
sixth Street; and before noon a fierce attack upon this building began. Many
factory-workers and employees of the street railroads joined the concourse. Fires
were set, flame and smoke enveloped the block, and when first the provost-
marshal's guard and then a detachment of police appeared, the mob overwhelmed
them and drove them to flight. That afternoon the disorders grew, until a great*

[334]

part of the upper East Side was in the hands of men inflamed by drink and
passion. Negroes were attacked wherever found, and toward evening, as Strong
records, the Colored Orphan Asylum on Fifth Avenue just above Forty-third
Street was sacked and set on fire.

July 13, MONDAY.   A notable day. Stopped at the Sanitary Commission office on my way downtown to endorse a lot of checks that had
accumulated during my absence, and heard there of rioting in the upper
part of the city. As Charley is at Newport and Bidwell in Berkshire
County, I went to Wall Street nevertheless; but the rumors grew more
and more unpleasant, so I left it at once and took a Third Avenue car for
uptown. At the Park were groups and small crowds in more or less
excitement (which found relief afterwards, I hear, in hunting down and
maltreating sundry unoffending niggers), but there was nothing to
indicate serious trouble. The crowded car went slowly on its way, with
its perspiring passengers, for the weather was still of this deadly muggy
sort with a muddy sky and lifeless air. At Thirteenth Street the track was
blocked by a long line of stationary cars that stretched indefinitely up
the Avenue, and I took to the sidewalk. Above Twentieth Street all shops
were closed, and many people standing and staring or strolling uptown,
not riotously disposed but eager and curious. Here and there a rough
could be heard damning the draft. No policemen to be seen anywhere.
Reached the seat of war at last, Forty-sixth Street and Third Avenue.
Three houses on the Avenue and two or three on the street were burned
down: engines playing on the ruins—more energetically, I'm told, than
they did when their efforts would have been useful.

The crowd seemed just what one commonly sees at any fire, but its
nucleus of riot was concealed by an outside layer of ordinary peaceable
lookers-on. Was told they had beat off a squad of police and another of
"regulars" (probably the Twelfth Militia). At last, it opened and out
streamed a posse of perhaps five hundred, certainly less than one thousand, of the lowest Irish day laborers. The rabble was perfectly homo-
geneous. Every brute in the drove was pure Celtic—hod-carrier or
loafer. They were unarmed. A few carried pieces of fence-paling and the
like. They turned off west into Forty-fifth Street and gradually collected
in front of two three-story dwelling houses on Lexington Avenue, just
below that street, that stand alone together on a nearly vacant block.
Nobody could tell why these houses were singled out. Some said a drafting officer lived in one of them, others that a damaged policeman had

taken refuge there. The mob was in no hurry; they had no need to be; there was no one to molest them or make them afraid. The beastly ruffians were masters of the situation and of the city. After a while sporadic paving-stones began to fly at the windows, ladies and children emerged from the rear and had a rather hard scramble over a high board fence, and then scudded off across the open, Heaven knows whither. Then men and small boys appeared at rear windows and began smashing the sashes and the blinds and shied out light articles, such as books and crockery, and dropped chairs and mirrors into the back yard; the rear fence was demolished and loafers were seen marching off with portable articles of furniture. And at last a light smoke began to float out of the windows and I came away. I could endure the disgraceful, sickening sight no longer, and what could I *do*?

The fury of the low Irish women in that region was noteworthy. Stalwart young vixens and withered old hags were swarming everywhere, all cursing the "bloody draft" and egging on their men to mischief.

Omnibussed down to No. 823, where is news that the Colored Half Orphan Asylum on Fifth Avenue, just above the reservoir, is burned. "*Tribune* office to be burned tonight." Railroad rails torn up, telegraph wires cut, and so on. If a quarter one hears be true, this is an organized insurrection in the interest of the rebellion and Jefferson Davis rules New York today.

Attended to business. Then with Wolcott Gibbs to dinner at Maison Dorée. During our symposium, there was an alarm of a coming mob, and we went to the window to see. The "mob" was moving down Fourteenth Street and consisted of just thirty-four lousy, blackguardly Irishmen with a tail of small boys. Whither they went, I cannot say, nor can I guess what mischief the handful of *canaille* chose to do. A dozen policemen would have been more than a match for the whole crew, but there were no policemen in sight.

Walked uptown with Wolcott Gibbs. Large fire on Broadway and Twenty-eighth Street. Signs of another to the east, said to be on Second Avenue. Stopped awhile at Gibbs's in Twenty-ninth Street, where was madame, frightened nearly to death, and then to St. Nicholas Hotel to see the mayor and General Wool. We found a lot of people with them. There were John Jay and George W. Blunt and Colonel Howe and John Austin Stevens, Jr., all urging strong measures. But the substantial and weighty and influential men were not represented; out of town, I suppose.

SANITARY COMMISSION HEADQUARTERS

GENERAL HOSPITAL, GETTYSBURG, JULY 1863

SANITARY COMMISSION LODGE FOR INVALID SOLDIERS

374 NORTH CAPITOL STREET, WASHINGTON

THE DRAFT RIOTS AT NEW YORK, JULY 1863

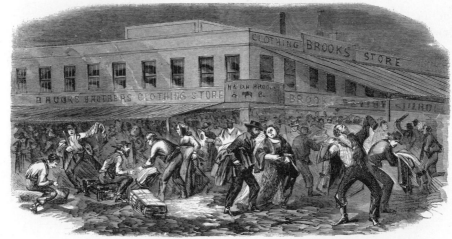

SACKING BROOKS BROTHERS' CLOTHING STORE
CATHERINE AND CHERRY STREETS

DRAGGING COL. O'BRIEN'S BODY THROUGH THE MUD   LYNCHING IN CLARKSON STREET

CHARGE OF THE POLICE ON THE RIOTERS AT THE TRIBUNE BUILDING

Their absence emboldened Gibbs and myself to make pressure for instant action, but it was vain. We begged that martial law might be declared. Opdyke said that was Wool's business, and Wool said it was Opdyke's, and neither would act. "Then, Mr. Mayor, issue a proclamation calling on all loyal and law-abiding citizens to enroll themselves as a volunteer force for defense of life and property." "Why," quoth Opdyke, "that is *civil war* at once." Long talk with Colonel Cram, Wool's chief of staff, who professes to believe that everything is as it should be and sufficient force on the ground to prevent further mischief. Don't believe it. Neither Opdyke nor General Wool is nearly equal to this crisis. Came off disgusted. Went to Union League Club awhile. No comfort there. Much talk, but no one ready to do anything whatever, not even to telegraph to Washington.

We telegraphed, two or three of us, from General Wool's rooms, to the President, begging that troops be sent on and stringent measures taken. The great misfortune is that nearly all our militia regiments have been despatched to Pennsylvania. All the military force I have seen or heard of today were in Fifth Avenue at about seven P.M. There were two or three feeble companies of infantry, a couple of howitzers, and a squadron or two of unhappy-looking "dragoons."

These wretched rioters have been plundering freely, I hear. Their outbreak will either destroy the city or damage the Copperhead cause fatally. Could we but catch the scoundrels who have stirred them up, what a blessing it would be! God knows what tonight or tomorrow may bring forth. We may be thankful that it is now (quarter past twelve) raining briskly. Mobs have no taste for the effusion of cold water. I'm thankful, moreover, that Ellie and the children are out of town. I sent Johnny off to Cornwall this afternoon in charge of John the waiter.

July 14. Eleven P.M. Fire bells clanking, as they have clanked at intervals through the evening. Plenty of rumors throughout the day and evening, but nothing very precise or authentic. There have been sundry collisions between the rabble and the authorities, civil and military. Mob fired upon. It generally runs, but on one occasion appears to have rallied, charged the police and militia, and forced them back in disorder. The people are waking up, and by tomorrow there will be adequate organization to protect property and life. Many details come in of yesterday's brutal, cowardly ruffianism and plunder. Shops were cleaned out and a black man hanged in Carmine Street, for no offence but that of Nigritude. Opdyke's house again attacked this morning by a roaming handful of

Irish blackguards. Two or three gentlemen who chanced to be passing saved it from sack by a vigorous charge and dispersed the popular uprising (as the *Herald*, *World*, and *News* call it), with their walking sticks and their fists.

Walked uptown perforce, for no cars and few omnibi were running. They are suppressed by threats of burning railroad and omnibus stables, the drivers being wanted to reinforce the mob. Tiffany's shop, Ball & Black's, and a few other Broadway establishments are closed. (Here I am interrupted by report of a fire near at hand, and a great glare on the houses across the Park. Sally forth, and find the Eighteenth Ward station house, Twenty-second Street, near First Avenue, in full blaze. A splendid blaze it made, but I did not venture below Second Avenue, finding myself in a crowd of Celtic spectators disgorged by the circumjacent tenement houses. They were exulting over the damage to "them bloody police," and so on. I thought discretion the better part of curiosity. Distance lent enchantment to that view.)

At 823 with Bellows four to six; then home. At eight to Union League Club. Rumor it's to be attacked tonight. Some say there is to be great mischief tonight and that the rabble is getting the upper hand. Home at ten and sent for by Dudley Field, Jr., to confer about an expected attack on his house and his father's, which adjoin each other in this street just below Lexington Avenue. He has a party there with muskets and talks of fearful trouble before morning, but he is always a blower and a very poor devil. Fire bells again at twelve-fifteen. No light of conflagration is visible.

Bellows's report from Gettysburg and from Meade's headquarters very interesting. Thinks highly of Meade. Thinks the battle around Williamsport will be tolerably evenly matched, Lee having been decidedly beaten a week ago, but not at all demoralized. But there's a despatch at the Union League Club tonight that Lee has moved his whole army safely across, except his rear guard, which we captured.

A good deal of yelling to the eastward just now. The Fields and their near neighbour, Colonel Frank Howe, are as likely to be attacked by this traitor-guided mob as any people I know. If they *are*, we shall see trouble in this quarter, and Gramercy Park will acquire historical associations. O, how tired I am! But I feel reluctant to go to bed. I believe I dozed off a minute or two. There came something like two reports of artillery, perhaps only falling walls. There go two jolly Celts along the street, singing a genuine Celtic howl, something about "Tim O'Laggerty," with a refrain of pure Erse. Long live the sovereigns of New York, Brian Boroo *redivivus* and multiplied. Paddy has left his Egypt—Connaught— and reigns in this promised land of milk and honey and perfect freedom. Hurrah, there goes a strong squad of police marching eastward down this street, followed by a company of infantry with gleaming bayonets. One A.M. Fire bells again, southeastward, "Swinging slow with sullen roar." Now they are silent, and I shall go to bed, at least for a season.

July 15. Wednesday begins with heavy showers, and now (ten A.M.) cloudy, hot, and steaming. Morning papers report nothing specially grave as occurring since midnight. But there will be much trouble today. Rabbledom is not yet dethroned any more than its ally and instigator, Rebeldom.

News from the South is consolatory. Port Hudson surrendered. Sherman said to have beaten Joseph Johnston somewhere near Vicksburg. Operations commencing against Charleston. Bragg seems to be abandoning Chattanooga and retiring on Atlanta. *Per contra*, Lee has got safely off. I thought he would. . . . Lots of talk and rumors about attacks on the New York Custom-house (*ci-devant* Merchants' Exchange) and the Treasury (late Custom-house). Went to see [John J.] Cisco and found his establishment in military occupation—sentinels pacing, windows barricaded, and so on. He was as serene and bland as the loveliest May morning ("so cool, so calm, so bright") and showed me the live shell ready to throw out of the window and the "battery" to project Assay Office oil-of-vitriol and the like. He's all right. Then called on Collector Barney and had another long talk with him. Find him well prepared with shells, grenades, muskets, and men, but a little timid and anxious, "wanting counsel," doubtful about his right to fire on the mob, and generally flaccid and tremulous—poor devil!

Walked uptown with Charley Strong and Hoppin, and after my cup of coffee, went to Union League Club. A delegation returned from police headquarters, having vainly asked for a squad of men to garrison the clubhouse. *None can be spared.* What is worse, we were badly repulsed in an attack on the mob in First Avenue, near Nineteenth Street, at about six P.M. Fired upon from houses, and had to leave sixteen wounded men and a Lieutenant Colonel Jardine in the hands of these brutes and devils. This is very bad indeed. But tonight is quieter than the last, though there seems to be a large fire downtown, and we hear occasional gun-shots.

At the club was George Biggs, full of the loudest and most emphatic jawing. "General Frémont's house and Craven's to be attacked tonight,

Croton mains to be cut, and gas works destroyed," and so on. By way of
precaution, I had had the bathtubs filled, and also all the pots, kettles,
and pails in the house. . . . Twelve-thirty: Light as of a large fire to the
south.

July 16. Rather quiet downtown. No trustworthy accounts of riot
on any large scale during the day. General talk downtown is that the
trouble is over. We shall see. It will be as it pleases the scoundrels who
are privily engineering the outbreak—agents of Jefferson Davis, permitted
to work here in New York.

Omnibusses and railroad cars in full career again. Coming uptown
tonight I find Gramercy Park in military occupation. Strong parties
drawn up across Twentieth Street and Twenty-first Streets at the east
end of the Square, by the G[ramercy] House, each with a flanking squad,
forming an L. Occasional shots fired at them from the region of Second
or First Avenue, which were replied to by volleys that seem to have done
little execution. An unlucky cart-horse was knocked over, I hear. This
force was relieved at seven by a company of regulars and a party of the
Seventh with a couple of howitzers, and there has been but a stray shot
or two since dark. The regulars do not look like steady men. I have just
gone over to the hotel with John Robertson and ordered a pail of strong
coffee to put a little life into them.

Never knew exasperation so intense, unqualified, and general as that
which prevails against these rioters and the politic knaves who are supposed to have set them going, Governor Seymour not excepted. Men
who voted for him mention the fact with contrition and self-abasement,
and the Democratic Party is at a discount with all the people I meet.
(Apropos of discount, gold fell to one hundred and twenty-six today,
with the city in insurrection, a gunboat at the foot of Wall Street, the
Custom-house and Treasury full of soldiers and live shells, and two
howitzers in position to rake Nassau Street from Wall to Fulton!!!!)

Every impression that's made on our people passes away so soon,
almost as if stamped on the sand of the sea-beach. Were our moods a
little less fleeting, I should have great hope of permanent good from the
general wrath these outrages have provoked, and should put some faith
in people's prophesyings that Fernando Wood and McCunn, and the
New York *Herald*, and the Brookses and others, are doomed henceforth to
obscurity and contempt. But we shall forget all about it before next
November. Perhaps the lesson of the last four days is to be taught us
still more emphatically, and we have got to be worse before we are

better. It is not clear that the resources of the conspiracy are yet exhausted. The rioters of yesterday were better armed and organized than those of Monday, and their inaction today may possibly be meant to throw us off our guard, or their time may be employed perfecting plans for a campaign of plundering and brutality in yet greater force. They are in full possession of the western and the eastern sides of the city, from Tenth Street upward, and of a good many districts beside. I could not walk four blocks eastward from this house this minute without peril. The outbreak is spreading by concerted action in many quarters. Albany, Troy, Yonkers, Hartford, Boston, and other cities have each their Irish anti-conscription Nigger-murdering mob, of the same type with ours. It is a grave business, a *jacquerie* that must be put down by heroic doses of lead and steel.

Dr. Peters and Charley Strong called at eleven P.M. They have been exploring and report things quiet except on First Avenue from Nineteenth to Thirtieth Street, where there is said to be trouble. A detachment of the Seventh Regiment, five hundred or six hundred strong, marched to that quarter from their armory an hour ago.

July 17.   The Army of Gramercy Park has advanced its headquarters to Third Avenue, leaving only a picket guard in sight. Rain will keep the rabble quiet tonight. We are said to have fifteen thousand men under arms, and I incline to hope that this movement in aid of the rebellion is played out.

The draft riots, which had filled four days with tumult and terror, were indeed ended. General Wool had thrown into the city about eight hundred United States troops, drawn from the forts in the harbor, the Navy Yard, and West Point. Though Governor Horatio Seymour played a dubious part in the affair, making a speech on Tuesday the 14th from the City Hall steps which was altogether too conciliatory and pacific, he cooperated with Wool by ordering all the militia within reach (commanded by General Sandford) to turn out and help maintain order. About two thousand policemen were brought into action and behaved with energy and courage. Moreover, as Strong reports, bodies of citizens organized themselves, obtained arms from the authorities, and with the aid of returned veterans took a hand in restoring order. Pitched battles occurred in Broadway, on Forty-second Street, and along the west-side avenues uptown. A strong set of barricades in Twenty-ninth Street had to be carried by storm. Many of the mob were slain—how many no one knew, for the Evening Post *recorded that many of the rioters were buried secretly at night, clandestine parties carrying the bodies across the East River. Some estimates of the total casualties on both sides ran as high as one thousand, while about $1,500,000 worth of private property was destroyed. The last sharp fighting took place near Gramercy Park, where on the evening of Thursday, the 16th, United States forces dealt severely with a body of rioters who were looting residences. Next day New York was quiet; and in August the drafting of men was resumed without difficulty.*

July 19, SUNDAY. Have been out seeking information and getting none that is to be trusted. Colonel Frank Howe talks darkly and predicts an outbreak on the east side of the town tonight, but that's his way. I think this Celtic beast with many heads is driven back to his hole for the present. When government begins enforcing the draft, we shall have more trouble, but not till then.

Not half the history of this memorable week has been written. I could put down pages of incidents that the newspapers have omitted, any one of which would in ordinary times be the town's talk. Men and ladies attacked and plundered by daylight in the streets; private houses suddenly invaded by gangs of a dozen ruffians and sacked, while the women and children run off for their lives. Then there is the unspeakable infamy of the nigger persecution. They are the most peaceable, sober, and inoffensive of our poor, and the outrages they have suffered during this last week are less excusable—are founded on worse pretext and less provocation—than St. Bartholomew's or the Jew-hunting of the Middle Ages. This is a nice town to call itself a centre of civilization! Life and personal property less safe than in Tipperary, and the "people" (as the *Herald* calls them) burning orphan asylums and conducting a massacre. How this infernal slavery system has corrupted our blood, North as well as South! There should be terrible vengeance for these atrocities, but McCunn, Barnard & Co. are our judges and the disgrace will rest upon us without atonement.

I am sorry to find that England is right about the lower class of Irish. They are brutal, base, cruel, cowards, and as insolent as base. Choate (at the Union League Club) tells me he heard this proposition put forth by one of their political philosophers in conversation with a knot of his brethren last Monday: "Sure and if them dam Dutch would jine us we'd drive the dam Yankees out of New York entirely!" These caitiffs have a trick, I hear, of posting themselves at the window of a tenement house with a musket, while a woman with a baby in her arms squats at their feet. Paddy fires on the police and instantly squats to reload, while Mrs. Paddy rises and looks out. Of course, one can't fire at a window where there is a woman with a child!! But how is one to deal with women who assemble around the lamp-post to which a Negro had been hanged and cut off certain parts of his body to keep as souvenirs? Have they any womanly privilege, immunity, or sanctity?

No wonder St. Patrick drove all the venomous vermin out of Ireland! Its biped mammalia supply that island its full average share of creatures that crawl and eat dirt and poison every community they infest. Vipers were superfluous. But my own theory is that St. Patrick's campaign against the snakes is a Popish delusion. They perished of biting the Irish people.

July 20.   Hot. Atmosphere mucilaginous. City quiet. Nothing special to record. Dined with Agnew at Maison Dorée, and spent a little time at the Club. I see a frequent placard bearing these two words, "Sam, Organize!" It plainly means that there is a movement to revive the old Native American party with its Know-Nothing Clubs; a very natural consequence of the atrocities just perpetrated by our Irish *canaille*. Talking with Americans of the middle and laboring class, even of the lowest social grade, I find they fully appreciate and bitterly resent these Celtic outrages. But the obstacle in the way of a revived Know-Nothingism is that it would be obliged to discriminate between Celts and Teutons. The Germans have behaved well and kept quiet. Where they acted at all, they volunteered against the rabble, as they did, most effectively, in the Seventh Ward. A mere anti-Hibernian party would have no foundation on principle, would seem merely vindictive and proscriptive, and would lead to no lasting result, I fear. For myself, personally, I would like to see war made on Irish scum as in 1688.

July 21. . . . Quiet continues, though the *Express* and that yet more beastly *World* are doing all they can to instigate outbreak.

A vehement south wind all day. Morgan's raid across the Ohio has failed very badly. His whole force is captured, artillery and all, and he escapes by slinking off while negotiations for surrender are in progress. Chivalric Morgan![1]

---

[1] John Hunt Morgan's cavalry, exhausted by its wild course through southern Indiana and Ohio, was surrounded and largely captured, Morgan himself surrendering July 26. His raid, however, had drawn Federal troops from East Tennessee, relieved the pressure on Bragg's army, and temporarily saved that area for the Confederacy.

July 25, SATURDAY. . . . The peace of this, our base community has continued unbroken, though we are dry-rotted by sympathy with treason, and long to lay our necks at the feet of Jefferson Davis and his genteel, "democratic," nigger-flogging aristocracy. It is amazing the amount of detriment done to our moral sense by the slavery system that has been legally and constitutionally forced upon us for so many years. I can safely predict that no one will be hanged for all this arson, murder, and treason. But there is great comfort in the current news from the South that has set in upon us for the last month—Lee's failure; Vicksburg, and Port Hudson, with their two or three hundred guns taken at last; the capital of Mississippi abandoned by Johnston with no end of railroad rolling-stock which rebeldom sorely needs and cannot replace; the great river reopened and freed from all but guerrilla warfare; the Virginia & Tennessee railroad cut at Wytheville, Virginia, and the bridge over the Tar River on the Wilmington & Weldon Line destroyed. All this run of fortune in our favor is of an importance that one can hardly overestimate. Still it does not justify the orgulous prophesyings of the newspapers. On the other hand, we seem to make little progress toward Charleston. There are rumors of repulse before Fort Wagner, and of the death of Colonel Shaw (Francis G. Shaw's son) who commanded a Negro regiment from Massachusetts. We must remember our many failures at Vicksburg, and keep on trying till the wicked little city that began the war is taken or destroyed.

What I most fear is that Bragg and Joe Johnston may have reinforced Lee and enabled him to turn on Meade with greatly superior force. There are little straws of rumor flying around, worthless individually, but agreeing in this, that Lee means to try his luck on this side of the Potomac once more if he can.

July 27. Edward Mitchell came in, a son of ex-judge William Mitchell, just from New Orleans. He has been spending several months there, and in the Teche country with Banks, as Sanitary Commission agent. His report on the state of affairs in the Southwest agrees with that of his chief, Dr. Crane, who returned with him. Mitchell says he went south conservative and constitutional and that he comes back radical and Abolitionist. No wonder, if all his stories of what he has seen be true. Both Crane and Mitchell speak highly of the discipline of our new black regiments. They report the plantation aristocracy generally inveterate in treason, its womankind specially virulent; New Orleans absolutely subjugated and submissive, however. The liberated Negroes, now working for wages, behave like Christians, bear no malice, and commit no outrages. Southern Cuffee seems of higher social grade than Northern Paddy. The generous and chivalric sons of Erin are under a cloud just now.

Dined with Murray Hoffman at Maison Dorée. Thence to Union League Club. Discoursed with Barney, the collector of this port. He thinks that Fernando Wood, nasty little Tucker the Surrogate, Butterworth, and McCunn,[2] with others, are at the head of a secret organization that did not fully shew itself in the late riots, but is held in reserve for a far more serious outbreak in aid of the rebellion, and that Fernandy Wood aims at being Doge or First Consul or something of New York. Barney is feeble and frightened, but we should be prepared for any violent, desperate move by Copperheads and Peace Democrats to get control of the city.

Talked over the position with Agnew and George F. Allen. We must make the clubhouse defensible, provide muskets, grenades, and the like. Its windows were darkened and its flag lowered during the riots, and such disgrace must not be incurred again. Long talk with Cisco this morning, from which I infer that Dix stands where he should and is no ally, open or secret, of Seymour's.[3]

July 31. Mr. Ruggles looked in, full of the success of the Pacific Railroad and prophesying that fifty miles of track will be laid before December. Ellie went with him to No. 24. I went to Union League Club, where were Agnew, Gibbs, Olmsted, and others. Gibbs has accepted the Rumford Professorship at Harvard, and is breaking up his establishment in Twenty-ninth Street preparatory to a flitting from New York. We lose a valuable man, thanks to the stupidity of our Columbia College trustees nine years ago. Much good have they got from the orthodoxy of McCulloh and Joy! . . .

People here are much puffed up with recent victory, expect speedy peace, and talk of North Carolina, Louisiana, and even Mississippi as

[2] All prominent Copperhead Democrats; Gideon J. Tucker had been Secretary of State in Albany, and Samuel F. Butterworth had been active in city politics. Fernando Wood, who was in Congress 1863–1865, had become bitterly anti-war, and was allied with Vallandigham in organizing the Peace Democrats.

[3] Governor Seymour, whose conduct during the draft riots had been fairly decent (for as soon as he reached the city July 14, he authorized the arming of the police and the citizens), had been accused of calling the rioters, in a speech at City Hall, his "friends." Actually he seems to have said to an orderly crowd there: "If you are my friends, you will go to your homes." But his speech was too mild (as we have said above) for the crisis, while his heated opposition to the Administration and the draft had encouraged disloyal action.

penitent and willing to come back to the Union the moment they are assured that their "constitutional rights" will be respected. This is all delusion, and God be praised that it is. Any overture from a rebel community should be received with an *Apage Satanas*. The disappearance of an acute symptom has tempted many a patient to renounce his treatment and his regimen and make a "compromise" with some deep-seated "constitutional" disease and has thus caused him to die and decompose. The virtue of this people is far from strong enough to resist an invitation to peace now at the cost of far worse and deadlier war hereafter. Lasting peace with Southern rebels can be attained only by subjugation and abolition. We see now that victory at Bull Run two years ago would have been a national calamity, and that statues of McDowell and Scott, saviors of the country, should be set up in every loyal village; McClellan making a third, perhaps, as a great public benefactor in a way he never dreamed of.

August 4, TUESDAY. Only news is the death of that notable scoundrel, W. L. Yancey, and the severe illness of the larcenous Floyd.[4] The gallows don't always get its due in this world, but the Devil commonly gets his in the next; and if men are to be judged by the quantity of mischief they have done and of misery they have caused, these deliberate authors of Civil War deserve a hot corner of Tophet. But I don't pretend to judge them. I would, of course, hang them or any of their tribe were I in authority and they in my power, but I would conclude my sentence with the usual formula of merciful aspiration.

August 5. . . . Bull Anthon has given up the Grammar School. From a pamphlet circular received this evening, it appears that he retains the title of Rector, and calls himself examiner in Greek—Drisler being examiner in Latin, Peck in mathematics, and Dwight in jurisprudence (!!!); but that one Rev. G. W. Bacon is principal. I suppose the connection Bull Anthon retains with it is nominal, and that this will lead to the repudiation of the school as an organ of the College. It has been Anthon's private school and nothing more for thirty years, and its title is and has been all that time a misnomer.

August 8. Newspapers brag far too loudly about our having "broken the backbone" of the rebellion and about the development of Union feeling in Tennessee, Mississippi, and North Carolina. The vertebrae

[4] Yancey, a member of the Confederate Senate, died in Montgomery on July 27; John B. Floyd, whose connection with dishonest contracts and embezzlements while Secretary of the Interior was remembered bitterly by Northerners, was mortally ill and died in Virginia on August 26.

of Southern treason still cohere, as we may yet learn to our terrible cost, especially if Lee reinforce himself with the debris of rebellion from the Southwest. And I would not give tenpence for all the loyalty that can be extracted from any slaveholding state except Maryland, Missouri, and Kentucky.

August 11. Symptoms reported of reaction toward loyalty, submission, or pacification in Mississippi and North Carolina. Southern newspaper quotations confirm them. Such reaction, if strong enough to determine the policy of any one rebel state, would do harm by strengthening the feeble brethren who would like to settle affairs by patching up any sort of compromise with rebellion. But if just *short* of that degree of importance, it is a most favorable symptom. Any rebel state negotiating about reconstruction at this time would weaken the North, but the more penitence and contrition among individual rebels the better, of course. And it would seem that those gracious tempers are becoming manifest in the Southwest.

We hardly appreciate, even yet, the magnitude of this war, the issues that depend on its result, the importance of the chapter in the world's history that we are helping to write. In our hearts we esteem the struggle as the London *Times* does, or pretends to. God forgive our blindness! It is the struggle of two hostile and irreconcilable systems of society for the rule of this continent. Since Mahometanism and Christendom met in battle this side the Pyrenees, there has been no struggle so momentous for mankind. I think that Grant and Rosecrans, Lee and Stonewall Jackson and Joe Johnston, and all the others, will be more conspicuous and better known to students of history A.D. 1963 than Wallenstein and Gustavus, Condé, Napoleon, Frederick, Wellington, and the late Lord Raglan; not as greater generals, but as fighting on a larger field and in a greater cause than any of them. So will our great-great-grandchildren look back on them a century hence, whatever be the result.

August 13. Nigger recruiting prospers. Rumor of a *Corps d'Afrique* to be raised here. Why not? Paddy, the asylum-burner, would swear at the dam Naygurs, but we need bayonets in Negro hands if Paddy is unwilling to fight for the country that receives and betters him in his poverty and transmutes him into an alderman and a wealthy citizen. If he back out, let us accept, with contrition and humiliation, the services of this despised and rejected race, and be thankful that it is willing to enlist in the cause of a nation from which it has received only contumely and persecution.

Experience of a New York "rough" who visited Boston for the purpose of assisting at the attempted anti-draft riot there, which was dispersed by a discharge of grapeshot from the arsenal or armory. "I've come away from Boston. Never saw such a damn place. Ain't a-goin' back to a place like that, I tell yer. Why, if a feller picks up a brick, they just heave a peck of shot at him." Bully for Bosting!

August 17, MONDAY. . . . Find both Mr. and Mrs. Ruggles somewhat indisposed. He came from Washington Saturday night, having been summoned thither by the ingenious Secretary Seward, who insists on his representing the U.S.A. in the Statistical Congress that's to gather at Berlin next month—a very imposing ecumenical synod, the members whereof are appointed by the states of Europe. Seward won't take no for an answer, and has sent Mr. Ruggles's commission after him. He wants the resources of this country announced to Europe in an official way by a competent man, and thinks it of great importance to our credit abroad and to the national cause that Mr. Ruggles should go and tell the story. But Mr. Ruggles is undecided. Pacific Railroad and other engagements are in the way.

It's said the draft is to begin next Wednesday. General Dix publishes a discreet and vigorous address to the people, recommending submission to the law on high grounds of morality and of patriotism and suggesting that there is enough grapeshot on hand to dispose of all who undertake riot or rebellion. Look out, O Paddy that hangest niggers, and thou, O Mike that burnest orphan asylums. This brutal savagery of our Celtic fellow-citizens but last month has made a deep impression on the community. I felt its effects at the Bank for Savings today. On former occasions I have handed out pass books to Bridget and Catharine and their husbands and brothers with a sense of philanthropic enjoyment in aiding the poor to save money, and have answered their stolid enquiries in the most affectionate, patronizing way, even as a good shepherd and trustee responds to the inarticulate baa-ings of his sheep and *cestuique trusts*. But I found myself today inclined to treat the Biddies and Mikes in a different spirit, and without a single spark of philanthropic sympathy.

August 18. At No. 24 I find Mr. Ruggles full of his mission to Berlin, and coruscating brilliantly with facts and figures and views. He will go next Saturday, barring accident, and I am glad of it; for he will do us credit. He is the very best man in the country, I suppose, for that particular job. The ultimate object he contemplates is to shew Europe that we can supply all the food and all the gold the world requires, and that we can do it better and cheaper than we could if disintegrated. To establish these two propositions will help and strengthen us abroad not a little. It's a pity and a shame that Seward gave Mr. Ruggles so little notice of his appointment and so little time for preparation.

At the Union League Club Henry Winthrop, Agnew (just escaped from the crowd and discomfort of Saratoga), Delano, Dudley B. Fuller, and others; also Colonel Howe, whose trumpet is in fine working order tonight. "By tomorrow noon there will be twelve thousand more troops here"—"two regiments of Sykes's corps"—"General Ayres, who is to take charge of the East Side of the city," and so on; blood and thunder in general. Government displays such force here that there will be no "muss" tomorrow, I think. The Copperheads cannot be strong enough to try that game a second time, nor have they forgotten the damage done their wicked cause by the little experiment they made a month ago. Treason and insurrection are distasteful to the meanest Copperhead, if he have taxes to pay. It's most fortunate that Governor Seymour is at least as much coward as traitor. Were he both bold and bad he could do fearful mischief; he might perhaps even succeed in degrading the country to his own level, by arraying this state against the Administration. But it's unwholesome to think too much about him or about the Woods, Brookses, Barlows, Duncans, and other vermin of his family. They will have their reward.

August 19. . . . Much importance attached to a very elaborate North Carolina newspaper publication, said to be the work of some noted chivalric and political magnate of that beggarly province. It does credit to its author's common sense, be he who he may; denounces secession as a crime and a blunder, administers pepper to the "Confederate" government, expatiates, *not* very ruefully, on the failing fortunes of the Confederacy, and clamors loudly for peace. People overestimate its significance, but it certainly proves that the chivalry of North Carolina is not a unit in favor of protracted resistance and death in the last ditch, and that there is a reaction at last among rational North Carolinians. Whether this seasonable minority is large or small doesn't appear.

The governor of Alabama orders a Negro conscription![5] *Eget mauri jaculis*, not being altogether *integer vitae*, probably. Two years of Southern hysterics and an inferior article of whiskey must have brought on softening

[5] A Confederate enactment of March 26, 1863, had legalized the impressment of slaves by the military authorities for work behind the lines, but this had to be done in conformity with state laws and regulations. Various states also impressed slaves for public purposes.

of his brain. These madmen have made a nice mess of their rebellion for the maintenance and extension of slavery. Every month weakens that blessed institution more and more fatally. Arming and drilling Cuffee in its defense seems likely to give it a final blow. Russell was right in calling the Southerners a strange compound of tigers and children—see his *Diary*. They are not tiger-monkeys like Revolutionary Frenchmen, but tiger-donkeys or tiger-goslings.

August 20. Called at No. 24 this evening. Saw Mr. Ruggles and Baron Gerolt, the Prussian Minister, who recommends that Mr. Ruggles take with him to Berlin some sets of Sanitary Commission reports and documents which he thinks will be appreciated. Thence to Union League Club. Committee on Admissions had a session. Surgeon-General Hammond was there with Van Buren, also General [Romeyn B.] Ayres, and others. Olmsted has completed his arrangement with the Mariposa people and is to busy himself for five years in a mountain gorge of California. We can ill spare him.[6]

August 21. Hotter. Ellie came to town to bid her father goodbye. He sails (steams, rather) for Hamburg tomorrow full of concentrated essence of America, railroads, grain, gold, production, transportation, continental nationality; he is charged with large sound propositions on all these matters in a highly condensed, concrete form, and I think he will shew his Old World colleagues that the gas of American brag can be solidified and made palpable and is *real matter* after all. Spent an hour with him at No. 24 this evening. Heaven prosper his mission and bring him safe home again!

At 823 were important letters. Dr. [Alden] March at Morris Island reports scurvy and wants more curried cabbage, which he finds a sure anti-scorbutic when potatoes and onions and lemon juice fail. Dr. Steiner,[7] our acting executive officer at Washington in Olmsted's absence, has confidential intelligence that there is to be a movement on Texas, led by General Dan Sickles, and wants a good inspector to send with it. Col-

[6] Olmsted, who felt that his main work of organizing the Sanitary Commission and fixing its lines of policy had been accomplished, was anxious to leave and resigned his position as General Secretary in September. His health had suffered under the strain; his nervous intensity had increased, and some friction with his associates had resulted; while he had been offered a lucrative position as superintendent of the Mariposa mines developed and partially owned by Frémont. He was succeeded by Dr. J. Foster Jenkins.

[7] Lewis Henry Steiner (1827–1892), physician and professor in the Maryland College of Pharmacy, was chief officer of the Sanitary Commission with the Army of the Potomac in 1863–1864.

lision with Louis Napoleon not impossible in that quarter! I suppose Sickles, with his one leg, among our best volunteer officers. His recuperative powers are certainly wonderful. Four years ago he was a ruined man in every sense, a pariah whom to know was discreditable. Story of Hon. [William Cabell] Rives of Virginia, when in some hotel on the Continent wanting a chambermaid to attend to something or other in his room, ringing and calling in vain and endeavoring to get his want supplied by telling the waiters loudly and distinctly, *"Je veux une pucelle— une pucelle—entendez-vous? une pucelle."*

August 22. Troops continue to arrive here from Meade's army, which must be seriously weakened. We have already more than enough to ensure the execution of the draft in this city, and I suppose these newcomers are to be sent to Texas or possibly to Morris Island. It looks hazardous and imprudent to withdraw so many men from the Potomac, but I suppose that Halleck and Stanton know what they are about.

Carlyle's "Ilias Americana," a summary of the American war in a London magazine, is an astounding concentration of blunders about matters of fact into a dozen lines.[8] Carlyle *has* had much influence on my notions about things in general for twenty years, but I have no more respect for and no confidence in the man who wrote this flippant little bit of falsehood and immorality. It's his misfortune to labor under a monomaniacal inclination to abase himself before strength when contending successfully with law and established system. He worships "the God of Force," not the God of Justice and Right. Hence his deification of Cromwell, Napoleon, and Frederick. See the third volume of his *Life of Frederick* for a specimen of the style in which he disposes of the rather important question whether that hero had or had not a right to seize and occupy and hold Silesia, whether his conflict with Austria was just or unjust. Frederick was able to make his rights, whatever they were, valid against "Owleries" and "Enchanted Wiggeries," and so on. That's all Mr. Carlyle can say or try to say in defense of his Hero's moral position. Natural enough and quite consistent that Carlyle should love the rebels, who are fighting against a Constitution, who have shewn most creditable pluck, and were seemingly in a fair way toward success when this dirty little squib was written.

[8] Carlyle's little parable in three paragraphs in *Macmillan's Magazine* for August, 1863, headed "Ilias (Americana) in Nuce," showed the North attacking the South because Southerners hired servants not by the week or month, but by the lifetime. It gave much offence in America, where Emerson's characterization "unfortunate" was thought mild.

August 24, MONDAY.   To the Union League Club, where were twenty or thirty members and C. A. Dana (whilom of the *Tribune*), who has been spending several months in some official or quasi-official position with General Grant and went through all the splendid campaign that ended with the surrender of Vicksburg and Port Hudson. Dana was under examination, the object of a concentric fire of queries, which he answered very intelligently and clearly. I don't know what his judgment is worth, but he thinks that rebellion in the Southwest has gone to eternal smash and that we have only to settle details of reconstruction and pick up the pieces. He says that many great slaveholding princes of western Mississippi have been and are doing their utmost to further Grant's operations, being satisfied that the cause of the Confederacy is hopeless and desiring only peace and order on any terms, with slavery or without it. Expects that Arkansas will soon formally secede from secession and return to her normal condition. Says that Grant doesn't drink. Tells an interesting story of characteristic ill-breeding, snobbishness, and arrogance displayed by General Pemberton and his chivalric pals during the negotiations for the surrender of Vicksburg, and so on. Northern manners are less showy and splendid than Southern chivalry, but sounder and better, nevertheless.

August 25. . . . Bache tells a lovely story of an army teamster whom he saw in front of the Treasury building (Washington) bothered with a fractious, balky team and blaspheming like a demon. A casual army chaplain, shocked by his profanity, accosts him. "My friend, do you know who it was that said, 'Thou shalt not take My name in vain?' " Teamster: "O go 'way with your damn conundruming. Don't you see I'm busy?"

August 26.   Long talk with G. W. Blunt[9] and others at club. It seems certain that the riot of July has damaged Seymour and his friends seriously in this city. It has stirred up also a feeling against Irishmen more bitter and proscriptive than was displayed by the most thorough Native American partisans in former times. No wonder. The atrocities those Celtic devils perpetrated can hardly be paralleled in the history of human crime and cruelty, and were without shadow of provocation or excuse.

August 31, MONDAY. . . . George F. Allen was free from disease Friday and gaining strength steadily all day. His friends began to think him safe, but that night a change took place. There were symptoms like those of Asiatic cholera; he began to sink hopelessly, and Saturday morning he died, leaving big vacancies hard to fill. I always thought I appre-

[9] George W. Blunt was a publisher who had been active in the free-soil cause.

ciated George Allen; I certainly prized him, but, as I now see, far below his real value. By whom can he be replaced in the Board of Columbia College, for instance, or at our Sunday evening supper table?

Home at one P.M. Arrayed myself in decorous black, went to 823 Broadway, attended to certain business, and proceeded thence to Horatio Allen's, 25 Clinton Place, being invited as pallbearer. The others were Bidwell, Augustus Craven, Dr. Lieber, Dudley B. Fuller, Clarkson Potter, etc. We marched from the house to Grace Church. Dr. Taylor mangled and bungled the service most hideously. Thence in carriages to Green-wood Cemetery. There were only pallbearers and relatives. It was a long drive. The lawns and shrubberies of the cemetery were lovely in the slant sunlight of the autumnal afternoon. Grecian temples, urns, obelisks, broken columns, and many other monumental enormities could not quite destroy their loveliness. Our carriages stopped at last; we got out and saw marks of recent laceration on the beautiful greensward of James Brown's lot. The coffin was brought forth from the hearse and went slowly down into the earth, and then came the terrible grating clatter of stones and sods on its lid. Poor Horatio Allen and his wife and others of George F. Allen's near relatives seemed to take it very hard, and no wonder. It seems hardly credible that George Allen's face and form, so familiar and so welcome in this house for many years, so full of geniality and sympathy, sagacity, keenest intelligence, high culture, appreciation of art, devotion to the nation and to the church, should now be lying under six feet of earth. He lies beside his two elder children, who died before 1854, and his brother, William. His wife and his third child rest fathoms deep in the ocean, near the sunken wreck of that fatal steamer, the *Arctic*.

Dined with Agnew at Maison Dorée, and went with him to Van Buren's, where was the Surgeon-General. He sails in the *Arago* tomorrow for Hilton Head and goes thence to New Orleans, under orders from the War Department. He thinks it's the first step in a scheme of Stanton's to supersede him, and he is probably right. Stanton shook him by both hands when he bade him goodbye, and it is generally understood at Washington that that mark of cordiality is the invariable precursor of some stab or blow at its recipient. Hammond says the regular regiments now in this city are destined for Texas, but under Joe Hooker instead of Sickles; that Mexico means to recognize the Confederacy, and will be thereupon invaded and that the prophets of Washington predict war with France. Not at all unlikely.

Death of Luther Bradish at Newport. He was our great exemplar of deportment, somewhat of a humbug, but on the whole, a truly respectable and valuable man. Much older than I thought him. Honorable John B. Floyd is defunct at Abingdon, Virginia; dishonorable J. B. Floyd, rather. *Sic transit infamia mundi.* The gallows has suffered heavy losses of late; Floyd, Yancey, Pemberton, and others. The South *will* keep repudiating its debts, even those due that time-honored institution.

September 1. Talk with General [Theodore] Read, introduced by Mr. Collector Barney. He has been serving under Grant. Has seen raw regiments of niggers under fire and thinks they behave as well as white folks. . . .

Everyone at the Club full of deep, sincere regret for George Allen's death. He is universally lamented. My thoughts keep constantly reverting to that grassy hillside. I find myself wondering whether it be really true that he is under it. No longer ago than Thursday night, the 20th, he was at the Union League Club in his usual health and spirits, presided at a meeting of Committee on Admissions, and was full of kind enquiries about Ellie and the children.

September 2. Newspaper gabble about the "backbone of the Rebellion" being "broken at last" is abundant and nauseating. I dread premature, insolent jubilations as a tempting of Providence. We have gained most important results since the first of July, of course, and God be praised for them, but the *Herald* and other journals talk in a strain that would be reasonable if we had taken Charleston, Mobile, and Wilmington, dispersed Lee's army, and occupied Texas, and if Jefferson Davis and one hundred of his chief rajahs had been severally committed to await the action of the grand jury.

George Anthon has returned from Newport, where he has been staying with George F. Jones. There has been much sickness at Newport, chiefly dysentery and disorders of that class. Bradish died of dysentery. . . . Professor Bull Anthon found a regiment of regulars the other day squatting on one of the vacant blocks of Columbia College property on the west side of Fifth Avenue about Fiftieth Street and accosted a tall sergeant.

Professor: "By whose authority, sir, have you taken possession of these premises?"

Sergeant: "By Abe Lincoln's authority, God damn you. What have you got to say about it? Sa-a-a-ay!"

The professor subsided and walked downtown.

Lincoln's judgment in refusing to postpone the draft in New York (as Governor Seymour urged him to do) had been vindicated. He now issued his famous Conkling letter of August 26 to the Union mass-meeting held at Springfield, Illinois, a letter explaining his war policy and calling for popular support. It contained some of his most eloquent and poetic phrases, and it expressed a fervent gratitude to all the loyal fighters for the Union who had stood so firm at Antietam, Murfreesboro, Gettysburg, and Vicksburg. "Thanks to all. For the great republic—for the principle it lives by and keeps alive—for man's vast future—thanks to all."

Meanwhile, Rosecrans, long inactive after the bloody battle of Murfreesboro, at last set his army in motion, and by able manoeuvring forced Bragg's Confederate army to abandon middle Tennessee. On September 9, he marched into Chattanooga, which as a great railroad and river center was as important a point as Vicksburg, Atlanta, or Richmond. At about the same time Burnside's troops (Army of the Ohio) pushed into East Tennessee and occupied Knoxville. Bragg, however, was very far from beaten. On the contrary, he was eager to attack Rosecrans. Mustering all his forces, with reinforcements from both east and west, he struck fiercely at Rosecrans on September 19—and thus opened the bloody struggle at Chickamauga. Of all this Strong was an eager spectator.

September 3. Dined with George Anthon this afternoon. Lincoln's little letter defending his war policy is very good; a straightforward, simple, honest, forcible exposition of his views, and likely to be a conspicuous document in the history of our times. There are sentences that a critic would like to eliminate, but they are delightfully characteristic of the "plain man" who wrote it and will appeal directly to the great mass of "plain men" from Maine to Minnesota. I think this little letter a brilliant, successful move. The squirmings of the *World* and *Express* are painful to behold.

Visited Barnum's this afternoon. His aquaria have just received a large accession of fish from Bermuda. Many of them very curious and beautiful.

September 8. Burnside and Rosecrans seem to have grabbed eastern Tennessee without serious opposition. Rebeldom asserts itself only in the Chattanooga region, and the decisive battle of this war may perhaps be fought there. But we have reports this afternoon from "authentic" deserters that the troops of Bragg, Buckner, Joe Johnston & Co. are demoralized, mutinous, deserting in squads, fleeing to the mountains, watching and waiting for the Old Flag. Maybe so. Maybe not. On Morris Island we hold our own and perhaps gain ground. But the shattered casemates of Sumter still live and require more pounding. The pluck and endurance of the handful of traitors that continue to hold it are admirable.

At 823 this afternoon with Agnew and Knapp. Discussed the grave question of filling Olmsted's place. Agnew wants Dr. Newberry. I rather incline toward Jenkins. Dr. Steiner has certain qualifications for the place. Dr. Douglas has not.

September 11. . . . . Evacuation of Chattanooga generally received as a decisive confirmation of reports that the rebels are dispirited and demoralized in the Southwest and as proof that there is no fight in them. But the felon-chivalry may have given up east Tennessee in order to concentrate its resources for an inevitable attack somewhere else; for example, on Washington. It would be a desperate move, like the sacrifice of a queen and two castles to secure a checkmate dimly worked out twenty moves ahead, and would do rebeldom special mischief by strengthening the "submissionist" or reconstructionist minority, which Southern newspapers begin to recognize and at which they scold as if it were not by any means insignificant. The indications, therefore, on the whole, favor the opinion that the "backbone of the rebellion" is badly cracked, though not yet broken.

Yet it seems unprecedented and unlikely that social and political questions so grave as those we are fighting about and involving all the destiny of so vast a territory should be settled by a single war. No issues of like importance to mankind have been submitted to trial by battle since the Saracen invasion of Western Europe was beat back by Charles Martel. And this, too, is a religious war. Two antagonistic creeds are struggling for possession of half a continent. For Mahometanism is nearer the common faith of Christendom than is the modern advanced type of Southern Christianity, so called. By their fruits ye shall know them. A church that inculcates antichristian ethics and makes crime and oppression a paramount duty, is to say the least no better than Christianity as promulgated everywhere else and in all past ages. They are repudiated at Canterbury, at Rome, Edinburgh, Geneva. Saint Chrysostom, Saint Ambrose, Saint Bernard, Cranmer, Laud, Calvin, Servetus, Wesley, Leo X, Luther, would agree in denouncing the practical Christianity of Richmond and Charleston as unchristian, heretical, and damnable. For nothing is more distinctive and characteristic of Christianity than its view of the relations of the poor—the working class—to the rich and to the whole community. It bids us to respect and honor the poor man and denounces woes on those who take advantage of their wealth to oppress and harm him. By implication, it requires the state to be diligent in doing what it properly can to elevate and comfort the poor by providing means of education and relief of every sort. But this new Southern gospel and its Southern missionaries say to the rich man: "Your place and your duty require you to own the poor man that works for you, to convert him (so far as you can) into a chattel and a brute, to appropriate the fruit of his labor (giving him in return such sustenance as will keep him in working order) to treat him as you treat your oxen and your mules, and to deny him every privilege and faculty of which he can be deprived by the legislation of tyrannous, selfish, wicked men. By all means give him Christian teaching, but remember that his wife and his children belong to you and not to him. It is your right and your duty to sell them off whenever you can thereby make money. Such is the true relation between capital and labor, rich and poor. Thus and not otherwise can the state be made prosperous. All other social systems are perishable."

September 12, SATURDAY.   We have undergone a repulse in Charleston harbor; boat attack on the ruins of Sumter beat off with loss, as, it seems to me, anybody might have known it would be.[10] People grumble at Dahlgren, and call him a marine McClellan; that is, a brave and capable man, but over-cautious, unwilling to encounter risks. [James Gordon] Bennett comes out against Governor Seymour. A good sign. The sagacious old rat knows when his ship is unseaworthy.

September 23, WEDNESDAY.   News Monday night that Rosecrans had been badly defeated at "Chickamauga Creek," if that's its name, and had fallen back on Chattanooga, after a two days' battle. It looked like a grave disaster and perhaps it is, but later news looks better. He has certainly had a severe fight, suffered heavy loss, and encountered a serious check. But rebel dispatches speak in subdued tone. It was probably a desperate but indecisive conflict, and every battle in which the rebels come short of complete victory is equivalent to a rebel defeat just now.

At 823 this afternoon. Our Sanitary Commission agents with Meade's

[10] Rear-Admiral John A. B. Dahlgren was cooperating with General Quincy A. Gillmore in operations against Charleston; Gillmore leading the land forces, Dahlgren the South Atlantic Squadron. The attacks reduced the batteries on Morris Island and Fort Sumter to ruins, and thus made it possible for monitors to come inside the bar and block the port. But a naval assault on Sumter, September 8, failed with material losses.

army call for a large consignment of chloroform, which was sent there. The call is suggestive of movement and battle in Virginia. Lee seems tending to fall back, step by step, toward the fieldworks before Richmond. Some portion of his army has been withdrawn southwestwardly and helped Bragg congest Rosecrans's advance into Georgia.

Chickamauga, the heaviest fighting of which occurred on September 20, was almost a Union disaster. Rosecrans had a large, admirably trained, and heroic army, which should easily have repelled Bragg; but at the critical moment the Northern commander lost his nerve. A momentary gap was opened in the front line by some confusion in the orders; and the Southern troops, rushing through it, drove a large part of the Federal forces in headlong flight from the field. Rosecrans fled to Chattanooga a dozen miles away and telegraphed Halleck that he had met defeat: "Enemy overwhelmed us, drove our right, pierced our center, and scattered troops there." But not all was lost. General George H. Thomas, commanding the left wing, stood fast; and by his intrepidity won the sobriquet of "the Rock of Chickamauga." His fine defense enabled the Union army to complete an orderly retreat to Chattanooga, where they hastily fortified themselves.

September 25. No precise information yet as to the result of Rosecrans's late battle. People take it for granted that it's all right, but I have misgivings, and our bits and scraps of intelligence from that quarter do not improve as they come in, but rather tend to assume a well-defined blue tint. I guess it will turn out that we were badly beat, but that it cost Bragg so dear that he cannot follow up his victory, and that Rosecrans is rapidly receiving reinforcements. The rebellion cannot afford victories of that sort.

From what Rosecrans told Captain Keteltas when he gave him his furlough, it seems certain that Rosecrans expected not only to occupy Chattanooga but to penetrate well into Georgia without a battle, and that he was confident that the bulk of Bragg's army had been sent to Charleston. This looks a little as if he had been outgeneralled, for Bragg's army seems to have been on the spot in full force and with a large detachment from Lee's army to help it.

Dined at Dr. Bellows's yesterday, with the Surgeon-General, Agnew, Van Buren, Norris of San Francisco, Dr. Bell of Louisville (terribly shattered by recent illness and reclining on a sofa all dinner time), Dr. Chapin, who is very entertaining, *et aliis*. Hammond has just returned from

Charleston harbor and is off to the West and New Orleans today. He lauds and magnifies the work of the Sanitary Commission on Morris Island. Says General Gillmore told him he had now accomplished all he undertook to do when he went there; namely, to drive the rebels off Morris Island and to silence Fort Sumter. The programme was that the iron-clads, when no longer endangered by the plunging fire of Sumter, would finish the work. But Dahlgren hesitates about encountering the hypothetical obstructions and submarine torpedoes of the inner harbor and is grumbled at as over-cautious. The Secretary of War assures pretty Mrs. Hammond that he never dreamed of ousting her husband from the Surgeon-Generalship. Maybe so. His instructions to Hammond for his western tour certainly look as if he were not to be displaced. Perhaps Stanton has been a little enlightened within the last month. A letter that appeared in the *Herald* some ten days ago purporting to come from an assistant surgeon of volunteers, but in fact written by Colonel Charles G. Halpine, is said to have made a sensation in the medico-military circles of Washington and to have satisfied Stanton that his manipulation of the Medical Bureau was watched.

September 26, SATURDAY.   I have forgotten to register for the benefit of Posterity the funniest incident of the riot week, gravely detailed to Ellie a fortnight ago by little Elbridge Gerry. You are doubtless aware, O Posterity, that Gerry lives with old Goelet, his uncle, in the big old-fashioned house on the corner of Broadway and Nineteenth Street, with a big courtyard around it. Old Goelet's business is the receipt of rents and the investment of capital. His relaxation is the culture of Gallinaceae. Everybody that passes his courtyard stops to look through the iron railing at his superb peacocks, golden pheasants, silver pheasants, California quail, and so on. Well, Gerry was telling all the great things he did, and all the tremendous things he was prepared to do last July: how he armed the servants, and barricaded the windows. He is a very grandiose young man. "One of the great objects at which I aimed," said Gerry, "was to make the house as little conspicuous as possible." "But," said Mrs. Ellie, "your house is always conspicuous; the beautiful birds in your courtyard always attract people's attention." "Ah," said Gerry, "I provided for that. Just as soon as the disturbances commenced, I sent for my coachman and I ordered him to pull out all the tails of all those birds. It is really quite remarkable," proceeded Gerry, "but the new tails have not grown yet, and whenever my peacocks hop up on the fence, they always lose their balance and teeter over forward."

September 28. Dined with George Anthon at Maison Dorée, after which solemnity we walked westward toward a lovely clear sunset that flooded the sky with amber and gold, and then back again to Broadway, where I took a bus and went downtown to a Trinity Church Vestry meeting. . . . Reverend J. H. Hobart resigns his assistant-ministership. He accepts a call to Grace Church in Baltimore. We dealt with him liberally; gave him complimentary resolutions and a present of solid cash.

September 29. Dr. 〔Alden〕 March, Sanitary Commission inspector from Port Royal and Morris Island, is in town. . . . He does not tend to overvalue his own services or to overstate his confidential intimacy with General Gillmore and his relation as patron and protector to General Gillmore's medical staff. His work on Morris Island has done the Commission the greatest credit. But he is possessed of a demon of criticism and cavil and depreciation.

He says among other things that we are farther from Charleston than we were six weeks ago. The "Swamp Angel" battery has been knocked to pieces, and its position cannot be recovered for the present.[11] It was nearer Charleston than is Cumming's Point, which we now hold. Gillmore doesn't shell Charleston for the sufficient reason that his guns will not carry so far. He can do nothing more without heavy reinforcements, which are promised him. Without the iron-clads, we could not hold Morris Island forty-eight hours. He is now erecting huge curtains and traverses to protect his force from the guns of James Island and Sullivan. He has made artillery practice at long range a specialty and understands it as well as any living man. But March evidently thinks his capacity as a general below the average. Our assaults on Wagner were ill-planned and murderously bungled, and so forth.

Jenkins is fresh from a visit to Culpeper, Meade's headquarters. His advance is on this bank of the Rapidan, some eight miles farther south; his force about forty-five thousand. Two divisions have just been withdrawn from him. One has gone over the Baltimore & Ohio Railroad under General Joe Hooker. Its officers grumble at serving under him. The other may be going the same way or may be going south. Transports are waiting at Alexandria for somebody.

October 1. . . . Did not go to Wall Street but proceeded to No. 823, much impeded by the crowd that blocked Broadway, spectators of the

[11] The "Swamp Angel" was an 8-inch 200-pounder Parrott rifled gun mounted in the swamp area of Morris Island, which began firing on Charleston August 22. It did much damage in the city before it burst on the thirty-sixth discharge.

reception of the Russian naval officers whose squadron is now in the harbor. This evening to the Club; a large assemblage, and a speech from a reverend Englishman, Dr. Massie, who is here to represent the anti-Southern feeling of England. He seems a sensible, venerable old codger, white as to his hair, nut-crackery as to his countenance, accurate as to his diction.

October 2. . . . Dr. March tells me that about a half hour after our repulse from Fort Wagner, an Ohio lieutenant gave him this little incident of the assault. The lieutenant was climbing the scarp, preceded by a South Carolina recruit of the 54th Massachusetts, under a galling fire, when the nigger dropped. He stooped and asked, "Are you hit?" He was answered, "Yes, Mas'r, I'm done gone, but go ahead and don't mind stepping on me." The lieutenant "didn't mind," and pushed forward, trampling on the prostrate body. Such stupid, soulless brutes are the black peasantry of the South!!! "None of them damn niggers shall speak to me, be Jasus." "Modern physiology, my dear sir, has, as you must be aware, demonstrated the essential inferiority of the black race and proved it to be anthropoid rather than human." Certainly. Why not? The Negro can be taught reading and writing and the first four rules of arithmetic, to be sure, and he is capable of keeping a hotel. He can fight like a hero and live and die like a Christian. But look at his facial angle, sir, and at the peculiarities of his skeleton, and you will at once perceive that his place is with the chimpanzee and the gorilla, not with man. Physical science is absolutely infallible, you know. No matter what the Church, or the Bible, or human instincts, or common sense may seem to say on any subject, physical science is always entitled to overrule them. It's very true that the science of 1863 has reversed or modified about 250,000 of the decisions it gave twenty years ago, but that makes no difference.

October 11, SUNDAY.   Went to Washington by the usual unavoidable railroad Monday, the 5th instant. Horace Binney and Charles J. Stillé boarded the train at Philadelphia. The ride presented no incidents, unless it might be the lovely glimpses of the arms of Chesapeake which the railroad traverses—beautiful bays, bordered by golden autumnal woodland. Genteel seceshdom has its hand along their sequestered shores and waxes fat on soft-shell crabs and canvasback ducks. But Maryland seceshdom is nearly played out. It will soon be what Jacobitism was in England sixty years ago or seventy, the sentimental tradition of a few old families. A new order of society is coming there, and the patriarchs must clear the track.

Our session at Washington lasted till Friday night and was highly satisfactory. Full reports came in from East and West. We spent some time in chasing the "igneous fatuous" executive organization that led poor Olmsted through so many thickets and bogs. We succeeded at last in putting on paper a scheme that he would pronounce loose, indefinite, and unsystematic, but which is as near completeness and precision as the nature of the case admits. It may perhaps work, and that is more than Olmsted's complex, laboriously elaborated paper programmes ever did or could. Newberry was satisfied, and we left him, I think, with all the soreness produced by his jars with Olmsted and with the executive committee worked out of his bones.[12]

We chalked out much work. An appeal to the public for more money must be issued at once. A Sanitary Commission periodical is to be started here, like Newberry's *Western Reporter*. Bellows is to go to the Pacific Coast, and if possible, stir up the pure minds of the Californians to the extent of another half million.

Visited the convalescent camp near Alexandria Thursday afternoon. A lovely drive. From beneath the ruins of the old Virginny civilization, as manifested in desolate old houses and barns stripped of half their wood for fuel and shanty-building, the germs of the New Order are springing up. There are "government farms" nicely fenced and worked by gangs of contrabands, good roads newly cut, substantial bridges, and other signs that the vandals of the North are at work. This convalescent camp has long been a most scandalous unsanitary nuisance and offense. But our remonstrances and petitions have prevailed, and it is now a model of neatness and order. It looks like a model New England village, with its long rows of comfortable white huts and shanties, its wide streets, well drained and perfectly policed, its pretty inclosures and evergreen groves. The men (about 8,000; it can accommodate 12,000) looked orderly and cheerful.

We gave a grand dinner to Seward Friday night at Willard's. Fifteen altogether. Sat next the Secretary and am satisfied there is more of him than I supposed. He is either deep or very clever in simulating depth, and discoursed of public affairs in a statesmanlike way, as I thought.

Professor McCulloh of Columbia College has sent in his resignation,

---

[12] It may be stated once more that Dr. John S. Newberry, one of the founders of the Sanitary Commission, was in charge of its Western Department with the rank of Associate Secretary. His ideas with respect to what should be done for the Western armies were usually put into effect by the Commission, for he was shrewd, experienced, and indefatigable. But he sometimes had to make a fight for them.

dated Richmond, Virginia!!! He "has gone over to the dragons" and we are well rid of him.[13] He has probably been offered a high price to come south to take charge of some military laboratory, having high qualifications (so says Professor Bache) for work of that kind. What a pity this sneak did not desert six months sooner, when poor George F. Allen was still with us and Wolcott Gibbs had not gone to Boston!

Dr. Heywood of Louisville brought in a favorable report from Rosecrans's headquarters. His army does not suppose that it has been defeated or repulsed. It fought its battle of Chickamauga for the possession of Chattanooga, and though severely handled in the contest, it holds Chattanooga and expects to hold it.

October 12. I went down to a Trinity Church Vestry meeting. The Rev. J. F. Young's[14] application for leave of absence (laid on the table at last meeting) was taken up. I moved to decline it and made a speech in support of the motion; a very superior style of speech, indeed. Swift and Cisco spoke on the same side. . . . The Rector read a letter from Young asserting himself loyal. It was a somewhat equivocal, ambiguous letter, but its professions of loyalty were very remarkably strong to come from a man who talks as Young does about "your fleet" being unable to open the Mississippi, and "your army" being badly defeated at Chancellorsville. It lowered Young in my opinion. The Rector affirmed Young's loyalty. Clergymen are clannish and always uphold each other. I acquiesced in a motion to lay the matter on the table again, so it is still undecided.

If the vestry grant this application, I will resign; but I don't expect it will be granted. As the reverend applicant has taken his passage for the first of November and the vestry does not meet again till the second Monday of that month, and as he married a wealthy old maid a few years ago and is, therefore, independent of the vestry, it is whispered that he will resign his assistant-ministership. Hope he will.

October 13. . . . Jonathan Nathan died the other day of Bright's disease, I believe. He was a favorite law student of my father's some thirty years ago.

What little war news we have is not star-spangled. Meade has fallen back to the Rappahannock. Of course, the movement is merely a masterly change of base, and brings Meade (strategically) much nearer Richmond, but it is liable to misconstruction. Rosecrans's long line of communication

---

[13] Richard S. McCulloh, the professor of physics, who had gotten the place that Strong wished given to Wolcott Gibbs, now joined the Confederate cause.
[14] The Rev. John F. Young (1820–1885) later became Bishop of Florida.

is threatened and bothered. Gillmore and Dahlgren were to have made a combined attack on something Sunday. If they did, I guess we shall hear that they were repulsed.

State elections came off today in Ohio and Pennsylvania. Their result is as important as that of any battle delivered since this war began. If it shew a Copperhead majority in either of those states, the national cause will be badly damaged. We shall know tomorrow. *Deus salvam fac Rempublicam!*

October 14, WEDNESDAY. . . . We are all jubilant over the good news from Ohio and Pennsylvania. The tail of the national Copperhead is out of joint. Ohio pronounces against the pinchbeck martyr to free speech, Vallandigham, by a majority estimated at near one hundred thousand. Curtin's majority in Pennsylvania is less multitudinous, but 'twill serve. McClellan has lowered himself sadly by an ill-advised letter supporting Judge Woodward, Curtin's Copperhead, anti-Administration, peace-on-any-terms opponent. I guess the McClellan pipe is nearly smoked out, and that McClellan is henceforth "out of this story"—to quote the delightful *Saga of Burnt Njal* as translated by Mr. Dasent. He may be a good general, but he is a bad citizen, doing all he can—ignorantly, I hope and believe—to weaken and embarrass the government and to help the public enemy. I think his name is losing day by day the potency it had a year ago, and that he is slowly settling down into obscurity. This miserable political letter of his, followed by the defeat of his candidate, gives him a heavy downward shove. He has lost the next presidency by want of common sense, by inability to see things as they are, and by misplaced confidence in men like S. L. M. Barlow and ex-General Fitz-John Porter.

October 15. Special meeting of College trustees, two P.M., was interesting. King read McCulloh's letter of resignation, dated Richmond, Virginia, and offered resolutions that he be *expelled* from his professorship, that his expulsion be noted in future college catalogues, and that the action of the board be made public in the daily papers. I am happy to say that Bishop Potter, Dr. Haight (who re-appeared after a long interval, and seems quite himself again), Morgan Dix, and Bradford expressed hearty approval. So did John Astor. The Bishop was very earnest and emphatic about it. William Betts was true to his rebel sympathies and thought our proposed action "violent," because McCulloh had probably acted "conscientiously." So he voted "no" all by himself. Dr. Beadle put out a feeler in the same direction, but drew in his horns and voted "aye." Then something was said about the way the published resolutions should be certified, and President King remarked, "I'll sign them if you like." "Very good," quoth Betts, "I'd rather not have anything to do with them." Whereupon Hamilton Fish, our chairman, got on his legs and proceeded, with more vigor and virility than I thought he possessed, to expatiate on the indecorum of our clerk's expressing any reluctance to certify officially any action the board might please to take on any subject. It was a severe rebuke, plainly spoken, and very unlike the usual placid urbanity of our proceedings. Betts looked as meek as a drowned earthworm and said he didn't mean anything by it, and would certify any resolution whatever. Gouverneur Ogden rubbed it into poor Betts by moving that the resolutions be published with the signatures of the chairman and *clerk*, which was carried. This action does the board credit. I did not hope for anything so masculine.

Then came up the question of filling the deserted chair, and the subject was referred to the ancient committee on the course, which consists of Morgan Dix (vice George F. Allen), Rutherfurd, and myself; to whom were added Bishop Potter and A. W. Bradford. It was freely discussed. Its decision involves large questions. The Bishop pronounced himself against physical science and in favor of "the humanities" as the base of training. I think the board will throw over Davies's higher mathematics and Davies himself with them. Rutherfurd favors Rood of Troy [University] as McCulloh's successor. So does Wolcott Gibbs by a letter received today.

October 22, THURSDAY. Tonight at the Academy of Music with Ellie, General Dix's handsome, buxom, bouncing daughter Miss Kitty, Jem Ruggles, George Anthon, and Johnny. We had Mrs. Little's box. *Macbeth* for the benefit of the Sanitary Commission, with Charlotte Cushman and Booth; a strong cast. Immensely crowded house. The Commission would have made ten thousand dollars but for the fact that the seats were bought up by speculators instead of being sold at auction as they should have been. They were selling at twenty dollars each in Wall Street today. The performance excellent. The sleep-walking particularly intense; indeed, Miss Charlotte Cushman is the best Lady Macbeth I ever saw—beyond all comparison. Macbeth died very game. His finale was made very effective. MacDuff was an importation from the Bowery.

Tuesday night the committee on College course met here and got over a good deal of ground. Conclusions generally right, I think, though Professor Nairne and Professor Davies will not think so. As to McCulloh's vacant place, Bradford is to confer with Joy and Peck and see whether they feel inclined to divide McCulloh's work between them. They incline to no such thing. Mobile papers, by the by, announce the arrival in that town of Brigadier-General McCulloh and tell how he called on Major-General [Dabney H.] Maury—the little snip of a Lieutenant Maury who was flirting so fearfully with Mrs.—— at West Point about thirteen summers ago.

Yesterday afternoon with the Reverend Morgan Dix and Cisco at Trinity Church as committee on the question of putting up a small organ near the chancel, or of removing the old instrument bodily from the organ loft to the other end of the church. Organ and choristers ought to be brought closer together, but I fear either method of remedying the discords their separation produces will cost more money than the vestry will appropriate.

Rosecrans is superseded by Grant! The change astonishes everyone—its alleged reasons are still more startling.[15] Opium-eating, fits of religious melancholy, and gross personal misconduct at Chickamauga are charged by newspaper correspondents. There has certainly been something queer and unexplained about his disappearance from the field during a critical period of that battle, but I cannot give up Rosecrans till something is clearly made out against him. (Banks and Franklin seem established at the mouth of the Rio Grande.) In Virginia, Lee is falling back, and we hear this afternoon that Meade is ordered to follow him up and force a battle. If so, we shall soon be conjugating the verb To Lick, in the passive voice, indicative present. But tonight, I bought five cents worth of extry *Herald*, containing a blind, apocryphal story of a Rebel raid on Chambersburg.

October 24.   General Lee has brought his army off without a battle and recrossed the Rapidan, probably. The roads and bridges behind him are destroyed so as to make rapid advance by Meade impossible, and Lee will probably send off large reinforcements to Chattanooga or East Tennessee. I think we shall never reach Richmond by that line.

[15] Stanton, meeting Grant at Indianapolis on October 17, handed him an order giving him command of the whole area between the Alleghenies and the Mississippi; and by Grant's own wish, the same order placed Thomas in command of the Army of the Cumberland in place of Rosecrans. A brave soldier and able strategist thus went into temporary retirement. Next year, however, Rosecrans as commander of the Department of the Missouri repelled a northward thrust by Sterling Price's army. George H. Thomas (1816–1870), the new leader at Chattanooga under Grant, had distinguished himself at Mill Springs, Perryville, and Murfreesboro before earning the title of "Rock of Chickamauga." He had come forward slowly, but he was destined to one of the highest places among American generals.

October 30.   At Agnew's till about midnight. Standing Committee of the Sanitary Commission met there, discoursed, and devoured. Wolcott Gibbs was added unto us. He likes his position at Harvard and the people about him, but says (what I was surprised to hear him say) that though there is more mental activity and culture in Boston than in New York, there is *less mental health.* No doubt he is right. Poor Mrs. Paulding's case is utterly hopeless, he says, but she may get through the winter. Sorry to learn from Dr. Bellows that Mrs. George Schuyler is sinking fast under uterine cancer. An admirable woman, inheriting somewhat of the genius of her grandfather, Alexander Hamilton.

Tonight's war news important. Gillmore's batteries have reopened at Sumter, Moultrie, and Johnson. The rebels seem to have been crowded and manoeuvred out of certain snug positions near Chattanooga, from which they threatened our fearfully long, vulnerable line of communications. They have given up "Lookout Mountain." A sharp battle has been fought on their left, which is claimed as a victory for Hooker.

Last Tuesday Miss Charlotte Cushman dined here; also Bellows, Van Buren, Agnew, and Dr. Weston. The tragedienne is a cultivated woman and made herself most agreeable. She looks far better off the stage than on it. Her performances of *Macbeth* at Boston, New York, Washington, and other cities, have brought the Sanitary Commission some eight thousand dollars. Yesterday, our College Committee on "School of Mines" met at William Betts's office. I think the board will agree to an experimental beginning on a small scale.

November 1, SUNDAY.   News that Gillmore has tossed a few more incendiary shells into Charleston. How English newspapers will howl and whine over Yankee barbarism—quite oblivious of the havoc English projectiles made among East Indian palaces and the shops and houses of Sebastopol a few years ago. I am confounded and bewildered by the ignorance and prejudice of educated Englishmen of the best class (for example, the university men and young barristers who write for the *Saturday Review*) as manifested in writing about American affairs. One of its contributors recently defined Burnside's execution of certain rebel officers caught within our lines, disguised and recruiting for the rebel army, as "the murder of officers enlisting subjects of their own government on their own territory." This article went on to investigate the causes that have produced the degeneration of an Anglo-Saxon race to the stage of barbaric cruelty and inhumanity reached by our Northern people and manifested in their conduct of this war. The sagacious investigator thinks "climate" has something to do with it—or may have—but that the true reason lies deeper. There has been an immense emigration into America. Emigrations are generally short of women. Hence, alliances between new settlers from the Old World and Oneida Squaws. Hence, a large infusion of "Red Indian" blood into the population of the North. Which unquestionable fact fully accounts for the fiendish atrocities and ruffianly brutalities Northern soldiers love to perpetrate and Northern communities approve, and also for the "milk in the cocoanut."

November 3. Election day. Only state and county officers to be chosen, but the result is of national importance. It will determine whether the reaction for government extends to New York. I think it does, and that we shall cut down the Copperhead vote, even if we fail to carry the state. The city is beyond hope. The seat of Samuel Jones, Duer, and Oakley is pretty certain to be disgraced by McCunn.[16] I stood in queue an hour and a half this morning in Nineteenth Street, waiting to get in my vote. All the respectability seemed to have turned out and was voting one way. Not a "friend" of Seymour's was visible. Many blackguards are afraid to vote for him, lest they should be put down for the next draft.

Have just come from the Union League Club, where I left an eager crowd waiting for returns which come in slowly and indicate that we have lost the city, as was to be expected, but by a greatly reduced majority.

November 7. Election turned out as I expected. The state repudiates Seymour by about thirty thousand majority. The disloyal vote of the city is greatly reduced, and that nasty sewer-rat McCunn gets in by only about one thousand six hundred. This change from last year's vote is a thing to be thankful for, but not to crow over. Anything short of substantial unanimity on the question before us is a public disgrace. But this fall's grand reaction, East and West, in support of nationality will do much good and shew Copperhead leaders like Seymour and the Woods that disloyalty is bad policy. It extends to every state. Every election has been a vote of confidence in government and in the national cause except in New Jersey, and even in that benighted region Copperheadism loses ground. Kentucky goes right by fifty thousand, and Maryland votes for unconditional Union and immediate emancipation! The world certainly moves. . . .

It seems certain that Richmond, Petersburg, and the region round about are suffering badly for want of food. The Russian Ball Thursday

---

[16] John H. McCunn was this year elected justice of the superior court of New York City, holding his place 1863–1872; he had a bad reputation.

night was well managed and successful. Ellie and I joined General Dix's party at his house, and went thereto in great glory, staff and all—half a dozen captivating creatures in epaulets—with nice Mrs. Blake and Miss Kitty. I like all that family very much. They seem up to the standard of the General and the Reverend Morgan Dix, and that is saying a great deal. The crowd was dense; shoddy, largely represented. I could find no one I cared to discourse with and soon sank into depths of boredom. The common phrase, "bored to death," is no hyperbole, but represents a very possible contingency.

The more patriotic citizens of New York correctly felt that Copperhead denunciations of the draft act, and Copperhead demands for peace, were largely responsible for the draft riots. Among many Republicans and Union Democrats, feeling against Governor Horatio Seymour ran high. Following the riots, the Governor had written Lincoln asserting that the enrollment of names for the draft ("this lottery for life") was unfair and partisan, declaring that the quotas set for New York City and Brooklyn were "glaringly unjust," and asking for a suspension of the law. When the draft took place late in the summer of 1863, Seymour refused to supply state militia to help execute it, and Federal troops had to be withdrawn from the front for that purpose. September found the political campaign in full swing, with only minor state officers to be chosen, but with intense interest in the repudiation or vindication of Seymour. The Democratic platform called for personal liberty, a free press, and maintenance of the writ of habeas corpus, and Democratic orators denounced the conversion of the war into a struggle for abolition and subjugation. The "Union" Party, as the opposition was called, attacked Seymour as disloyal and demanded a continuation of the war until rebellion was crushed. They made the most of Seymour's mild attitude toward the "red-handed" draft riot mob; they brought a great cohort of orators—Vice-President Hamlin, Governors Yates, Curtin, and Andrew of Illinois, Pennsylvania, and Massachusetts, Senators Henry Wilson, Zack Chandler, and John P. Hale, and Representatives Elihu Washburne, Schuyler Colfax, and Henry Winter Davis—into the state; and when election day approached they saw to it that an estimated 16,000 to 18,000 soldiers were furloughed to go home to up-state New York. The result was that the Union ticket triumphed by about 30,000 majority. Heavy Democratic losses in the metropolis indicated that the reaction against the draft riots had been marked. The new legislature was to have 21 Union men against 11 Democrats in the

Senate, and 82 Unionists against 46 Democrats in the Assembly. It would up-hold Lincoln loyally.

All along the line this fall (save in New Jersey) the Republican or Union Party won. In Ohio, where the egregious Clement L. Vallandigham was running for governor, local voters rallied behind John Brough, a war Democrat, to defeat him by 101,000 majority. In Pennsylvania, Andrew G. Curtin was reëlected governor. In Maryland, Delaware, Kentucky, and several Western States the Unionists won. "The elections," wrote John Lothrop Motley, "I consider of far more consequence than the battles." But on the battlefields, too, the tide of victory was now setting in with full force.

November 9, MONDAY.   Trinity Church vestry tonight. The Rev. J. F. Young's application for leave to go abroad was taken up. The rector backed it strongly, I regret to say, because he had much faith in the Reverend Mr. Young's efforts to promote Anglo-Americano-Muscovite intercommunion. Governor Dix thought Young's letter equivalent to a declaration of loyalty or quasi-oath of allegiance, which might reasonably satisfy us. So he went the same way. Tillou supported Young in a long speech, just as if he were arguing a special demurrer in the Common Pleas, and Samuel Davis delivered a long, rambling eulogy on the reverend applicant. Cisco, Ogden, and I opposed. We said that the man's sympathy with treason was notorious; that it was at least certain he would do harm abroad; that his talk, be its weight more or less, would tend *pro tanto* to counteract the efforts of agents sent by government expressly to en-lighten the English people about our efforts. But the motion was carried. Davis, E. M. Young, old Verplanck, Dunscomb, General Dix (!), Skid-more (!), Caswell, Bob Winthrop, and Tillou voted aye; Cisco, Sackett, Curtiss, Henry Youngs, and myself voted no. Ayes and noes were called for and recorded. This vote is disgraceful, and I have been inwardly vowing an immediate resignation all the way up in the omnibus. I shall be sorry to leave a board in which I have sat sixteen years and for which I have worked hard, but I don't want to belong to any concern that sends secession agents to England, or to be exposed to Tillou's oratory.

November 12.   Library Committee of Columbia College met at my office this morning. Mr. Jones as twitchy and tetanic as usual. . . . Prices are rising fast; bad for mortgagees and for all who depend on fixed incomes. We shall soon be even as the F.F.V.'s of Richmond, who go to market with their money in their baskets and come home with its purchases in their pocketbooks. Insolvency draws nearer daily. Never mind; I dare say I shall get along with it when it comes at last. Only let us succeed in asserting our national existence. Many insolvents of my acquaintance seem to get along somehow and to have, on the whole, a rather particularly good time. Workmen and workwomen of almost every class are on strike (and small blame to them) and among others the city railroad drivers. So our facilities for getting uptown and down are diminished, and all omnibi are being overcrowded. In the coal region of Pennsylvania the strike is combined with organized resistance to the draft and has attained serious dimensions.[17] It . . . is, in fact, a Copperhead insurrection that holds two or three counties. The insurgent strikers are mostly lewd fellows of the baser sort, and Irish at that, and are, of course, committing all manner of murderous brutality. Paddy has not done much to entitle his race to our sympathy and affection during the last six months. Pen Hosack tells me more about this than has appeared in the newspapers. He comes fresh from the seat of war, where are mines in which he holds an interest, and he came away very quietly, being warned that his stay in those parts might be dangerous. . . .

Ellie is spending the evening at Mrs. John Sherwood's, with whom Mrs. Carson is staying. Mrs. Carson is a daughter of Petigru (or Pettigrew)[18] the distinguished Charleston lawyer who stood faithful among the faithless as a Union man among the disunionists of that treasonous city till his death a few months ago. He was too eminent and respectable to be executed, so his death was in the course of nature. His daughter inherits his loyalty. It has cost her all her property, and she is absolutely destitute, supporting herself by the help of her friends and by her amateur talent for art.

November 17.   A great decisive battle said to be at hand in front of Chattanooga. Perhaps. From the southwest corner of North Carolina we have a legend of five thousand men, deserters from the rebel army and white trash, who have organized in the mountains, licked a rebel force sent out against them, and marched off to East Tennessee. Good luck go with them. Famine at Richmond seems a settled fact. I've no objection to have "the markets continue in scarceness," but this is very bad for our poor fellows in prison there. They are dying of starvation. The Sanitary Commission has obtained leave to send a consignment of food suitable to men in their

[17] The Ancient Order of Hibernians, later known as the Molly Maguires, were mainly responsible for this strike and draft-resistance. Schuylkill, Berks, and Cambria counties were seats of trouble, and a good many draft-evaders took refuge in the region.

[18] James Louis Petigru (1789–1863) was a Unionist who never abated his convictions.

condition, and government is sending clothing and ordinary rations. Strange as it may seem, General Neal Dow writes that these supplies have not been gobbled up *in transitu* by the Chivalries, but have actually reached their destination. But for a great many they will come too late. There is reason to believe that the famine is caused not so much by actual deficiency of hog and hominy as by the unwillingness of Virginia farmers to sell anything for which they must be paid in rebel paper. Want of lively faith in the value of rebel currency implies, of course, skepticism as to the ultimate triumph of the rebel cause. A British squadron has just been shelling a Japanese city of one hundred and eighty thousand inhabitants and laying it in ashes. With what refinement of humanity *they* make war, compared with us bloodthirsty Yankee barbarians! The squadron proceeded to attack certain Japanese coast batteries, but the batteries were not silenced and Britannia had to haul off badly punished. Can't say I'm very sorry.

November 21, SATURDAY.   Thursday night Ellie and I, with Bellows, his wife and daughter, went to Brooklyn Academy of Music. I rode outside on the box. The Rev. Henry Ward Beecher delivered an address about his experiences in England. Proceeds of the performance for the benefit of the Sanitary Commission. As representatives of the Sanitary Commission, we were received with distinguished consideration, admitted through the stage door, shewn into the Committee Room, introduced to the reverend, and accommodated in a special proscenium box. The house was large and intelligent. Capital address and enthusiastically applauded. Most agreeably disappointed in Beecher, whom I had supposed to be a cross between Friar Gerund and George Francis Train. His matter and his manner were excellent. I never heard so good a popular address. Beecher stands up for the English people and maintains that we have their sympathy. His speech was an argument against the bitter anti-Anglicanism now prevalent. He says that though we are hated by the aristocracy, the establishment, the universities, the plutocracy, and the larger portion of the leading non-conformists, the great mass of the people is with us.

Sorry to learn of the death of Miss Alice Jones at Paris—Mrs. Rebecca Jones's daughter. George Winthrop Gray also dead. He was old Griswold's son-in-law. Old John Allan, too, at a very advanced age.[19] What will become of his superb collection of illustrated books and bibliomaniacal oddities?

19 John Allan (1777–1863) was noted in his day as antiquarian and collector; his books, manuscripts, coins and curiosities were sold at auction in May, 1864, fetching some $37,000.

November 25. Thank Heaven for good tidings from Chattanooga! They are not very definite as yet, but there is no doubt that Bragg is beaten with heavy loss in guns and men after several days of sharp fighting. Burnside holds his own at Knoxville. He has twenty-two thousand men, according to Colonel Jem Strong, and [John G.] Foster, who is about to relieve him, will probably bring reinforcements. If Bragg be forced back, as seems likely, Longstreet, who is operating against Knoxville, may find himself in a tight place. . . .

Last evening H. W. Beecher spoke again at our Academy of Music. Proceeds for benefit of Sanitary Commission. The tickets had been put too high, three dollars for reserved seats, and it was a vile rainy night—rebel weather—so the house was thin and our net proceeds will not exceed two thousand one hundred dollars, or about one-half what we counted on. The speech was admirable and well received. I adjourned with Van Buren to Dr. Bellows's, where were the orator and some half-dozen others, including Mrs. Harriet Beecher Stowe, whom I found very bright and agreeable. Her brother is also a most interesting talker. We departed early after a slight supper. Ellie is appointed treasurer of the grand Metropolitan Fair. Heaven help her!

After this defeat in the bloody September battle of Chickamauga, Rosecrans had retired to Chattanooga, the important railroad center on the Tennessee River. Here he was closely invested by the Confederates under Bragg, who occupied Lookout Mountain and shortly cut off his direct line of supplies. Then in mid-October, as noted above, Rosecrans was replaced by Grant, who arrived at Chattanooga on the 24th. The new commander at once reëstablished a direct supply line and telegraphed Sherman to hurry his army to the scene. On November 15, Sherman reported in person at Chattanooga, and Grant was ready to carry out a well-laid plan of battle. Fighting began on the 23rd, and next day the spectacular "battle above the clouds" for the possession of Lookout Mountain took place. The ensuing struggle of the 25th for Missionary Ridge ended in the collapse and flight of the Confederate army, the capture of two thousand prisoners and thirty-seven guns, and the practical termination of Bragg's active military career. As Strong's diary indicates, Chattanooga was a victory which immensely heartened the Northern people and which for various reasons caught their imaginations. It was fought along a thirteen-mile line amid magnificent scenery; it brought together on the Union side troops from the three chief Northern armies, those of the Potomac, the Cumberland, and the Tennessee; it saw Grant, Sher-

man, Sheridan, and Thomas all engaged in victorious operations; and it
revealed an impetuous élan on the part of the Northern troops. The central line
of communication between the Confederate forces in the East and those in the
Mississippi Valley was finally broken; the way was now open for the invasion of
Georgia and Sherman's march to the sea; and the morale of the South, shaken
by Gettysburg and Vicksburg, was reduced to almost utter disheartenment.

Meanwhile, in New York plans were being laid for the great Metropolitan
Fair in aid of the Sanitary Commission which was ultimately held in 1864 in
buildings on Union Square and Fourteenth Street. The extensive military
operations of 1863 had placed a heavy strain on the Commission, and during
the last half of the year its disbursements were twice as great as its receipts.
Spending nearly $65,000 in December, 1863, it closed the year with a balance
of only $41,725. More money had to be found at once—and a series of fairs
provided part of it. The "Great Northwestern Fair" in Chicago in October–
November, 1863, yielded nearly $80,000 for the Chicago branch of the Sanitary
Commission. Boston followed in January, 1864. In the New York effort Mrs.
Strong was a leading figure.

November 27. The good news from Chattanooga amply confirmed,
and more than confirmed. Bragg's defeat is a rout, and Grant telegraphed
at ten A.M. that sixty guns were taken, at least, and that there was every
sign of flight and disorganization. He is pushing the shattered rebel columns hard, and there is probably much swearing this minute among the
Chivalry at several points far south of Chattanooga. God be praised for
this victory, which looks like the heaviest blow the country has yet dealt
at rebellion. . . .

Uptown early today, and at the new menagerie in the old Coster House
(afterwards "Chinese Buildings"), met Ellie, Miss Kitty Dix, Mrs. Blake,
and one Rice (manifestly dead in love with the young lady—and small
blame to him), also Johnny and Temple and little Albert and Jem Gallatin,
sons of my poor friend Albert. We had a rather refreshing time, though the
crowd was uncomfortable. It's an unusually interesting collection. I hope
the project of establishing it here permanently may succeed. There was
also an extra exhibition of a hideous fat woman and two revolting idiotic
"Australian children," whom I take to be the identical wretches that were
at Barnum's or elsewhere some years ago, and who were then called
"Aztecs."

Thence to Sanitary Commission rooms, 823, with Johnny and Temple.

Collins is in a twitter about a dreadful blunder Dr. Bellows was making; namely, publishing his *North American Review* article with all its slashing attacks on Mr. Secretary Stanton as a document of the Commission, No. 76. It would have been a most horrible blunder. "The Dominie," with all his tact, sagacity, and energy, needs watching. Left to himself, he can do the greatest mischief. Got this set straight this evening. . . . Bellows preached a sermon yesterday that aggravated and offended many who heard it. I don't know exactly what position he took, but it is called disguised Copperheadism, sympathy with the Rebellion, and so on. If he's a Copperhead, he is singularly wanting in the wisdom of the serpent.

Meade's army again reported in motion and across the Rapidan. It seems to have a grand opportunity just now. The nation needs one or two splendid victories by its Eastern armies to offset those gained in the West. Western sectionalism is already an established fact, and it may become no less mischievous than Southern sectionalism. All our Western Sanitary Commission correspondence foreshadows this danger. Chicago and Cincinnati feel sore because the Commission has thus far held no session at the West.

December 1, TUESDAY.   Voted this morning at charter election. It's a triangular duel between Orison Blunt, who is a decent citizen, and the Union candidate, Gunther, equally decent, but supported by Peace Democrats and Copperheads, and Boole, a disciple of Fernando Wood, a chief operator in "the Ring," and reputed a very clever, corrupt, swindling scoundrel. I thought his chance far the best, but at nine this evening full returns were received at the Union League Club, where I was with G. W. Blunt, Charles King, Colonel Howe, and others. . . . During the day Boole "was all the time undergoing his accomplishment," . . . or in other words, "his finish and quietus." He is *beat* and Gunther is mayor by about six thousand plurality in a vote of seventy thousand. Well, a Copperhead is perhaps as good as a thief, but it's a melancholy reflection that if Union men had not voted for Gunther as the only way of defeating Boole they could have elected Blunt.[20]

[20] In this triangular contest, Charles Godfrey Gunther received about 28,000 votes, Francis Boole about 22,000, and Orison Blunt, the Republican, only about 10,000. Boole, a builder, an alderman, a demagogue, and a reputed grafter, had appealed for the votes of Negroes by promising to protect their rights, and had thus estranged many Irishmen. Gunther was a Peace Democrat or Copperhead, who had been an original member of the Anti-Abolition State-Rights Association and had presided over a meeting in May, 1863, to protest against the arrest and imprisonment of Vallandigham. He was popular with German voters.

I find people at the Club and elsewhere full of wrath about this extraordinary sermon of Bellows's. It must be that it is misunderstood. Not more than ten days ago we were all lamenting his indiscretion and ultraism in consenting to preside at a series of meetings to be held under the auspices of the most advanced Abolitionists, intended to create a feeling in favor of a proclamation of emancipation everywhere—Border States and all. This caper of his, or this misconception as the case may be, will do the Sanitary Commission and this projected Metropolitan Fair in its aid serious damage which we can ill afford now, with a balance in the bank fast falling below ninety thousand dollars. . . .

Visit last evening from Tutor Van Amringe[21] of Columbia College and long discourse. He is a very intelligent fellow. Professors Davies, Peck, and Drisler have severally called here on the same errand to enlist me in favor of transferring Peck to the chair of physics made vacant by the flight, abdication, and consequent expulsion of "Brigadier-General" McCulloh. Davies sets all this in operation but will fail because he over-bores the trustees and also because his own agency is too manifest. Nearly every man in the board feels a vague, superstitious dread of his skill in manoeuvre and manipulation and of being thereby somehow seduced or coerced into voting for something against his own judgment and will. The chances now are that Rood will succeed McCulloh; Lewis Rutherfurd will carry with him Gouverneur Ogden and Hamilton Fish. The Rev. H. C. Potter of Troy, a nephew of the Bishop's, is a personal friend and admirer of Rood's, as appears by a letter received today. This accounts for the Bishop's tendency that way. The clerical vote of the board will be controlled by Bishop Potter. A. W. Bradford and Mr. Ruggles (now daily expected from Europe) and Edward Jones are likely to vote for him, and I predict he will be elected.

December 3. Weather still wintry. Columbia College library committee meeting in Wall Street this morning. At No. 823 thereafter. . . . From the Sanitary Commission office to Mrs. John Sherwood's in Thirty-second Street. I left with her a draft of a circular about the proposed Fair and sundry papers beside. After dinner Agnew came in, and we held council over the list of men to be invited to help the undertaking. We must take in Copperheads, I think, like Belmont and Willy Duncan. They will work the

[21] J. Howard Van Amringe (1835–1915) had been graduated from Columbia College in 1860. He took the chair of mathematics in the School of Mines in 1865, and was the very popular dean of Columbia College, 1894–1910.

harder for the sick and wounded because they are in a minority of opposition to the war and to government. . . . Meade has fallen back to Brandy Station. I guess he will be relieved, but by whom? His whole movement has been rather incomprehensible. Edge writes from England that English feeling about us improves, and quotes *tempora mutantur*, "the *Times* is changing."

December 6, SUNDAY.   Frosty. At Trinity Church this morning, taking Mr. Blackmore with us. Service impressed him. He thought it equal to cathedral services in England and was surprised to find the American prayer book so nearly identical with the English and "felt more at home" than he had done since he arrived here last Friday evening. . . .

Friday night our Sanitary Commission committee met at Dr. Bellows's. The doctor expatiated to us about his Thanksgiving Day discourse that has stirred up such a hornets' nest. He says the proposition he asserted was this: "Ours is a representative government and must be guided by the average instincts and wishes of the people, not by the aspirations of its more advanced intelligence and principle. The people want to see the rebellion squelched but care comparatively little about the slavery question; hence it is probable that our trouble will be settled without the absolute destruction of slavery and that the restored Union will include slaveholding states, though slavery will be shorn of its political power, in a declining, moribund condition." If this be all he said, it's very gratifying and encouraging that people are in such a fume over so moderate and reasonable a proposition.

Mr. Ruggles got home Friday morning from his Statistical Congress and Anglo-Graeco Church mission safe and sound, and unchanged save by the eruption of a grizzly mustache that is rather effective. He dined here yesterday with Mrs. Ruggles, Mr. Derby, Jem, and Blackmore. Blackmore is a Britisher, one of the agents or solicitors employed on our side in the *Alexandra* case in the Court of Exchequer, and seems a cultivated, thorough-bred man. He came over in the *Scotia* with Mr. Ruggles.

War news little or none. We are daily tossing twenty shells or so into the city of Charleston but make little progress toward reduction of its harbor defenses. There is uneasiness about Burnside and Knoxville; our latest information from East Tennessee is nearly a week old. Congress meets tomorrow. There are rumors of intrigue about its organization that may do immense mischief.

Despite Strong's uneasy prognostications, both the military and the political situations were now more favorable than at any time since the beginning of the war. In the West, the Mississippi was completely in Union hands; Arkansas had been wholly occupied by Federal troops, and was the seat of a well-organized reconstruction movement; Sherman followed up the great victory at Chattanooga by occupying Knoxville on December 3, and so bringing practically all of Tennessee under Union sway; and a force under General Banks had occupied the mouth of the Rio Grande in Texas. In the East, Meade's forward movement against Lee had stopped when it became evident that the Confederate army was strongly entrenched near Chancellorsville; but in December a Union force advanced into Southwestern Virginia, destroyed parts of the Virginia & Tennessee Railroad, and captured large quantities of stores. Charleston was under constant fire from General Q. A. Gillmore, who had built the "Swamp Angel" battery on Morris Island. All along the coasts the blockade was increasingly effective. The new Congress had an increased Democratic minority as a result of the elections of 1862. But the strength of the Administration (with 102 Republicans in the House as against 75 Democrats and 9 Border State men) was decisive, and Lincoln's prestige was much higher than at the close of 1862. As Strong says below, Uncle Abe was now the most popular man in the country. It was clear that victory was only a matter of time. Lincoln gave thanks in his annual message for "the improved condition of our national affairs," and declared: "It is easy to see that, under the sharp discipline of civil war, the nation is beginning a new life."

December 7. Cold for the season. Exceedingly busy all day. Columbia College trustees met at two. Committee on the Course reported. Their resolution to maintain a separate chair of physics passed *sub silentio*, and that of abolishing the calculus and higher analytical geometry (or rather, making them optional in the senior year) after a lively and really very able debate. Rutherfurd and Bradford supported it and Anderson opposed. He lost his temper just a little for the first time in his life, probably, said we were "making the physical course a farce," and got gently snubbed therefor by Bradford. It's very strange, but though Anderson is a man of great and varied acquirements, speaking with the authority of an expert on many subjects, personally most genial, kindly, and lovable, and endowed with the most subtle faculty of argumentation, he has less weight and influence in the board than any other of its members. . . .

December 11.   Visited by unknown author of *The New Gospel of Peace*, which has been attributed to a score of people, myself among them. The Cincinnati Sanitary Commission Fair people had written to his publisher, Tousey, to ask for the original manuscript that they might make merchandise thereof, whereupon, Mr. X. Y., the evangelist, came to me to say that our Metropolitan Fair could have it for the asking. I closed with the offer, for the manuscript will bring money. Though the squib does not seem to me very particularly clever, it has hit the average popular taste very hard. Seventy thousand copies of the first part and forty thousand of the second have been sold. The author is ⸺ [Richard Grant White]. Who'd have thought it!

President's message and proclamation of conditional amnesty to the rebels, certain classes excepted, finds very general favor. Uncle Abe is the most popular man in America today. The firmness, honesty, and sagacity of the "gorilla despot" may be recognized by the rebels themselves sooner than we expect, and the weight of his personal character may do a great deal toward restoration of our national unity.

Rebeldom has just played us a pretty prank; its audacity is wonderful. Sixteen "passengers" on the peaceful propeller *Chesapeake*, which left New York for Portland last Saturday, took possession of her during her voyage, killed some of her officers and crew, put the rest ashore near St. Johns, and then steamed off with their prize in triumph under Confederate colors. A whole armada has been sent in pursuit, but they won't catch her.

There is almost universal feeling that rebellion has received its death-blow and will not survive through the winter. It is premature, but being coupled with no suggestion that our efforts may safely be slackened, it will do no harm. The *soi-disant* Chivalry shews no sign of disposition to back down and is as rampant, blatant, and blustering as ever. The most truculent and foul-mouthed bravoes and swashbucklers of the South feel a certain amount of discouragement, no doubt, but they generally keep it to themselves. There will be no enduring peace while the class that has hitherto governed the South continues to exist. They are almost universally given over to a reprobate mind and past possibility of repentance. Southern aristocracy must be dealt with as the Clans were after 1745. Parton's life of Butler (a readable book) tells how that general treated their case in New Orleans.[22] Even his remedies were too mild, but they come nearer to what is required than any others yet administered. That book will do much to

[22] James Parton's *General Butler in New Orleans*, an "authorized" book, half history and half journalism, was published this year.

raise Butler in popular favor. It paints him as of that Jacksonesque type of beauty which we especially appreciate and admire. Parton colors very high and tries to make a demigod of his hero, but I have always thought Butler among the strongest men brought forward by the war.

December 13, SUNDAY.   Dr. Peters brings news of a bulletin at Union League Club announcing that A. H. Stephens, Vice-President of Rebeldom, has just presented himself once more at Fortress Monroe with a couple of colleagues as Peace Commissioners, that Butler refused to receive them in any official character, but offered to hear what they had to say as prominent citizens of Secessia, and that they thereupon went back again in a huff, sending a vindictive Parthian shaft behind them in the shape of a notification that they would no longer allow supplies to be sent our starving prisoners at Richmond.[23] If they have done this, it won't much help their cause abroad; but that's a small matter. Government should notify them that inasmuch as they have declared their inability to give their prisoners rations sufficient to sustain life, their refusal to allow us to make up the deficiency will be followed by the execution of the rebel officers in our hands *per diem*, till such refusal is revoked.

Message of Jefferson Davis, "anti-President," to the squad of malefactors now gathered at Richmond and styling themselves members of Congress from Kentucky, Tennessee, Missouri, and other states, is long and doleful and dull—a mélange of lies, sophistry, swagger, lamentation, treason, perjury, and piety. He admits that rebellion has been drifting to leeward during the past year, but refers his gang for consolation to the boundless capacities of the future. He is moral, also, and objects to any action inconsistent with the letter or the spirit of "the constitution we have sworn to obey." This is cool. He and probably the majority of his pals and councillors in Congress assembled had held not less than twenty offices apiece before they concluded to rebel. How many hundred broken oaths to uphold another constitution were represented on the floor while this pious message was being read? Could all these several perjuries have been combined in one colossal act of blasphemy, I think the earth would necessarily have opened and swallowed the perpetrator. Jefferson's act of hypocrisy is (time, place, and presence considered) of like enormity, though less criminal and black. I wonder the assembled peers of Secessia were not startled by a vast resounding guffaw from the Powers of Nature, reverberating from the Chesapeake to the Alleghenies. Jefferson Davis has outbrazened Louis Napoleon himself.

[23] This was a canard; Stephens was in Georgia.

December 15.   To Columbia College at three P.M. Committee on proposed School of Mines, and so on, met in the library; Betts, Rutherfurd, Torrey, Edward Jones, and I. We made good progress and found rooms that can be made available. Spent an hour with Professor Joy inspecting the splendid apparatus of McCulloh's physical room, probably the finest in the country, but thus far left unused behind its glass doors and in great part actually unpacked in the cases in which it came from Paris and Vienna. He shewed us that most striking and splendid of experiments which is mentioned in Tyndall's book on heat, the conversion of force into heat by the revolution of a copper disk between the poles of an electro-magnet. Who shall use this grand collection? I have thought Rood pretty sure of election, but Professor Davies is a most skilful and potent intriguer, and I fear "my son-in-law Professor Peck" will be put into the physical chair. . . .

Dined at Maison Dorée this afternoon with Ellie, Mr. Ruggles, Judd (Minister to Berlin), Dr. Lieber, Barney the Collector, and Parke Godwin. Very pleasant session and many good stories. I record one of Barney's attributed to Thackeray and illustrating our American appreciation of magnitude. A great six-foot Kentuckian sprawling about in a Louisville bar-room and spitting right and left and at very long range, and who has just returned from a visit to Europe, is asked by a friend, "How did you like it?" "Well, I liked it all pretty well except England. Didn't like England at all." "Why not?" "Why, I didn't dare to go out of the house nights for fear I should *step off.*"

Yesterday dined here Mrs. David Lane, Mrs. John Sherwood, Richard Grant White, Griswold Gray, and Agnew—a committee on the Metropolitan Fair. Memminger's report has appeared. He is secretary of that vast void, the rebel treasury. He reveals a fearful condition of vacuity and insolvency and reminds one of Mr. Micawber in *David Copperfield* expatiating on his own private impecuniosity. The difference between them is that while Micawber bewails a deficiency of the circulating medium, Memminger is suffering from its excess. Among his people a dollar is represented by about a peck of Confederate treasury notes and circulates with extreme difficulty, for Southern railroads are nearly worn out and unequal to the transportation of army supplies. So Memminger is in grand choler and proposes certain measures for financial relief that seem frantic and impracticable and unavailing if practicable. This paper is a confession that the Confederacy is *mired.* It may struggle out, for it has the fury and the energy of a cornered mad cat, but it is in a tight place. Foreign financiers will hold Memminger's statement and his propositions equivalent to a general assignment by a mercantile firm.

Reports of Union feeling in south and west Arkansas so multiply that we may begin to believe it exists there and is not only appreciable but important. So, too, in Texas, though not yet so distinctly manifested. If a reaction be once fairly established at any Southern point, it will spread like fire in a cotton factory, and the lawless, vengeful, half-savage Southern people will have a fearful settlement of accounts with their aristocratic rulers. The rebellion may be crushed that way—or may not.

December 19, SATURDAY.   Clear, windy, and wintry. Heard the *Pastoral Symphony* at the Academy of Music this morning; also, a nice concert overture of Gade's, entitled "The Highlands." His music is always melodic, genial, and suggestive. Stopped on my way uptown this afternoon to see John Wolfe's fine picture gallery on exhibition at the old Düsseldorf rooms and to be sold at auction next week. It's a good collection. There's not a picture in it that I positively covet, but all are above average merit. Their sale is a domestic tragedy. They are to Wolfe only not quite so precious as his wife and children. He had built a fine house on Madison Avenue with a fine large room for his collection just before the war broke out. Being a merchant with extensive business connections at the Sunny South, he suffered, of course, from the reluctance of chivalric Southern debtors to pay what they owed a mere Northern mudsill, and this sale is thus made necessary.

Thence to No. 823. Letters from Paris announce the organization of a European branch of the Sanitary Commission at Paris, under the presidency of the Rev. Dr. McClintock. Rather important. What a big thing the Sanitary Commission is getting to be, with all these great fairs at Chicago, Cincinnati, and Boston, and with its great money receipts and its recognized position as an auxiliary to the army system! When we began its work in June, 1861, we used to talk of what we could do if we could only hope to secure fifty thousand dollars for our treasury. I have already received about nine hundred and twenty thousand dollars, and our branches at Boston, Philadelphia, Cleveland, and other cities have doubtless received as much more.

After dinner, to Mrs. Hamilton Fish's. That lady sent for me to discuss certain questions about the Metropolitan Fair. Her drawing room was very nice. There was the ex-governor and his wife, and pretty blonde Miss Susy, and one or two young ladies beside, and a general aspect of wealth and refinement agreeable to behold. Discoursed with Mrs. Fish about the

Fair and Mr. Fish about the approaching election to fill the vacant Columbia College professorship. He is non-committal as to his own views. Hope Lewis Rutherfurd will make him vote right.

Last Wednesday night with Ellie, Johnny, and Temple to the Academy of Music and heard *Der Freischütz* once more. It's among the loveliest of operas. Poor little Temple was as white as a sheet when the curtain fell on the grand pyrotechnic tableau of the third act. It's a pity Auschütz's season should come to an untimely end, as it does next Monday. He made a blunder in taking so large a house, but only two cities have a larger German population than New York, and it ought to sustain a German opera.

Nothing material in public affairs except the recapture of the *Chesapeake* and Lincoln's last joke. He has had an attack of varioloid and told some condoling friend that the disease was rather a subject of congratulation. For the first time since he became President, he felt he had something to *give* every man who called on him.

The New York *Herald* has discovered that within a day or two General Grant is to be next President and expatiates on his claims and merits in slashing, slangy editorials. Its former pet, McClellan, seems forgotten. Grant is certainly our most successful general and might probably make a good President, but that the *Herald* takes him up so earnestly is against him.

December 21.   Cold and clear, but tonight is overcast and there are flying snow squalls. To Columbia College meeting (special) at two. Report to Regents read and approved. The Committee on proposed School of Mines reported, and its recommendations were adopted *nem. con.* So the whole subject is now in our hands, to prepare a scheme and to nominate a professor of mineralogy and instructors in French and German. Then Lewis Rutherfurd, from the committee to whom were referred the testimonials in favor of the several candidates for the chair of physics, read an elaborate report, very well drawn, giving an analysis of the barrel of letters, certificates, and so forth, that had come before the committee. He moved to print all the testimonials for the use of members of the board, but Bradford demurred to the motion and it was withdrawn. Draper's nomination was also withdrawn, so we had three candidates: Barnard, Peck, and Rood. The more important papers in support of each were called for and read. There seemed a general disposition to go into an election at once, and we resolved to do so. John Astor and I were tellers. The result was Rood twelve, Peck eight, Barnard two. So Rood is elected—a very satisfactory result. I telegraphed to him at once. Davies and Peck will be profoundly disgusted, and the former may resign, but I do not believe he will. Let him, if he wants to.

The Bishop asked Morgan Dix, Dr. Haight, Gouverneur Ogden, and myself to remain after the meeting as he wanted our advice about certain matters connected with that impecunious institution, the General Theological Seminary. He says that efforts to raise funds in its aid are coldly met by three classes of churchmen; first, of course, by the representatives of the old evangelical party of twenty years ago; second, by those who are indignant at the blundering (if not corrupt) mismanagement of its affairs under the old regime; third, by such strong High Churchmen as T. B. Coddington, Stephen P. Nash, Mumford, and D. A. Cushman, who will do nothing for an institution that employs rebel sympathizers like Seabury and Mahan as professors. This last, it seems, is the most serious objection the friends of the seminary have to meet. I'm surprised and gratified that it is. I advised the Bishop that this was not a political prejudice but a reasonable, well-founded disapproval. The institution through which the Church teaches and trains those who are to teach and train us and our children should be free from suspicion of sympathy with treason and rebellion, especially with a rebellion got up by systematic lying to support and strengthen a system of woman-flogging and children-selling and all manner of abominations.

To 823 a while and home to dinner late. After dinner with Ellie to Academy of Music. Gounod's *Faust*. House filled to its utmost capacity, so capricious and unaccountable are our audiences. The opera has its good points but is, on the whole, a bore. Gounod does his best, but he cannot write melodies, and three hours and a half of unmelodic music are severe. Mrs. Schuyler died yesterday in perfect serenity. . . .[24]

The official history of Columbia prepared in celebration of the one hundred and fiftieth anniversary of the founding of King's College discreetly glosses over Richard S. McCulloh's retirement to enter the service of the Confederacy. It says merely that he left in 1863 "to participate actively in the conflict." The vacancy was now admirably filled, as Strong records, by the election of Ogden N. Rood, a graduate of the College of New Jersey. He became a physicist of international eminence, and lived to lay the cornerstone of the new Physics Building on Morningside Heights in 1896; he died in 1902, at the age of seventy-one. He is best known for his work on optics.

[24] Eliza Hamilton Schuyler, granddaughter of Alexander Hamilton, wife of George Lee Schuyler, and mother of the well-known welfare worker Louisa Lee Schuyler.

December 23.   At 823 with Agnew and Bellows, and with them again tonight at Van Buren's. . . . We have had matters of some interest before us, and especially the great case of Mr. Secretary Stanton *vs.* the Surgeon-General, and we concluded tonight that we must at once begin operations on the Surgeon-General's behalf.[25] My belief is that they have been delayed too long already. We propose to open the campaign with an address to the President by the Sanitary Commission and perhaps to follow this up by a circular to a few leading Congressmen which is already in type and has been signed by Agassiz, Peirce, Hill, and Longfellow of Harvard, and by a lot of eminent New York and Boston doctors. It may be a serious struggle. The first gun will be fired in the next (fifth) number of the *Bulletin.* It is an anonymous letter purporting to come from an outsider, asking information as to the meaning of the Surgeon-General's banishment to Knoxville, which letter I concocted last night. Agnew read it to Van Buren and Bellows this evening, and they heartily approved it without knowing who wrote it, which fact titillates my vanity quite agreeably.

Professor Rood called just after dinner and spent half an hour with me in the dining room. I never saw him but once, and had quite forgotten what he looked like. He impresses me most favorably and seems a real man—honest, unaffected, straightforward, and full of enthusiasm and earnestness.

December 25, FRIDAY.   Christmas has passed off satisfactorily. It has been the clearest of clear days and not so cold as yesterday. After breakfast, the children were admitted to the beatific vision of their presents and made the middle parlor a bedlam for an hour. Then we went to church. Great crowd. Aisles full of standing people. Vinton's sermon respectable. Music good. Wonderful to relate, the anthem was the "Gloria" of Mozart's No. 12. Has a note of Mozart's ever been sung in Trinity Church before? The fresh young boy-voices were delightful in the anthem, and even Ellie's highly educated ear was satisfied with its execution. I sent Cutler my compliments and congratulations through Dr. Vinton. . . . No. 24 dined with us this afternoon, also Miss Julia Ruggles. Others looked in after dinner. I took in Mrs. Ruggles the elder, Ellie's invaluable and admirable grandmamma. I fear she will not be with us next Christmas. She has immense vitality. Van Buren, who was called to see her in consultation with Whiting, says it is almost unprecedented in his prac-

[25] The antagonism between Stanton and Surgeon-General William A. Hammond, destined to end in Hammond's dismissal, was now reaching its crisis.

tice. But this cancerous disease is slowly draining her life. She perfectly understands the fact, and says she thinks she has probably lived about long enough and doesn't want to live a day after she becomes unable to be useful. Her serenity and kindliness are unruffled. She is a wonderful old lady. . . .

That ill-conditioned, vicious, pragmatical brute, John A. Stevens, Jr., has just undergone an experience that may do him good. At a wedding party supper the other night (at Charles A. Heckscher's) he proclaimed in presence and hearing of several McClellanizing army officers that "of course, no *gentleman* ever did or ever could accept a position on Mc-Clellan's staff." Whereupon his host grabbed him by the collar and marched him to the street door. He apologized next day. His friends say this indiscretion should not be remembered against him because wholly due to temporary *surexcitation alcoholique*. Perhaps. But he is an ugly fellow, drunk or sober. His sister, Mrs. Peter R. Strong, continues to live at her father's as a *femme sole*. Peter R. Strong lives at Newtown with his mother. Many villainous stories are circulated as to the cause of their separation, all which I wholly discredit. I am sure she must be as pure and womanly as she is beautiful, and I know him to be a good, honest, warm-hearted fellow, with a foible or two to which no wife could have any trouble in accommodating herself. The probable explanation of the case is this: The loss of their little girl two years ago visited her with morbid depression. Insanity is in her family; it has appeared in one of her sisters and in her uncle, Dr. Alexander H. Stevens. There may be in her blood (though it can hardly be imagined of any woman) some trace or infusion of the malignity and hatefulness that makes her brother, John A. Stevens, Jr., so odious. This may have developed and become manifest when she was suffering under mental disease and may have shewn itself in morbid antipathy to poor Peter, founded on some of his little weaknesses; for example, his everlasting gabble about high art and tone, and about his own dreadful state of impoverishment and pauperism. Anyhow, this is a very sad state of termination of what was a most promising love-match. I shall never forget how sweet and graceful she looked ten years ago last spring, on her wedding day, and how desperately in love with her was poor Peter, now abandoned and left desolate.

December 29. Signs of reaction and reconstruction seem to multiply in Arkansas, Louisiana, Florida, and elsewhere. It is difficult to estimate their value or to be quite sure that they exist at all. But we had few, if any, stories of the kind a year ago. Charleston had a very merry Christmas. One hundred and thirty shells had been thrown into her up to afternoon church time. Her newspapers reluctantly admit serious damage—houses burned and lives lost. A pretty performance for Christmas day; snap-dragon in earnest. But she deserves it all. Sowing the wind was an exhilarating chivalric pastime. Shelling Anderson out of Sumter was pleasant; resisting the whirlwind is less agreeable; to be *shelled back* is a bore.

December 30. Mrs. Lane, Mrs. Sherwood, Macdonough, White, and Bellows spent the evening here in council over the Fair with the treasuress. I sat apart, representing the galleries and throwing in applause and groans at intervals. The debates were interesting. The male committee wants to hold the Fair in a building to be put up by the city on the Palace Garden lots in Fourteenth Street, and to be used afterwards as an armory for the Twenty-second Regiment, which already occupies part of the ground. Griswold Gray is manipulating the board of supervisors in a rather blundering way, and the plan smells of jobbery. The other locality, the Manice building (Broadway and Sixth Avenue), seemed to find favor tonight.

Committee on Columbia College School of Mines met today; Betts, Torrey, Edward Jones, and I at Betts's office. We agreed on young Egleston as our man for metallurgy and mineralogy, and I called on him afterwards, but he was out. . . . Southern correspondents of British newspapers begin to write darkly and despondingly of the prospects of slaveholding, woman-flogging Secessia, so dear to the gentry and the traders of Britain. In spite of myself, I feel more and more bitter against England every day for the moral support her ruling classes have given this atrocious rebellion and at the same time more and more sorry for her exposure and degradation. I had reverenced her so long and so heartily that this revelation of her insincerity and baseness is a shock to my moral sense. It's as if I were to discover that one of my most intimate and trusted friends was a humbug and a scoundrel.

December 31. 1863 A.D. is now *in extremis*. It has proved a far better year for the country than it promised at its birth. If its nascent successor prove half as propitious to the national cause, it will witness the downfall of rebellion. So at least things look *now*. But only a very bold man can prophesy for a whole year ahead in these times.

1864

GRANT ASSUMES COMMAND · BATTLE OF THE WILDERNESS ·
SHERMAN'S MARCH BEGINS · SANITARY COMMISSION'S
METROPOLITAN FAIR · HAMMOND'S COURT-MARTIAL

*T*he year opened with the armies of Meade and Lee confronting each other along the Rapidan, where they were to stay until spring. Since its defeat at Gettysburg, Lee's Army of Northern Virginia had suffered a perceptible decline of fighting spirit, though it was still a most formidable organization. The only other large Confederate force was that concentrated at Dalton, Georgia, under Joseph E. Johnston, who had succeeded Bragg. It was now possible for the Union command, for the first time in the war, to make detailed plans for the simultaneous and relentless movement of its forces toward the destruction of all the main Confederate units. The day of independent operations by various Northern armies was at an end. In token of this fact, Congress in February revived the grade of lieutenant-general and authorized the President to appoint an officer of that rank to command all the military elements. Grant was summoned east, and on March 9, meeting Lincoln for the first time, received his commission. Although he had at first thought of remaining in the West, he realized that this was impossible, and on March 26 established his headquarters at Culpeper, Sherman taking over the chief western command. A grand plan of campaign was laid out by which, as soon as spring weather made action possible, Ben Butler's Army of the James was to move against Petersburg, Meade's Army of the Potomac was to move against Lee, Sigel was to invade the Shenandoah, and Sherman was to advance in Georgia against Johnston.

Meanwhile, in February, Northern troops captured Meridian, Mississippi, destroying much Confederate property; and General Gillmore landed at Jacksonville, Florida, sending columns into the interior of the state, and before the end *of the month capturing Tallahassee. Under the Draft Act, great new levies were being poured into the Union armies. As the odds against the South lengthened, the debates in the Confederate Congress took on a note of desperation. Bills were passed early in 1864 to abolish many of the exemptions in the Southern conscription system and to employ Negroes, both free and slave, for labor with the Southern armies. The blockade was now a net of strangulating power, and the Southern railway system was fast wearing out.*

More of Strong's time than ever was consumed by his work as treasurer of the Sanitary Commission. For one reason, the battle between Surgeon-General Hammond, whose work the Commission greatly admired, and Secretary Stanton, was reaching its climax. For another, the finances of the Commission for the first months of the year were in a parlous state; and some of the officers of the monster money-raising fair organized early in the year were more zealous than discreet.

January 1, FRIDAY. By these presents, I wish a Happy New Year to all mankind except Jefferson Davis and his group. To them, I wish virtue enough to withstand urgent daily temptations to hang themselves.

Routed out of bed early (for me) to look over certain papers which Knapp had thought important enough to be sent from Washington by special messenger. They were about the Surgeon-General's case. Knapp has shown our letter to the President (No. 73, protesting against the Surgeon-General's removal without a hearing) to Nicolay, the President's private secretary, who raised certain objections to it, and dissuaded Knapp from handing it in. . . . They were founded on considerations of official propriety and etiquette. . . . But they did not convince me, nor have they convinced any of the committee. We telegraphed Knapp to hand in the letter and shall follow it up *totis viribus*. But we shall fail. Stanton is a strong man. He has made up his mind to commit this injustice, and we can hardly hope to prevent him. . . .

January 2. Governor Seymour has undertaken to remove our efficient Police Commissioners for making a "partisan" report about the July rioters, his particular "friends." He is an unprincipled politician, and I believe he deserves the infamous place he will occupy in our history. The validity of this official act will be questioned.[1]

[1] Seymour's attempt to remove Commissioners Acton and Bergen, who had dealt efficiently with the draft riots and in their report had censured the encouragement given the rioters by "newspapers and parties of influence and intelligence," broke down. The two men refused to quit office. In the end the legislature created a new four-headed commission which included the two officials, Acton being president.

January 5. . . . Archbishop Hughes is dead. Pity he survived last June and committed the imbecility of his address to the rioters last July. That speech blotted and spoiled a record which the Vatican must have held respectable, and against which Protestants had nothing to say, except, of course, "Babylon," "Scarlet Woman," and "anti-christ."[2]

Governor Seymour's message is understood to be a most copper-heady manifesto. Very likely. He seems strangely blind to the signs of the times. I supposed him sagacious and politic, though utterly base and selfish and incapable of any patriotic national impulse. But the manifestations of his malignity are those of a boor and not of a subtle politician.

January 7. Still this cold grey weather. There is every promise tonight of more snow. Met George Griswold this morning by appointment, and we called on General Dix to invite him to become president of the Union League Club, vice Robert B. Minturn resigned and gone to Europe. The General "will think of it," and probably say "no" at last. He is scrupulous about joining any organization that has any sort of *political* aspect while he is in government service. Apropos of clubs, the general election at the Century comes off next Saturday, and old Verplanck, its founder and its president since it was first organized seventeen years ago, is to be scratched as a Copperhead.[3] So are Edward Cooper and [William H.] Appleton the bookseller, who are on certain standing committees. Sorry for Verplanck, but *fiat justitia*. George Bancroft is put up as opposition candidate. William C. Bryant would have run better, for most people hold Bancroft an erudite ass. The opposition will be strong but probably unsuccessful. It will have my reluctant vote against Verplanck.

Downtown, called on by Richard Grant White and Frothingham of Brooklyn about fairs. There are many funny incidents in the history of the Metropolitan Fair, which I have no time to record. "Miss Leonora Jones," who got into the executive committee of ladies somehow, is now reported to be not only a very disagreeable old maid, but a suspicious character, and is (according to Acton) under surveillance by the police.

[2] Archbishop John Hughes, a zealous Union man, had labored in Europe to promote the national cause. His speech to the draft rioters, or rather to a general crowd, gently urging them to go home and live in peace, showed his failing mental powers, for he was an ill man.

[3] Gulian C. Verplanck (1786–1870), as lovable as he was versatile, had been out of public life since he left the State Senate in 1841, though he was still a regent of the University of the State of New York, and head of the Board of Commissioners of Emigration. He was distinguished for crotchety opinions and conservatism.

Pleasant. Told White to take the responsibility of leaving her name off the printed list. Then there is this delectable mess about poor Mrs. John Sherwood's high-falutin' circular, about Queen Victoria and Prince Albert, and "Humanity" as "a greater than" Queen Victoria, and so on, and how people guffawed over it, and how visitors on New Year's Day asked the lady who could have written that ridiculous circular, and how it was decided privily to suppress it, and how Mrs. Fish and Mrs. Lane spent a morning in burning up a cord or two of printed copies. All that is funny, but it's a sore mortification to the poor lady, whose role is to be clever and to have a literary salon and put little pomes into the *Atlantic Monthly* and be intimate with Everett and Longfellow. She is really intelligent and cultivated. How could she have made such a goose of herself?[4]

At half-past one, William Schermerhorn and I, with our tetanic librarian Mr. Jones, had a Columbia College library committee meeting in my office, and at two I went into William Betts's office for a meeting of the Committee on School of Mines: Betts, Edward Jones, and myself. We were harmonious. I took Jones to the office of the Copake Iron Works (Nassau Street) and introduced him to Egleston, and then went uptown to 823, where I had three hours of work over Sanitary Commission affairs. Our financial spasm was relieved yesterday afternoon, temporarily at least, by drafts for fifty thousand dollars from California, and the Commission has now about ninety thousand dollars in the bank. But our expenses for December were sixty-four thousand dollars, so this is a mere palliative. Home at six.

January 8. Thackeray is dead! It is an historical event. His *Snob Papers* and *Vanity Fair* and (probably) *Esmond* will live long. Only Tennyson, Dickens, and Carlyle are left in England to produce anything likely to be remembered fifty years hence, and I think Carlyle has survived his faculty for production.[5] I should think Dickens in like case but for his last Christmas story, *Mrs. Lirriper's Lodgings*, in which are gleams of humor worthy his best days.

[4] Mrs. John Sherwood, who had been Mary Elizabeth Wilson before her marriage in 1851 to a New York attorney, was a prolific author on social life and etiquette, and prided herself on knowing all the chief literary figures of the day. She was secretary of the Metropolitan Fair, Mrs. Hamilton Fish being president; Richard Grant White was secretary of the male auxiliary.

[5] Strong obviously wrote in haste. His diary shows ample appreciation of Browning, Kingsley, Trollope, and others. This very month he mentions reading Charles Reade's *Very Hard Cash*, "a novel of the special-abuse-corrective school" aimed at the English lunacy system, and gives it high praise.

January 9. Nothing noteworthy at No. 823 this afternoon. At Century Club tonight was the annual election and a great crowd; one hundred and seventy-six votes polled, an unprecedented number. It was understood this morning that Verplanck had been advised by his friends not to run and had decided to decline a reëlection. But unfortunately for him and for his personal friends like myself, he did not so decide, so I had to vote against him. The result was Verplanck 61, Bancroft 110, scattering 5. Considering Verplanck's popularity and his long identification with the Club, and Bancroft's foibles and snobbishness, this is an encouraging sign. Twenty people said to me tonight, in substance: "How unpleasant it is to vote for a snob like Bancroft, and against my old friend Verplanck! But Verplanck's Copperhead talk is intolerable." I think our Union League Club has done something toward educating people's moral sense up to this point.

Verplanck means to be and tries to be a loyal, patriotic citizen, after his kind. But he is naturally incapable of warm, hearty, generous impulses, except in his personal relations, and (like the Bourbons) he "learns nothing and forgets nothing." He does not see how times have changed and how fast they are changing. He looks on the great national movement that is growing stronger every day and already controls the conduct of the war just as he looked on the ravings of the little knot of philanthropes and infidels that constituted the Abolition Society twenty-five years ago.

January 11. . . . After dinner, and after giving Johnny a little Latin and a little algebra, which he has just begun and to which he seems to take kindly, I went to Trinity Church vestry meeting at Trinity Chapel schoolhouse on Twenty-fifth Street, a change of locality which seems like to be permanent. We agreed informally on the Rev. Mr. Wilson of St. Peter's, Albany, as Hobart's successor, but I doubt if he will give up his position as rector of an important parish for any subordinate position, even for that of assistant minister to an assistant minister in Trinity Church itself. The question about the new organ for Trinity Church was discussed and laid over. Dunscomb and Tillou brayed adversely. They are two most irritating and obstructive nuisances and waste much time at every vestry meeting. Their respective types of mischievous imbecility are beautifully contrasted; quite an elaborate and instructive essay could be written about them, a parallel, after the manner of Plutarch. I have time only to suggest the prominent distinction. Dunscomb cannot see that two and two are four, and confesses his inability with a frankness that would be touching but for its prolixity of expression. He deals mainly with the commonplaces of fogyism and dullness and relies on the danger of committing the vestry prematurely to this mathematical proposition, the possibility that it may be abused by designing men, the importance of taking time to consider it, and the fact that our predecessors have for many years past taken no action that expressly affirmed it. But Tillou, though fully equal to Dunscomb in argumentation of this kind, commonly asserts, also, that he "is not prepared to say" that two and two are not five, and on the whole, he thinks that "as at present advised" his "sense of duty as a member of this important corporation" will compel him to vote that they *are* five and possibly even five and a half.

January 16, SATURDAY.   To Washington Tuesday morning by the usual railroad; Agnew, Wolcott of Boston, and Harris on board. It was our first experience of the new arrangement that takes people around Philadelphia instead of carrying them by horse-car through its monotonous streets. We got to our journey's end two hours behind time. The delays and detentions were intolerable. But near us sat a lady with two children, both lovely, and I established a sentimental intimacy with the elder, a perfect little gem of a roley-poley, blue-eyed, curly-wigged creature some six years old, and we got on famously together. . . .

Willard's absolutely worse than ever; crowded, dirty, and insufferable. Agnew and I were put into one room in an obscure corner of the top story, accessible only by an enterprising and difficult escalade. It had the advantage of being traversed by certain steam pipes, connected with a large iron tank in the garret. They leaked and gave us the benefit of an atmosphere warmed by escaping steam and flavored with oleaginous vapors; also of a persistent noise, "as of a hidden brook in the leafy month of June," and somewhat as of frying sausages likewise. Dinner next day abominable, especially in point of attendance. Waiters a crowd of "What-is-it"-s or perhaps refugee field hands, incapable of being enlisted even as teamsters, cooks, or military bootblacks. I shifted my quarters last night to No. 244 F Street, where I got a good third story room and a comfortable bed. I took my meals out at Buhler's restaurant, a vile place (hippopotamus and cassowary served up as beef and turkey), and yesterday at "the Occidental," a degree or two better.

Our session was satisfactory, though Van Buren and Gibbs were missed. We elected Charles J. Stillé a full member. Bache and Newberry and Bishop Clark were with us.

Yesterday, I called on the Surgeon-General at his house in K Street.

He has just returned from Nashville and still suffers from the effects of his very serious fall downstairs. He can walk only on crutches, both legs being still paralyzed below the knee, but is gaining ground slowly and profoundly interested in the minute scientific observations and experiments he is making on his own case and diligently recording. Highly characteristic of the man. So is his talk about his feud with Stanton. The Secretary is manifestly hesitating before he pushes the case further. Our letter to the President and the circular to members of Congress (whereof more hereafter) shewed him that there was a hornets' nest in that bush, and that if he stirred it up, he might get stung. So being politic as well as arbitrary, he told a Senator to tell a surgeon to tell Hammond that he would abandon the persecution if H. would consent to let bygones be bygones. To which Hammond responded that he would be glad to do so if the Secretary would apologize, but that if the Secretary wouldn't, he must have a court-martial. From what Will Winthrop tells me (Theodore's brother, who is attached to the Judge Advocate-General's office), there will doubtless be a court, and probably an unfriendly one. The Surgeon-General gave me an outline of the case, and on *his* showing it is plain enough, of course. He proposed to try his own case, without counsel, against which preposterous course I gave him advice gratis, most emphatically.

As to the circular. It was signed by Agassiz and Peirce of Harvard, among others, and they were at Washington last week attending a session of the National Academy of Sciences. Stanton was asked to meet them at dinner, and replied Stantonically, "Meet them at dinner! I'd rather send them both to Fort Lafayette!!!" But when the Wise Men heard this, their hearts failed them and their knees became as water, because they had given offence to a great mandarin and a Cabinet member; so they declared it was all a forgery and a fabrication. They never signed the circular or did anything else that could be displeasing unto so sweet a prince—God forbid they should presume to take on themselves to do this thing! Did the Honorable Secretary suppose they didn't know their place? Of course, they knowed their place. Were they not even as dead dogs before our Honorable Secretary? Of course, they were; and that's my opinion, too.

Colonel (Dr.) Hamlin, a nephew of the Vice-President's, seems a remarkably clear, well-informed man. Much pleased, also, with a Colonel Andrews of Marietta, an intelligent man with a tawny, leonine beard, who has seen much service and talks strategy and geology.

Boston sends us fifty thousand dollars from the proceeds of her fair. This makes the treasury comfortable. I see clearly that the Commission is more generally recognized and appreciated than ever before. Senator Foster praised and magnified it as having become a great power in the land, which I think it be. But my role is to depreciate and diminish when I hear people talk that way. This, by the by, may be our last session at Washington. Talking with Bishop Clark in that crowded sty, the lobby of Willard's, and exchanging condolences over our respective experiences of dirt, discomfort, and inattention, I asked him WHY we should expose ourselves to these torments? What do we gain by meeting "near" the seat of government that would not be more than counterbalanced by the advantage of meeting elsewhere and shewing ourselves to our branches? The prelate received the suggestion as a shark gobbles a porgy and brought the subject forward next day. After much discussion, we agreed to hold a special meeting at Philadelphia in March, and our quarterly meeting at some point west of the Alleghenies, probably Cincinnati—whereat Dr. Newberry rejoiced greatly.

At Gettysburg, Lee used the cupola of the seminary, while his hospital flag was flying from it, to reconnoitre the field, and from that position went out the order for the final attack, which failed as it deserved. So Stillé was told by a theological student who was in the cupola when Lee and his staff came up here with their glasses.[6] Sich is chivalry. Lee would not have done this five years ago. Bad company has degraded him. No gentleman can fight two years to sustain the right of men to flog women, without damage to his moral sense.

January 17. . . . Intercepted rebel correspondence is entertaining and instructive. Rebel agents abroad are making and losing great sums in their blockade-running lottery, while their people at home suffer and starve. It is curious to observe how freely these agents of the Confederacy talk of assigning to Louis Napoleon Texas, or even Louisiana and Arkansas and everything west of the Mississippi, as a bribe that might at last induce one Power of Christendom to recognize the Confederacy and a new nation of women-floggers. Their first principle is the right of every state to secede whenever it pleases, but they are ready to make any state a colony of a foreign power if the interests of their dirty rebellion will be thereby promoted.

January 20. . . . George Anthon dined here. After dinner with him

---

[6] Lee watched Pickett's charge seated on his horse Traveller on low ground back of the Confederate batteries, now marked by the Virginia monument.

to German opera at the Academy of Music; Wagner's *Tannhäuser*. A crowded house. Much of the opera is a mere dilution of its very effective overture, and much of it is as unmusical as Robert Browning's hard, dry, crabbed, unmelodic rhymes are *unpoetical*. But there are good points in the second act.

January 22. . . . To 823 Broadway, where were Newberry and Bellows just from Washington. The Surgeon-General's court-martial is sitting. It refused an adjournment to allow him to bring on his most important witness, J. R. Smith, from Little Rock. But Hammond thinks well of the court and sees no symptom of prejudice or partiality. I do not expect an acquittal, though I am confident his case is honest and good. Some impulsive blunder of his will probably spoil it, and Stanton is an ugly adversary.

Went off by myself after dinner and heard Boïeldieu's *Dame Blanche* (in German) at the Academy of Music. It is a bright, sparkling, pretty opera, and I hope I may hear it again. The composer has worked in sundry phrases from old Scotch melodies, quite effectively, and has stolen from Haydn, as most composers of the second-rank used to do until the new generation arose which knows not Haydn and doesn't know enough of music to be aware that his conceptions are worth stealing. Stopped at Mr. Ruggles's for Ellie on my way home. Nothing talked of now but the Fair.

Extracts from rebel newspapers that are produced in our own are unusually interesting. The proposal to put every male adult into the rebel ranks, to make Jefferson Davis practically dictator, to repudiate the Confederate debt, and then to raise a few hundred millions by direct taxation, makes Southerners open their eyes wide. There are complaints and protests and signs of recalcitration. The statistical and chivalric DeBow himself, whilom apostle of slavery and First Gent-in-Waiting to the late King Cotton, has been suppressed and locked up because of an article in which for the first time in his life he uttered a little common sense. North Carolina is particularly disgusted and wants to know *why* North Carolinians should be legislated out of their houses and into the states they profess to represent and whose legislation is inoperative as against their own nominal constituencies. It is a pertinent inquiry. But Jefferson Davis has his foot on the neck of North Carolina and will be little embarrassed by editorials. Conscription will be vigorously pushed, and there will be a desperate convulsive effort to overwhelm us at some

weak point—probably in East Tennessee, where Longstreet seems offering battle already. A Captain Leggett (one of the Whitestone and Westchester County Quaker family), who was at 823 yesterday and seems
intelligent and trustworthy, is just from Knoxville and says our men
there and at Chattanooga are in most fearful destitution on much less
than half rations and with no hospital supplies at all. Hammerstein told
us something of the state of things there Sunday night, but it seems far
worse than I supposed. We have been straining hard to get supplies
forward, but transportation cannot be had in any way or on any terms.
Wagon trains are impracticable over the mountain roads, and the one
line of single-track railroad on which Grant's army depends is unequal
to the movement of ordnance stores alone. The road is worn out. Trains
traverse it at the rate of five miles an hour and run off the track on an
average twice a day. The country is stripped, and its loyal population is
perishing for want of food. What immeasurable misery this causeless
rebellion has brought on our people!

Thank God, the signs of reaction and reorganization grow stronger
every day. "Healthy granulations" appear in the mangled tissues at
last. Barring military disaster, we may expect to see Free State Governments established in Arkansas and Louisiana before next May. Maryland
and Missouri are fast developing into Free States, and I think Kentucky
and Tennessee will not be long behind them. But the rebellion is not yet
suppressed, by any manner of means, and we have yet much hard work to
do. God prosper it!

January 23. . . . . Walked uptown with George Anthon, who is very
full of complaint against the discipline of the College, and with ample
reason, I fear. A little Freshman named Fanshawe, an *élève* of his school,
has just been dismissed for illicit absences, or "sloping," as the boys call
it now. The practice was known in my day as "playing hookey." It was
exceptional then, but seems to have become general among our undergraduates. This boy has been absent from his college duties two days
out of three since the present session began, and no notice was given his
father. The indications are that the discipline of the College is only
nominal. Professor Bull Anthon says that he often has only seven or eight
in his lecture room out of a class or section of thirty. Professor Joy tells
me he ceased reporting absences some time ago, because it did no good.
I fear King has become utterly unfit for his place. Fanshawe *père* means to
bring this case before the trustees, and I think it will raise a storm.

George Anthon thinks Fanshawe *fils* unjustly treated, wants him reinstated, and is going about stirring up Fish and Edward Jones and others
of the board.

January 24, SUNDAY. . . . The confidence every one seems to feel in the
speedy downfall of rebellion surprises me. We shall have the hardest
fighting of the war before next June. Suppose the rebels move their seat
of government from Richmond to Columbia and send the bulk of Lee's
army to reinforce Longstreet and Bragg, leaving a small force in fortified
camps to retard Meade's pursuit through a difficult and desolate country.
They would hazard the loss of Virginia and North Carolina, but they
might annihilate our army in the Southwest.[7]

January 27. At two o'clock Columbia College Committee on School
of Mines at William Betts's office; Betts, Dr. Torrey, Rutherfurd, and
Edward Jones. Also, young Egleston, our proposed professor. All seem
to enter heartily into the plan, even the classical Betts himself. Session
was satisfactory and lasted an hour and a half. . . .

Eight P.M. at Bishop Potter's in Twenty-fourth Street, where was an
assemblage of some twenty-five, cleric and lay, convoked by the Bishop
to consider what can be done about the insolvent Theological Seminary.
There were the bishops of New Jersey and New Hampshire, the Rev.
Dr. Coxe (whom I decidedly like), S. P. Nash, George William Wright,
poor old Verplanck, Bayard Clarke (!), Mr. Ruggles, the Rev. Mr.
Morgan of St. Thomas's, John Caswell, Cyrus Curtiss, Kemble, Henry
Pierrepont, Professor Drisler, Samuel Davis, and others; also, a delegation
from the diocese of Western New York. Pierrepont, treasurer of the
seminary, read an elaborate and doleful financial statement. The Rev.
Mr. Morgan read a spirited letter from Bishop Delancey, and Bishop
Potter gave us an earnest and forcible address on the importance of
sustaining the seminary, which nobody can deny. But the disloyalty of
[Milo] Mahan and [Samuel] Seabury, two of its chief teachers, chills
my ardor in its cause. I cannot exert myself to raise money to support
two learned and able men in influencing—unconsciously perhaps, and

---

[7] This was not such an amateurish idea as it appears. The Union forces in the
West this winter were too widely scattered for safety. Thomas had part of the troops
at Chattanooga; John M. Schofield had others at Knoxville; Logan had still others at
Huntsville, Alabama; and some were at Meridian and Vicksburg in Mississippi.
Jefferson Davis and Lee both urged Joe Johnston to take the offensive and cut up the
Federal forces in detail. Indeed, Lee believed that if Johnston and Longstreet united
in an army reinforced from the East, they could move into middle Tennessee, divide
Thomas and Schofield, and then strike at each separately. But Johnston, always cautious,
rejected this plan.

certainly unintentionally—the next generation of our clergymen to sympathize with rebellion and slave-breeding and to underrate the value of our national life. I was among the first to come away, but the understanding seemed to be that the Bishop should call another and larger meeting to consider the case and organize a movement for general contributions by the laity. . . .

Nothing authentic from that vital centre of contest, the region of Chattanooga and Knoxville. Should we win another important battle there and dispose of Bragg or Longstreet, Seceshdom would be manifestly moribund and peace probably close at hand. But I count on no such good luck. We may be thankful if we escape grave retarding disaster at that most critical point.

January 28. Library committee of Columbia College at half-past one (Professor Anderson and William Schermerhorn), with our hysterical librarian, considering whether we can possibly so modify our regulations as to let the president and professors invade the library and carry off as many books as they please, whether the librarian be present to register the issue or not. King, being probably irritated by latent gout, made a little fuss about our "unreasonable restrictions" at the last meeting of the board. But we will not relax them "if the committee know itself, and it think it do."

Standing Committee of Trinity Church vestry met tonight at the vestry office. All the eight present. Sundry real estate matters disposed of. Ogden brought forward a proposition to raise temporarily the salaries of all assistant ministers having families, by reason of increased cost of living. This produced a discordant debate. Old Dunscomb ventilated his old speech about corporate debt and corporate expenses, to which I have listened two hundred and fifty times during the last sixteen years, and we were unable to agree on any recommendation to the vestry. This question of increasing debt and diminishing estate is a very grave and urgent question, nevertheless, and none the less serious because a blockhead bores us with prose and platitudes about it. I suggested that we might sell our unproductive real estate, or some of it, and assign the proceeds to some two or three of our number as trustees of a sinking fund in time for the payment of debt; and Cisco and Ogden and others received the suggestion very favorably. I must try to put the outline of resolutions to this effect on paper and see how they look and whether any such scheme can be devised that will hold water.

January 31, SUNDAY.   Mrs. Ellie is deep in Charles Reade's novel,

Very Hard Cash, and much interested. It is certainly the most artistic and effective sensation-novel I know.

Tomorrow's meeting of Columbia College trustees may prove important to the interests of the College. They need attention. If a Freshman can absent himself from recitations about three days out of four during the last four months and his parents know nothing of it; if it be not very unusual for Bull Anthon and Drisler to have about ten students attending their lectures out of a section of thirty; if Joy and other professors have ceased to report absences "because it does no good"; if notes excusing absence written by young sisters or forged by the young gentlemen themselves are practically sufficient to account for their default— then is the College a positive evil to the community. It would be far better for our undergraduates were they working at counting-house desks, where they would be obliged to be punctual, diligent, and attentive to their daily duties. The little smattering of Greek, physics, and so on which our average undergraduate gains . . . is no compensation for the relaxed moral sense, the indifference to the obligations of duty, the general slovenliness of character, whereby he is demoralized at the critical period and decisive turning-point of his whole life, by our defective discipline. I am not by any means sure that the endowment of Columbia College has not done the community more harm than good for the last ten years. I fear it is like "Dr. Dulcimer's suburban establishment for the idler members of the youthful aristocracy" of New York— *vide* Kingsley's clever *Water Babies* story.

February 1. Columbia College trustees met as usual at two o'clock, and it was an interesting session. The Bishop was absent and so was Rutherfurd. Minutes of the board (faculty) were read, disclosing its action in the case of Fanshawe the Freshman. A. W. Bradford thereupon made a quiet but very strong speech—very telling indeed—disclosing what he had heard of the case and of the discipline of the College and dwelling on our personal responsibility for whatever might be wrong. He offered two resolutions; first (as afterwards modified), that the faculty be recommended to reconsider their decision as to Fanshawe; and second, for a committee of investigation with power to examine professors and students. Edward Jones followed him up vigorously. Mr. Samuel B. Ruggles suggested that we ought not to act without hearing the President, who sat mute. So King made a statement of his views of the matter, and of the facts as he understood them. It was most candid, frank, and manly, but deplorably irresponsive and unsatisfactory. It was without his usual fire and spirit, listless and indifferent, as if it were a subject in which he felt no personal interest. The first resolution passed by a large majority, only Morgan Dix, Robert Ray, and one other voting no. I was surprised the negative vote was so small, for the precedent is mischievous and bad. If we undertake to sit as a court of appeals and revise decisions of the faculty, we weaken College discipline still further and shall be run down with personal application for redress whenever a contumacious Sophomore is sentenced to the penalty of admonition. This being disposed of, Fish put the question on Bradford's Resolution No. 2, or rather was about putting it, when King begged leave to say a single word. The passage of that resolution would be a vote of censure and would terminate his connection with the College at once. He was already contemplating resignation—had been for some time. Must confess he was growing old. Had lost some of his interest in the College. Did not feel equal to his official duties any longer. Must in any event tender his resignation, to take effect whenever the board should be ready to act upon it, provided such action were not delayed beyond next June. Great respect and regard for everybody and assurances of most distinguished consideration to every member of the board. Bradford made a kind little speech and withdrew his second resolution; thereby shewing he had more tact and presence of mind than I. For my first view of his course was that he was shewing absolute want of backbone and of sense of official duty. But I now perceive that it would have been ungracious and unnecessary to wound and affront the President after he had volunteered to do the very thing we all wanted of him. After he had decided on committing academic *hara-kiri* and announced his intention of so doing, it would not have been worth while for us to embitter this long-wished-for act of self-"abolishment."

We did a great deal of business beside. . . . The Grammar School of Columbia College *fuit*. It belongs to history alone. The foul, ill-ventilated den in which I was bullied, insulted, and tormented from October, 1832, to October, 1834, was pulled down years ago. The school itself ceased to exist this blessed afternoon. I signed the report recommending its abolition with a thrill of keen satisfaction and voted aye on the motion to adopt the recommendation with a feeling that long-cherished views of vengeance were fulfilled at last. In no decade of my life since 1834 has there been one hundredth part the sense of misery (oppression, terrorism, subjugation, tyranny) that I was wilting under every day of those two dark years of suffering at the Grammar School. Yet I was ambitious and interested in my work far beyond the average schoolboy standard, and was busying myself even during those brief but most lovely holidays at Whitestone in writing out Greek translations. I loved study, and a kind, sympathetic teacher could have moulded me into something quite respectable. But, O Charles Anthon, LL.D., and Dr. Jemmy Quin, and Mr. James Shea (now defunct), how blind and stupid you were—you and all your subordinates! Should we meet in purgatory hereafter, and should the duty be assigned me of attending to your moral discipline, I think it will be executed with diligence.

It seems that Fish called on King last week to talk over this Fanshawe matter; told him there were growlings and grumblings among the trustees against his administration and enquired casually and parenthetically, "Why don't you resign this vexatious position?" King said this afternoon that there was prospect of discord in the faculty growing out of Professor Rood's election, and that this was an additional inducement to resign. I suppose it is Davies and Peck *vs.* Joy and Rood.

February 4. . . . Rood looked in awhile after dinner, and I went downtown at eight to a Trinity Church standing committee meeting. We sat till near eleven, and did much business. We should have done more but for Dunscomb's weary, viscid, irrelevant prosings. Cisco's carriage brought Ogden and me uptown. I brought forward a hastily drawn series of resolutions providing for a large sale of real estate to pay debt and the creation of a sinking fund to be vested in trustees and just beyond the reach of our corporate generosity. To my surprise, the scheme was unanimously approved and recommended for adoption by the vestry with its details unchanged. If adopted and resolutely carried out, it may save the church from insolvency, toward which it has been steadily settling down for many years past. There was also the question of selling scores of pews in the church and downtown chapels for the unpaid pew rents that have been accumulating for decades. Dunscomb ventilated sundry profound legal doubts about "incorporeal rights." He suffered severe pain and oppression in doing anything about "incorporeal rights," and tried to express the precise seat and nature of his malaise at great length, but without success. We disposed of the matter, leaving his doubts for investigation hereafter. There was the question of raising clerical salaries, or of temporary subsidies to certain of our assistant ministers, who need a little help in these hard times, and this we disposed of by a compromise, for it was growing very late.

The Metropolitan Fair becomes interesting. Its administration brings up a great ethical question: is raffling sinful? The Standing Committee of the Sanitary Commission discussed it fully ten days ago and decided to advise the managers of the Fair to exclude and prohibit raffling. I acquiesced, not very heartily, for it seemed to me that there was more fuss about the matter than it deserved. Afterwards I saw Mrs. Fish and others and found that our advice was likely to offend sundry efficient and valuable people who were working for the Fair; so I wrote a note to Bellows Tuesday, begging him to do nothing about it, offer no advice, and allow the Sanitary Commission to occupy a position of neutrality. But he sent the letter I had previously signed to both managing committees yesterday morning. Richard Grant White tells me today that it came before the Gentlemen's Committee last night, was respectfully received, and was responded to by a resolution that the committee does not yet see sufficient reasons for prohibiting a feature that is recognized by usage as appropriate to all fairs intended to raise money for humane, charitable, or religious purposes. What the Ladies' Committee will do about it, I do not know and cannot guess. I predict they will agree with the gentlemen.

President King, who had guided the destinies of Columbia since 1849, had outlived his usefulness to the institution, and Hamilton Fish did well in making the rather brusque suggestion that he resign. On March 7, the resignation was formally offered and was accepted to take effect at the ensuing June commencement. King's presidency had been fruitful in changes, the principal of which was the removal of the College to its new Forty-ninth Street site. But he had failed to perform the great task that Dr. McVickar had outlined in an address on his inauguration: to create, as a public figure and former business man, "a new bond of sympathy between the College and the needs and wants of our great commercial metropolis." The gulf between the city and the College was nearly as wide as ever. Among the men now considered for the presidency, though never powerfully supported, was Strong himself. As Strong's pages show, even in the midst of the war the College was growing. The curriculum had recently been broadened and more time was allowed for modern literature, for Latin and Greek, and for moral and intellectual philosophy as distinguished from pure metaphysics. Above all, the School of Mines—the first in the United States—was coming into existence. Its principal founder, Thomas Egleston, graduate of the Ecole des Mines in Paris, in the spring of 1863 had submitted to the trustees, as above noted, a plan of organization. This was studied and approved; the decision to set up the school was taken in May, 1863; some six months later the trustees authorized the use of rooms in the College building and the appointment of a professor without salary; and now, in February, 1864, Egleston was named for the chair. He set about organizing a faculty. The plan contemplated a school as strong in mathematics as West Point, as thorough in physics, chemistry, and other general sciences as the German universities, and as expert in metallurgical branches as the Ecole des Mines. Aided by two energetic young men, Charles F. Chandler and Francis L. Vinton, who also accepted appointments without salary, Egleston had the school ready to begin operations in the fall of 1864.

February 6. . . . Story of Mrs. S. G. Howe, [author of] *Passion Flowers,* inviting the Hon. Charles Sumner to dinner "to meet" certain notables of lower grade than his own. Sumner responds languidly that he has been engrossed so long by grand public questions that he has quite lost all interest in individuals. Mrs. Howe replies that she is glad to hear of his progress, for the Almighty has not reached that point *yet.*

February 8. Diligent in Wall Street. Uptown to Forty-ninth Street for a meeting of the College library committee at eight o'clock. An hour's ride by Third Avenue railroad cars, and so much time wasted, for there was nothing of any importance to be done. But I adjourned from the library with William Schermerhorn to Rood's lecture room, where he received us very cordially and exhibited and expatiated on our splendid apparatus. Our big Ruhmkorff coil was on the table and a battery was working, though feebly, in the next room; so Rood put them into connection, darkened the windows, and gave us a gorgeous exhibition of voltaic electricity passing through glass tubes containing bisulphide of carbon vapor, uranium, glass bulbs, tubes immersed in solution of sulphate of quinine, and so on. The beaded streams of colored light, blue, rose-pink, and green, were most lovely—far beyond any fireworks I ever saw. Rood seems a brick. How much there is I don't know!!!

Thence downtown to No. 823. After dinner to Trinity Church vestry meeting. The sinking fund system distrusted and referred back to the Standing Committee; not unreasonably, being a new proposition, without precedent, and certainly open to plausible objections. We agreed, however, to make a large sale at once for payment of debt, and perhaps some other arrangement can be devised whereby the proceeds of such sale and of all subsequent alienations of our endowment shall be inviolably devoted to that object. James G. King and Bradford shewed absence of good sense in their discourse about this question, as usual. The Rev. Mr. Wilson of St. Peter's, Albany, declines to become the subordinate of a subordinate, as I knew he would. Other candidates for Hobart's vacated place were talked about, but we came to no decision. Tillou's absence was a thing to be thankful for. It saved fifteen of us half an hour apiece.

February 11. Have just glanced through volume two of Count Gurowski's *Diary*. He is Thersites still; not sharp-eyed, however, for his blue spectacles have won him the title of Gig-lamps and Count Goggleowski. As to the fury of his patriotism, it's but justice to say that I believe this savage, merciless censor of everybody and everything would be in the field at the front but for his age and obesity.

He growls, as we all do, at our slow progress toward suppression of slavery and rebellion. Is not this because he keeps his eyes fixed on the hour-hand of the clock? Look back at July, 1861, and then look where Maryland, Missouri, and Arkansas stand in 1864; at West Virginia, and at the Mississippi relieved from rebel strangulation. Our progress has been beyond what we had any right to hope for three years ago, in spite of the blunders he attributes (very justly, I suppose) to McClellan, Scott, Halleck, and others. He is humiliated because rebel generals—Lee, Jackson, and so on—shew energy superior to ours. But did he ever try to gag an infuriated tom-cat? If he ever did, he would do well to remember that he found the job troublesome, and that he did not feel inclined to give the tom-cat higher rank than his own on the scale of being because of its difficulty. . . .

Old Gurowski holds Lincoln and all his ministers and generals (except Wadsworth and one or two others) knaves or fools or both, and scolds more viciously and in worse language than any Russian count I've lately heard of. Many of his points are strong, but his style and temper are those of an enraged Tartar Khan, full of raw horse and bad liquor. This book will exert little influence. His epithets for the Woods, Barlows, Brookses, and all that race of vermin are various, novel, pungent, and sometimes unsavory. He deplores the probability of Lincoln's reëlection and thinks Stanton the man for the time. So don't I. Anyway that probability grows stronger daily.

February 15, MONDAY. Cold weather. Dyspeptic and atrabilious. Busy day, nevertheless. Columbia College Committee on School of Mines at Betts's office. Prospects good. Egleston may prove a great acquisition. He seems full of energy, enterprise, fire, and snap. At 823: the raffling question creates much talk. A long string of parsons sign a protest against the Fair in yesterday's *Times*. . . .

Our columns in the Southwest are moving, and newspaper strategists are racking their brains for good guesses at the plan of the coming campaign. But in East Tennessee, Secesh has the initiative and threatens Knoxville again. The Army of the Potomac is mired and stationary, as usual. There must soon be hard fighting in the Gulf States. Secesh would prefer to fall back, concentrating—its true policy. But the morale of its army is too low to bear this process. With a little more discouragement, such as retreat and abandonment of territory would produce, the cohorts of Bragg and Johnston would be disorganized by desertions and mutiny. So Secesh will have to fight. Defeat on a large scale will be damaging to us, though not irreparable, but to them it will be final and fatal. Rebellion can hardly survive another Gettysburg or Lookout Mountain. Guerrillas and rapparees would continue to steal cows and hang niggers for a season, but it would not be long. . . . In North Carolina there is increase of ferment. She seems tempted to kick out of the traces, if we can rely on indications from the Raleigh newspapers. But after all, their most minatory utterances are equalled by disloyal articles in the *Daily News* and other Northern treason-papers—or *newsance-papers*.

February 17.   Busy downtown today over various matters (resisting death by frost, among them). Afterwards at 823. Money still comes in from the Pacific Coast to sustain the Sanitary Commission. Another fifty thousand dollars received from San Francisco yesterday. That chrysogonous city has pledged twenty-five thousand dollars per month during 1864, and has paid up its first four instalments. Our monthly expenses for 1863 averaged forty-eight thousand dollars and seventeen cents. So we shall need further contributions. We shall probably get them from the Brooklyn Fair (February 22), and the Metropolitan Fair (March 28). Dwight Johnson at 823 this afternoon tells me the cash subscriptions to the former are one hundred and twenty thousand dollars. Deducting say ten thousand dollars for expenses, and thirty thousand dollars to be set apart to sustain the local (branch) work of accumulating stores and supplies, eighty thousand dollars is left for my central treasury, to which must be added the hundred or two hundred thousands that seem like to be raised by the Fair itself. We cannot yet foresee how the New York Fair will turn out. This nasty raffling question, and the question whether sufficient area has been secured, are embarrassing.

Special meeting of Trinity Church vestry tonight at schoolrooms of

Trinity Chapel in Twenty-fifth Street. We decided to sell some two hundred and fifty thousand dollars worth of real estate and apply its proceeds toward extinction of corporate debts. . . . Last evening Mr. Ruggles talked to me privately about what I could, should, or might do, were a certain offer made me. I admitted that it might possibly be made, and suggested that I might also be nominated as Minister Plenipotentiary to Tierra del Fuego, and that it was equally unprofitable to bother oneself about either contingency at present.

February 24. News from Sherman is anxiously looked for. He is making a most enterprising and splendid but hazardous move, marching from Vicksburg by way of Jackson, Meridian, and Quitman straight for Mobile, as we suppose—there to cooperate with a naval force. He is detached from his base, and "in the air," moving by forced marches and probably without a siege train, and breaking down bridges behind him as he advances. If he finds himself at last in front of strong fieldworks covering Mobile, he may come to grief, but his undertaking savors not only of audacity but of genius. When last heard from (through rebel reports) he was at Quitman, one hundred miles or so north of Mobile.[8] This was on the 18th. At other points, I see no signs of progress.

They have got up a little retail war of their own, on the other side of the Atlantic, about that two-penny Holstein-Schleswig controversy, which is just about big enough to come within the jurisdiction of the Supreme Court of this state, with Leonard or Barnard presiding at General Term. (I suspect that observation of being rather silly than otherwise.) Denmark has the worst of it so far. She is likely to be overwhelmed by Austria and Prussia unless some other great power intervene on her side. England wants to do it, but then war interferes so dreadfully with the regular profits of one's shop, especially when there are precedents of privateering *Alabamas*, which those cunning Yankees might use to one's disadvantage! But I'm a little mollified (toward England) by certain demonstrations of English sympathy with the Sanitary Commission in the form of large and liberal contributions of material aid.

Political cauldron begins to bubble. Lincoln will not be renominated unanimously. The *Tribune* comes out for a new man—for Chase, or possibly Frémont. On the other hand, many old Democrats, like Cisco and the

[8] This movement of Sherman's was a feint, designed to immobilize large Confederate forces in Alabama, demolish much of the Mobile & Ohio and Jackson & Selma Railroads, and if possible destroy General Forrest's cavalry. Sherman soon turned back north toward Canton and Vicksburg.

Cuttings, do strongly Lincolnize, and I should bet on Uncle Abe. It may result in a triangular duel between Chase, "radical"; Lincoln, "moderate"; and McClellan or some other extinct fossil "conservative." But the conservatives must nominate promptly or there will not be enough of them left to make a convention. Public opinion is "a-marching on" with seven-league boots, and the politicians observe its progress with lively personal interest. The Honorable James Brooks, for instance, has just ratted again and made an Abolition speech, congratulating the country and mankind on the death of slavery. Wonder if he supposes that anybody believes a word he says. The New York *Herald* crawled the same way some time ago. Probably the Woods and Winthrop Chanler, reptiles of the same genus, will soon be squirming after them.

The change of opinion on this slavery question since 1860 is a great historical fact, comparable with the early progress of Christianity and of Mahometanism. Who could have predicted it, even when the news came that Sumter had fallen, or even a year and a quarter afterwards, when Pope was falling back on Washington, routed and disorganized? I think this great and blessed revolution is due, in no small degree, to A. Lincoln's sagacious policy. But I do wish A. Lincoln told fewer dirty stories. What a marvellous change it is! Henry Clitz, Walter Cutting, and Jem Ruggles avowing themselves damn Abolitionists, and my little Louis singing after dinner, Sundays: "John Brown's bodies lies a-modrin' in the graves" just as if it were "The Star-Spangled Banner." Abolitionism established in the District of Columbia, and triumphantly rampant under state laws in Maryland and Missouri! *Mirifica Opera Tua.* God pardon our blindness of three years ago! But for our want of eyes to see and of courage to say what we saw, the South would never have ventured on rebellion.

February 26, FRIDAY.　An energetic day at Wall Street and at 823. Walked up Broadway and Seventh Avenue to parts unknown looking for eligible vacant blocks on which temporary buildings can be put up for the Metropolitan Fair. The Fourteenth Street building does not contain a quarter the room that will be wanted, and I fear that it is already too late to secure additional accommodations. It gives an area of fifty-five thousand square feet all told. Brooklyn occupies an area of forty-five thousand, and the managers are suffocating for want of room and lamenting their want of foresight. We need four times as much space as Brooklyn. Visited the Brooklyn Fair yesterday. A very pretty and lively spectacle, but the crowd was such that I could see no details and could have bought nothing, had I wanted to.

Last evening with Ellie and Mr. Blake to Artists' Reception at Dodworth's building on Fifth Avenue, in which George C. Anthon's school flourishes. Pleasant evening, but the collection of pictures exhibited was small trash. Grant is advancing from Chattanooga on Tunnel Hill and Dalton and seems well so far. Reports that Sherman is at Selma, Alabama, and that a naval attack on Mobile is in progress, are untrustworthy. . . .

February 27. Daniel Lord stopped me in Wall Street this morning to tell me how delighted he was to learn that I was to succeed King as President of Columbia College!!! He would accept no denial of his premises and said sundry things that were gratifying when said by so sharp a censor of men and things as Daniel Lord.

From all I hear about the views expressed by Anderson, King, John Astor, William Schermerhorn, and other trustees, I incline to think a majority of the board would put me into that place, marvellous as such action would be, provided I would consent to emigrate from 74 East Twenty-first Street to a frontier settlement in the "President's House" on Forty-ninth Street, where Ellie would be a mile away from all her friends, and the three boys as far from their schools, and all four in peril of typhus and malarial fever, as the vacant blocks of that region are dug up for improvement during the next ten years. That is among the things I will not do on any terms. Were this obstacle removed, I should still entertain such an office with hesitation. There must be somewhere men who possess all my qualifications, whatever they are, and who have rank in science and in letters, or hold position of some kind, whose appointment to the presidency would give dignity to the office and to the College. Barnard is a specimen of this class, but then he is absolutely disqualified for the place, as it seems to me, by his incurable deafness. The board may think otherwise, however, and I would never consent to run against him or anyone else and to get myself personally interested in an election and tempted to make an effort to secure votes for myself (the votes of Zabriskie and Beadle and Hutton and DeWitt, for instance!). It would be a positive degradation to which I would not submit, and I would decline any nomination unless it was made with evidence of substantial unanimity, which is about as probable as that a thousand-ton aerolite will tumble into Gramercy Park tomorrow morning.

February 29. No war news, except that our unlucky Army of the Potomac is said to be executing a movement. If so, its movement is probably *andante maestoso*—slow, and destined to cause mourning. I fear that army is paralyzed by the McClellanism impressed on it when it was organized two years ago. McClellan's voluminous report, just published, will not raise him in public estimation. Considered as a historical essay, or as a bit of autobiography contributed to the history of the war, it may have its value, more or less. But as the report of a general to his military superiors, it is worthless, or worse, and will do him harm. Its publication blights whatever hopes his friends may have entertained of making him President.[9]

March 2. . . . Tonight by invitation to a convention of boss carpenters at Clinton Hall (Astor Place) to organize a concerted movement in aid of the Metropolitan Fair. They wanted some representative of the Sanitary Commission to be present and give explanations as to the objects, methods, and results of the Commission. I got Agnew and Jenkins to attend, also. They were solid, respectable, intelligent, public-spirited men, as it seemed to me. James Renwick was chief manager. I was called on for "a few remarks" and favored the assemblage with an unpremeditated harangue that they must have found rather dull, but then there was a good deal of it. Agnew also spoke with spirit and effect, and we left the meeting busy over a subscription paper.

Gilchrist's *Life and Remains of William Blake*, "the mad painter," is an interesting study. Blake seems to me to have been a man of a high order of genius, arrested in its development at an early stage; to have been endowed with an organ of "vision" of artistic and moral truth and beauty given to few, but which became at an early period atrophied, myopic, and worthless; and to have been gifted with no corresponding "faculty divine" of expression. There are gleams of great splendor in his earlier poems, but in order to see them one must keep constantly in view the fact that they are the semi-articulate utterances of an apprentice in the machine shop of language. The "Song" on page 8, and the verses entitled "The Tiger" on page 89 are, to say the least, among the most vigorous bits of poetic thought that England produced during her Hayley period. But to appreciate even these, one must read them in the same spirit with which he would look for signs of inspiration in an ungrammatical ballad bought from the Park railings for one cent. Blake's anticipation of modern thought as to "Gothic architecture," "superstition," and sundry views of art

[9] McClellan's *Report of the Organization and Campaigns of the Army of the Potomac*, a volume of 465 pages, was issued by Sheldon & Co. of New York. In addition to the official report to the Adjutant-General on the Peninsular Campaign, it contained a brief essay on the campaign in West Virginia.

lately propounded by Ruskin and others as a new proclamation is worth remembering.

March 3. . . . People stop me in the streets daily to say that they are delighted to hear that I am to be next president of Columbia College and to express certain asinine delusions about my fitness for the place! This is certainly an era of small men. I have to tell them they err grossly and are deceived on both points. It seems incredible. How New York has fallen off during the last forty years! Its intellect and culture have been diluted and swamped by a great flood-tide of material wealth.

March 6, SUNDAY.   Yesterday to No. 823 at two o'clock to look after my report as treasurer to the Sanitary Commission meeting at Philadelphia next week, which I fear this very virulent cold will forbid my attending. Made my way with difficulty through the dense crowd that filled Union Square, for the first New York Negro Regiment was receiving its colors at the Union League Club House.[10] It has been organized by aid of subscriptions got up in this club. A second regiment of black New Yorkers will soon be sent off under the same auspices. Our labors of a year ago have borne fruit. The Union League has done something for the country. From the windows of 823 I saw this regiment march down Broadway after a spirited allocution by Charles King. The regiment was "black but comely," and marched well. General Wadsworth, who was in the office, said it was not below the average of new regiments. Both sidewalks and all the windows were full of applauding spectators. There was hearty cheering and clapping and waving of handkerchiefs, and I neither heard nor heard of any expression of sound, constitutional, conservative disapproval. Which is sad to think of!

This march will be the subject of cords of historical paintings before 1900 A.D. The flag presentation with Charles King and Colonel Bartram in the foreground is destined to spoil many acres of canvas. I have seen two memorable marches down Broadway: this one, and that of the Seventh Regiment in April, 1861. This transaction had far less material sublimity. The immense concourse was wanting, and so were the vague sense of awe and the fearful anticipations of coming woe, and the new thrill of national life and of patriotic resolution that stirred all the throng that cloudy, windy afternoon. It is among the most solemn memories of my

[10] The official designation was the Twentieth U.S. (Colored) Troops. They had been encamped on Riker's Island; the ceremony drew a hundred thousand spectators to the Union Square area.

life thus far. But I think yesterday morning's phenomenon—Ethiopia marching down Broadway, armed, drilled, truculent, and elate—was the weightier and the more memorable of the two.

March 8. Stopped at No. 2 Great Jones Street (Metropolitan Fair office) on my way down, and discoursed with Mrs. Lane and Mrs. D. D. Field, and Miss Nash and Mrs. Alexander Hamilton, Jr., all very charming and all as busy as bees; Mrs. Ellie among the busiest of the whole hive. The ladies have failed to convince their inert and stupid masculine colleagues that the Fair will be a disastrous failure and a disgrace to New York without at least four times the area yet secured for it. They were despondent and wanted—or said they wanted—to announce through the newspapers that the Metropolitan Fair was given up and would not come off at all. I suggested an appeal to the Standing Committee of the Sanitary Commission, which expressly reserved the right to decide between the two committees, male and female, in case of disagreement. The suggestion was well received. I was promptly served with written notice of disagreement and of appeal, and telegraphed as promptly to Philadelphia, where the Sanitary Commission is in session. I ought to be there in person, but I am made dead and voiceless and altogether inert and useless by this miserable cold.

It kept me from the regular Columbia College meeting yesterday afternoon. I hear from Mr. Ruggles that the board approved the action of the Committee on the School of Mines, and voted vehement thanks to me for sending the College a little collection of minerals several months ago. William Betts moved the resolution, and made certain statements about my admirable personal traits of character, for which I'm much obliged to him. King's resignation as President was formally accepted (to take effect after next commencement) under a heavy fire of complimentary speechification from Bishop Potter and others. Potter, Bradford, and Betts were appointed to a committee on the question of the succession. . . .

The great Brooklyn Fair has been a splendid triumph of public morality. Let Tyng and Spring rejoice. There was no "raffling," and nothing was disposed of by chance or lottery. The Brooklyn people (who are mostly down-Easterners and very smart) substituted an ingenious and absolutely unexceptionable process for the raffles and the Christian gaming tables Tyng and Spring used to wink at when used to raise money for Sunday School libraries and the like. People "subscribed" for an article. Each paid up his five dollars or ten dollars, and when the "subscription list" was full, the names of all the "subscribers" were put into a hat and one was drawn out. But the person thus drawn did not thereby "win" the article or become its owner. *O No!* He was merely selected by chance to decide which one of all the subscribers was, in his judgment, the most meritorious, pious, patriotic, public-spirited, and praiseworthy person, and as such best entitled to the prize. His nominee or appointee took it as a testimonial of the respect and affection of the whole corps of "subscribers." It is a striking illustration of the universal prevalence of *selfishness* in the human heart that the person whose name was drawn actually decided in every case that *he* was the most meritorious, and so forth, person in that crowd, and walked off with the property. All the others acquiesced most good-naturedly. But that does not affect the *principle*. Brooklyn Fair has been a glorious protest against gambling!

March 14. Committee on School of Mines at Betts's office at two o'clock, and satisfactory progress. Went with Egleston, Dr. Torrey, and Edward Jones to inspect a most showy and splendid collection of minerals on sale in Beekman Street, belonging to one Seymour. The superb crystals of fluor and quartz and baryte made my mouth water—in the interest of this School. Why am I not W. B. Astor? Echo answers, "Because you ain't," which is ungrammatical.

At 823 an important session. The sudden death of the Rev. T. Starr King makes it necessary for Bellows to go to California for six months to look after King's congregation and the interests of the Commission.[11] So he thinks, and he may be right. He is telegraphed for, most urgently. Then Van Buren will probably go off to Europe next month for a short spell of leisure, and if he do so, Agnew and I will be left to run this great machine! It's a rather grave prospect. . . .

The ladies of the Metropolitan Fair have taken the providing of additional space into their own hands. I saw Mayor Gunther on their behalf Friday morning, and he approved a "joint resolution" authorizing a large structure on the north side of Union Square. It was begun this morning. The Sanitary Commission guarantees payment of its cost by

[11] Thomas Starr King (1824–1864), who died suddenly of pneumonia, had been one of the principal pillars of the Union cause on the Pacific Coast and an invaluable supporter of the Sanitary Commission. It was his eloquence and organizing ability which were chiefly responsible for California's contributions of nearly one and a quarter millions to the Commission. Only four years earlier he had left the East, telling his Unitarian brethren that they did wrong in "huddling so closely around the cosy stove of civilization in this blessed Boston," and that he was "ready to go out into the cold and see if I am good for anything." At his death he was one of the most famous, influential, and beloved men in the West.

vote of Standing Committee during the Philadelphia session. Strange that I, with two or three other New Yorkers, should have the right to decide questions so large, confided to us somehow or other, nobody can exactly say how or by whom. This Brooklyn Fair, the Metropolitan Fair, and the Central Fair at Philadelphia may very possibly put more than a million into our treasury for Agnew and for me to use at our own sweet will during the next six months. It seems a most irrational and improvident arrangement. But it works and works well. At Olustee in Florida our agents had seven hundred wounded men on their hands for two days and provided for them, the medical staff being wholly without medical stores of any kind.

Death of Pelatiah Perit at New Haven.[12] He was a most worthy old gentleman. Professor Rood called last night, among others. He talked College, of course, and introduced the great College question now pending and King's views about it. Strange how generally the notion has spread that I am to be King's successor—and still stranger that it seems generally approved!! *Quam parva sapientia.* Barnard's friends push his claims vigorously. I am constantly receiving letters from Bache, Binney, President Woolsey of Yale, and others; all which I send in to the Committee on the presidency. Perhaps Barnard's friends are overdoing their work, as Wolcott Gibbs's backers did ten years ago.

Philharmonic rehearsal Saturday morning. Heard the Haydn Symphony again (it is numbered three on the programme). It is lovely. In spite of my stupefying cold, I appreciated it intensely. It was like a walk through sunshiny fields and pleasant wood paths in June, with Johnny and Temple in their highest feather for companions. I suppose musical critics would call the delicious phrases of the first movement and of the duo tame or childish, insipid, trivial. But nobody can write such things now. In one sense they certainly are childish—in their freshness and purity, so unlike anything to be found in the music of this day. Gade is the only living composer I know who tries to produce simple and beautiful musical thoughts. The grand object of all the rest seems to be to give an audience fits, which they don't. Heard also one movement of a very grand violin concerto of Beethoven's (opus 61, I think) and "Dove sono," sung by a Mme. Rotter.

[12] Perit (Yale 1802) had been a partner in the shipping firm of Goodhue & Co. He was for a decade president of the New York Chamber of Commerce, and during the riots of 1857, as Dexter, the Yale biographer, said, "was chosen by common consent to fill a vacancy in the Board of Police Commissioners and rendered, at much personal sacrifice, an important service in restoring the public security."

Jolly old Cozzens of West Point died yesterday very suddenly. I certainly met him in Wall Street Friday or Saturday. He was King of Hotelkeepers.[13] Lieutenant-General Grant supersedes Halleck as Commander-in-Chief. Probably a judicious change. Halleck abides at Washington as Chief of Staff, which seems equally judicious. Fitz-John Porter has recently gone to Colorado Territory as an agent of Eastern capitalists to inspect certain mines. Whereupon (according to newspapers) the Coloradians held a mass meeting of the Vigilance Committee or *Vehmgericht* type and requested Fitz-John Porter to depart from among them and quit those "diggin's." Poor Fitz-John Porter! That his conviction and disgrace should have been deserved seems incredible. But one damning fact is unexplained and undenied, so far as I know. He lay still for hours listening to the guns of a disastrous battlefield without an effort to help his comrades.

George Anthon has been discoursing with William Betts and A. W. Bradford and the Bishop about the question of the Columbia College presidency, in which he takes a lively interest. They say that the next president should be an alumnus of the College, and the Bishop and Betts seem to think a man of high scientific position undesirable. Bad for Barnard. But I do not think we ought to elect Barnard because he is a sufferer in the cause of loyalty. The College has been debilitated for nearly forty years, perhaps longer, from the fact that its presidents have not been chosen for fitness or from interest in the cause of education in this particular institution, but because they were excellent persons in want of a situation. So William A. Duer was elected, N. F. Moore probably, and Charles King certainly. . . .

March 18. Bad news for the household of Hamilton Fish. His beautiful daughter, Bessy, who married young d'Hauteville within the year, has died at Marseilles of puerperal convulsion in a premature confinement. God help those who suffer the catastrophe I so narrowly escaped fifteen years ago! The husband, d'Hauteville, is the same person whose custody was so contested when he was a baby in 1839 or 1840, his mother being an F.F. Bostonian, and his father a Swiss baron—*vide* pamphlets of that period. The mamma prevailed, of course, against all law and right, as it seemed to me at the time. It is hard to enforce law and right against a mother claiming her child—but right is right and wrong is wrong, nevertheless. If this poor young fellow had been otherwise disposed of in his

---

[13] William B. Cozzens, the much-liked hotelkeeper, 1787–1864.

infancy, as he should have been, he would have been reared on the other side of the Atlantic, and this lovely young lady would have escaped this crushing calamity which must color his whole after-life dark blue. It seems as if the sin of the mother were visited on the child; the sin being (as I remember the case) a distaste for her husband's family and excessive loyalty to her own and the abandonment of her husband because he insisted that she should try to identify herself with his people.

General Grant seems for the present in command of the Army of the Potomac as General-in-Chief without displacing General Meade. He will doubtless do or try to do something decisive in Virginia. But the road to Richmond is a *passage perylous, whereon have perysshed manie good Knyghtes;* for example, Syr Scott and Syr McDowell, Syr McClellan, Syr Burnside and Syr Hooker—to say nothing of Pope the Incredible Knyght, and Meade (*Le Noir Fainéant*) for the last eight months. A terrible ordeal for Grant. His path is whitened by the bones of popular reputations that perished because their defunct owners did not know how to march through Virginia to Richmond. I hope Grant may possess the talisman, "the seal of Solomon" that raises its possessor to capacity for his place, however large.

March 21, MONDAY.   Up Fifth Avenue this morning to call on Mrs. William Astor, and get instructions for drawing her will . . .

The great, hideous one-hundred-thousand-dollar Townsend-Sarsaparilla-Spingler house on the other side of Thirty-fourth Street has just been bought by A. T. Stewart, who has razed it to the ground and tells William Astor he is going to lay out one million on a new white marble palazzo.[14] I suppose it will be just ten times as ugly and barbaric as its predecessor, if that be conceivable.

This is a sign of the times. Another is Jerome's (not the Saint but the stockjobber) grand eighty-thousand-dollar-stable, with the private theatre for a second story, wherein the private theatricals "in aid of the Metropolitan Fair" are now being daily rehearsed.[15] The whole city is bubbling and fizzing with the Fair and the Sanitary Commission. I wonder people are not worn out with it, and that the words Sanitary Commission do not produce the effect of a heavy dose of tartar emetic. . . .

[14] The eminent merchant spent more than a million on his four-story white marble mansion at the northwest corner of Fifth Avenue and Thirty-fourth, for a time the most splendid private mansion in America. He lived there until his death in 1876, and in 1891 the Manhattan Club bought the house.

[15] Lester Wallack was stage manager for a dramatic committee which produced plays in connection with the Metropolitan Fair.

Talked with Gouverneur M. Ogden after the meeting about College affairs. He paid me the compliment of a frank expression of opinion on a matter in which I'm personally interested. Certain of my friends keep themselves very busy in this Columbia College business. I fear they will compromise me in sundry ways, and also that they will get me the credit of being an office-seeker now, and a defeated office-seeker next June.

Plans for the great Metropolitan Fair, as Strong indicates, were proceeding apace. The idea had been borrowed from Chicago, which held the first fair in October, 1863, raising $72,000 for the Western Department of the Sanitary Commission. Cincinnati followed with a fair that opened on Christmas day and produced a net return of about $225,000; while Boston, Cleveland, and Brooklyn all imitated the example. But the New York City fair was destined to eclipse all others. Early in 1864, two executive committees, one of women and the other of men, were set up. Plans were made to enlist trade, every profession, every branch of labor, and every important literary and artistic society. Cooperating committees were formed in London, Paris, and Rome. Two buildings were erected, one on Fourteenth Street, the other on Union Square. The former contained a great number of shops and stalls, a restaurant and dining hall, a library and bookstore, and a picture gallery. Nearly everything that could be found in a modern department store was on sale. The Union Square building contained the children's department, and an international department offering contributions from various parts of the world. At a cattle show connected with the fair, situated at Fifteenth Street and Seventh Avenue, numerous animals could be purchased, ranging from Shetland ponies to "a white ox from Livingston County weighing 3,602 pounds." Among the articles contributed by patriotic citizens to the fair were an original unpublished manuscript by Fenimore Cooper, the original bowie knife made for James Bowie of Alamo fame, autograph letters by famous authors (including a long account by Thomas Hughes of the sympathy of the British middle-classes and workingmen with the North), many oil paintings, and curios from the South Seas. The fair, as Strong records, had its formal opening on April 4, when the united chorus of the city and a military band performed "The Star-Spangled Banner," an Army Hymn written by Oliver Wendell Holmes was sung, General Dix on behalf of the men's Executive Committee presented the contents of the fair to the ladies, and Joseph H. Choate, on behalf of the women's executive committee, responded. The magnitude and attractiveness of the exhibits delighted all beholders, while the enthusiastic zeal

*of the women in charge (admirably expressed by a weekly magazine called
Spirit of the Fair) was infectious.*

*Meanwhile, Grant had assumed command of all the Union armies, and had
drafted his plan of campaign. He, with his powerful Army of the Potomac
(about 125,000 men), was to crush Lee's Army of Virginia; Sherman, with his
veteran Western army of about 100,000 men, was to destroy Joseph E. Johnston's command. On May 3, Grant crossed the Rapidan and moved forward
into the Wilderness; on May 6, Sherman's army left its positions in front of
Chattanooga and moved forward against the Confederates at Dalton. Mighty
hammer blows, from this time on, were to be delivered with unremitting vigor.*

March 22. Queer incident in the Hammond court-martial, communicated by H. to Van Buren. While he was off at Knoxville, under those
mysterious orders of the Secretary of War, a large number of papers disappeared from the files of the Surgeon-General's office—nobody knows how.
When charges were presented against him, Hammond found to his dismay that some of the abstracted documents were mostly quite essential
to his defense, especially his correspondence with a Dr. Cooper, medical
director at Philadelphia. Cooper, when put on the stand, swore emphatically that he never wrote or received the letters that make up this correspondence. A few days ago, Hammond received an anonymous note,
stating that its writer was in possession of these missing papers and would
deliver them up for a consideration, $1,500. He complied with the con-
ditions, I suppose, but at all events a package was left at his house containing most of them. One, of special importance, was missing. The anonymous person wrote that it had been taken from him. But Hammond thinks
that with the evidence he has thus secured he can convict Cooper of wilful
perjury, and also that he was sent to the West to give an opportunity of
ransacking his office and stealing his papers so as to leave him defenseless
against a conspiracy to ruin him. There are certainly signs of very sharp
practice by *somebody*.

March 26, SATURDAY. . . . To Law School Committee meeting at two
o'clock, 6 Wall Street. Nothing worth noting. Talk afterwards with
Gouverneur Ogden about the comptrollership and other matters. To No.
823. Then George Anthon dined here, and at eight I went to Van Buren's
for a committee meeting; Agnew, Bellows, Van Buren, and I. General
[E. D.] Keyes looked in at supper time and squelched our discussion of
the important question whether we can do anything indirectly toward

helping Hammond in the ruinous cost of this court-martial, which has already been sitting nine weeks and but just got through with the case for the prosecution. I am clear we can do nothing for him directly out of the funds of the Commission. This court is said to have cost the government $250,000 already, a heavy sum to be assessed on the country for the gratification of Stanton's personal pique and spitefulness, and rather oppressive on the Surgeon-General—with his pay and allowance of $3,500 per annum.

Got the School of Mines circular and so on from the printer today. I shall make a strong personal effort to raise the $20,000, or a good slice of it, though I never undertook anything of the kind in my life before. I have scarce a hope of success, but people are in a giving humor in these days.

Poor Mrs. d'Hauteville's funeral was at St. Mark's this afternoon, the body having been brought here across the Atlantic a few days ago. What a tragedy, when one remembers that lovely, stately, refined-looking Miss Bessy Fish moving through the ballroom an acknowledged princess of New York society, envied, courted, and admired, and thinks of the misery of her own household, and of her young husband! God help them! I had had the honor of being presented to this lady, but my acquaintance with her was only nominal. But she was among the most beautiful creatures I ever saw. What madness it is for a newly-married couple to go off careering over Europe! I contemplated that folly in 1848, but gave it up because of the signs of revolutionary trouble that began with the downfall of Louis Philippe. Heaven be praised I did so. Where should I be now if Ellie's visitation in April, 1849, had come upon her in some city of Europe? With all the help and appliances of home, she barely survived it. . . .

Mr. Ruggles had a conference with the Bishop last night about the presidency of Columbia College. The Bishop is kind enough to rate me much above my real value, and his talk indicates that he may very possibly prefer me for that position. Should I take it were it offered me? A grave question, but fortunately so remote and so unlikely to require an answer that I need waste no time over it tonight.

March 28. Stopped twice at No. 2 Great Jones Street (headquarters of the Metropolitan Fair) and inspected the building on the north side of Union Square. It is now nearly under cover. The quantity of gossip, intrigue, and personal pique that grows out of this Fair and its hundred committees is stupendous and terrible. Vast controversies have arisen, and immense issues, but I have not time to define them and record them. My general impression is that the executive he-committee has thus far proved a mere incumbrance to the executive committee of ladies. Griswold Gray, chairman of the former, and Lloyd Aspinwall, seem like to come out of the transaction without laurels and with positive damage. They have somehow affronted the ladies, whose husbands and brothers will, of course, side with them and adopt their views. Gray means well, but he is a mere successful trader, without culture or refinement, who has spent the best years of his life making money at Canton or Hong-Kong, and comes home to be petted by young ladies to whom he gives grand ostentatious dinners and suppers at Delmonico's, and five-hundred-dollar baskets (or colossal structures) of flowers occasionally. . . .

March 29.   Long conference and council at No. 823. Dined at William Schermerhorn's with Fred Sheldon and his wife. Stately little Miss Fanny and juvenile Miss "Chat" also convives, and "the baby," little seven-year-old Miss Annie, came in for dessert. We all had a pleasant evening, of course. The guests of that most charming and gracious Mrs. William C. Schermerhorn must be themselves in fault if they fail to enjoy their sojourn in Twenty-third Street. She has the most wonderful talent for making people feel comfortable, the most exquisite tact and delicacy in her methods of informing them that Mr. A. or Mrs. B. has casually said or done something that flatters their self-love.

Bache writes (with politic obscurity and diplomatic non-committal vague phrases) letters that shew that he expects Stanton's hostility to the Sanitary Commission to be about exploding at last. He is perturbed, anticipates some serious crisis, and talks of "withdrawing from any responsible position" in connection with the Sanitary Commission if there is to be a row. He is a most wary old practitioner, and will not stand by the Sanitary Commission a single day if he think himself thereby likely to endanger his influence with the Administration as Chief of the Coast Survey. I suppose him to be perturbed and alarmed by something or other that has been brought out in the Hammond court-martial. I cannot guess what it is; but signs and tokens from several quarters indicate that some attack on us is coming, probably inspired by Stanton's malignity and wrongheadedness. We are invulnerable, except possibly as to the arrangement for furnishing supplies to the hospitals of Washington and its vicinity, which was adopted while I was laid up last May and June. I have always maintained that this undertaking was unwise and wrong, no matter how practically beneficent, because it made the Commission a recipient of public money, buying mutton and poultry and vegetables in Pennsylvania and Maryland for which it was to be reimbursed from the "hospital funds" of Washington. I know the system has saved these hospital funds twenty-five per cent, at least, on the cost of their extra supplies, but it has mixed us up with money transactions that can be misrepresented and which I wish had never occurred.

March 30. . . . [At] 823. Much work of importance done, especially as to purchase of anti-scorbutics for the West. Large powers given Dr. Newberry. Nothing new as to the storm we are awaiting from Washington. I expect to find the Commission assailed some fine morning by a concentric fire from about forty Administration newspapers, east and west, as dishonest, imbecile, and disloyal. If so, we must roll up our sleeves and sail in.

April 1.   Dreary weather. Energetic in Wall Street, and at 823 from half-past three till near six. Standing Committee of Sanitary Commission met here at eight, and others of the Commission were with us. Bellows, Van Buren, Agnew, Wolcott Gibbs, Dr. Jenkins, Knapp, Professor Bache, Judge Skinner, and McCagg of Chicago, and Ellie and I sat down to our usual supper at ten, but kept steadily at business till after twelve, tolerating no talk that was out of order. (I forgot to count in Bishop Clark.) We disposed of much work. Bache's intimations of something wrong and alarming at Washington turn out to be moonshine. At least, he professed to know of no threatening signs in that or in any other quarter. That politic old gentleman is rather hard to follow. He talked oddly tonight, as if he thought of resigning his vice-presidency in case Mr. Bloor were transferred from the Washington to the New York office! It's very possible he "sees a hand we cannot see," that of Secretary Stanton, to wit, doubled up and ready to give us "one on the nob." But every other indication is that we are exceedingly strong at Washington just now, and much respected, in view of the presidential campaign just opening (politicians take it for granted, of course, that we are disposed to use our large machinery for political ends), and also that the Surgeon-General's case is progressing favorably, and that nothing has been brought out by the prosecution that reflects on the honesty of the Commission. Nevertheless, we shall probably send E. H. Owen to Washington next Monday to look into the case professionally and advise whether we are called on to do anything.

We are in collision with the "Gentlemen's Committee of the Metropolitan Fair." They were appointed as auxiliaries to the ladies, and as their advisers and aids in business matters which ladies could not be expected to deal with. But they have seen fit to thwart, snub, insult, and override the ladies' committee in the most disgusting, offensive, and low-bred way. Their general course has been snobbish and stupid. They have shown want of manners and of appreciation of the magnitude of the undertaking. Their chairman, Griswold Gray, is a well-meaning fellow enough, but a mere rich tradesman, without substantial culture and refinement, and his colleagues are mostly of the same stripe—men like Lloyd Aspinwall, whose bank accounts are all they can rely on for social position and influence. So far as I can discover, this masculine committee has been a positive drawback and damage and nuisance and calamity. By the original organization of this fair, with its binary system of two committees, male and female, the right was reserved to our Standing Committee (Sanitary Commission) of coming in as umpire in case of any difference of opinion between them. Such a difference arose about a question concerning tickets of admission, and Bellows being appealed to by the womankind, called me in to make a quorum of the Standing Committee, and we agreed on a letter to the gents yesterday morning most courteous in tone, but distinctly adopting and assuming the policy preferred by the women. This letter was laid before the gents at their meeting last night. It made a shindy. After much debate they resolved that it be returned to Dr. Bellows, and it was so returned accordingly under cover of an official note from "Richard Grant White, Secretary." I regret this. Dick White should have resigned his secretaryship and cut off several fingers of his right hand rather than consent to make himself responsible personally or officially for this piece of insolent, monied dirtiness. But I fear he is in fact a "poor shoat." I had thought he might make a good letter-writer and "literary secretary" for the Sanitary Commission during Dr. Bellows's absence in California, but he is clearly invertebrate and unavailable.

April 2, SATURDAY.   To the Academy of Music; Philharmonic extra concert in aid of Metropolitan Fair. It was a new experience to us. There were not 150 people in all the vast auditorium. But Eisfeld and his battalion came manfully up to their work and gave us the glorious ever-new Fifth Symphony (C Minor) in grand style. Eisfeld seemed to lead with special dash and freedom, I thought. . . . There were two American overtures also, "Columbus" by G. F. Bristow, and "Hail Columbia" by one Hohnstock, both creditable productions notwithstanding a certain amount of claptrap.

Coming uptown through the weather, I observe that the Seventeenth Street fair building is brilliantly lit up. They have a gang of men there working all night. Detmold, by the by, has resigned; a most excellent man, and he has worked indefatigably for the fair these two or three months, but he has somehow made himself generally odious. If this fair be wound up without any memorable calamity and catastrophe, I shall be thankful. What I most dread is fire, and I have been prosing and writing to everybody about the necessity of precaution against that danger for a month past. Suggested a preventive to White (architect of the Seventeenth Street shingle palace) this afternoon, which he cordially approved and said he would provide; a little embankment of earth or sand or rubbish of any sort all along the base of the structure, sufficient to prevent any malignant, devilish Copperhead or sympathizer from poking a little lump of cotton or of rags, saturated with camphene, under the floor through the crevices of the rough woodwork. Richmond papers would laud and magnify any such transaction, and there are many beasts in the community who would like to be concerned in it, could it be safely done. . . .

The war languishes and makes no progress. People naturally turn their thoughts, therefore, to questions of finance, taxation, and prices, and wonder whether gold will not soon be at 200 and butter a dollar a pound. I believe General Grant is working in his new place *ohne Hast, ohne Rast,* purging the Army of the Potomac of disaffected McClellanists in high command and bringing its morale into training for hard work in its next campaign against "Lee's Miserables." Stanton seems trying to interfere and thwart the lieutenant-general. So people say. If he is doing so, I hope Grant will tender his resignation and tell the country the reason why.

April 4.   Went at ten A.M. to the fair buildings in Fourteenth Street and spent a couple of hours there. The spectacle was interesting, but fatiguing to the spectator. A vast crowd of well-dressed men and women— our "best people"—were working their fingers to the bone, arranging and sorting material, directing decorative operations, receiving, acknowledging, unpacking, and distributing to their appropriate departments contributions from the four quarters of the earth. It was the busiest human anthill I ever saw. My self-assumed mission was to confer with the police department and the fire department about the fearful possibility of fire, panic, and slaughter. They seem fully aware of this peril, and have taken special precautions against it. Suggested one or two precautions that were favorably received. When I introduce myself as treasurer of the Sanitary Commission, I find every suggestion I offer cordially treated.

To Wall Street and then walked uptown with George Anthon. Grand parade and military spectacle in honor of the opening of the Metropolitan Fair. We inspected the column from the sidewalk of Astor Place. General Dix tells me tonight that 11,000 men turned out, and that this was the largest parade that New York Island has seen since 1814, when a large numerical force was assembled here to repel an expected invasion. Most of the warriors of this afternoon's pageant had been under fire. Many of their regimental flags were tattered and torn by rebel bullets. After dinner to the fair, calling for Mrs. General Dix and Mrs. Blake. Everything brilliant and handsome; a fine spectacle, creditable to the city and its dependencies. Crowd large but not oppressive. Police omnipresent and civil. They caught four or five pickpockets redhanded, and marched them backward and forward through the building with placards round their necks, defining their vocation in large capitals, and then haled them off to their appointed place. Poor devils, how shame and brazen impudence contended for the mastery in their mean faces! Some of our soft-hearted women thought the transaction "painful" and "cruel" and "humiliating" and "too bad," but to my common sense, it seemed a very goodly spectacle.

The ceremony of "inaugurating" the fair went off well. For Dr. Adams's opening prayer, General Dix's speech, and Mr. Choate's reply, I refer posterity to tomorrow's papers, where they will doubtless be found verbatim. Both orators are said to have been good, but they were inaudible to me. I did hear the bass part of the Hallelujah Chorus, however, which was bellowed into my ears by a battalion of bull-bassi, extinguishing and drowning the ensemble.

That he-committee is made up of louts and cubs and of a powerless minority of decent, well-bred men, like Marshall O. Roberts and Acton, the Police Commissioner. They made no provision for receiving General Dix tonight, and he had to get in as he could and find his way to the platform for himself. Nor was any place assigned to the ladies of the executive committee, to their intense mortification. Mrs. Astor, Mrs. Belmont, Ellie, Mrs. Lane, and others were almost tearful about it; while that indomitable Mrs. John Sherwood and that iron-clad little Miss Catherine Nash (what an appropriate sister-in-law for Agnew!) were not in the least tearful, but rather tended toward grimness. As I heard someone remark tonight, "I wouldn't be in Griswold Gray's boots for twice his assets." Gray, Lloyd Aspinwall, Detmold, Dick White, and others, have certainly shewn themselves in all this business not to be thoroughbred men. They may be severally most respectable and most useful and valuable in their several spheres, but they are *gentlemen* only in a conventional acceptation of that term.

[Richard Grant] White came here last night. I did not feel inclined to cut him, but I turned him a cold shoulder by formality of reception. He's a decorated, flamboyant gent. I hate to throw him over, for he has a certain amount of culture and is generally underrated and slighted, and was black-balled at the Century three or four years ago—I never knew exactly why. But he is clearly a second-rate fellow. I had intended to get him the position of "literary" or corresponding secretary to our Standing Committee during Bellows's absence (such an officer must be got somewhere), but it cannot be done. Both Agnew and Gibbs are "down upon" him to a surprising extent.

Called on Bellows last night in Twentieth Street and bade him goodbye with sincere regrets. We shall miss him sorely these coming six months, for he is most useful and efficient. He has his foibles, and they lead many people to underrate him. Though public-spirited and unselfish, farsighted and wise (never foolish if he give himself time to take counsel with slower men, like Van Buren, Agnew, Gibbs, or myself), he is conceited and he likes to be conspicuous. But what a trifling drawback it is on the reputation of a man admitted to be sagacious, active, and willing to sacrifice personal interests in public service, to admit that he knows, after all, that he is doing the country good service, and that he likes to see his usefulness made manifest in newspapers.

Mr. Ruggles dined here; and returning from the fair at eleven after a fearful bother about carriages, I found George Anthon here, having spent the evening at William Schermerhorn's. Both reported results of Columbia College meeting this afternoon, namely: *Nil.* The committee on the presidency reported no progress, except that they had heard of three candidates: Barnard, Coppée, whilom of West Point,[16] and (!!!) George T. Strong!!! Heaven help the board and its committees!

April 6. Had to wait a long while in Fourteenth Street this morning while Ellie, the treasuress, was endorsing the pocketful of checks I carried down to the Bank of America. It was a pretty sight: the throng of well-dressed people, the showy decorations, the stalls or counters loaded with all sorts of things, and especially the shoals of nice women with their

[16] Henry Coppée (1821–1895), a graduate of West Point, officer in the Mexican War, teacher at the military academy, and professor of literature and history in the University of Pennsylvania—which institution he left in 1866 to become the first president of Lehigh University.

graceful, diagonal, broad blue ribbons (a line generally wanting in our women's costume) all working in such deadly earnest.[17]

Though so much humbug, vanity, ostentation, and emulation are inherent in all fairs, there is a very deep feeling below them all in this instance, and its visible manifestation on so large a scale, with accessories so brilliant, appeals to me very strongly indeed. I confess it made my eyes fill this morning. Thank God for the hearts and the heads He has given the women of the country, and the men, too—after making every allowance for the baneful existence among us of vermin like the Woods and Brookses, and Winthrop Chanler and [Manton] Marble and Governor Seymour and J. G. Barnett, and of purse-proud snobs like George Griswold Gray.

Downtown and up again. Session at 823; Gibbs, Van Buren, Agnew, Jenkins, and I. Agnew brings forward a very large proposition, namely, to buy five hundred acres of land near Saratoga, where he has just been making a tour of inspection with Knapp, put up a sanitarium for disabled and discharged soldiers, a *Hôtel des Invalides* sufficient for (say) one hundred men, and to fund about $300,000 for its endowment. Much can be and was said in favor of the scheme, but my first impressions are strongly against it.

After dinner with Ellie to the opening of the Union Square department of the fair. Dense crowd, of course. We met in a little box of a room appropriated to the ladies' committee, and filed off to the stage or platform in the large room at the eastern end of the building, at eight. I took in Mrs. President King or Mrs. Sherwood, I forget which. King presided. The Rev. Morgan Dix made a brief prayer. Mr. Ruggles made a speech, inaudible to me, but well received by those whom the laws of acoustics permitted to hear it, and said to have been felicitous. Orchestra played the Overture to *Der Freischütz* (blessed be the memory of its composer!). King made a brief final allocution, and the meeting adjourned, and the concert went on. Put Ellie and Mrs. Sherwood into their carriage for the first of the private theatrical nights at Leonard W. Jerome's theatre, and then went down to the Fourteenth Street department with the Rev. Morgan

[17] The main buildings of the Metropolitan Fair were on Fourteenth Street, running through to Fifteenth. They contained the "grand hall" filled with numerous oval stalls for the sale of donated goods, sections devoted to fine arts, machinery, farm implements, and arms and trophies; and a restaurant. A large temporary erection on Union Square held the "international hall," the music hall, the children's department where entertainments for youngsters were given, and the "Knickerbocker Kitchen" fitted up in colonial style. The women attendants, dressed in uniform costume with white collars and diagonal blue sashes, seemed to sell every imaginable article—often at bargain rates; while the entertainments ranged from classical music to war dances in the Indian wigwam set up by the artist Bierstadt.

Dix and spent an hour or so as pleasantly as heat and crowd permitted.
Dix is certainly a brick of the first quality. I never knew a more genuine
man, or one who can be cultivated with more pleasure and profit.

The Union Square buildings are far more effective than those in Fourteenth Street. Their architect, White, has done his hurried job wisely
and well. Dick Hunt has put all his taste and all his indomitable energy into
their decoration, and has produced a series of most artistic and splendid
interiors at little cost.[18] The "international department" at the west end
is quite gorgeous with its banners and escutcheons, its fountain, and its
show of flowers. Who dreamed two years ago last June that the poor little
Sanitary Commission would ever make such a noise in the world?

Heaven grant the fair may pass off without any memorable catastrophe
from fire or crowd, and that Ellie may not be harmed by this long period
of excitement and hard labor! She is and for months has been steadily
working under a terrible pressure of steam. I have estimated the proceeds
of the Metropolitan Fair as probably not far from $700,000. But there are
bets on a million and a half, and all the indications of the last three days
point toward something larger than I anticipated.

April 7. . . . At half-past three to a meeting of the Columbia College
Committee on the Course at the Law School; Bradford, Rutherfurd, Potter,
and I. George Anthon's letter about qualifications for admission finds great
favor, and its suggestions will probably be recommended for adoption. Important session at 823. After dinner Mr. Ruggles appeared and we spent
an hour in the "Knickerbocker Kitchen" of the Fair.

April 10, SUNDAY.   Congress is doing bravely with its constitutional
amendment abolishing slavery. Think of Reverdy Johnson sustaining and
advocating it! "John Brown's soul's a-marching on"—double quick.

There has been a lovely little performance in the House. One Harris of
Maryland made an elaborate speech recommending that the Confederacy
be recognized at once.[19] A motion was made to expel him and a considerable majority voted for it, but not the two-thirds required (affirmative 81,
negative 58). Thereupon a resolution was introduced declaring Harris
"an unworthy member of this House" and that he "is hereby severely
censured"; carried 92 to 18. Good for the House. Fernandy Wood was one

---

[18] The architect Richard Morris Hunt (1827–1895) had opened a studio in New
York in 1858.

[19] This was Benjamin Gwinn Harris, who served two terms 1863–1867. Shortly
after Appomattox he was tried by a military court in Washington for sheltering two
paroled Confederate soldiers and sentenced to three years in jail and disqualification
from federal office.   President Johnson later remitted the sentence.

of the eighteen, of course; so was Winthrop Chanler, and with them voted John V. L. Pruyn, whom I have respected and esteemed for twenty years, but neither respect nor esteem any more. It is interesting to observe how eager such members of the opposition as can see beyond their own noses, even Cox of Ohio, were to set themselves right before the people on this question and to desert from Harris, in hope of saving the moribund old Democratic Party from the death and decomposition that seem to await it.

Law School Committee yesterday at Mr. Ruggles's office. Where and O where can we get an orator for next commencement? Professor Dwight himself will have to do the job, but it has suddenly occurred to me that Mr. Samuel B. Ruggles is of all others best able to do it. I must save up the suggestion for the commencement of 1865, if one side of my head do not drop off meanwhile.

April 14. Gold has been oscillating madly today. It reached 187! God help us. Things look very bad, but better men than I have died beggars, and we must endure every trial cheerfully if our national struggle can only be fairly fought out to the end. *Pro Ecclesia et Patria, et pereat Hopkinsius Episcopus cum Vallandighamio proditore!*

April 15. Weather comparatively decent. Twice at the fair. Drove thence in the morning with a jolly policeman, carrying some $25,000 to the Bank of America for the treasuress. Asked my companion if some of the people on the sidewalk wouldn't suppose I was in his custody, to which he replied, "Well, I reckon most on 'em think so, of course." On my afternoon visit, I invested a small amount in the only article of the Russian department that I cared for; one of the marvellous pictures of the Madonna and Child that are found in every Russian habitation, from the palace to the peasant's shanty. It's a most interesting symbol, representing not only the daily piety of so many millions of men and women, but also as coming down to us unchanged through a thousand years and more of faithful adherence to "old custom" in art, like certain usages in China.

Agnew, Van Buren, and Jenkins here tonight. An agreeable session. But I find myself in a minority of one on this proposition to establish sanitaria or *Hôtels des Invalides* for the *permanent* maintenance of discharged invalid soldiers. They are sorely needed. States cannot supply them for many reasons; relations between disease and climate among others. Pulmonary invalids should be sent to an inland sanitarium, typhoid patients shattered and disabled by typhoid malarial disease to some home on the seaboard. State institutions cannot thus discriminate. Government does nothing. Can we do anything? I fear not. Any considerable appropriation of our funds to this object would be a misappropriation—misapplication, breach of trust, constructive fraud—as it seems to me.

April 16.   Gold keeps at about 170 and exchange was bought today at 200! Insolvency is imminent. Congress is inefficient. The country seems drifting to leeward. I dread the newspaper attacks and queries and criticism to which the Sanitary Commission is about to be exposed on its receipt of the proceeds of this fair, and I have my doubts and difficulties about this question of our establishing sanitaria. Everything looks black and life is a failure today. . . .

Bostonians' joke about Whiting, now in high place in the War Department, and doing his duties most creditably, but while practising in the hub of the universe enjoying little reputation, and that bad. "First he got *on*, then he got *honor*, and at last he got *honest*."[20]

April 18, MONDAY.   O, Jupiter, how much there is to do, and how feebly I am doing it! Saw A. A. Low this morning and Jonathan Sturges about our Sanitary Commission Advisory Finance Committee; also, William H. Aspinwall. He is full of the plan, which public opinion is pressing on us, of funding part of the proceeds of the Metropolitan Fair for a *Hôtel des Invalides* or two, and made a magnificent suggestion on the subject, *en grand seigneur*. We will set apart half a million or so for that purpose, and he will turn over to us lands and buildings (*ci-devant* factories easily convertible to this new use) which must be worth $100,000 at least. It is very clear that we have got to meet this question, and it seems that we shall be compelled to fall in with Aspinwall's views, unless a great battle or two and the manifest urgency of calls for relief on the field divert public attention from the subject. That such battles are close at hand seems certain. The next two months are to be most momentous.

Took this opportunity to talk to Aspinwall about the School of Mines and to hint that he might make himself memorable as a "Founder." But it will do no good. I am met at every turn, in my endeavor to raise this fund, by the objection that the College is "endowed," and I begin to despair of success. The objection is absurd, as stated, for the simple reason that the College has to spend more than its income from all sources, endowment included. But it is the unconscious misstatement, the imperfect expression, of a very substantial objection that lies much deeper: that our trustees *feel* independent and above any appeal to public liberal-

[20] William Whiting, solicitor of the War Department, who did good service in checking fraud; the quip originated with Ebenezer Rockwood Hoar.

ity; that they are indifferent and apathetic, and disinclined to make any effort
to extend appeals to capitalists or to lovers of science. I have contributed
to it in money (*sit venia loquendi*) beyond what could have been expected
of a man of my humble income. No other trustee has subscribed a dollar,
or asked for a contribution, or made an effort to promote the undertaking.
John Astor, Edward Jones, Lewis Rutherfurd, Hamilton Fish, and Robert
Ray could do it by an hour's work each if they chose.

I suppose we must reconcile ourselves to the fact that New York is a
grand, commercial, money-making centre of the universe, and that learning and science are exotics which cannot be acclimatized. It's a first-rate
location for losing money, too. There is panic and smash in the stock
market. Sundry large fortunes gained by gambling during the first year
evaporated suddenly and quietly last Saturday and today. The great
Morse, whom General Van Alen knew last evening to be worth $2,500,000,
"went up" today and became a lame duck, having crippled himself on
Fort Wayne. (N.B. I don't clearly know what Fort Wayne is. Think it
is a railroad, but it may be a copper-mine for aught I can tell.) . . .

Tonight memorable for Ellie's debut at Leonard W. Jerome's
sumptuous private theatre in Twenty-sixth Street. This was the third
night of the season of private theatricals under the auspices of the dramatic committee of the Metropolitan Fair. Tickets are in great demand
at five dollars, the whole transaction being highly distinguished, aristocratic, and exclusive. House was full and everybody in the fullest tog,
men in white chokers and women in ball costume. The spectacle was
brilliant and pretty. First came *The Follies of a Night*, with handsome
Miss Isabel Rogers for Duchess, and Ellie as Mlle. Duval, her lady-in-
waiting. The men did very well, especially young Charles Fearing. So did
Miss Rogers. I trembled for Ellie, but she was perfectly self-possessed
and went through her subordinate but difficult part with wonderful grace,
dignity, and spirit. Her attire was most elaborate, and she looked lovely,
quite eclipsing her Duchess, as I thought, and so did others whose speech
I overheard. I was glad I took Johnny with me to witness his mamma's
triumph, and hear the applause she received. The whole performance was
strikingly *elegant*. Ladies and gentlemen have certain advantages over
professionals to compensate for their inexperience and their lack of stage
training.

April 20. Just from the fair, which I find much more crowded than
on any former visit. It closes next Saturday, I am happy to say. Called on
Major Halpine this morning at Dix's headquarters. He is about leaving

the service by reason of ill health, and there is talk of making him a paid "literary secretary" of the Sanitary Commission, about which step I doubt, though he is an unusually clever man.[21]

There was bad news this morning; another disaster had taken place, at least as damaging as Olustee and seemingly still more discreditable. The opening of this fearful campaign seemed to promise ill. But tonight in the third edition of the *Post* is a report of a second day's fight on the same ground (somewhere this side of Shreveport in the Red River country), in which we retrieved our fortunes, routed Seceshdom and took twenty guns. May it be true![22]

April 22. Our neighbor Mrs. D. D. Field died this morning after ten days of illness. . . . According to newspapers, both Mrs. Field and Mrs. Kirkland sacrificed their lives to overwork at the fair.[23] Both certainly worked very hard, but I doubt whether the death of either can be traced to this cause. The fair continues crowded, and its receipts are very large. Whether the final total will get up to a million is still uncertain, but it will not fall very far short of that sum.

Wall Street simmering with rumors. Fighting at Plymouth, North Carolina. Rebels repulsed, but certain of our gunboats sunk. We may have to evacuate Plymouth; Longstreet is moving down the Shenandoah Valley; Lee is crossing the Rappahannock or the Rapidan with 160,000 men (don't he wish he had them!); transmission of news from Washington stopped by the government, and so on. All this sent up gold sadly. Well, this much is certain, that the struggle of the campaign now just opening will be fearful and its results momentous. What if we fail?! Has this people faith and virtue enough to persevere after another season of failure or even of *partial* success?

Dr. Jenkins, just returned from Washington, brings back many

[21] Charles Graham Halpine was being forced out of the army by failing vision. He was a Protestant Irishman and graduate of Trinity College, Dublin, active for many years in journalism in Boston and New York. His burlesque poems in the assumed character of an Irish private, "Miles O'Reilly," were lively and popular. His war record was a brilliant one.

[22] The government was anxious to restore Federal authority in western Louisiana and in Texas, and Confederate forces under E. Kirby Smith and (more directly) Richard Taylor were stubbornly resisting an advance by Union troops under N. P. Banks and A. J. Smith. News from that remote quarter was tardy in reaching New York.

[23] Caroline Matilda (Stansbury) Kirkland was stricken in the Metropolitan Fair one crowded evening. She was the widow of Professor William Kirkland of Hamilton College, had resided in the West, and was the author of a dozen volumes of travels and belles-lettres.

important items of contraband intelligence about the Army of the Potomac and of the Cumberland, which I won't record. Good and hopeful on the whole; but we are not yet quite ready, and every day's postponement of the coming fight will be a great gain to the country.

April 23. . . . Received today proceeds of Albany Sanitary Fair— $80,000, minus $15,000 to be refunded the Albanians for their local work in getting up and forwarding supplies. Good for Albany! Though personally insolvent, I am quite flush for the present in my official character. . . . After dinner . . . took Ellie to Fourteenth Street Fair building. We ensconced ourselves in the "Floral Temple," a harbor of refuge from the dense crowd, mostly plebeian, of this final evening. Mrs. Ritchie was there in full-blown splendor; nice Mrs. George Betts; Mrs. Thorndike; Mrs. Robert Cutting; Mrs. Ronalds (one of our prettiest and cleverest women); her most sumptuous, fair-haired, beautiful sister (Miss Something Carter), whom I do not know at all, but whose presence is most worshipful to every one who appreciates a first-class blonde; also, Mrs. Gallatin, Mrs. Gentil, and others. Had to struggle through the crowd, like a fly in a pitcher of molasses, on sundry errands for the ladies, which were successfully achieved. At nine-thirty came the so-called announcement of the vote on the sword presentation, to Grant or to McClellan. The mob cheered madly and frantically over and over again for each candidate alternately. Asked forty people what was the result. Their contradictory answers were about equally divided. Rather guess McClellan has prevailed. It doesn't matter much. The suggestion of this vote came from Tiffany and does credit to his inventive faculty. It will add near $20,000 to the proceeds of the fair. Brought Ellie off at ten. Thank Heaven the fair is ended, and that Ellie is not yet broken down and seriously ill.

April 24, SUNDAY.   General Grant gets the sword after all, and by some 15,000 majority! Good. *Dignum et justum est.* The Union League Club subscription and other subscriptions in Grant's favor had been held back, judiciously, to the last moment. Belmont and Barlow looked in during the afternoon, satisfied themselves that McClellan was ahead, put in a little thousand just to give him a handsome majority, and went off. I hear they are full of wrath and confusion today. I am glad of this result, from no partisan feeling, but because Grant is in command and "little Mac" isn't, and because McClellan's success would have tended *pro tanto*, more or less, to weaken Grant in the estimation of his soldiers and of the people.

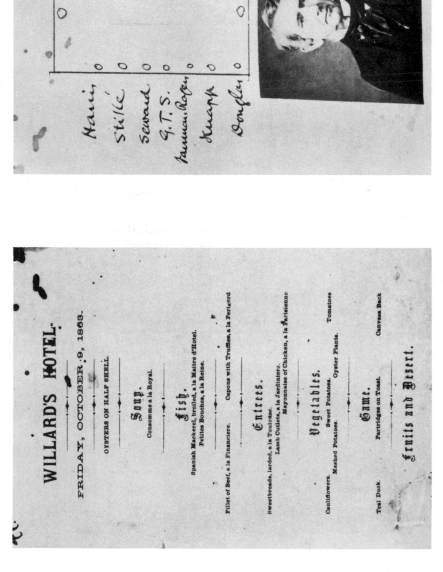

SANITARY COMMISSION DINNER TO SECRETARY SEWARD

FREDERICK NEWMAN KNAPP

FREDERICK LAW OLMSTED

It seems clear, or rather, *probable*, that Burnside's command has gone to Alexandria and is to constitute Grant's reserve. If so, the programme is *probably* that Burnside is to hold the defenses of Washington with 35,000 or 40,000 men, and thus enable Grant to turn Lee's entrenched position on the Rapidan without endangering the National Capital. A promising plan, if Burnside's force be strong enough to hold our fieldworks against an assault by Lee's whole army. But if Lee try that game, cannot Grant turn short round, follow him up, and put him between two fires?

April 26. . . . Curious story from George Gibbs, who spent the ten years preceding 1861 in California and Oregon. He met an old acquaintance from Steilacoom the other day who had arrived here by Panama steamer "night before last." "Why didn't you come and see me yesterday, old fellow?" quoth George Gibbs. "But I s'pose, of course, you were on a grand bust and went to every barroom in New York." "Not a bit," said he of the Pacific Coast; "I spent all yesterday loafing about in Trinity Church yard." To whom George Gibbs: "What the hell and damnation were you doing there?" "Well," said his friend, "I was going down Broadway to Wall Street, and I saw the old tombstones through the railings, and I have never seen before any work of man's hands that was older than myself, for I was raised on the Missouri frontier and have been pioneering among new settlements ever since I was born, and them old tombstones gave me a new sensation; so I asked leave of the sexton and just spent all day looking round among 'em." So there are communities that stand in the same relation to us that we occupy relatively to England and to the Old World generally.

In the Hammond court-martial, the evidence is closed. The Surgeon-General is to present his defense May 3rd. From all I can learn, it appears that there is nothing in the case to compromise the Sanitary Commission and that the prosecution has failed on every point. E. H. Owen, however (who called on me today to settle the judgment in Allen *v.* Schuchardt, wherein we got an affirmance from the Supreme Court at Washington), thinks there is a weak point in the defense as to a certain little contract for blankets. Four of the eight members of the court are understood to be positively hostile to Hammond, and I am confident the finding of the court will be short of full acquittal, at best, and that Hammond will thereupon resign in a huff, unless Van Buren can keep him within the bounds of reason.

April 27. J. J. Post duly married at Trinity Chapel to a Miss [Lucrie F.] Mahony, only child of a rich retired merchant in Twenty-third

Street. She's said to be a remarkably pretty little blonde girl of twenty. This is an age of signs and wonders. He is much more than a quarter of a century her senior and among the most peculiar of human beings. I wish them both all health and felicity, but unless the young lady possess uncommon tact and be among the best and most unselfish of women, she will have a troublesome time. Long talk with Cisco this morning at the treasury anent certain Trinity Church matters on which we are of one mind with the rector, and afterwards about public finance. All depends, he says, on the result of this campaign. Grant's failure or mere partial success will ruin us. His talk rather dyed me blue. I cannot bring myself even to hope for decisive victory by the Army of the Potomac under any chief.

Ellie's second appearance on any stage was this evening, at the Theatre San Jeronimo, in *The Follies of a Night*. Cast as before, house crowded, performance even better than before. Miss Isabel Rogers and Fearing, the most conspicuous personages, acted with more spirit and freedom, and Ellie went through her part with the utmost grace and delicacy of perception, looked and acted charmingly, and had a bouquet hurled at her by some unknown admirer—the first demonstration of the kind I have heard of as occurring in *aedibus hieronomycis*; no, *hieronomycensibus*, or *hieronomycalibus*. All this work is for a good and patriotic end, but the spectacle of lavish luxury tonight was a little suggestive of fiddling while Rome is in full blaze at its four corners. Raising a million by a fair and by auxiliary concerts and private theatricals for army relief is good and creditable to the community, but I should like to see somewhere a trace of the savage, indomitable resolution as of forty thousand tom-cats concentrated in one beleaguered corner, the ready endurance of privation, and the reckless disregard of consequences that are shewn by the cruel, semi-barbaric, treacherous leaders of the rebellion—or rather, by their people.

Long discussion this afternoon at 823 about the proposed removal of the Seventeenth Street Fair building to the Battery, to be used as a home and perhaps as an experiment, also, in the way of providing for discharged and permanently disabled men, if we can get the consent of our most honorable civic authorities. . . .

April 29. . . . Yesterday Ellie and I dined in state at John Astor's, with Mr. and Mrs. Carson Brevoort, Pinckney Stewart, Mr. and Mrs. Henry Day ("Lord's Day"), Cunards, Goold Hoyts, and others. Sat between Mrs. Cunard and Mrs. Camilla Hoyt. That lady grows stouter than is becoming, but her face is among the most splendid specimens of physical beauty—for form and color—I have ever seen. She is absolutely gorgeous to behold, though without much expression, if any. A model of her superb head in wax, under a glass case, would be just as good as the original.

Library Committee (Anderson and William C. Schermerhorn) at my office yesterday. General talk over college affairs. Professor Anderson brought up the presidency and *me* as one of the candidates and said sundry civil things. I made my usual reply to talk of that sort, and brought up the name of Professor Bull Anthon as eminently *the* man for the place. He is an alumnus, has served the College most faithfully forty years, more or less, and is the only member of its faculty who has done it much credit during that period. His promotion would therefore be natural and becoming and eminently proper if he be qualified for it. Now, admitting that he is defective in several important points, he has one qualification of the first order, namely, ability to establish and enforce discipline; and discipline is what the college now wants above all things. He is an old man and could not be expected to serve long, but if he held the presidency only four years, he could establish subordination and habits of obedience in the undergraduate corps and make the task of his successor comparatively easy. I urged this on Schermerhorn and Anderson and made some impression on them. Tried it on John Astor today, but he hates Bull and wouldn't tolerate the suggestion. As to my own claims and prospects, about which I hear people talking every day, I wouldn't give twopence for them. I have ceased to think about the matter.

April 30. No news from Virginia. Our Sanitary Commission Relief Corps is largely strengthened, and we are making heavy purchases of supplies. The collision must come soon. It will be nearly decisive. I fear it will be fatal. God help us!

May 1, SUNDAY. Mr. Ruggles came in at dinner time, just from Washington. Seward had sent for him to advise about a report or something as to a proposed line of telegraphic communication with Europe by way of Behring Straits and Asia. Afterwards appeared Wolcott Gibbs. Both Ruggles and Gibbs had much to say about the College and the presidency. I believe my own personal ambition on that question is understood—at least I hope so. I am sure it's an honest, well-defined, and unselfish position. . . .

I anticipate with resignation the calamity and trial of a journey to Washington tomorrow morning.

Strong's diary is here interrupted for a week; but he fills in the gap by his entries under May 8. During the interval Grant and Lee had fought the bloody battle of the Wilderness. Advancing into the tangled jungles of trees and bushes between the Rapidan and North Anna, the Army of the Potomac met there the whole force of the Confederates. Lee's veterans knew every part of the wooded battlefield, while the Northern troops were new to its thickets and morasses. Moreover, in the heavy cover the usefulness of the Federal artillery was much diminished. For two days, May 5 and 6, the battle swayed back and forth, first one side and then the other apparently successful. It was in the course of this hard-fought struggle that Lee, anxiously following a Texas brigade as it advanced into battle, was halted by the universal cry: "Go back, General Lee! Go back!" The battle was entirely inconclusive. Grant was disappointed in that his powerful army, more than twice as strong as Lee's, failed to deal the staggering blow for which he had hoped, while his losses (nearly 17,000) were far heavier than those of the Confederates. Lee was disappointed in that he had failed to out-manoeuver Grant as he had outgeneralled McClellan, Pope, Burnside, and Hooker, and in that he even failed to stop the Northern advance. For Grant, instead of falling back at the end of the exhausting contest, as other Union commanders would have done, lurched forward again. Turning to the left, he marched to Spotsylvania Court House—and Lee's tired forces, again placing themselves across his path, had to fight another bloody defensive battle. The North watched these movements with bated breath.

May 8, SUNDAY. I seriously incline to formally withdraw my name as a candidate for the presidency of Columbia College and put an end to the absurd aspirations of Charles King and Anderson of the trustees, and of George Anthon and other outsiders. The board meets again on the 18th and may then go into an election. I have not the smallest information as to the views of its members, but it seems to be the general belief that the lobby for Barnard (who is backed by the "ring" of the Academy of Sciences) has been active. His election would be a disaster. While I am in nomination, I cannot attend a meeting and vote against him, or urge the superior claims of any other candidate. Moreover, it seems questionable whether I could honorably decline the place were I elected, having had some two months' notice that I was talked of as a candidate and ample time, therefore, to make up my mind. But it is more than doubtful whether I would take the place were I unanimously asked to do so.

Got home from Washington last night at eleven after a day of weariness and starvation. A leather sandwich put into my stomach between Baltimore and Philadelphia was my sole aliment and accounts, under the circumstances, for today's infernal visitation of acute, nervous, restless, sick headache, and the heavy deadly somnolence that followed its partial relief.

News. Stanton's telegram to Dix, in our last extra, indicates a battle on the largest scale, and *victory.* Meade's medical director reports to Barnes, acting Surgeon-General, that six or seven thousand wounded men are to be sent into Washington. We have had the field, therefore. It would seem that Lee was forced to leave his intrenchments and attack, and that his attack failed, and that the woman-scourging chivalry was beat back with loss. But all our information on this point is vague. From the Peninsula we learn that Butler's and Baldy Smith's "change of base" from Williamsburg and West Point to the right bank of the James has been successfully executed. Strong naval force cooperating. Butler holds Petersburg. Sherman is moving from Chattanooga (that appears *aliunde,* by telegrams to Dr. Newberry), taking advantage of Longstreet's withdrawal from the southeast to reinforce Lee. Sigel, with Hooker (or more probably Couch) is marching up the Valley of the Shenandoah and threatening Lee's communications. It is long since our national prospects have looked so bright. But we may be fearfully "disillusionated" tomorrow morning, and find that an assault on Richmond has been repulsed and that Grant and Meade are falling back on Washington or "changing their base" to Fredericksburg and Aquia Creek.

Monday, the 2nd, by railroad to Washington, with Gibbs and Agnew. Pleasant ride enough. Woods and fields brighter and brighter with blossoms and greenery as we went southward. The orchards of Maryland lovely with apple and peach blossoms, and all the woodlands "a glad light green," contrasting with the red foliage that had survived the winter, and the dark coloring of cedar and pine trees. A heavy shower came up at sunset, and we reached Washington amid pouring rain. Drove to No. 244 F Street, where comfortable rooms awaited us, enabling us to eschew Willard's. We slept at 244 and took our meals out at Gautier's and Buhler's. Steiner, Knapp, and others estimate Meade's force at 125,000; Burnside's 20,000; Sigel's 16,000; Butler's 40,000, at least. *Quién sabe?* Everybody's utter ignorance about everything connected with the campaign is a most encouraging fact. Another is the relentless refusal of passes to the front.

Tuesday, the 3rd. The Commission met, with Bache in the chair. He has grown so deaf as to make an inefficient chairman. We were in small force, did only a little routine business, and adjourned early. With Bache and Gibbs to Navy Department, where we saw Admiral Davis, a most elegant, urbane, courteous old gentleman, but reported to be sly and selfish and ambitious of succeeding Bache in the Coast Survey, though a mere sciolist. Thence to the Smithsonian; went through the rooms with its superintendent, Professor Henry. Its museum is magnificent, but the laboratory and the working rooms look shabby, dusty, listless, and feeble.

Wednesday, the 4th. Loveliest weather. Spring manifested in ideal perfection. Genial warmth and bracing wind. The shady and the sunshiny side of the street each delightful. I crossed and recrossed F Street and 14th Street and Pennsylvania Avenue in voluptuous enjoyment of the change. Trees budding and visibly developing from hour to hour. The air full of little cottony pellets thrown off from the American poplar, copious as the flakes of a January snowstorm. Reports were (from our inspectors) that Meade's headquarters at Brandy Station broke up, and the Army of the Potomac moved at twelve last night, or at three this morning. Warren was to make a nocturnal movement and surprise the rebels at Germanna Ford.

Surgeon-General Hammond's defense was read yesterday. It seems conclusive, but Stanton will probably prevail against him. Hammond is confident of acquittal, but his anticipations are untrustworthy. . . .

Wednesday afternoon, attended a lecture to our corps of some thirty theological students from Princeton and from the General Seminary in Twentieth Street by Mr. Fay, mayor of Chelsea, who has been working on every battlefield from Fair Oaks to Chancellorsville. He is a rough diamond, and gave the corps a deal of sound advice. Then, to my dismay, I was called on for a "few remarks," which I emitted accordingly. My allocution had the merit of brevity, for it was comprised in about three sentences. I *loathe gas*, and I had nothing to say to these young men but to thank them, on behalf of the Commission, for responding to its call. They seem a fine manly lot of fellows, not like the divinity students of Harvard, whom Palfrey classified as "atheists, skeptics, and dyspeptics." During the leisure intervals between their lectures they were mostly "hallooing and singing of anthems"—also of secular melodies, *studenten lieder*, and nigger songs. "John Brown's body lies a-moulderin' in the ground" seemed a special favorite. Another of their "exercises" was in the back yard of 244, where pretty Miss Helen Gilson, Fay's ward,

who has shared all his labors, presided over a camp-kettle and lectured
"with experiments and illustrations" on the making of better coffee and
milk punch. The group would have made a nice picture. From the report
of Ellie on her Peninsular experiences of 1862 and of others, I suspect
this little New England girl of being a true heroine. Her manner in talking to her young pupils was admirable and delightful—self-possessed,
but modest, earnest, businesslike, perfectly simple, and wholly without
a trace of self-consciousness. News from Fort Monroe Wednesday
evening of an advance and coming battle, so we sent Knapp off to Baltimore to charter a steamer, and she was on her way down the Chesapeake
by two Thursday afternoon, heavily freighted with life-saving stores.
Our evening session was interesting. Agnew brought forward the report
of his committee in favor of establishing at least *one* sanitarium or *Hôtel
des Invalides* on a small scale. I was obliged to oppose the measure,
because this is not among our legitimate functions. We are appointed to
look after the national army. Binney backed this theory of our duty
quite emphatically, and raised the question whether our system of "pension
bounty and back pay" agencies, which we have been just extending and
enlarging, were not outside our proper sphere. We decided to take advice
of counsel in New York and Philadelphia. Whom can we consult in New
York?

Thursday, the 5th; long session. Grant is wholly detached from his
base with ten days' forage and fifteen days' rations. Rumors abound, but
there is no trustworthy intelligence. The general, absolute ignorance of
Grant's plans and movements is a good sign. The Commission adjourned
this (Thursday) evening.

Friday morning I spent mostly in letter writing. At half-past nine in
the evening, Agnew and I went to Governor (now Senator) Morgan's by
appointment, and with him to the War Department for an interview
with Secretary Stanton. Our object was to tell that terrible Turk in substance this: "Mr. Secretary, the Committee will have x plus y dollars to
spend for the aid and relief of your army and the promotion of its efficiency
during the campaign now just opened. Your cordial sympathy and cooperation will add fifty per cent to the value and effect of every dollar we
spend. We know we do not enjoy the light of your favor; on the contrary,
quite the reverse. You habitually denounce us and our work, and commonly talk of the Commission as a 'swindling concern.' Will you please
tell us what you mean by it, why you hate us, and what we can do to
appease your august disapprobation and secure for our unpaid, unofficial,

unrecognized private exertions for the benefit of your army the neutrality
—at least—of the War Department?"

After a little dangling in the antechamber, where we discoursed with
Chauncey McKeever, General Augur, and Senator Harris, we "sailed in"
to run Stanton's batteries under protection and convoy of Morgan, who
had no occasion, however, to "shell the woods" or gun-fire at all during
our two hours session. Our reception was on the whole rather grim, such
as a medieval saint would have vouchsafed to the Devil on receiving a
call from that functionary. We presented the resolution of the Commission appointing a committee to wait on the Secretary, on hearing
which the Secretary remarked, "Well, Sir???" Agnew proceeded thereupon to state from memoranda he had prepared an outline of our work and
our expenditure, which Stanton interrupted with inexpressible venom
and viciousness of manner. "I don't perceive any mention here of what
you must have paid for your scurrilous attacks on me and on the Administration through the public press." We could not guess what he meant,
and I humbly asked for light. We found that he referred to an article in an
early number of the *Bulletin* (signed "A Republican"), urging that the
Surgeon-General ought not to be displaced without a court-martial or an
investigation in some form. We submitted that this article discussed
fairly and temperately a question bearing directly on the efficiency of the
medical service and reminded him that it simply recommended him to do
what he did a month afterwards. Then he brought up the memorable
circular of last January. We said this was no act of the Commission, and
that the Commission was in no way responsible for it. But Stanton said
he had proof that it had been laid on the desks of members of Congress by
"our agent in Washington"—as to which fact we had no knowledge and
could say nothing. He dwelt with ferocious delight on the disgraceful
conduct of Peirce, Agassiz, and Hill, "whose signatures had been *fraud-
ulently obtained*—by whom he couldn't say."

It occurred to both Agnew and myself to tell him of the affidavits now
in New York, describing the deliberate reading of that paper and the
careful consideration of its purport, after which these gentlemen signed
it, but it also occurred to us both that it would be unwise to shew our
hand, and inexpedient to waste time in a squabble about details. So we
took the Secretary's fire with serenity, and his manner became less insolent
when he found we were not much frightened. Then he attacked our pension
and back-pay system as not within our proper sphere, but this position
(though his only strong one) he finally abandoned, admitting that the

work was useful and important, forced upon us in a manner, and subject only to a technical objection.

Next came a savage assault on our hospital supply system, kept up at Washington during the past year (but now wound up, I'm happy to say). "We had gone into the marketing business and made ourselves a trading association. Hammond's order that surgeons get their extra supplies through this channel was a gross violation of law, because all purchases were required to be by contract." There we *had* him. It was clear that the Secretary of War didn't know what a "Hospital Fund" is, or the regulations applicable to its disbursement. We enlightened him on this subject. He gasped and staggered, but soon came up again, and insinuated rather than asserted that the Commission had made money by the operation. "On the contrary, Mr. Secretary, our books and vouchers shew a balance against us of from $5,000 to $10,000." Whereupon the Secretary hit out viciously, but rather wild. "Then that amount of money has been lost—so much of the people's bounty wasted in this job." Our answer was obvious. This balance represents so much contributed to the hospitals, just as directly and effectually as if it had been used to buy them its equivalent in chickens, fresh eggs, and butter. The Commission has turned over the stores it bought and charged the hospital fund their cost price and no more, thus saving that fund not merely the profit of the middleman but also the expense of transportation. Of course the Secretary saw this, but he did not choose to say so, and changed the subject.

Agnew, who showed great tact, temper, and presence of mind throughout, said: "Well, Mr. Secretary, these criticisms are, after all, just what we have long wished to have the Department give us. What we want is the establishment of such relations with you as will secure our receiving your views and suggestions from time to time, and we shall, of course, and so on, always listen to your advice with—and so on." But this was among the things Stanton did not happen to want, and he withdrew himself at once, like a startled land-tortoise, or an irritated actinia. "You must execute your great trust in your own way, and on your own responsibility. I cannot advise you about it." So our interview ended at last, the Secretary taking leave of us with more civility than he had previously shewn.

He went out of his way more than once to declare his unbounded admiration and undying passionate affection for the Commission. He found fault only with the conduct of certain of its members or officers. He had done and always should do all he could to support and strengthen the

Commission itself. Strange, for he must have been aware that we knew this to be as big a bouncer as any that has passed over the telegraph wires during the last three years. It so demoralized me that I instantly replied "with effusion" that we couldn't possibly doubt it.

I was amazed by the discovery of our importance and that the Secretary of War keeps himself thoroughly posted as to our movements and our doings. Whenever he referred to any publication, he rang in his messenger, and said, "Ben! get me so and so of the Sanitary Commission," which the faithful but seedy creature did with admirable accuracy and promptitude. He failed only once, when he brought in a copy of the *Medical Times* instead. Whereupon the Secretary damned him and sent him back, soliloquizing, as it were, *sotto voce*, "It contains another attack on me. I suppose the Commission got *that* up, *too*." He was wrathful, also, over certain publications (I do not know what) in England, which he evidently credited to us and about the authorship whereof he designs to "have an investigation." This innocent design he announced in the tone with which a magistrate would notify a man charged with murder that his alleged alibi would be sternly scrutinized.

On the whole, this interview was a good thing, though without direct tangible results. We drew Stanton's fire and can estimate his weight of metal. It is not very heavy. He hates us cordially and would destroy us if he dared, but he fears our constituency. Public favor is the breath of his nostrils. He is not a first-rate man morally or intellectually. His eye is bad and cold and leaden and snakey, even when he is most excited. His only signs of ability at this conference were remarkable memory and capacity for details.

Pending our conference, the long, lean, lank figure of Uncle Abraham suddenly appeared at the door. Agnew and I rose. Stanton didn't. Lincoln uttered no word, but beckoned to Stanton in a ghostly manner with one sepulchral forefinger, and they disappeared together for a few minutes, going into a side room and locking the door behind them. We saw Abe Lincoln in the telegraph room as we entered the office, waiting for despatches, and no doubt, sickening with anxiety—poor old codger! But it's shameful so to designate a man who has so well filled so great a place during times so trying.

May 9, MONDAY. Thank God, Grant's victory seems established. Prisoners were taken on both sides. He lost one or two guns, and I do not hear that we captured any. But Lee is retreating and Grant is after him. Lee can hardly be making for Richmond. He, no doubt, means to fight again on the North Anna or at or about Hanover Court House. He shows no sign of demoralization. This battle of Thursday and Friday, nameless as yet, was a severe and close affair. Had not Lee retired, it would have been called a drawn battle. He seems to retire with his men well in hand, drawing no further from our base and our supports. That fine old fellow, General [James S.] Wadsworth, received a rebel bullet in his brain while leading his command into action. "Happy whom He finds in battle's splendor." We have lost a brave and useful man, but this is just the death Wadsworth would have ordered of the destinies had they consulted him on the subject.

During our vestry meeting, General Dix received and read the President's announcement of success and recommendation of public thanksgiving. If this good news *wear* a day or two longer, there should be a special service in Trinity.

Banks has come to grief. He is held responsible for our defeat and disaster in the Red River country and is condemned and denounced by everybody. General [E. R. S.] Canby supersedes him. People say he ought to be court-martialled and shot; poor Banks! Why will men of ability and reputation in civil affairs let themselves be deluded into the notion that they can handle armies? . . . Well, Heaven help the country and send us good news tomorrow! I think I would consent to be publicly executed in Union Square next Sunday after morning service if that ceremony would ensure success to Grant and Butler. Should their campaign fail, as it well may, our prospects both public and private are gloomy.

Another ill-starred campaign, as Strong notes, had come to a disastrous end. N. P. Banks, former Speaker of the House and Governor of Massachusetts, had been put in charge of the Red River expedition. This was a very dubious venture, for the river ran deep into Confederate territory. It roughly bisects northern Louisiana, flowing from Colorado, Texas, and Arkansas to run from Shreveport in northwest Louisiana to the Mississippi, which it joins near Port Hudson. Banks's orders were to ascend the stream and capture Shreveport, from which point he could invade northern Texas. This risky move was prompted by a number of reasons. Lincoln wished to make his newly reconstructed government in Louisiana effective throughout the state; Seward thought that, since a large French army had been landed in Mexico, it was important to restore the Union authority in Texas as soon as possible; and government agents believed that large stores of cotton could be seized along the stream. Banks advanced up the

*river with a force of nearly 30,000 men, supported by a fleet of gunboats under
Admiral Porter. But when he had almost reached Shreveport, the Confederates
fell upon his army, which was scattered for miles along the single road, and
fought two heavy battles with it (April 8, 9, 1864). In the first, at Sabine Crossroads, Banks was badly defeated; in the second, at Pleasant Hill, he stood fast.
But the stiff resistance he had met, joined with a failure of supplies, compelled
him to retreat. As he fell back, the gunboats were placed in a perilous position
by an unexpectedly early fall in the waters of the Red River, threatening to
leave them stranded. They would have been lost but for the fine expedient of a
military engineer in building a series of dams which furnished enough water to
carry them over the shoals. As Banks reached safer ground, Grant peremptorily
ordered him to send ten thousand men eastward; and the result was that he had
to give up Alexandria, Louisiana, on May 13. He was shortly superseded by
General E. R. S. Canby and returned to Massachusetts in discredit—though
then and since he has had not a few defenders.*

*But more momentous and heartening events were occurring in the East.
Grant's forward movement after the battle of the Wilderness had dismayed the
Confederates. As George Cary Eggleston writes, they felt "surprise and disappointment" when "he had the temerity to move by the left flank to a new position, there to try conclusions with us again." In the terrible fighting at Spotsylvania, closing May 12, Grant's losses were again much in excess of Lee's, for
the Confederates had entrenched themselves and the Northerners had to attack.
But the Southern army was hard hit—and Grant could easily replace his men,
while Lee could not. With grim tenacity the Northern leader, who had resolved
to fight it out on that line if it took all summer, simply made another flanking
march; and early in June he was ready for a new battle, that of Cold Harbor.
It was plain that the North had a commander of very different metal from
McClellan, Hooker, or Meade.*

May 10. . . . At Union League Club tonight, where was much people,
the tone of talk was grave and subdued. No one seemed particularly
jubilant or sanguine. The sad news of General [John] Sedgwick's death
(he was picked off by a sharpshooter at Spotsylvania) is depressing, and
then Lee shews such obstinacy and tenacity after his alleged defeat, and
our losses are so heavy! Twenty thousand men *hors de combat* already,
and the work only begun. Heaven help us! Agnew went to the front this
evening.

May 11. Little light from the morning papers, and that not particularly roseate. Their editorials are full of glowing prophecies about the moribund rebellion and the "doomed" city of Richmond, but that style of talk is stale and profitless. Their letters and despatches justify no vaporing. We seem to be holding our own—that's all. Were the case reversed, however, we should certainly feel more profoundly blue than we have felt this long while. If Grant were falling back toward Washington, fighting bravely and taking advantage of every defensible position, and Longstreet were in Maryland with from twenty to forty thousand men, feeling for a weak spot in the defenses of the Capital, and rebel gunboats controlled the lower Potomac, and some rebel chief were marching *up* the Shenandoah Valley (as Sigel is marching *down* the same), I think we should feel ourselves in a very tight place.

May 12. Call from Professor Anderson this morning. He "deplores" my withdrawal as a candidate for the presidency of Columbia College, and begs me to reconsider my resolution, which I shall not do.

Standing Committee meeting (Vestry of Trinity Church) tonight. Question of salaries of clergy fully discussed. We agree to recommend temporary donations rather than a permanent increase.

May 13. News from that fearful arena at and around Spotsylvania Court House is good, and has kept improving up to about three o'clock, when our latest tidings came and our last extra was issued. If these tidings be true, Grant and Meade have achieved what looks like material and perhaps decisive results, crushing and driving the larger portion of Lee's line of battle and taking thirty or forty guns and several thousand prisoners. Lee is out of ammunition and on short rations. The railroad lines that connect him with his base are cut or threatened. All this may be true. God grant it is! But we are so schooled in adversity that we presume all good news apocryphal. [General Rufus] Ingalls sends a jubilant telegram that "You may bet your pile" on complete victory, and Ingalls is a grave, business-like quarter-mastering officer, not ordinarily liable to sanguine spasms of exaltation. His despatch appears in this evening's *Post*, third edition. From Butler and Baldy Smith, operating on the right bank of James River, our intelligence is good, though indefinite and obscure. They would seem to be threatening Petersburg rather than Richmond, and to have cut the railroad that connects the two cities.

May 14. The bulletin boards of the *Post* and *Advertiser* at two o'clock were not dispiriting. Sherman holds Dalton after a fight in which he took twelve guns and five thousand prisoners. Schofield has beaten a rebel force out of East Tennessee into North Carolina, by way of "Bull's Gap," and is following up his victory. The killed and wounded Lee leaves behind him are 35,000. Among our prisoners is reported the notable Maryland renegade Bradley Johnson. Longstreet is reported dead and Lee severely wounded and in Richmond. All this looks well, but I do not believe that Lee's army is yet so demoralized as to be incapable of fighting, and Grant's force must be sorely reduced by the casualties of this terrible week of battle.

May 15. Whitsunday. A day of public thanksgiving for national victory, and a happy personal anniversary beside; so it has been a three-fold *Fest der Freude*, though chilly and rainy. . . .

Not much news. Sheridan (who is he?) is reported to have made a most brilliant raid in Lee's rear, tearing up miles of railroad, burning bridges, retaking prisoners, and destroying locomotives, cars, and commissary stores that Lee cannot well afford to lose. Tonight we hear of a despatch from Stanton to Dix that Sheridan is on the right bank of the James River with Butler, and that Grant has made a reconnaissance yesterday which disclosed that Lee was retreating westward—on Gordonsville, I suppose. I hope this may not tempt Grant to move on Richmond until he has put Lee beyond all power of doing mischief. Also, that very valiant rebel, J. E. B. Stuart, is said to be killed. Also, Sigel is at Woodstock, wherever that is, and censured for tardiness. It's said that he should have traversed the Shenandoah Valley and been rolling Dutch thunder on Lee's flank and rear a week ago. *Quién sabe?* All the prospect of this campaign is splendid beyond our hopes. But will it last? . . .

Strong had not watched the despatches from the West closely in 1863, or he would have been in no doubt as to the identity of Philip Henry Sheridan, who had taken part in numerous battles in Tennessee, and been promoted to the rank of major-general. This dashing West Pointer now commanded a cavalry corps in Virginia and had fought at Cold Harbor and Spotsylvania. By the daring raid he made behind the Confederate lines (May 9–25), he cut railroad communications, destroyed much property, and at Yellow Tavern defeated J. E. B. Stuart, the Confederate leader who had distinguished himself on many a field —First and Second Manassas, the Seven Days' Battles, Antietam, Fredericksburg, Chancellorsville, and Gettysburg. Resisting stubbornly at Yellow Tavern, Stuart was mortally wounded.

May 17. . . . Sorry to say that the feeling downtown today is despondent and bad. There is no news from the front to justify it, but people have taken up with an exaggerated view of Grant's hard-won success in opening the campaign, and now, finding that the "backbone of the Rebellion" is not "broken at last" into a handful of incoherent vertebrae, and that Lee still shews fight, "on the Po" or elsewhere, they are disappointed, disgusted, and ready to believe any rumor of disaster and mischief that the wicked ingenuity of speculators can devise and inculcate.

May 18, WEDNESDAY. Trustees of Columbia College met at two o'clock. Betts did not come in till late, so I acted as clerk *pro tem*. After reading minutes, we took up our special order, the question of the presidency. The Bishop handed in the report of the Committee on Nominations and requested that I read it. The document presented the names of Barnard, Coppée, Anthon, Vinton, Sam Eliot,[24] my own, and one or two more. I had never seen it before. Its second or third paragraph mentioned the high qualifications of myself as too well known to every member of the board to require any special statement! I read this with gravity and unction, and I hope without sign of self-consciousness or annoyance. Some little desultory talk followed, and I took the earliest opportunity of thanking the committee for the honor it had done me, and of withdrawing my name on two grounds: first, because it was so doubtful whether I should take the place even were it offered me that I should not be dealing fairly with the board if I consented to stand an election; and second, because the question before us was so vitally important that every trustee was bound to attend in his place and vote according to his best judgment, which I could not do while even nominally a candidate. I think this was well received, as I am sure it was sincerely said, and with a view to no interests but those of the College. Edward Jones made a kind suggestion that my withdrawal ought to appear on the minutes. Then Mr. Ruggles said somewhat in support of Eliot. But the Bishop responded with a decided attack on Eliot as having failed in his administration of the affairs of Trinity College, Hartford. He pronounced for Barnard and with more feeling and emphasis than he usually shews on any personal question. I had expected the election would be postponed, at least till June, but signs multiplied rapidly of the industry and success

[24] This Samuel Eliot (1821–1898) was a first cousin of the famous Charles W. Eliot so long president of Harvard. A public-spirited man of philanthropic bent and deep religious feeling, he was first professor and then president at Trinity College in Hartford until 1864, when he returned to Boston to devote himself to good works.

of the lobby for Barnard. Fish, Rutherfurd, Beadle, and Dr. Haight severally took the floor as his advocates. Reading of his "testimonials" was called for, and they were read. Certainly, if any faith can be put in the certificates of a man's friends, Barnard's qualifications are most preëminent, and his alleged disqualification of absolute deafness does not exist. He is only just a little hard of hearing. But such certificates are unfortunately not to be relied on. Mr. Ruggles and Bradford opposed the current—not very energetically. Morgan Dix professed himself to have been doubtful but to be satisfied, Dr. Torrey came out strong for Barnard, so we went into an election, Ogden and I tellers. Result: Barnard 14, Professor Bull Anthon 3 (Betts, Anderson, and I), Eliot 1 (Mr. Ruggles), and Dr. Vinton 1. I cannot guess who voted for Vinton, unless it may have been Zabriskie, who is apt to be eccentric and wrong in every vote he gives. King and Robert Ray were absent. They would have probably voted against Barnard.

So Barnard is president. We must give him all possible support in the performance of his duties, but I fear he will prove physically unequal to them, and that our action will be calamitous to the College. It is another instance of our electing men who want the place, instead of looking for men whom the place wants.

The new head of Columbia was one of the most distinguished educators of the time—though his gifts were certainly not equal to those of Charles W. Eliot, soon to become president of Harvard, or Andrew D. White, soon to be the first president of Cornell. Born at Sheffield, Massachusetts, in 1809, he had been graduated from Yale in 1828, and had made mathematics and chemistry his special fields. After teaching at the University of Alabama 1837–1854, he had gone to the University of Mississippi, of which he soon became head. His interests were wide, and he had written not only on mathematics, but on grammar, higher education, art education, and the Coast Survey. A man of great dignity, a thorough gentleman, a thinker of philosophic depth, and an executive of no little imagination, he was well fitted to preside over the College as it now slowly grew into a true university.

The Rev. Harwood of New Haven and Mr. Ruggles dined here. After dinner, to the Law School Commencement at the Historical Society Rooms in Second Avenue. Great crowd and great heat. Dwight's oration was good. . . .

Copperheadism perpetrated a most flagitious act of moral high treason this morning through the agency of the *World* and the *Journal of Commerce*. Those papers published a fictitious proclamation by the President that the situation in Virginia, our defeats in Louisiana (Banks, to wit), and our failure to reduce Charleston compelled him to call for three hundred thousand more men, and to suspend all aggressive operations till they should be enlisted and drilled into efficiency. This bogus despatch was announced to be a forgery on every bulletin board by ten o'clock, but it did its mischievous work and sent gold up to 184. At the Union League Club tonight with Mr. Ruggles, I rejoiced to hear that General Dix has taken possession, under martial law, of the offices of both papers. Public feeling will sustain him. In Wall Street this morning capitalists, lawyers, and sober citizens in general seemed inclined to prosecute the *Journal of Commerce* under the provisions of the Code of Lynch. Exasperation was intense, and it seemed taken for granted that this forgery was the work of Samuel Barlow.[25]

May 19. News from Virginia very good but not entitled to the least credit. Offices of *World* and *Journal of Commerce* still occupied by squads of men with guns and bayonets; a very grave proceeding, and involving very grave questions, but no one should criticize it now or until Lee is driven south of Richmond. Perhaps constitutional doubts about the action of government will then be in order. The obituary record of tonight's *Post* includes the name of Thomas Colden Cooper; Tom Cooper, my old college classmate, captain in the 67th New York, who fell while leading his command on the 6th "in the Wilderness." Poor Tom Cooper! From my recollection of his college ways, I can well believe he was doing his work with courage and with reckless audacity.

May 20. Very busy day. Nothing new from Grant. Am just from the Union League Club, whither I went at ten in pursuit of knowledge, after writing letters here all the evening. These are fearfully critical, anxious days. Their most trifling memories will be interesting hereafter. The destinies of the continent for centuries depend in great measure on what is now being done and suffered a few hundred miles south of Twenty-first Street. The howl of a newsboy may at any moment rise on the midnight air, announcing an extra with news of national success or ruin. At

---

[25] This outrageous forgery was concocted by a reporter on the New York *Times*, Joseph Howard, Jr., who hoped to make money from it on the stock market. He got three months in a military prison for his act. The *World* and *Journal of Commerce* were suppressed for two days by the Washington authorities for carelessly printing the forgery.

this very minute, it may be practically settled, at or about Spotsylvania Court House, whether American development is to be controlled by the ideas of New England and New York, or by those of South Carolina and Mississippi—whether an Algerine slaveocracy is or is not destined to bear sway from the Lakes to the Gulf and from the Atlantic to the Pacific for generations to come. Isn't it strange that one can make even a pretense of going through with the petty duties of common life, while these tremendous issues are *sub judice*? . . .

May 21. . . . Why did not government call for 200,000 more men, six months ago? They could have been got, and they might have been now strengthening the Army of the Potomac, enabling it to achieve decisive victory and averting the calamity of another unsuccessful campaign. But criticism is easier than administration.

We are working on a very large scale in aid of Grant's army, and making our mark there, as it seems to me. We spend $650 a day for river transportation by steamers, barges, and schooners chartered by Knapp. We are manning fifty or sixty wagons with four- and six-horse teams, and employing from 150 to 200 relief agents (all to some extent skilled laborers), and twice as many teamsters, servants, and contrabands, but I foresee a fearful time at hand of newspaper queries—"What has become of all this money?"—that may irritate me to suicide. No matter, if the money have been so used as to help save the country.

May 23, MONDAY. News from Sherman good, from Banks bad, from Grant obscure but not discouraging. Stanton's last published despatch to Dix, coupled with telegrams received at 823 today, and with the fact that Knapp is going up the Rappahannock in one of our supply steamers with a heavy cargo of stores, and with the vague reports of success that I hear of as prevalent downtown late this afternoon—all these things being put together seem to indicate that Grant has slipped quietly around Lee's right flank without a serious engagement, and that both are moving toward Richmond, side by side, Grant having the inside track, but Lee moving probably with fewer impedimenta and therefore faster; that there will be a decisive battle in the region of Hanover Court House; that Grant will establish his base on the Rappahannock below Fredericksburg, perhaps at Port Royal; that, and so forth. We shift our supply stations from Belle Plain to Aquia tomorrow, or perhaps did so today. The railroad from Aquia to Fredericksburg is restored or nearly so, and I suppose the hospitals of Fredericksburg are to be cleared out with all convenient speed.

We agreed tonight on large anti-scorbutic purchases ($25,000 worth of pickled cucumbers and preserved tomatoes), anticipating that the Army of the Potomac will be on our hands within a month in the same condition in which we found it at Harrison's Landing in July, 1862—every man sickening from exhaustion and hard work on the monotonous diet of fighting rations, hard tack and salt pork, to wit, and craving an onion or a raw potato or a hatful of sauerkraut, as an old drunkard craves his gin. . . .

The martyred newspapers, the *World* and *Journal of Commerce*, have been ungagged, and the former vomits acid bile most copiously. Two or three of its editorial columns are occupied by a letter to the President, full of protest and fury, signed Manton Marble (the name of a mercenary renegade); suggesting, *inter alia*, a parallel between Uncle Abe Lincoln and Charles the First! One might as well compare dirty little penny-a-lining Marble with Catiline. Will this most novel suggestion tempt Honest Old Abe to cultivate a peaked beard and long curls and to extend his shirt collar into a wide area of ornamental lace? Will he set about writing an *Eikon Basilike* in view of his possible dethronement by a convention and an election now at hand, and will such publication (should it ever appear) be discussed and fought over by literary critics, and its genuineness affirmed and denied with profound research and ingenious argument a century hence, by scholars who have been unfortunately unable to discover any more useful work for their scholarship to do?

May 25.   That demagogue, traitor, and scoundrel, Horatio Seymour, who is (for our sins) governor of this state of New York, publishes a letter to Mr. District Attorney Oakey Hall (*arcades ambo*), bewailing the lawless violence lately perpetrated on the *World* and the *Journal of Commerce*, and requesting him to get everybody responsible therefor duly indicted as soon as may be. The governor's official sense of the danger of violating law has improved since the memorable riots, arsons, and murders of last July. He dealt with rioters, house-burners, and murderers more kindly then; addressed them as his "friends," and said nothing about promoting any action against them by grand juries. But his "friends" of the *canaille* were working for the rebellion then and against the country. They were entitled to a degree of consideration which the national government cannot expect—from Horatio Seymour. Their violations of law were to be tenderly treated, but those of the Administration, though technical and not murderous, must be truly resisted. Seymour has blundered again, as men without principle are apt to blunder. Even War Democrats denounce him for seeking to commit "the party" to a position against the government. . . .

May 26. . . . War news looks favorable. Lee seems falling back on a position between the North Anna and South Anna rivers, or perhaps to Hanover Junction. . . .

May 27. Grant still goes *Vorwärts* as obstinately as old Blücher, and has crossed the North Anna after a sharp conflict, in which field-works seem to have been stormed in a style creditable to any soldier. . . .

May 28, SATURDAY. . . . Gold reached 189 today! We are in a bad way, unless Grant or Sherman soon win decisive victory. But I see no symptom yet of debility in the backbones of loyal and patriotic men, or, in other words, of the community minus Peace Democrats, McClellan-maniacs, mere traders and capitalists, and the brutal herd of ignorant Celts and profligate bullies and gamblers and "sporting men" that have so large a share in the government of our cities.

It is remarkable that every "sporting man" and every disreputable character, every employee of a gaming house, a policy shop, or a Lupanar is sure to be full of wrath against Abolitionists, to despise the Administration, to rate Southern pluck and capacity for fight far beyond our own, and to canonize McClellan as a martyr. Old "Hingland" takes the same view of the situation. I am thankful to be cured, at last, of the Anglo-philism that has oppressed me ever since I was a boy and made me forget or underrate my own people and my father's house.

May 29. News from Grant. He retired across the North Anna, but moved quickly down its left bank and down that of the Pamunkey, crossed it, turning Lee's position, and held Hanover (*not* Hanover C.H.) some twelve miles from Richmond on Friday. If this series of bold movements succeed, Grant will be held a great general. Should Lee be forced to cross the James River, rebeldom will totter to its base. God grant it! . . .

George Anthon came in, and Mr. Derby, Lewis Rutherfurd, Professor Joy, and Professor Rood, Mr. Ruggles, Wolcott Gibbs, John Sherwood, Richard Grant White, Kuhn, and others, and we had a full supper-table. An unusual amount of good talk, and I regretted Ellie's absence. She was obliged to retreat early with a headache. Rutherfurd had much interesting discourse with the other savants about astronomical matters, and then the great Darwin controversy came up. Gibbs argued for Darwin, not as a *Darwinian*, but as stating that side of the question. Gibbs's reply to the obvious objection that there is no evidence whatever for the development hypothesis is at first sight a poser—namely, that there is no sort of (scientific) evidence in support of the theory of successive acts of creation, and that both propositions, being equally without historical proof, must be estimated according to their relative internal a priori probabilities and consistency.

May 30.   News continues very good. May it prove *true*, also. Grant reported advancing, and close to Richmond. There has been a battle in Georgia resulting in our favor; "rebel loss 2,500, ours 300." Wonder whether these figures be strictly accurate? George Anthon dined here, and William Schermerhorn looked in to discuss the advantages of summer quarters at Quogue. To the Union League Club, but got no news. Gold reached 191 today! Union League Club people think Lee will not risk a battle outside the forts of Richmond, but will burrow in them and stand a siege. I think otherwise—that he will fight, and fight hard, and fall back on his earthworks if beaten.

June 1. . . . Cisco says that Mrs. Grant and a party of her friends came downtown the other day to see the Treasury Building, and that he escorted them through it. The lady is a simple-mannered, plain, quiet woman. "Is the General anxious?" "O no, not at all; the last afternoon he was in Washington, he spent a couple of hours on the floor playing with the baby." "He is confident of success then?" "Entirely so, of course; he knows it's his destiny to take Richmond." In reply to some suggestion about the White House and the next presidency, the lady said most emphatically that her husband would not think for one moment of accepting a nomination.

By the way, the Cleveland Convention or conventicle has nominated Frémont and John Cochrane for President and Vice-President. If Grant take Richmond, and Sherman take Atlanta, Lincoln's renomination by the Baltimore Convention is a tolerably sure thing.

The "Letter to a Whig Member of the Southern Independence Association" by Goldwin Smith of Oxford is among the best essays on this revolution so far; but it will make no impression on shabby old shop-keeping England. Her position among nations is to be estimated now only by the value of her assets in pounds sterling. The England I have venerated for so many years is dead of fatty degeneration and hypertrophied ledgers.

June 4, SATURDAY.   The Grant mass-meeting on Union Square is reported to have been large, earnest, and grave. Perhaps Union Square will be held a classical locality by our great-great-grandchildren and awaken historical associations.

Bulletin from Grant in this evening's papers announces a fight that began early yesterday morning. He attacked and was successful at every point, but "without decisive results." The moderate tone of all his despatches is a most favorable sign. It indicates that he is a man of business and work, that he knows the worth of facts and of results accomplished, and the importance of results not yet attained, and that he cares little for talk or for *telling* bulletins. I begin to rate Grant very high. He seems earnest and capable, stronger than Burnside and Hooker, and more single-minded than McClellan.

McClellan went into this work intending to do his *professional duty*. So did poor Fitz-John Porter. Both have come to grief because they were blinded by the situation of affairs, by old West Point traditions, and by the professional sympathies of the old military service before 1861. Neither saw the case and the duties the case imposed on him from a national point of view. They thought more of the good old Democratic party, of the infamy of abolitionism and the provocations of the South, of the worthlessness of volunteer generals compared with genuine West Pointers, and of their excellent but perhaps a little misguided West Point and army friends, such as Lee and Albert Sidney Johnston, than of the great national cause. Grant and Meade seem free from this mischievous taint, thank God.

June 7. English newspapers have heard of Grant's progress as far as Spotsylvania Court House. They are bothered by the news. Their faith in the final triumph of those dear, chivalric slave-breeders and girl-floggers is unimpaired, of course, but they are pained to discover that Grant, though a Northern general, must be admitted to possess a certain amount of military ability; that men in the national service can fight almost if not quite as well as the "patriot legions" of the South. . . . They think our battles, day after day, and night after night, without exhaustion, rather remarkable and interesting as compared with the history of European campaigns. By a curious coincidence with this discovery, the British government seems to have decided on buying the much debated rams, instead of letting them steam forth from a British post to butt open our blockade.[26]

[26] The Confederate agent James D. Bulloch had contracted with Laird Brothers, the great English shipbuilders, to build two iron-clad warships of formidable type, equipped with powerful beaks. These rams could break the Northern blockade. Begun in the summer of 1862, they soon aroused apprehension in America. Assistant Secretary Gustavus V. Fox of the Navy wrote that they must be stopped at all hazards, "as we have no defense against them." John Slidell, acting for the South, perfected a plan

June 8. Evening papers give Stanton's latest bulletins. Nothing new with Grant. But Grant reports that the Richmond papers say that General [David] Hunter (Sigel's successor) has defeated the rebels in the Valley of the Shenandoah, killed their General Jones (stationed at West Point in 1850, I think) and occupied Staunton. Excellent, if true, and a vast improvement on Sigel. The Baltimore Convention admitted the "radical" delegation from Missouri, excluding the "Claybank" or "Conservative" contestants, and nominated Uncle Abe Lincoln by acclamation. Well and wisely done—*me judice.* Who will be nominated as Vice-President? Either Hamlin, Dickinson, or Andy Johnson of Tennessee, probably. I should prefer Johnson. Mrs. Dix says the General was asked to be a candidate but declined. . . .

Frémont's nomination by the Cleveland schismatics seems to attract little attention. Their choice of a cypher like John Cochrane as their candidate for Vice-President is a confession of weakness. What will the Democrats do? Will they try to overbid their opponents by nominating some ultra anti-slavery and war-to-the-knife man, or allow their party name and prestige to be used by their peace-mongering brethren? They have a difficult game to play. Should they adopt the former policy and decide to be democratic in principle and reality as well as in name, they may endorse Frémont. That would be a revolution, indeed! But Frémont is not nearly as strong as he was in 1856, and will run badly. Who could be brought forward as a "Peace" candidate? Should Grant's campaign fail disastrously, McClellan stock might revive, but his name has lost much of its power, and it would be hard to make him an available candidate for any office. That pipe is probably smoked out at last. Governor Seymour would like to run as representative of a platform of treason and national disintegration, but his dallyings with the beastly rioters of last July could be used against him with fatal conclusive effect, I hope.

---

by which they should be delivered to a French house which would then resell them to the Confederacy. But the British government in September, 1864, issued orders to stop their departure.

LINCOLN'S CAMPAIGN AND REËLECTION · GRANT'S
SUMMER REVERSES AND AUTUMN SUCCESSES ·
SHERMAN TAKES ATLANTA

———————◦∞◦———————

*G*rant, *by the close of May, had pushed forward to Cold Harbor near
the Chickahominy River, nearly midway between Hanover Town and
Richmond. He was fighting now to reach the James River below Richmond and
to establish his base there, where he could easily be supplied by sea. Lee entrenched
himself strongly; and on June 3 Grant made the error of attacking his lines,
apparently in a final effort to destroy the Confederate army by a frontal assault.
The attack broke down with bloody losses. Grant, who later admitted that it
had been a costly mistake, then turned to the policy of approaching Richmond by
slow operations of a siege-like character. By now it was clear that Lee was
permanently on the defensive, and that Grant's steady blows would soon bring
him to a critical pass. In the West, Sherman had meanwhile advanced into
Georgia, driving Johnston's much weaker army before him; and on June 8 he
began the hard fighting about Kenesaw Mountain which, after three weeks of
battle, finally forced Johnston's withdrawal. Atlanta was being brought within
reach.*

*When the Union-Republican Convention opened in Baltimore on June 8,
Lincoln's nomination was a foregone conclusion. Prolonged cheers greeted every
mention of his name. On the first ballot (June 8) he was given a unanimous vote
—though twenty-two Missouri delegates temporarily supported Grant, then
changed their votes. The platform called for a victorious conclusion of the war,
without compromise, and for the full and final abolition of slavery by constitutional amendment. Lincoln's own choice for the vice-presidential nomination was
Andrew Johnson, who also was chosen on the initial ballot. But* **nearly all**

observers agreed that the success of the ticket would depend upon the fortunes of
war during the summer of 1864. Lincoln was popular at the North, but not so
popular that he could withstand crushing military defeats.

June 9.   After dinner to a session of that ancient and honorable
institution the Committee on the Course of Columbia College at Rutherfurd's in Second Avenue. Bradford was there and Barnard, our new
president, whom we elected trustee to fill George F. Allen's place last
Monday, and whom I met for the first time. We got through with our
work expeditiously. McVickar agrees to become an emeritus professor
at his present rate of compensation, "which is necessary to him" (!), and
Barnard will henceforth represent the Evidences of Natural and Revealed
Religion to the Senior class one hour weekly. After we got through,
Rutherfurd displayed his spectroscope and revealed to us the sodium
line and the lithium line, and so on. It seems a fine instrument, with care-
fully constructed carbide of sulphur prisms. The strontium lines were
gorgeous. Then I walked to Union League Club (monthly meeting) with
Barnard and left him there with his friends, Van Nostrand and G. W.
Blunt.

Barnard is manifestly a thoughtful, judicious, earnest, kindly man, of
high principle, intense loyalty, and great practice in all educational
questions. But he is *very* deaf, and his deafness will seriously interfere
with his official duties; and he has no presence to help him through. I fear
he will find his dealings with our insolent, unruly undergraduates painful
and difficult. But they may prove well-bred and magnanimous enough to
treat his infirmity with respect. If he possess great tact and win their
esteem and confidence, they are likely to do so. If not, they will soon
drive him out of the College, for he seems physically incapable of govern-
ing a disaffected, disorderly corps of students.

Baltimore Convention nominated Andy Johnson for Vice-President;
vice Hamlin dropped. Very well. Unanimity of these nominations encouraging. But it disgusts the *World* newspaper, which condemns and
denounces both Lincoln and Johnson as mere plebeians, utterly ungenteel
and excessively low. The *World's* editorial would make an effective
L. & J. campaign document. I suppose a certain amount of disapproval and
abuse by Marble and Hurlbut of the *World* and by such like coprophagous
insects to be as honorable as the Victoria Cross or the Order of the Garter.
Of course, its amount would have to be almost inconceivably large, its
authors being so despicable, but these renegade Copperheads dignify

and ennoble every loyal American by every epithet of indignity they apply to him.

No war news, except that the *Commercial* says Butler is about undertaking some great movement. I fear it will be a failure. Gold 197!!! People are blue. They have found out somehow that Grant will never get into Richmond after all. They may be right, but I do not see why they think so. Certain well-meaning friends of mine in Wall Street help depress public opinion and raise gold by going about bleating like forlorn desolate stray lambs. Take — for example. His daily talk when I ask the news is "Ba-a-a-a!" Snooks says he knows Grant's losses have been per-fect-ly tre-mendous.

June 13, MONDAY. . . . Much business at 823 this afternoon; Agnew, Jenkins, and I. A cord of big bills examined and passed. We are spending money fearfully fast, but I believe to good purpose, and from present appearances our disbursements for June will not much exceed $150,000. May cost us over $262,000! Apocryphal war news most abundant these four days. Newspaper reports, official telegrams, and our Sanitary Commission correspondence indicate one or two facts as established. Grant is destroying his communications with White House and changing his base once more, to the James River. Hunter's success in Western Virginia is fully confirmed and may prove important. Butler has been taking liberties with the city of Petersburg, Virginia, which would have been more completely successful had Gillmore's cooperation been more energetic.

It's a blessed sign that Richmond papers seem in a special fit or orgasm of rage, fury, spite, brag, and insolent indecency just now. The extracts we get from Southern newspapers seldom fail to be significant. They illustrate or indicate the mental and moral tone that slaveholding has given to our Southern aristocracy, falsely so-called. . . . By the by, the proportion of Celtic and Teutonic surnames in the daily newspaper lists of casualties is extremely small, and of those who bear (or who bore) these surnames, very many must have been born Americans. But the Richmond papers and the London *Times* would sneer at our armies "made up of hireling foreign scum," just the same, were every name on our muster-rolls pure Saxon or Norman.

June 15. Very weighty news was posted on the bulletin boards before noon today. Grant "changed his base" to James River on Sunday. He has crossed that river and his headquarters are at Bermuda Hundred.

Part of his force marched to White House and so round by water, down the Pamunkey and York, and up the James. This movement has been effected without molestation. That is its most remarkable feature.[1] After closely hugging the rebel lines for a week, Grant detaches part of his army for a long, roundabout detour, disengages the rest of it, somehow, and slides it along Lee's front by a most critical flank movement, and takes it across a difficult river. Yet Lee makes no attempt to follow him up or to destroy his divided army in detail. I do not understand the situation. Either Lee has made some demonstration of which we are not informed, *or*, he holds Grant's move a false one and disinclines (like Napoleon) to attack him while making it, *or* he is weaker and more seriously exhausted by these five weeks of fighting than we have supposed.

June 16. . . . "Little Mac" (very little; Napoleoniculus) delivered himself of an oration yesterday at West Point on the occasion of the founding of a monument to the memory of regular officers, thereby inviting comparisons between himself, the late Pericles, and the contemporaneous Edward Everett. It's a dull speech, and the symptoms of a latent Copperhead are dimly apparent here and there, under a pile of commonplace flowers of rhetoric. McClellan was serenaded by the cadets thereafter, and some of them called for three cheers for G. B. McClellan, "our next President," which cheers were given. Colonel Bowman and Clitz looked on and listened and let it pass. The official "visitors," also looking on, were much offended by this "affront to the Administration."

June 17. Grant *has taken Petersburg*, before the ink was dry wherewith its flatulent editors were recording their triumph over the failure of a late demonstration against that "gallant little city," and their full faith in its impregnability against "Lincoln the Baboon" and "Butler the Beast" and all the hordes of Yahooland. Heaven be praised. . . .

June 20. Our cackle over Petersburg was premature. What we did on Wednesday was merely to storm a difficult line of fieldworks, captur-

[1] Grant had determined, after his bloody failure to break the Confederate lines at Cold Harbor, to transfer his army south of the James and move on Petersburg and Richmond from the southeast and south. On June 14, Hancock's Second Corps began to cross the James, and by the morning of the 15th he had about 20,000 men beyond the river. The next step was to capture Petersburg, which would cut Lee's supply lines by the Southside and the Weldon railroads. Grant's movement was so rapid and efficient that for three days Lee was half bewildered by it. As late as the 17th, after being vehemently urged by Beauregard to lose no time in reinforcing the Confederate lines before Petersburg, he declared: "Until I can get more definite information of Grant's movements, I do not think it prudent to draw more troops to this side of the river."

ing prisoners, and sixteen guns.[2] Ethiopia, by the by, took six of the sixteen and came up to the scratch in the best style. On Saturday, we attempted another line and failed. Hence long faces in Wall Street this morning. . . .

June 21. Gold has reached 200 at last! . . .

June 22. . . . Gold has run wild under the Act of Congress meant to suppress speculation therein, and has been privily sold at 230!!! Pauperism probably awaits me and better men than myself. Let it come. I have lived much more than half my allotted term in ease and comfort, much beyond my deservings, and have no right to complain. Only let us all do our utmost to uphold the national cause, and let us not be disheartened by fear of poverty. . . .

June 24. Agnew, Van Buren, and Jenkins here in Standing Committee. Ellie came in late from her yachting party. I propose taking Johnny with me on our voyage—at his earnest prayer—but not without misgivings.[3] He will be at least as seasick as I, and then there are the chances of sharpshooting, torpedoes, flying field-batteries, and so on, for we are going into the heart of the enemy's country, and through miles of hostile river-navigation, more or less dangerous.

July 4, MONDAY. Home at eight A.M. Saturday, the 25th of June, was a most collar-wilting day. With Johnny to No. 823 Broadway; final arrangements made. Thence to propeller *Commander*, foot of Tenth Street, North River. Off at four in the afternoon. Hotter and hotter. Not till we were well down the Narrows did we cease groaning and begin to breathe freely. Our captain, Petrick, [was] obliging and kind and anxious for our comfort, but not efficient and ignorant of the coast. Mate a jolly, hirsute ruffian. Steward the embodiment of all stewardly virtues. Engineer (Peck) an exceedingly respectable person. The propeller seems a steady sea boat. All her appointments are good, save her boiler and engine, which are too small. She makes no more than six or seven knots, even

[2] Grant's Eighteenth Corps under General W. F. ("Baldy") Smith moved against Petersburg on June 15, and if it had been promptly reinforced by other Union forces south of the James and had acted with celerity, it could have overcome Beauregard's weak defensive lines and taken the city. But Smith did not get into position to attack until nearly seven in the evening, and Hancock's corps, tardily informed of the projected assault, did not arrive on the field until after dark. Smith's troops carried long lines of entrenchments, took some guns, and captured many prisoners. But during the night Beauregard was heavily reinforced, and the Union attack on June 16 broke down. Nine months were to pass before Petersburg was seized.

[3] Strong was leaving to visit the Sanitary Commission outfits before Petersburg and to talk with Grant at his field headquarters.

under sail. Our table very good, and reinforced by stores of our own
providing. . . .

Sunday, the 26th. Running slowly down the coast, which is sometimes wholly out of sight. "How fearfully hot it must be in town" (and
so it was). Watch ships, and an occasional sharkfin sailing slowly along. . . .
Up at five-thirty for a cup of strong coffee and breakfast well at nine.
Bluefish lines brought out and two tied to the taffrail. Agnew doubted
whether they be legitimate on "the Sabbath." Some sixteen chose to be
caught. . . .

Tuesday, the 28th. Cooler. Off Jamestown Island at eight A.M.
Ruined church a pregnant illustration of the difference between the
North and South. Had this building with all its historical associations
been this side of the Potomac and reduced by time or accident to its
present condition, how easily could any amount of money have been
raised to preserve or restore, or rather to rebuild it, for only the tower is
left, or rather the stump of its tower. . . .

Nine A.M. Past the mouth of the fatal Chickahominy—draw near to
Brandon—are passing Sandy Hill (or Point) Plantation. Pilot suddenly
discovers shoal water. Next minute we run into a tenacious mud-bank,
under full sail and thirty pounds of steam, at the top of a rather full flood-
tide. Back the engine. She budges not. "We must wait for tonight's
flood." We are four hundred yards out of the channel, and within three
hundred yards of a nicely wooded shore, an eligible position for sharp-
shooters. Our force is five deckhands, and our armament one revolver.
Rebels were in force ten miles above, last Friday. . . . Heavy thudding
of big guns audible Petersburg way. . . .

Thursday, the 30th. Our storeboat *Elizabeth* alongside at six in the
morning. Discharging cargo all day and lightened our *Commander* of
everything in the upper hold. Screw of the *Young America* cleared at last,
after hard work by men toiling up to their necks in water. We issued
certain bottles of whiskey for their comfort and restoration. The powerful sidewheel tug *City of Troy* (a quartermaster's boat) appears with Dr.
McDonald. Heavy guns near Petersburg very audible during the afternoon. Fire in the evening, supposed to be the nigger quarters on the
Allen plantation set by a boat's crew from the vessels. A little before
midnight the *City of Troy* takes hold astern and the *Elizabeth* aids on our
port side. After ten minutes' straining, off we glide at last. *Io triumphe!*
We are towed to an anchorage, having blown all the water out of our
boilers to lighten the ship. Drink of congratulation all round, and to bed.

Friday, July 1st. Up at daybreak with Johnny and Dr. McDonald and up the river by the *City of Troy*, leaving the *Commander* in charge of Lord to turn over the contents of her lower hold to the *Elizabeth* and then return to New York for another cargo of pickles and onions and curried cabbage. Most sultry. Below Harrison's Landing, where a force of cavalry raiders lately crossed, the air is black with innumerable turkey-buzzards; indeed, these foul birds are visible everywhere on the banks of the James River. Pass the rebel *Atlanta*, now converted into a loyal iron-clad, lying off Fort Powhatan. She looks like an ugly customer. City Point at nine.[4] The waters swarming with transports, hospital boats, tugs, gunboats, and light steamers and all manner of river craft. Land in a scene of matchless dust, confusion (apparent at least), and activity. They are repairing the railroad. Wagon trains are moving every way. Gangs of contrabands following mounted leaders who carry remarkably long riding whips— (*honi soit qui mal y pense*); docks are being built, officers riding about, and the usual nebula of stragglers, disabled men, and army followers is all-pervading. Everyone desperately in earnest about something. The shore is lined three deep, yes, six deep, with barges, and the like, steamers are screeching, corrals of mules braying—but I can do no justice to the sights and sounds of the place. All this is on or beside a strip of river shore. Back of this is a bank covered with fine trees and shrubs that were green once, but are now ash-colored and gray. Among them are tents of the same neutral tint. To your right, on the bank, there is a refreshing bit of warm color, the flag of Grant's headquarters. Looking still farther, you make out dimly through the yellow dust-saturated air the outline of a long series of pavilion hospitals, where 6,000 sick and wounded men (too sorely hurt or too ill to be on transportation) are stifling as they breathe the sluggish, heavy current of dust that keeps pouring in upon them. High up against the blue sky stand great columns of coppery dust, hardly moving and shifting their vague outlines slowly, like thunderheads as a storm blows up.

Join Agnew, and proceed at once to our headquarters (Sanitary Commission); sundry barges moored on the mud-bank of the shore, a festering expanse of filthiness. In all respects a most insanitary arrangement. Our men are so full of their work that they neglect themselves. No wonder more than twenty of our relief corps have broken down and gone home within so short a space. There is everything to produce disease,

---

[4] City Point lies at the junction of the Appomattox and the James; below it the James is broad and fairly straight, above it narrow and crooked.

not only in their work, but in their food and quarters. It is disgraceful
and murderous. We gave Douglass (in charge) our views about it, and
shall do so formally in writing, with definite orders for reform so far as
reform is possible. The situation is bad enough *per se* and cannot be changed
at present, but precautions can be taken against disease—and there are
none now. The Sanitary Commission needs a new Sanitary Commission
to look after the health of its small army of field agents, and our Executive
Committee must undertake the work instanter.

With Agnew to Grant's headquarters, taking Johnny with us that he
might enjoy a sight of *the* great man of the day—perhaps of the age.
Heaven grant it! Headquarters camp is pleasantly situated on top of the
bluff, among fine old trees, near the house of a runaway rebel named
Eppes. Ingalls has set up his quartermastering offices in the building. It
has been riddled and made nearly untenantable by shot and shell, having
been used as a trap to decoy some of our men under fire by a story of
some sick lady in it who wanted the attendance of a surgeon from our
fleet. Such is the story. Ingalls had three little niggers fanning him and
looked like a Rajah.

Call on Captain Jones, General Rawlins (chief of staff), and to General
Grant's tent. Most cordially received. Talk with him about transportation
of vegetables to the front, and so on. He's a man of few words, but gave
us clearest assurance of his readiness to help our work, and of his intelligent recognition of its importance. Whenever we want facilities of any
kind, we must come straight to him, or send Dr. Douglass, and he will
"see us through." Our discourse lasted some fifteen minutes. We made
it as brief as possible, though the General professed to be quite disengaged.
The impression he makes on me is favorable. He talks like an earnest
business man, prompt, clear-headed, and decisive, and utters no bosh. As
we were leaving, something was said about encouraging enlistments,
and the need of more men. "I think we shall want more men," said
Grant, "but there will be no difficulty in getting them."

His staff says his losses have been less than the estimate with which
the campaign began!—that Richmond and Petersburg are nearly *insulated* and cut off from railroad communication with mankind—that it
must be many days before these roads are repaired—that all the carts
and wagons that can be raised are doing their utmost to carry in supplies
—and that the results of these raiding expeditions are worth ten times
their cost in men and material. Also that the black troops fight well, and
take no prisoners. "Don't know how it is—we have made no enquiry—

somehow they give the Provost Marshal nothing to do. I suppose they
have to kill their prisoners before they can take them. When they go
into action, they yell 'Fort Pillow!' But it is queer they don't take any
prisoners, though they fight so well." Very queer, indeed.

Agnew, Greenleaf, and I set off for the front at twelve in a wagon
with a four-horse team. Frightful heat; dust unspeakable. After poking
about around General Baldy Smith's headquarters awhile, we came unexpectedly on my very estimable young cousin, Captain Horace Binney,
and were made much of; taken up to the top of an adjoining house, fed,
and shewn all that could be seen. Our position, near our extreme right,
overlooked a wide area of smiling landscape. The spires of Petersburg
rose from a sea of foliage at a distance of a mile and a half. Nearer us,
three lines of newly up-turned earth could be traced at intervals among
the trees. From the two farther, and from other points, little puffs of
smoke were breaking out, and there was a crackling sound, like that of
the squibs now going off in the streets, sometimes rather sluggish and
comparatively infrequent, and then rapid and multitudinous as when a
pack of crackers is fired at once. Every two or three minutes came the
smoke and the boom of a big gun from one side or the other, and every
fifteen minutes a special Parrott ("the Petersburg Express") went off
with a crash and a whoo-OO-oosh, and a shell burst in the city near the
railroad bridge. We were near enough to see the little spurts of dust
thrown up by the sharpshooters' bullets as they struck the ground a little
in advance of us. It would seem we can take the city whenever we like,
but it would be too hot to hold us while certain outside rebel works continue to command it.

Back to City Point, and a long discourse with Douglass, and others.
I meant to have taken Johnny to the front but am glad I did not. He was a
little headstrong in the morning, and the heat, dust, and discomfort of
the drive would have surely made him ill. I have seen the army smothering
in mud before, but never, till now, stifling in dust. Drought and travel
have done their work on this region and pulverized the soil to a "potency"
(as the homeopaths would say) beyond what I had dreamed possible.
Miles and miles of what were meadow and cornfield are now seas of
impalpable dust of unknown depth, and heated to a temperature beyond
what the hand can bear. Through this, and over such roads as are still
defined and distinct, though equally dusty, or worse, passes all Grant's
enormous transportation. Every horse raises a convoluted cloud of ropy

U. S. GRANT   W. T. SHERMAN

PHILIP H. SHERIDAN   GEORGE G. MEADE

METROPOLITAN FAIR.

THIRD

AMATEUR DRAMATIC PERFORMANCE

FOR THE BENEFIT OF

THE UNITED STATES SANITARY COMMISSION,

AT

MR. LEONARD W. JEROME'S PRIVATE THEATRE,

Under the direction of Mr. JOHN LESTER WALLACK.

MONDAY EVENING, APRIL 18th, 1864.

Will be presented the Comedy, in two acts, of

THE FOLLIES OF A NIGHT.

Duchess de Chartres,	Miss Rogers.
Mademoiselle Duval,	Mrs. George T. Strong.
Duke de Chartres,	Mr. Edward Henry Anderson.
Count de Brissac,	Mr. Peter Marié.
Dr. Druggendraft,	Mr. T. A. Emmet.
Pierre Palliot,	Mr. Chas. T. Fearing.

THE PERFORMANCE WILL CONCLUDE WITH THE FARCE, IN ONE ACT, OF

THE DEAD SHOT.

Capt. Cannon,	Mr. T. A. Emmet.
Hector Timid,	Mr. W. P. Talloys.
Mr. Wiseman,	Mr. J. F. Ruggles.
Frederick Thornton,	Mr. G. H. Bend.
Louisa, neice to Capt. Cannon,	Mrs. Harrison.
Chatter, her maid,	Miss Meert.

DRAMATIC COMMITTEE.

MRS. JOHN SHERWOOD.	MR. RICH'D GRANT WHITE.
Mrs. CHAS. E. STRONG,	Mr. LEONARD W. JEROME,
Mrs. J. C. PETERS,	Mr. JOHN LESTER WALLACK,
Mrs. WM. H. McVICKAR,	Mr. JOHN CORLIES WHITE,
Mrs. GEN. FREMONT,	Mr. WM. H. J. GRAHAM,
Mrs. J. K. WARREN,	Mr. WM. J. HOPPIN.
Mrs. RICHARD TIGHE,	
Mrs. GEORGE T. STRONG,	

smoke that comes up to his belly and steals away behind him for half a mile. A drove of cattle or a mule-train creates a fog so dense that in passing them this afternoon, our leaders were invisible. Though our teamster knew the ground perfectly, he had to stop within a mile of City Point, on the boundless area of naked yellow dust limited only by the circumambient haze and traversed by wagon ruts in every direction, and ask which way City Point lay. . . .

Yesterday at nine A. M. at Washington. Spent the day in council with Knapp over important matters. Off at 6:30 by railroad. Sleeping cars new and good, and I got through the night very comfortably. So did Master Johnny.

July 8, FRIDAY. . . . Bidwell's latest groan: "Well, Mr. Bidwell," said I, "do you think the destruction of the *Alabama* rather unsatisfactory and discouraging?" "*Why, of course, it is*," quoth Bidwell. "We have not caught Semmes, and besides, all our commerce is destroyed already." What can one do with people who talk that way? Edge writes me from London, just setting off for Cherbourg, where he is about investigating the details of that fight for embodiment in a pamphlet to be reprinted here. Saw Randolph on the subject this afternoon.

I dislike writing what looks like brag, but I believe the work of the Sanitary Commission with the army before Petersburg may materially influence the result of the campaign and the destiny of the country. Fifty thousand pounds of anti-scorbutics issued daily to an army that has begun to shew symptoms of scurvy, slight but generally diffused, are no insignificant contribution toward keeping up its health and efficiency.

July 9. . . . At 823 this afternoon as usual. Tonight at the Society Library awhile to look through magazines, and to the Union League Club. G. W. Blunt tells me Bache is recovering but slowly from his late shock. Many contradictory rumors about the invasion of Maryland; for example, that they have occupied Frederick, that our forces are retreating, that three rebel corps are across the Potomac, that they are marching straight on Baltimore, that a corps has been detached from Grant's army to meet them, and so on. I am sick and sore with long anxiety about the war. God send us victory and peace! There can be no lasting peace without victory and thorough subjugation of Southern barbarism.

Seymour, that Judas, seems deliberately endeavoring to bring this state into collision with the national government on questions growing out of the closing of the *Journal of Commerce* and *World* offices, but I doubt whether he possess the pluck to carry out his purpose. He is destined to unutterable infamy.[5]

The European conference about Denmark has accomplished nothing and hostilities are recommencing. I shall be sorry to see that plucky little old kingdom and nation destroyed, but prospects are bad. England scolds and blusters and pours out Billingsgate on Prussia.[6] When has England respected the weakness of a hostile power, or refrained from using all her brute strength against any foe, however feeble, for the maintenance of her pride or the extension of her trade? She *may* decide to intervene and save Denmark, even now, but I think she will not. She can make no money by the operation, and war would be inconvenient while the precedent she has set of fitting out *Alabamas* to prey on the commerce of a friendly power is fresh in our memory. I hope she may conclude to ally herself with Denmark. The navies of Austria and Prussia will find themselves largely reinforced by Teutonic privateers that have somehow managed to escape from American ports, and England will taste in legitimate war the treatment she has given us in our struggle with rebellion and slavery.

July 16. . . . Nothing special. Gold has fallen to 250, and there is a tight money-market. Sherman has crowded Joe Johnston across the Chattahoochee and must be very near Atlanta. The rebel kerns are withdrawing from Maryland with their plunder.[7]

July 18. Tonight Mr. Binney here, and Mr. Ruggles. Nothing new from Sherman or Grant, and time is so costly a commodity! But a long letter from Dr. Douglass this afternoon gave us a page of conflicting camp rumors that concur in indicating some important move by Grant as close at hand. General orders as to transportation and the like point the same

[5] Governor Seymour had violently denounced the temporary stoppage of the *World* and *Journal of Commerce*, and had called upon the District Attorney to prosecute anyone who had acted illegally; with the result that a Democratic judge issued warrants for the arrest of General Dix and others. Lincoln then directed Dix not to drop his command or brook any interference with his liberty because he had obeyed a military order of the President. Seymour carried the matter no further.

[6] Prussia and Denmark had fallen out over the duchies of Schleswig-Holstein, which were populated mainly by Germans but ruled by the King of Denmark. When Christian IX, violating an agreement of 1852, tried to incorporate the duchies in the kingdom of Denmark, the Germans interfered. In a brief war, the Prussians and Austrians compelled the Danes to give up the disputed territory.

[7] General Jubal A. Early, taking command of the Confederate forces in the Shenandoah in mid-June, marched down that valley, crossed the Potomac into Maryland, and on July 11 reached the outskirts of Washington; then, as the Union defenders of the capital were reinforced, he retreated into Virginia. Grant thereupon sent Sheridan to the Shenandoah, and a brilliant series of Union victories ensued.

way. There are predictions that Grant will suddenly change his front and march straight down into the Carolinas to put himself in rapport with Sherman, leaving Lee to follow him or to move northward at his discretion. Not very likely.

July 23, SATURDAY. Today's atmosphere unwholesome. People seem discouraged, weary, and faint-hearted. They ask plaintively, "Why don't Grant and Sherman do something?" "How can we raise 400,000 more men under Lincoln's last call?" . . . And so forth. Such is the talk of not only Copperhead malignants, but of truly loyal men with weak backbones. . . . To be sure, a stiff upper lip can be maintained in these days only by the liveliest faith, such as removes mountains (would that mine could remove a few fieldworks I could mention!). But I will not let myself doubt the final issue. What further humiliation and disaster, public and private, we must suffer before we reach the end, God only knows; but this shabbiest and basest of rebellions cannot be destined to triumph. . . .

July 26. News from Atlanta looks well, though not yet clear and positive enough to forbid the *World* cavilling and doubting and suggesting that "something is probably kept back." Hood, Joe Johnston's successor, seems to have attacked Sherman on Wednesday and again on Friday last, in great force, and to have been beat back with loss numerically more than double ours. But General [James B.] McPherson fell—one of our best officers. We seem to occupy part of the city or of its defenses—not clear which. It was under fire Saturday, and Hood was apparently burning his depots and withdrawing. All this comes through several and distinct despatches (not official, however), and there are no counter stories of disaster. If it be true, rebellion comes out of this round with a very black eye.

It seems, also, that a raiding column of accursed Abolitionists has defiled that great city, Montgomery, Alabama. *Per contra*, we hear this afternoon that Crook, Averell, Hunter & Co. have come to grief in Western Virginia, and that another foray into Maryland is imminent. . . .

July 28. Received this evening from Edge at London advance sheets of his pamphlet on the *Kearsarge* and *Alabama* combat, which I must get reprinted here at once. Nothing from Atlanta, except that we seem working with the spade. Lee has certainly made some kind of movement on the James River. There seems to have been a "muss" there. The demonstration was apparently against Butler at Bermuda Hundred, and against Harrison's Landing. Result unknown.

July 30. Death of Mrs. Arabella Barlow (who was Miss Arabella Griffith) at Washington of typhus is announced in last evening's *Post*.

She was ill when I was last at Washington, poisoned by disease contracted during her hospital work at Fredericksburg and Belle Plain. She did great service there. She was a very noble woman. . . .

A rebel cavalry raid, possibly on a large scale, has crossed the Potomac and occupied Chambersburg, Pennsylvania. Will these feeble, fat Pennsylvanians ever learn to establish a militia system and do a little to protect themselves? I almost hope Harrisburg may be harried—the lesson would be useful. At Atlanta, the rebel general Hood claims a victory. I rather think he lies. Untruthfulness is characteristic of his tribe. Southerners seem unable to perceive any virtue or value in veracity. But the silence of the War Department gives a certain color to the rebel story. Grant has had a fight on this side of the James River, seemingly successful; "four" or "six" guns captured, and prisoners. . . .

July 31, SUNDAY.   Hottest day of this burning summer, according to my sensations, if not by the thermometer. Have stayed within doors till tonight, steaming with perspiration and vainly dawdling over Horace Greeley's *History of the War*, Vol. 1.[8] At two o'clock came an extra. News important, the precursor possibly of decisive events. At four o'clock yesterday morning Grant's mines in front of the Ninth Army Corps were sprung, and one of the Petersburg redoubts was blown up. Heavy firing was instantly opened along the whole line, under cover of which the Ninth Corps carried two lines—or else one line—of entrenchments "with severe loss." The latest despatch purports to have been written yesterday afternoon and reports that we are in line of battle—only an artillery duel so far—and that a general engagement is impending, forced on Lee by Grant's strategy. I suppose Grant's move to the north side of the James may have been a feint for the purpose of withdrawing part of Lee's force from Petersburg to Richmond. Well, it's safe to say that matters might look much worse than they do. Atlanta is probably at least as vital a point as Richmond, and I think we have established a firm grip on both. The former is the new centre of rebellion, the latter its right arm; Charleston, its organ of generation.

Strolled down to the Union League Club this evening and found Mr. Ruggles there, Lieber, William Hoppin, George Anthon, and others. Discourse of the Petersburg news and of poor Mrs. Arabella Barlow. I am not sanguine about Petersburg. We have no right to expect speedy victory in this war, or to ask that rebellion be suppressed till we have

[8] This first of two volumes called *The American Conflict*, dedicated to John Bright, carried the story to the end of 1861.

suffered more than we yet have done by way of atonement for the many years of servility and of anesthetic processes applied to our moral sense, without which the South would have never dared rebel.

August 1.   No news from Petersburg this morning. But we have news by the afternoon papers. Grant 'has delivered his grand coup, and has failed. He exploded his mines, opened his batteries, and pushed forward his columns, but had to withdraw them or to let them withdraw themselves, with severe loss, it would seem. Never mind. Attacks on Vicksburg, Port Hudson, and Sebastopol failed ignominiously, but all three fell at last. Copperheads, sympathizers and traitors will rejoice over this news, but their joy may yet be turned to mourning and the country saved. . . .

Petersburg was now under close siege by Grant, with Meade in direct charge of the investment of the city, it being Grant's purpose to coop up Lee's army and to effect its destruction or capture. Burnside's Ninth Corps held the right of the line. In July, Burnside, who had a regiment largely made up of Pennsylvania coal miners, had excavated a tremendous mine under the Confederate works in front of Petersburg. Its central gallery was more than five hundred feet long, a number of lateral galleries ran forty feet to the sides, and its eight chambers held a ton of powder each. At five o'clock on the morning of July 30, the mine was exploded, throwing soldiers and debris high in air, and leaving a huge crater. The breach in the Confederate lines was fully four hundred yards wide. If Union troops had been instantly thrown into this gap, they might have broken through to take Petersburg. But their assault was delayed; the Confederates rallied; and when Burnside's men advanced, a mass of bluecoats were held in the crater under a deadly fire. In the end, the Northern forces were thrown back with terrible losses. A fiery altercation ensued between Meade and Burnside, and Grant ordered a military court of inquiry. This censured Burnside severely, and although the Congressional Committee on the Conduct of the War supported him, he resigned from the service. The Battle of the Crater was more spectacular than important, but it was an episode which caused discouragement at the North, and elation at the South.

August 5.   To Quogue by eight-thirty morning train Wednesday. . . . Find the Rev. Mr. Morgan Dix the life of the house, keeping everybody entertained (don't I envy him his social faculty!), introducing "croquet," leading the simple games that make the evening pleasant, and so on. The

General, his papa, arrived last night. General Dix brought a rumor that Grant was about giving up this Richmond and Petersburg job and coming back to the Potomac! A most lamentable result it would be. Today's papers refer to the existence of this rumor. It is founded on the notion that our repulse last Saturday has proved to Lee the fact that he is able to hold his lines with part of his force, and that he will, therefore, certainly detach the rest of it to take Washington. I am no strategist, but I think it improbable that Lee will venture on that move.

Conundrum by the rector of Trinity Church: "What is the difference between a vestryman and a street loafer?" Reply: "The former passes the saucer, while the latter sauces the passer"!!! Most horrible. What effect would this atrocity produce on Dunscomb, Gouverneur Ogden, and Skidmore if brought to their knowledge?

August 6. Showery morning and a hot day. Have just returned from a sultry stroll and a visit to the Club, where I find no news. Saw Collins at 823 this afternoon. He has been spending a couple of days at City Point. Says Grant was so certain of succeeding last Saturday that he had made all his arrangements for moving headquarters into Petersburg, and that his disgust at this failure brought on a sharp bilious attack. Collins was on the mail boat when it was fired on near Harrison's Landing. There was no little consternation on board. Telegram that one of our young "auxiliary relief agents" has been picked off by a guerrilla-shot from the banks of the James River. It seems quite clear that this last attack on Petersburg failed because of somebody's criminal bungling, and that "somebody" ought to be court-martialled and shot. But nobody will be. Whether "somebody" is Meade or Burnside, I do not know.

Most seriously perturbed by what I hear from independent trustworthy sources about the increasing prevalence of discouragement, and of aspirations for peace "at any price." Our slow progress, wretched finances, and difficult recruiting can be endured or remedied; but if the national backbone become diseased and degenerate into cartilage or gelatin, we are a lost people. Peace dictated by a rebel general at Albany or Boston would be less humiliating. Calm, dishonorable, vile submission, with half one's strength still unemployed, is worse than fighting it out and getting pounded to death at last. Let us hope for better things. Could we but inspire our people with one-hundredth of the earnestness and resolution the rebel leaders shew, all would be well, and that right early.

August 7. Long walk tonight, bringing to at the Union League Club, where were Mr. Ruggles and Botta, who has a story that Grant has gone to Harper's Ferry, taking the bulk of the Army of the Potomac with him, and giving up Richmond and Petersburg as a bad job. Perhaps. I am tending toward a desperate frame of mind, and feel like going south in disguise as the modern Charlotte Corday and shooting Jefferson Davis. This desperation is mainly due to a fit of dyspepsia now ravaging my inward parts. I acknowledge value received therefor, having dined on roast onions—a forbidden fruit, on which I seldom venture except when solitary and alone, as now.

August 8, MONDAY.   One of the bluest of many blue days. Charley Strong spent Sunday on a visit at Throg's Neck, where he fell in with Franklin and Baldy Smith. Both generals think themselves aggrieved by Grant or the government or somebody, and both talk dismally of everybody's incapacity and of the failure of this campaign, and the gloom of the military situation, East and West; all which Charles E. Strong detailed to me with a ghoulish gusto worthy of Bidwell himself. But there seems a woeful plausibility in the evil prophesyings of these discontented chieftains. If Grant's progress be effectually barred, and Lee can hold Richmond and Petersburg with a quarter of his army, why should he not send off the other three-quarters to hang Pennsylvanians, or (if he be wise) to reinforce Atlanta and compel Sherman to a retreat like that from Moscow fifty years ago? . . . O Abraham, Uncle of thy People, why didst thou not provide a trifle of two hundred thousand more men in season for this crisis?

Then, as if this were not enough, the Political Caldron is seething, as if it were much nitric acid in contact with boundless copper filings. There is fearful evolution of irritating offensive gas, and Heaven only knows what compound will be generated by the furious reaction of which we now see only the beginning. Peace Democrats and McClellanites are blatant. McClellan, it's said, will accept no nomination except on a war platform. Good for McClellan. But I guess the Vallandighams will control the Democratic nominating convention, and that we shall have a well-defined struggle next fall between those who want to fight for our national life and the Northern friends of the rebellion. A momentous struggle it will be!

How well I remember an afternoon in Wall Street in 1842, when I turned over the pages of the just-published *Poems on Slavery* by H. W. Longfellow with Henry Cram, both of us rather sniffing at the book as a remarkable avowal of "Abolition" sympathies by a poet, a scholar, and a gentleman, and how we were amused by the impractical, sentimental notion embodied in its last stanza. (The identical copy is before me now. Much has changed since that October afternoon.)

> There is a poor blind Samson in this land
> Shorn of his strength and bound in bonds of steel,
> Who may, in some grim revel, raise his hand,
> And shake the pillar of this Commonweal,
> Till the vast Temple of our Liberties
> A shapeless mass of wreck and rubbish lies.

Longfellow may have been a prophet after all.

Wolcott Gibbs, Dr. Jenkins, and Dr. Douglass here tonight. Much business done. Our (Sanitary Commission) relations with army surgeons in the Army of the Potomac need looking after. I fear some of its medical staff (for example, one Lowenthal) pervert the supplies we issue.

August 9. Farragut has passed the outer forts of Mobile Harbor, probably after a severe fight, and captured at least three ships or steamers of the rebel flotilla there. Its admiral, Buchanan, is a prisoner, all but one leg, carried away in action. Farragut is "approaching the city." We get this news through a despatch to Richmond from little Massey, now a traitor and a major-general. His despatch contains not a single word of brag, but he says the monitor *Tecumseh* was sunk. We seem to have landed a force (under Asboth?) to take Fort Gaines in the rear. This looks well, but there are, no doubt, heavy earthworks around Mobile itself, and it's said our iron-clads draw too much water to reach them. And how is Farragut to get out again if he be repulsed?

August 11. Good news from Mobile by rebel despatches to Richmond. They refer to our "victory over" their iron-clads (of which felon fleet only one seems to have escaped), and inform us that Fort Powell has been evacuated and blown up, and Fort Gaines surrendered under circumstances discreditable to its chivalric commandant, a "high-toned Alabama gentleman," Anderson by name.[9] He is evidently in bad odor just now with his chivalric military superiors, and suspected of cowardice or treachery. Poor Anderson! *Per contra*, people talk darkly of the failure of Grant's campaign and of Sherman's.

August 16. Grant is again reported to have begun a grand strategic

---

[9] Mobile was defended by Forts Morgan and Gaines at the entrance to her long bay, and Fort Powell farther in, while the Confederates had a small naval force there under Franklin Buchanan, the chief unit of which was the iron-clad ram *Tennessee*. On August 5, Farragut, lashed in the rigging of the *Hartford*, braved a double row of mines to take his fleet past the forts and disperse the Confederate flotilla. The forts soon surrendered, though the city still held out. This feat, equal to his victory below New Orleans, earned for Farragut the rank of vice-admiral.

move of the deepest and deadliest character. Do not know what it is, but one of its elements is a canal that is to cut off a great bend of James River. May it prove more prosperous than his mine!

The great election of next November looks more and more obscure, dubious, and muddled every day. Lincoln is drifting to leeward. So much is certain. There is rumor of a move by our wire-pullers and secret, unofficial governors to make him withdraw in favor of Chase, or somebody else, on whom the whole Republican party (if such a thing exist) can heartily unite. Frémont's nomination is coldly received here, though it may find favor in Missouri. John Jay (!!!) and a few others are denouncing Lincoln for making abolition of slavery the object of the war, and insisting that he ought to aim only at restoration of the Union with or without slavery.[10] A strange position for John Jay! But he is by nature factious, unable to work with others or to accomplish anything. His only talent is that of criticising and retarding the efforts of his own friends and allies to carry out his own principles.

August 17.   Charley Strong just from Saratoga, and Agnew, with whom I dined at Maison Dorée and who is just from New England and the northern and western parts of this state, agree in a bad report of the general feeling. Great complaints, even by the most loyal men, of the shortcomings and mistakes of government, and the "Peace Democrats" vocal and truculent in threats of vengeance on Black Republicans and Abolitionists and in talk about revolution and repudiation of the war debt —all which will do them no good. That blatant traitor, Walter Church, is the representative of this school.[11] *Maledicti Pacifici* just now. It is

[10] A wave of pacifism was throwing up its crest at this moment. Greeley in the *Tribune* was writing of "our bleeding, bankrupt, and almost dying country" stretching out its hands for peace and trembling at the "prospect of new rivers of human blood." The Peace Democrats, delighted to receive aid from the Peace Republicans, were redoubling their outcries. During July and August, Greeley was humbugged into lending himself to the machinations of some petty Southern schemers ensconced at Niagara Falls who pretended to be agents from the Confederate government authorized to negotiate for peace. Lincoln knew that the sole object of these schemers was to dupe and divide the North. He shrewdly checkmated both them and the editor by authorizing Greeley to visit them in Canada, to talk with them, and to bring them to Washington if they had from the Confederate government any written power to treat "for peace, embracing the restoration of the Union and abandonment of slavery." Greeley, posting to Niagara, found that the Southerners had no credentials and no honest purpose. But he continued to abuse the President for rejecting a hope of peace, and weak-kneed and traitorous men continued to echo him.

[11] Walter S. Church was allied with Horatio Seymour, S. J. Tilden, and August Belmont as a conservative Democrat.

satisfactory to know that these scoundrels have no love for the popular
hero, McClellan, but denounce him and Uncle Abe alike. Agnew, generally
so hopeful, is deeply, darkly, hideously blue. Thinks both Grant and
Sherman on the eve of disaster for want of men, because the Administration is afraid to go vigorously forward with the draft, lest it lose a few
votes next November!

Grant seems doing well with his last move. Nothing new from Sherman or Farragut. Sheridan may be about delivering an important battle
in the valley of the Shenandoah, that "dark and bloody ground."

August 19. . . . Pauper et miserrimus! I see no bright spot anywhere.
Rebeldom is beginning to bother Sherman's long line of communications.
We may expect to hear any day that he is fighting his way back to Chattanooga and that Grant has bid Richmond good-bye. I fear the blood and
treasure spent on this summer's campaign have done little for the country.
This is the kind of talk to which I respond with "thrasonicall huffe-snuffe"
. . . whenever I hear it, but it certainly has a dismal plausibility. Then
these infernal peace-mongers—how busily and malignantly they are working to spread their own foul disease of baseness and disloyalty, and how
omnipotently they will be despised and execrated hereafter! They are
moral lepers, necessarily but unfortunately allowed free range and permitted to do what they can to infect the whole community. Whether they
succeed or fail, they will be gibbetted in the history of these times, and
no one despises them, even now, more heartily than the rebel leaders for
whom they are humbly pimping. They have not yet corrupted the people
to the point of surrender, but the people may be deluded into electing
some so-called War-Democrat who will betray the country.

Lincoln's blunder in his letter "to all whom it may concern" may cost
him his election. By declaring that abandonment of slavery is a fundamental article in any negotiation for peace and settlement, he has given
the disaffected and discontented a weapon that doubles their power of
mischief. It's wonderful what an ill savor the word *Abolition* has acquired
during our long period of constitutional subjugation by the slaveholding
caste. One would think it a good word, and likely to be popular with a
free people, but it isn't. I never call myself an Abolitionist without a
feeling that I am saying something rather reckless and audacious. So it
will be for this generation at least. People have not yet learned the lesson
those three years should have taught them. They need more flogging,
and seem likely to get it.

The nomination and platform of the (pseudo) Democratic Convention at Chicago on the 29th instant are anxiously looked for. Can the two wings of that party, the Peace Democrats and the War Democrats, work together at all? Is not schism inevitable? Will the convention nominate some obscure man and run him without committing him or his party for or against the war?

McClellan, the inevitable, is talked of as nominee. So is Grant. Iscariot Seymour is in active squirm and wiggle for the nomination. Should either be nominated I shall expect to meet some great revivified lizard or saurian from the loess formation marching along Quogue beach some fine morning on his way to Washington to report to the chief of the Smithsonian Institution. Then there is Judge Nelson, a learned lawyer and full-blooded Copperhead, but he will not make a good, popular, available candidate.

If the Chicago Sanhedrim have sagacity and patriotism enough to nominate John A. Dix, I believe he will be elected. Many Republicans would vote for him. Possibly I should do so, though I object to "swapping horses while you are crossing a river" (*vide* facetia by A. Lincoln). But General Dix is too honest and true to find favor with politicians. Even if they recognize his availability, the question remains, for everyone of the gang, "*Cui bono?* Suppose he is sure to be elected, what good will his election do me? He won't give me a foreign embassy or anything else for supporting him in convention. So I had better support the claims of the Honorable Judas Jobbinger, who knows how to take care of his friends."

August 22. Grant has made a new move, extending his left and occupying the Weldon Railroad. Lee was compelled to come out and attack. Sharp fighting. Results rather mixed in quality. We have lost heavily, but seem to hold our new position, a position it much concerns Lee to recover if he can. . . .[12]

"O General McClellan, he is the man; He licked the Rebels at Antietan" is a popular song now. One hears its very good Celtic melody whistled everywhere, as just now by someone whom it helps defy the rain. A various reading devotes this lyric to Grant and makes him "lick the rebels wherever he can," which is equivocal praise.

August 23. . . . At 823 I find a letter from Hammond full of fight. He has published a card announcing a review of the case and is not in the

[12] On August 18 Grant sent General G. K. Warren with troops to attack the line of the Weldon Railroad, hoping to cut that supply artery and to draw off Confederate forces from the Shenandoah. Warren tore up some track, but was attacked by A. P. Hill, and after losing about 3,000 men was forced to entrench himself well back of the railroad, which was not effectively cut until December.

least cast down. His promised appeal to the people will need careful revision by some clear cool eye, or it will do him yet further damage. He sends on a copy (official) of the findings. I am glad to see that the adverb *corruptly* and other words and phrases in the charges and specifications are expressly excepted in the finding as not proven. So he stands convicted of little more than the technical sin of purchasing supplies too freely, and not in the way technically sanctioned by some act of Congress half a century old. His conviction looks like a base tyrannical outrage on law and right effected by the vast power of the man at the head of the War Department who hates Hammond, and whose hates are as unscrupulous as they are bitter and dangerous.

The *New York Times* published a savage editorial about Hammond this morning, but without Raymond's knowledge, as I hear. It is to change its base tomorrow and be more moderate.

Dr. W. A. Hammond's court-martial had resulted, as Strong indicates, in his dismissal from the army on the ground that he had been responsible for irregularities in the letting of contracts for hospital supplies. Actually, such irregularities as he countenanced were for the good of the army and the country; and the true reason for his dismissal was that he and Stanton could not get along together. Two men so masterful in temper, so autocratic in method, and so intent in different ways upon efficiency, were certain to clash. Both personally and officially they had come to detest each other. But Hammond's career was only at its beginning. Going to New York, he became a leader in the new field of neurology, treating great numbers of patients at a standard fee of ten dollars for a consultation. He was lecturer on nervous and mental diseases in the College of Physicians and Surgeons from 1864 to 1867. A chair of nervous and mental diseases was created for him in the Bellevue Hospital Medical College in 1867; he occupied it until 1874, when he transferred to the same professorship in the Medical Department of the University of the City of New York. He was one of the founders of the New York Post Graduate Medical School and Hospital in 1884. He wrote a long list of books, including not only the first text on nervous diseases in English, but novels and plays. He and his friends chafed under the stigma placed upon him by the court-martial, and in 1878 Congress authorized the President to review the proceedings of the tribunal and to restore him to the army rolls if an injustice had been done. As a result, he was vindicated and placed upon the retired list with the rank of brigadier-general. Hammond is remembered as founder of the Army Medical Museum, as chief initiator of the Medical and Surgical History of the War of the Rebellion, *and, along with S. Weir Mitchell and W. W. Keen, as a great pioneer in American neurology.*

Strong does not exaggerate the gloom and despondency which ruled at the North during July and August. The terrible losses of Grant's army, with casualty lists that sickened thousands of communities; the slow and uncertain progress of Grant, and until September, of Sherman; the financial straits of the country, so desperate that gold sold at 250 during most of July and August; the fast-rising cost of living—all these factors depressed the nation. Greeley wrote on August 9 that nine-tenths of all Americans, both North and South, "are anxious for peace—peace on almost any terms—and utterly sick of human slaughter and devastation." He wrote ten days later that "Lincoln is already beaten"; "he cannot be elected"; "we must have another ticket to save us from utter overthrow." The President himself for a time thought his defeat at the polls all but certain. In mid-July he had given his Secretary, John Hay, the above-noted letter to be shown to Greeley and transmitted by him to certain Confederate "peace commissioners." Addressed "To Whom It May Concern," it laid down two prerequisites for peace: the integrity of the whole Union, and the abandonment of slavery. As Strong states, many people thought that the latter ought not to be insisted upon in so dark an hour. But even as the Democrats met in convention at Chicago on August 29, with Seymour as permanent chairman and Vallandigham active on the floor, the tide of the war was about to turn. On the heels of Farragut's great victory over the Confederate fleet in Mobile Bay, culminating in the capture of Forts Gaines and Morgan and the sealing-up of that valuable port, came triumphant news from Sherman. On September 5 the newspapers printed his despatch: "Atlanta is ours and fairly won."

August 25.   After being severely repulsed in his attacks on our new position across the Weldon Railroad, Lee seems to have given that up as a bad job. So far so well. But Lieber tells me tonight in confidence that he receives most glowing letters from Halleck. I rank Halleck among the least of small potatoes, but he knows more about the state of affairs than I do. The peace faction grows more and more rampant and truculent. I predict that Belmont and Barlow will manipulate the Chicago convention into nominating McClellan on a non-committal platform, and that if elected, he will betray the country.

August 26.   It looks more and more likely that the Chicago Convention will nominate McClellan by acclamation next Monday and adopt an obscurely worded, doubtful, non-committal programme of resolutions under which the nominee will be able to disintegrate and destroy the country like a gentleman and a statesman. If so, they will try to appease the Peace Democracy traitors by nominating some Vallandigham or Seymour for Vice-President. They may win, though Heaven forbid! for the Administration has damaged itself fearfully of late. I fear the *World* and *Express* do not lie (for a wonder) when they say the post office is no longer safe. Jenkins told us tonight that his recent letters from Hammond seemed to have been tampered with.

August 27. . . . Lincoln manifestly loses ground every day. The most zealous Republican partisans talk doubtfully of his chances. Sorry for it, though it would be great gain to the country to unseat Stanton. Symptoms of an "independent" movement to nominate General Dix. Mr. Samuel B. Ruggles talked it over with the General last night. He would probably *go in*, for a free fight, if nominated by any respectable party or organization. But getting up any such machine is a large job. I suppose the very best thing that could befall the country next November would be the election of so honest and able a man as Dix to the presidency. I know he veered about between 1848 and 1856 in his views about certain matters and has been abused therefor. But no one ever questioned his integrity or his patriotism.

August 28, SUNDAY. Tried vainly for an after-dinner nap, and went to the Union League Club this evening, where were Mr. Ruggles, Lieber, Coit, the inevitable G. W. Blunt, Governor Andrew of Massachusetts, Frank Howe, and the Hon. Isaac Sherman, *cum aliis*. Talk rather good. A despatch came in announcing that the Richmond papers say Fort Morgan is "in possession of the enemy." Another (from the *Tribune* office) that there is nothing new before Petersburg. Lieber told me in great confidence a large story about a "reliable gentleman" who has arrived in town from North Carolina via Nassau and is now on his way to Washington with overtures to the government from the Union men of North Carolina and Georgia, and (I think) Alabama, proposing to announce for the Union and rebel against the Rebellion, if they can be assured their states will be readmitted as states. I put no faith in the story and less (if possible) in the hypothetical emissary and his constituents. Lieber told of his going to church at Charleston, South Carolina, just after the Nullification fuss there and taking up a prayer book, on the margin whereof he found pencilled opposite the prayer for the President of the United States, "D—

the Scoundrel." And of a talk with Calhoun, who became furious when
Lieber suggested that one of our national wants was a national name. He
said we were not a nation, and that this want of a name was conclusive
proof of it, that we ought not to be a nation, and that if a name could be
devised and generally adopted, comprehending the aggregation of states,
it would be a public calamity. I suppose that up to 1861, the maleficent
names in our history are Arnold, Jefferson, Burr, and above all, Calhoun.
Lieber thinks we should try to revive the old Norse appellation of *Vin-
land*. I rather like *Alleghania*, shortened to *Alghania*, and that we should
call ourselves *Alghans*. But Calhoun's vision may be dismally verified
within six months, which will save us the trouble of considering questions
of a name for the country by abolishing and extinguishing the country
itself. General impression tonight that McClellan will surely be nominated at Chicago, and that he will not run well. I think A. Lincoln would
find him a most troublesome antagonist.

August 29. To office of Provost Marshal of my district this morning
(Captain Manierre), where, after waiting an hour, I purveyed myself a
substitute, a big "Dutch" boy of twenty or thereabouts, for the moderate
consideration of $1,100. Thus do we approach the almshouse at an accelerat-
ing rate of speed. My *alter ego* could make a good soldier if he tried. Gave
him my address, and told him to write to me if he found himself in the
hospital or in trouble, and that I would try to do what I properly could to
help him. I got myself exempted at this high price because I felt all day as
if some attack of illness were at hand, and as if it might be unsafe to leave
my liability to draft unsettled.

At Wall Street and at 823 as usual, and a solitary dinner at Maison
Dorée. Home for a cup of coffee, and then to the Union League Club,
where I spent an hour or two in talk over the premonitory symptoms of the
Chicago Convention. They look well for the country and ill for the Democratic party. The Convention has approved a Committee on Resolutions,
of which Vallandigham and Franklin Pierce and other pediculi of the same
species are members. If this action indicate the policy of the Democratic
party, the country is safe, for the people are not yet so degraded and disheartened as to tolerate it. We are not yet prepared to listen to proposals
for recognition and disunion.

September 2. . . . The Chicago Convention has nominated McClellan.
That was expected. But the baseness of the platform on which he is to
run was unexpected. Jefferson Davis might have drawn it. The word
"rebel" does not occur in it. It contemplates surrender and abasement. If

McClellan consent to be its representative, he condemns his name to infamy. So shameful an avowal of dishonor has never been made by any political party north of the Potomac, nor even south of it. General Dix thinks McClellan will decline a nomination on such terms. We shall see. I have little faith in McClellan's principles. I could write at least a page of indignation about the insult these Chicago resolutions have inflicted on the country, were it not rather late, and were I not rather tired. If the people should endorse them next November, the country is not worth saving; the title "citizen of the United States" is equivalent to that of coward, fainéant, serf, and craven, and I will emigrate and become a citizen of some community of gregarious blue baboons in South Africa. It's a hopeful indication, however, that General Dix (who does not love the Administration) denounces these resolutions as shameful and scandalous. He tells me there will be no draft next Monday. So I expected. But I do not regret the $1,100 I paid for a substitute. The big Dutchman therewith purchased looked as if he could do good service.

The Democratic Convention nominated McClellan on the first ballot, and selected George H. Pendleton of Ohio as its candidate for the vice-presidency. The platform contained a plank which Vallandigham had inserted, and which merited all the scorn and indignation poured upon it by Strong. It declared that "after four years of failure to restore the Union by the experiment of war," with the Constitution "disregarded in every part and public liberty and private right alike trodden down," immediate efforts should be made to bring about a cessation of hostilities, "with a view to an ultimate convention of the states" to restore peace on the basis of Federal Union. This was a demand for a negotiated peace with the enemy. McClellan promptly repudiated this plank, declaring in his letter of acceptance that "the Union must be preserved at all hazards." He could not look his gallant comrades of the army and navy in the face, he added, and tell them that the Union had been abandoned. In this stand, as Strong indicates below, all right-minded and truly loyal Democrats supported him.

September 3, SATURDAY.   Glorious news this morning—*Atlanta taken at last!!!* It comes in official form, seemingly most authentic, but there are doubters who distrust it, and the appearance of no additional intelligence since morning gives a certain plausibility to their skepticism. So I suspend all jubilation for the present. If it be true, it is (coming at this political crisis) the greatest event of the war. It would seem that Sherman moved to the south of Atlanta, leaving one corps to guard his communications and cutting off Hood's; that Hood thereupon left his entrenchments, gave battle, and was beat, more or less, and that pending the battle, his reserve corps walked into the beleaguered city by its back door. We shall probably know more tomorrow. God grant our first news prove true.

Dined with George Anthon at Maison Dorée. Glad to learn that all but the most inveterate malignant Copperheads denounce and repudiate the Chicago platform. Even the *Herald* condemns it. They say McClellan will come out with a letter repudiating it and consenting to run as an "independent candidate." This may be part of a politic scheme intended to secure the votes of both Peace and War Democrats. McClellan is in the hands of Belmont and Barlow, and I fear they can manipulate him as they please.

At the Union League Club tonight, watching for news. None came. Told Mr. Ruggles that I would be glad if he could somehow hint to his special friend, the Hon. Washington Hunt, member of the Chicago Convention, that he was not particularly wanted as a visitor on these premises Sunday evenings or week days or at any time.

September 5. Two days of cold easterly storm. Thank God the fall of Atlanta is fully confirmed. We hardly dared believe it till today. Its importance, both moral and military, is immense. Hardee is said to be killed, and two less notorious rebel generals. He is no great loss to Secessia.[13] Hood seems to have destroyed much rolling stock and stores, which he could not carry off. We have news that the rebel privateer, *Georgia*, has been bagged by the *Niagara* (her name makes the event a coincidence, for I suppose Sherman's success gives us mastery of nearly all that state) and there is some reason to fear a complication with England, as the *Georgia* was sailing under British colors.

Dined with Agnew after a busy day. He is overworked and may be in danger of breaking down, which would be a grave misfortune.

The general howl against the base policy offered for our endorsement at Chicago is refreshing. Bitter opponents of Lincoln join in it heartily, and denounce the proposition that the country should take its hands off the throat of half-strangled treason, go down on its knees before its prostrate but insolent enemy, and beg it to do a little friendly negotiating. The audacious infamy of the Chicago traitors seems likely to produce a reaction

[13] A false report; W. J. Hardee survived to fight more battles.

and make the Administration party vigorous and united once more. Friends of the government have been somewhat languid and disheartened for a couple of months, always on the defensive, and apologetic in the tone of their talk. Chicago has put new life into them.

> Is all our travail turned to this effect?
> After the slaughter of so many peers,
> So many captains, gentlemen, and soldiers,
> That in this quarrel have been overthrown,
> And sold their bodies for their country's benefit,
> Shall we at last conclude effeminate peace?

Lord help us and save us from ourselves, our own deadliest enemy!

September 6. . . . Belmont tells Charley [Strong], who returned from Newport this morning, that McClellan's letter of acceptance will be most satisfactory even to the most resolute "War Democrats," and will secure his election. He may succeed in mystifying people with plausible generalities and commonplaces. If he take his stand on the Chicago platform, without some attempt at a protest, my faith in his honesty and loyalty will be shattered. Major Halpine (Miles O'Reilly) tells —— that he and Jem Brady and others are urging "little Mac" to say in substance: "I accept the nomination, and I adopt the platform. I want negotiation, armistice, and peace as badly as anybody. My policy will be to expedite them by a very vigorous prosecution of the war, which must soon put us in a position to negotiate with advantage for settlement, reconstruction, and pacification." Halpine is a very shrewd fellow, and on the fence till McClellan shall distinctly define his ground. He wants to support him, which he can do most efficiently—provided McClellan set himself right and repudiate the Vallandigham wing of his party. He thinks the defeat of Lincoln would give the rebels "a canoe to come ashore in"; that we cannot hope they will consent to scuttle their own ship and founder at sea, even after many calamities like the loss of Atlanta; that they are tired of war and will come back if we do something that looks like compromise. Perhaps. It would be a most hazardous experiment.

A new danger looms up, larger and darker every day. It is nothing less than civil war in the Northwest States! They are honeycombed by secret societies, working in aid of the rebellion, and controlled by reckless, desperate traitors for whom the gallows is far too good. The navigation of the Mississippi is still closed to ordinary trade, and that fact enables these "Knights of the Golden Circle" (more properly caitiffs of the Hempen Circle) to spread disaffection among western farmers and tradesmen. Both parties seem to be arming.[14]

The great experiment of democracy may be destined to fail a century sooner than I expected in disastrous explosion and general chaos, and this our grand republic over which we have bragged so offensively may be cast down as a great milestone into the sea and perish utterly—and all this within sixty days from the date of these presents. So much for traitors, demagogues, and lunatics! All the South and half the North are absolutely demented. Neither Lincoln nor McClellan is strong enough to manage so large and populous an asylum. Who is? Satan seems superintendent *de facto* just now. Old Fuller wrote two hundred years ago, when civil war was ravaging English homes: "Our sins were ripe. God could no longer be just if we were prosperous."

September 8. Political indications furnished by our Quogue family are encouraging. A fortnight ago Blake and Charley Lawrence expected to stump the state for McClellan. But the Chicago platform has changed their views. They cannot support McClellan, no matter what he says in his letter of acceptance. If he accept the nomination, he is bound by the resolutions that define the policy he is nominated to represent; and how can his co-nominee for the Vice-Presidency (George H. Pendleton, an avowed peacemonger), and members of Congress and governors of states nominated by the same party convention or by affiliated conventions, be disposed of? Must they each and all write letters denouncing their own party principles, or explaining them away? Blake insists that Lincoln possesses neither ability nor honesty, but he cannot oppose him *now*. He undervalues Lincoln, but no matter. Lincoln is an honest man, of considerable ability (far below the first grade), but made odious by the vagaries and the arbitrary temper of Mr. Secretary Stanton. As for McClellan, approved by Vallandigham and the London *Times* and the asylum-burning rioters, who hurrahed for him in July, 1863, *noscitur a sociis qui non noscitur ab ipso.* His name generates what old Fuller calls (in his *Worthies of England*) a most "valiant and offensive" stench. But there are men among us base enough to support him and to

> Sue for bondage, yielding to demands
> As impious as they're insolent and base.

[14] Joseph Holt, the Judge Advocate-General, had just concluded an investigation of the strong treasonable organizations in Ohio, Indiana, Illinois, Missouri, and Kentucky, and on August 8 had reported to the government that they were well armed, and ready to raise a revolt. Now in Indiana, Governor Oliver P. Morton was arresting a covey of Copperhead leaders on charges of treason and conspiracy.

September 9. McClellan's letter of acceptance is in the morning papers. Will it help him much? It is made up of platitudes floating in mucilage, without a single plain word against treason and rebellion. It has no ring of true metal, and no suggestion of magnetic power in word, phrase, or thought. But it is artfully drawn and may do its work, especially if Grant or Sherman be badly defeated any time before November. Its artificers know how to face both ways; to use language for the concealment of thought, and to humbug and seduce the sovereign people as well as any demagogues in history. Wonderful to consider how much study has been expended on every word of this lamentable, lifeless epistle by at least a score of eminent, politic, experienced Copperheads! Its flatness is due in some degree, no doubt, to the labor it cost, but still more to its constructors' ignorance of any sincere, patriotic purpose. McClellan wrote none of it. I suppose him far more honest than the scoundrels who are using him, but he is as putty in the hands of Barlow & Co., and the majority of that set would rather see Jefferson Davis President today than Abe Lincoln.

Said one of the orators at last night's ratification meeting, in substance: "When we have elected McClellan, we will bring back the Prodigal Son to his home and tell him we have subjugated the common enemy that alienates us and caused all these calamities, namely, the opponents of slavery extension into the territories, whom it is convenient to call Abolitionists." In other words, let us carry this election and then hang Horace Greeley and Henry Ward Beecher and put ourselves wholly under the feet of the prodigal women-flogging, fire-eating, law-breaking member of the family. Where in all history is one to look for a political party base enough for a comparison with our Copperheads? . . .

The Rev. H. W. Bellows has been making a Sanitary Commission speech at San Francisco, and told his audience, *inter alia*, that he had the minutes of our Standing Committee's daily meetings sent to him by every steamer, because "when the cat's away, the mice will play." Very cool indeed. Want of self-appreciation is not among the Dominie's faults. Confound his impudence!

Gold falls, but is still about 230. Stream of recruits to the front reported steady and large. Rumors from City Point are hopeful. Rebels said to be massing on our left for another effort to dislodge us from our position on the Weldon Railroad, which position is said to be strong in men and in fieldworks. Private letters to No. 823 indicate that Grant is stronger than is generally thought. The largest estimate of his force is 117,000, including

7,000 in the hospital, of whom a certain number, more or less, will become fit for duty every day. But we rather discourage the transmission of information on points of this sort by our inspectors.

Now that Atlanta has fallen, rebel newspapers discover that it was not worth holding and declare that Sherman's occupation of it is quite a blow to the Federal cause and equivalent to a rebel victory. Nothing is so characteristic of Southerners as brag (self-assertion, tall talking, and loud lying). Were they thoroughly squelched and subjugated tomorrow, they would say and swear that they never dreamed of establishing an independent Confederacy and that they had been fighting for "the old flag" ever since they opened fire on Fort Sumter.

Rumors continue of overtures by the state of Georgia or by somebody professing to represent that *soi-disant* nation for her return to the Union. These rumors are so persistent that I begin to think some dim shadow of some small fact may have set them going. Any move that may be even a respectable minority of any one "seceded" state would probably give rebellion its *coup de grâce*. But I fear the slaveholding aristocracy is still omnipotent in every Southern State.

September 12.   Last night Governor Andrew here, among others. He talks confidently and hopefully. Also that dubious cosmopolite M. Harrisse, the lyric philosopher of Quogue.[15] He seems a diluted Gurowski, a learned pig like the expatriated Count; much less learned and a little less irritable. "I do desire we may be better strangers."

Committee on School of Mines met at Betts's office at one P.M. Proposition to appoint Chandler of Union College professor of analytical chemistry, which position he would accept if guaranteed $1,500 salary for two years. Doubtful whether the board ought to give such guarantee. Rutherfurd said he would be willing to make one of a small party of outside guarantors. Betts demurred to this with some feeling, because "it would be a bad precedent that might be abused to force incompetent men on the College," and so on. A characteristic specimen of the blind, stupid policy according to which the College has been administered these sixty years, and which has kept it alienated from the rich and liberal community around it. The whole subject was referred to the board at its meeting next Wednesday.

At two o'clock to the Committee on the Course at the Law School;

[15] This is apparently Henry Harrisse (1829–1910), a French-born bibliographer and author of books on Columbus and John Cabot, who was helping Samuel Latham Mitchill Barlow to collect his famous library of Americana.

Bradford, Barnard, Morgan Dix, Rutherfurd, and I. Results satisfactory. Suggestions of George Anthon's little pamphlet on qualifications for admission recommended for adoption by the board. Barnard is fearfully deaf. Every word addressed to him at this meeting had to be roared out, and was understood only after two or three roarings. He is liable also to slips of the tongue and spoke of "a tragedy by Aristophanes" one time and another "by Aeschines" the next!

September 13, TUESDAY. . . . A great and decisive battle may be fought in Virginia before this week ends. There will be a murder grim and great, for Lee's hungry cohorts will fight their best. Hundreds or thousands of men, enlisted to maintain and enforce the law of the land, will perish by the violence of masterful rebels. Our Copperheads, anti-Administrationists, Peace Democrats and their candidates and leaders, McClellan and George H. Pendleton, Winthrop Chanler and F'nandy Wood & Co., are answerable for the death of every national soldier who dies in his duty. For it is only their factious opposition that keeps the rebellion alive. Were we united, Jefferson Davis himself would be at a parley. Washington Hunt, Barlow, Belmont, and the like, are the rebels' last hope.

At No. 823 with Agnew and Jenkins. Much business. Fear we must throw Knapp over, but it's a great pity. The Washington office is utterly insubordinate and unruly. . . . We had to record something like a plain vote of censure on Knapp this afternoon, and as he is already in a state of hyperaesthesia and wounded dignity, it will probably make him resign. We ought never to have appointed him an associate secretary. He was admirable as superintendent of special relief, but he is incompetent to run the Washington office, which is fast becoming chaotic under his slip-shod government. Moreover, strange as it seems, we hear that he "seems to have lost all interest in the business of the Commission." If he has, it is because of the wound we gave his official feelings when we ordered the chief inspector at City Point to report directly to the Standing Committee at New York and not through the associate secretary at Washington, and, also, when we put a check on his wild way of purchasing supplies at Washington. Who could have dreamed that that best of men, F. N. Knapp, so wholly free from selfishness, so single-minded and devoted to duty—a combination, as I have often thought, of Mark Tapley and Tom Pinch (*vide Martin Chuzzlewit*)—could be upset by these wretched little personal piques and morbid suspicions of affront?

September 14. Columbia College trustees met at two o'clock at the Law School. Session long but rather apathetic and dull. King attended and

seems quite convalescent. McVickar resigned the professorship he has held
for forty-seven years and was made an emeritus professor, whatever that
means. Recommendations of the Committee on the Course adopted, *nem.
con.*, including the change suggested by George C. Anthon in subjects
of entrance examination. Proposition to raise the age of admission to
sixteen or fifteen found little favor, and was tabled. Recommendations of
Committee on School of Mines adopted, except as to Professor Chandler of
Union College, which lies over to another meeting. Betts wants Joy to be
professor of analytical chemistry in the School. Joy would make trouble and
does not suit at all. Barnard, seen for the first time by the majority of the
board, shewed to great disadvantage. He was manifestly as unable to hear
what the board was doing as if he had been seated at the antipodes. Every
question or remark specially addressed to him had to be roared into his
ears more than once and was sometimes answered as Mrs. Peg Sliderscrew
answered Mr. Squeers in *Nicholas Nickleby*, "It's a fine evening," said
Mr. Squeers. "So they used to say in that part of the country where I come
from," said Peg, "but I think soap's better." Poor Barnard had certain
motions to make about changes and improvements in the College buildings
and talked a good deal about them. His talk was loose, flaccid, bungling,
rambling, and irritating. He has no "magnetism" to commend him to our
undergraduates, and he is likely to prove a failure. Our administration
of that great trust is imbecile, if not fraudulent. We, the trustees as a
body, come far short of our duty. Columbia College should be far ahead of
Yale and Harvard, but it is not by any manner of means.

September 16. . . . At our Sanitary Commission session were Agnew,
Van Buren, and Jenkins. We decided, among other things, to put Dr.
Parrish in charge of the semi-monthly *Bulletin* and to publish it henceforth
in Philadelphia. After we had got through with the business of the evening,
Jenkins asked a hearing and proceeded to state that he had now been general
secretary just a year and that he considered his administration a failure. He
was satisfied at last that he had not capacity equal to his duties as our chief
executive officer and wanted to bring his deficiencies to our notice. This
was said in the most single-minded, candid, honest way. We told him
frankly that he was mistaken; that the embarrassments of the last three
months were caused by a vicious organization and by insubordinate
officials at Washington and elsewhere, and that he would come to the same
conclusion if he took a blue pill tonight and a few quarts of Congress
water tomorrow morning. . . .

Spent last night looking over proof sheets of first half of *ci-devant*

Surgeon-General Hammond's pamphlet. It is too long, but he will not shorten it, and rather vehement and intemperate, but I have weeded out some of the hard words. It will not be generally read, but it will furnish texts for damaging editorials against Stanton in opposition newspapers. He deserves them, and Hammond has been treated most oppressively and infamously. But I hate to be anyhow privy to any attack on the Administration just now.

Farragut has pushed his gunboats to a point within shelling distance of Mobile. But we have indications that the co-operating land force is to be withdrawn and transferred to the other side of the Mississippi. . . . Horatio Seymour renominated at Syracuse as governor of New York. If any Democratic nominee can be beat, he can.

The Democratic Party in the state was in bad odor, and its chances of success were poor. A report had gained ground that Horatio Seymour would decline a renomination on the ground of ill health and the necessities of private business. But when the convention nominated him by acclamation, the governor stated that since the party insisted upon it, he would accept the honor! Many observers regarded his action as a trick. He had deceived the delegates, they said, luring them into tendering him a vote that was meant only to be complimentary; then, when it was too late for them to draw back, he had taken the nomination that they really hoped to give to William F. Allen of Oswego, or Amasa J. Parker of Albany. It was generally believed that Seymour, with his bad wartime record, would run a weak race. The Republicans named as his opponent a sterling citizen of western New York—Reuben E. Fenton of Chautauqua, an astute business man with a strong instinct for politics; and they entered upon the canvass with exuberant confidence. On the heels of Seymour's nomination came the thrilling news of Sheridan's decisive defeat of General Early at the battles of Winchester and Fisher's Hill; a defeat so complete that the Confederate army was put to total rout and was saved from destruction only by darkness. He struck the Southerners at Winchester on the 19th, taking 2,500 prisoners; and when they rallied, attacked them again at Fisher's Hill, took the remainder of their artillery, and sent them flying headlong. Here was an ironic commentary on the declaration of the Chicago platform that the war was a failure!

September 17, SATURDAY. Nothing new. Finest possible weather. At Union League Club tonight and strolled about awhile with George Anthon inspecting the outskirts of the great McClellan meeting on Union Square

and the tributary streams of banners, lanterns, transparencies, Roman
candles, and rabblement that were flowing up Fourth Avenue and Broadway. Governor Seymour's friends of July 1863 turned out in force. Meeting
very large and showy with its lights and fireworks; its appliances cost
a large sum. Belmont must have bled freely. Strange to see these working
men carrying banners on which Lincoln is held up to ridicule as a "rail-
splitter." *Swinish* is the appropriate adjective for the multitude. Even our
comparatively intelligent mechanics (or many of them) are too brutally
stupid to see that Lincoln is their representative and is fighting their
battle against "Little Mac," the champion of sympathy with and concession
to a rebellion that asserts the rightful supremacy of capital over labor.

Peace-at-any-price party is holding its little conferences and considering whether it should bolt or not. Its open hostility would do McClellan
little harm. But there will be no bolt and no nomination of anyone pledged
to recognize rebel independence. Wood and Washington Hunt and their
respective tails will sneak back into the ranks after making a few wry faces
and will support the patriot who locked up the Maryland legislature, the
general whose soldiers shattered the columns of our brethren at Malvern
Hill. That was an unconstitutional proceeding, to be sure, and seems at
first sight to have tended toward strengthening abolitionism. But the
general had nothing to do with it, for he swears he cannot remember
whether he was on the field or on board a gunboat miles away. His lieu-
tenents have better memories and swear he was on the gunboat and not
with his soldiers. I don't see why Wood & Co. should make much fuss
about swallowing McClellan. There is a very small modicum of war in his
concoction and abundant tenderness for treason.

It's certainly hard to vote for sustaining an Administration of which
Stanton is a member. He is a ruffian and will always abuse the power of his
great place to purposes of arbitrary, vindictive tyranny. His adulators may
possibly dishonor the memories of the Earl of Strafford and the Duke
d'Alva by comparing him with them, but the part he would play if he dared
to is that of Doctor Francia, dictator of Paraguay, or of the Committee of
Public Safety during the Reign of Terror. Still it is a plain duty to uphold
Lincoln, even with this millstone round his neck, as against the Chicago
platform, McClellan, and Pendleton. Pendleton is as rank a traitor and
secessionizer as Vallandigham himself. Though he be nominated only for
the Vice-Presidency, the President is mortal.

"An apoplexy, catarrh, or cough of the lungs" may carry off the valiant
McClellan any day, and then Vice-President Pendleton would be President

of the United States, and John Doe would become charged with the duty of conducting the case of Richard Roe. *Ab omni stultitia et dementia, Libera nos, Domine.*

"Mac" will carry this city by a great majority, but it will be made up in great measure of what Milton calls "the ragged infantine of stewes and brothels, the spawn and shipwreck of taverns and dicing houses," and of ignorant emigrant *gorillas* (Governor Seymour's "friends") to whom our fatal laws concede the right of suffrage, for abuse and mischief. It is certain, however, that many weak-backed men of respectability will go the same way, as for example, Hamilton Fish and W. H. Aspinwall.

September 19. . . . Last night Agnew and Jenkins came in with a report of Bloor's. Bloor has been grumbling for some time because his salary was not raised and his furloughs lengthened. In this report, he relieves himself by an attack on the Standing Committee. It is not intelligible, for Bloor delights in dignified, diplomatic, circumambulatory phrases, and is wholly gratuitous, but it is manifestly a deliberate act of insolence and insubordination. So we instructed Dr. Jenkins (who went to Washington this morning) to dismiss Mr. Bloor incontinently, unless he give us a full withdrawal and apology in writing.

Walked through Central Park yesterday afternoon with George C. Anthon. The lower park is finished now, all but the trees, which have twenty years of work before them yet, and it is certainly most attractive and creditable. The structures—bridges, and so on—are all good, some of them very good. Strange that of all these various, elaborate structures not one should be an absolute monstrosity. Dick Hunt and that scamp Wrey Mould are clever architects. . . .

Mr. Ruggles has just looked in a moment. There is a projected Lincoln ratification mass-meeting intended to counterbalance the great McClellan mass-meeting of Saturday night. He (Mr. Ruggles) thinks it politic to postpone this meeting for a fortnight or so for the sake of a great victory which somebody says General Scott thinks must happen within that space.

September 20. Fall weather cannot be finer than this. It has been worthy of the news today brought us. The howl of "Extry-a *Herald*" resounded through Wall Street at one o'clock. Extras are not common now. Their appearance indicates something of gravest importance, and I sent out for the news with fear and trembling. *Gratias Deo* for what was brought back. Sheridan attacked Early yesterday and after fighting all day drove him twelve miles with the loss of 2,500 prisoners, 5,000

killed and wounded, and five guns, pushing him into Winchester and
through it and out of it, and promising to resume his pursuit this morning. Hurrah for Sheridan and Sherman! If Grant can but do as well as his
lieutenants have done, the rebellion will be played out before November.
The military value of this victory is great, but it is worth still more as
influencing the political campaign and contributing to the determination
of the fearful issue that campaign is to decide: nationality or anarchy. It
will be known in history, I suppose, as the "battle of Berryville" or of
"the Opequon." It is priceless under any name. . . .

I feel comparatively jolly tonight, for the first time this long while,
and inclined to say with somebody in Beaumont and Fletcher, "I have
money and meat and drink before hand till tomorrow at noon. Why
should I be sad?" The wisest thing Sydney Smith ever uttered was his
maxim, "Take short views." Wish I could act on it.

September 21. At Union League Club tonight after a long walk.
Mr. S. B. Ruggles there. He applies Burns's lines:

> So Fare-ye-weel, auld Nickie Ben! (Ben Wood!)
> O wad ye tak a thought an' men
> Ye aiblins might—I dinna ken—
> Still hae a stake.
> I'm woe to think upon you, Ben,
> E'en for your sake!

A dismal den of political infamy (and without offices) it will be, unless
their people be stricken with judicial blindness and a mania for national
suicide. Historical infamy is inevitable anyway. The destruction of our
armies and our conquest and subjugation by the South would be less
shameful to us as a people than a public endorsement of the Chicago
platform and the election of a cold-blooded traitor like Pendleton to the
Vice-Presidency. God defend us from such dishonor. I am not sure we the
people are wise enough and patriotic enough to defend ourselves from it.

Sheridan seems doing much to help our defense. His victory of the
19th grows bigger and higher as we learn more about it and about his
way of following it up. It was a hard-fought battle, decided at last by a
heavy cavalry charge. That is a new feature in our battles, I think. Another new feature is that he seems to be pushing the retreating army
vigorously, even as Blücher after Waterloo, and was when last heard
from near Strasburg, thirty miles from his original position. No victorious army, rebel or national, has heretofore made what seemed a
prompt effort to secure the fruits of victory by pressing on the heels of

its losing adversary; that is, Beauregard after Bull Run, and McClellan after Antietam.

Richmond papers (before the 19th) brag and bluster, of course, but there is a trace of anxiety mingled with their savage thrasonism. One of them urges non-combatants to leave the city because there is a remote possibility that it may be shelled. Grant is certainly being reinforced, and largely; whence I know not. Dr. McDonald reports the arrival of ten transports at City Point one day last week and of six the next. . . .

Sorry to hear from Blunt tonight (G. W. Blunt), as from Professor Torrey the other day, that Professor Bache is failing. Brown-Séquard, and other physicians who have seen him, diagnose disease of the brain, softening or some other morbid condition, and the disease seems progressive. He is too irritable now to receive his friends or attend to any business. It's a hopeless case, I fear, and this kind, genial, but most politic old gentleman will assist at no more sessions of the Sanitary Commission.

September 26, MONDAY. Finest autumnal weather. Went to West Point (Cozzens's) by the *Mary Powell* Friday afternoon, the 23rd, a dull showery day with gleams of sunshine at longer and longer intervals. Find Donna Elena in the best of spirits, enjoying much, and looking and feeling quite well. That wonderful young woman grows prettier every day; so much for cheerfulness and a contented spirit. They keep her as fresh as she was sixteen years ago, and these years have made her even more bright and attractive than she was when I struck my colors to her. . . .

Came off at noon today by railroad, leaving Ellie to make her way to Cornwall, unescorted. I had a Trinity Church vestry meeting tonight, which I could not shirk. Attended it, but there was no quorum. Not displeased, for this enabled me to go to Van Buren's, where was a special session of the Standing Committee of the Sanitary Commission; Van Buren, Agnew, and I. We had business of importance. Our people at City Point expect a battle within a fortnight. Grant's reinforcements average 4,000 a day, raw men mostly. Jenkins writes from Harper's Ferry and Winchester. We send large consignments to that quarter and to City Point. Also, we expunge Mr. A. J. Bloor's name from our roster, on which it has stood long and honorably.[16] Sorry for it; but quite in-

---

[16] Alfred Janson Bloor, a young architect of note, was assistant secretary of the Sanitary Commission. He resumed his architectural practice; became a trustee and secretary of the American Institute of Architects and editor of its publications; and was one of the founders, in 1870, of the Metropolitan Museum of Art. He also published a book on *Women's Work in the War* (1866). The exact date of his birth is not known, but he died in New York in 1917.

dependent of the insolence of his late report (for which he makes no apology, but which he tries to explain away by verbal criticism) and more than sufficient to justify his dismissal, are matters that have come to light since last Sunday. *Malum Ovum.* He may try to avenge himself by a public assault, for he has a *cacoëthes scribendi*, but whatever he writes is so verbose, polysyllabic, and obscure that it will do us no great mischief.

Poor old General Scott is quite infirm and very gracious. He answered my reverent enquiry as to his health and my congratulations on his apparent improvement since I saw him last. He looks much better than in the summer of 1863. "My health, sir, is, on the whole, good. It is true, sir, that I am at present suffering from a *suppression of urine*, but it is without pain, sir, without pain." He is a delightful compound of strength and weakness—a grand old general and a good man, kept down from his due place in public respect by petty foibles.

Friday, about nine o'clock in the evening, I was sitting and smoking on the piazza with Talboys, when a youthful vendor of newspapers appeared and said, "*Express* and *Post*, sir?" I returned an indolent negative, having read the *Post* on my way up the river. "Fourth edition, sir, on'y ten cents." "Well, let me have it," said I with a sense of reckless extravagance in a small way. Nothing new, of course, that's of any importance, but there may possibly be some scrap of news in the third and fourth editions beyond the intelligence conveyed by the first and second. What a ten cents' worth I secured! Was such news ever bought so cheap? Sheridan attacked Early's retreating column at Fisher's Hill, an "impregnable" position near Strasburg, Thursday, the 23rd, at four o'clock, doubled up its left flank and assailed it in front. Early ran and left some twenty guns behind him. He seems to have been utterly broken, routed, and demoralized. General Scott says, "Sheridan's two battles seem to me to have been among the *most finished* affairs of this war." The General defines them accurately as an artist in tactique and strategy.[17]

September 27. Much work with Agnew at No. 823 [Broadway] this afternoon. Report of our committee appointed to investigate the

---

[17] Sheridan, who had a great superiority in both infantry and cavalry, was pressing Early hard. Late on the 22nd, at Fisher's Hill, he struck the Confederates first on the left and then along the whole line. "After a very brief contest," wrote Early later, "my whole force retired in considerable confusion." He extricated his trains but lost eleven guns. Union losses in the two battles of Winchester and Fisher's Hill were slightly larger than those of the enemy; but the Confederates could ill afford any losses at all, and the depletion of their artillery was sorely felt.

treatment of prisoners by the rebels. The report leads one straight to conclusions inexpressible in ordinary speech. It confirms the findings of the Congressional committee on the same subject. Those findings needed confirmation. They were incredible till confirmed by the investigations of men quite outside the political field, such as Dr. Mott, Dr. Delafield, and Gouverneur M. Wilkins.

This report will have a position in history. It establishes the proposition that Jefferson Davis's policy is to starve and freeze and kill off by inches the prisoners he dares not butcher outright. To cut their throats at once would be more merciful, but the proceeding might alienate outsiders, perhaps even Englishmen. Safer and pleasanter to destroy them by slow torture, especially as they are thus kept available for exchange, and the shattered, semi-idiotic wreck of a Northern boy can thus be made useful in restoring to the rebel ranks some prisoner who has been gaining flesh and strength and efficiency ever since he was captured. God grant this war may last till these fiends are exterminated from the surface of God's earth, no matter what insolvency it may bring on *me* for one! The *noyades* and fusillades and the Republican baptisms of the French Revolution were acts of mercy and charity compared with the lingering death Secessia is inflicting deliberately and with murderous malice and forethought on thousands of prisoners of war. We *cannot* retaliate, it is said; but why can we not and *should* we not take a dozen or a dozen score aristocratic rebel colonels and majors and subject them to the same treatment and regimen which our soldiers have to endure when in rebel hands?[18]

After dinner with Johnny and Temple to Academy of Music; *Don Giovanni* done in German, and rather badly done. Mme. Johannsen is hardly equal to Donna Anna's music, and Karl Formes (Leporello) is not what he was six years ago. But I enjoyed the evening much. Johnny's criticisms are sensible. . . .

General Philip Sheridan has knocked down gold and G. B. McClellan together. The former is below 200, and the latter is nowhere. But a reverse or two before November would bring him up again. With gold goes down the price of dry goods, pork, and flour. It seems well established that during these late battles our men cheered for Lincoln, and the rebels hurrahed for "little Mac." They feel by instinct that he and his

[18] This passage, though indicative of general Northern conviction, does injustice to the South. Grant this year had stopped the exchange of prisoners. If Union prisoners were nearly starved, so were many Confederate soldiers.

supporters are the allies and friends of rebellion and help it by a "fire on the rear" of the army from Boston, Cincinnati, and New York.

September 29.   Letters from Dr. March at Morris Island and from one of General Foster's staff urging us to send supplies to prisoners in Charleston and assuring us that there is every reason to believe the rebel authorities will faithfully and honestly apply them to the relief of our men. Clothing is urgently needed. Many of these poor fellows are in absolute nakedness. We (Agnew and I) sent the papers to Van Buren for his opinion. I think we shall have to risk it and send the supplies, but I have very little faith in the promises of these cruel, treacherous caitiffs. Their very peculiar "chivalry" is devoid of honor and humanity. . . .

News this morning that Sheridan's advance cavalry occupies Staunton, Virginia. Tonight, that Grant has made a move on Richmond, seemingly successful as far as it goes, carrying works on the Newmarket road and taking some fifteen guns. The operation, whatever it is, is still in progress at the date of his despatch, and a column is in motion toward Richmond. Weighty news may be looked for hourly. There have been tokens for several days of Lee's intention to shatter his lines by abandoning Petersburg. This move may expedite the contraction.

The "overtures by the state of Georgia" for a separate peace and return to the Union, about which so much has been said, are now pretty generally understood to be bogus and bosh.[19] Glad of it. Propositions from Vice-President Stephens and Governor Brown and Robert Toombs would probably be made in bad faith, and meant only to embarrass the Administration, divide the North, and help their friends McClellan and Pendleton into power. While Sherman, Sheridan, and Grant keep up their present rate of progress, we can do without peace overtures; but I am horribly afraid the tide will turn and there will be some fearful, disheartening reverse before November.

Governor Dix has come out strong against the Chicago platform. *Good* for Dix!

October 1, SATURDAY.   Standing Committee at Trinity Church at two o'clock. Dr. Higby, Morgan Dix, Eigenbrodt, old Floyd Smith, and

[19] The Georgia legislature in March, 1864, adopted "peace resolutions" based on a recognition of Southern independence and a Border-State plebiscite. On September 14, some Georgia citizens sent Alexander H. Stephens a letter inquiring whether it was not possible and expedient to begin a movement for the restoration of peace. In replying, Stephens affirmed the principles of the Georgia resolutions, but spoke hopefully of the idea of a convention of the states to submit some final plan for readjustment. Georgia was now almost helpless before Sherman's march.

the sagacious Strong. Helped create one bishop (of Kansas) and a small batch of presbyters. Then walked uptown through byways on the west side, and at No. 823 found Collins returned from Baltimore. Sanitary Commission seems doing a specially good work in the hospitals of Winchester, and others. Century Club tonight; monthly meeting. Professor Rood and Professor Joy, Rutherfurd, Van Nostrand, Henry Winthrop, [William S.] Haseltine, and others; also, Winthrop Chanler, the "Honorable," but I dodged that traitorous second fiddler to Fernando Wood successfully and saved myself the humiliation of speaking to him.

Grant and Sheridan seem doing well, thank God. May they continue to prosper. The rebels have fought the battles of the last ten days without much sign of vigor. Can it be their rank and file are discouraged and demoralized?

October 6, THURSDAY. To Cornwall on the beautiful clear, cool, still evening of Tuesday, by the *Mary Powell*. Fall foliage never lovelier. It comes late this year, and the woods are just bursting into full autumnal glory. Read on my way *The Trial*, a sequel to *The Daisy Chain*, by that admirable Miss Charlotte Yonge, who wrote *The Heir of Redclyffe*, *Heartsease*, and the *Landmarks of History*. This is the best thing the lady has written for a long while. In it she tries her hand at American life, both at New York and the backwoods, for the first time; and though she gives full prominence to our social foibles, roughness, and shortcomings, she does not caricature them and deals lovingly and kindly with her American characters, bringing out the goodness and warm-heartedness of the independent, ill-regulated, overdressed young lady fresh from an "educational institution" at the last, and of the wild women who call themselves "helps" in a frontier settlement at the West. She can hardly touch any type of character not absolutely reprobate from the decorous Anglican proprieties which her books shew to be her atmosphere, without making it beautiful. I am ashamed of being so much gratified by this little kind voice from sordid old England.

October 7. . . . Tidings from the war are good, as far as they go. Grant seems extending his left southwest of Petersburg and to have got within a short distance of the Southside Railroad, thereby compelling Lee to a corresponding extension. If Lee be outnumbered as we suppose he is, this extension must sooner or later attenuate his lines to dangerous weakness.

The attempt to cut off Sherman's communications seems to have failed. There has been hard fighting at or near Allatoona, and Rebeldom seems to have been badly punished. If I could only be sure that faction Copperheadism and party sympathies with Southern treason had not so demoralized the North as to make it lay down its arms next November, I should feel sanguine of national triumph at no distant day. Our most dangerous public enemy is not Jefferson Davis with his army, but the party of malcontents at home—traitors represented by "little Mac"clellan and Pendleton, H. Seymour, Vallandigham, [S.S.] Cox & Co.

Jefferson Davis has been making a queer oration at Macon, Georgia. I should take it for a fraudulent invention, did not Southern newspapers quote and condemn it. Surely the oration and the newspaper comments cannot all be forgeries, together! Seward and Stanton are hardly equal to so bold a stroke as that would be. If this *be* Jeff's latest utterance, he confesses Rebeldom a failure, admits it crushed, declares that it has called out its last man, deplores the "absence without leave" of many thousand men who have deserted their rebel regiments, and howls for old men and boys to volunteer and defend the Confederacy against Sherman and Grant. This speech would be a *cognovit*—and a surrender—but for the hopes still left to Rebeldom by the possibility that their allies may get control of the North next November. God grant we may be true to ourselves and to our duty.

October 8. With Dr. March at No. 823. Yellow fever is fearfully prevalent in North Carolina. News from before Richmond this afternoon. Butler's lines attacked yesterday at six-thirty in the morning, in great force, and I suspect, surprised. [General August V.] Kautz's cavalry driven back with loss of guns. [General David B.] Birney pushed forward thereupon, checking the attack, recovering the ground lost, and possibly more ground; and Butler's despatches claim a victory and loss to the enemy far exceeding ours. I am glad *Butler the Beast* has fought a battle and won it. But even a drawn battle is a victory just now, for Rebeldom is exhausted, outnumbered, and suffocating—*teste* rebel newspaper articles, general orders, and Jefferson Davis's Macon speech.

On my way uptown I treated myself to a Bunsen's burner and a few inches of magnesium wire. Ignited the latter in the flame of the former after dinner, to the great delectation of Temple and Louis.

October 9, SUNDAY.   After dinner, Mr. Ruggles came in, bringing Judge [Dudley] Selden to look at some of my old books. The Judge is fervent in patriotism and eager for the restoration of our degraded profession to its due place. He expects much from Columbia College Law School. May he not be disappointed! He thinks that Lincoln will be reëlected—God grant it!—and laments his own want of early training and his inability to read Latin, German, and French. Tells me that one of his earliest legal recollections is a brief of my father's for some motion before a vice-chancellor at Rochester or thereabouts in 1829 or 1830.

October 10. Cold. War news not much, but of a good sort. Sheridan seems to have harried the Valley of Virginia like a Viking. . . .

Visit from Hammond this morning, who wanted advice about a school for one of his children. I recommended George Anthon. Hammond's defense is out. Reads better than I expected and has made a favorable impression. He has been shamefully treated, but there is just a little bit of ground for hoping that the tyranny of the Secretary of War will soon be over and past. . . .

At 823 this afternoon. Agnew missing, so I could do nothing. Long talk with Dr. March, who can't get transportation to New Bern. Yellow fever and a congestive "country fever," still more deadly, are making havoc there. Our troops in that quarter have ample supplies, so the quartermaster's department holds it safest to keep the infected district insulated and to send down no boats from the post or from Fortress Monroe.

October 11. Dispatched much work at No. 823 this afternoon. After dinner to Club. Committee on Admissions sat and passed on a score of names. Coming down stairs from the committee room, we find the lower rooms crowded with members waiting for news from Pennsylvania. Bulletin up announcing Union gain in Philadelphia and prospect good. Cheering in the street from a circumambient procession, the vanguard of which entered our front door to exhibit a lantern, bearing the legend "Pennsylvania safe by 20,000 majority! How are *You*, Little Mac?" Most important if true, but let us see what tomorrow's papers have to say. If that great state have, in fact, expressed decided disapproval of the proposal that we lie down in the mud to be kicked by Jeff Davis, spit upon by England, and irked by F. Wood, our chance of escaping calamity and national infamy next November is doubled.

Our friend, Bishop Clark, has been making a fool of himself at Newport, writing a political pamphlet that Belmont and William Beach Lawrence praise and which his loyal friends have hardly saved him from the sin of publishing. Hoppin tells me tonight that loyal churchmen in Rhode Island were beginning to look darkly on their bishop, that invitations to dine were growing fewer, and that he preached a vigorous war sermon last Sunday morning. I supposed his spinal column to be made of sounder stuff.

Eleven-thirty P.M. George Anthon just rang at the front door to announce that the Pennsylvania news is confirmed and that Indiana and Ohio are reported (by despatch from the *Tribune* office at the Club) to have *gone Union* by great majorities. May it be true! If these state elections have come out right, thousands of men like Hamilton Fish, Gouverneur Ogden, Cisco, and others, will review their decision to vote for McClellan and Pendleton. Waiters on Providence, like James Gordon Bennett, will declare they have always been on the winning side, and the Administration will be sustained unless some great military disaster occur before November 8th and a period of discouragement set in.

Throughout the late summer the chances of Republican victory, as Strong's diary indicates, had seemed small. On August 22, Henry J. Raymond, editor of the New York Times *and chairman of the Republican National Executive Committee, had written Lincoln that he heard from all sides but one report: "The tide is setting strongly against us." This apparently confirmed what the astute Thurlow Weed had already told the President. The political situation reflected the discouraging military position. Grant appeared at a standstill before Richmond and Petersburg, unable to make progress; his first assaults on the Petersburg lines had been repulsed with shocking losses; the Confederates were still strong in the Shenandoah; it was by no means clear that Sherman might not have to turn back from his attempted march to the sea. Reports became current in the North that if McClellan won at the polls in November, his supporters would insist that he take immediate charge of the government. Lincoln feared that he might soon have to face the task of administering affairs during four dark and troublous months while the nation waited for a successor determined to make an ignoble peace. On August 23 he wrote on a sheet of paper two sentences defining his duty and purpose in such an event, and folding it, at the ensuing cabinet meeting asked all the department heads to endorse it without reading the text. The two sentences ran: "This morning, as for some days past, it seems exceedingly probable that this administration will not be reëlected. Then it will be my duty to so cooperate with the President-elect as to save the Union between the election and the inauguration, as he will have secured his election on such ground that he cannot possibly save it afterwards."*

Happily, the situation immediately thereafter changed. Sherman's telegram of September 3, "Atlanta is ours, and fairly won," gave the nation new confidence. Farragut's naval occupation of Mobile Bay shut off another port

*through which supplies had reached the hard-pressed Confederacy. Sheridan's
series of victories in the Shenandoah aroused popular enthusiasm. In September,
the elections in Vermont and Maine showed that the Republican Party still had
great strength. The price of gold fell; the credit of the United States in Europe
improved. On October 2, Secretary Chase wrote John Sherman that not the
slightest doubt concerning Lincoln's reëlection remained. "The only question is,
by what popular and what electoral majority. God grant that both may be so
decisive as to turn every hope of rebellion to despair!" Now state elections took
place on October 11. In Ohio the Union ticket triumphed with a majority of
54,751; in Indiana the efficient Oliver P. Morton defeated his Democratic
opponent by 20,883 votes; and in Pennsylvania a larger number of Union
Representatives were chosen. Maryland, by a narrow majority, adopted a
constitution which made her a free state. Altogether, the Union strength in
Congress was increased by twenty men.*

October 13. . . . Wall Street and No. 823 as usual, and tonight at a
meeting of Club. Reports from our Committee on Enlistment. They have
done the country substantial service, and the Club was not organized in
vain.

Results of the October elections not yet quite clear. Ohio and Indiana
are all right, but the "home vote" in Pennsylvania is very close, and both
sides claim it. The army vote will carry the state for the Administration,
however, for the army is Republican ten to one. On the whole, things
look well for Abraham, but Pennsylvania disappoints me a little.

One of the commonplaces of Republican talk is that the exhausted
rebels are only holding out in hope of McClellan's election, and that if
they see four years more of Lincoln and war coming next November,
they will instantly collapse. I doubt it. The pride and rage of their
leaders makes surrender unlikely under any circumstances. We have got to
destroy their military force and occupy their territory. When that is done,
and after a year is spent in doing military execution on bushwhackers
and guerrillas, we shall have peace.

The Hon. old Roger B. Taney has earned the gratitude of his country
by dying at last. Better late than never. I had begun to fear he was a
Struldbrug. Even should Lincoln be defeated, he will have time to appoint
a new Chief Justice, and he cannot appoint anybody worse than Taney.
Chase may very possibly be the man. Curious coincidence that the judge
whose opinion in the Dred Scott case proved him the most faithful of

slaves to the South should have been dying while his own state, Maryland, was solemnly extinguishing slavery within her borders by voting on her new anti-slavery constitution. (There seems no doubt it has been adopted.) Two ancient abuses and evils were perishing together. The tyrant's foot has rested so long on the neck of "Maryland, my Maryland," that she has undergone an organic change of structure, making it necessary for her to continue under that pressure, or in other words, loyal to the national government. The Confederacy will have nothing to say to Maryland as a free state.

October 14.   Grand rumpus at the Club meeting last night after I left it. The Executive Committee reported and recommended for adoption a preamble and resolution, whereas-ing the infamy of the Chicago platform and inferring the duty of the Club to use its influence and means to promote the election of Abraham Lincoln. There was some little disposition to table the resolution at first. That oracular donkey, the Rev. [Samuel] Osgood, thought its passage would convert the Club into a mere political machine. John Jay, who is always a stumbling block in the way of his own hobbies, by some inscrutable, mysterious law of his factious nature thought so, too. There was a lively debate. The supporters of the resolution had it all their own way, and the resolution was carried at last without audible dissent. But I hear that a few members talk of resigning. Let them depart in peace. A "mere political machine," indeed! What subject of human thought and action is higher than politics, except only religion? What political issues have arisen for centuries more momentous than those dependent on this election? They are to determine the destinies—the daily life—of the millions and millions who are to live on this continent for many generations to come. They will decide the relations of the laboring man toward the capitalist in 1900 A.D., from Maine to Mexico.

October 15.   Walk tonight and look in at the Club, seeking news and finding none. Mr. Ruggles looked in before dinner. Just returned from Washington. Abraham, the Venerable, says to him, "It does look as if the people wanted me to stay here a little longer, and I suppose I shall have to, if they do."

October 18.   Weather is lovely. Tonight at Dr. Bellows's. He has returned from the Pacific Coast and appeared at No. 823 yesterday afternoon. Tonight there were also Van Buren, Jenkins, and Agnew. The doctor delivered a most instructive and entertaining monologue on his observations and experiences of the last six months in California, Oregon, and Washington Territory, held the floor without much interruption from half-past seven till five minutes ago (eleven-thirty P.M.), and was not in the least tedious or prosy. He has gone deep into the philosophy of California manners and morals, and his view of the probable future of the Pacific States is not discouraging. He expatiates on the Yosemite Valley, the marvellous trees, "the cascades" of the Columbia, and the like. Olmsted is living in great state and dignity as chief of Mariposa. Our (Sanitary Commission) hold on California seems fully confirmed.

Matters political and military look hopeful. Elections in Maryland and Pennsylvania have apparently come out right by small majorities. The Copperheads try to crow over Pennsylvania, but it dies in their throats. News from Grant and Sherman is satisfactory, but I suppose the War Department is in no hurry to give the public, just at this crisis, any news but such as is hopeful.

After prolonged hesitation, the political tide had turned and was flowing ever more strongly in Lincoln's favor. The presidential canvass had been quiet, for both Lincoln and McClellan maintained a dignified silence. After the September and October elections, it was clear that, as Seward remarked, "Sherman and Farragut have knocked the bottom out of the Chicago nominations." Everyone now took Lincoln's victory for granted; and the chief interest of the final weeks of the campaign centered in the question whether Seymour would be reëlected governor of New York. Lincoln himself, resenting a speech by Seymour in Chicago charging that the Administration had been a party to fraud, earnestly desired the governor's defeat; and the Republicans exerted every nerve and sinew in behalf of Fenton, who was making an admirably thorough campaign.

Once more Phil Sheridan made a splendid contribution to Northern confidence in victory. His force had been ravaging the fertile Shenandoah Valley, gathering the ripe crops and driving herds of cattle before it. But Early, after his two defeats, obtained reinforcements, and at dawn of October 19, covered by darkness and fog, delivered a stunning surprise blow. Sheridan that night sent Grant a despatch narrating the result: "My army at Cedar Creek was attacked this morning before daylight, and my left was turned and driven in confusion; in fact, most of the line was driven in confusion with the loss of twenty pieces of artillery. I hastened from Winchester, where I was on my return from Washington, and found the armies between Middletown and Newtown, having been driven back about four miles. I here took the affair in hand and quickly uniting the corps, formed a compact line of battle just in time to repluse an attack of the enemy, which was handsomely done about one P.M. *At three* P.M., *after some charges of cavalry from the left to the right flank, I attacked with great vigor, driving and routing the enemy, capturing, according to the last report, forty-three pieces of artillery and very many prisoners." As he put it, disaster had been "converted into a splendid victory." T. B. Read celebrated one incident of the event in his poem "Sheridan's Ride."*

October 20, THURSDAY. *Laus Deo.* Another victory by Sheridan. News came at noon today. Early's successor, the redoubtable Long-street, attacked our Shenandoah Army at daybreak yesterday, between Strasburg and Winchester, with alarming vigor. He had probably been reinforced from Richmond. By twelve o'clock we had been driven four miles down the valley, with loss of guns and prospect of disastrous defeat, which might have cost the campaign and the election. At this stage of the transaction, Sheridan appeared on the field from Winchester on his way back after a visit to Washington. Then the tide of battle turned. The retreating lines were halted and formed again: the rebels were repulsed, and at three o'clock Sheridan became the assailant, and drove them back through Strasburg with loss of forty-three guns! He seems a brilliant practitioner, and our best fighting general. There are few cases in history of battle lost, and suddenly restored and converted into complete victory within six hours by the advent of a commander, *sicut deus ex machina.* Of course, the affair may look otherwise when we learn more about it, but our intelligence is official, and this looms up *now* as the most splendid battle of the war. Either we fight better of late, or the rebels fight worse. . . .

Nothing very notable at 68 Wall Street or at No. 823 Broadway. Weather fine. Johnny enters his teens today, through his thirteenth birthday. He still abstains from school and work, but seems better. Meeting of Library Committee (Columbia College) at No. 68. Received a telegram from Knapp at No. 823 and authorized purchase of $10,000 worth of supplies for the hospitals of Sheridan's army, in addition to our stores at Winchester and Harper's Ferry. None too much to provide the "supplementary" relief that's needed, no doubt, by thousands of brave men, lying mutilated, lacerated, and in misery this minute. Victory at Cedar Creek cannot have been recovered without fearful cost. And the Medical Bureau is as worthless now as it was three years ago. Surgeon-General Barnes is an amiable nonentity.

At Union League Club awhile this evening. Discoursed with Captain Marshall, Charles E. Butler, Parke Godwin, and others. Godwin is disposed to protest against confidence in the result of the election. He does not despond, but maintains the necessity of hard work by all loyal men. That is sound doctrine. Every symptom now apparent is unfavorable to the aspirations of G. B. ("Gun Boat") McClellan, and of "Peace and surrender at any price" Pendleton, but the damnable traitors who support them may be keeping some revolutionary movement in reserve for the day of election. The best thing I know of Stanton is that he wanted to send Governor Seymour to Fort Lafayette in July, 1863, and that his colleagues of the Cabinet, and Lincoln himself, hardly kept Stanton from doing it.

I would walk several miles to see Seymour duly and lawfully hanged— as convicted of treason. He is an avowed traitor—*traitoro-phile.*

October 22.   Johnny went with Charley this morning to Point Judith for a couple of days' sojourn. That young scamp has actually been *smoking* on the sly—the premature ruffian!—and has been duly and severely lectured therefor. Nothing very special in Wall Street.

Heard the *Eroica* rehearsed at the Academy of Music, with Ellie. A slovenly performance, but the strength and beauty of the symphony was apparent nevertheless. I suppose it excelled by no extant orchestral work but the peerless C Minor. From beginning to end, it is an intense manifestation of that highest art which cannot be embodied in rules or canons of art. No critic can analyze its wonderful power, and tell why this or that passage is so pungent and burns itself so deep into one's memory and recurs to one so often, solacing a walk uptown or a railroad ride. So Shakespeare's "Come unto these yellow sands" cannot be scientifically distinguished from doggerel, and in "Hark, Hark, the lark at Heaven's gate sings," English grammar is sacrificed to rhyme. But those two songs live and are loved and long will be, because there is in them the same occult vital power that inspires the *Eroica.* I admit, however, that I do not yet appreciate a certain *scratch-cat* passage in the first movement, and the doleful, long-lingering fugue in the second. But faultfinding is ungracious. Is there anything, in all music, instrumental or vocal, fuller of pathos and majesty, more touching and stately than the melody that occurs toward the close of the fourth movement? . . .

At 823 as usual this afternoon, and at the Club tonight. G. W. Blunt gives a bad account of Professor Bache's health. Dr. Lieber talks of probable row and riot here at the November election, and is uneasy because

the Democrats are so desperate. But they have no principle, no convictions, no idea to fight for. They are struggling only for possession of
the official crib. To be sure, there are among them many Southern refugees
and desperadoes. But the Democratic Party as a whole will not try to
get up a row. Its leaders are none too good, but they know better.

October 23. . . . Sheridan reports himself pursuing the routed rebels up
the valley, and that they are throwing away their arms, and that considerable bodies of them are breaking up and taking to the mountains.[20] This
looks as if the character of the war were changing. So does a late article,
quite elaborate, that appeared in some Richmond paper. It says in substance, "We have no cavalry, though the South is a people of horsemen.
We have only mounted men, useful as scouts and skirmishers, like the
Cossacks, but unequal to conflict with the masses of trained cavalry the
Yankees have somehow been able to put in the field. Most of them have
actually thrown away their sabres. They always run when attacked by
Yankee horse. They are not worth their cost, and three-fourths of them
should at once be dismounted and put into infantry regiments." A significant confession. It would seem that the estimate generally received
at the beginning of the war of the qualities and relative value of a Northern
and a Southern soldiery was just and true, but that its worth was not
developed till both armies had experienced three years of battle. In July,
1861, a Northern mob and a Southern mob came into collision at Bull
Run, and the North was routed. In 1864, Northern veterans are meeting
Southern veterans in Georgia and on the Shenandoah, and the case is
altered.

October 31, MONDAY. Let me register the notabilia of last week's
Sanitary Commission campaign at Washington.

Thither Monday the 24th, by the eight A.M. train. Woods still in full
autumn beauty. Ride as dreary and tedious as usual. Bishop Clark joined
me at Baltimore, and his lively talk helped me through the last two hours.
He seems indisposed to commit himself as to his present views on public
affairs. Probably they are of no great importance to anybody. I detected
nothing worse than a little pardonable uneasiness about the duration of
the war. At 244 F Street, I found a good room awaiting me (poor Bloor's
quarters), and a commissariat department fully established for the benefit
of this session; so we all breakfasted and dined together. The experiment

[20] Resistance in the Shenandoah was now practically ended, and many of Sheridan's
troops were soon fighting before Petersburg.

is not wholly successful, but it is an improvement on feeding at Willard's or at Buhler's cockroachy restaurant, and the symposia, though plain and frugal, were jolly.

Session closed Friday night, or rather Saturday morning. There were Bellows, Agnew, Newberry, Clark, Harris, Binney, Stillé (whom we added to the Standing Committee), and Wolcott of Boston. Also a very strong-minded Miss Abby W. May, an elect lady from the patriotic womankind of Boston, who had invited us to invite her attendance. She was attentive, interested, and silent, but her presence obliged us to "go into executive session" now and then, for the discussion of sundry personal questions, and to "clear the galleries" (the sofa in the corner, to wit). Then we lit our cigars. . . .[21]

General Grant wrote us for copies of the report on rebel prisoners to be sent to General Lee. We appointed a committee on my motion (for the sake of perfecting our record, but with no hope of accomplishing anything), to visit City Point and to see whether the rebel authorities could be shamed into allowing us to send supplies to our starving men in their wicked, tyrannous hands, and agents to distribute them and protect them from misappropriation. The President authorized the committee to make the experiment, but just as it was setting off for James River, news came that the rebels had themselves made overtures that way!!! So Bellows, Stillé, and Wolcott concluded to postpone this journey, especially as Grant was making a movement and was likely to be too busy to attend to them. (N.B. This movement failed, and was a worse failure than the newspapers indicated.) I believe these rebel overtures are due to this report by men like Dr. Mott, Dr. Delafield, and others known abroad as entitled to credence and respect and free from all partisan taint. Lee, Davis & Co. see that it is likely to raise a howl throughout Christendom against their barbarism, and hasten to open negotiations on the treatment of prisoners. It is a most important paper. Significant that Lord Lyons asked Bellows for copies to distribute in England.

We had an interesting visit to the Military Cemetery, near the old

[21] Abigail Williams May (1829–1888), member of an old Boston family well known for religious and social reform activities, was herself energetic in behalf of her community. She was a founder and chairman of the executive committee of the New England Women's Auxiliary Association, an affiliate of the Sanitary Commission. She had entered the Commission's hospital transport service in 1862 and no doubt had contributed much, both in money and work, to the organization. As she was also a staunch woman's suffrage worker, a species Strong abhorred, it is easy to understand his grudging acceptance of her part in the Commission's affairs.

"Soldiers' Home," where Uncle Abe has his summer quarters; 6,500 walnut headboards painted white, numbered, and recording the name, company, and regiment of the dead soldier sleeping below. These ghastly shapes crowd the beautiful greensward. Suppose the chivalric and venerable Robert Ruffin, who fired the first gun on Sumter, could have seen this sight in a trance or a vision the night before. Would he have touched off his piece without misgivings? We adjourned Friday night. . . .

November 2. . . . Visit from Vinton of the School of Mines this morning —*ci-devant* General Vinton.[22] He is hopeful about the School and seems energetic. It is to open on or about the 15th. Barnard's administration as president of the College is thus far most successful, in spite of his deafness. I predict he will prove the most efficient president we have had for thirty-five years. He must possess singular tact, for Professor Anthon likes him and speaks of him with respect, though he has never before had anything good to say of an official superior.

Standing Committee of the Sanitary Commission tonight at Dr. Bellows's. Newberry with us. The moment election is over, we must declare war against the Medical Bureau, which has been steadily retrograding for six months. If we were to proclaim what we know of its general efficiency and recklessness and of its murderous non-feasances in the Valley of the Shenandoah, the facts could be used by Copperheads so as seriously to weaken Lincoln's chance of reëlection. Of course, we must hold our peace a little longer.

The New York *World* scolds venomously over last night's meeting of War Democrats, and is very hard on General Dix. He is nobody, and a tool of the Administration besides. McClellan stock is low just now, though gold is high, and the *News* and *World* are therefore roaring their loudest.

November 3. Have just returned from the Broadway Theatre after a pleasant evening with Ellie and George Anthon. How long is it since I have taken her to the theatre? This is what used to be Wallack's, in what is now the remote, obscure, downtown latitude of Broome Street. Very good performance of *The Victims* and *Solon Shingle*. One Owens is

[22] Francis L. Vinton (1835–1879), a graduate of West Point in the class of 1856 and of the *Ecole des Mines*, had fought bravely in several campaigns, attained the rank of brigadier, and been so seriously wounded at Fredericksburg that he was unfit for further duty. His friend Egleston was now bringing him into the Columbia School of Mines, where for the next thirteen years he was to be an efficient professor. A man of great personal charm as well as culture, he was to become an intimate friend of Strong's.

the special attraction. His impersonation of an honest old garrulous codger from some rural district of New England or of Suffolk County, Long Island, whose father "fit into the Revolutionary War," is the *ne plus ultra* of histrionic photographing. Every movement and intonation seems carefully studied from a living model.

Nothing notable in Wall Street or at No. 823. Seward telegraphs Gunther the Mayor to beware of a conspiracy to burn this and other Northern cities on or about November 8th. The community is infested by rebel refugees and sympathizers. There are doubtless rebel agents among them, eagerly watching their opportunity to do mischief. Seymour's "friends" are ready to emerge from their tenement-houses and cellars and suburban shanties and from every gambling shop and brothel in the city whenever there shall be an opening for pillage, arson, and murder like that of July, 1863. But I predict no serious breach of the peace next week, though Rebeldom and Copperheadism are cornered and desperate and none too good to bring fire and knife into the streets of New York and Philadelphia, if their wicked cause would be helped thereby, or even for the mere gratification of their malignant spite against us. It looks as if the Administration would be sustained by next Tuesday's election. God grant it!

November 4. . . . At No. 823 this afternoon. Bellows tells me that Governor Morgan tells him "he considers the election over—and won." May he be sustained by the result! This prognosis of a coming election is as trustworthy as that of any political practitioner I know. N.B. The New York *World* is disgusted with Bellows—says he is making "Lincoln speeches" at "corner groceries" (meaning thereby the Cooper Institute), and that if the Sanitary Commission do not get him out of its presidency forthwith, it will be universally recognized as a mere "Black Republican Club."

Meeting of Committee on School of Mines at William Betts's office this morning. Prospects very hopeful. After dinner to Union League Club, and thence with George C. Anthon to inspect the grand Union torchlight procession. It was large, enthusiastic, and most brilliantly pyrotechnic with its rockets and Roman candles. What is more important, it was made up of voters. There were comparatively few boys of sixteen and upwards. Perhaps the Secesh majority in this city may be less than people expect.

[August] Belmont has been publicly invited in the newspapers to take up a bet of two to one that Lincoln will be reëlected. He replies by offering to bet that if Lincoln be reëlected, the war will last through his term of office, and that if McClellan be elected, there will be peace and reconstruction. Very significant as to Herr Belmont's (or Schönberg's) views of the case. The Democratic Party must be short of strong men when it has to put this Dutch banker at the head of its Executive Committee. I have a sort of respect for him as being beautiful Mrs. Belmont's husband, but he is, in fact, a mere successful cosmopolite adventurer and alien, who has made money as the agent of foreign capitalists and has no real affinity with our country or people. They *do* say, moreover, that he is a Jew, half-converted and conforming outwardly; a political Joannes Pfefferkorn (*vide Epist. Obsc. Virorum*). Don't know about that, but his setting himself up as one of our guides and governors is a piece of audacious impudence, whether he be Jew or Christian.

November 5. . . . The city is full of noises tonight. There is a grand McClellan demonstration in progress. Little "Mac" was to "review" his hordes of Celts and rebel sympathizers in person from the balcony of the Fifth Avenue Hotel. I have still respect enough for him left to believe that he must feel himself in a horribly false position. A general who commanded at Malvern Hill and Antietam in 1862 must be tempted to doubt his own identity when he hears Governor Seymour's "friends" hurrahing for him in 1864.

November 6, SUNDAY. General Butler in town. He commands the United States forces here, reporting to General Dix. I hear he proposed issuing an order last night that all officers of state militia regiments report to him. Dix objected and Stanton was telegraphed for a decision. Such an order would be disregarded by Seymour's Copperhead colonels, and they would have the law on their side. It would promote collision with state authorities. But General Butler's personal presence next Tuesday will do no harm. The rabble of New York is not generally well informed, but it knows Butler's name as suggestive of vigorous action against rebels at New Orleans and elsewhere—action hampered by very few scruples about form and legal right and thus far successful. The *World* and *News* and *Express* have raved about Butler "the Beast," the tyrant, the lawless minion of a profligate Administration, till such of their party as can read print regard him as the Covenanters regarded Claverhouse; a wholesome fear and dread of Butler underlies all the rebel and Copperhead denunciation of his corruption and abuse of power. It is quite natural that rats should hold terriers unconstitutional and scandalous.

November 7. Rainy day. Columbia College meeting at two. I hope much from Barnard's administration. The new measures he is taking promise to strengthen discipline and raise the moral tone of the undergraduates. There are already signs that the inner life of the College is gaining vigor. Then he appreciates the importance of our getting the hold on the community we ought to have, and is pushing out organic filaments that may become roots; for example, our proposed relations with the Lyceum of Natural History, over which we have pottered at intervals for two or three years, were brought up for action this afternoon, and a committee appointed. This may result in our securing a valuable ally and auxiliary, strengthening our scientific school, and getting control of a very considerable scientific collection.

November 8, TUESDAY. So this momentous day is over, and the battle lost and won. We shall know more of the result tomorrow. Present signs are not unfavorable. Wet weather, which did not prevent a very heavy vote. I stood in queue nearly two hours waiting my turn. A little before me was Belmont, whose vote was challenged on the ground that he had betted on the election. The inspector rejected it unwillingly, and Belmont went off in a rage. Very few men would have been challenged on that ground, but this foreign money-dealer has made himself uncommonly odious, and the bystanders, mostly of the Union persuasion, chuckled over his discomfiture. . . .

This election has been quiet beyond precedent. Few arrests, if any, have been made for disorderly conduct. There has been no military force visible. It is said that portions of the city militia regiments were on guard at their armories, and that some 6,000 United States troops were at Governor's Island and other points outside the city, but no one could have guessed from the appearance of the streets that so momentous an issue was *sub judice.* . . .

In this city the Democratic strongholds have enlarged their Copperhead majorities, but the total majority seems not to exceed 35,750, which is less than was feared. News from Westchester County looks rather ill, but there is not much of it. Philadelphia reported to have improved upon last month's state election. Baltimore and Maryland right by a large vote. Indiana ditto. Gain in New Jersey; Massachusetts all one way. Prospect good in Connecticut. George Anthon has just looked in on his way homeward from the Club. Says the feeling there is that Lincoln is certainly reëlected, but that this state is doubtful and is claimed at the Copperhead headquarters by 5,000 majority. That would be a serious offset against the results of victory. I hope better things.

VICTORIA! Te Deum laudamus. Te Dominum confitemur.

November 9. Laus Deo! The crisis has been past, and the most momentous popular election ever held since ballots were invented has decided against treason and disunion. My contempt for democracy and extended suffrage is mitigated. The American people can be trusted to take care of the national honor. Lincoln is reëlected by an overwhelming vote. The only states that seem to have McClellanized are Missouri, Kentucky, Delaware, and New Jersey. New York, about which we have been uneasy all day, is reported safe at the Club tonight. The Copperheads are routed—*Subversi sunt quasi plumbum in aequis vehementibus.* Poor "little Mac" will never be heard of any more, I think. No man of his moderate calibre ever had such an opportunity of becoming illustrious and threw it away so rapidly. Notwithstanding a certain lukewarmness in the national cause, his instincts and impulses were, on the whole, right and loyal. Had he acted on them honestly and manfully, he would have been elected. But his friends insisted on his being *politic*, and he had not the strength to resist them. He allowed Belmont and Barlow to strike out of his letter of acceptance a vigorous sentence declaring an armistice with armed rebels out of the question, and to append to it its unmeaning finale (which imposed on no man) stating that he assumed the views he had expressed to be what the Chicago Convention really meant to say in its treasonous resolutions. *Fuit* McClellan, Napoleoniculus. Five years hence people will wonder how such a fuss ever came to be made about him.

A very wet, warm day. Copperheads talk meekly and well. "It's a terrible mistake, but we have got to make the best of it and support the government." The serene impudence of this morning's *World* can hardly be matched. It says the mission of the Democratic Party for the next four years will be to keep A. Lincoln from making a dishonorable disunion peace with the South. So a gentleman who has just received a sentence of four years in the State Prison might (if cheeky enough) inform the court and jury that their unjust decision would oblige him to be especially careful during his term that law and order were maintained throughout the state and that no crime failed to meet prompt punishment. The *World* is, moreover, uncommonly proud of the "Democratic masses"

(Governor Seymour's "friends," the liquor dealers, roughs, and brutal Irishry of the city) because they committed no disorders yesterday, *though* so easily tempted to make a general row by the offensive and insulting presence of General Butler with sundry regiments to back him. . . .

George Anthon dined here, and we proceeded to the Union League Club, where was much folk. Discoursed with General Banks among others. It would seem that William E. Dodge is defeated by James Brooks, that most coprophagous of Copperheads, in this congressional district. A great pity, but Dodge's election was hardly hoped for. Would we were quite sure that Seymour is beaten! John Astor says he thinks Seymour's election would be more mischievous than McClellan's, and he may be right. Seymour and McClellan are weak men, but the latter means well. Seymour's instincts are all evil. He is quite as bad as Fernando Wood.

Lincoln's victory was as sweeping as his best friends could have desired. After being a minority President for four years, he now had the satisfaction of receiving a majority of almost 495,000 in the popular vote. He had 212 electoral votes, while McClellan was left with only 21, these being furnished by New Jersey (McClellan's own state), Kentucky, and with a very narrow margin, Delaware. In New York State the result was for several days in doubt, but it finally appeared that Fenton had won the governorship by a margin of 8,293 over Seymour. Never had the American electorate appeared to better advantage. Lincoln, in a felicitous little speech to a crowd of serenaders, made precisely the right comment. "The election, along with its incidental and undesirable strife, has done good," he remarked. "It has demonstrated that a people's government can sustain a national election in the midst of a great civil war; until now, it has not been known to the world that this was a possibility. . . . It shows, also, to the extent yet known, that we have more men now than we had when the war began."

November 10. Election returns improve. New York seems secure by from 5,000 to 7,500, Seymour running a little behind his ticket, and Missouri is claimed for the Administration, leaving poor McClellan only three states. If his wife and her mother, Mrs. Marcy, had not allowed themselves to be talked over by Belmont and Barlow, and brought household influence to bear upon him, he would not be in this plight. They prevailed on him to disregard General Dix's earnest advice and to try to ride two horses, Peace and War, at once. I should not wonder if the old

Democratic party were killed with its candidate—though it has immense vitality. It would be curious if that old and potent organization should die of this election, the result of which has been in great measure determined by the fireside talk of an amiable young wife and a strong-minded mother-in-law. That party can hardly survive another four years of exclusion from office under the national government and in almost every state. Its extinction would be a great blessing. It has been an ancient *imperium in imperio* with its own settled rules, usages, and traditions of political immorality, not worse perhaps than those of other parties, but better established, more powerful, and more fruitful of public mischief.

November 11.   No material news, except that it is positively asserted that "Little Mac" has resigned his commission in a pet, and by way of spiting an unappreciative people. . . . By the by, the most infamous paper of the last four years appeared in yesterday's *Daily News*: a congratulatory address to our Mayor, Gunther (an abject Copperhead), on his refusal to approve a resolution of the Common Council recommending illuminations in honor of Sheridan's victories and the fall of Atlanta. It fills two columns with treason and baseness. Charles O'Conor signs it (and it's evidently his handiwork), Horace F. Clark, S. F. B. Morse, [Gideon] Tucker the Surrogate, John W. Mitchell, Hiram Cranston, John McKeon, Richard O'Gorman, and a lot of others (mostly unknown to fame), among whom is the urbane William Betts. May their names be remembered!

I shall find it hard to meet Betts after this at our College committees on the Law School and the School of Mines without letting him know that I think him as infamous as his very small capacity can make him. This flagitious document bears the date October 20, but was suppressed till after the election—an unconscious compliment to the honesty and patriotism of the people. It should be remembered, however, that Betts inherited a large amount of treasonable impulse through his wife, a descendant of the Colonel Beverley Robinson of the last century who was mixed up with Arnold's treason. Betts got his social position by his marriage (I believe he was an adventurer from Jamaica or some other British Colony), and he has dutifully adopted the anti-American tradition of his wife's family. Fortunately, he has no more weight or influence than his cat. He is an attorney and conveyancer of small calibre, with a small amount of literary culture and scholarship on the strength of which he looks down upon the community at large with a supreme disdain. . . .

At the Union League Club tonight. Majority in the state promises to exceed our hopes. This election, peacefully conducted in a time of such bitter excitement, and with a result quietly recognized and acquiesced in by a furious malcontent minority, is the strongest testimonial in favor of popular institutions to be found in history.

November 12.   This morning spent at breakfast (Union League Club) in honor of Professor Goldwin Smith of Oxford.[23] About seventy sat down. I was between William C. Bryant and Lieber, and of course had an agreeable time enough. After a period of deleterious deglutition came speeches by Charles Butler, John Jay, General Butler, Evarts, George William Curtis, and others—and the professor, of course. He is a tall, thin, grave man, and speaks slowly but accurately, with intonation a little monotonous but agreeable. He is evidently a scholar and a thinker. General Butler's speech was telling, though a little artificial or stagey in delivery. The Rev. A. C. Coxe spoke, made certain very good points, and shewed his usual want of tact. Avowed that he had little sympathy with the English Liberals (of whom Professor Smith is representative), and said he was "not a political clergyman" and that "he never voted." This little dab at political clergymen brought the Abbé Bellows down on him and when Bellows's turn came, he delivered an opinion that "cocks that didn't fight and didn't vote ought not to crow." Quite smart, but not in the best taste.

Lieber says he wants to have the event of Tuesday known in history as *The Great and Good Election of 1864.* He is always saying things.

Tonight to an adjourned monthly meeting of the Century Club for election of members. Attendance large, as it was understood our minority of Copperhead members meant to blackball Parke Godwin of the *Evening Post.* He was triumphantly elected. Ned Bell, [Francis F.] Marbury, William E. Curtis, and others could not muster half the one-third required to defeat him. . . .

Poor, pretty, little loyal Mrs. Belmont, whom Ellie met tonight at the concert in aid of that everlasting "Nursery," declares herself made very unhappy by newspaper flings at her husband.

November 13, SUNDAY.   Vinton preached at Trinity and summed up

[23] The brilliant English publicist and scholar (1823–1910), who had played an important rôle in university reform, was one of the principal leaders in the struggle to place British sentiment squarely behind the North. His incisive pamphlets, articles, and speeches had attracted wide attention on both sides of the Atlantic. When the London *Times* pleaded a religious sanction for the peculiar Southern institution, Smith issued a telling pamphlet, "Does the Bible Sanction American Slavery?" His position as Regius Professor of History at Oxford, his slashing style, and his determination made him highly useful to the Union. In his tour of the North in 1864 he met an enthusiastic reception.

strongly against "the esoteric sentimentality of modern pantheism." He does so bounce and swagger in the pulpit and uses such big words that most of his congregation regard him with singular awe. But he would rise still higher in their respect and regard if his sermons lasted less than forty minutes. Tonight Miss Puss here, Charley, D'Oremieulx and wife, Dr. [J. Charles] Peters and wife, John Sherwood, Murray Hoffman, [Charles F.] Blake, Mr. Ruggles, and Charley Post.

A distinguished delegate to the Chicago Convention expatiated to Blake (a fortnight ago) on the dignity and weight of that body. "It was made up, sir, of the most loyal and influential Democratic leaders from Illinois, from New York, from New England, from Ohio, and from Canada. In fact, it represented the whole Democracy." Quite true, no doubt. Had fewer Canadian Democrats (that is, plotting Southern refugees) assisted at that convention, it might have adopted a more patriotic platform, and its party might have escaped absolute annihilation.

> Please to remember the *Eighth* of November,
> Copperhead Treason and Plot.
> We know no reason why Copperhead Treason
> Should ever be forgot.

This election of last Tuesday is quite as important an event in our history as the miscarriage of the Gunpowder Plot in that of Great Britain. Both indicate progress in the same way.

November 14. Uptown at two P.M. with William Schermerhorn to Forty-ninth Street, where the College Library Committee met. Nothing done except to pass on the purchase of a very few new books. We cannot afford to buy many. Dr. Anderson rather objected to the purchase of a very cheap copy of Foxe's *Actes and Monuments* which the librarian had smelt out in some obscure book store, and so did *I*; for that lying, vulgar, narrow-minded old martyrologist is entitled to little respect. But as his book has acquired a certain position in history which entitles it to a place in every collection as a curiosity (on the same shelf with Pinto and the *Malleus Maleficarum*), I proposed that we buy it and that we also import the Rev. S. R. Maitland's *Letters* shewing its worthlessness; which was agreed to. Maitland's book is valuable as a specimen of what can be done by minute, accurate criticism, and we shall have the bane and antidote together. From the library to the School of Mines; Professors Vinton and Egleston there, at work over their arrangements and confident of success. The Gilmore Collection presented by Kemble proves worth far less than its cost, but it is an acquisition, nevertheless. . . .

November 15. . . . . Rebel editors and Congressmen are in great heat over the question whether they shall arm a few thousand slaves, offering them freedom as a reward for a certain term of military service.[24] The chief objection to doing so seems to be that they would thereby admit that freedom is a boon to the field hand, whereas slavery is its highest blessing, and emancipation a penalty and a curse instead of a reward. The policy proposed, therefore, violates first (Southern) principles. They don't want to stultify themselves, but necessity will probably outweigh logic in the end, and their most sacred and inviolable theories will have to be violated. The most pious pirate would consent to raise the Devil to help him when in extremity, but the Devil is not to be depended on as an ally. *There* is the real stress of the question. When Cuffee is armed and equipped and under orders to march on Maryland, he will be very apt to march at double quick, and perhaps to march back again in the pay of the "Gorilla Despot." . . .

November 16. Gold falling, inopportunely, as I had $16,000 worth from California (Sanitary Commission) to dispose of. Why it falls is a mystery. Some say it's because General Butler talked about offering an amnesty at the Fifth Avenue Hotel Monday night. But the Southern newspapers are, if possible, more truculent and thrasonical than ever, and more earnest than ever about the necessity of dying in the very last ditch, if it can be reached, and of dying in any ditch rather than give up, now that they know of A. Lincoln's reëlection. The air is full of rumors that Sherman has made a grand movement from Atlanta.[25] Nobody knows what or whither. They are severally contradicted, but I shall not be surprised if something important has in fact created them. Sherman *may* be striking out for Augusta, Montgomery, Mobile, Savannah, Charleston or Lynchburg.

November 19, SATURDAY. Committee on School of Mines met this

[24] As the South scraped the bottom of its barrel for white recruits, voices were raised suggesting that slaves be enlisted. General Pat Cleburne suggested such action early in 1864, and General Joseph E. Johnston among others approved the idea. Now, in his November message to Congress, Jefferson Davis hinted that the Confederacy might have to use slaves for soldiers, and threatened to press the measure if he could not get enough white men. Several governors and a good many newspapers advocated this desperate measure, but for obvious reasons it met embittered resistance. Not until March 13, 1865, did the Confederate Congress pass a law for Negro enlistments.

[25] Sherman had obtained Grant's permission on November 2 to begin his march to the sea; and after burning Atlanta, his army of nearly 70,000 set out on November 15. Although he had little resistance to fear, his cutting loose from his base of supplies seemed to many a dangerously bold venture.

morning. Barnard with us, Egleston, and Chandler. The School opened on the 15th with twenty students and more are coming. Its success seems almost sure now. I hear it talked of out-of-doors, and it is plainly finding favor with the community. Could we but raise a trifle of $50,000 or so and give it a complete outfit!

Thence to Philharmonic rehearsal; Mendelssohn's Symphony, *vulgo vocento* the "Scotch Symphony"—why Scotch rather than Welsh I cannot say. Very delightful work. No end of talent, taste, culture, skill, fertility of resources, copiousness of musical language. Every movement beautiful and original and full of splendid points. No fault can be found with it, except that it is without the surpassing, almost supernatural, vigor and beauty that Mozart and Beethoven make an orchestra express. It is first-rate work of the second order, and different *in general* and not merely in degree from work of the first order. But the scherzo is marvellous, and so is the finale. . . .

Union League Club tonight. A hundred or more of its members came together to meet Lieutenant Cushing, who finished the rebel ram *Albemarle* with a torpedo-boat in the waters of North Carolina, thereby not only doing the country most substantial service, but shewing the most distinguished personal gallantry and daring.[26] He blew up his own boat with the iron-clad, and saved himself by swimming. According to our abominable national usage, somebody had to make a "few remarks" on the occasion; and John Jay was happy to make them and belabored this modest, boyish-looking young hero with ten minutes of eulogy. He blushed and looked uncomfortable, but made his inevitable reply, simply and briefly, and passed this ordeal as creditably as the other, which I dare say he found hardly more trying. He seems a most charming young fellow; handsome, intelligent, and dignified in his bearing, though very young (twenty-two) and looking much younger.

The Hon. John Sherman of Ohio was also present, and he had to make a "few remarks," too, of course. What he said was much to the purpose, and the evening was uncommonly satisfactory.

[26] Lieutenant W. B. Cushing, U.S.N., had fitted a torpedo to a long spar on a launch, ascended the Roanoke River, and blown up the Confederate iron-clad ram *Albemarle*, which had previously done much damage to the Union fleet in Albemarle Sound. This was one of the most daring feats of the war, for to reach the *Albemarle* Cushing had to drive his launch over a log boom under a hail of shot and shell. The back of his coat was torn out by buckshot, the sole of one shoe was carried away, and the rest of his clothing was riddled by bullets. Then, still under heavy fire, he managed to swim across the cold river (the date was October 27), and after many vicissitudes, reached a Union vessel in the Sound.

November 20.   Reports from Sherman more or less authentic (probably *less*) place him seventy miles south of Atlanta on the 14th, and "advancing toward the Savannah River," eating his way, living on the country, and leaving a track of desolation behind him. May God prosper his march and help and comfort the homes which right and justice, whose minister he is, oblige him to lay waste! It is sad to think of the misery rebellion has brought upon Rebeldom, of the many thousand households it has ruined and is starving. They have brought it on themselves in the great majority of cases. . . . They deserve no sympathy. But think of the poor little children who do not know good from evil! Think of the thousands of little people, each "like an angel, with bright hair," who have pined and wasted and perished under privation and exposure inflicted on them by this war. Think of them, and then say what doom can meet the deserts of the wicked men who forced war upon us in mere arrogance of self-will. Treason so groundless and gratuitous cannot be found in the history of man. The children have to suffer for the sins of their fathers—poor little souls. But the nation should execute justice on the guilty all the more sternly because their crime has inflicted so much suffering on the innocent.

November 22. . . . Grant declares that he does not know on what point Sherman is moving. . . . Sherman's orders were indefinite. He was merely directed to move into the "bowels of the enemy's country"; whereupon somebody remarked that we should in that case hear of operations and evacuations before long. Grant was nervous and anxious, unusually so, according to Burnside, in consequence of telegrams from Sheridan that the enemy had disappeared from his front, and reports from rebel deserters that all rolling stock had been moved westward from Richmond, and that Lee, reinforced by Early, was contemplating a grand attack on our lines. On the other hand, we have reports from City Point of issues of rations and ammunition, indicating a forward movement from our side. . . .

Burnside wants a command, and called on the President about it. Charley [Strong] and Tom Goddard were present at the interview. Lincoln said he must wait and consent to be under a cloud a little longer. He must not resign. Burnside seems to acquiesce. Charley is full of admiration of his unselfish, magnanimous disposition. He reports Meade unpopular and morbidly sensitive about his personal reputation; for example, when directed by Grant to issue a certain order, Meade demurs because "if this move succeed, you will get all the credit, but if it fail, I shall have to bear all the newspaper criticism." Bad for Meade, if true. Perhaps utterly untrue. "I tell the tale as it was told to me." Charley reports the Army of the Potomac and of the James in the best possible heart and highest confidence, according to his observation.

At No. 823 [Broadway] this afternoon. An anxious discussion. Renewed it with Agnew at the Union League Club this evening. Sanitary Commission is in trouble. I fear we must throw overboard either Knapp, or Jenkins and Collins, to save the ship from foundering. Very unfortunate, but these men cannot work together.

November 23.   At No. 823 this afternoon, and tonight at Dr. Bellows's with Agnew, Van Buren, and Gibbs. Jenkins not present by request, being interested in the personal embroilments and jealousies we had to discuss. There are three grave questions now before us, each requiring much sagacity and a large range of view for its decision. First, there is this miserable but most perilous disagreement and discord among our chief officers. Second, the apportionment of our expenditure, and the settlement of its monthly amount, which is necessary, inasmuch as we have probably seen our best financial days and can hope for no more millioniferous Metropolitan Fairs. Third, our policy of peace or open war with the Medical Bureau, which has relapsed nearly to its condition of three years ago. It has already opened a campaign against us in the New York *World*, which has published two editorials against us, evidently inspired by Copperheads' hostility to Bellows as a recent speaker in support of the government, but using material as evidently furnished by Satterlee or some other representative of the fossil fogyism of the Bureau. We were mostly occupied with the first of these, and agreed on a new disposition of our staff, sending Jenkins to Washington. It is a mere palliative at best, postponing the inevitable explosion a month or two. But Jenkins will probably refuse to try the experiment and decline all further official relations with Knapp. Jenkins thinks himself unequal to his work; naturally enough, for his rôle is altogether exceptional and indefinite, and this makes him morbid, dissatisfied, and irritable. If he resigns, whom can we put in his place? Dr. Douglass and Dr. Parrish were talked of. Douglass declines the Associate Secretaryship, but might consent to become General Secretary.

My chief anxiety is about Collins's possible defection. He is certainly cross-grained and crotchety, but without a lieutenant of his unquestionable honesty and reliability, I should not dare to make myself responsible for the really large and complex money operations of the Commission as its treasurer, and I do not see how we can replace him. I shall have been the depositary of near four millions of trust money before the work is wound up, if I live so long—an hundred-fold more than I ever dreamed of handling when I consented to take the treasurership. I take it for granted that I shall be charged with stealing some of it, and I don't very much mind the prospect for myself. But I don't want the name of Johnny's, Temple's, and Louis's Papa mixed up, twenty years hence, with vague rumors of "something wrong about that great Sanitary Fund," and a thoroughly trustworthy aid like Collins is my chief dependence and reliance against such rumors. With him to help me, I am sure I can squelch those just as fast as they spring up. None has sprouted yet, thank God.

November 25. [Eliakim] Littell, the Boston publisher, called in Wall Street about the cheap edition of the report on rebel prisons which he is getting out and for the expense of which he is raising money by subscription. A single Bostonian, A. A. Lawrence, I think, agrees to pay for three or four thousand copies to be sent to England. Littell wants to be enabled to send a copy to every clergyman and every newspaper editor in the Northern States. He thinks it will influence the coming campaign on the anti-slavery constitutional amendment question, as displaying most clearly the barbarizing and maligning effect of slavery on slaveholding communities; and says he knows Eastern Copperheads who have apologized for every crime rebels have committed, but now confess the rebel treatment of our prisoners inexcusable and criminal beyond precedent.

Uptown early at Egleston's request to visit the School of Mines, now fully at work—with twenty-nine pupils!!![27] Everything looks well, save our account with the Trust Company, which is much too small. Our $2,400 is nearly used up, and at least $5,000 more is needed for indispensable outfit and equipment. Can we get an appropriation from the College? The School seems managed by Egleston, Barnard, Vinton, and Chandler with the utmost energy, economy, and judgment. With a little judicious stimulation and nutrition, it can be developed into a most important centre of practical training in science. O for $50,000! Dr. Haight, Dr. Dix, and Mr. Ruggles were there, with Egleston and Chandler.

From Forty-ninth Street to No. 823. Then home, and after dinner, a Sanitary Commission (Standing Committee) session; Bellows, Jenkins, Agnew, Gibbs, Van Buren, Stillé. Mainly devoted to discussion of our

---

[27] Instruction in the School of Mines had begun this fall, with Thomas Egleston in charge, and with Professors Francis L. Vinton, Charles F. Chandler, Charles A. Joy and others on the as yet unpaid faculty. Chandler supported himself by working as chemical analyst in a sugar refinery for two hours each morning before arriving at Columbia at eight A.M. Egleston had private means. Joy was paid for his teaching in the College, which soon became known as the School of Arts.

relations with the Medical Bureau and of the propriety of undertaking a Congressional campaign in the hope of promoting reform in the Bureau and preventing Barnes's confirmation as Surgeon-General. We incline that way, though Van Buren declares he will not go to Washington on any terms, and Agnew has crotchets I do not understand. Our application to Barnes for authority to renew our inspection of hospitals is formally disapproved by order of the Secretary of War on the ground that official inspectors were appointed by the Act of 1862. This is a subterfuge, for the corps of government inspectors has notoriously proved a nullity. They have no authority, their reports and recommendations are studiously ignored, and they are systematically snubbed. Stanton's policy as to the Sanitary Commission almost makes me wish myself a Copperhead and a traitor that I might freely deliver myself of my opinion as to a member of the Administration whom duty compels every loyal man, in these critical days, to uphold, or at least, to tolerate, and silently to acquiesce in as a necessary evil that will doubtless be somehow overruled to good ends in the course of God's good Providence. But his arrogant, official discouragement of aid from the unexampled bounty of the people, through the Commission, in his duty of saving the lives of our soldiers and economizing the life-blood of the country is a crime almost without precedent. Its sole provocation (that I can discover) is some little squabble with Bellows in 1862, when Bellows called on him to object to the appointment of one Tucker as an Assistant Secretary of War, because the said Tucker was reported corrupt and untrustworthy.

November 26.   George Anthon dined here and spent the evening. He tells me that according to the talk of the New York Club the harlotry of the city is largely reinforced by Southern refugee women who were of good social standing at home, but find themselves here without means of support and forced to choose between starving and whoring. Mortal man will never know the whole amount of sorrow, suffering, bereavement, devastation, and crime for which the secession conspirators of 1860 A.D. are answerable. It seems a just retribution on the Southern slaveholding chivalry who have been forcing their female slaves—black, mulatto, and quadroon—to minister to their pleasures that their rebellion should drive their wives and daughters to flee northward and prostitute themselves to Northern "mudsills," plebeian "Yankees." All the North is full of these refugees, male and female. One of them tried to seduce Burnside the other day at Washington and nearly succeeded, but as she was turning down the gas he remembered Molly (Mrs. Burnside) and fled the room. These scoundrels tried to burn the city last night. I heard the melancholy bell of Calvary Church tolling the alarm again and again at short intervals during our Sanitary Commission session, but I did not know what it meant. They fired the old United States Hotel ("Holt's Hotel" of thirty years ago, corner of Fulton and Pearl Streets), the St. James Hotel, Barnum's Museum, the St. Nicholas, the Lafarge, the Metropolitan, Lovejoy's (twice), the Belmont House (Fulton Street), Tammany Hall, the Howard House, and the "New England Hotel," corner Bowery and Bayard Streets. This morning they tried to fire the Astor House and the Fifth Avenue Hotel. Tonight Calvary Church bell clanked awhile, but I do not know why. All these incendiary efforts have been made by unknown lodgers securing rooms, saturating their beds with camphene, depositing a stick of phosphorus to promote combustion (which it wouldn't), and then disappearing.[28]

November 28, MONDAY. . . . Our news from Sherman through rebel channels indicates that he is marching on—ploughing a deep furrow many miles wide through Georgia and destroying a vital nerve-system of railroad; that he has passed by Macon, has harried Milledgeville, and is threatening Savannah. But rebel editors judiciously keep back most of their information about his movements, and what scraps of intelligence we get from them reach us through a distorting, refracting atmospheric stratum of falsehood and bluster. . . .

November 29. . . . At the Union League Club tonight; Emmet, Osborn, Marshall, Butler, and others. Rebeldom is sorely perturbed by Sherman's march south-eastward. But rebel newspapers are sure he will be destroyed before he can reach the coast, "if every man will only do his duty." They comfort themselves also with the reflection that his movement is really a retreat, though it does not look like one when superficially considered, being the wrong way, and that he is in fact driven out of Atlanta. So Napoleon drove the Allies out of Leipsic toward Paris.

I am satisfied that the South is thoroughly rotten, and the Confederacy a mere shell. It's a white-hot crust that can burn the fingers that try to break it, but there is nothing to support it—nothing below its surface.

[28] This incendiary attempt was devised by Jacob Thompson, whilom member of Buchanan's Cabinet, who had been living in Canada, plotting with leaders of the Knights of the Golden Circle, and trying to help Confederate prisoners escape. With the help of R. M. Martin, a body of eight men was organized, sent to New York, and directed to fire eleven large hotels and Barnum's Museum with its attached theatre. Had their "Greek fire" not proved a failure, many innocent people might have perished.

Its weakness lies mainly in the utter debasement of its poor whites. The original fire-eating, revolver-flourishing, aristocratic "chivalry" of 1861 is nearly used up and worn out. The material to replace it is scanty. Railroad tracks and rolling stock are in like case, and still harder to replace. . . . And there seems reason to believe—though it's a horrible suspicion to record—that a large class of Southern women has been demoralized and corrupted by the war. Not only in New York, but at Nashville, Cairo, New Orleans, Washington, and other places I hear of activities of Southern ladies whose husbands and brothers are in the rebel army and who live by the profits of sin. It is said that Sherman decided to order all inhabitants of Atlanta to leave their homes mainly because he knew the health and efficiency of his soldiers would be seriously impaired if any women were left in Atlanta! This seems incredible, but all the foundations of Southern society have been shaken or destroyed for three years and upwards.

November 30. Long consultation with Egleston this morning about the School of Mines, and another after dinner with William E. Dodge, Jr., who, being wise and public-spirited, sees the importance of this undertaking and wants to aid it by work in any capacity, however subordinate. May the College trustees be inspired to close their eyes a few moments to their own corporate dignity and to allow a few of their fellow citizens humbly to help them in work to which they are confessedly unequal. But I hardly hope for it. We, the trustees, are "enclosed in our own fort." The notion of active, earnest effort to promote the usefulness of the College has never occurred to three-fourths of us. We think we are doing a great deal if we attend a monthly meeting that lasts two hours. Now that we can enlist a score of first-rate business men and lovers of science in the energetic development of the most hopeful undertaking, we shall probably be paralyzed by doubts as to whether it is becoming to ask help from outsiders, whether the trustees ought not to attend to their own business, and whether there are not various considerations by which the organization of an important School of Science can be retarded, dwarfed, and killed. I fear a majority of the board will devote itself to the question of "how *not* to do" anything for the College, and for the community. But I am satisfied that if this school can be kept alive through the winter, it will succeed, and that two years hence its supply of educated metallurgists and engineers will begin to add millions to our national resources for the payment of our national debt.

December 1. . . . Up to Forty-ninth Street at three P.M. for the Committee on the School of Mines, which met in the president's room; Betts, Rutherfurd, Edward Jones, Torrey, and I, with Professor Egleston and Chandler. I proposed that we recommend an appropriation of $2,500 or thereabouts, which was agreed to, and then brought forward a plan for enlisting outside aid. As I expected, it was most unfavorably received, except by Torrey, who had discussed it with Egleston, and by Barnard, who was as unconscious of what we were talking about as if he had been in Kamschatka. But the rest came round, after some demur, and a recommendation was adopted substantially such as I wished. Good! Now if we can only carry it through the board, I shall feel that our germ of a school is safe. . . .

"Extray" at noon today, announcing victory at Franklin, Tennessee (eighteen miles south of Nashville), yesterday. Hood's rebels attacked Schofield (one of Thomas's lieutenants) at four P.M., fought till dark, and were defeated, losing "6,000 killed and wounded," and 1,000 prisoners; our loss only 500. The news is confirmed by official despatch in evening papers. The result is very probably overstated, but it looks like a substantial success at a most important point of conflict, and any serious check is a disaster to Hood.[29] Thank God. Rebel papers tell nothing definite about Sherman, and talk of his movements only in the style of vague bluster and brag with which a New York Bowery boy mentions the movements of his adversary.

December 4, SUNDAY. . . . Friday Egleston, Chandler, and Vinton of the School of Mines dined here, with Jem Ruggles. A most satisfactory session. Vinton made a great impression. Ellie is enthusiastic about him. He left the service, in consequence of a wound received at Fredericksburg, having risen to the rank of brigadier-general, and shewn distinguished merit while in the army. He is fluent, vivacious, clever, and earnest— somewhat like Dick Hunt. Three young men so accomplished in science and so full of self-devotion and disinterestedness would be hard to find in New York. In my enthusiasm I turned over my Nachet Binocular of 1859 to the School, and Egleston called and carried it off tonight. It's no sacrifice, for I have not looked into it for four years. These young gentlemen are actually making the fires in their lecture-rooms and carrying their own coal. Two of them are graduates of the *Ecole Impériale* of Paris.

[29] At Franklin the Confederates under Hood were defeated after some of the fiercest fighting of the war. They lost one-tenth of the men engaged slain on the field, and another two-fifths wounded or captured. In this battle the Union troops under Colonel John S. Casement used magazine breech-loaders with terrible effect. Thomas was now preparing his final blow for the annihilation of Hood.

Chandler has given up a permanent salaried place in Union College to aid this experiment of a scientific school in New York. Rood and Joy are working with them most heartily.

Men like William E. Dodge, Jr., and F. H. Delano are ready and anxious to work with us in raising funds for the School if the College will give them leave. The community wants such a school and is eager to contribute, deterred only by the fact that Columbia College "has an endowment." If appealed to by new men not identified with our respectable fogyism, it will give abundantly. When I mentioned the matter to Talboys this evening, he instantly asked whether we would receive so small a contribution as $100. The College never had such a chance of establishing a hold on the capitalists and business men of New York, getting out of its shell, and identifying itself with the interests of the community. . . . The meeting of the board tomorrow . . . may determine whether we are still to be a mere mediocrity, or to become an important centre of education and science. I think Egleston, Vinton, and Chandler can redeem it. If the board turn them a cold shoulder and neglect this opportunity, I shall be tempted to believe the College hopelessly reprobate and to decline trying to do any more for it.

December 5.   Good weather, and a good day altogether. College board met at two. Not a full meeting. Our chairman, Hamilton Fish, was kept away by illness. . . . Betts read the report I had drawn on the School of Mines, and to my surprise and delight the resolutions recommended were unanimously passed. Betts, Haight, Barnard, and I said something in the way of explanation and advocacy, but there was not a word of opposition. Ogden, who feels bound as treasurer to oppose all increase of outlay, had been privily brought round by Rutherfurd, and I think Haight's views were changed by my suggestion that there was now a good chance for churchmen to beat the Calvinists of Yale and the Unitarians of Harvard on their own ground. So the School has got its appropriation of $2,250; its light and fuel, and what is far more important, leave to ask public-spirited men to work with its committee as associates. They must be most carefully chosen. . . .

This may prove our most important meeting for ten years past. Hooray! I see an annual corps of skilled engineers and metallurgists going out to develop our mineral wealth, now so wastefully used, on which we must so largely rely for payment of our swelling national debt; or, in other words, to defray the cost of saving our nation. I see capitalists and stockholders in mining companies enlisted in the cause of the College. I see a splendid collection of all manner of minerals, including the most magnificent quartz crystals, the loveliest agates, and the biggest beryls. I see pterodactyls and megatheria. What don't I see? Much of my vision is out of sight, I fear, like that of the heroine of *The Critic* when she raved about the Spanish fleet. But the prospects of this undertaking are reasonably good.

December 6. Voted at charter election all by myself. Small vote polled. Gave mine against our neighbor, old Gerard, as school commissioner. We want no Copperheads in office, high or low.

The President's message seems characteristically sensible and straightforward. Chase said to have been nominated and confirmed as Chief Justice of the Supreme Court. Not a bad appointment. We hear nothing about Sherman or Thomas.

At the Union League Club tonight. Committee on Admissions. Discoursed with F. H. Delano afterwards as to School of Mines. W. E. Dodge, Jr., called this morning on the same subject. We must rope them both in as associates. It is most marvelous that the trustees should have condescended to authorize us to use them. It's contrary to all our precedents, a departure from all our corporate policy. Fossil trustees seem to have been suddenly inspired with new life and sense when called on to further a collection of their kindred fossils, "Paleontology." All things, however remote from each other in time or space, are bound together by mysterious sympathies and relations. Betts, Ogden & Co. must be connected by unknown ties with the saurians and ganoid fishes and rodents of remote geological ages.

December 7. Dr. McDonald (from City Point) tells me that Grant is quietly establishing heavy guns in a position four miles from Richmond and will soon be pitching shell into that nest of treason. Nothing from Sherman, about whom there is deep anxiety. The President's message is well received.

December 8. A windy night and growing colder after a cold day. Much concern felt about Sherman. His failure would be a fearful calamity. Even Richmond papers seem not certainly to know what has become of him. Perhaps he will never be heard of again, like King Arthur and Don Sebastian. He should be very near the coast by this time, unless he has come utterly to grief. . . .

December 9. . . . At No. 823 this afternoon, and tonight at Van Buren's with Agnew, Jenkins, and Dr. Parrish. Suggested a plan for putting our protest against the mismanagement of the Medical Bureau on record (for the sake of our own credit hereafter, not with any hope of doing any good) by formally calling its attention to the suffering and waste of life caused by the want of splints on the field. And then, our suggestion being of course ignored, by asking Congress to legislate, which it of course will not take the trouble to do. A series of such moves, each directed against some flagrant abuse, and each made public at the time, may stir up the people at last to demand action and reformation. Surgeon-General Barnes seems to behave as if his object were to demoralize the Medical Bureau and destroy its usefulness. He is sending all his best men, like Cuyler, for instance, off to remote posts, and studiously assembling all the worst subjects of the medical staff at Washington and putting them in the most responsible places.[30]

No positive intelligence from Sherman. Rebel newspapers report that he has been badly defeated at this point—repulsed with heavy loss at that point. His march is a failure. He shews himself at last irresolute. He has manifestly lost his head, if he ever had any, and does not know which way to turn. His army is disorganized, men and animals are worn out and exhausted. But on Mr. X's plantation we saw horses, apparently of fine stock, that had been wantonly slaughtered by the invaders!!! Why did the invaders slaughter these noble animals, and why did they not put saddles on their backs if the national Rosinantes were used up? "The roadside is thickly strewn with corpses of Negro women and children," murdered by these ogres from Yankeeland. There must be Southerners capable of believing such stuff, or it would not have been written.

December 10. Committee on School of Mines at Betts's office. Betts, Edward Jones, Barnard, and I. We appointed fifteen "associates" under the power given us at the last meeting of the board. I brought a list with me, which was approved, and then suggested as possible matter for consideration hereafter that the committee and its associates might perhaps some of these days incorporate themselves under the general act as trustees of the School, reserving to the trustees of the College such power of control, veto, and so on as might be thought expedient. My suggestion was most timid and tentative, and I was delighted and surprised to find it favorably received by the rest of the committee; and the more I think of it the more feasible it seems.

December 11, SUNDAY. . . . Re-read Kingsley's *Water Babies* story. It has been little read on this side of the Atlantic, and, so far as I know, has been

---

[30] Joseph K. Barnes (1817–1883) had been appointed surgeon-general in August, 1864, after the ouster of Hammond. He gathered a brilliant staff and furnished a creditable administration.

pronounced by its few readers an unintelligible, preposterous extravaganza. But it seems to me one of the best things Kingsley ever wrote. . . .

December 12.   Spent part of the morning in looking up sundry of the associates appointed. Saturday saw Lewis Delafield, Percy R. Pyne (Moses Taylor's son-in-law), William E. Dodge, Jr., and Giraud Foster; all glad to serve, and eager to work. Pyne promised to turn over to the School his very valuable suite of fossils from the coastal region of Pennsylvania. Old Major Delafield promised contributions from his collection at Trinity Church vestry this evening. The future of the School is *couleur de rose* just now. May it continue! The incorporation of the committee and its associates into an independent body will make its success nearly certain. Talked with Ogden of that project tonight and made some progress in removing his first instinctive adverse judgment; also, with Morgan Dix, while walking down with him from the vestry meeting. Dix sees the importance of the step instanter, and I think will favor it. It's most fortunate that Egleston, Vinton, and Chandler are churchmen.

December 14.   Sherman was, when last heard of through Richmond papers, within five miles of Savannah, "with a large force in his front, and a great battle imminent and every prospect of our (rebel) complete success." About $15,000 worth of supplies ordered south, coast-wise, this afternoon, to meet him. Rumored repulse of Hood; very doubtful. The St. Albans raiders and bank robbers discharged by the Canadian court for want of jurisdiction; whereupon General Dix issues a stringent order to military authorities along the Canadian frontier, bidding them to be watchful and militant, and requiring them in case of another raid to pursue the raiders across the line. This is right and sustained by British precedent in the case of the *Caroline*, when American sympathizers were aiding provincial rebellion. It may lead to complication and war with England, but we must take that disaster, if it comes, as in our day's work. It's a great inducement, of course, to Southern refugees and agents in Canada to repeat the St. Albans experiment, but I think the Canadian government is honestly trying to prevent its repetition.

Sorry to find William Schermerhorn a little doubtful on first thought about my plan for incorporating the trustees of the School of Mines. But he is sensible and open to conviction. I must see Rutherfurd, Fish, Torrey, and Haight on that matter. It is a vital point. No money can be raised for Columbia College.

December 15.   Fine morning. At two o'clock with William Schermer-

CHARLES SUMNER

SALMON P. CHASE

HORACE BINNEY, JR.   CHARLES JANEWAY STILLÉ   BISHOP THOMAS MARCH CLARK

horn to Forty-ninth Street for a meeting of Columbia College Library Committee. Barnard with us. Anderson missing. We passed on the application of the faculty of the School for temporary transfer of certain scientific books to its reading room from the library proper, referred to us at last meeting of the board, and then I took Schermerhorn through the laboratory and lecture rooms of the School. Egleston and Chandler were there. A most satisfactory visit. Everything in that wing of the College building tingles with life and smokes with energetic movement and progress. During our inspection, a cart drove up laden with boxes containing the Pyne collection of coal fossils. Egleston was rending his garments and declaring there was no place to put them. Indeed, we have outgrown ourselves in every member. Our collections threaten to exceed our capacity to display them, and more students apply than we can accommodate with laboratory room. If the fogies of the board do not throttle or dwarf the School, it is likely to become great.

  December 16. Today's news important. Thomas attacked Hood in front of Nashville yesterday and drove him, taking 1,000 prisoners and sixteen guns. This was reported last night, but not believed. It comes officially now. Battle would probably be renewed today, but we have no later tidings. Nothing whatever from Sherman. Butler has left City Point with his whole force, Ethiopians excepted, gone down the James, and sailed from Hampton Roads with a great naval escort for parts unknown, Wilmington most probably. The latest of the facetiæ generated by the war is that Butler ordered an offending officer before a court-martial, which found him guilty and sentenced him to two years hard labor on the Canal at Dutch Gap! Whereupon Butler disapproved finding and evidence, dissolved the court, and bade the culprit go and sin no more.

  The war, as Strong realized, was now entering its final phase. General George H. Thomas, commanding the Union army at Nashville, had been so slow in attacking Hood's much weaker force in front of the city that he aroused Grant's anger. Thomas had about 48,000 men; Hood only 26,000. On December 15, Thomas finally struck a mighty sledgehammer blow, which at a cost of fewer than 3,000 casualties, utterly crushed the Confederates. Hood's army, as an organized force, simply ceased to exist. The remnants of his command were hotly pursued, and fewer than 15,000 of his infantry crossed the Tennessee to temporary safety. Throughout the North the jubilation was unbounded. And as the people rejoiced over this destruction of one of the enemy armies, Sherman, who had been hewing his way from Atlanta eastward through the heart of Georgia, was about to make a Christmas gift of the city of Savannah to the nation.

December 17, SATURDAY. *Gratias agimus Tibi!* Glad tidings from all quarters. Official despatch as to the second day (16th instant) of fight before Nashville. Hood worse clawed than on Thursday the 15th, driven from one position after another, with loss of thirty guns and many thousand prisoners. He must be much cut up. Thomas has been deliberately and steadily reducing him into a tight place, and has assailed him at last in overwhelming force. Newberry's letters satisfy me of this. We had not less than 63,000 men engaged yesterday and the day before, besides the garrisons of Murfreesboro and other points. Thomas commands 100,000 men at least. Canby has been helping him by cutting Hood's railroad communication with his base, in which work certain nigger regiments did themselves credit. Stoneman is making a stir in Southwest Virginia. Sherman has stormed Fort McAllister, the stronghold commanding Savannah harbor which was vainly shelled by our iron-clads eighteen months or more ago. Probably Savannah cannot long hold out. Rebellion has bad luck in December 1864, A.D. May it not be so very bad as to lead to a reaction and a run the other way! . . .

This morning to Philharmonic rehearsal by sloppy, slippery streets under a dull, grey sky. Mendelssohn's symphony. Overture to *Zauberflöte*, very lovely. Overture to *King Lear* by Berlioz, mere rubbish and rot. Shakespearean overtures by galvanized anthropoid Parisians are becoming a nuisance. I could write overtures as good as theirs to any play by Shakespeare, Massinger, Victor Hugo, Joanna Baillie, Kotzebue, Grillparzer, or Dion Boucicault on the shortest notice and produce a "notice" afterwards quite as discriminating and profound as any that has appeared among the musical criticism of the *Tribune* or *Herald* for a year past.

December 20. At No. 823 this afternoon I find myself running the Sanitary Commission machine all alone. Bellows and Agnew were summoned to City Point by telegram from Fry that arrived yesterday. It was obscure and alarming: "Grave charges against officers of the Commission demanding immediate investigation." We concluded that some of our people had been getting the Commission into a scrape with the military authorities; so Bellows and Agnew posted off this morning most enthusiastically, and today comes a letter from Fry, more plain-spoken than his telegram, and indicating that he charges McDonald, inspector at City Point, with drunkenness and immorality. I don't believe a word of it.

December 21. Union League Club tonight—special meeting. Proposed act of incorporation discussed and approved. Proposition to change name to National or National Union Club voted down. It would have been better to adopt the former title at first, and I urged it at that time. But the Club has done a certain amount of public service under its present title, and we may as well keep it for that reason.

December 22. With Ellie and Johnny to Winter Garden to see Booth as Hamlet. He does it well, very well—his readings are good and carefully studied; his bearing is that of a gentleman, even in his difficult, ambiguous dealings with poor dear Ophelia. Possibly overdoes a little now and then. Notable that the grave-digger's facetious remark that Hamlet's madness would do him no harm in England, for "there the men are as mad as he," brought down the house. N.B. Shakespeare uses words as nobody but Beethoven has ever used musical notes, conveying the most intense impressions in the most unaccountable way.

What news we get is good. Thomas is following up his victory, and Hood is unable to make a stand anywhere. Foote of Missouri has been letting out a doleful speech in the rebel senate, the purport whereof is that the Confederacy must soon come to grief, and that he means to return to private life.

Details come in of Sherman's grand adagio movement through Georgia, and most interesting they are. That seems to have been among the best and boldest conceptions of the war and to have been most triumphantly executed. Savannah is fully invested now by land and water. Rebel newspapers have not the least misgivings as to the safety of that city. Even if it should capitulate, or be stormed, nobody need be much concerned. Indeed the surrender of Savannah—should strategic considerations lead thereto— would probably give the final blow to the Yankees.

December 24. Tackled A. W. Bradford in Wall Street and converted him fully to my School of Mines project. To Trinity Church at three o'clock, the annual Children's Festival. Crowded congregation. Everybody in a pleasant kindly form of mild excitement. . . .

The New York *World* publishes a savage editorial against the Sanitary Commission this morning—one of a series. Collins thinks that Agnew's friend and patient "Private Miles O'Reilly" writes the attacks, hoping that he may be engaged by the Commission to answer them. Halpine is a

Bohemian, a free lance, and a professional member of the press gang, but I do not believe he would descend to work quite so dirty.

Yesterday, Ellie and I dined at General Viele's in Twenty-eighth Street: also Admiral Farragut and wife; Mrs. Jessie Frémont; James T. Brady; Fred Sheldon; Dr. Barker; George Bancroft; Belmont; Pierrepont Edwards; John Van Buren; William C. Bryant; and General Dix. A queerly mixed assemblage, characteristic of our hostess, though she is much toned down now and is quiet, having outgrown her oddities. She retains much of her cleverness and originality, however. As I sat between Sheldon and Jem Brady, with the Admiral just opposite, and Mrs. Teresa Viele next to Brady, I had a better time than I usually have at these solemn feasts.

No one would recognize the Admiral by acquaintance with his portraits. I know his photograph well, but when I saw him talking with Belmont before dinner, I asked General Dix what was the name of that naval officer. Though I knew Farragut was to be present, I never dreamed it could be he. I find him a most jolly, conversible, genial old boy; clear-headed, well informed, and perhaps a little dogmatic, but not much. He does not talk shop, so we gained no insight into the counsels of the Navy Department. He seems fond of science, though professing to know nothing about it, and to be an uncommonly sharp observer of nature, making up no theories of his own, but fond of using what he has seen to upset the theories of others, however generally received. He announced himself skeptical tonight as to certain geological propositions enunciated by Viele (when half a dozen of us were tippling Clos de Veugeot after the ladies had gone upstairs), and did not venture to deny them, but had observations of his own which he thought justified him in declining to believe them. I think Farragut is built on a large pattern. His wife is young-looking and attractive, though not pretty at all. Her manner is most kindly, simple, and cordial. Fred Sheldon is the first man I have seen who gives Kingsley's queer, fanciful *Water Babies* story the credit I think it deserves.

December 25, SUNDAY. . . . An extra went screeching through the streets at seven o'clock this evening. It announced the surrender of Savannah and of Wilmington, I'm told, on the authority of "a very reliable" contraband, or Southern Union man, who has sought refuge within our lines and brings this story with him from Richmond. Bogus. Don't believe it. When Wilmington is choked, the whole Confederacy will be asphyxiated and perish. I cannot hope for that result quite yet. But it must come, sooner or later, in God's good time. There are already signs of demoralization at Richmond. Senator [Henry S.] Foote ("Hangman Foote") seems to have ratted.

Hood's army is so shattered that the rebels have no substantial force east of the Mississippi except at and about Richmond.

December 26. Great news today, official and indubitable. Savannah surrendered to Sherman last Wednesday with 120 guns, storehouses full of cotton worth eighteen millions, and other goods. Hardee stole away with the bulk of his army, 15,000 more or less, through some unguarded loophole of retreat. But the city is reclaimed and occupied by the national army. Its people seems quite resigned to the change, and we have secured a new and most valuable water-base for operations on the Gulf States and on South Carolina. *Laus Deo!* So much for Sherman's desperate enforced retreat to the coast and for the braying and bragging and *outre-cuidance* of all rebel newspapers. Their statements have ceased to affect me at all when favorable to their own wicked cause. They out-lie any Northern paper I know.

December 27. Bellows and Agnew reported at No. 823. They found our work at City Point well and economically conducted. They had a long interview with Grant just after dinner. Bellows thought the General might have taken "just a little too much soup." According to his judgment, much of Grant's strength lies in his singleness of purpose, his entire devotion to his work, his freedom from political aspirations, and his readiness to avail himself of the talent and energy of any subordinate without pausing to consider whether his own personal renown may not be thereby endangered. He spoke of Sherman, frankly and naturally, as "altogether our best General," and as "loose at Savannah," giving Bellows to understand that this march through Georgia was Sherman's own conception, and that Sherman's next move would be at his own discretion. Very good for Grant. If not only able, but unselfish and single-minded, we may hope much from him. He says Hood is smashed and powerless for the present, that he expects little from the Wilmington expedition (he seems to hold Butler rather cheap), that there is much division at Richmond just now, and that he is on the lookout for Jefferson Davis trying to pass our lines in disguise on his way to Europe. He made this statement seriously and says that every refugee, in breeches or petticoats, is scrutinized with a view to the chance of detecting a fugacious Confederate rebel pseudo-president!

December 28. We have no information but through Richmond papers. They reveal that Fort Fisher was vigorously attacked Christmas Eve, that the attack was vigorously maintained Christmas day, and that Butler had succeeded in lodging some 10,000 men between this Fort and Wilmington itself—which movement is distasteful to them. A certain alleged hypothetical "torpedo boat," carrying x plus y tons of gunpowder, either has or has not been successfully exploded close to Fort Fisher and crushed its casements and embrasures into pi. Probably *not*. I never thought that device promising. George W. Blunt is ready to bet that Fort Fisher falls and blockade-running into Wilmington is finally suppressed before next Monday. May he be, in fact, as sagacious and infallible as he thinks himself! If we can close the harbor of Wilmington, we shut off the slave-breeding and woman-scourging rebels from the illicit aid England has been giving them ever since they rebelled, and but for English sympathy and comfort, this most flagitious of rebellions would have collapsed and perished long ago.

December 29. At the Club tonight. Mr. Ruggles brought out a proposition about a grand Petroleum Company, which looks well, but will come to nothing. Professor Egleston has boldly contracted to buy the whole of that magnificent Seymour collection, now in Beekman Street, for the cabinet of the School of Mines, at $2,000, relying on funds being raised somehow. I'm no judge of its scientific value, but it is unrivalled as a *show collection*. Unscientific visitors will be astonished by its enormous specimens of crystallization—its huge cubes of fluor, and so on—and will be thereby stimulated to contribute what they may have, for to him that hath shall be given. I have certainly never seen such big, brilliant, generous, noble specimens anywhere. A meeting of the College Committee on the School is called for tomorrow at Betts's office. If it agree to amend the plan of incorporating the School, a most important point will have been secured. Should that plan fail, I shall feel tempted to give up both School and College as beyond human help. . . .

Agnew has been conferring with [Manton] Marble of the *World* about his attacks on the Sanitary Commission, and calling him to account. Marble can only say that somebody or other told him so-and-so. His gross, broad charges of fraud and corruption among our agents and of great fortunes made by some of them out of their relations with the Commission have nothing tangible to rest on, though his renegade Copperhead paper has published these charges just as if their truth were notorious and agents of the Commission were generally conceded to be as profligate as members of the Common Council of New York. Agnew is more or less prejudiced in Marble's favor. I am not. Marble seems to me one of the dirtiest of our dirtiest dogs.

December 30. School of Mines Committee met at Betts's office—Betts, Torrey, Edward Jones, and I; Egleston and Chandler assessors.

Elected Lucius Tuckerman, George Cabot Ward, and Baron Osten-Sacken associates. I introduced a memorandum of a scheme for our incorporation in connection with the College. After a long talk it was substantially approved, and Betts is to draw the report. I would rather have drawn it myself but did not like to volunteer. He has a peculiar distaste for clear, definite, distinct allegations and a habit of circumlocution that will make his report feeble and provoke discussion in the board. . . .

Standing Committee of the Sanitary Commission tonight; Bellows, Agnew, Gibbs, Van Buren, Jenkins. We despatched much business and discussed our relations with the Secretary of War and the late Surgeon-General at great length, over a very modest supper-table. Mrs. Ellie intervened, *sicut dea ex machina*, pending our symposium, took her seat as the honorable member for the opera house and her share in the debates—a most ornamental accession. How pretty she did look!

We were repulsed at Wilmington, that is clear. May this not be the beginning of a turn of the tide and a run of bad luck! There has been a want of concert between the army and navy, it would seem, and Butler has gone back to the James River, more or less damaged—probably *more*. The fleet seems disposed to stay and try a little longer, but we can hardly hope it will accomplish anything. We must trust to Sherman to squelch Wilmington by a northward march from Savannah, calling at Charleston on his way. The announcement by a Savannah newspaper of Hardee's abandonment of that city and its probable occupation by the national army is peculiar in its tone. It counsels submission to a "magnanimous" enemy that is likely to hold the place "for an indefinite period."

December 31, SATURDAY. . . . At No. 823 this afternoon were Bellows, Agnew, and Gibbs. Seward wants 30,000 copies of the report on rebel treatment of prisoners for circulation in England. It should be translated into French and German and scattered over Europe.

Harvey resigns. A great loss. He wants to enter the School of Mines next fall and to get up his mathematics meanwhile. Knapp also expects to resign before next spring, his "self-respect" being damaged by sundry orders in the Special Relief Department of the Commission. But he will not resign if I am a prophet and he have common sense. He is not so silly as to renounce his place in the Commission's staff merely because he is found to be without certain "business" qualifications for work in another department as far out of his line as the presidency of a bank would be outside that of Florence Nightingale. . . .

Thus passeth away into history this memorable year 1864. Much has

been done toward destroying rebellion in these twelve months. It is far
weaker tonight than it was a year ago. God aid our efforts to put it down
and establish unity and peace this coming year as the last! *DEUS SAL-
VAM FAC REMPUBLICAM*—and may God bless and preserve my
wife and our three little boys. Success to the Sanitary Commission and to
the School of Mines. For one result of the coming of this New Year we may
cordially be thankful in advance. Seymour will no longer be governor of
this state. We are fairly entitled to assume it impossible that his successor
Fenton (we know but little about him) can prove base, maleficent, and
disgraceful as Seymour. The less said about him the better for us. Let us
hope historians will overlook his official existence and ignore the disgrace
he has inflicted on the state of New York. If he be not forgotten he must
be named in the same category with Benedict Arnold and Aaron Burr. From
Horatio Seymour and his tribe during 1865 A.D., *et in secula seculorum,
Libera nos, Domine.*

BATTLES BEFORE RICHMOND · FIVE FORKS AND APPOMATTOX ·
END OF CIVIL WAR · ASSASSINATION OF LINCOLN ·
THE WHITE HOUSE FUNERAL

*T*he dawn of 1865 found the North strong in the confidence of victory.
New levies of men had been called in December, and cities, towns, and
counties were busy making up their quotas. Sherman, after capturing Savannah,
prepared his army (which soon numbered 60,000) for an advance northward
through the Carolinas to reach the area of Grant's main force, and to attack
Richmond from the rear. He could move almost at will, for the Confederate force
under Johnston opposing him numbered only 30,000, and was badly furnished with stores and munitions. Grant and the Army of the Potomac were
spending the winter on the banks of the James; reinforcements were constantly
arriving, and the harbor at City Point was kept full of vessels laden with supplies.
It was plain that Lee's army was doomed. Only the wretched condition of the
roads prevented Grant from beginning offensive operations at once. In Washington, Lincoln had reaffirmed his stand on emancipation, about which Strong
had been so needlessly uneasy; and he pressed Congress to take up the Thirteenth
Amendment abolishing slavery throughout the nation and lay it before the states.
Debate began early in January, and on the last day of that month, the amendment was carried in the lower chamber by a two-thirds vote. Thereupon, "in
honor of the immortal and sublime event," the House adjourned for the day.
A general feeling of relief, of thankfulness, and of confidence in the future pervaded the North.

Strong's legal affairs were prosperous, and his household happy, with the
three boys and his wife in excellent health. The Sanitary Commission was now
at the apex of its usefulness. Its average monthly expenditures had for some

[537]

time exceeded a quarter of a million dollars, it maintained a force of more than five hundred in the field, and it was supporting a wide array of "homes and lodges." It had its own flotilla of steamers, its own hospital cars, and its own wagon trains. Over its finances, sustained by a steady stream of popular contributions, Strong presided with efficiency and credit. Only the affairs of the infant School of Mines failed to advance as he wished. He wanted it given a separate incorporation, but other Columbia trustees objected.

Strong was also giving much time to the Union League Club. As the record shows, he carried on his campaign to interest men of wealth and influence in the School of Mines by enlisting a number of his Union League Club friends as Associate Members. Among them were William Earl Dodge, Jr., N. Pendleton Hosack, Robert L. Kennedy, Franklin H. Delano, Samuel W. Bridgham, George Cabot Ward, and of course his intimate friend, George C. Anthon.

January 2, MONDAY. On New Year's Day duty from eleven till near five, my field bounded by Forty-ninth Street (Mrs. Professor Joy) and Hudson Square (Morgan Dix). It was a pleasant day's work as usual. Mrs. Professor Joy, Mrs. Sam Whitlock, Mrs. William Schermerhorn, all the Dixes, Mrs. Rutherfurd, the Rev. Coxes, were as charming, kindly, and gracious as I have always found them. So were Mrs. Serena Fearing and Mrs. Laura Field. It is really a great privilege to be cordially received once a year by half a dozen such nice women.

At Bishop Potter's, I discoursed with that prelate about the School of Mines. Mrs. Talboys (West Eleventh Street) was very pleasant; Mrs. Augustus Schermerhorn and Miss Ellen in University Place, ditto, as usual. Mrs. Lucretia Heckscher (née Stevens) has been living out of town, and I have not seen her for three years. I established an intimacy with two boys of hers, the elder of whom confided to me, in a fearful whisper, his doubt whether there was any Santa Claus at all. Our usual New Year's dinner table was thus wise:

Mrs. G. T. Strong

Gen. Vinton		Gen. Viele
Miss Kitty Dix		Mrs. Blake
Willy Graham		Col. McMahon
Charley Post		Capt. Bankhead, U.S.N.
Miss Fanny Staples		Mrs. Viele
Charles Blake		Jem Ruggles

Mr. Strong

McMahon has more culture and refinement than I have given him credit for.[1] Viele is much interested in this nascent School of Mines; thinks we should have a professor of physical geography and would not refuse to fill that place. He would probably fill it well, for he talks of the subject as a lover of his mistress and seems full of public spirit and devotion to science.

Miss Fanny Staples spent the day with Ellie, and they seem to have had a good time together. The bouquets and baskets contributed to Mrs. Ellie's drawing room by her admirers (myself included) far surpassed any display of flowers I saw today, and I saw several that were notably sumptuous and splendid. I think New Year's Day visiting has been rather less generally attended to this year than usual. The streets were bad for pedestrians, and a hack cost thirty dollars!! Then our repulse at Wilmington has produced more depression than it should, considering that Nashville and Savannah and the salt works and lead mines of Virginia can be offset against it.[2] I think the Southern Confederacy is destroyed. It may or may not save itself from subjugation by arming its niggers. But if it do thereby sustain itself in existence for a time, it abolishes the institution for which it rebelled and will soon begin to wonder for what it is fighting. The talk of Vinton, Viele, McMahon, and Bankhead tonight about their several experiences, if put in writing, would be absolutely priceless fifty years hence. . . .

Morgan Dix told me this morning that he actually had to lay down Doré's *History of Holy Russia* (which Mrs. Ellie sent him as a Christmas present) after looking over four or five pages, because acute physical pain warned him that laughing any more might be dangerous.

January 4.   Conciliabulum here tonight on the School of Mines. Rutherfurd, Edward Jones, and I of the trustees; Egleston and Chandler of the faculty; and of the associates, George Anthon, Otis Swan, Pen. Hosack, Franklin H. Delano, Lucius Tuckerman, Baron Osten-Sacken, James Renwick, William E. Dodge, Jr., Percy R. Pyne, Temple Prime, Dr. Agnew. They made me chairman, and the chair addressed the meeting with more

[1] This was apparently Martin T. McMahon, who became brevet major-general after fighting bravely on many Virginia battlefields, and who later wrote some interesting articles on the war.

[2] Wilmington was the last port through which blockade-runners could bring in European supplies. In December a joint land and naval expedition under General Ben Butler and Admiral David D. Porter was fitted out against it. Just before Christmas the fleet attacked with a day-long bombardment, and troops were landed who after a reconnaissance reported that the place could not be taken. To the disgust of Northerners, the expedition ingloriously sailed home. But a new attack on Fort Fisher with a fresh commander, General Alfred H. Terry, was at once planned.

or less dignity, lucidity, and coherency. Our session came to no definite conclusion, but it was satisfactory as shewing an earnest disposition to support the School on the part of all present. Adjourned to a slight supper at ten. Pleasant evening enough.

Rutherfurd is crotchety. He looks coldly on the plan of incorporating the School, and sees objections. They ought to disappear on closer view, and I hope they will. But if the trustees disapprove this plan, I think I shall decline further effort to establish any school whatever. I will spend no more time on the organization of the weak, struggling, starveling, dead-alive school, supported by reluctant appropriations from the College treasury—as inadequate as unwilling.

News from Savannah, *possibly* of first-rate importance. Its mayor and sundry civic notables seem to have been prominent at a public meeting that passed resolutions declaring that community subject to the laws of the United States, praising General Sherman, deploring further war, averring that bygones should be bygones, and calling on the governor of Georgia to convoke a convention that shall restore his state to her lawful and constitutional relations with the Union! Did this meeting represent any respectable minority of Savannites? Or was it got up by Sherman? If genuine, it is an event of first order. One Arnold is, or seems to be, mayor of the city, and his name will give the sons of Belial who write for newspapers at Richmond much occasion to blaspheme.

January 5. . . . Richmond papers (especially the *Sentinel*, Jeff Davis's peculiar mouthpiece) are blue and dismal. They lament the prevailing discouragement, and endeavor to cure it by discussing the advantages of emancipating Cuffee and making a soldier of him, and then asking France, Spain, and England to be kind enough to receive the rebel states as colonies! Of course, these measures are mentioned "only as a man in good health talks of his will." It can obviously do no harm to think of what the Confederacy could, would, or might do, if it should meet any serious reverse hereafter, though it is hardly necessary to say that everything is now most uncommonly serene and all the future most hopeful and brilliant, and so on. This is stimulus and encouragement of most inferior quality. The most sanguine and chivalric rebel in Richmond must have needed six drinks instead of five after being *thus* cheered and upheld by his morning paper. What a falling off is this from the bluster of every editorial bravo in Secessia four years ago!

The signs of healthy reaction in Savannah are stronger than they seemed. A certain respectable minority, at least, declares publicly for peace and reunion, and so commits itself on that side as to be without hope of mercy should it fall hereafter under the paws of the rebellion. And there is no show in Savannah of the furious spite and inveterate hatred encountered by the army when it occupied New Orleans. This may be the germ of an entirely new Southern party; *may* be—and may be not.

January 6. Bellows called for me after dinner, interrupting a game of chess with Prince John (to Johnny's regret, for his position was quite hopeful), and we waded up the Fifth Avenue to Agnew's and held our Sanitary Commission council, and waded back at eleven. Many interesting letters and reports produced by Jenkins, especially a report from one of our relief agents (Hoblett), who accompanied Sherman's column on its memorable march to Savannah. He seems to have had little to do. The army took care of itself and its sick and wounded. Its ambulances and medical stores were abundant and well managed. It lived on turkeys and chickens, fresh beef and pork, sweet potatoes, honey, and sorghum molasses, and carried droves of milch cows with it for the benefit of its invalids. The land it traversed was flourishing with milk and honey, and all manner of good things. Hence, I deduced (1) further proof of the barbarity and cruelty of Slave-Ownia in starving its prisoners at Andersonville, Millen, and other towns, and (2) a doubt whether the farmers and planters of Georgia, whose barnyards, pigpens, and storerooms unwillingly issued all these delicacies, are likely to feel much love for national soldiers, or for the Union, in the name whereof their homesteads have thus been harried. But the grip of Richmond officials may have been as bad, or even worse.

January 7, SATURDAY. With Bellows at No. 823, and afterwards Agnew, horribly disgusted because Dr. Bellows has given a certain Dr. Fisher an official letter of recommendation without first consulting his medical colleagues; the said Fisher being a low-caste practitioner. Dr. Bellows is too apt to do this sort of thing without due pause. Fisher, it seems, wants Governor Fenton to make him superintendent of the state "Soldiers' Relief" establishment in Howard Street.

To the Century Club tonight, where I put up the names of Professors Egleston and Vinton, but the vacancies are so few and the nominations so many that their chance of immediate election is bad. Thence to the Union League Club, and thence back to the Century with Dodge and Roosevelt for a conference about their plan for a corps of commissionaires to be made up of invalid soldiers. Dodge is certainly among the best men we have. He must spend nearly all his time in undertakings for the public good, in which he is most useful, without the least self-seeking or ostentation, keeping himself always in the background as far as may be. His manners are refined and attractive. He is likely to become a very prominent man.

January 9. At two to the Columbia College meeting in Lafayette Place. Betts read the report of our Committee on the School of Mines; a most weak, non-committal, indefinite kind of document, merely hinting at the possibility that members of the committee and their "associates" might feel inclined to incorporate themselves under the Act of 1848, and that should they do so, they might hereafter propose to the College to do something or other in the premises. I did not expect this to pass *sub silentio*, but I had no doubt that after a few objections and explanations, the board would acquiesce in the proposal of certain outsiders to try to raise half a million for it, and sit still, at least, while they were trying.

Betts called on me for a statement of the position of affairs, which I made at some length, and must have done very badly, to judge from the profound misconceptions of the whole case that were afterwards displayed by members of the board. I represented very briefly that postponement was death—the movement would cool off and die if retarded. This made matters rather worse and was construed as an attempt to coerce the board into action without time to think. Ogden and Haight brought forward the usual platitudes of fogyism. The Bishop and Hamilton Fish went further and seemed to suspect some sort of conspiracy or underhand manoeuvring to get the School out of the hands of the College. A majority of the trustees present were in favor of the plan. Morgan Dix, Barnard, Mr. Ruggles, and Edward Jones said a little each in its favor, but a proposal to put off anything cannot be successfully opposed in that body, and I did not feel willing to be factious. So I merely said a word or two more, contradicting or explaining away certain of the more preposterous assertions of the chairman and the Bishop, and the whole subject was laid over to our February meeting. Then came sundry routine business, and then I asked to be excused from further service in the committee, because it was evident that leading members of the board took a view of the case that was doubtless correct but which I could not understand, and so forth. This brought out sundry expressions of opinion as to the value of my services, and a motion to lay my application on the table. I pressed it as far as I could without wasting too much time and finally withdrew it. But I give up all further effort to help the undertaking and shall be prevented from attending any more meetings of the committee.

Thus ends the most hopeful movement made in my time to strengthen Columbia College by bringing it into relations with the interests and the wants of the community. It is squelched by our traditional sense of corporate dignity and distrust of help from without, by the unwillingness of Fish, Ogden, and Haight to let any little bit of power and patronage escape them, and by the unaccountable foolishness of the Rt. Rev. the Bishop of New York, who certainly talked more like a goose this afternoon than any American bishop before him. I see now why the position of Columbia College is so unlike that of Harvard and Yale and Princeton. It's a consolation to remember that I should have been fearfully overworked for months to come, had not the trustees decided to choke and suppress this movement. But it is a *great pity*, nevertheless, and a public calamity. So much might have been done; so strong a school established, and such proof given that physical science can be taught under church influence.

January 14, SATURDAY. To Washington, Tuesday the 10th. . . . Took refuge in one of Anthony Trollope's novels (*The Bartrams*), a good quiet story, and at half-past six emerged from the depot into the national mud flats. Made my way to 244 F Street, where a comfortable room awaited me. Bellows, Jenkins, Binney, Stillé, Harris, and Newberry there; also, Dr. Gould of Cambridge, and Dr. Parrish. Skinner and Mc-Cagg of Chicago appeared next day. Our session ended yesterday morning. Its business was mostly routine; hearing reports, and so on, of which several were important. We appointed Knapp general superintendent of special relief, under the general secretary, Jenkins, but declined to create a separate bureau or department of special relief. This will, I trust, appease Knapp's wounded dignity. We cannot afford either to lose his services or to give him an independent position with money to spend.

Weather at Washington was cold but sunshiny and genial. Left it at seven-thirty last night with our three western colleagues and Gould. My berth in the sleeping car most unfavorable to slumber. Waked uncomfortably all night, caught cold from a slender current of air that found its way into the hot ill-ventilated car and got home at eleven this morning, hours behind time, tired, jaded, and sore. . . .

Authentic story about E. B. Elliott, whilom actuary to the Sanitary Commission. He has much talent for mathematics and a great faculty of working with entire concentration on abstract questions, but he is quite without common sense. He called on Dr. Woodward, United States Army, to find fault with certain blanks Dr. Woodward has been issuing to army surgeons calling for information as to the medical history of the war.

"Dr. Woodward," said Elliott, "I have looked over these forms of yours very hastily, but I am shocked to discover at the first glance omissions in your list of diseases that must deprive the returns of all scientific value." Woodward requests to hear it, and begs for particulars. "Why, sir, in your catalogue of fevers—malarious, typhoid, and so on—you have omitted and overlooked a most important form of fever, a fever which according to foreign statistics constitutes 8.2376948" (or whatever it may be) "per cent of the aggregate of febrile cases. What will foreign statisticians think of us if we publish returns founded on so imperfect a classification???? I have studied the subject thoroughly and exhaustively and feel it my solemn duty to warn you that this oversight destroys the worth of all your work."

"Gracious goodness!" said Woodward. "You don't mean it—do tell me what species of fever has been forgotten." "Why, puerperal fever," said Elliott, "and here are the tables that shew the percentage," and so on. "But soldiers cannot have puerperal fever," quoth Woodward. "I don't see why they are not as much exposed to it as civilians," replied Elliott, and Woodward told him why, in very vigorous Saxon English. Elliott fled in consternation.

Missouri is a free state if a constitutional convention can make her free by a vote of sixty to four! Tennessee drifts fast the same way. Kentucky and Delaware feel the current and will soon be drawn into it. Certainly John Brown is marching on. What a *nunc dimittis* would the valiant old man have sung under the gallows tree had he foreseen this day!

January 16. . . . At Union League Club tonight. They propose a club meeting about the lamented Everett, and some of them wanted me to second sundry resolutions and "make a few remarks," which I respectfully declined to do, as I am not an oratorical undertaker by profession or practice.[3] I suggested Hamilton Fish as exactly the man for the job, and that malicious suggestion was cordially and enthusiastically received. Fish is just the weak-backed, timid man of expedients and plausibilities

[3] Edward Everett, one-time Cotton Whig and long a timid man on slavery, had died January 15. During the war he had shown more nerve, and had been president of the Union Club in Boston.

who ought to pronounce Everett's eulogy. But it must not be forgotten that Everett has sustained government as manfully as his organization allowed him to support anything for the last four years, or since April, 1861, at least. Therein, by the by, he has the advantage of the Hon. Pisciculus Minor, who has been cold and fishy all the time—very fishy, except in his mischievous croakings. I feel more respect for fully-developed avowed, venomous Copperheads than for the class to which he belongs, and they are less dangerous, for they are recognized public enemies and deceive nobody.

January 20. . . . I fear our poor School of Mines is getting into deep water. Its faculty seems to have been ordering work and making purchases without much reference to the amount of funds on which it could depend. Chandler sent me this morning a batch of bills that totted up $700, and a respectable carpenter named Humes, whose little account is $1,300 and upwards. The balance of unexpended contributions (from without) in my hands is only about three hundred and fifty dollars (exclusive of $100 specially contributed for the purchase of minerals from the Seymour collection), and the College appropriation is $2,250. So the School will probably be swamped before the end of its first term, next May, by want of money, thanks to those *Asinucci*, Fish, Ogden, Haight, and the Bishop (*sit venia loquendi*). Had they not shewed themselves lamentably wanting in common sense last Monday week, the School would have had its circulars out before now and committees at work calling for contributions and stirring up the whole community. What short-sighted, narrow-minded blockheads they are!

Betts sends me a reminder, by the by, of another meeting of the committee tomorrow afternoon. It may be better that I should attend it. If I do so, I shall press no plan of organization and merely report myself as present in the course of duty to help make a quorum. I shall insist on being discharged from further service on the committee at the next meeting of the board. Notice is given of a meeting of the board next Monday, the 23rd, though our last adjournment was certainly to the first Monday of February.

January 21, SATURDAY. . . . The Committee on the School of Mines met at the Law School this afternoon; Barnard, Betts, Rutherfurd, Edward Jones, and I. Barnard brought in an estimate of expenses of the School for the next year, footing up some $30,000, which was pottered over and criticized and at last referred to Barnard and Torrey as a subcommittee to screw down its items. They may reduce it a little, but it will give our enlightened treasurer a cold chill when he hears it. What a blind, narrow concern is this distinguished board of ours! It seems a little scrap of the Chinese empire or the Papal court, let into this energetic, progressive American community. I held my tongue during the meeting, disheartened by our shortsightedness and sickening to see so splendid an opportunity so drivelled over and wasted.

Edward Jones earnestly opposes my declining further service on the committee, and his advice is entitled to great respect, but I have lost all hope of success on any considerable scale, and do not care to spend my time in nursing and propping a dwarfed and weakly school kept from health, vigor, and greatness by the fatuity of my colleagues.

Tonight with Johnny and Temple to the Broadway Theatre. *Solon Shingle* was not quite so funny this second time. But *The Live Indian* was excruciating. Laughed myself sore.

The Hon. George P. Marsh contributes to the treasury of the Sanitary Commission $500, being proceeds of copyright on his very able work, *Man and Nature*. Work is unequally paid in this world. This octavo volume of 550 pages, full of thought and research, brings its author $500. Success in developing a batch of petroleum wells gives some Snooks or Snobkins an income of $25,000 per annum.

January 22. Burnside dined with Charley Strong today. Just from Washington. Is promised a command forthwith. Says Grant, whom he met at Washington, is the happiest man he has seen for many days. It is thought best that Sherman should not take Charleston, unless it be quite necessary to have a water-base at that point, because it will be impossible to save the city from utter demolition if once occupied by our men, and its destruction would injure us at the South and abroad. I don't see it in that light myself. But we can postpone this question until Charleston is within our grasp, which it is *not* as yet. Burnside says Butler had just got through with his evidence before the Committee on the Conduct of the War, and with that branch of it which proved that Fort Fisher was impregnable, when the news came in the committee room that the fort had fallen! He uttered an ejaculation of delight but has been "much chopfallen" ever since. Poor Butler! I should fully acquiesce in his being shelved, but for the joy it gives all Copperheads. What they so heartily approve must be wrong.

We get no material war news today. Everything still looks most hopeful. Everybody thinks Rebeldom in *articulo mortis* at last. Grant himself tells Burnside he looks for no more serious fighting, and Burnside's only fear is that the rebels may give in before we have shewn them that we can drive Lee out of Richmond. May all this sanguine feeling not prove premature!

I think old Blair's coming and going between Richmond and Washington shew that there are the negotiations for a settlement or efforts to open such negotiations. They may do the greatest mischief, but I have faith in Uncle Abe's sagacity and honesty and in Stanton's vindictiveness. They will favor no pacification that leaves the sources of this war still open and the Slaveocracy in existence to recover its strength and rebel a second time. They know that peace and union cannot be secured without utterly squelching slavery and slaveholders. Blair's unofficial diplomacy will probably produce no result, unless the story be true that he was charged with the duty of informing Jeff Davis that the government of the United States would put no obstacles in the way if he should feel inclined to take a foreign tour for the benefit of his health. I wish Jeff Davis would abscond to foreign parts, for we should not hang him if we caught him. We should let him run, and he would be a United States senator within a year or two.

Francis P. Blair, Sr., head of the great Border State family and intimate friend of Lincoln, had made a journey to Richmond in the closing days of December. He held a confidential interview with Jefferson Davis on January 12. In this he declared that he was not a diplomatic representative of the North, but that he had a proposal of his own for stopping the war of brother against brother. It was that the North and South cease fighting, join hands, and move against Maximilian and the French in Mexico in common defense of the Monroe Doctrine. Davis made a favorable response, saying that he was ready to negotiate for peace and to send commissioners for that purpose. Lincoln did not approve of the suggested expedition into Mexico, but he went so far as to write Blair (January 18) that he would receive agents informally sent to him. On the 28th, three Confederate commissioners, Alexander H. Stephens, R. M. T. Hunter, and John A. Campbell, were admitted to Grant's headquarters. The result was a conference held on February 3 aboard a steamboat off Fortress Monroe, President Lincoln and Secretary Seward talking for several hours with the Confederate emissaries. But it came to nothing. Lincoln insisted that the full and unconditional restoration of the Union must take precedence over all other terms, and that he would not grant an armistice of any kind until the South consented to this restoration. The Confederate commissioners returned to Richmond, where Jefferson Davis announced that the North had offered only such terms as "the conqueror may grant," and that the South would fight on defiantly.

January 24.   At the Union League Club tonight. Mr. Ruggles just from Washington. Reports everyone there full of confidence and spirit except Butler. . . .

Special meeting of trustees of Columbia College yesterday was called to pass on a question of leasing certain Greenwich Street property. Nothing else came up. After the meeting, our venerable diocesan shuffled and sidled up to me to say that he had used the word "plot" in his foolish philippic of a fortnight ago in its "dramatic sense" only. He is not very wise, but this was kindly meant. Had a little talk also with Anderson and with Edward Jones about organization of School of Mines, and sent Jones today at his request a memorandum of a scheme of organization under the Act of 1848. Anderson appreciates most keenly the platitudes and imbecilities that were uttered on that subject at the last previous meeting and was very funny over them in his own peculiar, solemn way.

January 25.   After dinner Egleston came in, and we had a long discourse over the School of Mines. He and his colleagues have got wind somehow of the debate of our regular January meeting and are in deep discouragement. They have overestimated the importance of our inaction at that meeting, and I succeeded in satisfying him that all *might* be set right at the meeting next month. I do not expect it will be set right, however. Egleston went away much comforted. What an opportunity the dunces of our board are losing us! . . .

January 27. . . . Am just from the Sanitary Commission Standing Committee session at Bellows's. Jenkins just back from Washington. We talked over poor Knapp's fancied grievances and came to the conclusion that if he will be foolish enough to leave us, we must let him go in peace. He is not the first good, earnest, and disinterested man that has been bewildered by that delusive, unmeaning word *self-respect*, and misled by pride and selfishness disguised under that title to abandon his unselfishness and sacrifice his duty.

January 30.   State dinner at John Astor's in honor of White and his two colleagues of the Senate Committee. There were The Astor (William B.) and D. D. Lord, Harry Day, John Weeks, F. H. Delano, Judge Hoffman, Mr. Ruggles, and others; some twenty altogether. Very splendid dinner. Sat next to White and like him much. But our occasional little gatherings at home spoil me for parties abroad. Nobody has Ellie's faculty of bringing pleasant people together, setting them at their ease, and drawing them out.

January 31. . . . Committee on School of Mines at Betts's office; Betts, Edward Jones, Torrey, and I. Also Barnard, who heard nothing that was said. The case is hopeless. The committee is paralyzed by its chairman, Betts. Nothing can be done with him. He meets every movement toward any tangible result with some obscure oracular expression of disfavor, which the committee has not power to meet. Edward Jones means right but is overcautious and slow. Torrey seems timid, and will not say what he thinks. I do not choose to go single-handed into the fight and to fret myself into a brain fever by entering on a campaign against the impregnable stolidity of Gouverneur Ogden, Betts, Hamilton Fish, the Rev. Haight, Martin Zabriskie (!) & Co. (to say nothing of the Rt. Rev. the Bishop), and undertaking to impress on them the duty of thinking a little more of the interests and the development of the College and a little less of our two-penny "corporate dignity," and our manifest ability to manage our own affairs without help from any quarter.

February 1, WEDNESDAY. The constitutional amendment prohibiting slavery within the United States passed the House yesterday by a vote of 119 to 56, a little more than the required two-thirds. Sundry Democratic members helped it, but James Brooks and Winthrop Chanler voted *no*, as might have been expected of them. So did John V. L. Pruyn, I am sorry to say. The Senate has already passed on it, but three-fourths of the states must endorse the amendment before it can become part of the Constitution. Unless affairs change greatly for the worse within six months, it will surely be ratified. The current sets steadily that way; witness this vote as compared with the last, 95 to 65, when the measure failed for want of a two-thirds majority. No one expected it to prevail in this Congress. Who thought four years ago that John Brown would march so fast? And here has the Supreme Court of the United States just been admitting a colored person one of its attorneys and counsellors, on motion of Charles Sumner!!! I can scarce believe the evening papers. The dust that was Roger B. Taney must have shivered in its tomb when the motion was granted, and Sumner must have felt an acute but pleasing titillation in all those portions of his manly form that were contused by the Hon. Brooks's chivalric bludgeon, nine years ago come next May.

At Law School this afternoon to attend a meeting of the College Committee on the Course, whereof notice had been given as for "important business." That committee has been ordered by the board to report without further delay, having dragged along for many years without result. But there was no quorum. Barnard and I talked over matters an hour or so and came off. Here is another illustration of the inability of the board of twenty-four busy men to manage the College proper, and *a fortiori* to undertake the additional work of organizing a school of science. Sixty years ago, when New York was a dozy little town, and the College had half a dozen professors at most and a handful of students, two dozen respectable citizens, our predecessors, had leisure to spare for the thorough and diligent execution of their trust. But times are changed. The College has grown (by the increased value of its landed endowment, and no thanks to its board therefor), and multiplied duties—public, private, and professional—have been imposed on every trustee; for example, Astor, Fish, Rutherfurd, and William Schermerhorn have as much as they can do to care for great private estates. Betts and Bradford are under constant heavy pressure of legal work. The clerical members, from the Bishop down, are engrossed by official duties. Mr. Ruggles has irons in the fire at Albany or Washington or somewhere that must be looked after and kept hot all the time. The rest are mostly fainéants, in the usual proportion. Trustees willing to work for the College and anxious for its development can give it only the odds and ends of their time and thought. Hence its weakness.

The board is made up, on the whole, of good and valuable men (we'll say nothing about Ogden, Betts, and Zabriskie), but it has less working power than any board I ever knew. To this want, and to its hypertrophied sense of its own corporate power and grand air, is due its failure to secure any hold on the community around it, such as Harvard, Yale, and Amherst rejoice in. Our own alumni give us a cold shoulder, and small blame to them. Their poor little "alumni association" has, from time to time, appointed its committee to attend the College examinations and has once or twice ventured to send us their reports. They have been received with alarm and studiously suppressed on our minutes, because it was so dangerous to concede to outsiders any privilege of criticizing our operations.

February 3. . . . Lincoln is at City Point this minute talking peace with A. H. Stephens and his two colleagues, who deserve hanging for treason if ever men deserved it, and Stephens above all, who has sinned against the clearest light. This negotiation will come to no good. It is undignified for Lincoln to make a long expedition for the purpose of arguing with a little delegation of conspirators representing an armed and truculent rebellion. But if the palaver had to be held, it will be less mischievous at City Point than at Washington, where these wily legates *a latere diaboli* would have contrived to open privy communication with Copperheads and with invertebrate national men and with political caitiffs of every grade, from that of Fernandy Wood up. The claims of the rebellion and of the nation seem incapable of compromise or adjustment by concession. . . .

Mr. Ruggles handed me this evening a certificate for 10,000 shares of the stock of the "Kenzua Mining Co." (petroleum) issued to me as director thereof. I suppose them worth about as much as so many shares would be in a land company organized to develop the mineral resources of the intertropical regions of the planet Jupiter, but they may prove worth five dollars or even fifty, and I don't know why I should decline the chance of getting fifty dollars for Mrs. Ellie. I undertake only to look into the management of the company. It is understood that there shall be no advertising, and that no director is expected to ask his friends to take stock. A working capital is to be raised by certain Philadelphians, and all I shall have to do will be to see that the work is honestly done. The work may produce a prize or a blank. If a blank turn up, as is altogether probable, nobody will be hurt.

February 6. Columbia College trustees met at two o'clock. Betts read the report he had drawn for the Committee on the School of Mines. It stated that a quasi-separate organization was inexpedient; that to sustain the School to the end of its present term, a certain minimum amount was required, and a certain other for the next year—both estimates on a quarter-ration basis. I declined to sign it. It made no recommendations, and the omission was noticed. Much discourse followed, and its tone was encouraging. I held my tongue, being determined to repeat my motion to be relieved from service on the committee when we should reach "miscellaneous business." But the others came out with the strongest avowals of their faith in the School and their conviction that we must sustain it *somehow*. It appeared also that the notion of a subordinate corporate organization had been working in the minds of several and gaining ground. It was all one way, except that Martin Zabriskie objected, of course, that he had not attended certain former meetings, that the subject was new to him, and that, therefore, it ought to be postponed —to give his intellect time to grapple with it. The Bishop, by the by, made a very handsome and kind disclaimer of any meaning injurious to me personally in his speech at our regular January meeting and spoke of *me* in terms much beyond what that dirty, despicable subject deserves.

The result was this: An appropriation to carry the School through this term. A vote pledging the board to carry it through the next year, till May, 1866. Refusal to vote a specific sum for this latter purpose because it might prove better economy to *build* than to refit the shaky, dilapidated, east wing of the College. The report referred back to the committee with instructions to make definite recommendations at the next meeting. Hamilton Fish added to the committee. Result, on the whole, satisfactory. Our fogies are more thoroughly stirred up and awakened than they have been on any subject these ten years. Dix and Haight begin to see the real dimensions of the question. Dix sees the case fully and clearly, and did good service by a vigorous statement of it. He is a most valuable man.

Went from meeting to No. 823 and thence down to Egleston's, to let him know that our action had been satisfactory. Egleston had called on me this morning in deepest despondency. . . .

The peace negotiations seem to have proved a failure. *Laus Deo.* Lincoln and Seward have come back to Washington *re infecta.* Gold rises, of course, and that is bad, but nothing could be so bad as a parley with Rebeldom.

February 8. . . . Not so clear but that the Hampton Roads Conference has done good after all by silencing or converting Peace Democrats. Fernandy Wood has changed his base and made a speech breathing battle, murder, and sudden death, and protesting against talk of pacification till peace is won by force of arms. Opposition papers incline the same way and say in substance, more or less distinctly, "Since the South refuses to negotiate about peace, except on the basis of recognition and disunion, there is nothing left but to fight it out." Strange they have been so long in coming to that conclusion. It has been self-evident for three years. The course of Southern leaders is unaccountable. They are astute, experienced politicians and subtle negotiators. They must see that an offer to compromise would divide and paralyze the North, and that in the discussions to which it would lead they would get the ascendancy and be able to make their own terms of settlement and secure the means of ultimate disunion and independence. Probably they dare not trust their own people and fear that if negotiations were once opened, they would be forced to consent to reconstruction, and would forfeit place and power.

February 9, THURSDAY.   There was fighting southwest of Petersburg,

near "Hatcher's Run," Monday; results "mixed." We held the positions
gained on Sunday, but one division was stampeded in attempting a
further advance. Meade commanded in person. His reputation tends to
wane. . . .

The Columbia College Committee on the Course met at the Law
School at three P.M.; Barnard, the Bishop, Morgan Dix, and I. We are
so ancient a body and have slept so long that we felt like a congregation
of revived myths. We listened dreamily to a large amount of prosing by
Barnard and hastened to adopt a report, which, I hope, will be final and
enable the committee to go to its last rest. Barnard is sadly tedious and
diffuse in speech, but he seems to make an excellent president. At four
the Committee on the School of Mines met at the same place; Betts,
Barnard, Fish, Edward Jones, Dr. Torrey, and I. Much work chalked
out and two subcommittees appointed to report a fortnight hence, on
finance and on organization. I'm unfortunately on both. Tone of our discussions not unpromising. When Barnard asked whether there was any
objection to the names of the associates appearing on a circular now in
press, he was cordially and promptly answered in the negative. Betts
was narrow, petty, and formal, of course, but the rest, Fish included,
talked sensibly and seemed to appreciate the work we have in hand.
They do not yet fully see it, but the fact is that our admission of a corps
of associate outsiders to work with the College trustees in any capacity
and for any purpose is the most hopeful step the College has taken in
our time.

February 13. At two o'clock resigned myself to one of those foul,
overcrowded, mephitic Third Avenue railroad cars, which took me to
Forty-ninth Street for a meeting of the Library Committee. After dis-
posing of our little business, Barnard, Schermerhorn, and I went downstairs and met Egleston by appointment in the School of Mines; also
George C. Anthon. Every sign there of an energy and directness of purpose and faculty for doing things most remote from our corporate traditions. Much progress has been made. Egleston and his colleagues are full
of enthusiasm and activity, and the atmosphere of the rooms is pervaded
by a bracing, almost rejuvenating flavor of life and strength.

The finest things from the Seymour collection are secured. Such a
group of specimens is hard to match. We understand the suite of Fluors
to be the most splendid extant. They are certainly most noble and marvelous to behold, and so are certain gigantic, ponderous crystals of Baryta.
Egleston expatiated on their importance as illustrating certain recondite

crystallographic laws, but they have a special value beside in that they will astonish unscientific barbarians, like myself, with the brute force of lustre and magnitude, and tempt thereby to further contributions. One "wonders and no end of wondering finds" over those magnificent cubes of purple fluor, partially encrusted with crystals of quartz or of galena, or of some metallic carbonate (iron?) that stimulates a deposit or growth of organic matter.

February 14.   Clear and only a little less cold than yesterday. Sub-committee (on organization) of Committee on School of Mines met at Betts's office (Betts, Fish, Jones, and I), and spent two hours and a half without substantial results. Half our time was spent in settling certain regulations for the faculty, merely embodying on paper what the faculty now does. This was surplusage, though harmless. There was disposition to legislate still further, but we came to the wise conclusion that while the School is in its present stage of rapid development as a reality, we had better let it grow in its own way and enact nothing that can be left without enactment. Then we took up the ticklish question of the relations of the committee and the associates. It was talked over candidly and reasonably. Fish and Betts do not see the position aright, I think. Betts cannot be expected to see it, but Fish ought to know better. Still, one must not be pig-headed and opinionated. I am not quite infallible after all, though this case does seem as clear as daylight. I brought in two schemes, one for a subordinate incorporation, and another making the associates members of the committee, which were discussed and laid over to an adjourned meeting a week hence. Fish's plan is that the College appro-priate $250,000 to the School, including in that sum the value of the portion of the College grounds on Forty-ninth Street that would be occupied by the new building, provided the associates raise the same amount. This sounds munificent, but it amounts to this, that we give the School say $17,000 per annum, of which the nominal rental of its premises forms part, and receive the fees of (say 100 students at $160) $160,000 per annum, thereby making an actual profit; and in consideration of this most liberal and public-spirited action, invite the public to give the Col-lege a quarter of a million. I fear it would be *no go.*

February 17.   Almost a spring day. Street crossings deep and danger-ous; a black torrent of muddy water flowing down Wall Street; Broad-way a long series of lagoons. Nothing special downtown. Called on [Sydney Howard] Gay of the *Tribune* about the School of Mines. Inter-view most satisfactory, but I shall send the *Tribune* no editorials on that subject till I have spoken with some of the College trustees. They are so jealous of their corporate dignity and so sensitive about any outside action that one must move with the utmost caution. I might give mortal offense and scandal to Fish, Betts, Ogden, and others if I "dragged the College into the newspapers," by securing a *Tribune* editorial commending the School of Mines to public favor and support.

Dined with Ellie at William Astor's (Jr.) very sumptuously; some twenty convives—General Dix, lovely Mrs. Belmont, Fred Sheldon and wife, John Astor, Mrs. Thorndike (née Delprat), and others. Sat between Mrs. Sheldon and Mrs. Cunard—nice women both—and got through the solemnity better than I had any right to expect.

General Dix tells me that Lincoln has postponed the execution of Beall, the pirate and spy, as predicted.[4] We treat rebels, traitors, spies, and assassins with unprecedented delicacy and mildness. It seems wrong, but the fact may have important bearing on the future course of history. . . .

The Raleigh *Progress* and the Charleston *Mercury* publish remarkable editorials. Their sound is as the dying howl of a suppressed ram-cat with a shattered spine. The former demands peace on any terms—the best obtainable, but peace now. Both indicate helplessness and utter inability to oppose Sherman's advance. Both denounce and vituperate Richmond and Jeff Davis as savagely as they ever abused Washington and the Illinois baboon, and both seem to look sideways at subjugation and reconstruction as possibilities that can no longer be ignored. Per contra, the New York *World*, carrying out its policy of disheartening and discouraging, thinks that when we have taken Charleston, Wilmington, and Richmond, and occupied all the rebel seaboard, the war will have but begun in earnest. Lee will withdraw to an interior position, entrench himself in the western strongholds of Virginia and the Carolinas, and bid us defiance. Perhaps. Would he were there now! His companies would have to issue rations of smoked nigger, and when they were exhausted, his men would have to disband and become bushwhackers. When we reach that stage of the war, we shall be prepared to treat bushwhackers as they deserve, and then peace will be very near.

[4] This refers to another of Jacob Thompson's machinations. He laid a plot to capture the armed steamer *Michigan* on Lake Erie and use her to free the Confederate prisoners on Johnson's Island in Sandusky Bay, these men then to attack Cleveland. John Y. Beall, a Virginian, headed a crew of Confederates who seized the *Philo Parsons* on Lake Erie, and scuttled another vessel, but failed of their main object. They fled into Canada; but Beall was later caught near the Niagara Suspension Bridge making an effort to derail a passenger train. He was eventually hanged.

February 20, MONDAY. . . . At two came an extra—"Evacuation of Charleston!" Grant telegraphs Stanton that the Richmond papers say Charleston was abandoned last Tuesday. We are of little faith, and do not fully receive these good tidings until officially announced. Washington is said to accept them with jubilation, but we distrust them.

February 21. Yesterday's doubtful news confirmed by the *Fulton*, which left Charleston on Saturday night. Charleston was entered and occupied Saturday morning, and the national flag floats over the ruins of Sumter. The Chivalry did not stay to exchange shots with mudsills, but flitted Friday night after firing their cotton storehouses. . . . My deluded Southern friends, who would hear of no compromise four years ago, "not even if you had *carte blanche* to dictate its terms," and who shook hands with effusion and drank cocktails in Charleston bar-rooms on the night of April 12th, 1861, after you had fired the Southern heart and hurled a proud and scornful defiance at Abe Lincoln and his Northern scum by beginning a causeless Civil War, and who telegraphed in the exuberance of your jollity to Washington "With mortar cannon and petard, We tender old Abe our Beau-Regard," what do you think about that day's job now? But I suppose a large majority of the young gentlemen who got more or less gloriously tipsy that memorable night are in their graves before this. Heaven forgive them their share in the colossal crime that has cost so many lives. Wiser, cooler, and better men might have been as blind, mad, and criminal had they grown up as members of a slaveholding caste in a woman-flogging and a baby-buying country. Of course, the whole city has been lit up with flags all day.

Long meeting at two of the subcommittee of Committee on School of Mines; Betts, Rutherfurd, Fish, Jones, and I. Much of our talk deplorably dense and fatuous, but the result, on the whole, not unsatisfactory, and we report in the course of red tape to the "mother committee" on Thursday, and then it will report to the board some of these days.

Sherman's hard-bitten and superbly confident army, leaving Savannah on February 1, was so overwhelmingly superior to the Confederate forces in front of it that it met little opposition as it marched northward. The worst obstacles were the bottomless mud of the roads, the flooded streams, and the ill-mapped swamps. Five large rivers had to be crossed. As General Jacob D. Cox wrote, the problem was one of "bridging chaos for hundreds of miles." Sherman made gestures which convinced the inhabitants of Charleston on the right and Augusta on the left that both were threatened. But actually he marched straight through to Columbia, which he entered over a pontoon bridge on February 17. That night a great conflagration destroyed much of the capital city. Sherman always contended that huge piles of cotton fired by the retreating Confederates were responsible for the holocaust. "Before one single public building had been fired by order, the smouldering fires set by Hampton's order were rekindled by the wind, and communicated to the buildings around. About dark they began to spread and got beyond the control of the brigade on duty within the city." The Confederates blamed the Union troops—who, Sherman admits, "may have assisted in spreading the fire after it had once begun."

Sherman's movement had flanked and isolated Charleston, and on February 21 the little Southern army of 14,000 under Hardee evacuated the city. While the North rejoiced over the humiliation of the starting-point of the "rebellion," General Q. A. Gillmore on February 21 took possession of it, with more than four hundred and fifty cannon and large stores of ammunition. The American flag had gone up over Fort Sumter at nine o'clock on the morning of February 18, when a small boat was sent out from Cumming's Point for that purpose. Sherman's forces now rapidly pushed forward to Goldsboro and Wilmington, North Carolina. Meanwhile, Grant continued his preparations for an irresistible movement against Petersburg and Richmond; and Sheridan was active in the Shenandoah Valley. The first blow of the year in Virginia, in fact, was struck by Sheridan on March 5, when, encountering Early's remnant force between Staunton and Charlottesville, he smashed it to bits, captured most of the survivors, and almost took Early himself. Thunder ringed the Confederacy, and to such passionate patriots as Strong the days were bright.

February 23.   Committee on School of Mines at Law School at half-past three o'clock; Fish, Barnard, Betts, Rutherfurd, Edward Jones, and I. We agreed on our report to the trustees. I fear the measures we recommend will bear no fruit, but I have said my say and done my duty. Fish and the rest seem to me to be (rightly or wrongly, and it is possible I am wrong) blind to self-evident considerations. What is worse and more surprising, they seem influenced by no feeling of ambition to develop and strengthen the College. When I tell them that our associates think they would be far more successful in raising funds for an organization affiliated with the trustees and governed by them, but nominally independent, than for the treasury of Columbia College, Fish replies, "Very good; then let them go to the 'University,' or set up a school on their own account." Outside wealth and influence and public spirit to help the College, when that help is respectfully offered, does not strike Fish and his colleagues as desirable.

Meeting at Union League Club tonight. We are now duly incorporated.

It is painful to think what Columbia College might become were half a dozen of its trustees earnestly desirous to promote its development. I can do nothing alone. Mr. Ruggles is full of other affairs. The rest are mostly indisposed to get out of their old, well-worn ruts. Having been inert since 17—, they feel bound by corporate traditions and a due sense of corporate dignity to be inert and inefficient and a scandal and offense that deters and repels all rich men who would like to promote the cause of education from giving a dollar to help them.

February 25, SATURDAY. Mrs. Ruggles the elder, Ellie's grandmamma, the noblest of old ladies, died at five this morning. Poor Ellie brought in the news before I was up. I did not in the least expect it, for though Mr. Ruggles spoke to me of the patient last evening as much prostrated and unlikely to survive very long, I thought her immense vitality would carry her on for weeks or months. . . .

February 27. . . . The Rebel Senate declines nigger soldiers by a close vote. Rebel editors are furious and hint that Lee might advantageously "purge" the rebel parliament. The New York *World*'s Baltimore correspondent, "Druid," favors mankind this morning with special and exclusive intelligence as to Lee's intentions. Lee means to seize Jeff Davis and put that potentate in irons. That's step No. 1. For No. 2, he proposes to march on Washington, cross the Long Bridge, march past Willard's Hotel, capture A. Lincoln, and put him in irons. His third move will be to proclaim himself dictator, and in that capacity to call a convention to restore the Union. A very politic and hopeful programme.

March 1. . . . Dr. Peters at the Union League Club tonight, just returned from a seven weeks' exploration at Beaufort, Savannah, and Charleston and Sumter the day after the rebels left it. Conflagration and rifled cannon have left about three-quarters of Charleston standing, but the city is dead. Only low-caste whites and their Ethiops remain there. "Obstructions in the harbor" have been a delusion for many months. There has always been an opening half a mile wide through the piles that barred the channel. This opening *was* obstructed with rope-net entanglements, but they were carried away by tides and currents, and the rebels got tired of replacing them.

Many of the better-most, blue-blooded Savannites still abide in
Savannah. Of these one-third secessionize strongly; the rest hate U.S.A.
and C.S.A., the Nation and the Rebellion, more or less impartially, and
pant for peace after the restoration of law and order anyhow and on any
terms. Peters supposes Sherman to be striking for Wilmington as a new
base, with 60,000 men as a minimum estimate, and thinks Beauregard
cannot confront him with more than 30,000.

March 2, THURSDAY. Trinity Chapel well filled this morning for the
Russian service. Part of the chapel was reserved for Russians, Greeks,
and Orientals, of whom there were fifty or sixty. The officiating priest,
Father Agapias, was in handsome robes. . . . Ogilby says this is the first
time the Liturgy of St. Chrysostom has been heard in a Western church
(excepting, of course, chapels of embassies at Paris and other Western
capitals) since the great schism between Eastern and Western Christendom. If so, this was a very remarkable transaction. It may prove—
possibly—a little step on the road toward Catholic unity. There certainly
seems to be a moving on the face of the waters just now. Our diocesan
committee minutes of every meeting record Congregationalists and
Presbyterians applying to become candidates for orders in the church.
Even the Unitarians are to hold a council here next month to consider
whether they do not believe *something* after all, and if so, to define it in
some symbol of faith. . . .

McVickar tells me he found the hard-headed old Scotch sexton of
Trinity Chapel quite sulky this morning over the proposed service.
Clarke thought it was to be something Popish, and felt conscientious
scruples about being accessory thereto. Whereupon Professor McVickar
opened a heavy fire on him, with the Council of This and the Council of
That, the "Mother Church of Jerusalem" and the "Mission Church of
Rome," and the orthodoxy of the Oriental communities and their enmity
to the Pope. Clarke was satisfied, or stunned, and said he was glad to learn
it was all right, and said he would be happy to countenance the service.

March 4. Standing Committee of Sanitary Commission here this
evening; Bellows, Agnew, Van Buren, Stillé, with Wolcott, Jenkins, and
Knapp. Appropriated $100,000 for immediate investment in battlefield
stores. Made progress with organization of our little *Hôtel des Invalides*
in Grove Street. The lease of its building has been taken in my name. We
have published an advertisement announcing our intention to use funds
for that object, and thus get around Professor Dwight's opinion as to the
trusts on which our funds are held.

March 6. The news of Early's defeat by Sheridan was telegraphed by Grant to Stanton, and by Stanton to Dix. . . . It took me an hour to work my way uptown through the crowded streets to our Columbia College meeting at the Law School in Lafayette Place at two o'clock. Little more than a quorum present. Only important business was the report of the Committee on School of Mines. Rutherfurd supported its recommendations forcibly and well. So did Mr. Ruggles. Ogden opposed them ex officio as too *costly*, but withdrew his objections and acquiesced. Zabriskie opposed them in his usual addle-brained way because they were not costly enough to succeed, because they were too costly for the College treasury, and because we ought to inquire and ascertain what professors were paid at Freiburg and Paris before venturing to employ professors in New York. The Bishop made a characteristic speech on both sides of the question. I said a little in confirmation of Rutherfurd. The result was that our resolutions passed without an audible dissenting vote, namely: the conditional pledge of $250,000 to the School and the recognition of the associates as colleagues of the committee. Very well. Now it remains to be seen whether we can get the *other* $250,000 out of the public for the treasury of Columbia College. I have my doubts. Wrote to Egleston this evening.

Today's grand jubilation was a splendid affair, more so than it would have been if held on the fourth, for there are anti-Lincolnites who would have kept aloof lest they should seem to do honor to Lincoln by making the day of his re-inauguration a festival. The crowd was enormous. Even Wall Street was thronged with Brooklynites from the Wall Street ferry. From the Park to Madison Square all New York seemed in the streets, at the windows, or on the housetops. We saw great crowds in the spring of 1861, and when the Prince of Wales honored us with a visit, but that of today seems to me bigger than any of them—perhaps because the impression is more fresh. The procession was three hours and a half long; that is, in passing any one point. I saw portions of it. After dinner, spent an hour at Union Square looking at fireworks. The jets of fire balls—red, white and blue; a dozen or twenty in the air at once—were very brilliant and beautiful. All this extravagant, exuberant rejoicing frightens me. It seems a manifest omen of mishap.

Sorry to say that Andy Johnson, Vice-President of the nation, whom I have held in great respect for four years past, seems to have been disgracefully *drunk* last Saturday and hardly in a condition to take part in the inaugural ceremonies of the new Administration. He has given the

JOHN STRONG NEWBERRY   G.T.S.   CORNELIUS REA AGNEW

WASHINGTON, OCTOBER 1863

NORTH.

Admit the Bearer to the
EXECUTIVE MANSION,
On **WEDNESDAY,** *the*
19th of April, 1865.

STRONG'S CARD OF ADMISSION TO LINCOLN'S FUNERAL

LINCOLN FUNERAL PROCESSION ON PENNSYLVANIA AVENUE

World and the *News* lamentable occasion to blaspheme. Those news-papers denounce and deride the inaugural address by A. Lincoln. It is certainly most unlike the inaugurals of Pierce, Polk, Buchanan, or any of their predecessors; unlike any American state paper of this century. I would give a good deal to know what estimate will be put on it ten or fifty years hence.

It is remarkable that Strong, with his highly cultivated literary taste, should have felt any doubt as to the verdict of history upon the most religious and most eloquent of all Lincoln's state papers, the second inaugural; a piece of prose that will live as long as the English language. It is not so remarkable that the World *and* News, *two embittered Democratic organs, should have been deeply irritated by the President's statement that it might be God's will that the war continue "till all the wealth piled by the bondman's two hundred and fifty years of unrequited toil shall be sunk, and until every drop of blood drawn with the lash shall be paid by another drawn with the sword." Lincoln's "re-inauguration," as Strong calls it, was attended by scenes of patriotic rejoicing throughout the North. Numerous cities, including New York, witnessed the pageantry of grand military and civic parades; while in Washington a huge throng gathered under the shadow of the Capitol dome, now completed with the bronze statue of Liberty surmounting its crest as a symbol of the triumphant vindication of the principle of Union. Before Lincoln delivered his address and took the oath of office administered by Salmon P. Chase, the new Chief Justice, Andrew Johnson was sworn in as Vice-President in the Senate Chamber. This ceremony was unduly prolonged by his own half-maudlin utterances; but he was not to be judged as harshly as Strong's passage implies, for, just recovering from a grave illness, and suffering from fatigue and a bad cold, he had indiscreetly taken too large a glass of stimulant. Vice-President Johnson, far from being addicted to drink, was an eminently temperate man.*

March 8.   Wet evening after a fine day. Poor Bob LeRoy's funeral was at Trinity Church at ten o'clock. Ellie went with me; that true little woman never forgets an old friend. I was glad to see so many in attend-ance. . . . Poor fellow, he came home on furlough a fortnight ago, having suffered since June from camp diarrhea of unusual severity, but seemingly not at all pulled down by it. General McCook spoke of him as among the bravest and coolest men he ever knew, and as having utterly abstained from stimulants while on his staff. Poor Bob spoke of his own reformation.

lamented the prevalence of drunkenness among officers in the army, and referred to himself as a living proof that the habit could be broken, no matter how far it had gone (he had suffered at least two attacks of delirium tremens). A day or two after, while he was waiting at a railroad depot to receive Mrs. Charles E. Strong and escort her to her hotel, the morbid appetite came on him suddenly with a force he found absolutely irresistible. This is what he stated on his death-bed. He went involuntarily to the nearest grocery and swallowed two or three glasses of whiskey, one after another, and then adjourned to his club to continue the treatment. Mrs. Charles E. Strong found her way to her hotel without escort as best she could, and Bob returned to his father-in-law's house while the family was at dinner, his wife included, and dropped on the rug before the dining-room fire. He was carried up to bed and resumed the same practice the next day, and the next. But after some four or five days of hard, steady drinking—last Wednesday, I think—he had to give it up and take to his bed, for his diarrhea was much aggravated. His physician (Neill) did not think him dangerously ill till last Saturday morning, when he reported that there was a sudden and alarming change, and that he would call again in an hour or two. He did so, and pronounced the case hopeless. The patient was sinking and stimulants were positively inert. The patient saw the grave looks of those about him and called on his doctor to "speak out like a man" and tell him the truth. "Was he going to die?" Yes. "Would he live through the day?" Probably not. . . . Poor Bob LeRoy! What might not have been made out of him twenty years ago by even the least effort to train him aright? . . .

Kenzua Petroleum Co. Directors sat a couple of hours yesterday afternoon at Mr. Ruggles's office. We commence boring forthwith. May we "strike ile"!

March 9. . . . To School of Mines, where I spent an hour; then to No. 823, where was Marcus L. Ward of Newark, also Mrs. Hoge and Mrs. Livermore of Chicago, who are here working for the Great Northwest Sanitary Fair that is to be opened next June and to surpass all fairs that have been held since the universe was a universe. They are fearful and wonderful women, whose horsepower is to be expressed in terms of droves of horses.

We send a first-class propeller to Wilmington Saturday, as the *Uncas* does not return yet from her last trip, and we cannot delay supplies to that point any longer. I should go with her but for this confounded School of Mines. The next fortnight is a critical period in our *accouche-*

ment of that bantling, and I ought not to go away. Egleston and Chandler spent the evening here, settling drafts of certain circulars.

March 10. . . . Richmond newspapers are in a special spasm of fury beyond any fit they have yet suffered. We must not attach too much weight to what these sensitive, excitable, high-toned, chivalric creatures rave when in nervous exaltation, whether arising from patriotic or from alcoholic stimulus. But this particular paroxysm certainly resembles the death flurry of a whale. The editorial utterances are violent, desperate, incoherent, hurried, and objectless. They amount in substance to this, that there is somewhere a class of "whipped seceders" and "whipped croakers" who desire subjugation and have an appetite for infamy—that these caitiffs want Davis to abdicate, and their pressure is sufficient to make it worthwhile to expend much bad language on them—that they will not succeed in these base designs, because Southerners never, never, *never* will be slaves, and because "our women" ought to take up their broomsticks and drive these wretches into the James River, and so on. There are certainly signs in Secessia of incipient decomposition. The rebellion has, at the very least, another year's fight in it, but it may die of inward disease within thirty days. I trust it will not die too soon and that it will be killed, not merely "kilt." I long for peace, but only for a durable peace, of material that will wear. John Bright writes F. M. Edge that he hopes our war will not end till its work is done, and he sees the case aright.

The rebel hosts continue to be seriously drained by desertion. Not less than fifty deserters have taken refuge within Grant's lines every day for many weeks past, and their average number is probably nearer one hundred than fifty. Companies come in, led by their company officers. All tell the same story of compulsory service, hardships, failure of pay and of clothing and of rations, and of general despondency. The Confederacy has "gone up," they say. "We all know it, and we know it is useless to fight any longer." Lee's soldiers would throw away their arms and disband tomorrow if they dared, and so on. Such statements made by deserters are worth much "less than their face." But when made by hundreds, and corroborated by the actual desertion of thousands, at imminent risk of life and with certain and conscious loss of honor, they are worth a great deal. It is likely, moreover, that for every rebel who flees within our lines, two flee the other way and take sanctuary in the hill country or the "piney woods," supporting themselves by levying contributions on all and sundry as sovereign powers so far as their own personal sovereignty can be made practically available, and thus carrying out the doctrine of secession to its

ultimate results. Many counties of Virginia, the Carolinas, and the Gulf
States are said to swarm with these banditti, and they are admitted to be
even more savage and reckless than the vandal hordes of the North.

The Rebel Congress seems to have reconsidered its refusal to arm the
slaves and to have decided, reluctantly, and by a very close vote, that
there is no help for it and that Cuffee must be conscripted and made to
fight for his chivalric master. So much for the visions of glory the South
saw in 1860. This sacrifice of the first principles of the Southern social
system is a confession of utter exhaustion; a desperate remedy and a most
dangerous experiment. And the experiment is tried at least a year too
late. It will take six months to drill and equip any considerable *corps
d'Afrique*, and Sherman, Sheridan, Thomas, and Grant are likely, with
God's blessing, to give rebellion its death blow within that time.

But the measure has its immediate effects. It disgusts and alienates
many slaveholders and many fanatical theorists about slavery, and it is
received as an affront by the rebel rank and file—an affront that justifies
desertion. They will feel it not only as an affront, but as a disheartening
surrender of the principle for which they have fought. They learn that
niggers are now to be armed and put into the field as the allies of Southern
gentlemen; "that it will depend on the nigger's pluck and muscle and
endurance how far he is to share with white men the glory of upholding
the Southern cause. It will depend on that and nothing else. Moreover,
he is to be rewarded for good service by freedom." But the first of all
Southern axioms has been for thirty years past that freedom was a punishment to the slave, servitude his normal condition, and that he loved and
looked up to and depended on his owner as a good dog does on his master,
and that he despised and rejected emancipation just as a good dog would
dislike being discharged from his duty of guardianship and kicked into the
street to get his own living as best he could.

March 13.   Did little in Wall Street. Committee on School of Mines
met with the associates at the Law School this afternoon. Chandler,
Egleston, and Vinton attended, some sixteen in all. It was a kind of preliminary meeting, and no important action was taken. All depends now
on the success of our subcommittee on ways and means, as to which I'm
not in the least sanguine. . . .

March 15, WEDNESDAY.   Egleston spent the evening here, and after
talking of the School of Mines, diverged to his experiences abroad, Trinity Church, theology, religion, theories of education, and so on. His
earnestness and enthusiasm are remarkable, and his intensity of feeling as

to religion and science both is a phenomenon almost unexampled in these times.

Yesterday brought tidings from Sherman, at last; at Laurel Hill, North Carolina, the 8th instant, and "all right." Gold dropped. Today at noon came news that he was at Fayetteville, North Carolina, and had opened communication with Wilmington. This let gold down to 174⅓; a very deep descent and sudden fall. It almost makes me suspect that operators have further information of an esoteric nature. Bragg has retreated across the Neuse. Sherman seems steering for Raleigh. If he get there safe, his entry may be the signal for a hearty counter revolution. Loyal men abound in Raleigh, and are kept quiet only by Davis's bayonets. And if Bragg stay where he is, he may find it a tight place. He will probably make for Raleigh, too, with Schofield after him. All which looks very nice and hopeful, but let us put off exultation a little longer.

Moreover, the morning papers say that there is sore panic in Richmond and that the evacuation of that pseudo-metropolis is positively in progress at last. This must be the 750th time we have been so informed, on the authority of "escaped prisoners" or "reliable gentlemen" or "intelligent contrabands." I should not think the story worth noting had I not a scrap of information from a disgusted New York Secesher which tends to confirm it. . . .

March 18. Very energetic in Wall Street. Walked off with George Anthon at two, crossed at Wall Street ferry, and explored sundry new districts of Brooklyn. Visited "Fort Greene," a noble public square with fine views in every direction. I hereby prophesy that in 1900 A.D. Brooklyn will be the city and New York will be the suburb. It is inevitable if both go on growing as they have grown for the last forty years. Brooklyn has room to spread and New York has not. The New Yorker of Thirty-fifth Street already finds it a tedious and annoying job to make his way downtown to business and home again. How will the New Yorker of One-hundredth Street get about forty years hence? Brooklyn must outnumber this city before very many years, and then places of amusement and fashionable residences will begin to emigrate across the East River. New York will become "the city" in the London sense of that word. Its Belgravia will be transferred from the Fifth Avenue to King's County. A like change is within my own memory. When I was a boy, the aristocracy lived around the Battery, on the Bowling Green, and in the western streets below Chambers; in Wall Street, Cedar Street, and Beekman Street, on the east of the town. Greenwich Street, now a hissing and a desolation, a place of lager beer saloons, emigrant boarding houses, and the vilest dens, was what Madison Avenue is now. There were the Griswolds in Chambers Street, Philip Hone in Broadway below Park Place, Mrs. Cruger at No. 55, and so on. Between 1828 and 1832, emigration to the regions of Fourth Street, Bond Street, and Lafayette Place set in, and the centres of fashion were moved again, for we are a nomadic people, and our finest brownstone houses are merely tents of new pattern and material. Brooklyn has advantages, too, that will speed the change. The situations on the Heights overlooking the bay can hardly be matched in any great city of Christendom. How often have I wished I could exchange this house for one of them, and that I could see from my library windows that noble prospect and that wide open expanse of sky, and the going down of the sun every evening! . . .

At No. 823; $11,000 in gold from San Francisco. Sold the draft at 164. No war news. No fighting around Richmond. Davis sends his Congress a message, almost equivalent to a *cognovit* of failure and ruin. Southern newspapers are unhappy about the conflagration that destroyed Columbia, South Carolina, when the rebels walked out and our army walked in. It would seem to have been caused by the firing of cotton stored there, and to have been suppressed, at last, by the exertions of our soldiers. But it is attributed to Sherman's "unprincipled diabolism."

George Anthon dined here. After dinner to meeting of the finance subcommittee of the Committee on School of Mines at the Law School, 37 Lafayette Place; Delano, Fish, Dodge, Jones, Tuckerman, Ward, and others. Return rather discouraged. Raising our $250,000 will be uphill work. This fall in gold will depress values, produce a sense of impoverishment, and tell against us. I shall not willingly become interested in the organization of anything *pro bono publico* again. It costs me more worry, anxiety, despondency, and general wear and tear than my feeble work for the public good is worth. For the last few months, I have been as unhappy about the School of Mines as if it had been one of my own children. Let it fail and come to naught and let me devote myself to my own personal interests. But then think of the admirable enthusiasm and self-devotion of Egleston, Chandler, and Vinton! Never was such material put within the control of our board. Not to improve it and make it felt in the community is a breach of trust.

March 21. . . . Great dismay in Wall Street; gold down to 156. It touched 152, I hear. So stocks are down, and men's hearts fail them for fear of a revolution and collapse. United States securities can be bought for less than their face, taking accrued interest into account. This fact will throw cold water on the new 7–30 loan, a curious consequence of our late triumphs and of the general conviction that rebellion is stricken with death.

Fifth Avenue from Forty-ninth Street down was absolutely thronged with costly new equipages on their way to Central Park this bright, bland afternoon. It was a broad torrent of vehicular gentility, wherein profits of shoddy and of petroleum were largely represented. Not a few of the ladies who were driving in the most sumptuous turn-outs, with liveried servants, looked as if they might have been cooks or chambermaids a very few years ago. . . .

Jeff Davis's message seems of graver and more doleful import the longer it is looked at. "Was ne'er prophetic sound so full of woe." He tells his Congress that he and they and all Rebeldom are in a desperate case, and that it is difficult to imagine a worse extremity than theirs, and urges remedies that are not only desperate but impracticable and that would be ruinous if practicable. His Congress has dispersed without administering these remedies or any of them. Strange this paper should have been published. Some say he means to resign, and run—having no doubt put away a pot of money in London or Paris—and to become an illustrious exile, and that this manifesto is meant to justify his abdication. Let him run, if he will. I hope he may get off safe, for if we caught him, we should not hang him, and our omission to do so would be discreditable. . . .

March 23. . . . Jeff Davis's Congress, being snubbed by that potentate in his last message and charged with the responsibility for all the present troubles of the Confederacy, jaws back through a committee report adopted just before adjournment (not on ayes and noes), "sasses" Jeff Davis, and says it's all his fault. As between Jeff Davis and his peers, I believe myself quite impartial, like the spectator of the fight between skunk and rattlesnake. I think that on the face of the papers, Congress has the best of it, and Jeff Davis gets a black eye. Anyhow, Satan is certainly divided against himself, and that is a hopeful sign.

March 24. Sanitary Commission session here tonight; Bellows, Van Buren, Jenkins. Agnew still in North Carolina. Jenkins gives no good account of Knapp's ways at Washington; thinks him cunning, evil-disposed, and untrue. It seems incredible this should be his character, but I fear he is not the embodiment of single-mindedness and unselfishness I used to suppose him. Jenkins has just had a long, semi-confidential talk with [William] Whiting of the War Office, and certain of our western agents have held like discourse with high officials of Thomas's army as to the coming campaign and the points at which we should set about accumulating supplies. Their letters and reports read tonight were interesting. As far as they go, they confirm Whiting's statements, which are generally none the worse for a little confirmation.

Taken together they are encouraging. Sherman and Schofield are about 100,000 strong; Grant 140,000; Sheridan has 15,000 cavalry in southern Virginia; Hancock (or Torbert?) a like force at Winchester and some 8,000 infantry beside.[5] Thomas has 150,000 (I suppose this means our whole force from Nashville and Knoxville to New Orleans). He is to send 50,000 toward Lynchburg and Danville, the Winchester column moving in concert up the Valley, and is to command in person a column of 40,000 marching on Selma. The department thinks it quite likely that Lee will have to capitulate without a battle. The draft and the volunteering thereby stimulated have already mustered into service nearly 100,000, and of these 30,000 are now under arms. We are 100,000 stonger than this time last year.

I hope all this may be true. If we have near 400,000 men in the field, Secessia must be outnumbered two to one, at least, to say nothing of discouragement, discord, financial collapse, and the closing of rebel ports to supplies from abroad. May we get through the next sixty days without any serious reverse or blunder!

March 25, SATURDAY. . . . At Philharmonic rehearsal at three o'clock; Beethoven's Ninth Symphony (the *Choral*), of which I have not heard a note for about five years. A rough performance. Though Eisfeld was not extreme to mark what was amiss, the raps of his baton for the repetition of an ill-rendered passage were many; so many that the orchestra spent an hour and forty minutes on the symphony, though they skipped all the long passage of melodic plain sailing that immediately precedes the "Marcia" subdivision of the fourth movement. On the whole, this great but unequal work gained on me. Its demerits were more distinctly visible, but its merits still more. Never before did I fully recognize the vigor and dash of the second movement, or the noble gravity, the serious sweetness, of the third. That movement is not matched. To me it seems to embody the sentiment of "When to the sessions of sweet silent thought."

March 27. . . . I must record the movements of two chips, because they shew which way the tide is setting. First: The Baltimore correspondent of

---

[5] Better authority credits Grant with 124,000; but Lee's army was reduced to about 50,000.

the New York *World*, and a bitter secessionist, who has long been prophesying woes to the country and victory to Jeff Davis over the signature of
"Druid," writes that within a few weeks or months the Confederacy must
cease to exist. It will no longer have a government, an army, or a capital.
Its leaders made several mistakes at the outset, and among others this,
that the cause of self-government and freedom must be destined always
to prevail. Does this statement invite one to vehement cachinnation or to
profuse nausea??? Second: At the recent debates in the House of Commons,
Palmerston and Disraeli and others were of one mind with Mr. Bright,
commending the energy and discretion of Lincoln's Administration under
the most trying circumstances, and the most creditable spirit it has shewn
in all its dealings with foreign powers! Poor, mean, shabby, fallen, old
England restores us the tribute of her shop-keeper's civility and compliments the moment she discerns that we may win our unpromising lawsuit,
after all; may "come to our own again," and be a profitable customer or
an expensive enemy next year.

March 28. . . . The Kenzua Petroleum Co. directors met at Mr. Ruggles's office this afternoon. Cresson of Philadelphia and Moses H. Grinnell
added unto us. Prospects of the company seem good. If it "strike ile,"
my 10,000 shares of stock may prove worth something, more or less,
which would be gratifying. But I expect nothing, and am therefore incapable of disappointment. My stock has cost me nothing, so I have nothing
at stake, and any oil of gladness that may flow therefrom, if only half a
pint, will be so much clear gain.

Gold seems to have stuck fast in the neighborhood of 154. The prophets
of Wall Street are prophesying that it will not soon sink much lower.
They hold that we have discounted victory, that the late rapid decline
represents the common belief that rebellion is as good as dead already,
and that gold will stay where it is for some time after rebellion is actually
defunct and gibbeted in chains as a warning to posterity. I do not think so.
The wisest financier can only guess how it will be, for the equation is too
complex and includes too many unknown and variable quantities—too
many chances and contingencies—to be worked out by human wit.

The fray of the 25th before Petersburg was no small affair.[6] Had
Lee's veterans fought as they fought last May it might have been a bad

[6] Seeing that he would soon be compelled to evacuate Petersburg and Richmond,
Lee determined upon a last attempt to drive Grant back in his immediate front. On
March 25, General John B. Gordon in a surprise assault captured Fort Stedman, one
of the Union strong points. The Union forces then rallied and drove the Confederates
out with heavy losses.

business. But after that first brilliant and successful dash at our line, they shewed little sign of their ancient pluck and tenacity. When once inside "Fort Stedman," many of them seem to have withdrawn into bomb-proofs in spite of their officers and thus to have secured an opportunity to surrender by dint of great resolution. Lee cannot afford many experiments like this. It must have cost him ten per cent of his available force. But what can he do? Grant has him by the throat. Sherman, reinforced by Schofield and Terry, was at last accounts threatening Raleigh, North Carolina, and steadily approaching the last duct that brings nutriment to the garrison of Richmond.

March 29. Committee on School of Mines met at Law School this afternoon and sat near two hours. Certain recommendations to the trustees. Satisfactory meeting. But it is clear one of our associates was a bad choice, Mr. Lewis L. Delafield to wit. He is talkative, conceited, pragmatical, and disputatious. He carries no weight, however, and is only an annoyance.

Afterwards at No. 823. Agnew made a long and interesting report (verbal) on what he did and saw at New Bern and Wilmington. Our supplies sent by the *Chase* reached Wilmington just at the right moment and saved scores of lives. His account of the condition of hundreds of returned prisoners, founded on personal inspection, is fearful. They have been starved into idiocy—do not know their own names, or where they are, or where their home is. Starvation has gangrened their extremities —destroyed their instinctive sense of decency, and converted them into irrational, atrophied, moribund animals. No Bastille and no Inquisition dungeon has ever come up to the chivalric rebel pen for prisoners of war. I do not think people quite see, even yet, the unexampled enormity of this crime. It is a new thing in the history of man. It infinitely transcends the records of the guillotine and concomitant *noyades* and *fusillades*. The disembowelment and decapitation of all men, women, and children of a Chinese city convicted of rebel sympathies is an act of mercy compared with the politic, slow torture Davis and Lee have been inflicting on their prisoners, with the intent of making them unfit for service when exchanged.

I almost hope this war may last till it become a war of extermination. Southrons who could endure the knowledge that human creatures were undergoing this torture within their own borders, and who did not actively protest against it, deserve to be killed.

March 30. . . . Gold touched 149 today. Military matters are as they were. Sherman's army is taking a rest at or near Goldsboro and trying on its new shoes. Lee has made another push at Grant's lines, a small affair compared with that of the 25th, and took nothing by his motion. Sheridan is on the rampage somewhere south of the Appomattox. A column from Thomas seems moving Lynchburg-ward. We are closing in upon Richmond, but Lee has his back to the wall and will fight like a rat in a corner if his men be kept to their work. I do not believe it possible for him to carry his army to Danville or Lynchburg if he wants to. His only hope is in the chapter of accidents. Something may turn up. Richmond editors keep up their spirits, however, and also their vocabulary.

March 31, FRIDAY.   Gold 151. News that Mobile was attacked on the 21st. Result not yet known. Also that Grant opened an important movement at three A.M. on the 29th. Sheridan seems to have marched toward Dinwiddie Court House, backed by a strong infantry force. Object probably to cut the "South Side Railroad," and perhaps to draw Lee out of his forts. I hope this rain may not have spoiled the party. We may expect weighty news any minute. There has already been a lively little collision, of which the rebels had the worst. Though all the chances are in our favor, I am anxious, for we are in a premature stage of jubilation that invites disaster.

Agnew opened more of his budget from Wilmington and New Bern. He tells us Sherman's officers say that their campaign was made possible by the order of the rebel government that corn be planted instead of cotton. Four years ago the army could not have been fed. As it was, they marched through a land of groaning corn cribs and granaries, and their men and their animals entered Savannah in better flesh than when they left Atlanta. A notable statement. . . .

From observation at Wilmington, Agnew thinks the Southern "masses" an effete people, unable to take care of themselves now that their slaveholding lords and magnates are gone. A "local committee" at Wilmington is feeding four thousand Wilmingtonians on rations issued by the government. The white trash of even North Carolina is helpless and imbecile, unable to work or to reorganize the community.

So much for that. To come nearer home, the bill for a paid fire department, superseding our ancient, rowdy organization, has passed both houses of the state legislature, to the great disgust and wrath of the existing engine companies. Some of them are reported to say and swear that they will not turn out in case of fire. That is quite enough to justify the change. But as the new department does not yet exist, and the old one is disaffected and mutinous, a large fire might be a very serious business just now. There has been no act of the legislature, in my time, that will work so great a change in this city's daily life.

April 1, SATURDAY.   Noon brought an extra, with despatches from Grant, in substance: "Hard fighting yesterday. We took the Boydton plank road, lost it, recovered it, and hold it; also took four battle flags." Not bad so far as it goes, though it leaves much to the imagination. According to Charley Strong, who has returned from City Point and the front after three days there, our officers say the rebels have clearly lost heart, that they fight coldly, run readily, and surrender joyfully. To be sure, this hard pounding on the 31st looks unlike it. But he talked with a Major Miller of General Kimball's staff, who was bagged by the rebels during the Fort Stedman fight. Their commanding officer ("Louisiana Tiger, G–d–you") instantly demanded the major's overcoat, watch, money, and horse, which were surrendered, and hailed the orderly who was taking off the quadruped. "Recollect, now, that's *my* horse, don't you go and turn him over to anybody." After this business transaction, the major asked his captor's name and rank, received the answer above quoted, and was ordered to the rear. But it "rained blue beans," as the Germans say, and also iron cocoanuts and watermelons all along the way to the rebel lines. The fire from both sides was a *feu d'enfer,* and the major's guard preferred taking him into one of the bomb-proofs of Stedman and waiting there till the storm should abate a little. The bomb-proof was already crowded with rebel soldiers. The major proceeded to call the attention of those nearest him to a few leading facts. "The Confederacy had gone up. If they went back to their own lines and took him along, it would be unpleasant for him, but would it be a good thing for them? They would have to do more fighting and probably be bagged at last. Whereas, if they were only in *our lines,* they would be well treated and get not only abundant rations, but twenty dollars each for their arms and accoutrements." They listened eagerly, but they did not like to desert. "Very becoming and proper," said the major, "but why can't I take you in as my prisoners?" The suggestion was received with favor, so he formed them in column by threes and double-quicked them into our lines, 204 men, each with his musket.

The Confederacy was now in its death-throes. Grant on March 24 had issued orders for the grand final movements against Lee to end the war. Though he had now besieged Richmond and Petersburg since the summer of 1864, he did not control the lines west and southwest of these cities; and he feared that

Lee's army would break out along the route of the Richmond & Danville Rail-road, and then either join forces with Johnston's troops or effect its escape into the mountains. A union of the two Confederate armies, he feared, would result in a bloody and painful campaign consuming most of the summer. Grant there-fore thrust forward his left wing, south of Petersburg, in order to cut the branch railroad leading from Petersburg to the Richmond & Danville and seal up the Confederates in that town. Heavy rains slowed down the movement. But on April 1, the Union troops under Sheridan came into collision with the Con-federates at Five Forks, southwest of Richmond; and they carried everything before them. By nightfall the victory was complete. Pickett's troops were routed in utter disorder, and nearly six thousand of them were taken prisoner. This left the main Confederate army, stretched out in a long thin line, in a dangerous position; and next day (April 2) Grant ordered an assault at dawn along the entire front. The Confederate leaders already knew that the struggle to hold their capital was lost. In the first hours of the general assault the Union forces proved irresistible, and before noon Lee had telegraphed to Jefferson Davis: "I see no prospect of doing more than holding our position here till night. I am not cer-tain that I can do that." The Union forces had actually cut his army in two and thrown a powerful wedge between the segments. On the night of April 2, the Confederate forces filed out of Richmond and Petersburg. It was still Lee's hope that he could get away along the southwesterly roads and join hands with Johnston; but April 3 found Grant's army in hot pursuit. So little did Norther-ners grasp the mighty power of Grant's blows that as late as April 1 Strong feared that the Union forces might yet retreat; but, he added, "Grant knows what he is doing."

April 2, SUNDAY.   There is reason to hope this day may long be re-membered. To Trinity with Ellie and the two boys. After service (com-munion), we asked General Anderson (of Fort Sumter) to ride up with us and stopped at the *Tribune* office to look for news. There was an extra with a despatch from Lincoln at City Point to Stanton—brief but weighty. Read it to the general, and his *Thank God* was fervently uttered and good to hear. . . .

April 3.   Petersburg and Richmond! *Gloria in excelsis Deo.*

New York has seen no such day in our time nor in the old time before us. The jubilations of the Revolutionary War and the War of 1812 were those of a second-rate seaport town. This has been metropolitan and worthy an event of the first national importance to a continental nation and a cosmopolitan city.

The morning papers disclosed nothing decisive. There were two short despatches from City Point giving later news of yesterday's great battle, which looked well, but I omnibussed downtown expecting only to learn during the day more positively that the South Side Railroad was cut; that Lee had returned to his entrenchments badly punished, and that it was confidently expected that he would have to evacuate them at some future period.

Walking down Wall Street, I saw something on the *Commercial Advertiser* bulletin board at the corner of Pine and William Streets and turned off to investigate. I read the announcement "Petersburg is taken" and went into the office in quest of particulars. The man behind the counter was slowly painting in large letters on a large sheet of brown paper another annunciation for the board outside: "Richmond is"— "What's that about Richmond?" said I. "Anything more?" He was too busy for speech, but he went on with a capital C, and a capital A, and so on, till I read the word *CAPTURED*!!! Finding that this was official, I posted up to Trinity Church to tell the sexton to suggest to Vinton to ask the Rector's permission to set the chimes going (which was duly done). When I came back, all William Street in front of the *Advertiser* office was impenetrably crowded, and people were rushing together in front of the Custom House (the *ci-devant* Merchants' Exchange), where Prosper M. Wetmore and Simeon Draper were getting up a meeting on the spur of the moment.

An enormous crowd soon blocked that part of Wall Street, and speeches began. Draper and the Hon. Moses Odell and Evarts and Dean (a proselyte from Copperheadism) and the inevitable Wetmore, and others, severally had their say, and the meeting, organized at about twelve, did not break up, I hear, till four P.M. Never before did I hear cheering that came straight from the heart, that was given because people felt relieved by cheering and hallooing. All the cheers I ever listened to were tame in comparison, because seemingly inspired only by a design to shew enthusiasm. These were spontaneous and involuntary and of vast "magnetizing" power. They sang "Old Hundred," the Doxology, "John Brown," and "The Star-Spangled Banner," repeating the last two lines of Key's song over and over, with a massive roar from the crowd and a unanimous wave of hats at the end of each repetition. I think I shall never lose the impression made by this rude, many-voiced chorale. It seemed a revelation of profound national feeling, underlying all our vulgarisms and corruptions, and vouchsafed to us in their very focus and centre, in Wall Street itself.

I walked about on the outskirts of the crowd, shaking hands with everybody, congratulating and being congratulated by scores of men I hardly know even by sight. Men embraced and hugged each other, *kissed* each other, retreated into doorways to dry their eyes and came out again to flourish their hats and hurrah. There will be many sore throats in New York tomorrow. My only experience of a people stirred up to like intensity of feeling was at the great Union meeting at Union Square in April, 1861. But the feeling of today's crowd was not at all identical with that of the memorable mass-meeting four years ago. It was no less earnest and serious, but it was founded on memories of years of failure, all but hopeless, and on the consciousness that national victory was at last secured, through much tribulation. . . .

After dinner to the Union League Club. Vast crowd, enthusiasm, and excitement. Meeting organized upstairs, Captain Marshall in the chair, and "a few remarks" made by a score of people. Honest, downright old Judge Vanderpoel[7] was very good. "Gentlemen," said the judge, "I tell you that for years before this rebellion, we at the North lived under the tyranny of the slaveholders. I see now that when I was in Congress, almost every important vote I gave was dictated by them and given under the plantation lash. I confess it with shame, and humbly ask pardon of this meeting and of all my fellow-countrymen."

Hamilton Fish was at the Club—I never saw him there before— beaming and gushing, and shaking everybody's hands with fervor. Two years ago he talked nothing but discouragement and practical disloyalty. But (as Sydney Smith irreverently said of bishops), "If you want to know which way the wind blows, throw up Hamilton Fish."

It seems like a Fourth of July night—such a fusillade and cannonade is going on. Thus ends a day *sui generis* in my life. We shall long remember that the first troops to enter Richmond were niggers of Weitzel's corps. It is a most suggestive fact. It's said there were abundant signs of Union feeling in the city. Lee, Davis, & Co. are supposed to be making for Burke's Junction. Lynchburg or Danville is doubtless their proposed harbor of refuge. May Sheridan's cavalry be fresh enough to deal with them according to the example of Blücher after Waterloo. The government of the "Confederate States" has become nomadic. Its capitol and its depart-

[7] Aaron Vanderpoel (1799–1870) had been a Democratic member of Congress in Van Buren's presidency, and later was judge of the superior court in New York.

ments of state and of war are probably in a dirty, damaged, worn-out railroad car, and its "seat of government" probably rests on the saddle which Jeff Davis bestrides.

April 4. Ellie set off for City Point on the steamer *George Leary* with a large pleasant party: Mrs. Paran Stevens and Miss Fanny Reid, John Van Buren and his pretty daughter Miss Annie, Captain Comstock and his daughter, Arthur Leary, Griswold Gray, and Colonel Stoughton. Wish I could have gone. I consented with sore misgivings, but she had earned this little spree by her faithful service on hospital transports on the Pamunkey and the James in 1862. I fear she and her party will be disappointed after all and unable to visit Richmond.

Broadway is a river of flags. Poor Frederic Winthrop was shot through the lungs and is dead. He rose from the ranks to a brigadier-general's brevet. He was a cousin of Theodore Winthrop and brother of Frank Winthrop, with whom I walked uptown after the College meeting yesterday. It's said another despatch came last night, after Howard Potter had left town, announcing the death of General Robert Potter. Tonight's *Post* mentions the report as probably true. God help poor Miss Stevens![8] At Life & Trust Co. meeting this morning, and at three o'clock to a meeting of the Kenzua Co. directors at their new office, 36 Wall Street. Tonight at Union League looking over the collection recently bought by the club of foreign books and tracts on the Rebellion. Nearly all one way, of course.

No news from the front up to half-past one. Everybody was sallying out to look for news every ten minutes and coming back disappointed and wondering whether something hadn't gone wrong. At last came announcements on bulletin boards and an extra with despatches. They indicate that Lee is damaged and demoralized. The country is full of stragglers. We bag prisoners in large handfuls. Lee's course is marked by abandoned artillery and by burned or charred wagons and caissons. Great store of war material found at Richmond, including railroad rolling stock. Unofficial statements are that we have 15,000 prisoners at City Point, that Fort Darling and the rebel iron-clads on the upper James have been blown up, that the Union feeling of North Carolina is so star-spangled as to be actually oppressive, that Sherman's men are so cocky and Johnston's rebels so depressed that three of our foragers commonly form in line of

---

[8] Brigadier-General Robert B. Potter, a son of Bishop Alonzo Potter, was sorely wounded in the assault on Petersburg April 2, but recovered to live until 1887. He married Abby Austin Stevens.

battle when they encounter not more than thirty seceshers, and always drive them; also, however, that the communication between Goldsboro and Sherman's base is thought to be just a little endangered by Wade Hampton's cavalry.

Guns popping off in every direction tonight. A salute of one hundred guns fired at the foot of Wall Street this morning, and another in front of the Union League Club tonight. Surely the slaveholders' rebellion, with its capital lost, its best army defeated, its soldiers demoralized, its people broken-spirited, and its ports closed to contributions from sympathizing Britons, and its president and chief general both running for their lives, cannot sustain itself or claim to be called a nation much longer. But heaven save us from overtures of peace and reconstruction for the next six months. May Pharaoh's heart be hardened yet a little longer!

April 5. . . . Despatches are still bright. They report Lee's grand army crippled and in great measure disorganized. Unless newspaper correspondents lie most exorbitantly, it is used up and done for. . . .

April 6. . . . Today's news is good and full of promise. Lee is retreating perforce toward Lynchburg. He cannot make for Danville or try to join Johnston in North Carolina, because Sheridan and Grant are moving on a parallel line south of his, and are seemingly ahead of him. He has been obliged to take the wrong side (the north bank) of the Appomattox. . . . Jeff Davis made a moonlight flitting Sunday night and is believed to have taken a special train for Danville. Like the missing Massa in the "Year of Jubilo" [Kingdom Coming]:

> He saw the smoke 'way down the ribber, where the
>   Linkum gunboats lay,
> And he picked up his hat, and he left bery sudden,
>   an I 'spec he's run away! . . .

April 7. . . . At noon came more good news. Lee's army again routed yesterday. More guns and wagon trains captured, and several thousand prisoners, among them Kershaw and Ewell and half a dozen rebel generals beside. Sheridan confident that Lee, with the debris of the "Army of Northern Virginia," will soon be bagged. . . .

April 8, SATURDAY. . . . For the first time in my life, I think, I have heard two of Beethoven's symphonies within twenty-four hours. The Ninth was rehearsed by the Philharmonic corps at the Academy of Music at three o'clock, and this evening I heard the Seventh at Irving Hall with George Anthon, who dined here. It was the last of Theodore Thomas's "symphonic soirées" (why does Mr. Thomas repudiate the English language?). We heard a "Passacaglia" by Bach (whatever that is) "arranged for full orchestra by H. Esser" (whoever he is); the "first time in America." Would it be a serious blow to be told it was the *last*? I honor Bach's name and works, but this seemed a mere exercise in counterpoint, clear and compact, but without significance or interest. Mozart's Symphony for Violin and Viola, with orchestra, was beautiful exceedingly, though there was little orchestra but the strings and hardly a trace of color from the wind instruments. Schumann's Overture to *The Bride of Messina* was rubbish and rot. . . .

April 9. Not a word from the army. This naturally makes one a little anxious. Nor have I yet any news from Ellie and her party. I rather infer from her silence that they have penetrated to Richmond. . . .

★ ★ ★ ★ ★

LEE AND HIS ARMY HAVE SURRENDERED! *Gloria in Excelcis Deo. Et in Terra, Pax hominibus bonae voluntatis.*

April 10, MONDAY. A series of vehement pulls at the front door bell slowly roused me to consciousness soon after I hurried in last night and routed me out of bed at last. I made my way downstairs in my dressing-gown, half awake, and expecting to find Ellie returned from her James River trip. But it was George C. Anthon come to announce The Surrender and that the rebel army of the Peninsula, Antietam, Fredericksburg, Chancellorsville, The Wilderness, Spotsylvania Court House, and other battles, has ceased to exist. It can bother and perplex none but historians henceforth forever. It can never open fire again on loyal men or lend its powerful aid to any cause, good or bad. There is no such army any more. God be praised!

To bed again, but sleep was difficult. Up early, stimulated thereto by the enthusiasm of John R. Strong, Esq., who was hallooing all over the house, hurrahing for Grant and "singing of anthems" after a fashion; that is, making well-meant efforts to chant "John Brown" and "The Red, White, and Blue." Find the correspondence between Grant and Lee in the morning papers at the breakfast table. It is creditable to Grant, who opened it, and not discreditable to Lee. Lee made a decent shew of coyness, and wrote quite a large number of notes. He was not altogether prepared to admit his position quite hopeless. But he accepted Grant's terms at last. They are most generous. Officers and men to be paroled, officers retaining their side-arms and private property. My first thought was that Grant had been too liberal. I would have waited a day or two longer, when Lee would have been without ammunition and without rations and ready to surrender at discretion. But I was wrong. Grant understands his business. Every officer and every private who goes home on parole under this arrangement will report, for his own credit's sake, that the surrender was unavoidable; that the Confederacy was overmatched; that fighting was useless waste of life; that the rebel cause was hopeless. Each will be a fountain of cold water on whatever pugnacity and chivalry may yet survive in his own home and vicinage. Thus ends Grant's most memorable campaign of eleven months.

Binney came in after breakfast. Then to Wall Street, where appeared at noon tidings (unofficial and not to be counted upon) that Sherman has occupied Raleigh, North Carolina, and a column of Thomas's army penetrated far into Alabama and burned Selma. If untrue they are merely premature, I think; facts a little irregular as to the accident of time.

It has rained hard all day; too hard for jubilant demonstrations out of doors. We should have made this Monday something like the 3rd of April, 1865, I think, had the sun shone, and could we have congregated in the streets without umbrellas. Guns have been firing all day in spite of foul weather. Uptown at two o'clock with William Schermerhorn to Forty-ninth Street for the Library Committee of Columbia College. Discourse with Barnard, Egleston, and Chandler thereafter about the School of Mines. Egleston subject to severe paroxysms of despondency.

On April 7, Lee's army was cut off. It was moving along the road which ran by the way of Appomattox Court House to Lynchburg; and leading elements of Grant's force, crossing the Appomattox River, planted themselves in front of the Confederates and brought Lee to bay. That day Grant sent the Southern commander a polite summons to surrender, and a series of communications passed between the two leaders. Lee knew that his ill-fed, ill-clad, exhausted army was rapidly falling to pieces, and that any battle with the great Union forces gathering in front and on the flank would be hopeless. Further bloodshed would have been criminal, and an interview was finally arranged on April 9. Lee waited in a little house on the outskirts of Appomattox Court House; and a little after noon Grant, accompanied by Sheridan and Ord, was ushered in. The Union general sat down and penned a letter offering to parole all Lee's men, and to permit them to keep their side-arms, baggage, and horses. Lee, donning his glasses, read it, and as he handed it back, he remarked, with what Grant later thought was "some feeling," that the concession as to side-arms would have a happy effect upon his army.

Though small Confederate armies under Johnston and Kirby Smith remained in the field, their surrender was now certain; and the North rejoiced over the triumphant close of the bloody struggle and the dawn of a brighter era. On April 14, at noon precisely, Strong's friend Robert Anderson raised above Fort Sumter, in the presence of a distinguished group, the very flag he had lowered four years before. But before the news of this symbolic act was printed in the morning journals next day, it had been thrown into insignificance by a catastrophic event.

April 11. No further tidings from Ellie, and none from the army. Our appetite for news has been gratified with such powerful stimulants of late that a single day without intelligence of great victory or gain somewhere seems a disappointment.

To Trinity Church at half-past twelve. A meeting of business men yesterday resolved on a *Te Deum*, and arrangements for a service of thanksgiving had accordingly been made, as far as they could be made on such short notice. I found the church already packed, and made my way up the crowded south aisle as certain marine mollusca bore into sandstone. Encountered Miss Kate Wolfe and handsome Miss Mary Ulshoeffer, and got them chairs from the vestry room. Service began a little after one o'clock. The church was then jammed to its utmost capacity, and (I am told) there was a dense crowd at its doors. It was an irregular, special service, conforming to no rubric, but the great assemblage joined in it heartily. The "lesson" was the Beatitudes. Vinton made a very short and a very judicious little address from the pulpit, enforcing the duty of forgiveness and charity. In alluding to the President, he used terms that do his insight credit: "Wise, merciful, resolute, Christian," or their equivalent. Many loyal men hold Lincoln a sensible, commonplace man, without special talent, except for story telling, and it must be admitted that he sometimes tells stories of the class that is "not convenient" and does not become a gentleman and the holder of the exalted place. But his weaknesses are on the surface, and his name will be of high account fifty years hence, and for many generations thereafter. The choir had been largely reinforced and did well, considering there had been no time for rehearsal. . . . The old *Gloria in Excelsis*, the old chant familiar to me since boyhood, was taken up by a thousand voices, sustained by both organs. It was most touching, noble, awe-ful to hear. The "nave-organ" played the assemblage out of church with Handel's "Hallelujah Chorus," "Hail Columbia," and "The Star-Spangled Banner," *fortissimo.*

To No. 823. Much work there. May we hope to wind up soon and muster ourselves out of service? After dinner to the Union League Club, where I presided over the committee on admissions. Copperheads of two years ago, and men who supported Seymour and McClellan last fall, are applying for admission. We rejected half a score of them this evening. Barlow and Belmont, O'Conor and Betts will soon be sending in their names, I suppose. We are discovering now with some surprise that everybody, little Ned Bell included, has been an "uncompromising Union man from the first." What a pity we had not known this a year ago; we should have been saved much uneasiness.

People hold the war virtually ended. It looks so. Lee is out of the game. Napoleon could hardly save Joe Johnston's army. . . . When Joe Johnston is disposed of, Lincoln should announce by proclamation that from and after the —— day of —— next, the Confederacy will be no longer practically recognized as a belligerent power, and that men thereafter taken in arms against the country will be treated as criminals and not as prisoners of war. He might properly do so forthwith, for the so-called Confederate government seems to have abdicated and to be concealing itself with intent to avoid the service of process. That power is reported to have emerged from a railroad car at Danville, Virginia, Monday evening (3rd instant), represented by Davis *Imperator* and two of his pals, all three dusty, deliquescent, and much demoralized. Since that date we know nothing of it. . . .

A rather lively theoretical controversy has arisen of and concerning Jeff Davis: Shall we hang him, when and if we catch him, or shall we let him run? Weight of opinion is clearly for hanging him, but he will save his neck somehow. Justice requires his solemn public execution. Sound policy would probably let him live, in prison or exile. I should vote to hang him. "We'll hang Jeff Davis on a sour apple tree, as we go marching on."

This choral promise and vow, so often repeated by so many thousand soldiers and civilians, should be performed at the first opportunity. Bidwell has long predicted that Jeff Davis, when finally cornered, would kill himself. The best disposition destiny can make of the scoundrel would be to let him be grabbed by some one of the organized bands of deserters and refugees who hold the hill country of North Carolina and Virginia. They would award him a high gallows and a short shrift, and so dispose of a troublesome question.

Even the *World* and the *Daily News* say that Secessia is now conquered, crushed, subjugated, and under our feet. They whine for forbearance and magnanimity toward their friends and fellow-conspirators. To be sure, we should be as merciful as we *safely* can be. The punishment already inflicted on the Southern people is fearful to think of. The death of their best (or worst) and bravest; the devastation, the breaking up of their social system, general destitution, the bitterest humiliation of the most arrogant of mankind, the most splendid and confident expectations disappointed, universal ruin, bereavement, and shame—these are among the terms of the sentence God has pronounced and is executing on rebellious slaveholders. Never, in modern times, at least, has so vast a territory been so scourged. Think, for example, of the scores of hundreds of families, prouder than Lucifer, worth their millions only *four* years ago, whose women and children and old men are now sustaining life on the rations of Yankee charity, whose plantation homesteads have been plundered and burned, whose husbands, brothers, sons, cousins have been killed, and who have to see soldiers that were once "their niggers" mounting guard in the streets of Savannah, Charleston, or Richmond, and prepared to suppress every Southern lady or "high-toned" gentleman who walks his or her own streets without a pass from some Yankee mudsill provost marshal.

April 12. Letter from Ellie at Washington. She has had a glorious time at City Point and Richmond. . . .

April 15, SATURDAY. Nine o'clock in the morning. LINCOLN AND *SEWARD ASSASSINATED LAST NIGHT! ! ! !*

The South has nearly filled up the measure of her iniquities at last! Lincoln's death not yet certainly announced, but the one o'clock despatch states that he was then dying. Seward's side room was entered by the same or another assassin, and his throat cut. It is unlikely he will survive, for he was suffering from a broken arm and other injuries, the consequence of a fall, and is advanced in life. Ellie brought this news two hours ago, but I can hardly *take it in* even yet. *Eheu* A. Lincoln!

I have been expecting this. I predicted an attempt would be made on Lincoln's life when he went into Richmond; but just now, after his generous dealings with Lee, I should have said the danger was past. But the ferocious malignity of Southerners is infinite and inexhaustible. I am stunned, as by a fearful personal calamity, though I can see that this thing, occurring just at this time, may be overruled to our great good. Poor Ellie is heart-broken, though never an admirer of Lincoln's. We shall appreciate him at last.

Up with the Black Flag now!

Ten P.M. What a day it has been! Excitement and suspension of business even more general than on the 3rd instant. Tone of feeling very like that of four years ago when the news came of Sumter. This atrocity has invigorated national feeling in the same way, almost in the same degree. People who pitied our misguided brethren yesterday, and thought they had been punished enough already, and hoped there would be a general amnesty, including J. Davis himself, talk approvingly today of vindictive justice and favor the introduction of judges, juries, gaolers, and hangmen among the dramatis personae. Above all, there is a profound, awe-stricken feeling that we are, as it were, in immediate presence of a fearful, gigantic crime, such as has not been committed in our day and can hardly be matched in history.

Faulkner, one of our Kenzua directors, called for me by appointment at half-past nine, and we drove to the foot of Jane Street to inspect apparatus for the reduction of gold ore by amalgamation, which he considers a great improvement on the machinery generally used for that purpose. Returned uptown and saw Bellows to advise about adjournment of our Sanitary Commission meeting next week. Thence to Wall Street. Immense crowd. Bulletins and extras following each other in quick, contradictory succession. Seward and his Fred had died and had not. Booth (one of the assassins, a Marylander, brother of Edwin Booth) had been taken and had not. So it has gone on all day. Tonight the case stands thus:

Abraham Lincoln died at twenty-two minutes after seven this morning. He never regained consciousness after the pistol ball fired at him from behind, over his wife's shoulder, entered his brain. Seward is living and may recover. The gentleman assigned to the duty of murdering him did his butchery badly. The throat is severely lacerated by his knife, but it's believed that no arteries are injured. Fred Seward's situation is less hopeful, his skull being fractured by a bludgeon or sling shot used by the same gentleman. The attendant who was stabbed, is dead. (Is not.)

The temper of the great meeting I found assembled in front of the Custom House (the old Exchange) was grim. A Southerner would compare it with that of the first session of the Jacobins after Marat's death. I thought it healthy and virile. It was the first great patriotic meeting since the war began at which there was no talk of concession and conciliation. It would have endured no such talk. Its sentiment seemed like this: "Now it is plain at last to everybody that there can be no terms with the woman-flogging aristocracy. Grant's generous dealing with Lee was a blunder. The *Tribune's* talk for the last fortnight was folly. Let us henceforth deal with rebels as they deserve. The rose-water treatment does not meet their case." I have heard it said fifty times today: "These madmen have murdered the two best friends they had in the world!" I heard of three or four men in Wall Street and near the Post Office who spoke lightly of the tragedy, and were instantly set upon by the bystanders and pummelled. One of them narrowly escaped death. It was Charles E. Anderson, brother of our friend Professor Henry James Anderson, father of pretty Miss Louisa. Moses H. Grinnell and the police had hard work to save him. I never supposed him a secessionist.

To Trinity Church vestry meeting, specially called, at half-past three at the rebuilt vestry office, corner Fulton and Church. A series of resolutions was read, drawn by the Rector. They were masculine and good, and they were passed *nem. con.*, though Verplanck and Tillou were in their seats—Copperheads both. I looked at the record of our action when Washington died sixty-six years ago. It was a mere resolution that the church and chapels be put in mourning. Our resolutions of today went, naturally, much further. I record to the credit of Gouverneur Ogden, whom I have always held cold-hearted and selfish, that he broke down in trying to read these resolutions, could not get beyond the first sentence, and had to hand them back to the Rector. There was a little diversity of opinion whether we should put our chancel into mourning tomorrow, being Easter Sunday, or postpone it a day longer. We left it to the Rector's discretion. No business was done today. Most shops are closed and draped with black and white muslin. Broadway is clad in "weepers" from Wall Street to Union Square. At 823 with Agnew, Bellows, and Gibbs. George Anthon dined here; with him to Union League Club. Special meeting and dense, asphyxiating crowd. Orations by George Bancroft and by the Rev. (Presbyterian) Thompson of the Tabernacle.[9] Both good; Thompson's very good. "When A. Johnson was sworn in as President today," said the Rev. Thompson, "the Statue of Liberty that surmounts the dome of the Capitol and was put there by Lincoln, looked down on the city and on the nation and said, 'Our Government is unchanged—it has merely passed from the hands of one man into those of another. Let the dead bury their dead.

---

[9] The Rev. Joseph Parrish Thompson (Yale 1838), scholarly Congregationalist minister of the Broadway Tabernacle, and one of the first Americans to attain high rank in the study of Egyptology, was esteemed for his eloquence.

Follow thou Me.' " Burnside tells me this morning that he ranks Johnson very high.

Jeff Davis has at last issued a manifesto. It is from Danville, before Lee's surrender and is full of fight.

April 16. An Easter Sunday unlike any I have seen. Drove downtown very early with Ellie, Johnny, and Temple. Nearly every building in Broadway and in all the side streets, as far as one could see, festooned lavishly with black and white muslin. Columns swathed in the same material. Rosettes pinned to window curtains. Flags at half mast and tied up with crape. I hear that even in second and third class quarters, people who could afford to do no more have generally displayed at least a little twenty-five cent flag with a little scrap of crape annexed. Never was a public mourning more spontaneous and general. It is like what we read of the demonstrations that followed Princess Charlotte's death, but with feelings of just wrath and aspirations for vengeance that had no place there.

Trinity was never filled so full, not even last Tuesday. The crowd packed the aisles tight and even occupied the choir steps and the choir itself nearly to the chancel rails. The outer doors, by the by, were in mourning, and the flag on the spire edged in black pursuant to my suggestion yesterday. Within the church, the symbols of public sorrow properly gave place to those of Easter. When we came to the closing prayers of the litany, Vinton proclaimed, "I bid you all unite with me in prayer for all the bereaved and afflicted families of this land, and especially for that of Abraham Lincoln, late President of the United States, recently destroyed by assassination," and read the proper prayer for those in affliction. He then prefaced the usual prayer for a sick person by a like bidding "for the Secretary of State and the Assistant Secretary of State, now in peril of death from wounds inflicted on them by an assassin." The effect of these formulas introduced into the service was telling. The anthem (Hallelujah Chorus) represented the ecclesiastical aspect of the day and was admirably well done. Vinton's sermon, or rather address, was far the best I have heard him deliver; extemporaneous, as he told us afterwards, when Ellie asked him for a copy. He blended the Easter sentiment with that of public grief most skillfully, or I should rather say by presenting suggestions of deep-lying truths that harmonized them. He brought out clearly the thought that had occurred to me and to many others: Perhaps Lincoln had done his appointed work; his honesty, sagacity, kindliness, and singleness of purpose had united the North and secured the suppression of rebellion. Perhaps the time has come for something beside kindliness, mercy, and forbearance, even for vengeance and judgment. Perhaps the murdered President's magnanimity would have been circumvented and his generosity and goodness abused by rebel subtlety and falsehood to our lasting national injury. Perhaps God's voice in this tragedy is "Well done, good and faithful servant. Thou hast done thy work of mercy. To others is given the duty of vengeance. Thy murder will help teach them that duty. Enter thou, by a painless process of death, into the joy of the Lord."

Southern barbarism has largely promoted our ethical education. What should we have said four years ago of Vinton earnestly enforcing on us the duty of hewing the (Southern) Agag in pieces before the Lord, not from personal animosity, but as a sacred obligation to be neglected only at peril of divine punishment, public and private? The whole service was a new experience to me. Men and women (poor Ellie among them) were sobbing and crying bitterly all around. My own eyes kept filling, and the corners of my mouth would twitch now and then in spite of all I could do.

Tonight Osten-Sacken, little Kate and her papa, George Anthon, and Colonel Howe, with a pocket full of telegrams from Washington. Seward and his son seem doing well. Sorry to say that neither assassin has yet been caught. There are reports that our policy at Richmond is to be changed, that the proposed convocation of Virginia rebels will be dispersed, and that some of them will be held as hostages against further attempts at assassination of presidents and cabinet officers.

There is intense exasperation. I hear of a dozen households whose Celtic handmaidens have been summarily discharged for some talk of rejoicing at Abe Lincoln's death. The New York Hotel was protected by policemen last night and today on its proprietor's petition. The President's funeral is to be Thursday next. Gramercy Park House dismissed a batch of waiters today, at Howe's instigation, for blind, foolish, Celtic talk approving Lincoln's murder. Horace Greeley, the advocate of pacification and amnesty, is as unpopular as General Lee. I directed my waiter to stop the *Tribune*. There are hopeful signs that the community may be ready at last for action against its Barlows, LaRocques, Belmonts, and Duncans.

April 17. Very busy in Wall Street, and at two to Columbia College meeting. A little progress made in the ancient undertaking of the "new statutes." Did any one of the pyramids take so much time to build? Also we passed and ordered published a series of resolutions on the assassination. Barnard drew them. They are plain-spoken and radical enough, declaring this atrocity, like the attempted incendiarism of last November and the systematic starvation of 60,000 prisoners of war, due to the brutalizing influences of slavery. They seemed diffuse, and too abundantly peppered with vehemence of adjectives, but it is hard to find words too strong for this case. Betts and Zabriskie recalcitrated, of course; doubted, demurred, and did not like the resolutions a bit. But they passed without a division. Thence to No. 823, making arrangements for the Sanitary Commission session at Washington, for which I expect to leave town tomorrow.

All over the city, people have been at work all day, draping street fronts, so that hardly a building on Wall Street, Broadway, Chambers Street, Bowery, Fourth Avenue is without its symbol of the profound public sorrow. What a place this man, whom his friends have been patronizing for four years as a well-meaning, sagacious, kind-hearted, ignorant, old codger, had won for himself in the hearts of the people! What a place he will fill in history! I foresaw most clearly that he would be ranked high as the Great Emancipator twenty years hence, but I did not suppose his death would instantly reveal—even to Copperhead newspaper editors—the nobleness and the glory of his part in this great contest. It reminds one of the last line of Blanco White's great sonnet, "If Light can thus deceive, wherefore not Life?" *Death* has suddenly opened the eyes of the people (and I think of the world) to the fact that a hero has been holding high place among them for four years, closely watched and studied, but despised and rejected by a third of this community, and only tolerated by the other two-thirds.

To Mr. Ruggles's after dinner. He's laid up with a very severe cold that has threatened to become inflammation of the lungs. He says, "the one consolatory fact connected with Lincoln's death is that he cannot pardon his murderer." Seward's throat was saved from the assassin's knife by the wire apparatus applied by his surgeons to his broken jaw. He is said to be improving. Edwin Booth, the actor, reputed an honest and loyal man, is said to be in the deepest affliction and humiliation over his brother's crime and to have declared that he will never appear in public again. He is in town and sent for Bellows to come and see him tonight as a spiritual adviser. Marie, little Louis's nurse, who used to take charge of poor Booth's little Edwina, called at his house, as she often does with Louis (who was quite a pet of Booth's it seems), but found only signs of consternation and misery. None of the family could be seen. Mrs. John Sherwood told Ellie today that she knew the late Mrs. Edwin Booth (a very charming, admirable young woman, who died some two years ago), and once asked her about the several members of her husband's family who had appeared on the stage. The lady spoke kindly and affectionately of them all, save and except this wretched caitiff, J. Wilkes Booth. Him she declared the most false, malignant, wicked man she had ever known, and this astounding declaration she made so frankly and earnestly as almost to take away poor Mrs. Sherwood's breath. Such is her story.

April 28, FRIDAY. The best part of an expedition even to Richmond itself is the getting home again and finding Ellie and the children safe and well, as I did at six o'clock. Dr. Vinton's nice son, Frank, was dining here, and there was reading from Haydn's second and sixth Masses and Mozart's No. 1 after dinner that refreshed me after my day of railroading. Tonight's papers announce that Johnston has surrendered everything from Raleigh to the Chattahoochie on the same terms that were given Lee. People will grumble. Sherman opened these negotiations several days ago and brought himself into sore disfavor. His popularity is gone for the present. . . .

Little business has been done in town these ten days. Never, I think, has sorrow for a leader been displayed on so great a scale and so profoundly felt. It is very noteworthy that the number of arrests for drunkenness and disorder during the week that followed Lincoln's murder was less than in any week for very many years! The city is till swathed in crape and black muslin.

[Here follows Strong's record of his trip.]

Tuesday the 18th, to Washington by early train. Called for the Rev. Bellows, and then we picked up Miss Louisa Schuyler and drove through two miles of silent, black-draped streets to the Jersey City ferry, where we found Wolcott Gibbs, Agnew, and his sister-in-law Miss Nash (a chief engineer of last year's Metropolitan Fair). We were invited to take seats in the special car set apart for the delegations on their way to the funeral. There were Moses Grinnell, Colonel Howe, Charles H. Russell, John Jay, William E. Dodge, Judge Pierrepont, and others; also Governor Andrew, with Adams and Ritchie of his "staff." A generous lunch was provided at noon, and the car being "select" was not overcrowded and comfortable; so our journey was less afflicted than usual. . . . In Copperhead New Jersey, few buildings—public or private—shewed sign of public mourning; but Baltimore was all in black. The humble shops and houses, past which the train runs, displayed almost without exception some little black rag, and every street we looked up as we went along was a vista of flags and drapery. I am told the traitorous mansions on Monument Square and the aristocratic quarters generally were profuse in weeds of woe. Perhaps they were put on as mere matter of prudence; perhaps Baltimore aristocracy sees that the cause it favors is hopeless now and finds in this great crime, committed in the interest of that cause and stimulated by Southern teaching, a good opportunity to change its front.

We entered Washington on time, for a wonder. Everywhere like insignia of sorrow. I got a breezy room high up among the higher ranges of Willard's by special favor, for the city is very full. Sanitary Commission met in F Street at eight P.M. Jenkins was plainly unhappy, nervous, and unstrung; he had no quarterly report. He had tried to write his report but had been in a state of mental torpor that made it impossible. Three ladies attended our session, Miss Schuyler and Miss Nash of New York, and Miss Abby May of Boston.

Wednesday the 19th was a bright cloudless day. All places of business closed, of course. Learned that members and officers of the Sanitary Commission (and of the *soi-disant* Christian Commission also) had places on the official programme and were expected to attend the ceremonial in the East Room, a privilege eagerly sought by all sorts of people but not solicited or invited by any of us. We went in a body to the office of the Secretary of the Treasury in the Treasury building. A delegation of our "Christian" friends reported at the same place, including that evangelical mounte-bank and philanthrope, Mr. G. H. Stuart of Philadelphia. They were an ugly-looking set, mostly of the Maw-worm and Chadband type. Some were unctuous to behold, and others vinegary; a bad lot. A little before twelve we marched to the White House through the grounds that separate it from the Treasury, were shewn into the East Room and took our appointed place on the raised steps that occupied three of its sides—the catafalque with its black canopy and open coffin occupying the centre. I had a last glimpse of the honest face of our great and good President as we passed by. It was darker than in life, otherwise little changed. Personages and delegations were severally marshalled to their places quietly and in good order; the diplomatic corps in fullest glory of buttons and gold lace; Johnson and the Cabinet, Chief Justice Chase, many senators and notables, generals and admirals, Grant, Farragut, Burnside (in plain clothes), Davis, Porter, Goldsborough, and others. About 650 in all.

The appearance of the assemblage was most distinguished. Most of those present were men of visible force and mark, with whom the bedizened diplomats contrasted unfavorably. The latter looked like gorgeously liveried flunkies. Of the religious service, the less that is said the better, for it was vile and vulgar; Bishop Simpson's whining, oratorical prayer most nauseous. When this was finished, the coffin was lifted and the assem-blage followed it silently, reverently, and in perfect order. All that was perfectly and admirably managed and executed, and it was all most solemn and decorous, save and except the spoken words. So ended the most memorable ceremonial this continent has ever seen. I count it a great privilege to have been present. There will be thousands of people ten years hence who would pay any money to have been in my place.

After standing nearly four hours, we were too tired for a march in procession to the Capitol. So we slipped off, and Gibbs and I watched the latter half of the funeral cortège as it moved thither along Pennsylvania Avenue. A great body of freedmen brought up the rear, marching in well-ordered ranks and looking quite as respectable as the Caucasian civilians who preceded them. We dined at Nelcker's (Buhler's) and held an evening session.

Two incidents in the East Room were worth noting: the Italian Minister (who looked like a green and gold scarabaeus on its hind legs) leaving his place to march across the room and shake hands with Grant in a very marked way; and Johnson, stepping quietly up to the side of the coffin, looking down a few moments solemnly and thoughtfully upon the dead face—a subject for some future Delaroche.

Thursday the 20th was wholly given to business. After the evening session adjourned, there was a conference about Jenkins. Knapp and he dislike and distrust each other so thoroughly as to neutralize each other and demoralize the Washington office. Jenkins is among the best and most unselfish men, but he has little executive ability. He knows it, and the knowledge frightens and paralyzes him. He wanted to resign six months ago. We decided to let him know his resignation would be accepted now. Newberry should succeed him, but he declines the appointment. Knapp would not do. We must take Blatchford, who has been long in our service at Boston and for the last few months at Washington. He is efficient and accurate, but so formal in manner and quiet in speech that I have not rated him very high. We called at Seward's today; he is doing well.

Friday the 21st. "Executive session"; that is, the three ladies were locked out. Jenkins resigned. I am sorry for him. He shewed himself morbid and sore and thinks Knapp has ousted him by some subtle intrigue, which is a great mistake. Blatchford elected and accepts.

Bellows, Stillé, Binney, and I waited on Andrew Johnson, *Gratia Dei* President, at two o'clock by appointment at his temporary executive chamber in the Treasury building. Before its door hang the two flags that decorated Lincoln's box at Ford's theatre that fatal Friday night. One of them shews a rent several inches long made by the assassin's spur as he leaped down on the stage. We discoursed [with] Maunsell Field a few minutes while waiting for admission to our audience. Field was present during Lincoln's last hours. Being admitted, we find fat Preston King and a couple of military men with Johnson. We were graciously received. Bellows said a few words as to who and what we were, and the President replied in substance that he knew all about the Commission and would further its operations by all the means in his power. We made our interview as brief as might be. Most favorably impressed by Johnson. The "incoherency" of the 4th of March is doubtless correctly accounted for as an accident, for he looks utterly unlike a free drinker. He seems dignified, urbane, and self-possessed; a most presentable person. Heaven prosper his handiwork. Left cards for Seward; he is improving. Mr. Fred Seward is not out of danger. Our Sanitary Commission session closed tonight.

Agnew brought away many anecdotes of Lincoln after a talk with Dr. Stone, his friend and physician. The story of his dream the night before his death as retailed in the papers, is true. It was of a "fine ship entering harbor under full sail." He had had that very dream before every great national success—before New Orleans, Gettysburg, Fort Fisher, Charleston, and other successes—and he was certain he should hear of some great piece of good news within forty-eight hours. A poet could make something out of that. When one McKim, a notable abolitionist, complimented him on some thought or phrase in his Emancipation Proclamation, Lincoln said very slowly, "Well, I should be a quack if I accepted any praise for that. It was Chase gave me that notion."

Saturday the 22nd of April unsettled and showery in the morning. Went at two o'clock with Newberry (Johannes Neuleigendis) to the government mail boat, the *City Point*, and down the river, stopping at Alexandria. Great crowd. . . . At one A.M. there was a knocking at stateroom doors and general commotion. Everybody tumbled up and turned out. A picket boat had brought us to and was lying alongside. Officers came on board and searched every stateroom for Booth and some of his accomplices, but in vain. We were all inspected and called on to shew our papers.

Sunday the 23rd, up early. Stopped at Fortress Monroe and then proceeded up the James River. . . . At City Point, we transferred ourselves to the *Red Jacket*, a boat of lighter draft, and went forward. On to Richmond at last. . . . Landed at Rocketts at seven o'clock in the evening. We found the Spottswood Hotel after a march of a mile and a quarter at double-quick, mostly through the burned district, a wide area of ruin still smoking. Just before we got there, we heard a familiar voice behind us. It was a small newsboy, evidently an enterprising emigrant from Wall Street or Chatham Street, tearing madly up "Main Street" and yelling " 'Ere's the New York *Tribune* and a-*Errald!*" I looked at him with profound respect as a missionary and a harbinger of civilization. Find the hotel rather full, but we got a room and what was called tea, and after a short stroll through the silent, sombre streets, I went to bed. Many secesh officers on parole infest the public rooms of the Spottswood. They are in uniform, but they have no other clothes. They have been ordered not to appear with their side-arms on penalty of arrest. They are silent and downcast. The sight of the greyback uniform and buttons seems to irritate our officers, whose feeling against Rebeldom has become bitterly intensified. They now seem to regard rebels as mortal enemies, unscrupulous, malignant, faithless, and unfit for any treatment but stern repression. Had they but begun to do so three years ago!

Monday the 24th was cloudless and cool, but direct sunshine even in April is far more potent at Richmond than at New York. After breakfast we proceeded to the Sanitary Commission office on Broad Street and spent an hour or two there. One Williams in charge. As there are very few sick or wounded in the military hospitals, he is issuing medical stores to civilians on medical certificates. The office was crowded with applicants, mostly women in black, with baskets. They were receiving Northern charity with little shew of gratitude, much as a hungry, sulky, ill-conditioned hound accepts a bone—uncertain whether to gnaw the donation or to bite the fingers of the donor. The women were arrogant and sour, but there were poor little children with wan faces and pitiful stories of sick mothers and of privation and misery endured for months. We decided to stop these issues pursuant to the resolutions adopted last week. It seems hard and cruel, but providing tea and sugar for sick rebels is no part of our legitimate work, and it strengthens Southerners in their delusions about their own supreme dignity and the duty of Yankees to take care of them.

Long walk out of town to Jackson and Winder general hospitals. They provide for five thousand patients and are well organized. Talked with rebel surgeons and patients and found abundant evidence to confirm what we had heard in Washington; namely, that while our men were dying by the thousands of slow starvation on Belle Island and in Libby Prison, these hospitals were lavishly supplied, more abundantly than ours. Their hospital ration was just double ours. They had dairies, ice-houses, and a great staff of official "matrons" with assistants. They had fewer luxuries—jellies, sugar, and so on—than our patients, but a more liberal issue of subsistence. Talked with many of the patients, Tennesseans, Lousianians, and Carolinians. All looked well fed and had suffered no recent privation. All wanted to go home, hoped there would be no more fighting, and shewed no sulkiness. The (rebel) Dr. Hancock in charge (associated with our Dr. Quick) felt the same way very strongly. Asked him if he'd ever happened to hear of Willy Alston. He said, "Yes. He died in my arms in that room, August 11th, of pyaemia after amputation at the shoulder joint." It may be some other Willy Alston, for the name is common in South Carolina. After returning, we walked through the ruined district and along the riverside, looked at Belle Island and the rapids, talked with natives—middle-class people who denounced and damned Jeff Davis with the most heartfelt sincerity of manner—and looked for bookstores; all burned up. After dinner went through that execrable Folter Haus, Libby Prison, now being cleared out; saw Turner's ugly mug peering out of a hole in the door of his underground cell. Walked to Rocketts and explored the hilly suburb in its rear. Lovely view of the city and down the river.

Richmondites are cowed and broken in spirit. The only utterance of Secheshdom I heard was from a party of little boys in an out-of-the-way street, who hurrahed for Jeff Davis as Newberry and I walked by; then set up a song how "Jeff Davis rides on a whi-ite horse, and so does General Lee." The former is running away as fast as he can, and the latter is living on rations issued by our charitable government. I hope he will go abroad and stay there. He can take service under the King of Dahomey, who sells his prisoners of war into slavery, or the Emperor of China, who disembowels them. No power (now that the Confederacy has exploded) can be found that starves them to death, so Lee will have to put up with a milder discipline and a more "humanitarian" rule than he has been used to.

Saw not the least sign of the spite and fury manifested by the women of Nashville and New Orleans when the vandals entered those cities, but perhaps the most aristocratic and blue-blooded of the daughters of Richmond kept within doors. . . .

Tuesday, the 25th, more explorations of the city and its surroundings. Grand review by Generals Ord and Devens. Lines extended near the whole length of Main Street—black regiments and white, alternating like the keys of a piano. Newberry and I sat in a shady place on the pretty capitol grounds and watched the performance, the intervening block or two of buildings having been burned down. It was a most significant spectacle. Opposite to us, that is, on the other side of the gravel walk sat a boy of eighteen in the uniform of a rebel captain, an olive-complexioned Southerner, with features that suggested Jewish blood. He was gazing over the ruins of the rebel capital, on the long line of victorious regiments parading in triumph, with their bands playing and their men bursting out in cheers now and then—regiments of liberated slaves among them—and he did not look as if he liked the spectacle! Occasionally, he would give us a furtive side glance, such as a subjugated wildcat gives a spectator whom it would bite if it dared. It was a look of malice and of curiosity. . . .

Dined frugally at the Sanitary Commission office and went down the river at two o'clock on the *Trumpeter*. Pleasant voyage. Landed at City Point at five o'clock and found quarters for the night on our Sanitary Commission barges. Benson J. Lossing and Greble of Philadelphia (Lieutenant Greble's father of Big Bethel memory) were guests of the Commission, and after a good plain supper, we spent the evening in good talk. Our work at City Point seems systematic and efficient, though it is growing smaller, I fear; Dr. McDonald is wearing out.

Wednesday the 26th, Newberry took our tug and steamed over to Bermuda Hundred to look for the famous "Bermuda Clay," but returned without any. Off for Washington at ten o'clock in the morning in the *George Leary*. Many refugees from Richmond and Petersburg on board, Americans and Germans, Amster-"dam Dutchmen" (*vide Blackwood's*); all most bitter against Jeff Davis and secheshers. . . .

To Washington at eight o'clock on Thursday morning, too late for day train to New York. Spent day at 244 F Street dining and breakfasting with Newberry at Nelcker's. City full of reports about Booth and Herold. . . . Interrogated on the train today by an officer of the Invalid Corps, and I produced papers to prove my identity. Very glad government is so watchful.

"No war news!" exclaimed Strong on May 2. At long last, the orgy of battle, death, and destruction seemed ended. Some fear existed, as May began, that Kirby Smith might still attempt a bitter resistance west of the Mississippi, but on the 26th his army surrendered. This sudden cessation of war gave the diarist a strange sense of vacuity. "War and rebellion have been the one great subject of my hopes and fears every hour for four years past. I feel strangely tonight and hardly recognize myself from the absence of anxiety about McClellan or Buell or Burnside or Hooker or Grant; from a new sense of indifference to the devices of Beauregard, Bragg, Lee, and Joe Johnston." Strong was little

interested even in the flight of Jefferson Davis southward, believing that his escape to some foreign land would be a blessing. "Catching and hanging him would be a national luxury, but it would be enervating. Our good-natured people would feel that justice was satisfied and would instantly begin treating Southern rebels with hyper-charitable magnanimity and inviting them to resume their old place and crack the plantation whip." Carried along in the wave of anger that overswept the North after Lincoln's murder, Strong believed in dealing severely with the South—so severely that it would feel no temptation to keep the Negro in a partial servitude, or to start another rebellion. President Johnson on May 2 issued a proclamation which accepted the charge that Davis, Jacob Thompson, and ex-Senator C. C. Clay of Alabama had been implicated in the assassination of Lincoln and the attack on Seward. Like perhaps most Northerners, Strong thought that the President would not have made such a statement without strong grounds. "If there be such grounds, even though legally and technically defective, rebeldom is not only dead, but damned."

Carried slowly back to Illinois, Lincoln's body was buried at Springfield on May 4. For twenty days the acts and principles of the dead President had been uppermost in men's minds. "It would be hard to find in history," wrote Strong, "an instance of mourning for a ruler so spontaneous, heartfelt, and general, and so conspicuously manifested." New York was strangely quiet, with business all but stopped and citizens subdued by the nation's loss. It seemed to the diarist specially significant that all along the 1600-mile route taken by the funeral train, marked respect had been paid to the organizations of colored people who joined the processions. No cheering was permitted, but Strong was told that whenever these groups passed, the sidewalks and windows became white with waving handkerchiefs.

Tokens of peace now appeared on all hands. Gold sank early in May to 136. Army corps were moving in to central points to be paid off and mustered out, and the demobilized soldiers began to crowd trains. In City Hall Park, which had been a desolation during the past four years, the recruiting shanties were torn down and grass plots laid on their sites. Despite all the shedding of blood, the private mourning for the dead, and the impoverishment of large groups, this was one of the nation's happiest springs.

May 11, THURSDAY. There is much dissatisfaction because the assassination plotters are tried by a military court and not by ordinary public methods of criminal law. The *Tribune*, *Times*, and *Post* are of one mind with the *News* and the *World* in this matter. There may be reasons for the course adopted of which we know nothing, but it seems impolitic and of doubtful legality. I hope nothing will be done to revive discord in the North. We have an era of good feeling now. Copperheads are silent even if still unconverted. It's a Golden Age after four years of Iron, preceded by a long period of Pewter and Pinchbeck. May it last unbroken, at least till we are fully reconstructed and Southern Congressmen return to the bosom of Willard's Hotel; then we shall have trouble again, of course.

English newspapers are full of comments on the assassination. It has clearly produced a feeling in London, Manchester, Liverpool, and other cities, never before created by the death of any foreign ruler. Hearty sorrow and indignation seem universal throughout all England. After reviling Lincoln for four years as a bloodthirsty clown, Albion has suddenly discovered that he was a merciful, honest, wise ruler, and that his death is a calamity to mankind. Now that he is dead and gone, her editors can afford to admit that he was a great and good man. But they prove to their own satisfaction that our success in putting down rebellion was wholly due to his sagacity and honesty and that the country must come to grief without him and with a "drunken mechanic" as his successor. They grasp at any straw of hope for their friends, the slave-dealers. To do them justice, they admit—or some of them admit—that this assassination, the hotel-burning plot of last November, and the robbery and murder plot at St. Albans, Vermont, do no credit to the cause in the interest whereof those atrocities were perpetrated. More atrocious than all of them together has been (I think) the starvation, on system, of 60,000 prisoners of war.

May 13. . . . News from abroad, a day or two later, shews that the heart of England has been most deeply stirred by this villainy. English newspapers handle the distinguished Mason's published letter on the subject without gloves.[10] They ask, rather pertinently, whether he really

[10] Former Senator James M. Mason of Virginia, Confederate envoy in England, had published in the London *Index* a letter dated April 27 in which, after declaring that the murder of Lincoln could not have been planned by Southern leaders and that the South would regard it with abhorrence, he added: "but they (the people of the South) will know, as will equally all well-balanced minds, that it is the necessary offspring of those scenes of bloodshed and murder in every form of unbridled license which have signalized the invasion of the South by the Northern armies, unrebuked certainly, and therefore instigated by their leaders, and those over them."

means to say that shooting an old man from behind and getting access by lies to the sick room of another man and cutting his throat in the presence of the women of his family while he is disabled and in his bed are "necessary consequences of Civil War"; whether he must not hold them justifiable since he declares them necessary; whether slaveholding ethics are not peculiar; and whether his statement does not imply that he believes the crime to have been perpetrated by rebels in the interest of rebellion. All which is bad for the Honorable Mason, F.F.V., after his four years' quest of recognition as a representative of a Christian power (so called). May these comments inspire him to another letter or two, and may he write without help from any brain less muddled and adipose than his own. Edge at London and Fisher at Paris write me under the deepest feeling. Edge thinks the people of England and of America "will shake hands over the grave of A. Lincoln."

May 14, SUNDAY.   Jeff Davis has been bagged at Irwinsville, Georgia! Kirby Smith hears of Lee's surrender but thinks it of no consequence and proclaims his intention to fight for the Southern cause in Texas and Louisiana.[11] Meetings are held and defiant resolutions passed in that benighted region. A Texan Flournoy pronounced a eulogy on Booth as the Brutus of America! Reporters admitted yesterday to the trial of the assassin at Washington. Their report is of little interest. A passage at arms occurred between a member of the court and Reverdy Johnson of counsel for some one of the caitiffs on trial. It shewed no high sense of dignity and propriety on the part of the judge. But the Honorable Reverdy Johnson has lost his taste sadly of late, and no one will regret that he got snubbed. . . .

Bowles (just from Paris), Lee, Colonel McMahon, Graham, and others, here this evening. Much good talk around the little supper-table. McMahon, who is on Dix's staff, accompanied the funeral cortège of Lincoln from this city to Buffalo. He says nothing in all this unprecedented manifestation of public mourning has impressed him so much as the sight that was frequent along the line of the railroad of some solitary husband-man laying down his spade or hoe or stopping his team half a mile away, taking off his hat, and remaining uncovered while the train passed by and as long as he was in sight. No prince, no leader of a people, was ever so lamented as this unpolished Western lawyer has been and is. His

[11] Jefferson Davis was captured May 10 by men of the Fourth Michigan and First Wisconsin Cavalry. E. Kirby Smith, commanding in the Trans-Mississippi Department, did not surrender until June 2, 1865.

name is Faithful and True. He will stand in history beside Washington, perhaps higher.

May 15. . . . There is a universal guffaw over Jeff Davis's involuntary abdication of his high place as hero, champion, patriot, and statesman, and his appearance in the new character of comic gentleman, running through bush and through briar, in the cumbrous disguise of hooped skirts that were the property of Mrs. Davis. His declaration after capture that he had thought the government too magnanimous to chase women and his wife's suggestion to his captors that they had better be careful or Mr. Davis would hurt them, provoke much laughter; so does Barnum's telegram to Stanton, offering $500 for the petticoats in which Jeff Davis was captured.[12] Barnum is a shrewd business man. He could make money out of these petticoats if he paid $20,000 for the privilege of exhibiting them.

May 17. Bowles with us at No. 823 this afternoon. His parts of speech are marvellous and would be past endurance if one forgot his energy and patriotism.

Another long letter from poor Edge, who is offered the secretaryship of the English Reform League, which advocates "manhood suffrage" and he wants to take the office.[13] But he is in debt $440, and this fact stands in his way. His debts have been incurred by fighting our battles by a series of effective pamphlets, and he thinks we on this side should help him. So we should; but raising the money would be uphill work. He says the effect of Lincoln's murder on English feeling toward this country astonishes him. Southern sympathizers hold their tongues, and the cause for which Lincoln died stands at last with Englishmen where it ought to have stood these four years. One of his statements is very remarkable: that though the words "democrat" and "democracy" have heretofore been almost as odious, even to English Liberals, as "abolitionism" and "abolitionist" were in this country before 1861, they are now freely and openly adopted by the Reform party. If so, the influence

[12] When Davis surrendered he wore male attire; with a shawl which Mrs. Davis had thrown over his shoulders. But the New York *Herald* printed a story of his "ignominious surrender" in his wife's clothing, and cartoons were soon current showing him in skirts and bonnet. One popular caricature pictured Mrs. Davis standing by and declaring: "Don't irritate the 'President'—He might hurt somebody!" She had never said anything of the sort. Barnum was soon making money out of a life-sized figure of Davis in woman's garb, resisting Union soldiers.

[13] Frederick Milnes Edge, a London journalist who had been in the United States during the war as special correspondent of the *Morning Star* and who had warmly supported the Union cause.

of America on England is far more direct and potent than I ever dreamed, and the sympathy of English aristocracy with any movement likely to divide and destroy us—even with a rebellion for the sake of slavery—is fully accounted for.

Another notable symptom is Mr. Punch's frank, ·self-condemning palinode. A more manly confession and recantation could hardly be written, and it is the finest tribute to Lincoln's memory that has yet been framed in verse.[14] It would be ungenerous to consider whether it is prompted by perception that the tide has turned. Let Mr. Punch have full credit for it, and it entitles him to a great deal.

May 18. With Ellie tonight to "Testimonial Concert" to Theodore Thomas at Irving Hall. Uncommonly well-flavored programme. It included the *Tannhäuser* and *Midsummer Night's Dream* overtures; Weber's *Invitation to the Waltz*, "instrumented" for orchestra by Berlioz (and for a wonder not flashy and flagrant); two movements from a piano and violin sonata by Beethoven; and the delightful little Allegretto of his Eighth Symphony. There was also a movement from one of Schumann's symphonies, handsome, elaborate, and artistic in form, but without a trace of life or genius that I could discover, though I conscientiously tried to find it. People who know more of the matter than I give his works high rank, but not one of them has ever interested me, nor have I carried away from them the memory of a single phrase, save one, a scrap of jig tune (not at all fresh or original) that he has worked into a laborious scherzo. . . .

May 19. . . . George Anthon says his clerical brother, Edward, has received a letter from a Georgetown clergyman enquiring for some vacant parish farther north. He says he can't stand it any longer where he is, because the ladies of his congregation are carrying about little card photographs representing Booth's head crowned with laurel. Can this be true? If so, how should such women be disposed of?

May 20. This evening at the Union League Club with Bowles, Professor Egleston (lately promoted to be a married man), and George Anthon. Private conference with Egleston. As usual he is full of tremor and perturbation about something the trustees either will or won't do about the School of Mines. With all his admirable zeal, energy, and

---

[14] The reference is to Tom Taylor's noble poem:
> "Yes, he had lived to shame me from my sneer,
> To lame my pencil and confute my pen—
> To make me own this hind of princes peer,
> This rail-splitter a true-born king of men. . . ."

disinterestedness, he is not a comfortable man to work with. Though he always has success and progress beyond our hopes to report, I always leave him with a sense of despair and disgust that we are doing so little. Bowles had much to tell about the dirty doings of Anglicizing and Gallicizing Americans of the Copperhead persuasion in London and Paris. I wish his statements could be printed. If they were, George Peabody and other notables of like grade would never dare shew themselves in their own country.

May 22. . . . After dinner to the Union League Club, where I spent an hour turning over volume one of Mr. Townsend's fifty or sixty dumpy folios filled with newspaper cuttings illustrating the history of the war. This volume covered December, 1860.[15] It seemed like reading the records of some remote age and of a people wholly unlike our own. So many notions were then put forward as axioms which are now seen to have been preposterous, and so many men were molluscous and invertebrate who were so soon thereafter transmuted into mammalia that we have forgotten their indecision and gelatinous quiverings of but little more than four years ago. . . .

May 23. College Trustees at two o'clock. I believe we finished the statutes at last. A medal should be struck to commemorate the event. Nothing very important came up. We were notified of a large donation to the library, a complete body of Japanese literature! One thousand dollars was appropriated to fit up the old buildings east of the College (heretofore leased as a paper-hanging factory) for the use of the School of Mines.

I think it will not be long before I make up my mind, unwillingly, to resign my trusteeship. The work that comes in my way interests me so much, but for that very reason I leave three meetings out of every four with a keen sense of depression and pain and disgust because the board is so amazingly inefficient and so unfit for its work; and there is no remedy during the life of a large majority of trustees. Many of that majority are severally energetic and intelligent, but they are so combined as to nullify each other and produce an inert and stupid compound, just as caustic potash and oil of vitriol unite to form a compound far less energetic than either of its components. . . .

[15] The Townsend Library, later extended to over a hundred volumes, was the work of Thomas Seaman Townsend. Efforts to purchase the scrapbooks for the Library of Congress failed, and they were acquired by F. Augustus Schermerhorn, who presented them in 1895 to the Columbia University Library.

May 25. . . . Newspapers full of the grand parade and review at Washington preliminary to mustering out a large part of the armies of Atlanta and Richmond. Two hundred thousand men, it's said, marched past the White House in column twenty-one miles long during two days amid vast crowds of spectators. . . .

May 29. . . . PEACE.

Peace herself at last, for Smith and Magruder have surrendered, if General Canby's dispatch to the War Department be truthful. So here I hope and believe ends, by God's great and undeserved mercy, the chapter of this journal I opened with the heading of *War* on the night of April 13, 1861. We have lived a century of common life since then. Only within the last two months have I dared to hope that this fearful struggle would be settled so soon. . . .

What a time it has been, say from December 21, 1860, when we heard that the process of national decomposition had set in with the secession of cantankerous little South Carolina, on through disaster and depression for four years and nearly six months, till today, with its tidings that the last army Rebeldom has organized out of the many hundred thousand men it has seduced or coerced into fighting for its felonious flag, exists no longer. As I look back now to Bull Run, Fort Donelson, the Seven Days, Antietam, Gettysburg, Chancellorsville, and other battles, I wonder my thoughts have not been even more engrossed by the developments of the great tragedy, that I have been able to pay any attention to my common routine and to be interested in anything outside the tremendous chapter that history has been taking down in shorthand.

APPENDIX

Strong's letter to Francis Lieber, dated from New York July 12, 1862 (now in the Henry E. Huntington Memorial Library), explains the need for a voluntary relief organization.

"1. The old Medical Bureau was, by the universal consent of all but its own members, the most narrow, hidebound, fossilized, red-tape-y of all the departments in Washington. It was wholly incapable of caring for the army when the war broke out. It was without influence or weight with Government. Lincoln actually did not know last September who the surgeon-general was. He said so in my presence.

"2. The Bureau was reorganized to some extent by Congress last April and an energetic young vigorous ambitious man put at its head. He is working hard. But the appointment of the new officers and additional surgeons under this act has been most criminally delayed, and without them the new surgeon-general is almost powerless.

"3. Government has heretofore relied on the Hospital Fund system —i.e., purchase of hospital stores with proceeds of commutation of rations. This has worked well with regulars, but our volunteer regiments have not had experience enough to get this system adopted among them very generally, or in good working order.

"4. In fact, I believe the sufferings on both sides during the last Italian war exceeded those of our men. They certainly did so in the Crimea.

"5. The social status, education, and so forth of our volunteer rank and file, the life they have been used to at home, the attention they expect in sickness, make things necessary for them which would be extravagant luxuries to the rank and file of any foreign army, and which it is questionable whether Government ought to supply.

"6. It is out of the question for Government to do all that is to be done immediately after severe fighting. It cannot be done even with volunteer aid. For instance, a regiment 1,000 strong after a day's fighting leaves say 250 wounded men scattered over a mile square. To attend to these there are a surgeon and assistant, perhaps a hospital steward, a couple of ambulances at most, and the band (if any) to take charge of them—all unskilled laborers except the surgeon and assistant. The medical stores are at some depot four miles off. Is it not clear that a day must often elapse before these men can all be brought in and even looked at by their surgeon? Of course Government can do something toward alleviating all this—for example, it can increase the supply of ambulances and can make the medical staff numerically stronger. Both these measures are being pushed with the utmost vigor by Surgeon-General Hammond. But even with *four* surgeons to a regiment it seems clear that there must be more work after a severe engagement than they can possibly perform. Government cannot establish and keep in pay such a force as will make its medical department fully equal to such an emergency. Hence the absolute necessity of volunteers during active operations.

"But Government is responsible for the most abominable neglect, and deserves the severest censure for allowing a state of things to exist among troops when at *rest*, when *no* fighting is going on, which renders volunteer aid necessary even then. That it should depend on private charity for the supplies for its hospitals at Washington is a disgrace. That it should put 2,000 *typhoid* cases at Yorktown in charge of a surgeon who could say, in answer to a question from one of our agents whether he had stimulants enough, 'Yes—that is, I have not got any *now*. They were used up very fast, they are all gone, and I have not made a requisition for any more. No, I thank you, you needn't send me any from your stores. The men die as a general rule anyhow'—that it should allow such a man to remain in its service one hour is a national crime."

INDEX

Abbot, Samuel Leonard, 275
Abingdon, Va., 354
Abolitionism, 3–4, 8, 54–55, 57, 62, 66, 69, 76, 84, 94, 105, 120, 128, 136 n., 160, 194, 204, 209, 216, 264, 282, 283, 298 n., 300, 344, 376, 392, 408, 452, 454, 467, 471, 473, 474
Academy of Design, 20, 21
Academy of Music, N.Y., 11, 15, 16, 19, 22, 36, 43, 47, 48, 65, 74, 91, 232, 310, 365, 373, 383, 384, 396, 494, 504, 577
Acland, Sir Henry Wentworth, 51
Acton, Thomas C., 389 n., 390, 424
Adams, Charles Francis, 107
Adams, John Quincy, II, 588
Adams, William, 277, 424
Adams House, Washington, 186
Adelaide, 155, 157
Agapius (Honcharenko), Father, 559
Agassiz, Louis, 6, 9, 215, 385, 394, 440
Agnew, Cornelius Rea, ix, 160, 162–164, 166, 168, 175–178, 182–184, 190, 191, 193, 194, 197, 198, 201, 203, 209, 211, 215, 220, 221, 223, 224, 226, 231, 233, 238, 239, 253–255, 257, 258, 265, 269, 280, 290, 292, 293, 298, 303, 305, 306, 312, 314, 316, 317, 320, 343, 345, 349, 353, 356, 358, 367, 376, 381, 385, 393, 410, 413, 414, 418, 421, 424–426, 428, 437, 439–442, 444, 458, 460–464, 473, 481, 486, 487, 490, 492, 493, 495, 501, 506, 519, 521, 526, 530, 531, 533–535, 539, 541, 559, 567, 570, 571, 584, 588, 591
Aigner, Philip, 184 n.
Alabama, 63, 72, 80, 90, 95, 108, 110, 113, 114, 142, 349, 407, 478, 579, 595; secedes, 83
Alabama, C.S.S., 311, 312, 465–467
Alabama, University of, 448
Alamo, 417
Albany, N.Y., 101, 432, 470, 488; wounded sent to, 231; draft riots in, 341
Albany Law School, 27
Albemarle, C.S.S., 517

Albemarle Sound, 206, 517 n.
Albert, Prince Consort, 391
Alden, Colonel, 141, 144, 147
Alexander, Appoline (Mrs. F. P. Blair), 151
Alexander, Harriet L. (Mrs. Joseph Henry), 88
Alexandra case, 377
Alexandria, La., 444
Alexandria, Va., 149, 152, 153, 177, 190, 195, 220, 248, 252, 324, 360, 362, 433, 591; occupation of, 146, 147, 151; hospital at, 172–173
Alexandria-Fairfax turnpike, 212
Algeria, 252
Allan, John, 372
Allatoona, Ga., 496
Allen, salesman, 36
Allen, George Featherstone, 65, 107, 110, 115, 117, 158, 168, 178, 192, 267, 286, 292, 293, 298, 309, 312, 316, 345, 363, 365, 457; death of, 352–354
Allen, Mrs. George Featherstone, 353
Allen, Horatio, 292, 353
Allen, Mr. and Mrs. Philip, 76
Allen, William F., 488
Allen's regiment (Troy), 156
Allen v. Schuchardt, 433
Alpha Delta Phi, 7 n.
Alston, William Algernon, 22, 62, 134, 140, 593
Alva, Fernando Alvarez de Toledo, Duke of, 489
Alvord, government agent, 212
Amboy, N.J., 88, 191
Ambrose, St., 356
American Institute of Architects, 492 n.
American Medical Association, 219
Amherst College, 550
Ancient Order of Hibernians, 371 n.
Anderson, commandant of Fort Gaines, 472
Anderson, Abel Tyler, 37
Anderson, Charles Edward, 584
Anderson, Elbert Ellery, 132

Anderson, Henry James, 263, 378, 399, 409, 435, 436, 445, 448, 515, 529, 548, 584

Anderson, Louisa, 584

Anderson, Robert, 74, 75, 81, 82, 85, 88, 96, 108, 114, 116, 118–121, 125–128, 133, 140, 277, 387, 573, 580

Anderson, Mrs. Robert (Elizabeth Clinch) 120

Andersonville Prison, 541

Andrew, John Albion, 129, 156, 164, 369, 478, 485, 588

Andrews, Colonel, of Marietta, Ohio, 394

Annapolis, 134, 185

Anne, Queen of England, 44

Annie, servant of Mrs. G.T.S., 230

Anthon, Charles, 100, 304, 346, 354, 397, 400, 402, 435, 447, 448, 507

Anthon, Edward, 599

Anthon, Emily, 251

Anthon, George Christian, ix, 3, 5, 12, 20, 21, 40, 41, 43, 48, 61, 65, 68, 73, 78, 99, 106, 117, 126, 134, 136, 145, 200, 208, 223, 226, 237, 245, 249, 251, 267, 268, 270, 292, 304 n., 305, 321, 354, 355, 360, 365, 395, 397, 398, 409, 415, 418, 423, 425, 427, 436, 452, 453, 468, 481, 486–488, 490, 498, 499, 507, 508, 510, 512, 521, 538, 539, 553, 565, 566, 577, 578, 584, 586, 599

Anthon, Henry, 87, 99, 304

Anthon, Mrs. Henry (Emilia Corré), 251

Anthon, John, 303–305

Anthon, Philip Hone, 305

Anthon, Mrs. Philip Hone (Theresa Hotchkiss), 305

Anthon, Reginald, Mrs., 251

Anthony, Henry Bowen, 87, 107, 112

Anti-Masonic Party, 282

Antietam, Battle of, 256, 290 n., 326, 355, 446, 475, 492, 509, 578, 601; battlefield, 325; visited by G.T.S., 260, 261

Antioch College, 232

Apollo Rooms, Broadway, N.Y., 315

Appleton, D., & Co., 9, 36

Appleton, William H., 9, 321, 390

Appomattox Court House, Va., 579

Appomattox River, 462 n., 571, 577, 579

Aqueduct Bridge, Washington, 212

Aquia Creek, 221, 239 n., 246, 248, 278, 318, 324, 437, 450

Arago, 353

Archibald, Edward M., 34, 51

Arctic, 353

Arkansas, 100, 102, 112, 140, 193, 208, 210, 214, 268, 352, 378, 382, 386, 395, 397, 405

Arkansas, C.S.S., 247

Arlington Heights, Va., 141, 149; occupation of, 146

"Arlington House," 154, 195

Armstrong, Kosciusko, 14, 306

Armstrong, Margaret Rebecca (Mrs. W. B. Astor), 73, 117

Army of Northern Virginia (C.S.A.), 328, 388, 418, 577

Army of the Cumberland, 366 n., 373, 432

Army of the James, 388, 519

Army of the Ohio, 355

Army of the Potomac, 184, 185, 196, 208, 211, 240 n., 242, 290 n., 308, 327 n., 330, 331, 350 n., 373, 388, 406, 409, 410 n., 416, 418, 423, 432, 434, 436, 438, 450, 451, 471, 472, 519, 537

Army of the Rappahannock, 300

Army of the Tennessee, 373

Army of Virginia, 168, 248, 250

Arnold, Benedict, 291, 479, 513, 536

Arnold, Major, 139

Arnold, Mayor, of Savannah, 540

Asboth, Alexander, 472

Ashley, drillmaster, 139, 159

Ashley, Elizabeth——(Mrs. J. J. Critten-den), 111

Ashmun, George, 27

Aspinwall, Lloyd, 132, 133, 420, 422, 424

Aspinwall, William Henry, 86, 101, 125, 203, 277, 293, 299, 429, 490

Astor, John Jacob (1763–1848), 9 n.

Astor, John Jacob (1822–1890), 20, 36–38, 73, 139, 194, 195, 239, 287, 295, 306, 364, 383, 409, 430, 434, 435, 512, 548, 549, 555

Astor, Mrs. John Jacob (Charlotte Augusta Gibbes), 73, 137, 140, 306, 424, 434

Astor, John Jacob (1864–1912), 222 n.

Astor, Laura (Mrs. F. H. Delano), 306 n.

Astor, William, 37, 73, 138, 222 n., 306, 416, 555

Astor, Mrs. William (Caroline Webster Schermerhorn), 18, 222, 416

Astor, William Backhouse, 39, 46, 73, 95, 117, 139, 306, 413, 548

Astor, Mrs. William Backhouse (Margaret Rebecca Armstrong), 2, 73, 117

Astor House, 101, 133, 137, 235, 522

Astor Library, 19, 30, 37, 46, 192; ghost in, 14–15
Astor Place, 41
Astronomy, 452, 457
Atlanta, 339, 355, 453, 456, 466–468, 471, 518, 522, 523, 571, 601; capture of, 477, 480–482, 485, 499, 513; burning of, 516 n.
Atlanta, C.S.S., 462
Atlantic Dock, Brooklyn, 29
Atlantic Monthly, 391
Augur, Christopher Colon, 440
Augusta, Ga., 516, 556
Aunt Polly, slave, 212, 213
Auschütz, Carl, 310, 383
Austria, 57, 407
Averell, William Woods, 467
Ayres, Romeyn Beck, 349, 350

Bach, Johann Sebastian, 578
Bache, Alexander Dallas, ix, 154, 159–60, 165, 167, 173, 180, 190–192, 195, 210, 211, 275, 280, 352, 363, 393, 414, 420, 421, 438, 465, 492, 504
Bachelors' Balls, 20
Bacon, George Washington, 346
Baillie, Joanna, 530
Baker, Edward Dickinson, 112, 148, 189, 190
Balch, Lewis Penn Witherspoon, 136
Ball, Black & Co., 141, 338
Ballet dancing, 74
Ball's Bluff, Leesburg, Va., Battle of, 189, 190, 206, 260
Baltic, 125, 134
Baltimore, 86, 129, 131, 132, 136–138, 140, 144, 150, 155, 157, 163, 166, 167, 172, 177, 181–182, 227, 237, 257, 259, 268, 324–326, 329, 330, 439, 496, 505, 510, 558, 568, 588; Clippers, 257; Constitutional Union Party Convention (1860), 26; Democratic Convention (1860), 24, 35–36; Lincoln assassination plot, 102 n.; Sixth Massachusetts regiment attacked in, 126, 130; Union-Republican Convention (1864), 453, 455, 457
Baltimore & Ohio R.R., 360
Baltimore & Washington R.R., 172
Bancker, Edward, 63, 67, 78
Bancroft, George, 20, 139, 291, 292, 307 n., 315, 321, 390, 392, 532, 584
Bank for Savings, N.Y., 33, 104, 105, 132, 246, 348
Bank of America, N.Y., 425, 428
Bank of Commerce, N.Y., 94

Bankhead, of N.Y. Club, 45
Bankhead, John Pine, 296, 538, 539
Banks, Nathaniel Prentiss, 22, 163, 170, 177, 184 n., 209, 226–228, 231, 240 n., 250, 279, 280, 305, 309, 324, 344, 366, 378, 431 n., 443, 449, 450, 512
Barbarities of the enemy, 174
Barclay, Matilda Antonia (Mrs. Francis Robert Rives), 73
Barker, Fordyce, 532
Barlow, Francis Channing, 132, 261, 328
Barlow, Mrs. Francis Channing (Arabella Griffith), 132, 261, 328; death, 467–468
Barlow, Samuel Latham Mitchill, 268, 297, 330, 349, 364, 405, 432, 449, 477, 481, 484–486, 511, 512, 581, 586
Barnard, of N.Y. Rifles, 148
Barnard, Frederick Augustus Porter, ix, 383, 409, 414–15, 425, 436, 447, 457, 486, 487, 507, 510, 517, 520, 523, 525, 527, 529, 542, 545, 549, 550, 553, 557, 579, 586; elected President of Columbia, 448
Barnard, George G., 342, 407
Barnes, of N.Y. Rifles, 148
Barnes, Joseph K., 174, 437, 503, 521, 527
Barnett, J. G., 426
Barney, Hiram, 312, 339, 345, 354, 381
Barnum, Phineas Taylor, 31, 143, 207, 598
Barnum's Museum, 12–13, 31, 355, 374, 522
Bartram, Colonel, 411
Bates, Edward, 26, 205, 304
Bates, Joshua H., 275
Baton Rouge, La., 241, 247, 324; occupied, 223
Battery, The, N.Y., 133, 434, 565
Battery No. 1, York River, 222
Baxter, George, 62
Bayard, George Dashiell, 279
Beach, Moses Yale, 9 n.
Beadle, Edward Langdon, 364, 409, 448
Beall, John Y., 555
Beaufort, N.C., 214
Beaufort, S.C., 193, 558
Beaumont, Francis, 491
Beauregard, Pierre Gustave Toutant, 116, 138, 158, 161, 168, 169, 171, 177, 213, 216, 223, 228, 229, 326, 459 n., 460 n., 492, 556, 559, 594
Beecher, Henry Ward, 372, 373, 484
Beekman, James William, 89, 164, 189, 203, 299
Beekman Street, N.Y., 565

Beethoven, Ludwig van, 11, 15, 16, 19, 22, 23, 91, 232, 267–268, 315, 320, 414, 422, 504, 517, 531, 568, 577, 599
Behring Straits, 435
Belden, Laura (Mrs. Dudley Field, Jr.), 32, 36, 538
Bell, Edward, 296, 310, 321, 514, 581
Bell, Isaac, 60, 139
Bell, John, 26, 41–43, 59, 60, 121 n.
Bell, Theodore S., 298, 299, 358
Belle Island, Richmond, 592, 593
Belle Plain, Va., 450, 468
Bellevue Hospital Medical College, 476
Bellini, Vincenzo, 23
Bellows, Henry Whitney, ix, 5, 101, 115, 131, 150, 151, 159, 161, 164, 166, 168, 172, 173, 178, 181–185, 187, 189–192, 198, 201, 203, 204, 207, 209–211, 213, 215, 217, 218, 223, 226, 230–232, 234, 239, 248, 249, 252, 253, 257, 258, 265, 266, 270, 275, 277, 280, 291, 292, 293, 298, 302, 303, 307, 313, 314, 316, 321, 325, 329, 332 338, 358, 362, 367, 372, 373, 375–377, 385, 387, 396, 403, 413, 418, 421, 422, 425, 484, 501, 506–508, 514, 519–521, 530, 533, 535, 541, 543, 548, 559, 567, 583, 584, 587, 588, 590, 591
Bellows, Mrs. Henry Whitney (Eliza Nevins Townsend), 223, 225; and daughter, 372
Belmont, August, x, 36, 73, 256, 268, 297, 300, 301, 376, 432, 473 n., 477, 481, 482, 486, 489, 498, 508–512, 532, 581, 586
Belmont, Mrs. August (Caroline Slidell Perry), 36, 73, 424, 509, 514, 555
Belmont Hotel, N.Y., 522
Benham, Henry W., 101, 234
Bennett, James Gordon, 121, 357, 499
Benson, Robert, 110
Benton, Charlotte N. (Mrs. Alfred Schermerhorn), 27, 137
Benton, Jessie (Mrs. J. C. Frémont), 28, 532
Berdan, Hiram, 222
Bergen, John G., 389 n.
Berkshire County, Mass., 260, 335
Berlin: International Statistical Congress (1863), 348–350, 377
Berlioz, Hector, 315, 530, 599
Bermuda clay, 594
Bermuda Hundred, Va., 458, 467, 594
Bernard, Claude, 34 n.
Bernard of Clairvaux, St., 356

Berrian, William, 2, 44, 118, 124, 276, 288; death, 272–273
Berrian, Mrs. William (Jane L. C. Dayton) 21
Berryman, Catherine (Mrs. L. C. Jones), 28
Berryman, Georgiana, 296
Berryville, Va., 491
Betts, George, 167
Betts, Mrs. George, 432
Betts, William, 12, 26, 38, 61, 98, 364, 365, 367, 381, 387, 391, 398, 405, 412, 413, 415, 447, 448, 485, 487, 508, 513, 524–527, 534, 535, 553–557, 542, 545, 549–551, 581, 587
Betts, Mrs. William (Anna Dorothea Robinson), 513
Bever, 20
Beveridge, Isabella (Mrs. H. D. Noyes), 230
Bidwell, Marshall Spring, x, 29, 61, 117, 124, 142, 283, 295, 335, 353, 465, 471, 581
Bierstadt, Albert, 21, 426 n.
Big Bethel, action of, 158, 160 n., 161, 166, 234, 278, 594
Biggs, George, 339
Binney, Horace (1780–1875), 86 n., 288
Binney, Horace, Jr. (1809–1870), x, 38–39, 85–86, 135, 147, 172, 191–192, 203, 257–261, 275, 280, 361, 414, 439, 466, 506, 543, 579, 590
Binney, Mrs. Horace, Jr. (Eliza Johnson), 86
Binney, Horace, III, 260, 261, 464
Birney, David Bell, 497
Bishop, Anna, 65
Bishop, Mary Richmond (Mrs. A. E. Burnside), 521
Bishop, Nathan, 311
Black, Jeremiah Sullivan, 74 n., 84
Black Republican Party, 58, 255, 473, 508
Blackburn's Ford, Va., 212, 213
Blackmore, British solicitor, 377
Blackwood's Edinburgh Magazine, 193, 594
Blaikie, Jane Currie (Mrs. A. H. Hoge), 562
Blaine, James Gillespie, 323 n.
Blair, Francis Preston (1791–1876), 547
Blair, Francis Preston, Jr., (1821–1875), 149, 151, 154, 162, 210
Blair, Mrs. Francis Preston, Jr. (Appoline Alexander), 151
Blair, Montgomery, 304
Blake, Charles F., 409, 483, 538

Blake, Mrs. Charles F. (Elizabeth Dix), 369, 374, 424, 538
Blake, William, 410
Blankman, Mrs. (Fanny White), 69, 73
Blatchford, John S., 590
Bleecker, Anthony J., 16, 111
Blenker, Louis, 151
Bletham, Captain, 220
Bliss, George, Jr., 132
Bliss, Zenas R., 224
Blockade of Southern ports, 127, 144, 145 n., 193, 210, 214, 329, 395, 454 n., 539 n.
Bloor, Alfred Janson, 231, 232, 421, 490, 492–493, 505
Blücher, Gebhard Leberecht von, 169, 246, 491, 575
Blue Ridge Mountains, 271
Blunt, George William, 336, 352, 375, 457, 465, 478, 492, 504, 534
Blunt, Orison, 375
Boïeldieu, François Adrien, 268, 396
Bomba (Ferdinand II of the Two Sicilies), 42, 55
Bond Street, N.Y., 566
Boole, Francis I. A., 375
Boonville, Mo., action of, 149, 160
Booth, Edwin, 76, 365, 531, 583, 587
Booth, Mrs. Edwin (Mary Devlin), 587
Booth, Edwina, 587
Booth, John Wilkes, 583, 587, 588, 591, 594, 597, 599
Border States, 64, 75, 90, 92, 95–97, 103, 104, 112, 117, 119, 121–123, 140, 271, 376, 378, 547
Borodino, Battle of, 213
Boston, 22, 55, 113, 129, 152, 156, 158, 164, 180, 197, 255, 275, 333, 347, 348, 367, 374, 385, 393, 395, 413 n., 415, 429, 447 n., 470, 495, 506, 520, 544 n., 589, 590; draft riots, 341, 348
Boston, 130
Bostwick, Mary, 4
Botta, Vincenzo, 470
Boucicault, Dion, 530
Bourbon, House of, 42, 392
Bowdoin, young, 18
Bowery, The, 41, 109, 128, 241, 587
Bowery boys, 524
Bowie, James, 417
Bowles, Charles B., 597–600
Bowling Green, Ky., 201
Bowling Green, N.Y., 565
Bowman, Alexander Hamilton, 459
Boyd, Lieutenant, 156
Boydton Plank Road, Va., 572

Brace, Charles Loring, 166
Bradford, Alexander Warfield, 16, 295, 364, 365, 376, 378, 383, 400, 401, 405, 412, 415, 427, 448, 457, 486, 531, 550
Bradish, Luther, 43, 44, 161; death, 354
Bradish, Mrs. Luther (Mary Eliza Hart), 338
Brady, James Topham, 29, 164, 482, 532
Brady, John, 164
Bragg, Braxton, 138, 285, 326, 339, 343 n., 344, 355, 358, 373, 374, 388, 398, 399, 406, 565, 594
Brandon (Bridge), Va., 461
Brandy Station, Va., 377, 438
Brannan, Mrs. John M., 17
Breadstuff, King, *vs.* King Cotton, 244
Breckinridge, John Cabell, 41–43, 52, 59, 112, 121 n., 247, 255, 330
Brevoort, James Carson, 46, 434
Brevoort, Mrs. James Carson (Elizabeth Dorothea Lefferts), 434
Brevoort House, 125
Brian Boru, 339
Brick Presbyterian Church, N.Y., 128 n.
Bridgham, Samuel W., 538
Bright, John, 468 n., 563, 569
"Brightwood," Washington, 178
Brignoli, Pasquale, 41
Bristed, Charles Astor, 298
Bristow, George F., 422
Broadway, 32, 33, 43, 45, 51, 53, 57, 59, 73, 100, 101, 125–130, 132, 134, 135, 137, 138, 144, 151, 162, 170, 177, 208, 216, 260, 274, 307 n., 313, 315, 320, 336, 341, 359, 360, 387, 411, 433, 489, 554, 566, 576, 584, 585, 587
Broadway railroad, 313
Broadway Tabernacle, N.Y., 584 n.
Broadway theatre, 507, 546
Broadwell, S. J., 275
Brodhead, John Romeyn, 143, 161
Brooklyn, 6, 271, 353, 565
Brooklyn Heights, 566
Brooklyn, U.S.S., 96
Brooklyn Academy of Music, 372
Brooklyn Navy Yard, 114, 116, 341
Brooklyn Zouaves, 152
Brooks, Erastus, 123 n., 256, 300, 333, 340, 349, 405, 426
Brooks, James, 58 n., 123 n., 256, 269, 302, 340, 349, 405, 408, 426, 512, 549
Brooks, Preston Smith, 103, 243, 549
Brookville, Ky., 254
Brough, John, 370
Brown, Sexton, 48
Brown, Clarence S., 151

Brown, James, 353
Brown, John, 1, 3, 8, 9, 11, 42, 84, 91, 94, 120, 128, 205, 216, 226, 266, 427, 544, 549
Brown, Joseph E., 495
Brown, Rev. Mr., of St. George's Chapel, 17
Brown, Stewart, 201, 203
Brown-Séquard, Charles Edouard, 492
Browne, William M., 89, 90 n.
Brownell, Francis E., 147
Browning, Robert, 391 n., 396
Bruce, General, 50
Bryan, Thomas Jefferson, 33, 306
Bryant, William Cullen, 312 n., 390, 514, 532
Buchanan, Franklin, 472
Buchanan, James, 1, 26, 54, 58, 59, 67, 69–71, 74–76, 78–80, 82–85, 87, 89, 95, 103, 104, 106, 108, 115, 138, 199, 292, 319 n., 561
Buck, Gurdon, 302, 318
Buckner, Simon Bolivar, 207, 355
Buel, W. P., 184 n.
Buell, Don Carlos, 202, 216, 258, 594
Buhler's restaurant, Washington, 393, 437, 506, 590
Bulkley, Ellen (Mrs. Philo Ruggles), 320, 385, 386; death, 558
Bull Run, Battle of, 168–172, 179, 180, 188, 195, 234, 264, 268, 278, 346, 446, 492, 601; reaction in England and France, 176–177; visit of G.T.S. to battlefield, 211–213; second battle of Bull Run, 249–251, 287 n., 446
Bull's Gap, Tenn., 446
Bullitt, Diana Moore (Mrs. Philip Kearny), 252
Bulloch, James Dunwody, 454 n.
Bunsen's burner, G.T.S. purchases, 497
Burgoyne, John, 329
Burke, Edmund, 8
Burke's Junction, Va., 575
Burkett, Colonel, 267
Burlington, N.J., 191
Burns, Mrs., 15
Burns, Robert, 491
Burnside, Ambrose Everett, x, 122, 153, 179, 185, 200, 202, 206, 223, 230, 243, 254, 276–282, 290, 296, 297, 308, 355, 367, 373, 377, 416, 433, 436, 437, 454, 469, 470, 518, 521, 546–547, 585, 589, 594
Burnside, Mrs. Ambrose E. (Mary Richmond Bishop), 521
Burr, Aaron, 479, 536

Burrill, John E., 29
Burrowes, 142
Butler, Benjamin Franklin (1818–1893), 155, 156, 158 n., 166, 167, 173, 176, 179, 192, 200, 215, 228, 283, 284, 305, 323, 379–380, 388, 437, 443, 445, 446, 458, 459, 467, 497, 509, 512, 514, 516, 529, 533, 535, 539 n., 546, 548; "Woman order," 283, 305
Butler, Charles, 297, 309, 514
Butler, Charles E., 223, 504
Butler, Rosalie, 223
Burden, Helen (Mrs. Irvin McDowell), 195
Butler, Sarah (Mrs. O. J. Wister), 209
Butterworth, Samuel F., 345
Byng, John, 289
Byron, George Noel Gordon, Lord, 92

Cabot, John, 485 n.
Cairo, Ill., 313, 523
Caleb Cushing, 326
Calhoun, John Caldwell, 479
California, 67, 80, 148, 191, 245, 290, 350, 433, 501, 502; contributions to Sanitary Commission, 267, 269, 274, 277, 279, 362, 391, 406, 413 n., 502, 516, 566
Calvary Church, N.Y., 266, 268, 302, 328, 522
Calvin, John, 356
Calvinism and Calvinists, 12, 525
Cam, 120
Cambreleng, Churchill John, 235
Cambreleng, Stephen, 235
Cameron, Alexander, 43
Cameron, Mrs. Annie, 117
Cameron, James, 188
Cameron, Simon, 112, 159, 162, 165, 169, 173, 176, 181, 182, 187, 188, 190, 195, 200, 201, 203, 207, 228, 259
Campbell, John A., 547
Campbell, Malcolm, 29
Canada, 1, 40, 473, 522 n., 528, 555 n.
Canby, Edward Richard Sprigg, 443, 444, 530, 601
Canterbury, 356
Canterbury Music Hall, N.Y., 73–74
Canton, Miss., 326, 407
Cape Sable, 326
Carey, Arthur, 117
Carey, Henry Charles, 192
Carey, John, 117
Carlisle, Pa., 259
Carlisle Barracks, Pa., 129
Carlyle, Thomas, 36, 351, 391

Carnes, Jessie (Mrs. R. S. Willis), 315
Caroline affair, 528
Carpenter, Mrs., of Philadelphia, 17
Carpenter, Charles L., 305
Carroll, Alfred L., 6, 51–52, 61, 75
Carson, Mrs., William A. (Caroline Petigru), 64, 68, 223, 371
Carter, Miss, 432
Carter——(Mrs. Ronalds), 432
Carter, James Coolidge, 315
Carter *v.* Taylor, 124, 142
Cary, Miss, 25
Casement, John S., 524
Cass, Lewis, 74, 84
Castle Garden, 224
Caswell, John, 370, 398
Cecil Dreeme (Winthrop), 158, 163 n.
Cedar Creek, Va., Battle of, 502–503
Cedar Street, N.Y., 565
Cemetery Ridge, Gettysburg, 331
Central Park, 30, 31, 106, 160, 175, 225 n., 251, 274, 490, 567
Centreville, Va., 170, 171, 202, 211 n., 214, 251; skirmish, 181; G.T.S. trip to, 211–212
Century Club, 113, 115, 201, 296, 309, 310, 315, 390, 392, 425, 496, 514, 542
Chain Bridge, Washington, 155
Chamber of Commerce, N.Y., 129, 143, 162, 167, 414 n.
Chamberlain, William, 212, 221, 232, 253
Chambers, Ezekiel Forman, 176
Chambers Street, N.Y., 565, 566, 587
Chambersburg, Pa., 259, 366, 468
Chancellorsville, Va., 309, 378; Battle of, 261 n., 316, 317, 321, 322, 326, 363, 438, 446, 578, 601
Chandler, Charles Frederick, 404, 485, 487, 517, 520, 524, 525, 528, 529, 534, 545, 562, 564, 566, 579
Chandler, Zachariah, 369
Chanler, John Winthrop, 270, 271 n., 290, 408, 426, 428, 486, 496, 549
Chanler, Mrs. John Winthrop (Margaret Ward), 2, 117
Chantilly, Battle of, 252
Chapin, Edwin Hubbell, 358
Chapman, Elizabeth (Mrs. T. B. Lawrence), 111
Charles I, 451
Charles Martel, 356
Charleston, S.C. (and Harbor), 86, 88, 105, 108, 115–121, 144, 229, 234, 236, 284, 308, 310, 312, 317, 329, 339, 344, 354, 356–360, 367, 371, 377, 378, 387, 468, 478, 495, 516, 535, 546, 555–558, 582, 591; Democratic Convention (1860), 22–25, 35
Charleston *Mercury*, 97, 555
Charlestown, W. Va., 266
Charlotte, Princess, 585
Charlottesville, Va., 557
Chase, 570
Chase, Carlton, 398
Chase, Salmon Portland, 26, 162, 205, 214, 230, 269, 280, 312, 407, 408, 473, 500, 526, 561, 589, 591
Chattahoochee River, Ga., 466, 588
Chattanooga, Tenn., 285, 339, 355–358, 363, 366, 367, 397–399, 409, 418, 437, 474; Battle of, 371, 373, 374, 378
Chautauqua, N.Y., 488
Cheeseman's Creek, Va., 221
Cheever, George Barrell, 4
Chelsea, Mass., 438
Cherbourg, 465
Chesapeake Bay, 130, 166, 361, 439
Chesapeake incident, 379, 383
Chetwood, Bradbury Chandler, 179
Chicago, 502; Republican Convention (1860), 26–28; Democratic Convention (1864) and platform, 474–475, 477–483, 488, 489, 491, 495, 501, 511, 515
Chickahominy River, 456, 461
Chickahominy swamp, 247
Chickamauga, Battle of, 355, 357, 358, 362, 366, 373
Chickering's Rooms, Broadway, 315
China, 56; state papers, 144
"Chinese Buildings," N.Y., 374
Choate, Joseph Hodges, 342, 417, 424
Choiseul-Praslin murder case, 2 n.
Christian IX of Denmark, 466 n.
Christian Remembrancer, 214
Christianity, early, 408
Christmas, 197, 282, 385, 387
Chrysostom, St., 356
Chrystie, William Few, 68, 76, 108, 121
Church, Frederick Edwin, 21, 110
Church, Walter S., 473
Cincinnati, Ohio, 252, 326, 495
Cisco, John Jay, xi, 43–44, 49–51, 124, 143, 162, 339, 345, 363, 366, 370, 399, 402, 407, 434, 453, 499
City Hall Park, N.Y., 270, 335, 560, 595; barracks in, 133
City of Troy, 461, 462
City Point, Va., 462, 464, 465, 470, 484, 486, 492, 506, 518, 526, 529–531, 537, 550, 551, 572–574, 576, 591, 594

City Point, 591
Clark, Alonzo, 34, 201
Clark, Horace Francis, 513
Clark, Lizzy, 137
Clark, Thomas March, x, 172, 178, 179,
    181, 186, 188, 209, 215, 257–259, 265,
    275, 296, 297, 393, 395, 421, 498, 505,
    506
Clarke, Bayard, 398
Clarke, Rutherford, 559
Clason, Augustus Washington, 106
Claverack, N.Y., 68, 73
Claverhouse, John Graham of, Viscount
    Dundee, 509
Clay, Clement Claiborne, 595
Clay, Henry, 91
Cleburne, Patrick Ronayne, 516 n.
Clerke, Thomas W., 21, 29
Cleveland, Army chaplain, 221
Cleveland, Ohio, 555 n., Frémont Re-
    publican Convention (1864), 453, 455
Clinch, Elizabeth (Mrs. Robert Ander-
    son), 120
Clinton, Charles A., 193
Clinton, De Witt, 193
Clinton County (N.Y.) volunteers, 162
Clinton Hall, N.Y., 410
Clitz, Henry Boynton, 235, 243, 245,
    327, 408, 459
Clymer, Meredith, 164, 218
Cobb, Howell, 54, 55, 100, 109
Cochrane, John, 177, 453, 455
Coddington, Thomas B., 384
Cogswell, Elizabeth (Mrs. James Dixon),
    86
Cogswell, Joseph Green, 14–15, 46, 192
Cogswell, Milton, 189
Cogswell, Mrs. Milton (Susan Lane), 189
Coit, Henry Augustus, 478
Cold Harbor, Va., 456, 459 n.; Battle of,
    444, 446
Coleridge, Samuel Taylor, 21, 23
Colfax, Schuyler, 369
College of New Jersey. *See* Princeton
    College
College of Physicians and Surgeons. *See*
    Columbia College
Collins, of U.S.S.C., 375, 470, 496, 519,
    520, 531
Collins, Wilkie, 41
Collyer, Robert, 194
Colorado, 415
Colson, Pauline, 7
Columbia, S.C., 398, 557, 566

Columbia College, 3, 7, 13, 28, 31, 34, 38,
    58, 61, 77, 98, 100, 110, 117, 232–233,
    263, 267, 269, 276, 288, 304, 312, 316,
    346, 353, 354, 362, 364–365, 367, 370,
    376, 378, 381, 383, 384, 391, 397,
    399–401, 403, 404, 409, 411, 412, 414,
    415, 417, 419, 427, 429–430, 435, 436,
    445, 447, 449, 457, 485–487, 503, 510,
    515, 523, 525, 528, 535, 538, 542–543,
    548–555, 557–558, 560, 576, 586, 600;
    Alumni Association, 550; Botanic Gar-
    den property, 38, 354; Christian Asso-
    ciation, 276; Commencement, 36; fenc-
    ing at, 263; fraternities, 7; G.T.S.
    mentioned for president of, 403, 407,
    409, 411, 414, 417, 419, 425, 435, 436,
    445, 447; Law School, 3, 7, 8, 12, 13, 16,
    17, 21, 22, 25–29, 31, 62, 65, 111, 117,
    146, 179, 269, 276, 288, 322, 418, 428,
    448, 497, 513; Library, 370, 391, 399,
    435, 503, 515, 529, 553, 579, 600 n.;
    Medical School (College of Physicians
    and Surgeons), 31, 34, 38, 316 n.,
    476; post-graduate scientific course,
    34, 38, 39, 316 n.; presidency, 397,
    401, 403, 407, 409, 411, 412, 414, 415,
    417, 419, 425, 435, 436, 445, 447–448;
    President's House, 7, 13, 98–99; School
    of Mines, 316, 367, 376 n., 381, 383,
    387, 391, 398, 403–405, 412, 413, 419,
    429, 485, 487, 507, 508, 510, 513, 515–
    517, 520, 523–529, 531, 534–536, 538–
    540, 542–543, 545–546, 548–557, 560,
    562–564, 566, 570, 579, 599, 600;
    University Course (1858), 316 n.
Columbia County, N.Y., 25, 85
Columbia Grammar School, 346, 401–402
Columbia River, 502
Columbia University, 30
Columbus, Christopher, 485 n.
Commander, 460–462
Commodore, 220
Commodore Nutt, 207
Comstock, Captain, and daughter, 576
Conciliation efforts to avert Civil War,
    64, 71, 75, 77, 83, 87, 88, 90, 91, 94,
    102, 103, 107, 156 n., 160
Condé, Prince de (Louis Joseph de Bour-
    bon), 347
Confederacy, Southern, 81, 83, 84, 95, 96,
    99, 102, 107, 113
Confederate Congress, 380, 389
Confederate Treasury, 381–382
Congregationalists, 40, 559, 584 n.
Conkling, Frederick Augustus, 271 n.
Conkling, James C., 355

Conkling, Roscoe, 271 n., 332
Connecticut, 19, 66; elections, 310, 510
Conolly, medical student, 221
Conscription. *See* New York City, Draft, Draft Riots
Constitutional Union Party, Baltimore Convention (1860), 26
Contest for national anthem, 142–143, 161–163
Continental Hotel, Philadelphia, 172, 191
"Contrabands," 155, 156, 192, 207, 212, 213, 462
Coon, H. P., 267 n.
Cooper, Edward, 115, 310, 390
Cooper, George Edward, 418
Cooper, Henry Woodward, 29, 65
Cooper, James Fenimore, 249, 417
Cooper, Peter, 40, 47, 52, 115 n.
Cooper, Thomas Colden, 138, 449
Cooper, William B., 29
Cooper Union, 55, 150, 310, 508
Copake Iron Works, 391
Cope, Caleb, 192
Coppée, Henry, 425, 447
Copperheads (Defeatists, Dirt-Eaters, Peace-Democrats), 87, 285, 286, 289–290, 294, 296–300, 303, 306, 307 n., 309–310, 319, 321, 324, 330, 337, 344, 345, 349, 363, 368, 369, 371, 375–377, 390, 392, 423, 449, 451, 457, 459, 467, 469, 471, 473, 475, 478, 481–484, 486, 497, 502, 507–512, 514, 519–521, 526, 534, 545, 546, 551, 552, 582, 584, 587, 588, 596, 600
Copperopolis, Cal., 277
Corcoran, Michael, 32, 132, 146, 155, 165, 169
Corday, Charlotte, 471
Corinth, Miss., 223, 228–231; Battle of, 321 n.
Cornell University, 448
Cornwall, N.Y., 337, 492, 496
Cornwallis, Charles, second Earl, 329
Corré, Emilia (Mrs. Henry Anthon), 251
Cortesi, Adelaide, 31
Corwin, Thomas, 66, 102 n., 107
Corwin resolution, 107
Coster, young, 239
Coster house, N.Y., 374
Cottenet, Annie Laight (Mrs. W. C. Schermerhorn), 2, 420, 538
Cottenet, Francis, 120
Cotton, 146, 178, 196, 244, 396, 443
Couch, Darius Nash, 329, 437
Cowen, Esek, 13
Cowles, Edward Pitkin, 151

Cowper, William, 92, 311
Cox, Jacob Dolson, 287 n., 556
Cox, Samuel Sullivan, 428, 497
Coxe, Arthur Cleveland, 302, 398, 514, 538
Coxe, Mrs. Arthur Cleveland (Katherine Cleveland Hyde), 538
Cozzens, William B., 415
Cozzens's Hotel, West Point, 492
Cram, Clarence, 110, 151, 195
Cram, Henry Augustus, 145, 286, 471
Cram, Thomas Jefferson, 337
Crane, Charles Henry, 17, 344
Crane, Dr., U.S.S.C. inspector, 260
Cranmer, Thomas, 356
Cranston, Hiram, 123, 513
Crater, Battle of the, 469
Craven, Alfred Wingate, 339
Craven, Augustus, 353
Cresson, John Chapman, 569
Crichton, British Guardsman, 223
Crittenden, S. B., 298
Crittenden, John Jordan, 77, 83, 87, 90, 94, 106, 107
Crittenden, Mrs. John Jordan (Elizabeth ——Ashley), 111
Cromwell, Oliver, 351
Crook, George, 467
Cropsey, John W., 46
Cruger, Mrs. Harriet (Douglas), 2, 566
Cub Run, Va., 212
Cuba, 77
Cullum, George Washington, xi, 47, 174, 180, 186, 191
Culpeper, Va., 213, 360, 388
Culpeper County, 146
Cumberland Gap, Tenn., 231
Cumming's Point, Charleston, 360, 557
Cunard, Edward, 434
Cunard, Mrs. Edward (Mary McEvers), 434, 555
Curtin, Andrew Gregg, 259, 364, 369
Curtis, Burrill, 280
Curtis, George William, 4, 27, 114, 143, 163, 280, 514
Curtis, Joseph Bridgham, 280
Curtis, Samuel Ryan, 268
Curtis, William E., 514
Curtiss, Cyrus, 370, 398
Cushing, Caleb, 54
Cushing, William B., 517
Cushman, Charlotte, 51, 365, 367
Cushman, D. A., 384
Custis, George Washington Parke, 155
Custom House, N.Y., 574, 583
Cutler, Henry Stephen, 125, 385

Cutler, Peter Y., 21, 29
Cutting, Mrs., 46
Cutting, Francis, Brockholst, 120, 151, 160, 254, 408
Cutting, Hayward, 151
Cutting, Robert Livingston, 65
Cutting, Mrs. Robert Livingston, 432
Cutting, Walter Livingston, 3, 20, 36, 41, 68, 75, 94, 105, 108, 120, 136, 223, 255, 328, 329, 408
Cutting, William, 27, 67, 151
Cuyler, John M., 166, 220, 260

Dahlgren, John Adolphus Bernard, 357, 359, 364
Dahlgren guns, 87
Dalton, Ga., 388, 409, 418, 445
Dalton, John Call, 34, 292
Daly, Charles Patrick, 16, 26, 29, 117, 202, 207, 296, 306
Dana, Charles Anderson, 197, 201, 352
Daniel Webster, 220, 224, 225, 231, 238, 239, 243
Danville, Va., 568, 571, 575, 577, 581, 585
Darwin, Charles, 9–14, 89
Darwinian theory, 452–453
Dasent, Sir George Webbe, 364
David Copperfield (Dickens), 381
Davidson, Harriet (Mrs. D. D. Field), 412, 413
Davies, Charles, 100, 365, 376, 381, 383–384, 402
Davies, Henry Eugene, 117
Davis, Charles Augustus, 306
Davis, Charles Henry, 438, 589
Davis, Henry Winter, 369
Davis, Jefferson, 77, 87, 88, 93, 100, 102 n., 103, 109, 113, 117, 120, 124, 136, 139, 141, 177, 223, 228, 253, 256, 264, 272, 283, 292, 294, 295, 308, 313, 323, 326, 336, 340, 344, 354, 380, 389, 396, 398 n., 471, 479, 484, 486, 494, 497, 498, 506, 516 n., 533, 540, 547, 548, 555, 558, 563, 565–567, 569, 570, 573, 575–577, 581, 583, 585, 593–595, 597, 598
Davis, Mrs. Jefferson (Varina Howell), 113, 598
Davis, John Chandler Bancroft, 139, 166
Davis, Samuel, 370, 398
Day, Henry, 434, 548
Day, Mrs. Henry (Phebe L. Lord), 434
Dayton, Jane L. C. (Mrs. William Berrian), 21
Dayton, William Lewis, 113, 293

Dean, 574
Deas, George, 141, 145, 160
De Bow, James Dunwoody Brownson, 396
De Koven, Henry, 19, 69, 71, 73, 74
De Koven, Mrs. Henry (—— Le Roy), 18
Delafield, Edward, 34, 38, 494, 506
Delafield, Lewis Livingston, 528, 570
Delafield, Richard, 47, 528
De Lancey, William Heathcote, 398
Delano, Alice Howland (Mrs. J. A. Weeks), 2
Delano, Franklin Hughes, 302, 305, 306 n., 307, 321, 349, 525, 526, 538, 539, 548, 566
Delano, Mrs. Franklin Hughes (Laura Astor), 306 n.
Delano, Sara (Mrs. James Roosevelt), 306 n.
Delaplaine, Isaac Clason, 90
Delaroche, Paul, 590
Delaware, 544; elections, 370, 511, 512
Delmonico's, 37, 39, 132, 245, 297, 420
Delprat, Henrietta (Mrs. J. S. Thorndike), 432, 555
Democracy, G.T.S. doubts on, 483
Democratic Party, 1, 22–26, 30, 33, 35, 39, 41, 56, 90, 106, 112–114, 117, 119, 120, 135, 151, 163, 165 n., 256, 262, 264, 270, 271, 279, 285, 286, 294, 296, 298, 330, 334, 340, 345, 369, 370, 375, 378, 407, 428, 454, 455, 466 n., 471, 473–475, 477, 479, 480, 482, 488, 500, 505, 507, 509–511, 513, 515, 561, 575 n. *See also* Baltimore, Charleston, and Chicago Democratic conventions
Demoralization of the Volunteers, Report on the, 180
Denio, Hiram, 33
Denmark, 407, 466
Dent, Julia (Mrs. U. S. Grant), 453
Derby, Elias Hasket, 13, 134, 377, 452
Desportes, Laure (Mrs. H. M. Field), 2
Detmold, William, 422–424
De Trobriand, Régis Denis de Keredern, 20
De Trobriand, Mrs. Régis Denis de Keredern (Mary Mason Jones), 88
Devens, Charles, 593
Devlin, Mary (Mrs. Edwin Booth), 587
De Witt, Thomas, 409
Dexter, Franklin Bowditch, 414 n.
Dickens, Charles, 391; *David Copperfield*, 381; *Martin Chuzzlewit*, 111, 184, 486; *Nicholas Nickleby*, 487; *Oliver Twist*, 237
Dickinson, Daniel Stevens, 35, 455

Dillon, Robert James, 307
Dimmock, Charles, 156
Dinwiddie Court House, Va., 571
Disasters, 1–2, 4, 6
Disraeli, Benjamin, 569
District of Columbia, Emancipation in, 216, 217
Dix, Charles Temple, 2, 21
Dix, Dorothea Lynde, 165, 173–174, 182, 260
Dix, Elizabeth (Mrs. C. F. Blake), 369, 374, 424, 538
Dix, John Adams, xi, 2, 27, 39, 70, 74, 84, 89, 102, 108, 124, 129, 133, 143, 161, 182, 264, 307 n., 325, 345, 348, 365, 369, 370, 390, 417, 423, 424, 430, 437, 443, 446, 449, 450, 455, 466 n., 469, 475, 478, 480, 495, 507, 509, 512, 528, 532, 538, 555, 560, 597
Dix, Mrs. John Adams (Catherine Morgan), 424, 455, 538
Dix, Kitty, 365, 369, 374, 538
Dix, Morgan, xi, 15, 16, 273–4, 276, 287, 363–366, 369, 370, 384, 401, 426–427, 434, 448, 469, 470, 486, 495, 520, 528, 539, 542, 552, 553, 574, 584
"Dixie's Land," 53, 121
Dixon, James, 66, 305, 308
Dixon, Mrs. James (Elizabeth Cogswell), 86
Dodge, William Earl (1805–1883), 512, 538, 588
Dodge, William Earl, Jr. (1832–1903), 523, 525, 526, 528, 538, 539, 541–542, 566
Dodworth's Building, N.Y., 2, 408
Doré, Gustave, 214, 261, 539
Dorr, Henry Crawford, 192, 296–297, 315
Dorr, Thomas Wilson, 142
Dorsey, Dr. and Mrs., of Hagerstown, 260, 261
Douglas, Jonathan Hancock, 177, 184 n., 190, 231, 356, 463, 464, 466, 472, 519
Douglas, Stephen Arnold, 22–24, 26, 35, 36, 41–43, 52, 58 n., 59, 67, 94, 121 n.; death of, 157
Dow, Neal, 372
Dower, George, 205
Dower, Mrs. George (Ellen), 205
Downing's Oyster Cellar, 21
Draft, 244, 246, 348, 349, 355, 369, 389
Draft Riots of July 1863, 332–343, 389, 390, 451
Draper, Mrs. John Christopher, 230
Draper, John William, 383
Draper, Simeon, 139, 158, 574

Dred Scott decision, 23, 500
Drinking, 18–19, 22, 23, 25, 166, 335, 352, 531, 533, 560–562, 591
Drisler, Henry, 346, 376, 398, 400
Ducachet, Henry William, 192
Duels, 33, 286
Duer, John, 368
Duer, William Alexander, 415
Duffie, Cornelius Roosevelt, 29
Dumas, Alexandre, 41
Dumont, Captain, 156, 157
Duncan, William Butler, 55, 71, 73, 120, 121 n., 301, 319, 349, 376, 586
Duncan, Mrs. William Butler (Jane Percy Sargent), 73
Duncan, Sherman & Co., 55, 71
Duncombe, British guardsman, 223
Dunmore, Charles Adolphus Murray, seventh Earl of, 223
Dunmore, John Murray, fourth Earl of, 223
Dunscombe, William Ellsworth, 44, 46, 50, 118, 140, 273, 274, 370, 392, 393, 399, 402, 470
Du Pont Samuel Francis, 190
Du Pont de l'Etang, Pierre, 333
Durand, Asher Brown, 21
Duryee, Abram, 155, 156, 166, 182, 320 n.
Duryee's Zouaves, 235, 320
Düsseldorf Gallery, N. Y., 382
D'Utassy, Frederick George, 151
Dutch Gap Canal, Va., 529
Dwight, James McLaren Breed, 61
Dwight, Theodore William, 13, 25, 28, 29, 33, 146, 269, 276, 286, 292, 293, 316 n., 322, 346, 428, 448, 559

Early, Jubal Anderson, 466 n., 488, 490, 493, 502, 503, 518, 557, 560
Ecole des Mines, Paris, 316 n., 403, 404, 507 n., 524, 560
Edgar, Mrs. William (Betty Rhinelander), 2
Edge, Frederick Milnes, 377, 465, 467, 563, 597, 598
Edinburgh, 356
Edwards, Henry, 87
Edwards, Lewis, A., 218
Edwards, Pierrepont, 532
Eggleston, George Cary, 444
Egleston, Thomas, xi, 316, 387, 391, 398, 403–405, 413, 507 n., 515, 517, 520, 523–525, 528, 529, 534, 539, 541, 548, 552, 553, 560, 562, 564–566, 579, 599
Egyptology, 584 n.
Ehninger, John Whetten, 3, 21, 99

Eigenbrodt, William Ernest, 495
823. *See* United States Sanitary Commission (823 Broadway)
Eisfeld, Theodore, 422, 568
Elections and campaigns, 19, 22, 41–44, 52–59, 70, 263, 264, 266, 269–272, 364, 368, 375, 407, 453, 455–457, 471, 473–484, 486, 488–491, 498–502, 504, 508–512, 526
Eliot, Charles William, 447 n., 448
Eliot, George, 9
Eliot, Samuel, 447, 448
Eliot, Thomas Dawes, 88, 210
Eliot, Thomas Stearns, 189 n.
Eliot, William Greenleaf, 188–189
Elizabeth, 461, 462
Elizabeth City, Va., burned, 206
Elliott, Ezekiel Brown, 180, 543–544
Ellsworth, Ephraim Elmer, 137, 146, 147, 149, 152
Ellsworth's "Fire Zouaves" (11th N.Y. Regiment), 137, 149, 152, 169, 174, 180
Elm City, 231
Elmendorf, "Unadilla," 3
Emancipation: of slaves, 192, 216, 217, 226, 242, 264, 368, 540; Proclamation, 257, 261–262, 268, 286, 299, 591; Bureau proposed, 288
Emerson, Ralph Waldo, 351 n.
Emory, William, H., 195
Enfield rifles, 133
England, 201, 282, 342, 381; contributions of, to U.S. Sanitary Commission, 407; G.T.S. disillusionment with, 262, 387, 452, 453; misinformation of, on U.S. affairs, 367–368. *See also* Great Britain
Englehart, Duke of Newcastle's private secretary, 48, 51
English language in America, 197
English Reform League, 598
Epistola Obscurorum Virorum, 509
Eppes, runaway rebel, 463
Ericsson, John, 210
Ericsson, U.S.S. *See Monitor*
Erie R.R., 20
Erskine, Thomas, Baron, 311
Esser, H., 578
Euterpe, 231, 243
Evarts, William Maxwell, 101, 117, 139, 514, 574
Everett, Charlotte Brooks (Mrs. H. A. Wise), 153

Everett, Edward, 26, 41, 42, 59, 153, 282, 391, 459, 544, 545
Ewell, Richard Stoddert, 577

Fabbri, Inez, 56, 65
Faile, Thomas Hall, Jr., 231, 317
Fair Oaks, Battle of (Seven Pines, Va.), 228–230, 232 n., 438
Fairfax Court House, Va., 160, 161, 164, 168; G.T.S. at, 212; skirmish at, 154, 155
Falmouth, Va., 281, 318
Faneuil Hall, Boston, 123
Fanshawe, George A., 397
Fanshawe, William Snell, 397, 398, 400, 402
Farragut, David Glasgow, 224 n., 225 n., 228, 310, 472, 474, 477, 488, 499, 502, 531, 589
Farragut, Mrs. David Glasgow (Virginia Loyall), 531
Faulkner, Kenzua director, 583
Faulkner, Charles James, 208
Fauntleroy, Charles M., 160
Fay, Francis Ball, 438
Fayettville, N.C., 565
Fearing, Charles, 430, 434
Fearing, Daniel Butler, 5, 15, 18, 91, 105, 254
Fearing, George, 254
Fearing, Henry Seymour, 41, 63, 327
Fearing, Mrs. Henry Seymour (Serena Mason Jones), 2, 538
Fearing, Kate, 121
Federalists, black cockade, 299
Felton, Cornelius Conway, 151
Fenton, Reuben Eaton, 488, 502, 512, 536, 541
Ferdinand II of the Two Sicilies, 42, 55
Fessenden, William Pitt, 291
Field, Cyrus West, 2 n., 47, 162
Field, David Dudley (1805–1894), 2 n., 76, 103, 338
Field, Mrs. David Dudley (Harriet Davidson), 412, 431
Field, Dudley, Jr. (1830–1880), 32, 36, 133, 338
Field, Mrs. Dudley, Jr. (Laura Belden), 32, 36, 538
Field, Henry Martyn, 2 n.
Field, Mrs. Henry Martyn (Laure Desportes), 2
Field, Jenny, 32
Field, Maunsell Bradhurst, 40, 43, 44, 101, 142, 161, 163, 591
Field, Rachel, 2 n.

Fifth Avenue, 2, 45, 46, 114, 117, 125, 274, 335–337, 409, 416, 567
Fifth Avenue Hotel, 43, 49, 50, 125, 509, 516, 522
Fillmore, Millard, 49
Financial worries of G.T.S., 182, 201, 370–371, 460
Finley, Clement Alexander, 173, 181, 182, 184–188, 190, 193, 194, 196, 197, 204, 217, 306 n.
Fire engines, steam, 6
Fires, 6, 16, 87, 335–340, 522
Fish, Elizabeth Stuyvesant (Mrs. F. S. G. d'Hauteville), 279, 415–416, 419
Fish, Hamilton, xi, 20, 33, 38, 43, 47–8, 73, 77, 87, 96, 101, 117, 129, 143, 161, 233, 299, 305–306, 365, 376, 382, 383, 398, 401–403, 415, 430, 448, 490, 499, 525, 528, 542–545, 549, 550, 552–558, 566, 575
Fish, Mrs. Hamilton (Julia Kean), 382, 391, 403
Fish, Sarah Morris (Mrs. Sidney Webster), 33
Fish, Susan Le Roy, 382
Fisher, 597
Fisher, Dr., 541
Fisher's Hill, Va., Battle of, 488, 493
Five Forks, Va., Battle of, 573
Flags, display of, 135
Flax cotton, 178
Fletcher, John, 491
Flint, Austin, 234
Florence, Ala., 206
Florida, 63, 79 n., 83, 226, 280, 386
Florida, 293
Floyd, John Buchanan, 26, 82, 92, 99, 100, 109, 115, 199, 207, 243, 346; death, 354
Flushing, L.I., 266
Folsom, George, 101
Foote, Henry S., 531, 532
Ford's Theatre, Washington, 590
Formes, Karl Johannes, 56, 65, 494
Forrest, Nathan Bedford, 407
Forsha, a quack, 304
Forsyth, John, 114
Fort Adams, R.I., 247
Fort Darling, Va., 576
Fort Donelson, Cumberland River, 206, 208, 216, 236; capture of, 199, 207, 601
Fort Ellsworth, Alexandria, 173, 195
Fort Fisher, N.C., 533, 534, 539 n., 546, 591
Fort Gaines, Mobile, Ala., 472, 477
Fort Greene Park, Brooklyn, 565

Fort Hamilton, Brooklyn, 114, 115, 243
Fort Henry, Tennessee River, 206, 216; capture of, 199, 205
Fort Jackson, La., 224 n.
Fort Johnson, Charleston Harbor, 367
Fort Lafayette, N.Y. Harbor, 206, 394, 504
Fort Leavenworth, Kans., 87
Fort McAllister, Ga., 530
Fort McHenry, Baltimore, 131, 150, 163, 182
Fort Macon, N.C., surrender of, 223
Fort[ress] Monroe, Old Point Comfort, Va., 155, 156, 166, 167, 173, 185, 187, 199, 209, 210, 216, 220, 222, 238, 246, 316, 380, 439, 498, 591
Fort Morgan, Mobile, Ala., 116, 472 n., 477, 478
Fort Moultrie, Charleston Harbor, 58, 72, 74, 78, 81, 82, 116, 126, 367
Fort Pickens, Pensacola Bay, 114–116, 195, 292
Fort Pillow, Tenn., 464
Fort Powell, Ala., 472
Fort Powhatan, Va., 462
Fort Pulaski, Savannah, 116
Fort St. Philip, La., 224 n.
Fort Stedman, Va., 569 n., 570, 572
Fort Sumter, Charleston Harbor, 81, 82, 84, 85, 96, 100, 104, 105, 107–110, 114–117, 122, 292, 310, 312, 356, 357, 359, 367, 387, 408, 485, 507, 558, 573; bombardment of, 116, 118–119, 583; surrender of, 120; flag of, 126; reoccupied, 556, 557; Anderson raises U.S. flag again, 580
Fort Wagner, S.C., 360, 361
Fort Washington, Md., 220
Fort Wayne R.R., 430
Foster, Jacob Post Giraud, 63, 166, 528
Foster, John Gray, 278, 310, 325, 330, 373, 495
Foster, Mrs. John Gray, 209
Foster, Lafayette Sabine, 87, 107, 108, 111, 114, 209, 395
Foster, Mrs. Lafayette Sabine (Martha Lyman), 114, 209
Fouqué, Friedrich, Baron de la Motte, *Sintram*, 237; *Undine*, 237
Fourth Avenue, N.Y., 587
Fourth Street, N.Y., 566
Fowler, Dr., of Montgomery, Ala., 267
Fowler, Isaac Vanderbeck, 26, 27, 31, 39
Fox, Gustavus Vasa, 116, 454 n.
Foxe, John, 515

France, 353, 540; intervention of, 205, 206, 236, 238; U.S. relations with, 279, 299; Army of, in Mexico, 443, 547; Protestant clergy of, oppose slavery, 313; Reign of Terror in, 489; Revolution in, 494

Francia, José Gaspar Rodriguez, 489

Francis, John Wakefield, 99

Frank Leslie's Illustrated Newspaper, 3

Franklin, Tenn., Battle of, 524

Franklin, William Buel, 221, 254, 277, 290, 297, 366, 471

Frederick, Md., 253, 256, 324, 465

Frederick the Great, 347, 351

Fredericksburg, Va., 230, 246, 277, 308, 316, 318, 437, 450, 468, 507 n., 524; Battle of, 279 n.–282, 285, 297, 578

Free-soilers, 1, 8, 76, 352

Freedmen, 590

Freiburg School of Mines, 560

Frémont, John Charles, 28, 177, 182–184, 188, 189 n., 191, 228, 231, 240 n., 250, 289, 339, 350 n., 407, 453, 455, 473

Frémont, Mrs. John Charles (Jessie Benton), 28, 532

French, Lewis, 328

French, William Henry, 329

Friar Gerund, 372

Front Royal, Va., 227

Frothington, of Brooklyn, 390

Frothington, Octavius Brooks, 2

Fry, James Barnet, 530

Fry, William Henry, 111, 113

Fugitive Slave Law, 64, 68, 77

Fuller, Dudley B., 349, 353

Fuller, Thomas, 483

Fulton, U.S.S., 556

Furness, William Henry, 192

Gade, Niels Wilhelm, 315, 382, 414

Gaines's Mill, Va., Battle of, 235

Galena, U.S.S., 225

Gallatin, Mrs., 432

Gallatin, Albert, 374

Gallatin, Albert, Jr., 374

Gallatin, James, 374

Gambling. *See* Raffling

Garibaldi, Giuseppe, 33, 42

Garibaldi Guard, 151

Garter, Order of the, 457

Gautier's restaurant, Washington, 437

Gavitt, Joseph F., 5

Gay, Sidney Howard, 554

General Theological Seminary, 37, 176, 295, 384, 398; students, 438

Geneva, 356

Gentil, Theodore, 144, 147

Gentil, Mrs. Theodore, 432

George III of England, 47

George Leary, 576, 594

Georgetown, D.C., 599; hospitals at, 172–173

Georgia, 8, 57, 58, 62, 63, 74, 78, 83, 90, 99, 110, 142, 193, 226, 358, 374, 388, 453, 456, 478, 485, 495, 505, 522, 530, 531, 541. *See also* Sherman, W. T.

Georgia, C.S.S., 481

Gerard, James Watson, 32, 526

German regiments, 317

German, Theatre, N.Y., 265, 268

Germanna Ford, Va., 438

Germans in U.S., 6, 55, 96, 111, 142, 144, 151, 343, 375 n., 383, 458, 479, 480, 594

Gerolt, Friedrich von, Baron, 350

Gerry, Elbridge Thomas, 359

Gettysburg, Battle of, 327–332, 338, 355, 374, 388, 395, 405, 446, 591, 601

Gettysburg Seminary, 395

Ghosts, 14–15

Gibbes, Charlotte Augusta (Mrs. J. J. Astor), 73, 137, 140, 306, 424, 434

Gibbs, George, 172, 292, 433

Gibbs, Laura Wolcott (Mrs. T. M. d'Oremieulx), 515

Gibbs, [Oliver] Wolcott, xii, 5, 19, 37, 158–160, 162–164, 166, 167, 171, 172, 177, 178, 182–184, 190, 192, 198, 201, 209, 211, 215, 217, 223, 226, 231, 232, 257, 265, 275, 276, 280, 286, 288, 292, 293, 298, 303, 305, 307 n., 314, 317, 336, 337, 345, 363, 365, 367, 393, 414, 421, 425, 426, 435, 437, 438, 452, 471, 519, 520, 535, 584, 588, 590

Gibbs, Mrs. Wolcott (Josephine Mauran), 336

Gibert, Frederick E., 200

Giddings, Joshua Reed, 67

Gilchrist, Alexander, 410

Gillmore, Quincy Adams, 357 n., 359, 360, 364, 367, 378, 388, 458, 557

Gilman, Chandler Robbins, 34, 38, 39

Gilman House, Baltimore, 172

Gilmore collecton, School of Mines, 515

Gilson, Helen Louise, 238, 438–439

Gimbrede, Joseph N., 44

Girard House, Philadelphia, 85

Gist, William H., 59, 68

Goddard, Mrs., 315

Goddard, Robert Hale Ives, 153

Goddard, Thomas Poynton Ives, 518

Godwin, Parke, 381, 504, 514

Goelet, Peter, 359
Goethe, Johann Wolfgang von, 17, 92
Golden Gate, 245
Goldsboro, N.C., 557, 570, 577
Goldsborough, Louis Malesherbes, 589
Goodhue & Co., 414 n.
Gordon, Charles George, 301 n.
Gordon, John Brown, 328 n., 569
Gordon, Nathaniel P., 208–209
Gordonsville, Va., 243, 258, 278, 446
Gosse, Philip Henry, 35
Gottschalk, Louis Moreau, 207–208
Gould, Benjamin Apthorp, 325, 543
Gould, Charles, 297–298, 312, 319
Gouley, John William Severin, 275
Gounod, Charles François, 384
Governor's Island, 114, 115, 121, 259, 510
Grace Church, Baltimore, 360
Grace Church, N.Y., 288, 353
Graham, William, 278, 538, 597
Gramercy Park, 132, 208, 291, 338, 340–342, 409
Gramercy Park House, 340, 586
Grant, Ulysses Simpson, 199, 208, 216, 217, 285, 287 n., 309, 311 n., 313, 321, 324, 326, 332, 347, 352, 354, 366, 373, 374, 383, 388, 397, 409, 415, 416, 418, 423, 432–434, 436, 437, 439, 442–447, 449, 450, 452–456, 458–460 n., 462–472, 474, 475, 477, 484, 491, 492, 494–497, 499, 502, 506, 516 n., 518, 526, 533, 537, 546, 547, 556, 557, 560, 563, 564, 568–573, 577–580, 584, 589, 590, 594; G.T.S. visits, 463
Grant, Mrs. Ulysses Simpson (Julia Dent), 453
Gray, Dr., 298
Gray, George Griswold, 381, 387, 420, 422, 424, 426, 576
Gray, George Winthrop, 372
Great Barrington, Mass., 37, 38, 41, 179
Great Bethel. *See* Big Bethel
Great Britain: U.S. relations with, 52, 72–73, 143, 145–146, 192–194, 196–198, 201, 205, 209, 214, 226, 236, 299–300, 311–313, 315, 377, 417, 452–455 n., 466, 481, 494, 498, 506, 514 n., 520, 528, 534, 535, 540, 569; reaction to Lincoln assassination, 596, 598. *See also* England
Great Eastern, 37
Great Northwestern Fair, Chicago, 374
Greble, John T., 594; father of, 594
Greek fire, 522

Greeley, Horace, 76, 103, 109, 120, 270, 285, 468, 473 n., 477, 484, 586
Green, John Cleve, 61, 65
Greenleaf, Charles R., 464
Greenwich Street, N.Y., 565
Greenwood Cemetery, Brooklyn, 353
Grierson, Benjamin Henry, 324
Griffin, Francis, 29–30
Griffin, Mary, 3
Griffin, Teresa (Mrs. E. L. Viele), 532, 538
Griffin, Mrs. William Preston (Christine Kean), 3, 136, 221, 224 n.
Griffith, Arabella (Mrs. F. C. Barlow), 132, 261, 328; death, 467–468
Grigsby, a Virginian, 212
Grillparzer, Franz, 530
Grinnell, Moses Hicks, 78, 133, 139, 569, 584, 588
Griswold, George, 302–305, 307, 321, 325, 372, 390, 566
Grouchy, Emmanuel de, Marquis, 169
Grymes, Dr., 221, 232
Gunpowder Plot, 515
Gunther, Charles Godfrey, 375, 413, 508, 513
Gurowski, Adam, 72, 279, 405, 485
Gustavus II. Adolphus, 347
Guyot, Arnold, 22

Habicht, Claudius Edward, 101
Hackett, James Henry, 267, 268
Hackley, Charles William, 87
Hagerstown, Md., 254, 259, 332
Haight, Benjamin Isaacs, 273, 364, 384, 448, 520, 525, 528, 542, 543, 545, 549, 552
Haight, David H., 97
Haight, David Lewis, 221
Hale, John Parker, 112, 369
Hall, Abraham Oakey, 451
Hall, General, 125
Halleck, Henry Wager, 210, 228, 239 n., 249, 250, 252, 255, 258, 271, 276, 285, 309, 329–331, 351, 358, 405, 415, 477
Hallock, Gerard, 123 n.
Halpine, Charles Graham ("Miles O'Reilly"), 359, 430–431, 482, 531
Hamilton, Alexander (1757–1804), 367, 384 n.,
Hamilton, Alexander (1815–1907), 151, 154
Hamilton, Mrs. Alexander, Jr., 412
Hamilton, Eliza (Mrs. G. L. Schuyler), 20
Hamilton, James Alexander, 151

Hamilton, John Church, 151
Hamilton, Mary Morris (Mrs. George Lee Schuyler), 5, 20
Hamilton, Schuyler, 151
Hamilton College, 431 n.
Hamlin, Adjutant, 156, 157
Hamlin, Augustus Choate, 394
Hamlin, Hannibal, 28, 57, 139, 282, 369, 394, 455, 457
Hammond, William Alexander, xii, 185, 187, 218–220,227,231,234–5,240,249, 257, 275, 304, 306, 314, 350, 353, 358, 359, 385, 388, 393–394, 396, 418–421, 433, 438, 440, 441, 475–478, 488, 498, 527 n., 535, 604
Hammond, Mrs. William Alexander (Helen Nisbet), 359
Hampton, Va., 167; G.T.S. at, 156–157
Hampton, Mrs. Sally (Baxter), 55, 62
Hampton, Wade, 557, 577
Hampton Roads, 190, 210, 529
Hampton Roads conference, 547, 550–552
Hancock, Dr., 593
Hancock, Winfield Scott, 459 n., 460 n., 568
Handel, George Frederick, 382
Hanlon brothers, athletes, 208
Hanover Court House, Va., 443, 450
Hanover Junction, Va., 452
Hanover Town, Va., 452, 456
Hardee, William Joseph, 481, 533, 535, 557
Hare, John Innes Clark, 192, 203, 257, 258, 280
Harlem R.R. Co., 313
Harney, William Selby, 144
Harper's Ferry, Va., 128, 129, 145, 148, 149, 155, 158, 177, 227, 253 n., 256, 258, 261, 471, 492, 503
Harper's Magazine, 19
Harriet Lane, U.S.S., 118
Harriot, John, 30
Harriot & Henry, 30
Harris, Mrs., of Philadelphia, 260
Harris, U.S.S.C. agent, 312
Harris, Benjamin Gwinn, 427, 428
Harris, Elisha, xii, 150, 184, 209, 251, 258, 393, 506, 543
Harris, Ira, 440
Harris, Isham Green, 208
Harris, Townsend, 31
Harrisburg, Pa., 102, 259, 261, 324–327, 468
Harrison, William Henry, 41, 43
Harrison's Landing, Va., 237–239, 240 n., 242, 243, 247, 451, 462, 467, 470

Harrisse, Henry, 485
Harsen, Jacob, 150
Hart, Mary Eliza (Mrs. Luther Bradish), 338
Hartford, draft riots in, 341
Hartford, U.S.S., 472 n.
Hartford Convention, 299
Hartington, Spencer Compton, Marquess of (afterward eighth Duke of Devonshire), 300–301
Hartshorne, Edward, 189, 192, 221, 260, 261
Harvard University, 151, 166, 325, 367, 385, 394, 447 n., 448, 487, 525, 543, 550; Divinity School students, 438; Law School, 276; Rumford Professorship, 345
Harvey, of U.S.S.C., 535
Harwood, Edwin, 448
Haseltine, William Stanley, 11, 309, 496
Hatcher's Run, Va., 553
Hauteville, Frederick Sears Grand d', 415–416
Hauteville, Mrs. F. S. G. d' (Elizabeth Stuyvesant Fish), 279, 415–416, 419
Hauteville, Paul d', 415–416
Hauteville, Mrs. Paul d' (Ellen Sears), 415–416
Havelocks, 137
Havre de Grace, Md., 150
Hawkins, George Sydney, 88
Hawks, Francis Lister, 20, 25, 262, 266, 268, 302
Hay, John, 477
Haydn, Joseph, 91–92, 96, 99, 109, 126, 267, 396, 414, 588
Hayes, Isaac Israel, 20
Hayes, Rutherford Birchard, 476
Hayley, William, 410
Haynes's Bluff, Vicksburg, Miss., 285
Hayward, Mrs., of South Carolina, 55
Heckscher, Charles Augustus, 386
Heckscher, John Gerard, 301
Heckscher, Lucretia (Stevens), 538
Heenan, John C., 24, 32
Heintzelman, Samuel P., 318
Helper, Hinton Rowan, 1, 3
Henry, Joseph, 88, 210, 438
Henry, Mrs. Joseph (Harriet L. Alexander), 88
Henry, Robert, 30
Henry Hill, Battle of Bull Run, 171
Herold, Davy, 594
Herrmann, Alexander, 208
Hewitt, Abram Stevens, 101, 120, 309
Heywood, John Healy, 363

Hickok, Laurens Perseus, 110
Higbee, Charlotte, 315
Higbee, Edward Young, 2, 13, 15, 16, 125, 133, 176, 183, 266, 273, 495
Higbee, Mrs. Edward Young, 16
Higbee, Mrs. Joseph Milnor (Angelina Lloyd), 315
Hill, of Davenport, Iowa, 329
Hill, Ambrose Powell, 475 n.
Hill, Nicholas, Jr., 13
Hill, Thomas, 385, 440
Hills, Mrs., 315
Hilton, Henry, 234
Hilton Head, S.C., 323, 353
Hinchinbrooke, Lord, 47
Hitchcock, Roswell Dwight, 277
Hoadly, George, 167, 274, 278, 280
Hoar, Ebenezer Rockwood, 429 n
Hobart, John Henry, 273
Hobart, John Henry, Jr., 16, 273, 360, 392, 405
Hobart, Mrs. John Henry, Jr., (Elizabeth Riggs), 16
Hoblett, U.S.S.C. relief agent, 541
Hoboken Battery (of E. A. Stevens), 210
Hoffman, Charles, 145
Hoffman, [David] Murray, 146, 292, 548
Hoffman, Murray, xii, 3, 12, 14, 21, 61, 68, 75, 76, 78, 93, 109, 113, 147, 192, 265, 268, 270, 293, 305, 307 n., 345, 515
Hoffman, Richard, 315
Hoffman, Wickham, 65, 68, 150–155, 157–158, 160
Hoge, Mrs. A. H. (Jane Currie Blaikie), 562
Hogg, 74
Hohnstock, composer, 422
Holly Springs, Miss., raid on, 321 n.
Holmes, Oliver Wendell, 417
Holstein-Schleswig controversy, 407, 466 n
Holt, Joseph, 291, 483 n.
Holt's Hotel, N.Y., 522
Homer, 46
Honcharenko, Agapius, 559
Hone, Philip, 99 n., 566
Hone, Robert Swartwout, 73
Hone, Mrs. Robert S. (Eliza Rodman Russell), 73
Honolulu: contribution to U.S.S.C., 293
Hood, John Bell, 467, 468, 481, 524, 528–531, 533
Hooker, Joseph, 277 n., 281, 290, 300, 308, 309, 312, 313, 315–319, 321, 323–326, 353, 360, 367, 416, 436, 437, 444, 454, 494

Hooker, Richard, 311
Hope Chapel, N.Y., 147
Hopkins, John Henry, 265, 428
Hoppin, William Jones, 15, 292, 325, 339, 468, 498
Hosack, Nathaniel Pendleton, 306, 371, 538, 539
Hotchkiss, Theresa (Mrs. P. H. Anthon), 305
Hotêl des Invalides, 426, 428, 429, 439; Grove Street, N.Y., 559
Houston, Sam, 42, 115
Howard, Joseph, Jr., 449 n.
Howard, Oliver Otis, 318, 322
Howard Hotel, N.Y., 522
Howe, Frank E., 164, 329, 336, 338, 342, 349, 375, 478, 586, 588
Howe, Samuel Gridley, 159, 186, 280
Howe, Mrs. Samuel Gridley (Julia Ward), 404
Howell, Varina (Mrs. Jefferson Davis), 113, 598
Howland, Mrs. 221
Hoyt, Goold, 434
Hoyt, Mrs. Goold (Camilla Scott), 48, 49, 434–435
Hudson, N.Y., 38, 69, 73, 74
Hudson & Berkshire R.R., 38
Hudson River, 38, 50, 54
Hudson River R.R., 101
Hughes, John, 390
Hughes, Thomas, 417
Hugo, Victor, 530
Humes, a carpenter, 545
Humphreys, Andrew Atkinson, 281
Hungarians in U.S., 151
Hunt, Richard Morris, 3, 321, 427, 490, 524
Hunt, Seth P., Jr., 298
Hunt, Washington, 4, 5, 20, 42, 94, 265, 481, 486, 489
Hunt, Mrs. Washington (Mary Hosmer Walbridge), 46, 50
Hunter, David, 169, 226, 234, 455, 458, 467
Hunter, Robert Mercer Taliaferro, 22, 94, 547
Huntington, Charles B., 8 n.
Huntington, Daniel, 138
Huntington, Samuel Howard, 88
Huntington (Henry E.) Library, 603
Huntsville, Ala., 398 n.
Hurlbert, William Henry (born Hurlbut), 163, 201, 457
Hutchings, Robert Chadwick, 29
Hutton, Mancius Smedes, 409

Huxley, Thomas Henry, 9
Hyde, Katherine Cleveland (Mrs. A. C. Coxe), 538
Hygeia Hotel, Old Point Comfort, Va., 155, 166
Hyslop, Robert, 44, 46, 50

Ideas (North or South) to control America, 450
Illinois, copperheads in, 482–483 n.; elections, 271; Lincoln stories, 204–205
Illinois Central R.R., 123
Indiana, 343 n.; copperheads in, 482–483 n.; elections, 499, 500, 510
Indians, 214
Ingalls, Rufus, 221, 445, 463
Ingraham, Daniel Phoenix, 26, 29
Ingraham, Duncan Nathaniel, 58
International Statistical Congress, Berlin (1863), 348–350, 377
Ireland, St. Patrick and snakes in, 343
Irish in U.S., 6, 22, 32, 51, 132, 137, 144, 146, 157, 169, 313, 334–339, 341–343, 345, 347, 348, 352, 371, 375, 452, 458, 475, 509, 512, 586
Irving, Mrs. John Treat (Helen Schermerhorn), 223
Irving Hall, N.Y., 215, 577, 599
Irwinsville, Ga., 597
Island No. 10, 214, 250
Italian Minister, 590
Italians in U.S., 151
Iverson, Alfred, 87

Jackson, Miss., 321
Jackson, Andrew, 79, 86, 109, 204, 278, 380
Jackson, James T., 146, 147, 149
Jackson, Thomas Jonathan (Stonewall), 171, 227 n., 228, 232 n., 239, 250, 252, 253 n., 255, 256, 318, 323, 347, 405; loses arm at Chancellorsville, 321; death, 322
Jackson & Selma R.R., 407
Jackson General Hospital, Richmond, 592
Jacksonville, Fla., 388
Jacobins, 583
Jamaica, B.W.I., 513
James, Frederick P., 77
James I of England, 47
James Island, S.C., 234, 236, 360
James River, 225, 229, 232 n., 235–240, 245–248, 437, 445, 446, 452, 456, 458–460 n., 462, 467, 468, 470, 506, 529, 535, 537, 563, 576, 591; canal, 473
Jamestown, C.S.S., 225

Jamestown, Va., ruined church at, 461
Jamestown Island, 461
Japan: visit of ambassadors of, to U.S., 31–34, 36, 37, 45, 100, 110; literature of, given to Columbia Library, 600
Jardine, Lieutenant-Colonel, 339
Jarvis, Nelson, 295
Jay, John (1817–1894), 42–43, 57, 307, 308, 336, 473, 501, 514, 517, 588
Jefferson, Joseph, 78
Jefferson, Thomas, 479
Jefferson City, Mo., 149
Jefferson Medical College, 240 n.
Jenison, a Virginian, 155
Jenkins, John Foster, 192, 210, 350 n., 356, 360, 410, 421, 426, 428, 431, 457, 460, 472, 478, 486, 487, 490, 492, 501, 519, 520, 526, 535, 541, 543, 548, 559, 567, 589, 590
Jerome, Leonard W., 416; private theatre of ("Theatre San Jeronimo"), 426, 430, 434
Jersey City, 37, 264
Johannsen, Mme., singer, 310, 494
John (waiter at G.T.S. home), 337
"John Brown's Body," 205, 408, 438, 574, 578
Johnson, Andrew, 140, 427 n., 455–457, 560–561, 584, 585, 589, 595; G.T.S. interview with, 590–591
Johnson, Bradley Tyler, 335
Johnson, Bushrod Rust, 207
Johnson, Dwight, 406
Johnson, Eastman, 2, 21–22, 157
Johnson, Herschel Vespasian, 41, 42
Johnson, Judge, 301–302
Johnson, Julia, 86
Johnson, Reverdy, 77, 427, 597
Johnson, William H., 12
Johnson, Mrs. William Templeton (Laura Winthrop), 158
Johnson's Island, Lake Erie, 555 n.
Johnston, Albert Sidney, 207, 208, 454; killed, 216
Johnston, Joseph Eggleston, 168, 169, 171, 211 n., 214 n., 220 n., 229, 230 n., 255, 326, 339, 344, 347, 355, 388, 398 n., 406, 418, 456, 466, 467, 516 n., 537, 573, 576, 577, 580, 581, 588, 594
Jones, Alice, 372
Jones, Captain (Grant's headquarters), 463
Jones, Edward, 18, 276, 306, 376, 381, 387, 391, 398, 400, 413, 430, 447, 524, 527, 534, 539, 542, 545, 546, 548, 549, 553, 554, 556, 557, 566

Jones, George Frederic, 354
Jones, Mrs. George Frederic (Lucretia Stevens Rhinelander), 2
Jones, Mrs. Isaac Colford (Rebecca Mason), 372
Jones, Leonora, 390–391
Jones, Mrs. Lewis Colford (Catherine Berryman), 18, 28
Jones, Mary Mason (Mrs. R. D. de K. de Trobriand), 88
Jones, Samuel, 368
Jones, William Alfred, 370, 391, 399, 515
Jones, William E., 455
Jones House, Harrisburg, Pa., 259
Joy, Charles Arad, 7, 34, 345, 365, 381, 397, 400, 402, 452, 487, 496, 520, 525
Joy, Mrs. Charles Arad, 538
Judd, Norman Buel, 381
Jullien's Hotel, N.Y., 18
Junca, Marcel, 7

Kalorama, Washington, smallpox hospital at, 196
Kane of Baltimore, 163
Kansas, 1, 8, 67, 319 n.; Bishop of, 496
Kautz, August Valentine, 497
Kean, Christine (Mrs. W. P. Griffin), 3, 136, 221, 224 n.
Kearny, Philip, 252
Kearny, Mrs. Philip (Diana Moore Bullitt), 252
Kearny, Philip R., 53
Kearsarge, U.S.S., 467
Keedysville, Md., 261
Keen, William Williams, 477
Keene, Laura, 39, 78
Keese, Oliver, Jr., 114
Kemble, Fanny, 209
Kemble, Gouverneur, 398, 515
Kenesaw Mountain, Battle of, 456
Kenly, John Reese, 227
Kennedy, John A., 45, 46, 50, 90
Kennedy, Robert Lenox, [104], 305, 538
Kenny, Peter Duncan, 322
Kensett, John Frederick, 21
Kent, William, 87
Kentucky, 68, 75–77, 89, 92–95, 110, 123, 139, 140, 142, 149, 178, 182, 183, 193, 202, 252, 298, 347, 380, 381, 397, 544; Copperheads in, 482–483 n.; elections, 368, 370, 511, 512
Kenzua Petroleum Co., 551, 562, 569, 576, 583
Kerlin, U.S.S.C. agent, 312
Kernochan, Francis Edward, 323
Kernochan, Mrs. John, 48

Kernochan, Joseph, 106, 256, 293, 323
Kernot, salesman, 36
Kershaw, Joseph Brevard, 577
Ketchum, Morris, 167
Keteltas, Henry, 358
Key, Francis Scott, 574
Keyes, Erasmus Darwin, 178–179, 195, 418
Kimball, Gilman, 166, 167, 173
Kimball, Nathan, 572
King, Augustus, 267
King, Charles, 7, 20, 29, 34, 47, 98, 117, 139, 143, 144, 191, 246, 297, 364, 365, 375, 397, 399–403, 409, 411, 412, 414, 415, 436, 448, 486
King, Mrs. Charles (Henrietta Liston Low), 98, 426
King, James Gore, 405
King, John Alsop, 20
King, Preston, 86, 87, 102, 165, 591
King, Thomas Starr, 267 n., 413
"Kingdom Coming," 577
Kingsland, British guardsman, 223
Kingsley, Charles, 178, 391 n., 400, 527–528, 532
Kingston, Ont., 40
Kinsley, 136
Kirkland, Caroline Matilda (Stansbury), 431
Kirkland, William, 431 n.
Knapp, Frederick Newman, 183, 184, 190, 194, 220, 221, 230, 356, 389, 421, 426, 437, 439, 450, 465, 486, 503, 519, 535, 543, 548, 559, 567, 590
Knickerbocker, 224, 236, 238
Knickerbocker Kitchen, Metropolitan Fair, 426 n., 427
Knights of the Golden Circle, 482, 522 n.
Know-Nothing lodges, 40, 343
Knoxville, Tenn., 355, 373, 377, 378, 385, 397–399, 406, 418, 568
Kossuth, Louis, 57
Kotzebue, August von, 530
Kuhn, Charles, 239, 262, 267, 452
Kuhn, Mrs. Charles, 262
Kuhn, Hamilton, 239

Lafarge House, N.Y., 522
Lafayette Place, N.Y., 566
Lafitte, of N.Y. Club, 110
Laird Brothers, 454 n.
Lake Erie, 555 n.
Lamb, Dr., 181
Lamson, of Boston, 155–157
Lander, Frederick William, 215

Lane, Mrs. David, 221, 381, 387, 391, 412, 424
Lane, Helen, 11
Lane, James Henry, 87, 165
Lane, Joseph, 42
Lane, Susan (Mrs. Milton Cogswell), 189
Langdon, Walter, 306
Larocque, Joseph, 268, 586
Laud, William, 356
Laurel Hill, N.C., 565
Law, George, 313
Lawrence, Mass., 1–2, 4
Lawrence, Amos Adams, 520
Lawrence, Charles, 483
Lawrence, James, 136
Lawrence, Mrs. James (Julia Montaude-vert), 136
Lawrence, Joseph, 53
Lawrence, Timothy Bigelow, 111, 113
Lawrence, Mrs. Timothy Bigelow (Elizabeth Chapman), 111
Lawrence, William Beach, 136–137, 498
Lawson, Thomas, 173
Leary, Arthur, 143, 576
Leary, Charles, 52
Leavenworth, Annie, 2, 3, 30, 43
Lecompton Constitution, 319 n.
Le Conte, John Lawrence, 203
Lee, David Bradley, 597
Lee, Robert Edward, 138, 154, 223, 228, 230 n., 232 n., 235, 236, 247 n., 250, 252 n., 253 n., 255–257, 259, 281, 312, 313, 316–318, 324–332, 338, 339, 344, 347, 354, 358, 366, 378, 388, 395, 398, 405, 418, 431, 433, 436, 437, 442–447, 449, 450, 452–454, 456, 459, 467–471, 475, 477, 486, 495, 496, 506, 518, 537, 547, 555, 558, 563, 568–582, 584–586, 588, 593, 594, 597; surrender of, 578–580
Leech, John, 50
Leesboro, Md., 254
Leesburg, Va., 177, 209; Battle of Ball's Bluff, 189, 190
Lefferts, Colonel, 144
Lefferts, Elizabeth Dorothea (Mrs. J. C. Brevoort), 434
Legal Tender Bill, 201, 205
Leggett, Captain, 397
Lehigh University, 425 n.
Lemmon case, 57
Leo X, Pope, 356
Leonard, William H., 28, 32, 407
Le Roy, Jacob Rutgers, 18, 19, 25, 68, 69, 71–74, 85

Le Roy, Mrs. Jacob Rutgers (I) (Helen Otis), 71
Le Roy, Mrs. Jacob Rutgers (II), 68, 69, 71, 72, 73, 85, 92
Le Roy, Robert, 18, 19, 22, 23, 25, 68, 69, 71, 72, 73, 85, 319–320, 561–562
Le Roy, Mrs. Robert (Amelia Lewis), 18, 19, 22, 23, 25, 71, 320, 562
Letcher, John, 140, 142
Letterman, Jonathan, 231, 240, 321
Leutze, Emanuel, 3, 21, 151
Levy, Captain, 135
Lewinsville, Va., action of, 181
Lewis, card-engraver, 304
Lewis, Amelia (Mrs. Robert Le Roy), 18, 19, 22, 23, 25, 71, 320, 562
Lewis, Henry H., 87, 107, 134, 138
Lewis v. Anthon, 303
Lewisburg, W. Va., 227
Lexington, Battle of, 126
Lexington, Mo., skirmish, 182
Libby Prison, Richmond, 592, 593
Library of G.T.S., 497
Lieber, Francis, xii, 3, 13, 20, 28, 55, 61, 113–115, 117, 150, 223, 236, 276, 298, 302, 309, 315, 353, 381, 468, 477–479, 504, 514, 603
Lieber, Hamilton, 236
Lieber, Oscar Montgomery, 55, 236
Lincoln, Abraham, xiii, 26, 27; nominated for President, 28; 30, 33, 36, 41, 42, 44, 45, 52–55, 57–63; elected President, 60; 61–63, 67, 74, 76, 77; first Inaugural Address, 85, 105–108; 92, 94, 99, 100; G.T.S. sees A. L. in N.Y. procession, 101; Baltimore assassination plot, 102; 103–109, 112, 114–116, 119; calls for volunteers, 120; 121, 127, 130, 138, 139, 144, 145 n., 151, 153 n., 156, 159, 164, 173, 177, 187; G.T.S. visits A. L., 188; 190, 199–201; G.T.S. and Dr. Bellows visit A. L., 204–205; 207, 209, 210, 216; signs D.C. emancipation bill, 217; 218, 219, 223, 225, 231, 232 n., 233, 235, 236, 240 n., 242–246, 250, 253, 255; and Emancipation Proclamation, 257, 261–262, 282, 283, 286; 259, 264, 269, 271, 272, 278, 279, 281–287, 289, 290 n., 291 n., 292, 293, 298 n., 304, 308, 309, 312 n., 314–315, 319n., 324, 327 n.; announces victory at Gettysburg, 331; 332, 334, 337, 354, 355, 369, 370, 378, 379, 383, 385, 388, 389, 394, 405, 407, 408; G.T.S. sees A. L. in Stanton's office, 442; 443, 449, 451, 453; renominated, 455, 456; 457,

459, 466 n., 467, 471, 473–475, 477–
479, 481–483, 489, 490, 494, 497–502,
504, 506–510; reelected President, 511–
512; 516, 518, 526, 537, 547; peace
talks, 550–552; 555, 556, 558; and
Second Inauguration, 560–561; 569,
573, 580, 581; assassinated, 582–583;
584–588; G.T.S. attends funeral of,
at White House, 589–590; 591, 595,
596; funeral cortege, 597; G.T.S.
estimate of A. L., 597–598; *Punch*
tribute, 599; 603
Lincoln, Mrs. Abraham (Mary Todd),
104, 255, 583
Littell, Eliakim, 520
Little, Mrs., 365
Livermore, Mary Ashton (Rice), 562
Livingston, Anson, 20
Livingston, John Robert, Jr., 16
Livingston County, N.Y., 417
Lloyd, Angelina (Mrs. J. M. Higbee),
315
Lockport, N.Y., 4, 5, 11
Logan, John Alexander, 287 n., 398 n.
Lombardy, 252
London *Index*, 596 n.
London *Morning Star*, 598
London *Times*, 166, 170, 171, 193, 200–
201, 347, 377, 458, 483, 514
Long Bridge, Washington, 152, 153, 165,
169, 173, 174, 178, 211, 213, 558
Longfellow, Henry Wadsworth, 385, 391,
471–472
Longstreet, Augustus Baldwin, 326, 373,
397–399, 431, 437, 445, 446, 503
Lookout Mountain, Tenn., 367; Battle of,
373, 406
Lord, Daniel, 101, 409
Lord, Daniel De Forest, 132, 548
Lord, James Couper, 132
Lord, Phebe L. (Mrs. Henry Day), 434
Loring, Judge, 292
Lossing, Benson John, 594
Louis Philippe, 419
Louisiana, 80, 83, 92, 99, 323, 345, 386,
395, 397, 443, 597
Louisville, Ky., 298 n., 299, 326, 381
Lovejoy's Hotel, N.Y., 522
Low, Abiel Abbot, 429
Low, Frederick Ferdinand, 267 n.
Low, Henrietta Liston (Mrs. Charles
King), 98, 426
Low, Nicholas, 99
Lowell, Mass., volunteers of, 166
Lowell, Charles Russell, 195
Lowenthal, army surgeon, 472

Lowndes, of South Carolina, 68
Loyal Publication Association, 297
Loyall, Virginia (Mrs. D. G. Farragut),
531
Luther, Martin, 356
Lydig, Philip Mesier, 2
Lyman, George Hinckley, 218
Lyman, Martha (Mrs. L. S. Foster), 114,
209
Lynchburg, Va., 516, 568, 571, 575, 577,
579
Lyon, Caleb, 221
Lyon, Nathaniel, 149, 160, 174–175, 182
Lyons, Richard Bickerton Pemell, second
Baron, 46, 49, 50, 506

Macbeth (Shakespeare), 365, 367
McCagg, Ezra Butler, 421, 543
McCall, George Archibald, 232 n.
McChesney, Colonel, 166
McClellan, George Brinton, xiii, 149, 158,
167, 168, 170, 177, 181–183, 185–188,
190, 192, 194, 195, 199, 202, 203, 206–
208, 214–217, 220 n., 222, 225–233,
235–237, 239, 240, 242–248, 250, 252,
254–258, 260, 261, 265–268, 271,
277 n., 279, 282, 287, 289, 290, 297,
298, 301, 306, 317, 324, 330, 346, 357,
364, 383, 386, 405, 408–410, 416, 423,
432, 436, 444, 452, 454, 455, 459, 471,
475, 477–484, 486, 488–490, 492, 494–
495, 497–500, 502, 503, 507, 509, 511–
513, 581, 594; G.T.S. at McClellan's
headquarters, 226
McClellan, Mrs. George Brinton (Mary
Ellen Marcy), 512, and baby, 265
McClellan, John Hill Brinton, 192, 203
McClernand, John Alexander, 309
McClintock, John, 382
McCook, General, 561
McCulloch, Ben, 175
McCulloh, Richard Sears, 34, 345, 362–
366, 376, 381, 384
McCunn, John H., 340, 342, 345, 368
McCurdy, Robert H., 162, 201
McDonald, Dr., 461, 462, 492, 526, 531,
594
Macdonough, Augustus Rodney, 296,
309, 387
McDowell, Irvin, 154, 168, 169, 171, 174,
179, 183, 188, 195, 208, 213, 214, 217,
227 n., 228, 230, 232, 240 n., 250–252,
254, 255, 289–291, 346, 416
McDowell, Mrs. Irvin (Helen Burden),
195

McEvers, Mary (Mrs. Edward Cunard), 434

McIlvaine, Charles Petit, 265, 266

Mack von Leiberich, Karl, 333

McKeever, Chauncey, 440

McKeon, John, 513

McKim, James Miller, 325 n., 591

Maclure, British guardsman, 223

McMahon, Martin T., 538–539, 597

McMichael, Morton, 258

Macmillan's Magazine, 351 n.

Macon, Ga., 497, 522

McPherson, James Birdseye, 309, 467

McVickar, John, 100, 304, 403, 457, 487, 559

Madison Avenue, N.Y., 566

Madison Square, 49, 312, 560

Magruder, John Bankhead, 160, 161, 220 n., 245, 601

Mahan, Milo, 384, 398

Mahometanism, 194, 356, 408

Mahony, John H., 433

Mahony, Lucrie F. (Mrs. J. J. Post), 433–434

Maine elections, 500

Maison Dorée, Union Square, 168, 245, 336, 343, 345, 353, 360, 381, 473, 479, 481

Maitland, Samuel Roffey, 515

Malleus Maleficarum, 515

Mallory, Stephen Russell, 157

Malvern Hill, Battle of, 235, 245, 489, 509

Manassas Junction, Va., 148, 158, 160, 161, 163, 168, 171, 249, 250, 253, 255; G.T.S. trip to, 211–213

Manhattan Club, 416 n.

Manice building, N.Y., 387

Manierre, Benjamin F., 479

Mann, Mary A. (Mrs. R. B. Marcy), 265, 512

Mansfield, Joseph King Fenno, 154

Mansion House, Alexandria, 152

Marat, Jean Paul, 583

Marble, Manton, 300, 333, 426, 451, 457, 534

Marbury, Francis F., 514

March, Alden, 312, 350, 360, 361, 495, 497, 498

Marcy, Mary Ellen (Mrs. G. B. Mc-Clellan), 265, 512

Marcy, Randolph Barnes, 306

Marcy, Mrs. Randolph Barnes (Mary A. Mann), 265, 512

Marie (Lewis's nurse), 587

Marié, Pierre, 105

Marine Band, 153

Mariposa mines, Calif., 350, 502

Markoe, Thomas Masters, 234, 318

Marsh, George Perkins, 546

Marshall, Charles Henry, 298, 504, 575

Marshall House, Alexandria, Va., 146, 152

Martin, R. M., 522 n.

Martin Chuzzlewit (Dickens), 111, 184, 486

Martinez, restaurateur, 245

Martinsburg, Va., 164

Mary Ann (housekeeper of J. R. Le Roy), 69, 71

Mary Powell, 492, 496

Marye's Heights, Va., Battle of, 281

Maryland, 77, 89, 93–95, 104, 123, 136, 138, 139, 231, 249, 252–257, 259, 325, 347, 361, 397, 405, 408, 421, 427, 437, 445, 446, 465–467, 489, 500, 501, 516, 583; invasion of, 326; elections, 368, 370, 502, 510; legislature locked up, 182

Maryland, University of, 219

Maryland College of Pharmacy, 350 n.

Mason, Henry, 18, 135

Mason, James Murray, 5–6, 192–196, 198, 596, 597

Mason, Lily, 18, 48

Mason, Rebecca (Mrs. Isaac Colford Jones), 372

Massachusetts, 78, 325, 443, 444; elections, 510; nurses from, 167; volunteers, 123, 126, 129, 178

Massachusetts regiments: 6th, in New York, 124, attacked by mob in Baltimore, 126, 130; 22nd, 165; 54th, 344, 361

Massey, Major General, C.S.A., 472

Massie, James William, 361

Massinger, Philip, 530

Mathews, Albert, 17, 302

Matthews, William, 44

Mauran, Josephine (Mrs. Wolcott Gibbs), 336

Maury, Dabney Herndon, 366

Maximilian, Emperor of Mexico, 547

May, Abigail Williams, 506, 589

May, Edward Harrison, 22

Maynard carbine purchased by G.T.S., 90

Maynard rifles, 87

Mazzini, Guiseppe, 57

Meade, George Gordon, 326–332, 338, 344, 351, 357, 360, 363, 366, 375, 377, 378, 388, 398, 416, 437, 438, 444, 445, 454, 469, 470, 518, 553

Medical Association for Furnishing Hospital Supplies, 150
Medical Times, 442
Meigs, Charles Delucena, 192
Meigs, Montgomery Cunningham, 173, 187, 207, 249, 257, 276
Memminger, Charles Gustavus, 381, 382
Memphis, Tenn., 313, 321
Menagerie, 374
Mendelssohn-Bartholdy, Jacob Ludwig Felix, 315, 517, 530
Mercantile Society Library, N.Y., 232
Merchants' Exchange, N.Y., 339, 574, 583
Mercier, Henri, 293
Meridian, Miss., 388, 398 n., 407
Merrimac (afterward *Virginia*) C.S.S., 157 n., 187, 214, 216, 221, 247; engagement with *Monitor*, 210; blown up, 225
Messenger, Daniel, 17, 110, 121, 151, 152, 155
Metcalfe, John T., 71, 125
Metropolitan Hotel, N.Y., 34, 522
Metropolitan Museum of Art, 492 n.
Meurer, Augustus W., 141, 252
Mexican War, 252; Second, 16
Mexico, 77, 353, 547; French army in, 443
Meyer, Tom, 107, 121
Michigan, U.S.S., 555 n.
Michigan regiment: 4th, 597 n.
Microscopy, 5, 182, 524
Middletown, Va., 502
Mignot, Louis Remy, 21, 223
Miles, Dixon S., 258, 261
Milford, Pa., 20
Military Cemetery, Washington, 507
"Military policy" of G.T.S., 193
Mill Springs, Kentucky (Logan's Cross Roads), Battle of, 366 n.
Milledgeville, Ga., 522
Millen, Ga., 541
Miller, Major, 572
Mills, Alice Fenner (Mrs. Fernando Wood), 95
Mills, Clark, 86, 111
Mills, Drake, 95
Milton, John, 311, 490; *Paradise Lost*, 308
Mineralogical specimens, 412, 413, 534, 545, 553–554
Minié balls, 173
Minturn, Robert Bowne, 43, 73, 101, 125, 133, 201, 203, 277, 299, 303–307, 321, 390
Minturn, Mrs. Robert Bowne (Anna Mary Wendell), 73

Missionary Ridge, assault on, 373
Mississippi, 58, 63, 79 n., 80, 83, 90–92, 95, 113, 114, 142, 290, 309, 326, 344, 345, 347, 352, 363, 449
Mississippi, University of, 448
Mississippi River (and Valley), 95, 99, 294, 308–310, 326, 374, 378, 482, 488; Campaign, 144, 201, 215; opened to North 332, 405
Missouri, 77, 80, 92, 95, 100, 112, 142, 144, 149, 174, 177, 182, 183, 193, 208, 210, 252, 283 n., 347, 380, 397, 405, 408, 455, 456, 473, 531, 544; Copperheads in 482–483 n; elections, 511, 512
Missouri, Department of the, 366 n.
Missouri Compromise, 66, 67, 72, 77; line, 103
Mitchel, Ormsby McKnight, 217
Mitchell, Edward, 344
Mitchell, John W., 513
Mitchell, Silas Weir, 477
Mitchell, William, 344
Mobile, Ala., 280, 284, 329, 354, 366, 407, 409, 488, 516, 571
Mobile & Ohio R.R., 301 n., 407
Mobile Bay, Battle of, 472, 477, 499
Molly Maguires, 371 n.
Monitor, U.S.S., 216; engagement with *Merrimac*, 210
Monroe Doctrine, 547
Montaudevert, Julia (Mrs. James Lawrence), 136
Montgomery, Ala., 267, 467, 516; Convention, 83
Moore, Nathaniel Fish, 415
Morgan, Catherine (Mrs. J. A. Dix), 424, 455, 538
Morgan, Edwin Denison, 158, 264, 439, 440, 508
Morgan, Mrs. Edwin Denison (Eliza Matilda Waterman), 48, 49
Morgan, George C., 295
Morgan, John Hunt, 343
Morgan, William Ferdinand, 398
Morris Island, Charleston, 350, 351, 356, 357 n., 359, 360, 378, 495
Morse, Lemuel W., 430
Morton, Oliver Perry, 483 n., 500
Moscow, retreat from, 471
Motley, John Lothrop, 370
Mott, Alexander Brown, 39, 166
Mott, Louisa Dunmore (Mrs W. H. Van Buren), 238
Mott, Valentine, 161, 234, 277, 301, 302, 494, 506
Mould, Jacob Wrey, 490

Mount Vernon, 143, 220
Mount Vernon Ladies' Association, 143
Mowatt, Anna Cora (Ogden)(Mrs. W. F. Ritchie), 20, 296, 452
Mozart, Wolfgang Amadeus, 262, 385, 517, 578, 588
Mulligan, James A., 182
Mullin, Joseph, 28
Mumford, trustee of General Theological Seminary, 384
Mumford, William B., 283 n.
Munson's Hill, Va., skirmish at, 190, 195
Murray, David Colden, 65
Murray, Mrs. David Colden (Mary Sherwood), 2, 65, 111, 207
Murray, James B., 101
Murfreesboro, Tenn., 241, 287, 386, 530; Battle of Stone's River, 285, 355, 366n.
Musicale Club, 315
Mutual Life Insurance Co., 175
Myers, Theodorus Bailey, 89

Nachet binocular microscope, 524
Nairne, Charles Murray, 13, 21, 28, 100, 110, 312, 365
Naples, 42
Napoleon I, 347, 351, 459, 581
Napoleon III (Louis Napoleon Bonaparte) 11, 206, 238, 293, 297, 299, 300, 351, 380, 395; mediation effort in the Civil War, 286
Nash, Catherine, 412, 424, 588, 589
Nash, Stephen Payn, 384, 398
Nashville, C.S.S., 214
Nashville, Tenn., 241, 285, 394, 523, 529, 530, 539, 568, 593
Nathan, 262
Nathan, Jonathan, 363
Nation, The, 325, 327
National Academy of Sciences, 394, 436
National anthem contest, 142–143, 161–163
National Club. *See* Union League Club
National Hotel, Washington, 111, 166
National name, 479
Native American Party, 343, 352
Naval Brigade, 167
Neale, 18
Negro soldiers, 283, 291, 305, 312, 313, 324, 344, 347, 354, 361, 460, 463–464, 516, 529, 530, 539, 558, 564, 575, 582, 593.
Negroes, 3–4, 12, 26, 35, 52, 54, 55, 57, 60, 66, 76, 91, 128, 155–157, 179, 209, 222, 244, 284, 334, 335, 337, 341–345,

348, 349, 361, 375 n., 389, 411, 527, 549, 555, 558, 595. *See also* Abolitionism, Slavery
Neill, Dr., 562
Neill, Samuel M., 33, 151
Nelcker's restaurant, Washington, 590, 594
Nelson, Samuel, 33, 35, 475
Neurology, 476, 477
Neuse River, N.C., 565
Nevada silver, 277
New Bern, N.C., 310, 498, 570, 571
New England, 54, 473, 508; ideas, 450
New England Hotel, N.Y., 522
New England Women's Auxiliary Association, 506 n.
New Gospel of Peace, The, (White), 379
New Haven R.R., 8 n., 17
New Jersey: Copperheadism, 588; elections, 271, 368, 370, 510–512; waterlogged countryside, 85
New Orleans, 99, 283 n., 284, 305, 344, 353, 359, 379, 472, 509, 523, 541, 568, 591, 593; Union demonstrations in, 208; expedition, 200, 215, 224–225; capture of city, 223–225, 228
New Year's calls, 2, 538, 539
New York & Harlem R.R. Co., 313
New York City: bombing of, feared, 196; Colored Half-Orphan Asylum (Association for the Benefit of Colored Orphans), 335, 336; Common Council, 292, 534; and Draft Riots of July, 1863, 332–343, 389, 390, 451; paid fire department, 571; Post Office, defalcation in, 26; residential changes, 565–566; Riots of 1857, 414 n; Southern sabotage plot, 89, arson plot, 522; Superior Court, 368; victory celebrations, 573–576
New York Club, 18, 39–41, 63, 107, 110, 119, 122, 125, 126, 134, 140, 141, 144–145, 147, 160, 200, 201, 286, 521
New York *Commercial Advertiser*, 72, 76, 207, 327, 445, 458, 574
New York *Courier and Enquirer*, 97, 108, 120, 125, 153, 164, 174, 294
New York Daily News, 123, 175, 337, 406, 507, 509, 513, 561, 582, 596
New York *Day-Book*, 120, 123
New York Evening Post, 87, 105, 115, 119, 141, 237, 297, 327, 341, 431, 445, 449, 467, 493, 514, 596
New York Express, 42, 58, 76, 105, 121, 123, 296, 300, 343, 355, 478, 493, 509

New York Herald, 42, 55, 76, 81, 105, 117–122, 270, 296, 329, 338, 340, 342, 354, 359, 366, 383, 408, 481, 490, 530, 591, 598 n.
New-York Historical Society, 8, 29, 146, 272, 448
New York Hospital, 224
New York Hotel, 55, 57, 123, 586
New York Journal of Commerce, 84, 120, 123, 175, 449, 451, 465, 466 n.
New York Life Insurance & Trust Co., 40, 53, 59, 63, 106, 293, 520, 576
New York Lyceum of Natural History, 510
New York Post-Graduate Medical School 476
New York Regiments: 5th, 133, 155, 320; 7th, 87, 101, 125–127, 129–131, 134, 135, 138, 140, 144, 146, 324, 340, 341, 411; 8th, 132, 170; 9th, 152; 11th, 137, 149, 152; 12th, 122, 152, 335; 14th, 152; 22nd, 387; 28th, 155; 67th, 449; 69th, 32, 132, 155, 169; 71st, 170; 79th, 173, 174; 84th, 271 n.; 1st Negro (20th U.S.), 411
New York Rifles, 122, 130–132, 134, 135, 137, 138, 141, 144, 147, 148, 159
New York Society Library, 61 n., 214, 315, 465
New York State: Court of Appeals, 117; Regents of the University, 383, 390 n.; Soldiers' Relief Establishment, 541; Supreme Court, 27–29
New York Times, 96, 97, 117, 142, 193, 194, 196–198, 226, 264, 270, 271, 317, 323, 327, 406, 449 n., 476, 499, 596
New York Tribune, 1, 19, 26, 28, 41, 45, 99, 102, 111, 117, 120, 129, 141, 164, 168, 170, 196, 201, 208, 225, 257, 270, 286, 316, 327, 329, 336, 352, 407, 473 n., 478, 499, 530, 554, 555, 573, 584, 586, 592, 596
New York University, 61 n., 557; Chapel, 306; Law School, 21, 27, 29; Medical College, 219, 476
New York World 159, 163 n., 193, 194, 205, 270, 296, 300, 309–310, 338, 343, 355, 449, 451, 457, 465–467, 478, 507–509, 511, 519, 531, 534, 555, 558, 561, 569, 582, 596
Newberry, John Strong, 160, 161, 186, 279, 356, 362, 393, 395, 396, 421, 437, 506, 507, 530, 543, 590, 593, 591, 594
Newcastle, Henry Pelham Fiennes Pelham Clinton, fifth Duke of, 40, 46, 48, 50
Newell, Robert Henry, 300
Newmarket, Va., 495
Newport, R.I., 136, 245–248, 262, 272, 335, 354, 498
Newport News, Va., 187, 243; G.T.S. at 167
Newtown, Va., 502
Niagara, U.S.S., 481
Niagara Falls "Peace Conference," 473 n.
Niblo's Pantomime and Horse-Opera, 40
Niblo's Saloon, 207
Niblo's Theatre, 267, 268
Nicholas Nickleby (Dickens), 487
Nicolay, John George, 389
Nightingale, Florence, 130, 535
Ninth Army Corps, 468, 469
Nisbet, Helen (Mrs. W. A. Hammond), 359
Norfolk, Va., 144, 149, 216, 223, 279; Navy Yard, 145; surrender of, 225
Norris, of San Francisco, 358
North American Review, 375
North Anna River, 436, 443, 452
North Carolina, 78, 108, 122, 193, 310, 323, 345–347, 349, 371, 396, 398, 406, 446, 478, 497, 517, 564, 567, 571, 576, 577, 582; Union movement in, 330
North Carolina, U.S.S., 116
Northwest States, Copperheads in, 482–483
Noyes, Mrs. Henry Drury (Isabella Beveridge), 230
Noyes, William Curtis, 8, 12, 17, 103, 298

Oakley, Thomas Jackson, 368
O'Brien, Fitz-James, 215
Occidental restaurant, Washington, 393
O'Conor, Charles, 33, 117, 310, 513, 581
Odell, Moses Fowler, 574
Odenheimer, William Henry, 398
Offenbach, Jacques, 109
Office-seekers in Washington, 111
Ogden, Anna Cora (Mrs. James Mowatt, Mrs. William F. Ritchie), 20, 296, 432
Ogden, Gouverneur Morris, xiii, 12, 25, 38, 61, 98, 118, 124, 140, 273, 365, 370, 376, 384, 399, 404, 417, 418, 448, 470, 499, 525, 526, 528, 542, 543, 545, 546, 549, 550, 555, 560, 584
Ogden, J. H., 74
Ogden, James De Peyster, 60, 104
Ogden, Samuel Gouverneur, 20
Ogilby, Frederick, 15, 125, 133, 559
O'Gorman, Richard, 265, 513

Ohio, 324, 343 n.; Copperheads in, 482–
    483 n.; elections, 271, 364, 370, 499,
    500
Old Point Comfort, Va., 149, 158, 166,
    215, 220, 222, 231; G.T.S. at 155–156
Oliver Twist (Dickens), 237
Olmsted, Frederick Law, xiii, 160, 161,
    164, 166, 172, 175, 177, 180, 183–185,
    190, 191, 194–196, 198, 207, 211–213,
    215, 220, 221, 230, 231, 240, 243, 248,
    267, 276, 278–280, 291, 303, 304, 307
    n., 325, 327, 329, 332, 345, 350, 356,
    362, 502
Olustee, Fla., 414, 431
Opdyke, George, 167, 168, 196, 201, 251,
    277, 336, 337
Opequon Creek, Va., 491
Opera, 6, 12, 22, 31, 41, 56, 65, 104, 265,
    268, 310, 383, 384, 396; German opera,
    383
Orange & Alexandria R.R., 318
Orange Court House, Va., 244
Orangemen, 40
Ord, Edward Otho Cresap, 579, 593
Ordronaux, John, 28, 201
Oregon, 80, 433, 501
O'Reilly, Miles. *See* Charles Graham
    Halpine
Oremieulx, Theophile Marie d', 5, 61,
    94, 515
Oremieulx, Mrs. Theophile Marie d'
    (Laura Wolcott Gibbs), 515
Oreto, 293
Origin of Species The (Darwin), 9–11,
    13–14
Orpheus C. Kerr Papers, 300
Oscanyan, Christopher, 8, 111
Osgood, Samuel, 201, 501
Osten Sacken, Carl Robert Romanovich
    von der, Baron, 278, 535, 539, 586
Oswego, N.Y., 488
Otis, Helen (Mrs. J. R. Le Roy), 71
Otis, James W., 18
Owen, Edward H., 421, 433
Owens, John E., 507–508
Oxford, University of, 453, 514
Oxford Tracts, 9

Pacific Mail Steamship Co., 197
Pacific R.R. *See* Union Pacific R.R.
Pacifism, 473, 474, 477, 480, 483
Paez, General, 47
Page, Dr., 238
Palace Gardens, N.Y., 37, 56–57, 387
Palfrey, John Gorham, 438

Palmerston, Henry John Temple, Vis-
    count, 569
Paltock, Robert, *Peter Wilkins*, 237
Pamunkey River, 231, 235, 236, 238, 248,
    452, 459, 576
Paradise Lost (Milton), 308
Parish, Daniel, 307
Parish, Henry, 304
Parish & Co., 106 n.
Park Place, N.Y., 566
Parke, John Grubb, 296
Parker, Miss, 315
Parker, Amasa Junius, 27, 488
Parker, Theodore, 40–41
Parker, Willard, 34, 38, 302, 306
Parkyn, Mrs. Fanny (Rogers), 137
Parrish, Joseph, 487, 519, 526, 543
Parrott guns, 360, 464
Parton, James, 379, 380
Patterson, Robert, 164, 168–170, 179
Patti, Adelina, 6–7, 41
Paulding, Mrs., 367
Paulding, James Kirke, 20
Pea Ridge, Ark., 268; Battle of, 210, 214
    321 n.
Peabody, George, 600
Peace: feelers from South, 380; overtures,
    495; negotiations, 547–548; Hampton
    Roads Conference, 547, 550–552
Peace Democrats. *See* Copperheads
Peacocks and pheasants on Broadway, 359
Peck, engineer, 460
Peck, William Guy, 100, 346, 365, 376,
    381, 383, 402
Peirce, Benjamin, 151, 385, 394, 440
Peirce, Ebenezer Weaver, 161
Pell, Alfred, 101
Pell, Laura, 27, 28, 223
Pemberton, John Clifford, 309, 326, 332,
    352, 354
Pemberton Mill, Lawrence, Mass., col-
    lapse of, 1–2, 4
Pendleton, Edmund Henry, 20
Pendleton, George Hunt, 480, 483, 486,
    489, 491, 495, 497, 499, 504
Peninsula, The, 250, 437, 578
Peninsular Campaign, 199, 215, 216,
    220 n., 228, 230, 232 n., 235, 242, 246,
    250, 268, 290 n., 410 n.
Penniman, James F., 168
Pennington, William, Jr., 6, 39, 113
Pennington, William, Sr., 1, 6, 86, 113
Pennsylvania, 147, 253, 256, 258, 331,
    337, 420, 468, 471; coal miners, 469;
    elections, 44, 45, 265, 266, 271, 364,
    498–500, 502; invasion of, 324, 336;

Militia, 259, 327; State House, 259; strikes in coal regions, 37; volunteers, 126

Pennsylvania, University of, 425 n.

Pennsylvania Avenue, Washington, 106, 107, 130, 438, 590

Pennsylvania R.R., 188 n.

Pennsylvania regiment: 118th, 260, 261

Pequoson Bay, 221

Perit, Pelatiah, 43, 47, 414

Perkins, Augustus Thorndike, 22

Perry Matthew Calbraith, 36

Perryville, Ky., Battle of, 366 n.

Personal Liberty Laws, 64, 65, 66

Peter Wilkins (Paltock), 237

Peters, Charles, 65, 248

Peters, John Charles, 3, 5, 39, 65, 68, 75, 88, 161, 166, 168, 197, 329, 341, 380, 515, 558, 559

Peters, Mrs. John Charles (Georgiana Snelling), 3, 6, 7, 22, 55, 56, 88, 137, 515

Petersburg, Va., 244, 368, 388, 437, 445, 458–461, 463–465, 468–471, 478, 495, 496, 499, 505 n., 552–553, 557, 569, 572–574, 576 n., 594; captured, 574; G.T.S. visits battlefront, 464; Petersburg mine (Battle of the Crater), 468, 469

Petrigru, Caroline (Mrs. W. A. Carson), 64, 68, 371

Petrigru, James Louis, 64–65, 68, 86

Petrick, Captain, 460

Petroleum, 534, 551, 562, 569, 576, 583

Pfefferkorn, Joannes, 509

Phelps, Royal, 78

Phelps, William Walter, 323

Phelps, Mrs. William Walter (Ellen Maria Sheffield), 323 n.

Philadelphia, 22, 85, 88, 127, 147, 167, 172, 191–192, 255, 260, 324–326, 329, 330, 361, 393, 395, 411, 487, 498, 551, 589; elections, 510; hospital, 22

Philharmonic Society concerts and rehearsals, 11, 15, 16, 18, 22, 91, 96, 267, 272, 315, 414, 422, 517, 530, 568, 577

Phillips, Wendell, 84, 91, 94, 246

Philo Parsons, 555 n.

Pickens, Francis Wilkinson, 76, 96, 109

Pickett, George Edward, 331, 395 n., 573

Pierce, Franklin, 479, 561

Pierrepont, Edwards, 117, 588

Pierrepont, Henry Evelyn, 398

Pike, Benjamin, & Sons, 38

Pillow, Gideon Johnson, 207

Pinckney, of N.Y. Club, 45

Pinkerton, Allan, 102 n.

Pinto, Fernão Mendes, 515

Piracy, 208–209

Pittsburg, 324

Pittsburg Landing, Tenn., 215–217

Pius IX, Pope, 11

Pleasant Hill, La., engagement at, 444

Pleasanton, Alfred, 329

Plutarch, 392

Plymouth, N.C., 431

Point Judith, R.I., 504

Polk, James Knox, 561

Polly, Aunt, slave, 212, 213

Pope, John, 240, 243, 244, 246–254, 287, 289, 290, 298, 299, 408, 416, 436

Port Hudson, La., 308–310, 324, 339, 344, 352, 469

Port Royal, S.C., 226, 312, 360; expedition, 190, 193, 200, 202

Port Royal, Va., 450

Porter, David Dixon, 444, 539 n., 589

Porter, Fitz-John, xiii, 235, 250, 254, 255, 260, 261, 287, 289–292, 297, 364, 415, 454

Portland (Me.) Harbor, 326

Post, Charles, 515, 538

Post, Jehiel Jaggar, 433–434

Post, Mrs. Jehiel Jaggar (Lucrie F. Mahony), 433–434

Potomac River, 239 n., 245, 249, 250, 253–256, 260, 271, 326, 329–332, 344, 351, 445, 465, 466 n., 468, 470

Potter, Alonzo, 192, 576 n.

Potter, Clarkson Nott, 353

Potter, Henry Codman, 376

Potter, Horatio, 2, 101, 183, 265, 364, 365, 376, 384, 398, 400, 412, 415, 419, 427, 447, 538, 542, 543, 545, 548–553, 560

Potter, Howard, 325, 576

Potter, Robert B., 132, 576

Potter, Mrs. Robert B. (Abby Austin Stevens), 576 n.

Potts, George, 2

Powel, Samuel, 192

Powell, Miss ("Justitia"), 194, 204, 226

Powhatan, U.S.S., 116

Praslin, Duc de, 2

Prentiss, Benjamin Mayberry, 216

Pre-Raphaelite paintings, 21

Presbyterians, 49, 322, 559; General Assembly (O.S.), 128 n.

Price, Edward, 208

Price, Sterling, 175, 208, 366 n.

Prime, Nathaniel, 130, 132

Prime, Temple, 223, 539

Prince of Wales (afterward Edward VII), Visit to U.S., 1860, 1, 12 n., 32, 34, 39, 40, 42–52, 101, 145, 560
Prince Rupert's drops, 35
"Princeton, Battle of" (Leutze painting), 3
Princeton College (College of New Jersey), 384, 543; John C. Green School of Science, 61 n.
Princeton Theological Seminary students, 438
Pringle, Southerner, 62
Pringle, Sir John, 161
Prisoners, Rebel treatment of, 494, 520, 535
Privateering, Southern, 124
Protestant Episcopal Church: General Convention of 1862, 262, 263; High Church-Low Church controversy, 384; House of Bishops, 262, 265; N.Y. Diocesan Convention, 42–43, 183; Strong's disgust with, 262–263
Protestants, 40
Prussia, 407, 466
Pruyn, John Van Schaick Lansing, 428, 549
Pugh, George Ellis, 24
Pumpelly, Josiah Collins, 322
Punch, 50, 107, 120, 191, 599
Puritanism, 153
Pyne, Percy Rivington, 528, 529, 539
Pyne, Smith, 87, 111

Quick, Dr., 593
Quin, James M., 402
Quitman, Ark., 407
Quogue, L.I., 453, 469, 475, 483, 485

Rabelais, François, 295, 300
Rachel (Elizabeth Rachel Felix), 52
Radical Republicans, 242
Rae, John, 117, 120
Rae, Mrs. John, 120
Raffling, 403, 405–406, 412–413
Raglan, Fitzroy James Henry Somerset, first Baron, 347
Railroad travel, 4–5
Raleigh, N.C., 406, 565, 579, 588
Raleigh *Progress*, 555
Rams, Confederate, 454, 455 n.
Randolph, Anson D. F., 465
Rapidan River, 247 n., 360, 366, 375, 388, 418, 431, 433, 436
Rappahannock River, 247 n., 248, 277–281, 290, 309, 316–319, 323, 363, 431, 450, 471
Rawlins, John Aaron, 463

Ray, Robert, 98, 401, 430, 448
Raymond, Captain, 306
Raymond, Henry Jarvis, 194, 196, 197, 226, 264, 271, 476, 499
Read, Theodore, 354
Read, Thomas Buchanan, 503
Reade, Charles, 399–400, 391 n.
Red River, 444; expedition, 443
Regents of the University of the State of New York, 383, 390 n.
Reid, Fanny, 576
Renwick, Edward Sabine, 288 n
Renwick, Henry Brevoort, 288 n.
Renwick, James, Jr., 288, 539
Renwick, James, Sr., 288 n., 296, 410
Report of the Demoralization of the Volunteers, 180
Republican (and Union) Party, 1, 8, 22, 26–28, 30, 36, 41–45, 52, 55–60, 66–68, 71, 75–77, 83, 89, 91, 94, 98, 102–104, 106, 108, 109, 151, 163, 165 n., 168, 197, 264, 270, 281, 369, 378, 455, 473, 475, 478, 488, 499, 500, 502
Revolutionary War, 508
Reynolds, John Fulton, 278, 327
Rhett, Robert Barnwell, 73
Rhinelander, Betty (Mrs. William Edgar), 2
Rhinelander, Lucretia Stevens (Mrs. G. F. Jones), 2
Rhode Island, 247, 498; volunteers, 123
Rhode Island Regiments: 1st, 153, 280; 2nd, 178, 180
Rice, 374
Rice, Edmund, 86
Rice, Henry Mower, 165
Richmond, Va., 138, 168, 176, 208, 215, 225 n., 227–229, 231–233, 235–237, 239 n., 243, 245, 246, 271, 279, 294, 316, 318, 332, 355, 356, 358, 363, 364, 366, 368, 370, 371, 380, 398, 416, 423, 437, 445, 446, 449, 450, 452, 453, 455, 456, 458, 459 n., 463, 468, 470–472, 474, 478, 492, 495, 497, 499, 503, 505, 518, 526, 532, 533, 537, 540, 541, 547, 548, 555–557, 563, 565, 566, 569, 571–576, 578, 582, 586, 601; capture of, 574; G.T.S. visit to, 588, 591–593
Richmond & Danville R.R., 573
Richmond *Enquirer*, 138, 294, 323
Richmond *Examiner*, 323
Richmond *Sentinel*, 540
Riggs, Elizabeth (Mrs. J. H. Hobart, Jr.), 16
"Ring, The," 375
Rio Grande River, 366, 378

Rip Van Winkle, 267
Rip Van Winkle, 38
Ritchie, Harrison, 588
Ritchie, Mrs. William F. (Anna Cora (Ogden) Mowatt), 20, 296, 432
Rives, Francis Robert, 73
Rives, Mrs. Francis Robert (Matilda Antonia Barclay), 73
Rives, William Cabell, 73, 351
Roanoke Island: expedition, 200; occupation of, 206
Roanoke River, 517 n.
Roberts, Marshall Orme, 167, 424
Robertson, John, 340
Robinson, 142
Robinson, Anna Dorothea (Mrs. William Betts), 513
Robinson, Beverley, 513
Rochester, N.Y., 498
Rockaway, L.I., 247
Rocketts, Richmond, Va., 591, 593
Rockville, Md., 254
Rogers, of Boston, 211, 212
Rogers, Fanny (Mrs. Parkyn), 137
Rogers, Isabel, 430, 434
Roman Catholic Church, 40, 390
Rome, 356
Ronalds, Mrs. (née Carter), 432
Rood, Ogden Nicholas, 365, 376, 381, 383–385, 402, 404, 452, 496, 525
Roosevelt, 541
Roosevelt, Franklin Delano, 306 n.
Roosevelt, Mrs. James (Sara Delano), 306 n.
Roosevelt, James John, 57, 101, 133, 256
Ropes, John Codman, 287 n.
Rosecrans, William Starke, 170, 185 n., 285, 286, 290, 294, 313, 326, 347, 355, 357, 358, 363, 366, 373
Ross microscope, 5
Rossiter, Thomas Prichard, 2
Rossini, Gioachino Antonio, 23, 315
Rothschild, Baron, 40
Rotter, Mme., singer, 414
Rudd, Erastus Barnes, 323
Ruffin, Robert, 507
Ruggles, Ellen Caroline. *See* Strong, Mrs. George Templeton
Ruggles, George, 324
Ruggles, Mrs. Herman, 264
Ruggles, James Francis, 3, 5, 12, 56, 61, 78, 111, 125, 130, 134, 137, 178, 267, 365, 377, 408, 524, 538
Ruggles, Julia, 385
Ruggles, Mrs. Philo (Ellen Bulkley), 320, 385, 386; death, 558

Ruggles, Rosalie, 37, 38, 81, 90, 96, 120, 125, 128, 137, 207, 262, 265, 278
Ruggles, Samuel Bulkley, xiv, 4, 5, 11–13, 20, 25, 29–31, 34, 36, 38, 43, 46, 49, 50, 53, 57, 63, 65, 66, 68, 72, 80, 84, 86, 87, 94, 110, 113, 120, 125, 126, 128, 129, 134, 147, 164, 167, 168, 178, 183, 191–193, 201, 205, 223, 229, 237, 244, 246, 262, 265, 266, 276, 278, 291–293, 302, 305, 323, 329, 345, 348–350, 376, 377, 381, 385, 396, 398, 400, 407, 412, 419, 425, 426–428, 435, 447–449, 452, 466, 468, 470, 478, 481, 490, 491, 497, 501, 515, 520, 542, 548, 550, 551, 558, 560, 562, 569, 587
Ruggles, Mrs. Samuel Bulkley (Mary Rosalie Rathbone), 4, 55, 110, 225, 348, 377
Ruhmkorff coil, 404
Ruskin, John, 39, 411
Russel, William Channing, 319
Russell, of N.Y. Club, 145
Russell, Charles Handy, 101, 588
Russell, Eliza Rodman (Mrs. R. S. Hone), 73
Russell, Helen, 49
Russell, Isaac, 311
Russell, Lord John, 145
Russell, William Howard (afterward Sir), 166, 170, 171, 177, 198, 200–201, 350
Russia, 539
Russian Ball, N.Y., 5 Nov. 1863, 368–369
Russian ikon, G.T.S. purchases, 428
Russian naval squadron in N.Y. harbor, 361
Russian service at Trinity Chapel, 559
Rutherfurd, a Glaswegian, 173
Rutherfurd, Lewis Morris, 2, 26, 31, 107, 110, 120, 221, 263, 316, 365, 376, 378, 381, 383, 398, 400, 427, 430, 448, 452, 457, 485, 486, 496, 524, 525, 528, 538–540, 545, 550, 556, 557, 560
Rutherfurd, Stuyvesant, 221
Rynders, Isaiah, 26

Sabine Crossroads, La., engagement at, 444
Sackett, Adam Tredwell, 370
Saga of Burnt Njal, 364
St. Albans, Vt., raid, 528, 596
St. Anthony, Falls of, 244
St. Denis Hotel, N.Y., 16
St. George's Chapel, N.Y., 17, 61, 118, 122

St. Germans, Edward Granville Eliot, third Earl of, 49, 50
St. James Hotel, N.Y., 522
St. John, Samuel, 38
St. John's Chapel, N.Y., 262, 265, 287
St. John's Church, Washington, 87, 111, 195
St. John's Park, N.Y., 15, 288
St. Lawrence County, N.Y., volunteers, 162
St. Louis, Mo., 149, 188–189; street fighting in, 142
St. Mark, 228, 230, 231, 233, 234, 236, 238
St. Mark's Church, N.Y., 99, 272, 305, 419
St. Nicholas Hotel, N.Y., 336, 522
St. Paul's Chapel, N.Y., 132, 225, 272, 273
St. Peter's Church, Albany, 392, 405
St. Thomas's Church, N.Y., 101, 398
Salisbury, Robert Arthur Talbot Gascoyne Cecil, third Marquis of, 301 n.
San Francisco, 265, 277, 406, 484, 566
San Francisco, 154
Sandeau, Léonard Sylvain Jules, 27
Sanderson, of U.S.S.C., 165
Sandford, Charles W., 88, 151, 341
Sands, Austin Ledyard, 14–15
Sands, Henry Berton, 318
Sandusky Bay, 555 n.
Sandy Hill (or Point) Plantation, Va., 461
Sandford, Henry Seymour, 112
Sanitary Commission. *See* United States Sanitary Commission
Saratoga Springs, 349, 426, 473
Sargent, Jane Percy (Mrs. W. B. Duncan), 73
Satterlee, Richard Sherwood, 193, 218, 226, 234, 519
Saturday Review, 193, 299, 367
Savannah, Ga., 516, 522, 528, 530, 531, 535, 539–541, 556, 558, 559, 571, 582; capture of, 532, 533, 537
Savannah River, 518
Savin Rock, New Haven, 167, 182
Sawyer guns, 167
Sayers, Tom, 24, 32
Scharfenberg, William, 96, 126, 315
Schell, Augustus, 101
Schermerhorn, Abraham, 18, 222
Schermerhorn, Alfred, 27
Schermerhorn, Mrs. Alfred (Charlotte N. Benton), 27, 137
Schermerhorn, Anna White (Mrs. Charles Suydam), 222

Schermerhorn, [Archibald] Bruce, 222
Schermerhorn, Caroline Webster (Mrs. William Astor), 18, 222
Schermerhorn, Edmund, 17, 63
Schermerhorn, Ellen, 2, 18, 538
Schermerhorn, Helen (Mrs. J. T. Irving), 223
Schermerhorn, Henry Augustus, 27
Schermerhorn, Mrs. Peter Augustus, 2, 27, 538
Schermerhorn, William Colford, 20, 27, 58, 63, 100, 391, 399, 404, 409, 420, 425, 435, 453, 515, 528, 529, 550, 553, 579
Schermerhorn, Mrs. William Colford (Annie Laight Cottenet), 2, 420, 538
Schiller, Johann Christoph Friedrich von, 17
Schleswig-Holstein controversy, 407, 466 n.
Schoepf, Albin, 202
Schofield, John McAllister, 398, 446, 524, 565, 568, 570
Schroeder, Francis, 192
Schumann, Robert, 96, 578, 599
Schuyler, George Lee, 20, 101, 139, 202, 384
Schuyler, Mrs. George Lee (Eliza Hamilton), 20, 46, 367; death of, 384
Schuyler, Mrs. George Lee (Mary Morris Hamilton), 5, 20
Schuyler, Louisa Lee, 384 n., 588, 589
Schuyler, Robert, 8 n.
Scotia, 377
Scott, Camilla (Mrs. Goold Hoyt), 48, 49
Scott, Cornelia (Mrs. H. L. Scott), 49, 61 n., 191
Scott, Henry Lee, 61, 74, 114, 191, 195
Scott, Mrs. Henry Lee (Cornelia Scott), 49, 61 n., 191
Scott, Russell, 37 n.
Scott, Thomas Alexander, 187, 188n., 259
Scott, Sir Walter, 51–52
Scott, Winfield, 20, 22, 39, 43, 57–58, 61, 70, 74, 76, 81, 86, 87, 99, 115, 138, 144, 147, 149, 151, 164, 168, 169, 170, 171, 174, 183, 188, 190–192, 195, 208, 226, 233, 246, 247, 346, 405, 416, 490, 493, 600 n.
Seabury, Samuel, 96–97, 384, 398
Sears, Ellen (Mrs. Paul d'Hauteville), 415–416
Sebastopol, Siege of, 367, 469
Secession (and disunion), 1, 45, 52–54, 56–58, 60–67, 69–72, 74–84, 90, 94–97, 100–102, 105, 112, 114, 192

Secor, Charles A., & Co., 125
Sedgwick, Charles Baldwin, 209
Sedgwick, Mrs. Charles Baldwin (Ellen C. Smith), 209
Sedgwick, John, 318, 444
Selden, Dudley, 497–498
Selma, Ala., 409, 565, 579
Semmes, Raphael, 465
Sermon on the Mount, 286
Servetus, Michael, 356
Seton, of N.Y. Club, 45
Seven Days' Battles, 228, 232 n., 236, 446, 601
Seven Pines, Va., Battle of Fair Oaks, 228–230, 232 n., 438
Seward, Frederick William, 583, 585, 586, 591
Seward, William Henry, xiv, 26–28, 42, 56, 71, 76, 77, 86–89, 91, 94, 102, 105, 120, 127, 139 n., 144, 154, 162, 176, 235, 238, 242, 269, 272, 279, 281, 282, 286, 291–293, 312–315, 348, 349, 362, 435, 443, 497, 502, 508, 535, 547, 552, 582, 583, 585–587, 590, 591, 595
Seymour, Horatio, 35, 263–265, 269–271, 296, 299, 307 n., 333, 340, 341, 345, 349, 352, 355, 357, 368, 369, 389, 390, 426, 451, 455, 465, 466, 473 n., 475, 477, 478, 488–490, 497, 502, 504, 509, 512, 536, 581
Seymour Collection of Minerals, 413, 534, 545, 553–554
Shafter, William Rufus, 222 n.
Shakespeare, William, 17, 268, 311, 504, 530, 531; first folio, 46; *Macbeth*, 365, 367
Sharps's rifles and revolvers, 137, 147
Sharpsburg, Battle of. *See* Antietam, Battle of
Sharpsburg, Md., 260, 261, 265
Sharpsburg turnpike, 260
Shaw, Francis George, 344
Shaw, Robert Gould, 344
Shea, James, 402
Shedden case, 20
Sheffield, Mass., 448
Sheffield, Ellen Maria (Mrs. W. W. Phelps), 323
Sheffield, Joseph Earl, 323 n.
Sheldon, Annie, 420
Sheldon, Miss "Chat," 420
Sheldon, Fanny, 420
Sheldon, Frederick, 296, 420, 532, 555
Sheldon, Mrs. Frederick, 18, 296, 420, 555
Shenandoah Army, 503

Shenandoah Valley, 228, 388, 431, 437, 445, 446, 455, 466 n., 474, 475, 499, 500, 505, 507, 557, 565
Sheridan, Philip Henry, 374, 446, 466 n., 474, 488, 490, 491, 493–496, 498, 500, 502–504, 513, 518, 557, 560, 564, 568, 570, 571, 573, 575, 577, 579
Sheridan's ride, 503
Sherman, Isaac, 478
Sherman, John, 6, 500, 517
Sherman, Thomas West, 152, 190–192, 200
Sherman, Watts, 55
Sherman, William Tecumseh, 285, 309, 339, 373, 374, 378, 388, 407, 409, 418, 437, 445, 450, 453, 456, 466, 467, 471, 472, 474, 477, 481, 484, 485, 491, 495–497, 499, 502, 516, 518, 522–524, 526–530, 533, 535, 537, 540, 541, 546, 556, 557, 559, 564, 565, 568, 570, 571, 576, 577, 579; March to the Sea, 516 n., 518, 522, 527, 531, 533
Sherwood, John, 108, 145, 391 n., 452, 515
Sherwood, Mrs. John (Mary Elizabeth Wilson), 46, 371, 376, 381, 387, 391, 424, 426, 587, 588
Sherwood, Mary (Mrs. D. C. Murray), 2, 65, 111, 207
"Sherwood Forest," 156
Shiloh, Battle of, 215–216, 217, 228
Shinplasters, 245
Ship Point, 220
Shipman, William Davis, 268 n., 305
Shiras, Alexander Eakin, 165, 180, 186
Shooter's Hill, Alexandria, 152
Shreveport, La., 431, 443, 444
Sickles, Daniel Edgar, 323, 328, 350, 351, 353
Sigel, Franz, 175, 254, 278, 388, 437, 446, 455
Silliman, Benjamin Douglas, 47
Simmons, James Fowler, 107
Simpson, Matthew, 589
Sintram (Fouqué), 237
Sixth U.S. Cavalry, 195
Skidmore, Samuel T., 124, 141, 370, 470
Skinner, Mark, 210, 259, 275, 421, 543
Slave Code, 1, 23, 24, 57, 91
Slave trade, 43, 68, 208–209
Slavery, 1, 3–4, 23, 24, 27, 52, 55, 57, 60, 67, 69, 72, 73, 77, 83, 91, 92, 93, 97, 99, 105, 106, 136 n., 146, 179, 191, 192, 194, 197, 214, 216, 217, 229, 283, 299, 342, 344, 350, 377, 408, 427, 450, 471, 473, 474, 477, 501, 516, 521, 537, 549, 586; *See also* Emancipation

Slaves, uprising of, 58
Slidell, John, 192–194, 196, 198, 454 n.
Slocum, John, 179
Smith, 155
Smith, A. K., 260
Smith, Andrew Jackson, 431
Smith, Caleb Blood, 291 n.
Smith, Charles, 152
Smith, Edmund Kirby, 179, 431 n., 580, 594, 597, 601
Smith, Ellen C. (Mrs. C. B. Sedgwick), 209
Smith, Floyd, 495
Smith, Francis Gurney, Jr., 192, 203
Smith, Goldwin, 453, 514
Smith, Gustavus Woodson, 229, 230 n.
Smith, J. R., 396
Smith, Richard Somers, 130, 151
Smith, Sydney, 491, 575
Smith, Truman, 112
Smith, William Farrar ("Baldy"), 437, 445, 460 n., 463, 471
Smithsonian Institution, 86, 88, 153, 182, 210, 316 n., 438
Snelling, Andrew S., 7
Snelling, Frederick G., 39, 75
Snobs, 45, 319, 392, 422
Snoring, 213
Soldiers' Home, Washington, 507
Somers, John, Baron Somers, 311
Sothern, Edward Askew, 78
South (U.S.) and Southerners, *passim;* arson plot in New York, 522; barbarism of, 586; brag, bluster, and bad rhetoric, 8, 42, 53, 56, 59, 60, 68, 91, 330–332, 379; chivalry, 8–9, 103, 170, 352; Christianity, 356–357; fire-eaters, 23, 52, 58; newspaper abuse of Lincoln and the North, 138, 144; refugee women in New York, 521; reign of terror, 58; vigilance committees, 8, 9, 42
South Anna River, 452
South Carolina, 44, 52, 54, 57, 58, 60, 62–65, 68, 72, 73, 75, 76, 78, 79, 81–86, 88, 91, 95, 96, 99, 100, 108–110, 114, 116, 136, 138, 140, 142, 214, 226, 268, 274, 296, 450, 533, 564, 593, 601; regiments: 1st, 312
South Side R.R., 459 n., 496, 571, 574
Spain, 540
Spalding, 231, 233, 238, 239
Spanish-American War, 222 n.
Speakership contest, House of Representatives, 1, 3, 7
Spectroscope, 457
Speculation, 26

Spencer, Herbert, 9
Spies, 157, 163, 190, 555
Spingler, 416
Spirit of the Fair, 418
Spotswood Hotel, Richmond, 591, 592
Spotsylvania Court House, Battle of, 436, 444–446, 450, 454, 578
Spring, Gardiner, 127–128, 412
Spring Hill, Tenn., 321 n.
Springfield, Ill., 355, 595
Stadt Theatre, Bowery, 109
Stahel, Julius, 252
Stansbury, Caroline Matilda (Mrs. William Kirkland), 431
Stafford Heights, Va., 281
Stanton, Edwin McMasters, 70, 84, 188 n., 203, 207, 208, 218–220, 226, 227, 230, 231, 235, 237, 239, 242, 243, 246–249, 251–253, 256, 258, 272, 276, 279, 281, 284, 306, 313, 314, 321, 323, 351, 353, 359, 366 n., 375, 385, 389, 394, 396, 405, 418–421, 423, 437–439, 446, 450, 455, 476, 478, 483, 488, 489, 497, 498, 504, 509, 521, 535, 556, 560, 573, 598; G.T.S. interview with, 440–442
Staples, Fanny, 538, 539
Star of the West, 84, 88, 89
Staunton, Va., 455, 495, 557
Steilacoom, Washington Territory, 433
Steiner, Lewis Henry, 350, 356, 437
Stephens, wife-poisoner, 6
Stephens, Alexander Hamilton, 380, 495, 547, 550
Stevens, Abby Austin (Mrs. R. B. Potter), 576 n.
Stevens, Alexander Hodgdon, 386
Stevens, Edwin Augustus, 210
Stevens, John Austin (1795–1874), 61, 63, 94
Stevens, John Austin, Jr. (1827–1910), 76, 298, 302, 303, 312, 336, 386
Stevens, Lucretia (Mrs. Heckscher), 538
Stevens, Mrs. Paran, 576
Stevens Battery, 210
Stewart, 87
Stewart, of N.Y. Club, 45
Stewart, Alexander Turney, 307 n., 416
Stewart, A. T., & Co., 274
Stewart, William Pinckney, 434
Stigelli, opera singer, 7, 56, 65
Stillé, Charles Janeway, xiv, 180, 184 n., 203, 221, 275, 280, 282, 288, 361, 393, 395, 506, 520, 543, 559, 590
Stockton, Calif., 277
Stone, Dr., Lincoln's physician, 591
Stone, Charles Pomeroy, 206

Stone, William Oliver, 2, 20
Stone Bridge, Manassas, 212, 213
Stone Creek, 229
Stone Fleet, 221
Stone's River, Murfreesboro, Tenn.,
  Battle of, 285, 355, 366 n.
Stoneman, George, 316, 530
Stoughton, Colonel, 576
Stowe, Harriet Beecher, 84, 94, 373;
  Uncle Tom's Cabin, 68
Strafford, Sir Thomas Wentworth, first
  Earl of, 489
Strasburg, Va., 491, 493, 503
Strauss, David Friedrich, 9
Strong, Charles Edward, xiv, 7, 18–19, 22,
  31, 39, 41, 45, 55, 61, 63, 73, 97, 104,
  107, 116, 121, 145, 161, 162, 168, 223,
  226, 244, 290, 296, 300, 301, 315, 321,
  335, 339, 341, 471, 473, 482, 504, 515,
  518–519, 546, 572, 586
Strong, Mrs. Charles Edward (Eleanor
  Burrill Fearing), 7, 18, 25, 31, 88, 107,
  121, 315, 319, 562
Strong, George Crockett, 305
Strong, Mrs. George Templeton (Ellen
  Caroline Ruggles), *passim*; birth of
  third child, 25; meets Prince of Wales,
  49; in Washington, 110–111, 194–195;
  makes havelocks, 137; serves as war
  nurse, 223–228, 230–233, 236–239,
  439; treasurer of Metropolitan Fair,
  373, 374, 412, 424–427, 430, 432; in
  Sanitary Commission theatricals, 430,
  434; trip to City Point after surrender,
  576, 582
Strong, George Templeton, Jr., "Temple"
  (1856–1948), 2, 6, 31, 46, 248, 262,
  324, 328, 374, 383, 414, 494, 497, 520,
  546, 585
Strong, George Washington, father of
  G.T.S. (1783–1855), 252, 304, 363,
  498
Strong, James Henry, 45, 63, 96, 373
Strong, John (Elder), 305
Strong, John Ruggles, son of G.T.S.
  (1851-1941), 2, 6, 22, 31, 46, 81, 120,
  128, 129, 225, 237, 248, 262, 267, 315,
  324, 328, 337, 365, 374, 383, 392, 414,
  430; Virginia trip, 460, 462–465; 494,
  503, 504, 520, 531, 541, 546, 578, 585
Strong, Josephine, 3
Strong, Kate Fearing (Miss Puss), 61,
  315, 515, 586
Strong, Lewis Barton (son), birth, 25;
  38, 205, 408, 497, 520, 587
Strong, Peter Remsen, 309, 386

Strong, Mrs. Peter Remsen (Mary Em-
  meline Stevens), 386
Stuart, Chaplain, C.S.A., 260
Stuart, George Hay, 589
Stuart, James Ewell Brown, 212, 248;
  killed, 446
Sturges, Jonathan, 201, 302, 429
Stuyvesant, Miss, 18
Substitute, G.T.S. hires, 479, 480
Suckley, George, 177
Suffolk, Va., 316
Suffolk Co., L.I., 508
Sullivan's Island, Charleston, 360
Sumner, Charles, 8, 67, 88, 103, 192,
  282, 286, 404, 549
Sumner, Edwin Vose, 290
Surgeon General of the U.S. *See* U.S.
  Army, Medical Department
Susquehanna, 254
Sutherland, Josiah, 28, 29, 32, 73
Sutter's Hill, Alexandria, 152
Suydam, Mr. and Mrs., 73
Suydam, Mrs. Charles (Anna White Scher-
  merhorn), 222
Suydam, James Augustus, 21, 309
"Swamp Angel," 360, 378
Swan, Otis Dwight, 302, 317, 539
Swift, surgeon, 176
Swift, John H., 122, 124, 363
Sykes, George, 349
Syracuse, N.Y., 264, 488

Tailer, Henry Austin, 166
Talboys, William P., 493, 525
Talboys, Mrs. William P., 538
Tallahassee, Fla., 389
Talmage, 132
Tammany Hall, 522
Taney, Roger Brooke, 500, 549
Tar River, 344
Taylor, Moses, 307 n., 528
Taylor, Richard, 431 n.
Taylor, Thomas House, 353
Taylor, Tom, 599 n.
Taylor, Zachary, 204
Techumseh, U.S.S., 472
Teesdale, Sir Christopher Charles, 50
Telegraph line, European, via Behring
  Straits, proposed, 435
Tennessee, 76, 89, 92, 95, 101, 140, 142,
  149, 193, 199, 202, 205, 208, 285, 308,
  323, 324, 326, 343 n., 346, 355, 356,
  366, 371, 377, 378, 380, 397, 398, 406,
  446, 455, 544
Tennessee, C.S.S., 472 n.
Tennessee River, 373, 529

Tennessee River Campaign, 201, 205, 206, 216

Tennyson, Alfred, Lord, 391

Tenth Street Studio Building, N.Y., 3

Terry, Alfred Howe, 539 n., 570

Texas, 58, 80, 103, 108, 115, 142, 280, 326, 350, 351, 353, 354, 382, 395, 443, 597

Thackeray, William Makepeace, 381, 391

Thanksgiving Day, 377

Thayer, William Sydney, 87

Thirteenth Amendment, 537, 549

Thomas, George Henry, 358, 366 n., 374, 398 n., 524, 526, 529–531, 564, 568, 571, 579

Thomas, Philip Francis, 74 n.

Thomas, Theodore, 577, 599

Thompson, Jacob, 522 n., 555 n., 595

Thompson, Joseph Parrish, 584

Thorndike, James Steuart, 27, 110

Thorndike, Mrs. James Steuart (Henrietta Delprat), 432, 555

Thorpe, 132

Thouvenel, Edward Antoine, 293

Throg's Neck, N.Y., 471

Tiffany, Charles Lewis, 432

Tiffany & Co., 43, 141, 274, 338

Tighe, Mrs. Richard, 113

Tilden, Samuel Jones, 56, 297, 473 n.

Tillou, Francis R., 370, 392, 393, 405, 584

Tippecanoe (Harrison) campaign of 1840, 41, 43

Titanic, 222 n.

Todd, Mary (Mrs Abraham Lincoln), 104, 255, 583

Todleben, Franz Eduard, 246

Tombs Prison, N.Y., 6

Tomes, Robert, 184 n.

Toombs, Robert, 8, 73, 77, 79, 87, 91, 103, 495

Torbert, Alfred Thomas Archimedes, 568

Torrey, John, 34, 38, 381, 387, 398, 413, 448, 492, 524, 528, 534, 545, 549, 553

Tousey, Sinclair, 379

Townsend, Eliza Nevins (Mrs H. W. Bellows), 223, 225

Townsend, John Joseph, 107–108

Townsend, Samuel P., 416

Townsend, Thomas Seaman, 600

Tracy, Charles, 315

Train, George Francis, 259, 372

Travers, John, 295

Trinity Cemetery, Manhattanville, 306

Trinity Chapel, 16, 392, 407, 559

Trinity Church N.Y., 15–16, 19, 21, 22, 44–46, 49, 50, 61, 75, 81, 99, 107, 118, 120, 122, 128, 135, 140, 141, 214, 240, 252, 265, 272–274, 287, 295, 306, 328, 360, 363, 366, 370, 376, 385, 392, 399, 402, 404, 406–407, 433, 434, 443, 445, 492, 495, 514, 528, 531, 561, 564, 573, 585; U.S. flag on tower of, 124–126; chimes, 574; Thanksgiving Service, 580–581

Trinity Church, Newport, 248

Trinity College, Hartford, 447

Trinity School, N.Y., 59

Tripler, Charles Stuart, 181, 184, 187, 190, 222, 230, 231, 240 n.

Trollope, Anthony, 391 n., 543

Trowbridge, William Petit, 154

Troy, N.Y., 192, 197, 376; regiment, 144, 156; draft riots, 341

Troy University, 365

Trumpeter, 594

Tucker, Gideon J., 345, 513

Tucker, John, 521

Tuckerman, Lucius, 535, 539, 566

Tunnel Hill, Ga., 409

Turkey-buzzards, 462

Turner, in Libby Prison, 593

Twiggs, David Emanuel, 103, 115, 116, 121

Tyler, Daniel, 170, 179

Tyler, John, 102 n., 156; abandoned home of, visited by G.T.S., 156–157

Tyndall, John, 9, 381

Tyng, Stephen Higginson, 412

Ucalegon, 147

Ulshoeffer, Mary, 580

Uncas, U.S.S., 562

Uncle Ned (coachman), 212

Uncle Tom's Cabin (Stowe), 68

Undine (Fouqué), 237

Union Club, Boston, 544 n.

Union Club, N.Y., 33, 63, 161

Union College, 312 n., 485, 487, 525

Union Defense Committee, 129, 130, 147, 158, 298 n.

Union Gun, Fortress Monroe, 187

Union Hotel, Georgetown, D. C., 172

Union League, 311

Union League Club, N.Y., 276, 286, 288, 292, 298, 299, 302–307, 312, 317–321, 325, 327, 329, 337–339, 342, 343, 345, 349, 350, 352, 354, 361, 368, 375, 376, 380, 390, 392, 411, 432, 444, 449, 453, 457, 465, 468, 470, 478, 479, 481, 488, 491, 498–501, 504, 508, 510–514, 517, 519, 522, 526, 531, 534, 538, 541, 544, 548, 558, 575–577, 581, 584, 599, 600

Union League Club, Philadelphia, 86 n., 286, 288, 302

Union Mass-Meeting, Union Square (20 April, 1861), 126–129, 241, 575

Union Pacific R.R., 72, 80, 84, 86, 87, 345, 348

Union Party, 41, 369, 370, 375

Union Square, N.Y., 53, 127–129, 168, 205, 241, 304, 307 n., 310, 328, 374, 411, 413, 417, 419, 426, 427, 443, 453, 488, 560, 575, 584

Unitarians, 188–189, 266, 413 n., 525, 559

United States Army: Medical Department (Medical Bureau), 150, 159, 173, 178, 180–182, 184, 185, 194, 196–198, 200–203, 207, 210, 215, 217–219, 226, 227, 234, 240 n., 254, 257, 275, 304, 314, 359, 472, 503, 507, 519, 521, 526, 527, 603; Medical Museum, 477; Quartermaster Department, 257

United States Capitol, G.T.S. visits, 86, 153

United States Christian Commission, 310–311, 589

United States Coast Survey, 154, 438, 448

United States Congress, Committee on the Conduct of the War, 546

United States Dragoons, 155

United States Government Loan of 1860, 53, 55

United States Hotel, N.Y., 522

United States House of Representatives, 427–428; Committee of Thirty-three, 102 n., 107; Military Committee, 203–204, 210–211

United States Navy Department, 183, 210, 214, 438, 532

United States Sanitary Commission, 86 n., 130–131; beginnings of 150, 151, 158; appointed by Sec. of War, 159; G.T.S. made treasurer of, 159; 160–164; room in Treasury Bldg., Washington, 164, 178, 186; 165–168, 171–173, 175, 177, 178, 180–185; moves to Adams House, Washington, 186; 187–204, 207, 209, 210, 212, 215, 217–221, 223, 224, 226; rents N.Y. headquarters, 498 (later 823) Broadway, 226; 227, 228, 230–234, 238–240, 243, 245, 248–249, 253–255, 257, 258, 265–267, 269, 270, 273–280, 286–288, 290–294, 298, 302–306, 307 n., 310–312, 314, 317, 318, 320–322, 332, 335, 336, 338, 344, 350, 353, 356–360, 362, 365, 367, 371–377,
382, 384, 385, 389, 391–397, 402–408, 410–414, 416–427, 429–435, 438–442, 450, 451, 458, 460, 462, 463, 465, 472, 475, 484–487, 490, 492, 493, 495–498, 500–508, 516, 519–522, 526, 530, 531, 533–538, 541, 543, 544, 546, 548, 552, 559, 566, 567, 570, 581, 583, 584, 587, 589–592, 594, 598

Branches: Boston, 382; Chicago, 374, 375; Cincinnati, 273–275, 277, 278, 280, 305, 375, 379, 395; Cleveland (Western Branch), 382; Paris, 382; Philadelphia, 382; San Francisco, 267, 269, 274, 277, 279, 362, 391, 406, 413 n., 502, 516, 566

Bulletin, 385, 440, 487

Fairs: Metropolitan Fair, New York (1864), 373, 374, 376, 379, 381–383, 387, 390, 391, 396, 402–403, 406, 408, 410, 412, 413, 416, 417, 419–431, 434, 588; Albany, 432; Boston, 382, 395, 417; Brooklyn, 406, 408, 412–414, 417; Chicago, 382, 417, 562; Cincinnati, 382, 417; Cleveland, 417; Philadelphia, 414

Western Division (St. Louis), 188, 189, 265, 274, 306, 362 n., 375

United States Senate: Committee of thirteen, 77; G.T.S. present in, 86–88, 112; Military Committee, 165, 203–204, 314; Seward's hired roughs in galleries of, 292

United States Supreme Court, 433, 500, 526, 549

United States Treasury Building, 589, 590

United States Trust Co., 53

United States War Department, 173 n., 181, 183–186, 188, 201, 206 n., 235, 237, 268, 314, 317, 353, 429, 439, 440, 468, 476, 502, 567, 601

Usher, John Palmer, 291

Vallandigham, Clement Laird, 285, 290, 299, 345 n., 364, 370, 375 n., 428, 477–480, 483, 489, 497

Van Alen, James H., 430

Van Amringe, John Howard, 376

Van Brunt, Henry, 20

Van Buren, Addie, 238

Van Buren, Annie, 576

Van Buren, John, 21, 48, 265, 272, 296, 532, 576

Van Buren, Martin, 264, 575 n.

Van Buren, Sally, 238

Van Buren, William Holme, 71, 114, 150, 159–167, 172, 175, 178, 182–184, 190–192, 198, 201, 203, 209, 211, 213, 215, 217, 218, 223, 224, 226, 231–234, 238, 245, 258, 265, 267, 275, 280, 287, 291, 298, 306, 350, 353, 358, 367, 373, 383, 385, 393, 413, 418, 421, 425, 426, 428, 433, 460, 487, 492, 495, 501, 519–521, 526, 535, 559, 567

Van Buren, Mrs. William Holme (Louisa Dunmore Mott), 238

Vanderpoel, Aaron, 120, 160, 309, 575

Van Dorn, Earl, 210, 241, 321

Van Evrie, John H., 123

Van Nostrand, David, 457, 496

Vatican, The, 390

Vermont, 66; elections, 500

Verplanck, Daniel Crommelin, 197

Verplanck, Gulian Crommelin, xv, 113, 140, 163, 197, 295, 309, 370, 390, 392, 398, 584

Vicksburg, Miss., 92, 285, 294, 298, 308–310, 321, 323, 324, 326, 327, 344, 352, 355, 374, 398 n., 407, 469; surrender of, 331, 332

Victoria, Queen, 44, 52, 391

Victoria Cross, 49, 457

Viele, Egbert Ludovickus, 225, 532, 538, 539

Viele, Mrs. Egbert Ludovickus (Teresa Griffin), 532, 538

Vienna, Va., 160

Vigilance Committees of the South, 8, 9, 42

Villafranca, Peace of, 1

Vinton, Alexander Hamilton, 99

Vinton, Francis, xv, 15, 19, 26, 75, 81, 120, 125, 189, 265, 273, 277, 321, 385, 447, 448, 514–515, 574, 580, 585, 586, 588

Vinton, Francis Laurens, 404, 507, 515, 520, 524, 525, 528, 538, 539, 541, 564, 566

Vinton, Frank, 588

Virginia, 3, 8, 64, 68, 75–77, 87, 89, 91–99, 101, 104, 106, 107, 112, 114, 122, 123, 134, 138–143, 149, 152, 162, 166, 174, 179, 206, 208, 211–213, 215, 222, 223, 227, 229, 231, 232 n., 233, 239 n., 243, 247, 268, 274, 290, 294, 316, 317, 323, 332, 351, 358, 362, 366, 371, 378, 395 n., 398, 416, 435, 449, 458, 466 n., 467, 486, 498, 530, 539, 555, 557, 564, 568, 582, 586

Virginia, C.S.S. *See Merrimac*

Virginia & Tennessee R.R., 344, 378

Volcano, Calif., 277

Vollum, Edward P., 218, 231, 234, 275

Volunteers' Association, 132

Wabash, U.S.S., 116

Wade, Benjamin Franklin, 76, 77

Wadsworth, James Samuel, 220, 263, 264, 270, 328, 405, 411; killed, 443

Wagner, Richard, 96, 396, 599

Walbridge, Hiram, 271

Walbridge, Mary Hosmer (Mrs. Washington Hunt), 46, 50

Walker, Presbyterian bookbinder, 49

Wall Street, 11, 13, 22, 31, 32, 36, 45, 46, 53, 54, 61, 63–65, 80, 97, 105, 112,114, 123, 125, 127, 137, 139, 141, 144, 147, 208, 230, 303, 318, 324, 325, 335, 340, 360, 365, 376, 404, 408, 409, 415, 421, 423, 431, 433, 449, 458, 471, 479, 490, 500, 503, 504, 508, 520, 554, 560, 564–566, 569, 574–577, 579, 583, 584, 586, 587, 592

Wallace, Lew, 216

Wallack, Lester, 416 n.

Wallack's Theatre, 265, 507

Wallenstein, Albrecht Eusebius von, 347

Walpole, N.H., 248

War Office, Washington, 153

Ward, George Cabot, 304, 535, 538, 566

Ward, Henry Hall, 63, 160, 286

Ward, Julia (Mrs. S. G. Howe), 404

Ward, Marcus Lawrence, 562

Ward, Margaret (Mrs. J. W. Chanler), 2, 117

Ward, Samuel (1814–1884), 2, 170, 200

Ward, Mrs. Samuel (Emily Astor), 2

Warren, Gouverneur Kemble, 182, 235, 438, 475

Warrenton, Va., turnpike, 213

Washburn, Emory, 151

Washburne, Elihu, 369

Washington, D.C., 86–88, 193, 238–240, 248–250, 252, 253 n., 258, 324, 326, 330, 356, 367, 420, 421, 431, 433, 437, 441, 445, 466–468, 470, 475, 486, 487, 490, 503, 519, 521, 523, 527, 537, 543, 546–548, 551, 552, 558, 561, 586, 590, 601, 603; attacks on, feared, 127, 128, 169; reinforcement of, 131; spring in, 438; G.T.S. in, 111–112, 149–155,164–166, 172–174, 178–182, 185–190, 194–196, 202–205, 209–213, 256–259, 275, 361–363, 393–395, 435, 437–442, 465, 505–507, 543, 587–591, 594

Washington, George, 32, 109, 584, 598; equestrian statue by Clark Mills, 111; Farewell Address, 286; proposed re-

moval of bones from Mount Vernon, 143; Washington's birthday celebration, 101
Washington, John Augustine, 143
Washington, John Marshall, 154; son captured at Fairfax Court House, 154
Washington *Constitution*, 89
Washington Monument, 112
Washington Parade Ground, N.Y., 135
Washington *Republican*, 197
Washington Territory, 502
Washington University, St. Louis, 189 n.
Waterloo, Battle of, 491, 575
Waterman, Eliza Matilda (Mrs. E. D. Morgan), 48, 49
Watson, James, 69, 71, 73
Watts, Robert, 234
Webb, James Watson, 125
Webb, William A., 121
Weber, Karl Maria von, 7, 56, 426, 599
Weber, Max, 167
Webster, Daniel, 91
Webster, Sidney, 33
Webster, Mrs. Sidney (Sarah Morris Fish), 33
Weed, Thurlow, 27, 42, 76, 105, 235, 312 n., 499
Weeks, Justice, 90
Weeks, Francis Henry, 7
Weeks (afterward Weekes), John Abeel, 7, 548
Weeks, Mrs. John Abeel (Alice Howland Delano), 2
Weitzel, Godfrey, 575
Weldon, N.C., 278
Weldon, R.R., 459 n., 475, 477, 484
Welles, Gideon, 129, 242, 287 n., 304
Wellington, Arthur Wellesley, Duke of, 347
Welsh, William, 203
Wen, William, 213
Wendell, Anna Mary (Mrs. R. B. Minturn), 73
Wendell, John Lansing, 13
Wenzler, Henry Antonio, Jr., 2
Wertherism, 92
Wesley, John, 356
West Point, 50, 54, 87, 91, 130, 151, 179, 191 n., 195, 247, 250, 279, 289, 306, 321 n., 327, 341, 366, 404, 415, 426, 446, 454, 455, 459, 492, 507 n., 600 n.; Southern plot to control, 108
West Point, Va., 437
West Stockbridge, Mass., 38
West Virginia, 139, 140, 142, 158, 167, 168, 177, 185, 193, 406, 410; admitted as state, 286
Westchester County, N.Y., elections, 510
Western Reporter, 362
Weston, Sullivan Hardy, 158, 292, 367
Wetmore, Edmund, 323
Wetmore, Prosper Montgomery, 297, 298, 312, 319, 574
"What-is-it?," 12, 31, 207
Wheaton, medical officer, 234
Wheaton, Frank, 178
Whetten, Harriet Douglas, 223
Whig Party, 1, 299
White, architect, 423, 427
White, Andrew Dickson, 448, 548
White, Mrs. Fanny (alias Mrs. Blankman), 69, 73
White, Joseph Blanco, 587
White, Richard Grant, xv, 142, 144, 147, 161, 163, 243, 379, 381, 387, 390–1, 403, 422, 424, 425, 452; *The New Gospel of Peace*, 379
White House, Va., 225 n., 231, 232, 235, 236, 458, 459
White House, The, Washington, 153, 589, 601
Whitestone, L.I., 402
Whiting, Alexander B., 385
Whiting, William, 314, 429, 567, 568
Whitlock, Mrs. Samuel H., 2, 538
Whitney, Stephen, 9
Whittingham, William Rollinson, 265, 266
"Wide-Awakes" (Republicans), 41, 43, 56, 57
Wigfall, Louis Trezevant, 87, 107, 108, 112
Wilderness, Battle of the, 328 n., 418, 436, 444, 449, 578
Wilkins, Gouverneur Morris, 494
Willard's Hotel, Washington, 86, 104, 106, 107, 111, 150, 151, 164–166, 181, 211, 258, 259, 275, 296, 362, 393, 395, 437, 506, 558, 589, 596
Willard Parker Hospital, N.Y., 34
William and Mary of England, 44
Williams, U.S.S.C. agent in Richmond, 592
Williams, Lawrence A., 68, 78, 81, 90–91, 94, 134, 137, 138, 190, 195, 243, 286
Williams, Thomas, 247
Williamsburg, Va., 246, 437; Battle of, 220 n., 236
Williamsport, Md., action at, 338
Williamsport, Pa., 329, 332
Willis, Nathaniel Parker, 153

Willis, Richard Storrs, 315
Willis, Mrs. Richard Storrs (Jessie Carnes), 315
Willoughby's Point, Va., 225
Wilmington, N.C., 354, 529, 532, 534, 535, 539, 555, 557, 559, 562, 565, 570, 571
Wilmington & Weldon R.R., 344
Wilson, Henry, 165, 173, 203, 369
Wilson, Mary Elizabeth (Mrs. John Sherwood), 46, 371
Wilson, William, 132, 137
Wilson, William T., 392, 405
Wilson Small, 240
Wilson's Creek, Mo., Battle of, 175 n.
Winchester, Va., 227, 492, 496, 502, 503, 568; Battle of, 488, 490–491, 493
Winder General Hospital, Richmond, 592
Winston, surgeon, 176
Winston, Frederick S., 175, 201, 203
Winter Garden, N.Y., 51, 531
Winthrop, Charles Francis, 576
Winthrop, Benjamin Robert, 370
Winthrop, Frederick, 576
Winthrop, Henry Rogers, 309, 315, 349, 496
Winthrop, Theodore, 130, 160, 161, 394, 576; killed in battle 158; *Cecil Dreeme*, 158, 163 n.
Winthrop, William Woolsey, 394
Wisconsin troops, 327 n., 597 n.
Wise, Henry Alexander, 8, 41, 58, 73, 99, 142; threatens invasion of Washington, 60
Wise, Henry Augustus, 153, 155
Wise, Mrs. Henry Augustus (Charlotte Brooks Everett), 153
Wister, Owen Jones, 209 n.
Wister, Mrs. Owen Jones (Sarah Butler), 209
Wolcott, J. Huntington, 275, 393, 506, 559
Wolfe, Catherine Lorillard, 580
Wolfe, John David, 101, 382
Wolseley, Garnet Joseph, first Viscount, 301 n.
Women, 283, 305, 343, 344, 521, 523
Women's Central Association of Relief, 150, 277
Wood, Benjamin, 123 n., 268, 270, 368, 408, 426, 491
Wood, Fernando, 45, 47, 95, 120, 123 n., 170, 196, 265, 268, 270, 272, 290, 302, 306, 310, 333, 340, 345, 349, 368, 375, 405, 408, 426, 427, 486, 489, 496, 498, 512, 551, 552

Wood, Mrs. Fernando (Alice Fenner Mills), 95
Wood, George, 16
Wood, Robert Crooke, 150, 159, 165, 180, 181, 186, 204, 218, 306
Woodruff, Lewis Bartholomew, 26, 29
Woodruff, Lockwood de Forest, 221
Woodstock, Va., 446
Woodward, George Washington, 364
Woodward, Joseph Janvier, 544
Wool, John Ellis, 139, 176, 225, 321, 336, 337, 341
Woolsey, Miss, 221
Woolsey, Theodore Dwight, 414
Wormeley, Katherine Prescott, 223 n., 224 n.
Wormley's, Washington, 166
Wright, C., 21
Wright, George, 283
Wright, George William, 398
Wright, Mrs. Isaac, 3
Wright, Joshua Butler, 298
Wright, "Poke," 136
Wright, Silas, 264
Wyandotte Constitution, 1
Wycliffe, John, 205
Wynne, James, 101
Wytheville, Va., 344

Yale College, 316 n., 414 n., 448, 487, 525, 543, 550, 584 n.; Law School, 276
Yancey, William Lowndes, 23, 41, 73, 79, 83, 91, 103, 346, 354
Yates, Richard, 369
Yellow Tavern, Va., Battle of, 446
Yonge, Charlotte Mary, 496
Yonkers, N.Y., draft riots, 341
York River, 220 n., 221, 222, 459
Yorktown, Va., 215, 216, 222, 228, 231–233, 236, 316, 604; hospitals at, 218
Yorktown, C.S.S., 225
Yosemite Valley, 502
Youmans, Edward Livingston, 9
Young, Edmund M., 295, 309, 370
Young, John Freeman, 307, 363
Young America, U.S.S., 461
Young Men's Christian Association, 311 n.
Youngs, Henry, 370
Yubaville, Calif., 277
Yznaga, Mrs. 301

Zabriskie, Martin Ryerson, 98, 233, 409, 448, 549–551, 560, 587
Zollicoffer, Felix Kirk, 202
Zouaves, 137, 146, 147, 149, 152, 156, 169, 174, 180, 182

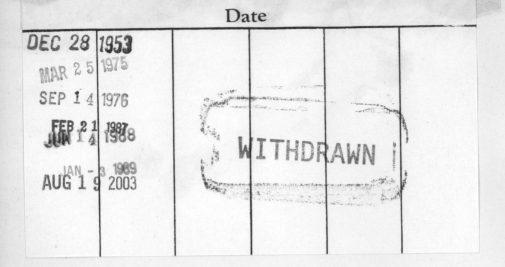